essential

JTAPI

JAVA™ TELEPHONY API

Design Telecom Projects with Java

ISBN 0-13-080360-X

Titles in the PH/PTR essential series:

Essential JNI: Java Native Interface
Essential JMF: Java Media Framework
Essential JTAPI: Java Telephony API
  Design Telecom Projects with Java

Series Editor Alan McClellan is co-author of the best-selling *Java by Example, Graphic Java: Mastering the AWT*, and *Automating Solaris Installations: A JumpStart Guide* (SunSoft/Prentice Hall). He is an award-winning software technical writer with over ten years of experience in the computer industry.

essential

JTAPI

JAVA™ TELEPHONY API

Design Telecom Projects with Java

S P E N C E R   R O B E R T S

Prentice Hall PTR
Upper Saddle River, NJ 07458
http://www.phptr.com

Library of Congress Catalog-in-Publication Data

Roberts, Spencer.
    Essential JTAPI: Java telephony API : designing telecom projects
with Java / Spencer Roberts.
        p.   cm. -- (PH/PTR essential series)
    Includes bibliographical references and index.
    ISBN 0-13-080360-X
    1. Telephone systems--Computer programs.   2. Java (Computer
program language)   I. Title.   II. Series.
    TK6421.R63   1999
    621.385'0285--dc21   98-45641
                                                          CIP

Editorial/production supervision: *Vanessa Moore*
Cover design director: *Jerry Votta*
Cover designer: *Scott Weiss*
Manufacturing manager: *Alexis Heydt*
Development editor: *Ralph E. Moore*
Technical editor: *Gary Gartner*
Acquisitions editor: *Gregory Doench*
Series editor: *Alan McClellan*
Marketing manager: *Kaylie Smith*

© 1999 Prentice Hall PTR
Prentice-Hall, Inc.
A Simon & Schuster Company
Upper Saddle River, NJ 07458

Prentice Hall books are widely used by corporations and government agencies for training,
marketing, and resale. The publisher offers discounts on this book when ordered in bulk
quantities. For more information, contact Corporate Sales Department, Phone: 800-382-3419,
Fax: 201-236-7141, Email: corpsales@prenhall.com
or write: Prentice Hall PTR
            Corporate Sales Department
            One Lake Street
            Upper Saddle River, NJ 07458

Printed in the United States of America
10   9   8   7   6   5   4   3   2   1

ISBN 0-13-080360-X

Prentice-Hall International (UK) Limited, *London*
Prentice-Hall of Australia Pty. Limited, *Sydney*
Prentice-Hall of Canada, Inc., *Toronto*
Prentice-Hall Hispanoamericana S.A., *Mexico*
Prentice-Hall of India Private Limited, *New Delhi*
Prentice-Hall of Japan, Inc., *Tokyo*
Simon & Schuster Asia Pte. Ltd., *Singapore*
Editora Prentice-Hall do Brasil, Ltda., *Rio de Janeiro*

*This book is dedicated to
my wife, Susie, and
"my three sons," Spencer, Weston, and Noah.*

CONTENTS

PREFACE

Background   xiv
Overview   xv
    Approach   xvi
    Content   xvii
    Audience   xix
About the Author   xix
Acknowledgments   xx
The Essential JTAPI FTP Site   xxi

PART I   TELECOM PROGRAMMING   1

CHAPTER 1   AN OVERVIEW OF COMPUTER TELEPHONY   3

Telecom Fundamentals   4
    The Telephony Problem Space   4
    JTAPI to the Rescue   11
Telephony Implementations   17

vi

Telephony Support in Hardware   17
Remote Communication   18
Telephony Configurations   19
Data Transport Protocols   21
Telephony Protocols   21
Summary   22

CHAPTER 2   TELEPHONY BUS ARCHITECTURES   23

Bus Architectures   24
Telephony Bus Architectures   25
The Espresso Approach   26
Trans-Bus Communication   27
Summary   29

PART II   TELEPHONY APIs   31

CHAPTER 3   JAVA'S SUITABILITY TO TELECOM PROGRAMMING   33

Toys and Tools of the Trade   34
Selecting a Programming Language   35
Smalltalk   36
Ada   37
C/C++   37
Java   38
Why Java for Telecom?   38
Packages   38
Interfaces   39
Java's Thread Model   41
Portability   41
The Reflection API   42
Java Event Management Models   42
Remote Method Interface (RMI)   43
Native Methods   43
Why Not Java for Telecom?   43
Garbage Collection   44
Performance   45
Summary   47

CHAPTER 4   A CLOSE LOOK AT JTAPI   49

JTAPI — Sun's Java Telephony Application Programming
   Interface   50
   The Java Standard Extension APIs   50
   The JTAPI Specification   54
   JTAPI Architecture   54
   JTAPI Security   55
   JTAPI Package Hierarchy   55
JTAPI — A Modular API   56
   JTAPI Packages   56
   JTAPI Interface Specification Practice   58
JTAPI Core Components   60
   Observable Core Telephony Interfaces   61
   Observer Core Telephony Interfaces   87
   Peer Core Telephony Interfaces and Classes   92
JTAPI Capabilities   99
   Static and Dynamic Capabilities   101
JTAPI — An Object-Oriented API?   103
   Implementing JTAPI Using Extension   103
   A Possible Object Diagram for javax.telephony   105
   Implementing JTAPI Using Linked Interfaces   106
   A Small Soapbox   108
JTAPI — An Event-Driven API   108
   JTAPI Events   108
   States, Events, and State Transitions   110
   JTAPI Core Events   112
   Is a Connection Event a Call Event?   116
JTAPI — An Exception-Aware API   117
   JTAPI Exceptions   118
Summary   122

PART III   IMPLEMENTING JTAPI   123

CHAPTER 5   TELEPHONY API OVERVIEW   125

What Is a Standard API?   126
Why Use Standard APIs?   127
   The Problem with Standards   127

The Benefits of Standards Compliance   128
Design Requirements for an API   129
   General API Requirements   129
   Telephony-Specific API Requirements   146
A Survey of the Leading Telephony APIs   148
   Enterprise Computing Telephony Forum APIs   149
   Novell and AT&T's Telephony Services Application Programming
      Interface   151
   A Dialogic Application Programming Interface   152
   Microsoft's Telephony Application Programming Interface   153
Does JTAPI Measure Up?   168
   JTAPI and General API Requirements   169
   JTAPI and Telecom-Specific API Requirements   171
Summary   173

CHAPTER 6   CONSTRUCTION OF A JTAPI LIBRARY   175

A Library Design Methodology   176
   Deciding Upon a Design Approach   176
JTAPI Library Architectural Components   177
   The Infrastructure Layer   180
   The API Layer   226
Summary   263

PART IV   TELEPHONY PROGRAMMING WITH JTAPI   265

CHAPTER 7   APPLICATION PROGRAMMING WITH JTAPI   267

Hello World in JTAPI   268
Implementing the Observer Interfaces   269
Revisiting the Phone Dialer Application with JTAPI-Lite   277
   Running the Application   284
   Glitches   289
Summary   290

CHAPTER 8   STANDARD EXTENSIONS TO THE CORE PACKAGE   293

Call Control Packages   294
   Call Control Core Components   294

CallControlAddress   298

CallControlCall   300

CallControlConnection   308

CallControlTerminal   313

CallControlTerminalConnection   316

The Call Control Observer Interfaces   319

CallControlAddressObserver   320

CallControlCallObserver   320

CallControlTerminalObserver   321

Call Control Events   322

Call Control Capabilities   324

Phone Packages   326

Phone Core Components   326

PhoneTerminalObserver   327

Component   327

Component Group   328

PhoneTerminal   329

PhoneButton   329

PhoneDisplay   330

PhoneGraphicDisplay   330

PhoneHookswitch   330

PhoneLamp   331

PhoneMicrophone   331

PhoneRinger   331

PhoneSpeaker   332

Phone Capabilities   335

ComponentCapabilities   335

ComponentGroupCapabilities   335

Phone Events   336

Media Packages   337

Media Core Components   337

Media Events   342

Call Center Packages   342

Call Center Core Components   343

Call Center Capabilities   368

Call Center Events   368

Private Data Packages   370

Private Data Core Components   370

Private Data Events 373
Private Data Capabilites 376
Summary 377

PART V REAL WORLD TELEPHONY PROGRAMMING 379

CHAPTER 9 EVENT MANAGEMENT IN JAVA 381

Event Management in a Nutshell 382
 A Brief Illustration 383
 A Set of Event Management Model Design Requirements 384
Dependency — The Java Observation Model 385
 Understanding the Observation Model 385
 Implementing the Observation Model 387
 Swallowing the Pill 389
 Requirements Satisfaction Using the Observation Model 391
Delegation — The Java Event Model 392
 Understanding the Delegation Model 393
 Trouble on the Horizon 394
 An Important Bunny Trail — True Events 395
 The Smalltalk Event Mechanism 396
 The Java Event Mechanism 397
 Requirements Satisfaction Using the Delegation Model 405
 *Morphing the Delegation Model into the Observation
  Model* 408
 Requirements Satisfaction Using Morphed Delegation 409
Enhancing the Observation Model 409
 Asynchronous Notification 410
A Java Message Management Idiom 413
 Understanding the Message Management Model 413
 Implementing the Message Management Model 415
 Asynchronizing the Message Management Model 417
 Is it Soup Yet? 418
 The CORBA Event Services 419
 Event Management in a Bombshell 420
Summary 421

CHAPTER 10   IDIOMS AND PATTERNS IN TELEPHONY   423

Idioms   424
  Idioms in Java   425
Patterns   446
  Java Component Patterns Useful in Telephony   447
  Server Telephone Patterns   470
  Implementing Persistent Graph Structures   474
Summary   478

CHAPTER 11   ORGANIZING A LARGE-SCALE TELECOM DEVELOPMENT PROJECT   479

Project Management in a Nutshell   480
  Requirements, Architecture, and Fabrication: The RAF Project
    Management Model   481
  Requirements Discovery   483
  Product Development   490
  Documentation Requirements   510
A Programmer's Perspective   512
  Distributed Programming   513
  Application, Library, and Systems Programming   514
  Planning a Telecom Project   514
Summary   517

PART VI   FUTURE TELEPHONY PROGRAMMING IN JAVA   519

CHAPTER 12   ALTERNATIVE JAVA TELEPHONY ENVIRONMENTS   521

Java and Consumer Devices   522
  The Web Phone and Other Consumer Devices   522
  Putting the Pedal to the Metal   523
  Where Does JTAPI Fit In?   523
Alternative Java Execution and Development
  Environments   523
  PersonalJava   524
  EmbeddedJava   524
  Java Sits on Top   525

Java and IP Telephony   526
    Who's Afraid of IP — and Why?   527
    How IP Telephony Works   527
    Where JTAPI Plugs into IP Telephony   527

APPENDIX A   TAPI SOURCE CODE   529

INDEX   559

PREFACE

Background

Telephony/telecom programming is essentially the practice of programming telephone services and integrating telecom devices with a computer. It is also known as Computer Telephony Integration (CTI) and other such terms. This application discipline encompasses everything from simple modem processing to the management of complex call routing strategies and switching systems used by the big carriers. Telecom programming involves using the largest distributed networks throughout the world.

By this definition, the major phone companies have been involved in telephony programming since their inception. For the workstation and midrange programmer, however, telephony programming has only recently moved from somewhat of a black art to more of a mainstream *software engineering* field. This has occurred as telephone service providers compete to deliver customized desktop systems to their clients. The phenomenal growth of the Internet in the 1990s has blurred the distinction among many of these types of services. This trend is likely to continue into the foreseeable future.

This book is about telephony programming. It is also about Application Programming Interfaces (APIs). APIs facilitate the development of robust software. As platforms, operating systems, and even programming languages converge, the requirement for universal vertical market APIs grows. To answer this perceived demand, a handful of companies have stepped up to the plate to offer their telephony API sets as potential *de facto* standards to the industry at large. Most notably, Microsoft Corporation, the ECTF, and Sun Microsystems have developed API sets and standards for the vertical telephony market. There are other players, but these three dominate the field.

Lastly (and probably most significantly), this book is about identifying and solving advanced programming issues that come up in a typical telephony environment, particularly using the telephony extensions of the Java programming language. This book is about the Java Telephony Application Programming Interface (JTAPI).

Overview

This is not a book championing a particular programming language or product over any other. Rather, it is written to address practical programming issues that arise in the design and construction of large and small telecom programs using Java. Its primary focus is to provide detailed coverage of implementing telephony applications using JTAPI, version 1.2. Along the way, related topics, and complementary and competing APIs are addressed and contrasted in an effort to aid the programmer in better understanding JTAPI. We actually implement a subset of a JTAPI telephony library. The techniques used here may be helpful to programmers implementing Java extension packages on Windows platforms.

What is JTAPI? JTAPI (Java Telephony Application Programming Interface) is Sun's telephony API implemented in the Java programming language. It is designed to ease platform-independent telephony software development. To this end, it is largely successful from the perspective of the application programmer. To the library programmers of the world, it presents much opportunity for employment! The first version of the JTAPI specification was released to the public on November 1, 1996. The updated specification, version 1.1, was released on February 1, 1997. The latest version 1.2 was released in October 1997. Further revisions are expected. However, they are not expected to change dramatically.

Why focus on JTAPI? There are three compelling reasons in no particular order. First, JTAPI is implemented in Java. Java is a modern object-oriented programming language that allows for the creation of quality software components. In addition, it provides for the development of platform-independent implementations and is designed to operate with software written in other programming languages, which is necessary in a telephony environment. Second, JTAPI is an API written for a vertical market. Standard software written for vertical markets hold the promise of software reuse and commonality not previously achieved. Third, the API itself is extremely well designed for the most part. Included are specifications for entities intuitively obvious in the telephony problem space. Therefore, telephony programming can be simplified if these standardized domain objects are used.

Approach

This is a different kind of programming book because JTAPI is a different kind of API. We approach the subject matter from a programmer's perspective as opposed to that of a "telephony expert's." We make every attempt to simplify complex (necessary, yet conceptually insignificant) details into common software abstractions. We agree with the approach taken by Sun Microsystems and others before them — that large segments of vertical markets can and should be modeled with standard software libraries that can be reused by large segments of the programming population.[1] We believe that telephony is a vertical market to be conquered by programmers. Although it is often presented that way, there is nothing inherent in a telephony solution that cannot or should not be expressed purely in software terms (as opposed to proprietary hardware, such as many PBX systems). We advocate the conversion of telephony systems from proprietary hardware to open software.

First, the book describes basic telephony programming by determining a set of fundamental services required of telephony applications. Standard telephony configurations are presented. It also covers general criteria for evaluating the suitability of any API and the ensuing design/usability trade-offs. The Java language is explored and compared to other suitable programming languages in an effort to aid the reader in determining if Java is a practical alternative for them to more traditional telephony programming approaches.

Second, this book describes existing telephony API sets, particularly Microsoft's TAPI. Microsoft's Windows NT is fast becoming the telephony platform of choice and the TAPI API is the industry standard for that platform. This "bunny trail" is a necessary prerequisite to discussing JTAPI in depth because JTAPI is designed so it may be implemented "on top of" TAPI, among other API sets.

Third, this book explores the JTAPI architecture in some detail and how well it satisfies typical telephony programming requirements. Telephony programming is currently a specialized field generally relying on home-grown code solutions, but Java can change all that for applications not requiring the speed of a compiled language. JTAPI vastly simplifies telephony programming by providing a protocol that is much simpler than most competing APIs. It also provides some level of portability in the form

---

1 This approach has been largely unsuccessful in the past, but that doesn't mean it's not the right thing to do.

of a platform-neutral API. There are drawbacks in that Java itself is interpreted; not to mention that JTAPI is usually layered upon TAPI on Windows platforms; other APIs on other platforms. And so, for some types of telephony applications, the Java approach may not be suitable due to performance considerations as well as nondeterministic garbage collection. But for the vast majority of applications, it will likely suffice, especially as both client and server-side processing power increases by orders of magnitude in shorter periods of time.

The portion of this book dealing with JTAPI is designed to be a companion to the online documentation provided by Sun Microsystems, not a copy of it. The Sun documentation is not required; this book is all that is necessary to gain a working and complete knowledge of JTAPI. However, Sun Microsystems has done an outstanding job documenting both the API and the design concepts behind the JTAPI architecture. And so this documentation is a nice complement to the book. However, we believe the background information and analysis as provided herein are still necessary for most programmers in order to properly understand how to make effective use of the product. If you are near a terminal, put down this book right now and download the JTAPI documentation and the specification itself from `http://www.javasoft.com`. Run a site search on the keyword "JTAPI" or "Java Media APIs" and follow the directions.

Fourth, a portion of this book describes what we are calling "real world" telephony programming issues. Although JTAPI makes code more understandable and simpler to use and maintain, it is designed using fairly advanced programming techniques and idioms. Although coding is easier once the API is understood, the learning curve may be a bit steep for those unfamiliar with advanced object-oriented design techniques. This excursion leads into both fundamental and advanced design topics and a thorough discussion of modern software engineering architectures. We even throw in some practical project management techniques tailored to telecom projects. This book is intended as a design guide as well as a practical reference for more advanced programming using Java and JTAPI.

Content

This book is organized in six principal parts:

Part I — Telecom Programming

Part II — Telephony APIs

Part III — Implementing JTAPI

Part IV — Telephony Programming with JTAPI

Part V — Real World Telephony Programming

Part VI — Future Telephony Programming in Java

Part I introduces telecom programming. Chapter 1 covers fundamental aspects of telephony processing environments, industry terminology, and provides an overview of the most popular API sets. We introduce JTAPI, the extension package to the Java programming language, developed by Sun Microsystems. In Chapter 2, we look at one important aspect of what distinguishes telecom programming from other types — namely, the hardware that programs control. Fundamental to how this hardware operates is an understanding of bus architectures.

Part II contains Chapters 3 and 4. Here, we provide an examination of the Java programming language. Issues surrounding the use of Java are explored as they pertain to telephony programming. Chapter 4 is an in-depth coverage of JTAPI. Featured is an exhaustive analysis of the JTAPI API, including sample code and the complete software definition of the core packages.

In Part III, we look at what it takes to create a JTAPI library. Although most implementations will leverage existing platform APIs such as TAPI, JTAPI is equally suitable for native implementations. In Chapter 5, we examine the importance of APIs; first in general, and then as they pertain to telecom programming. A few simple telephony applications are created using Microsoft's TAPI API. In Chapter 6, an approach to providing a Win32-JTAPI binding is presented and a partial JTAPI implementation is produced.

In Part IV, we finally begin application programming in JTAPI. We use the library we created in Chapter 6 to produce a simple JTAPI application in Chapter 7. Chapter 8 introduces the remaining packages provided with JTAPI — namely, the subpackages that are to provide capability beyond the core functionality of placing and receiving calls.

Part V covers real world telephony programming. In Chapter 9, we take an excursion into an area that is critical to providing a JTAPI implementation — the production of message management models. These models are used for providing registration and subsequent asynchronous notification of events. Chapter 10 draws on Doug Martin's extensive experience in the telephony field coupled with Spencer's application of some of these idioms and patterns in Java. Implementing a specification is not always as straightforward as understanding one. And so this section deals with these kinds of issues. In Chapter 11, we approach project life cycle and management issues as they relate to a typical telephony project and present a telecom design methodology.

Part VI, the final section, covers future telephony programming in Java. Chapter 12 provides a brief examination of related API sets as proposed for Java as standard extension packages. It discusses how these APIs may be used to complement and extend the use of JTAPI for consumer devices such as Web phones.

Audience

The primary audience for this book is experienced programmers familiar with object-oriented design concepts and programming languages. Some telephony background is helpful, but not required. However, the focus is on advanced Java programming and telephony programming issues. What we mean by advanced is that the material is not advanced in the sense that low-level telephony programming is advanced. We do not delve into programming RS-232 interfaces and UARTs; that is great advanced material but is not the focus of this book.[2] Nor do we delve much into the complexity resulting from nonstandard Computer Telephony Integration (CTI) product integration efforts (this seems to be the focus of most computer-telephony books). Instead, the material is advanced in three other senses.

First, we do not cover general telephony programming concepts except in a cursory sense in Chapters 1 and 2. Second, no fundamental programming material is presented. It is assumed that the reader is proficient with Windows programming as well as the C/C++ and Java programming languages. Discussions about the Java programming language focus on its strengths and weaknesses as a telephony programming and design language as well as those features of the language that may be capitalized on to gain maximum benefit in a telephony environment. Third, the material goes beyond programming into design concepts, which may be foreign to those not formally trained in software methodologies. In this sense, readers with exposure to operating system concepts and data modeling probably will not find the material challenging; but we hope to hold their interest as we apply it to the subject matter.

About the Author

This book is born of a collaboration between two programmers — one a contract application programmer and mentor (Spencer Roberts), and the other a domain expert telephony programmer and architect (Doug Martin).

Spencer Roberts aced his first computer class in 1976 at the University of California at San Diego, California in UCSD Pascal, FORTRAN, and COBOL with the help of a very smart friend, Charles Dahms. (Chuck, wherever you are, thanks.) He later went on to obtain a bachelor's degree in economics there, and a master's degree in software engineering with distinction at National University in San Diego. Mr. Roberts has been programming professionally since 1985 and is president of Titus Corporation, a freelance contract programming and consulting firm. He has worked with a wide range of both DoD and commercial systems ranging from engineering applications to business systems, C3 satellite systems, telecom systems,

---

2 This kind of programming is rarely done in the private sector; instead, libraries are purchased and linked into application code.

and medical systems. Mr. Roberts specializes in the design and construction of object-oriented distributed systems and concurrent programming in multiple languages with companies like MCI, ICS, and Micromedex. He may be reached at `spencer.roberts@titusoft.com` or through Prentice-Hall.

Although not an official author of this book, Doug Martin provided extensive input and feedback to the book. Without Doug's help, we never would have taken on the task! Doug earned a bachelor of science degree at the University of Colorado and a master's degree in computer science from the CIBAR Systems Institute. He is the chief technical officer and a principal of Interactive Communication Systems (ICS), Inc. Mr. Martin has been the primary system architect for some 50 different computer telephony systems developed by ICS. Prior to joining ICS, Mr. Martin held senior development engineering positions at TRW, where he developed applications and system software for command, control, communications, and intelligence systems used in major Air Force intelligence centers. He may be reached at `dmartin@icstelephony.com`.

Acknowledgments

Most books provide a dizzying array of names thanking folks for their contributions (you may include this among them, I suppose). But the primary contributions here, however, have been in the lost time a father could have spent with his children — time I will never be able to replace. I can only pray that this book will serve as a reminder to my kids as to what dad did "for a living" all day long and that it will provide a means for me to spend more time with my family.

First I would like to thank the technical editor of this series, Alan McClellan, for providing me the opportunity to write this book. Alan is not only a pleasure to work with, but he is a really great guy. I would like to thank the following colleagues for their technical contributions to this effort: Doug Martin of ICS for his concepts and overview of the telephony material. Doug is a premier expert in telephony programming. Along with his company ICS, Doug has developed some of the most advanced and scalable telephony systems in production today; David C. Hay for his technical editing of the object/data modeling section in Chapter Eleven. David is the expert in this field and we deeply appreciate his contributions. You need to pick up a copy of his book, *Data Model Patterns: Conventions of Thought*. Dave may be reached at `http://www.essentialstrategies.com`; Ralph and Vanessa Moore of Prentice-Hall for their efficient management of the production process; Greg Doench for his executive support; and Steve Farmer for technical editing. Steve is a poet in the bay area with some neat stuff that you should read. He's my twin brother and the *true* writer in the family.

I would like to thank my beautiful wife Susie and my children, Spencer, Weston, and Noah, for their patience and support during this project. Boys, I hope you will always be proud of your dad (I hear it gets harder as you get older). I would also like to thank Pastors Rick Brown, Bob Havenor, Chuck Swindoll, and Scott Donteville for their spiritual support. Most importantly, I thank Jesus Christ for His grace and a debt that can never truly be repaid.

We also would like to extend our gratitude to Rational Corporation for providing the Rational Rose OO modeling software used throughout the book. Rose is an indispensable tool in our daily programming arsenal. Visit them at `http://www.rational.com`.

The Essential JTAPI FTP Site

Source code for all of the examples in the book are available from the Prentice Hall ftp site, `ftp.prenhall.com`. This site is accessible via anonymous ftp.

A single ZIP file named `examples.zip` contains the source code for all of the examples in the book. After logging in, change directories to the `essential_jtapi` directory as described below and download `examples.zip` to your hard drive.

```
cd /pub/ptr/professional_computer_science.w-022/roberts/essential_jtapi
```

If you have any problem downloading the file, you can also access the source code for the examples via the Prentice Hall website. Go to `www.phptr.com`, search for Essential JTAPI, and follow the appropriate links to download the `examples.zip` file.

PART I

TELECOM PROGRAMMING

Telecom[1] programming is defined here as the integration and application of telephone networks and services with computer systems. These so-called telephony systems range in size and complexity from simple e-mail accounts on dumb terminals, to systems that integrate with large computer networks that host satellite and microwave links across the world. Of course, the telephone networks themselves are in fact computer systems — and so the distinction is sometimes blurry. Nevertheless, most telecom programs deal with either integrating phone services with an application or managing those services.

If this is telecom programming, what is telephony programming? Throughout this book, we often use the terms interchangeably because from our perspective, it really doesn't matter. However, we generally refer to telephony programming as a lower level of abstraction than telecom programming. At the same time, it is more general. *Telephony* programming might deal with programming a UART, implementing a telephony library, or writing an application program that uses a particular telephony library. While *telecom* programming also encompasses this last activity, it also addresses the design and construction of more large-scale applications that may encompass many different forms of distributed processing, not just telephony.

---

1 Telecom means *telecommunications*.

1

In Chapter 1, we investigate the telecom industry, its terminology, and some of the hardware used. We are introduced for the first time to JTAPI. Chapter 2 provides an overview of an interesting facet of telephony programming — namely, bus architectures.

Chapter 1   *AN OVERVIEW OF COMPUTER TELEPHONY*

"Thriving on Chaos"
Tom Peters

The computer telephony industry is a very large one, encompassing all the major telecom companies worldwide (MCI, AT&T, Sprint, TCI, and the like) as well as thousands of local carriers and service providers. It is a $200 billion industry that dwarfs the application software[1] industry by a few orders of magnitude. Currently, it is a curious blend of relatively archaic telephone technology and state-of-the-art computer technology. It is widely believed that these technologies will merge in the near future.

For decades, the telephone companies worldwide have held government-sponsored oligopolies[2] on telephone services. This has led to the creation of proprietary telephony systems that are standardized only to the extent that they benefit the implementation for a particular vendor or public utility. The large service providers have been generally indifferent to efforts to standardize systems — why should they?

In 1996, however, all that changed (at least in the United States). Congress began to deregulate the telecommunications industry. This has led to a revolution in competition. Indeed, there would now seem to be even less incentive than ever before for vendor cooperation and intersystem collusion. Yet, in a sense, we are seeing just the opposite occur. Software

---

1 Shrink-wrapped desktop application software like word processors.
2 Oligopoly: one of several quarantined monopolies.

3

giants such as IBM and Sun are teaming together with such telephony vendors as Lucent and Dialogic to produce common API sets. Industry user groups striving to lower overall development costs are spearheading these efforts. In Europe, cellular telephones are already in widespread use. It seems everyone has one and uses it regularly. Speech recognition software technology has finally reached a point where it is both reasonably accurate and cost-effective.

All of these factors seem to be pointing to a telecom market that has the potential to change the manner in which much commerce is accomplished today. This market will require skilled telephony programmers at all abstraction levels including the application, library, and system levels. Let's get started with some background material.

Telecom Fundamentals

Like any industry, telephony is full of its own terminology and acronyms. It is far beyond the scope of this book to fully describe the myriad of terms involved; yet it is essential to get a grip on some of the more fundamental concepts. We may proceed as we would normally in analyzing any development project. Let's examine the *problem space*.

The Telephony Problem Space

As programmers, we think in terms of understanding the problem space. In this sense, the telephony industry is no different than any other vertical market — it is best understood by attempting to model it. If we can model it, we can understand it; if we can understand it, we can code it.

High-Level Telephony Entities

We can intuitively guess many of the real world objects commonly used in telephony applications. All telephony applications must somehow model the following fundamental telephony abstractions at a minimum:

- Phone (a.k.a. handset, terminal)
- Address (a.k.a. phone number)
- Telephone Line
- Call
- Modem, Fax, or Board (optional device)

Voice- and data-recognition equipment can provide much more capability, but these are the fundamental services. Simply put, a user (or a machine) must at least be able to place and disconnect calls, and sometimes to answer them. More sophisticated applications manipulate calls as they are routed to their final destinations. In a more general sense, computers must be able to process information and communicate in a distributed environment using specialized auxiliary devices. All of these are design entities internal to the telephony problem space. But how do calls get from one endpoint to another? Via an external path known as the telephone network.

The Telephone Network

Telephony applications pass information over a ***telephone network***. From the time that the telephone call leaves its origination and reaches its destination, the data may have changed forms many times and may have passed through mediums of many different types. Specifically, the actual signals are typically converted back and forth between analog and digital and may be passed through twisted wire, microwave radio signals, fiber optics, multiplexers, and even satellite systems. From the application programmer's perspective, the telephone network is an external system; the ultimate black box, if you will. It is a puffy white cloud that moves the call from point to point. Usually, this transmission is completely out of the control of the programmer, although there are systems today that put a portion of this control in the hands of not only programmers, but also users.

The network may be of several different types including combinations of those types. By far the most common is Plain Old Telephone Service (POTS), which is your basic analog telephone line. POTS supports the transmission of video, voice, or data, but only one type at a time. In other words, a single call must transmit voice only or data only. In addition, POTS transmissions support one channel per line. Besides POTS, more advanced network connections are possible, including connections over Integrated Services Digital Network (ISDN) networks, CENTREX centers, and Private Branch Exchange (PBX) connections. ISDN transmission is 100% digital and is essentially a better POTS. CENTREX services allow users to log in to centralized telephony servers and utilize telephony services while using the server's specialized hardware instead of their own. The advantage of this is that the client only needs a means to communicate (usually a modem); they require no other specialized hardware.

In general, there are three types of these black-box interfaces with which a client application may communicate. The first and most common interface is depicted in **Figure 1.1** as the Home Use Path (for lack of a better name). It is best suited for home use and is comprised of an analog line pair-wire POTS setup called a loop start or a ground start. Here, the computer sends analog signals back and forth over two wires (red and green) to a junction box on the side of your house.[3] From there, it is sent either underground or overhead via telephone wires to the telephone company's central office (CO). From there, the CO does whatever it wants with the signals, passing them on to trunks and then to waiting ears (or other systems) everywhere. All desktop e-mail and browser applications (e.g., AOL

---

3 Check it out! Go over to your wall socket right now and find the colored wires.

and Microsoft Internet Explorer) that people run from their homes support this type of interface. Even though users are "surfing the net," they are almost always hanging ten over an analog phone line. In Windows, this is accomplished by way of Dial-Up Networking. As far as the programmer is concerned, the programming interface is either the vendor's API or a standard Computer Telephony (CT) API such as TAPI or JTAPI. The physical interface is the wall jack.

Figure 1.1 *Home and Business Analog Links*

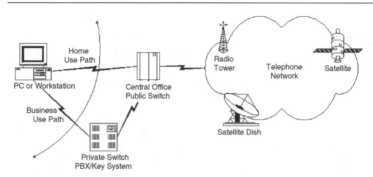

The second type of interface is what we call a Business Use Path (see **Figure 1.1**). The computer hooks to what is called a switch (either a PBX or a Key System). Most businesses go with this kind of system because it can offer them control over the routing, transferring, and parking of, say, customer calls, and it allows them to call each other in the same building without using public outside lines. PBXs support a "wall jack" interface just like the CO option, but many are also programmable. Unfortunately, these types of interfaces are usually proprietary.

The third type of interface is the server application. A server application can wrap a PBX or perform the services of a PBX and much more. For example, companies such as Interactive Communications Systems (ICS) create specialized server applications that process incoming calls at alarming rates. Client applications either write to their API or more typically send predefined messages understood by the server application.

CT in a Nutshell

In order for a CT system to do anything other than just place, hold, and disconnect calls, it must be able to process two types of information: Automated Number Identification (ANI) and Dialed Number Identification Service (DNIS). Caller ID service is a form of ANI (pronounced "Annie") information. Basically ANI tells which phone number is the calling party along with possibly other customer information. DNIS provides the other piece of the puzzle — the number dialed. This relationship is depicted in **Figure 1.2**.

Figure 1.2 *ANI and DNIS*

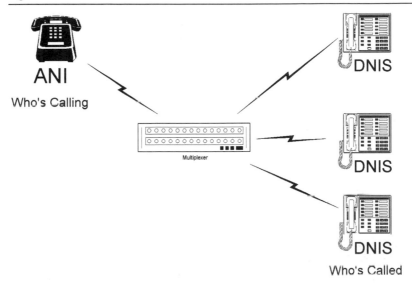

The lightning bolts in **Figure 1.2** represent ANI and DNIS data sent as a part of the call (say between rings of the phone) that may be captured by a CT system. Both ANI and DNIS are not provided automatically with standard phone services; they must be ordered and paid for as additional services.

Once the originating and terminating addresses have been determined, CT systems can provide an array of other services and functions. These include, but are not limited to, the following:

- Automated Fax Processing
- Banking
- Insurance Claims Processing
- Inventory
- Medical Records
- Order Processing
- Paging
- Registrations
- Speech Synthesis, Concatenation, and Recognition
- Time Reporting and Scheduling

Of course, many of these same functions may be accomplished on a computer alone. In truth, the telephone is merely a medium of information transfer. But, however more prevalent computers (as we know them today) are becoming in modern society, they are never likely to replace the telephone as a convenient and now portable medium of communication. Human beings (even programmers) will hesitate to turn on a computer and log into a system before they will pick up a phone. And therein lies the most compelling argument for becoming familiar with computer telephony in general.

Desktop vs. Server Applications

Most telecom applications may be loosely classified as either desktop or server applications. Desktop applications usually deal with the initiation, termination, and processing of a single telephone call at a time. Normally, these types of applications reside on workstations or PCs equipped with a single modem (although this physical configuration is not the determining characteristic). In contrast, server applications always answer telephone calls and must process multiple client calls, often simultaneously. In addition, server boxes usually house multiple telephony boards. They may also place calls just like desktop applications — but they usually do so only as a service to some client.

Although normally implemented in hardware, PBXs are conceptually primitive server applications. More modern server systems are implemented in software and may even take the place of a PBX. They are equipped with multichannel telephony boards utilizing specialized bus architectures. Server systems such as these are infinitely more flexible than PBXs because they are fully programmable. For these types of systems, call routing strategies and *coverage policies*[4] are essential. As one might expect, the line between desktop and server applications is often blurred. In a sense, desktop applications may be perceived as servers if they receive calls; conversely server applications may place calls and therefore exhibit desktop qualities.

In the past, some APIs (such as TAPI) have been criticized due to their desktop-centric focus. The argument says that they are fine for desktop applications but are wholly inadequate for server applications. This distinction is quickly disappearing as capabilities are added to these APIs as they mature. Further, there is a hint of wisdom in the evolution of these APIs. Both TAPI and JTAPI build their API sets upon a desktop-centric call model. Why? Because the services required of server applications also require these same fundamental capabilities — to place, disconnect, and answer calls. As we study the architectures of these more modern APIs, we will see this pattern evolve.

Threads and Telephony

Threads play an integral part in telephony programming, primarily because there is a constant interaction with one or more devices. In a device-centric

---

4 What to do when no one answers.

application, threads are essential because the communication between the application and the device is often a tenuous and time-consuming activity. No other process wants to wait for the handshaking and I/O to complete before continuing on; rather, they should be notified when such communication is complete. Delegating I/O to a separate thread also increases the fault tolerance of the application — if the subprogram invocation fails, the thread may be terminated and the application need not be terminated as well.[5] In order to accomplish this, some form of *asynchronous communication* must be used.

Threads are also used to implement asynchronous communication. In fact, they are the only practical way to implement truly asynchronous communication[6] on a single box. Before the widespread popularity of Windows NT, OS/2, and Linux, asynchronous communication had to be programmed from scratch. For example, in the DOS world, many board manufacturers implemented their own proprietary quasi-threaded APIs as interrupt-handling TSR callback routines. They had no choice; DOS is not multithreaded. However, the threaded landscape has improved significantly because nearly all major operating systems now provide direct programmable thread support.

Multitasking vs. Multiprocessing

Threads are awesome. It is important to note, however, that no matter the compiler's intent, *processing is actually sequential* on a single CPU system. Recall that on a single processor system, at any point in time only one thread may be executing. Access to the CPU is serialized because there is only one processor.[7] This is true even in the most parallel applications because the processor simulates concurrency by quickly interleaving thread execution. We are multitasking — not truly multiprocessing. In other words, we are executing concurrently, but not in parallel.

Due to the rapid influx of a potentially large number of inputs, telephony processing can actually push the processing limits of a single-CPU architecture. In 1996, ICS set a world record by being the first company to handle 240 lines concurrently on a single processor box. Using a threaded architecture, the system works as expected — in fact, it screams. But they believe there may be a limit to how many threads can run concurrently on a box before the degradation of excess context switching begins to surpass the benefits of using threads. This theoretical limit is depicted in **Figure 1.3**. Of course, as processor speed increases, this is theoretically less of a problem. The problem doesn't go away, it is merely less noticeable.

---

5 Of course this assumes a well-behaved device routine, one that does not bring down the entire operating system upon its own failure. Unfortunately, this seems to be the default behavior of far too many telephony device drivers.

6 This is not entirely true — one may also use separate processes. Threads, however, are preferred due to their lightweight nature.

7 Threads are neat things, but they cannot defy the laws of physics.

Figure 1.3 *Negative Effect of Threads on System Responsiveness*

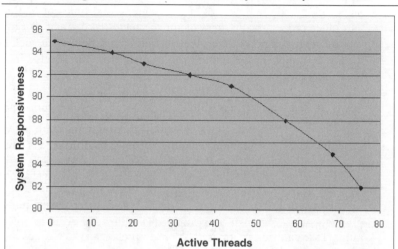

The only way to get true parallel processing is, of course, by using multiple processors. Intuitively, one might think that a multiprocessor machine would automatically improve things — that one would see linear improvement with each additional processor added. But this is not the case. Adding processors always increases performance, but at a rate always less than constant and always first rising and then diminishing at some point toward zero. Nevertheless, threads are so critical to telephony programming that they cannot be ignored.

The Challenge of Telephony

The biggest problem with telephone systems is that they have never been designed to integrate with computer systems. What this usually means is that the telephone hardware[8] was not designed to operate with computer software; thereby creating an integration nightmare. In retrospect, all telephony systems could have been implemented in software (albeit with a substantial performance penalty). Instead, most legacy systems in use today are implemented with hardware circuitry. They generally lack an adequate software interface. These types of interfaces can be made to work, but only by kluge. They encourage hacks and shaky handshakes between systems. This fact has heavily influenced the server side of the design of both TAPI and JTAPI.

In contrast, the desktop side of the house (where software emphasis is heavy) is more easily defined. The purchasing power of the masses has led to de facto standards in modem capabilities, which has enhanced commonality in the functionality provided by desktop vendors. Although the APIs are different, the capabilities are essentially the same.

---

8 Including both handset devices and server systems like PBX systems.

How in the world will this mess ever get cleaned up? Through a process of standardization of course. Enter the APIs ...

JTAPI to the Rescue

If the communication between CT systems can be standardized in software, the integration problems can be mitigated. The best way to standardize interfaces in software is to standardize APIs. JTAPI is an extremely high level standard API. Those programmers used to programming APIs such as Microsoft's TAPI will find application programming with JTAPI to be a delight. Those programmers coming from a traditional CTI background will be even happier; yet they may have a hard time understanding how such a high-level API can solve their problems. In some senses, it simply cannot. Many of the problems associated with integrating computers and telephones will be with us for a very long time. But the promises of the Java language telephony extensions lie not only in the solutions they imply but also in the decreased maintenance of evolving software. In the production of highly maintainable software, the ugly details associated with getting disparate systems to interoperate must be hidden from the application programmer just as it must be hidden from the ultimate user. JTAPI does not specify low-level solutions, although it does provide a standard mechanism for dealing with them (just as TAPI does). But how can a programming language help reduce complexity? With objects, of course.

Objects Aid Understanding Telephony...

Using a procedural mindset, it is easy to become overwhelmed with the vast amount of information necessary to comprehend the telephony problem space. Ditto for most telephony APIs. Object-oriented APIs such as JTAPI simplify telephony modeling by providing many of these objects (both logical and physical) for the application programmer. Procedural APIs (like TAPI) do not; however, the mapping is relatively straightforward for experienced modelers. But the object-oriented paradigm is vastly preferred. In this book, we demonstrate how the predesign of these problem space entities can simplify telephony programming if for no other reason than they help to "explain" the problem space to the developer. Although grasping the entire architecture is not necessarily a straightforward mental process for all programmers,[9] once the learning curve is complete, the development process can be greatly simplified. At the very least, it can be neatly compartmentalized into functional layers.

... And JTAPI Is Comprised of Objects

JTAPI approaches the telephony problem space in a unique manner. Fundamental capabilities are modeled and provided in a "core" telephony

---

9 That's why we wrote this book!

module called a *package*. As more capabilities are needed, they are provided in subpackages that build on the capabilities of the *core* package. The JTAPI core package provides what is known as a **call model** in telecom jargon.

JTAPI is comprised of a set of cooperating classes[10] that implement a call model. Each class instance (object) has a well-defined state and a set of correlated events that are triggered as a result of state transitions. The operations defined for these objects implement the call model. So JTAPI is essentially a set of predefined objects that transition between predefined states signaling predefined events at different layers of abstraction. Applications register for these events and then react accordingly (i.e., as they see fit). **Listing 1.1** shows a code snippet to introduce you to some of the classes used in JTAPI.[11]

Listing 1.1 *Sample JTAPI Classes*

```
Call aCall = aprovider.createCall();
Address phoneNumber = aProvider.getAddress("5551212");
Terminal[] telephones = phoneNumber.getTerminals();
Connection[] twoConnections =
    aCall.connect(telephones[0], phoneNumber, "5551212");
```

The simplicity of this programming interface is almost striking. Objects are intuitively named and the services they provide are expected. Those readers having experience with any other telephony API will appreciate the expressive power of this API. Those who have never programmed using a telephony API will quickly grasp the intuitive nature of this one.

Let's take a look at some of the sample code provided with the JTAPI API documentation. An outgoing call is presented as follows:

```
import javax.telephony.*;
import javax.telephony.events.*;
import MyOutCallObserver;

/* * Places a telephone call from 476111 to 5551212 */

public class Outcall {

    public static final void main(String args[]) {

        /*
         * Create a provider by first obtaining the default
```

---

10 Actually, most are Java interfaces, not classes — but this is a detail for now.

11 This is the only nonworking code in the book — it won't compile. This is intended to show the names of classes/interfaces without complicating it with exception handling and some other details we will get into later.

```
 * implementation of JTAPI and then the default
 * provider of that implementation.
 */

Provider myprovider = null;
try {
   JtapiPeer peer = JtapiPeerFactory.getJtapiPeer(null);
   myprovider = peer.getProvider(null);
} catch (Exception excp) {
   System.out.println("Can't get Provider: " +
     excp.toString());
   System.exit(0);
}

/*
 * We need to get the appropriate objects associated
 * with the originating side of the telephone call.
 * We ask the Address for a list of Terminals on it
 * and arbitrarily choose one.
 */

Address origaddr = null;
Terminal origterm = null;
try {
   origaddr = myprovider.getAddress("4761111");
   /* Just get some Terminal on this Address */
   Terminal[] terminals = origaddr.getTerminals();
   if (terminals == null) {
      System.out.println("No Terminals on Address.");
      System.exit(0);
   }
   origterm = terminals[0];
} catch (Exception excp) {
   // Handle exceptions;
}

/*
 * Create the telephone call object and add an observer
 */
Call mycall = null;
try {
   mycall = myprovider.createCall();
   mycall.addObserver(new MyOutCallObserver());
} catch (Exception excp) {
```

```
    // Handle exceptions
  }


/*      * Place the telephone call.      */
  try {
     Connection c[] = mycall.connect(origterm, origaddr,
        "5551212");
  } catch (Exception excp) {
     // Handle all Exceptions
  }
  }
}
```

A cursory glance at this code reveals the general nature of programming in JTAPI. The major hurdle using the API is not so much mastering the API as it is understanding the object model. Compare this code to any other telephony API. Even though the terms may be foreign at the moment, the code is easier to read than say a typical listing using, say, TAPI.

An incoming call is presented as follows:

```
import javax.telephony.*;
import javax.telephony.events.*;


/*
 * The MyInCallObserver class implements the
 * CallObserver and recieves all Call-related
 * events. */


public class MyInCallObserver implements CallObserver {

  public void callChangedEvent(CallEv[] evlist) {

     TerminalConnection termconn;
     String name;
     for (int i = 0; i < evlist.length; i++) {
        if (evlist[i] instanceof TermConnEv) {
           termconn = null;
           name = null;
           try {
              TermConnEv tcev = (TermConnEv)evlist[i];
              Terminal term = termconn.getTerminal();
              termconn = tcev.getTerminalConnection();
              name = term.getName();
           } catch (Exception excp) {
           // Handle exceptions.
```

```
        }
        String msg = "TerminalConnection to Terminal: "
                        + name + " is ";
        if (evlist[i].getID() == TermConnActiveEv.ID) {
            System.out.println(msg + "ACTIVE");
        } else if (evlist[i].getID() ==
              TermConnRingingEv.ID) {
            System.out.println(msg + "RINGING");
            /* Answer the telephone Call using "inner
             * class" thread */
            try {
                final TerminalConnection _tc = termconn;
                Runnable r = new Runnable() {
                    public void run()         {
                        try {
                                tc.answer();
                        } catch (Exception excp){
                                // handle answer exceptions
                        }
                    };
                };
                Thread T = new Thread(r);
                 T.start();
            } catch (Exception excp) {
                // Handle Exceptions;
            }
        } else if (evlist[i].getID() ==
              TermConnDroppedEv.ID) {
            System.out.println(msg + "DROPPED");
        }
      }
    }
  }
}
```

Looks easy, eh? Where's the DLL? Can't wait to download it and try it out, huh? Not so fast, Bucky. Unfortunately, using JTAPI means first finding a JTAPI implementation.

JTAPI Implementations

A JTAPI implementation is just that — an implementation of the JTAPI specification. On Windows platforms, we might expect to find a module called say, JTAPI.dll. But finding one (especially for free) can be a rather disappointing exercise. Many a computer telephony programmer has rushed excitedly to the Java Web site prepared to download some sample code and test it out only to come away very disillusioned. What they find is the sample code just presented and the JTAPI specification in all its glory — but no software to go with it. In other words, JTAPI is a specification and only a specification — no more, no less. Actually, this practice of providing an interface specification and no code is a very common one followed by almost all of the Java extension packages. More on this later, but does that mean we are hosed?

That depends upon your perspective. Once you cool down from the trauma of coming away empty-handed, you gather your senses and realize that there is actually no other alternative. To provide a JTAPI implementation, Sun would have to first pick a specific platform and even then the implementation would work for only a subset of the modems available. For example, they might target the Windows platform (not very likely due to the ill blood between Sun and Microsoft) and then find a way for the majority of modems on Windows to operate with the library. However, this task is not as daunting as it first seems. Why? JTAPI is designed from the ground up to be implemented "on top of" platform telephony libraries like TAPI.

JTAPI may be implemented in one of two ways. It may act as a Java interface to existing telephony APIs (e.g., TSAPI and TAPI), or it may be used as a Java interface to proprietary service packages of a particular board manufacturer (a.k.a. a native implementation). Of course, board vendors or third parties may provide both types of interfaces. Because the Java runtime is generally portable, JTAPI applications are equally as portable[12] with expected adjustments for hardware and platform peculiarities. Scalability is achieved by avoiding the specification of transmission protocols at the application-programming layer. This architecture frees the application programmer from the burden of dealing with distributed objects. This burden is now shifted to the library programmer providing the JTAPI implementation. Multitier architectures are encouraged but not directly supported by the JTAPI specification except in the sense that some objects operate at a lower level of abstraction than others.

Vendors are encouraged (but not required) to provide implementations that operate in one of two configurations: network computer (NC) or desktop. Note that the NC configuration usually requires the modem or telephony board be located on a server somewhere. In this case, the network is the computer — and so the telephone is the network!

The capabilities of a JTAPI implementation follow a service specification model similar to that of the Common Object Request Broker

---

12 We discuss portability later and find that it is a relative term with respect to telephony implementations.

Architecture (CORBA). Applications query a so-called *service provider* to determine the level of support or capability provided. This feature allows application programmers the ability to determine telecom support at run-time. Providers may be mixed and matched or even swapped out in real time. For example, if a switch goes down during an earthquake, an application may be able to determine this by simply querying the provider and swap it out for another provider's service.

Later we will delve into all the gory details of the JTAPI API. For now, let's shift our attention to some more general telephony information to round out our intentionally shallow coverage of computer telephony.

Telephony Implementations

Here, we discuss some implementation details common to all telephony setups. Regardless of the API used, these setup issues are either already in place or require some initial configuration before telephony processing can commence. We will investigate hardware configurations, remote communication, and telephony protocols. In many cases, the application programmer does not need to be concerned about these issues, but it is good information to know. In other cases, some telephony functions will not be possible unless a particular configuration is used. We begin by investigating the telephony support found in typical hardware products.

Telephony Support in Hardware

In general, telephony hardware support comes in three different levels: basic modem (Hayes/AT), voice-data modems (AT+V), and telephony cards. Basic modems support the placement of outgoing calls and usually the receipt of incoming calls. Voice-data modems add voice services such as parking calls, call forwarding, and caller ID. The "Lexus" version of telephony hardware support comes with telephony cards (ISA or PCI boards that provide extended telephony capabilities). This relationship is depicted in **Figure 1.4**.

For basic telephony services, a typical modem will suffice. But for any professional-quality telephony application (especially server applications), telephony boards are well worth the money and are in fact the only way to go. Most modems only support one phone line where telephony boards come in multiple-lines-per-board configurations. In addition, these products often supply proprietary bus interfaces to pass control signals between cards within a box. This allows for greater call throughput and increased call-handling parallelism capability.

Figure 1.4 *Telephony Hardware Support*

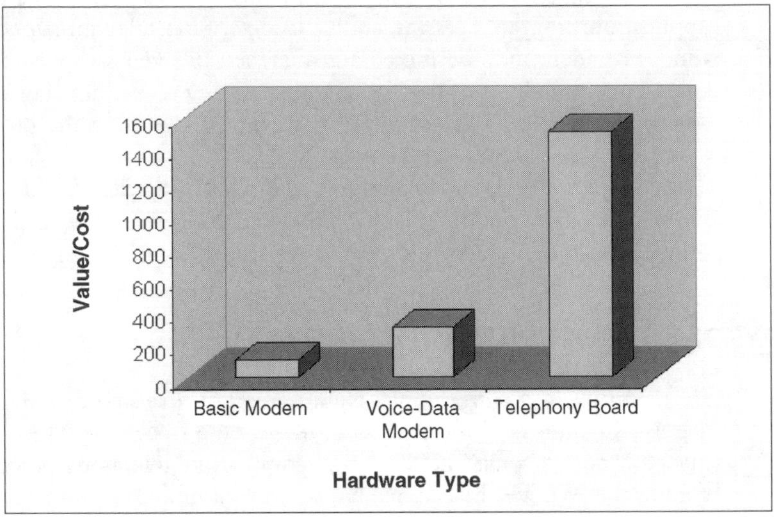

Remote Communication

Most telephony applications ultimately communicate over a modem device. The reason for this is that computers process information digitally while local loop phone service (that provided from the phone company "main office switch" to your location and back) is processed in an analog format.[13] In the near future, this may change as digital phone services replace current analog lines. But worldwide, analog service will be around for a very long time. **Figure 1.5** depicts a typical modem communication *event trace*.

In terms of remote communication, the primary difference between telephony programming and other types of distributed programming is the *medium* over which remote communication takes place. Keeping this in mind, distributed telephony systems can be designed in the same manner as, say, a corporate information network, subject to hardware constraints. In other words, the communication medium may be isolated to a lower layer of software — the data transport protocol. Properly designed, telephony communication medium becomes an implementation issue. Of course, the details at lower levels of abstraction will differ, but the architectural principles are the same. We'll revisit this subject shortly and again when we investigate the scalability requirements for telephony APIs.

---

13 Once the call reaches a switch point, it is usually converted to digital format by the phone company for high-speed transmission, then converted back to analog if the destination requires.

Figure 1.5 *Modem Communication*

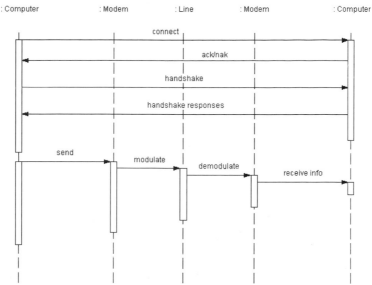

Although most small-scale desktop applications connect from a local modem, the actual telephony communication (from the computer to the telephone device and back) can occur on either a client or a server machine.

In the following section, we begin to look at the physical characteristics of a telephony environment. There are multiple ways in which telephones and computers may be configured. Each of these configurations affects the manner in which the system fundamentally operates.

Telephony Configurations

There are a variety of ways a computer may be configured with a telephone. These physical configurations determine certain capabilities and disallow others, regardless of the API or protocol used to communicate. The first and simplest configuration is the *phone-centric* configuration. Here, the service switch is connected to the telephone and the telephone is in turn connected to the computer. This configuration is depicted in **Figure 1.6**.

Here, the computer may monitor or control an incoming call *after* the telephone answers it provided it has gained access to the line prior to the call. We might call this the Watergate configuration. The computer may have a telephony board installed, or it may communicate in a more primitive fashion through the serial port using HAYES modem commands.

Figure 1.6 *Phone-Centric Configuration Taking an Inbound Call*

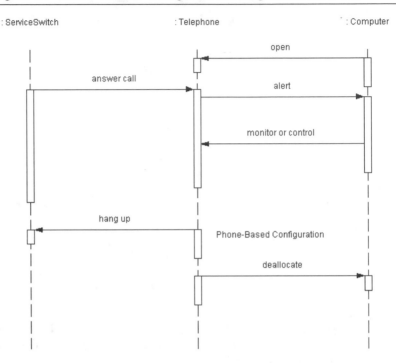

By far the most common setup is a *computer-centric* configuration (see **Figure 1.7**). Here, the computer is placed *between* the switch and the handset and actually answers the call instead of the telephone handset. The primary benefit of this configuration is that it allows for less human intervention. It is vastly more flexible as well. Once the computer has the call it can do just about anything it wants, providing the software supports telephony capabilities.

Both of the configurations investigated so far seem to be primarily desktop-centric. But as we said earlier, a telephony configuration certainly does not have to reside on one machine. There are also client/server configurations. A *LAN-based server* can tie multiple telephone-line connections to a single switch. Operations invoked at any of the client computers are forwarded over the LAN to the server, which houses one or more telephony boards. In this configuration, the server may use ***third-party call control*** between the server and the switch to implement the client's call-control requests. (Third-party call control is external control of the call itself regardless of the media. It is the process of connecting two or more calls together by an external entity.)

Figure 1.7 *A Computer-Centric Telephony Configuration*

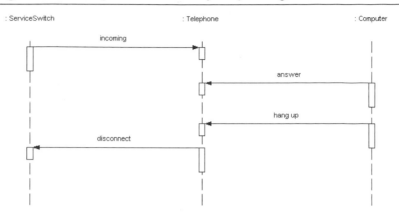

Data Transport Protocols

Again, communication between the client and the server can use any appropriate medium. Any programmable device can be used to transmit telephony information provided the telephony protocol supports the transmission of that media.

Because telephony information (like all other information) is ultimately a series of bytes transmitted in either analog or digital format, any transmission protocol that "understands" telephony can be used as the underlying data transport mechanism. This means that programmers are free to use CORBA, LDAP — Lightweight Directory Access Protocol, TCP/IP, X.25, or any other protocol provided the telephony service provider software supports the protocol.

In some cases, the telephony programmer (or development team) may have control over the entire communication environment, or at least a portion larger than the local handset. In these cases, further architectural considerations may be required regarding issues such as network security, firewalls, and so forth. But in most cases, the underlying data transport protocol is transparent to the telephony application programmer. This is not the case with telephony protocols.

Telephony Protocols

Telephony programs communicate with external systems (e.g., a PBX) or internal telephony boards using telephony protocols. These are well-understood processes of initiating, maintaining, and then terminating communications channels so that data can be processed in an orderly and efficient manner.

Telephony protocols are used to implement *call control* policies. A typical "conversation" with a T1 trunk might look like this:

1. Application waits for an event from the T1 signaling that an incoming call has arrived. This occurs when the A bit is set high. When the event arrives, a *handshake* process is initiated.
2. The application winks[14] back to the T1 signaling that it is ready to accept the call. This completes the handshake process.
3. The T1 begins sending a data stream to the application.
4. (Optional) The application signals the T1 when through.

Summary

This chapter has presented a brief overview of some general telephony programming concepts, including JTAPI. In the next chapter, we wrap up our overview of telephony programming by investigating one aspect of telephony systems that sets them apart from most other types of applications — telephony bus architectures.

---

14 A wink is the process of setting a bit and then immediately resetting it.

Chapter 2 TELEPHOHY BUS ARCHITECTURES

> "Too much, magic bus..."
> The Who

All telephony communication ultimately travels across a bus of some sort. Of course, so do all other computer signals — so what makes telephony different? Well, the bus, of course. Telephony computers are typically outfitted with vendor-supplied boards that handle most if not all of the telephony functions as well as providing a data transport and a telephony protocol. The board is outfitted with processors and buses (separate from the computer's main CPU and buses, of course) to handle all of the intelligence and resource management necessary for telecom processing. This same architecture generally holds whether the boards are supplied for a home computer or a massive call center.

For example, as calls are placed and answered, each telephone line is designated a unique channel for the duration of the call. The programmer's interface to the telephony board (essentially a black box) is typically provided by the board vendor in the form of a software API.

In this chapter, we peek inside the black box. We briefly explore telephony bus architectures to gain an elementary understanding of how telephony data travels to and from an application program.

Bus Architectures

A *bus architecture* is an architecture based on, well, a bus! Recall that a *hardware* **bus** is a set of electronic circuits that connect multiple devices together. On a computer, these devices are the processor, screen, printers, memory, expansion boards, and so forth. (A bus is distinguished from a *channel* in that a bus may be attached to many different devices, whereas a channel can be connected to only one.) All devices attached to the bus receive the same kinds of signals for that bus, yet only the device that is addressed will receive any particular set of signals (depending, of course, on the address sent).

Each bus can hold information that travels in parallel based upon the *bit size* of the bus. For example, an 8-bit bus can send 8 bits of information at one time along the bus. Generally the larger the bit size the more efficient the bus, although other design criteria are used to determine the optimum bus size based upon the particular processor architecture and the accompanying operating system.

Most computers have at least three buses: a *data bus*, an *address bus,* and a *control bus*. The data bus allows for the transfer of information deemed as data only. The address bus is used exclusively for passing memory addresses to and from memory devices (providing bus stops for the bus, if you will). Ideally a 32-bit computer would have a 32-bit address bus,[1] a 64-bit computer a 64-bit bus.

The control bus is used to pass control codes to devices that give instructions as to what to do with the data found on the data bus. The control codes may also be used to reference other control codes. For example, a control code could be used to tell a device to ignore the next three control codes coming on the control bus. Of course, the context of each code depends on how it is interpreted by the receiving device.

The control bus has a **read line** and a **write line** for signaling whether information passed along the various buses should be *retrieved* or *sent* to a particular device. For example, consider a memory read. The processor places an address on the address bus and then *sets* the read line of the control bus. The memory device then retrieves the data at that address and places it on the data bus for return to the processor (see **Figure 2.1**).

The neat thing about this architecture is that it is standardized. All PC and workstation CPU processors operate in more or less the same manner. This not only benefits hardware manufacturers, it also benefits programmers and software vendors. Programmers can be assured that when they declare a pointer variable and point it to a memory location previously set

---

1 Recall that early Intel processors used a 20-bit bus, which led to the need for near and far pointers to access segments and offsets into RAM memory. If the address bus on these computers had been 32 bits, this would have been unnecessary! Today, all modern processor architectures align the address (pointer) size with the bus size to create what is called a *flat memory model*.

with data that the runtime software will return a valid address pointing to that data. System programmers and compiler vendors can rely on this architecture as well.

Figure 2.1 *Reading Contents of RAM*

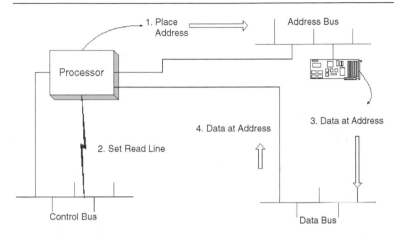

Telephony Bus Architectures

Telephony devices use buses that generally operate in the same manner as the standard PC and workstation buses. However, their architecture is not standardized; rather it is proprietary.[2] Normally all the intelligence to place and answer telephone calls and perform other telephony operations is housed entirely on the telephony board. This board has its own processor(s) and bus architecture even though it usually plugs into either an ISA (16-bit) or a PCI (32-bit) slot to allow for communication to and from the computer's CPU. Telephony buses are also referred to as "backplanes." A typical PBX will have a backplane bus implemented as a multiplexed line.

Because the bus architecture is proprietary we can only guess at how it works. A hypothetical architecture demonstrating voice transfer over a phone line is presented in **Figure 2.2**.

Let's walk through a scenario in **Figure 2.2** where a phone call is to receive data (this could be voice or data as in a modem connection). Initially, each phone line may be attached to a channel.[3] When the phone rings, the telephony software may associate an address (i.e., telephone number, not to be confused with a memory address!) with that unique line/channel (1). The telephony processor alerts the telephony board control bus by setting its write line (2). The data associated with the call is assigned a channel on the media bus (3). Somehow, the vendor's control bus is

---

2 Standardized bus architectures are available, but they are not often used.
3 This assignment can either be "hard-coded" or configured at run time.

"attached to" the CPU's control bus so that the incoming data from the media bus may be sent to the data bus of the CPU (4). The CPU responds by selecting a valid address to place the incoming data (5). And finally, the CPU control bus read line is set so that the application may read the data previously placed on its data bus (6).

Figure 2.2 *A Hypothetical Telephony Bus Architecture*

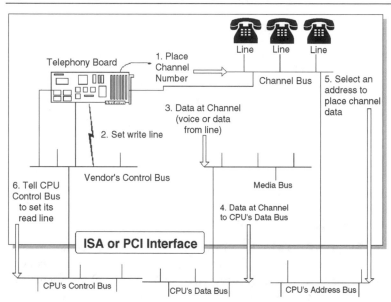

The Espresso Approach

The interface between the telephony board (or any other device) and the computer's processor (CPU) is normally specified in a set of I/O addresses known as *ports* and device signal transport channels called *interrupt request* (*IRQ*) lines.[4] Some programming languages (e.g., C, Ada, and some versions of BASIC) and all assembly languages provide a mechanism for reading and writing to these ports and responding to the IRQ line interrupts.

It should be noted that Java provides absolutely no support whatsoever for this level of programming. It is assumed that software at this level will be written in C and accessed as necessary through native methods. But usually the telecom programmer's interface to the telephony board capabilities is provided at a much higher level in the form of a vendor-supplied API. Even though telephone line inputs generate interrupts on the telephony board, these are normally translated into *software events* for retrieval through the vendor's API by the application program.

---

4 Actually the IRQ requests are sent to another chip called the Programmable Interrupt Controller (PIC) instead of the main CPU.

This is all great information, but why should an application programmer care? Well, normally they shouldn't. To them the telephony board is essentially a black box that manages all incoming and outgoing calls. The programmer is rarely given access to the address space of the device itself. Normally this works just fine, but there are cases where more low-level control would be advantageous.

One of these situations is the case of stringing multiple boards together on the same box. In this scenario some means of communicating between boards is necessary. Essentially, the capability to piggyback buses from each board together would be nice. Another situation is where we would like thread-level control over line channels. Such support is enabled via *trans-bus communication.*

Trans-Bus Communication

Most high-performance telephony boards come with some form of Inter-Process Communication (IPC) between multiple boards. Some use the existing ISA or PCI architecture; but normally this is offered via a proprietary bus interface over what is called an SC (Signal Control) bus. What this allows is the capability to pass control not only from the telephony hardware to the CPU, but also *between* boards on the same box.

The SC bus operates in a manner similar to an SCSI device chain. Each telephony board is physically "daisy-chained" to the other by a cable not unlike the ones used to attach hard drives to controller boards on a PC. You know those gray, wide, funny looking flat cables with a red stripe on one end that are always smashed up against a card somewhere — yeah, those. This configuration is pictured in **Figure 2.3**.

Figure 2.3 An SC Bus in Action

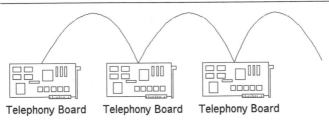

Telephony Board   Telephony Board   Telephony Board

Why would we want to do all this? One reason is to maximize the number of lines processed by a single application on a single box. Another is to allow for transfer of control to another box. Vendor APIs that use this architecture allow the application programmer access to the passing of control information but not data (at least not directly).

Figure 2.4 demonstrates how the application is hooked into this bus and how control may be provided.

Figure 2.4 *Voice and Network Resources Connected to a Telephony Bus*

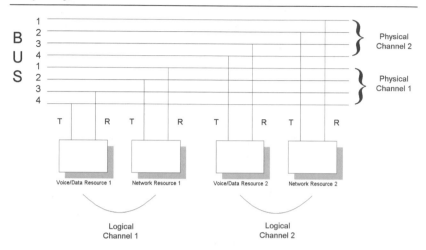

The programming interface to this architecture is provided by the logical abstraction of a *channel,* which represents the physical channels that make up the bus. Each logical channel is made up of a voice/data resource and a network resource. Each of these in turn are provided a *transmit* (T) and *receive* (R) line that is attached to the appropriate line on the bus (see **Figure 2.4**). The voice/data resource provides for the transmission and reception of voice and data (surprise!). The network resource provides services across the bus for specific telephony resources. An example would be an audio file. The assignment of a channel's receive line to the proper bus line would allow for the playing of, say, a greeting message for menu selection providing a caller with various prompts.

The transmit line is static in that the programmer cannot move from the line it is connected to. This way, callers can always be assured that a resource can be located at a valid, permanent address, and the telephony subsystem can always determine the origination of the call. The receive line is, however, configurable. For example, suppose a telephone call comes in and is assigned by the telephony subsystem to channel 1. Therefore, the channel is able to receive, say, voice on line 3. In order for a conversation to take place, however, at least two channels must be attached to the same receive line. This is depicted in **Figure 2.5**.

Other channels may join this conversation by simply assigning their receive lines to the same line, thereby creating a conference call. This works because each line is essentially a broadcast mechanism. The bus is implemented using a *time division multiplex* (TDM) architecture, whereby each channel is allotted a time slice over a shared line.

Figure 2.5 *Initiating a Conversation Between Two Channels*

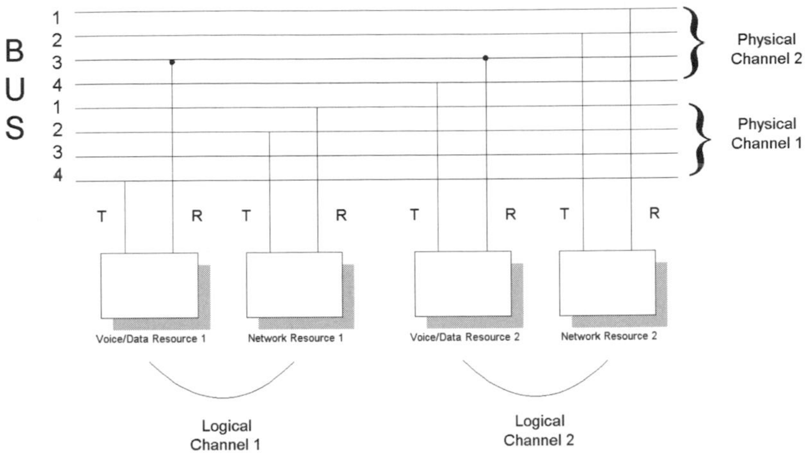

Summary

This completes the whirlwind tour of the telephony landscape we began in Chapter 1, "An Overview of Computer Telephony." We have provided a broad, yet admittedly incomplete, picture of computer telephony. To cover computer telephony in all its marvelous (and ugly) complexity is thankfully beyond the scope of this book. However, it is hoped that the reader has gained a feel for what CT is about. Next, we take a quick look at a question that any self-respecting programmer would ask — Is Java up to the task of telephony programming?

PART II

TELEPHONY *APIs*

Java is the Holy Grail.
Java is all hype.
Java is new!
Java stole every feature from another programming language.
Java performance is approaching that of C++.
Java is a performance pig.
Java is a design language.
Java is nothing more than the silver bullet of the late 1990s.

Well, we feel better now that we got all that out of the way.

In Chapter 3, we try to steer clear of the landmines that have come to define what Java is (or is not) and take an earnest look at how (or even if) it is appropriate for use in telephony programs. This is an important concern to telephony programmers used to the blinding speed of statically compiled C programs.

In Chapter 4, we examine exactly what Java's telephony library is and we explore what is provided to application programmers as a telephony library; namely JTAPI.

Chapter 3   *JAVA'S SUITABILITY TO TELECOM PROGRAMMING*

> "Good to the last drop."
> Maxwell House coffee commercial

In this chapter, we broach the subject of tool selection. We admit to a certain bias here. We are flatly against the notion of using *proprietary tools* for large-scale telephony programming. In our opinion, such an approach is short sighted. In contrast, selection of nonproprietary tools leaves open the possibility of taking advantage of economies of scale in such areas as flexibility, common skill sets, formal training, and maintainability. For these reasons, we ignore proprietary RAD tools and consider only viable standardized *programming languages* like Java.

In short, Java is a fully object-oriented programming language providing built-in support for concurrent programming. Java is really nothing new under the sun (no pun intended), borrowing all of its features from several other programming languages[1] as shown in **Table 3.1**.

---

1 Of course it can be said that the source languages themselves "borrowed" these features from other relatively obscure languages (e.g., Simula), but we choose to stop at some point.

Table 3.1 *Java's Borrowed Language Features*

Feature	Language
Exceptions	Ada
Packages	Ada
Syntax	C++ (similar)
Virtual Machine	Smalltalk
Root Object Inheritance	Smalltalk
Interfaces	Ada/Objective C
Threads	Ada
Events	Smalltalk

This chapter will explore most of the salient features that make Java a viable solution for telephony programming. It will also address those areas where Java may not be up to the task.

Toys and Tools of the Trade

Before we examine programming languages, we must first clarify our previous statement regarding proprietary tools. Many of these toys are in widespread use today for small applications. In this context, their use may be appropriate. Many small-to-middling CTI shops rely on these tools to provide small office solutions for their customers.

These tools are essentially *application generators* that provide visual development environments for developing canned telephony applications. They interface with one or more telephony boards and provide an "easy-to-use" mechanism for attaching sound files and switching logic to DTMF tones when a call is answered. A typical toy application would be similar to the automated voices that come with credit card activation centers — "Press One to activate your credit card ...." The developer supplies the voice prompt[2] and indicates either the next voice prompt to play or the next action to perform.

A typical toy development environment is comprised of a visual editor with icons representing voice prompts connected by lines indicating program control flow. The tool then generates the code necessary to implement the design. Although many advertisements claim the mantra "no programming required," this is ill-advised in all but the most trivial of applications. On the other hand, if I were a power-user (i.e., a nonprogrammer) opening my own office requiring a simple, well-defined phone-answering application, I might be tempted to give these tools a whirl. However, a seasoned programmer is always wary, not only of the spurious claims of marketers, but also of the future availability and upgradability of the product. But most

---

2 A voice prompt is nothing more than an audio file.

importantly, he is wary of the limitations placed upon the application due to the fact that the tool is *proprietary*. Although some of these toys generate real code, most come with their own (you guessed it) proprietary programming "language." Ever get the feeling someone was trying to lock you into something? Nah... they wouldn't do that, would they?

When power users grow up, they reach the conclusion that there is a valid need for programming languages after all. They grow tired of the endless empty vendor claims and tedium of having to learn yet another stupid proprietary programming language. They are ready for *real* tools, which can only be implemented using and interfacing with real programming languages.

Selecting a Programming Language

As computer science has matured, programming languages have continued to merge in terms of their capabilities. This assimilation process is inevitable. As programming languages evolve, they take on features found to be useful in other languages. This is evidenced by the fact that all new programming languages are object-oriented and all revisions of legacy languages are moving that way — if possible (e.g., COBOL to OOCOBOL, C to C++).

In the Preface, we promised not to dwell on the fundamentals of Java or any other programming language. It is, however, instructive to examine the fundamental capabilities provided to assure ourselves we've made the right choice in terms of suitability with telephony programming. Let's investigate some of the technical reasons for selecting (or not selecting) Java as a telephony programming language suitable for telephony programming. But first, let's check out the competition.

As we will see in later chapters, the selection of an API usually implicitly binds the programming language we must use. For example, the selection of TAPI and TSAPI force the use of C or C++. TAPI also binds an implementation to Microsoft platforms. TSAPI limits deployment options to Novell networks. We will always be forced to make an engineering tradeoff — flexibility in choice vs. functionality or, say, native capability vs. platform independence. But in certain circumstances, we don't have to be bound quite this tightly. What if we could find a programming language we liked that also directly supported a telephony programming API that could run on any platform? In addition, it would be nice if the language were object-oriented (although this is not necessarily a requirement, it is strongly advised). Let's see if we can.

Any programming language selected for serious telephony programming should support the following requirements:

- Concurrent programming
- Interfacing with other languages (particularly C)

- Distributed programming
- Callback capability
- Portability (optional)

Concurrent programming is implemented with *language-level support* of threads. Modern telephony applications require the use of threads for maximum efficiency in both single and multiple processor implementations. Effective asynchronous processing cannot be accomplished without threads. Interfacing with other languages is critical for maximum *flexibility*. Further, most telephony libraries are written in C, and so a C callable interface is often required. Support for distributed programming allows for an interface to or implementation "on top of" a communications protocol. It is vital — without it there is no telephony programming. The capability to make callbacks is often required for *asynchronous notification* and to again maximize processor resource utilization. Portability is only required if a particular application requires it — but without such support in the programming language, it is extremely difficult to retrofit.

Given this set of requirements, we can rule out several programming languages. The only programming languages that *directly* support our first requirement are Ada, Smalltalk, and Java. In addition, these three languages support the remaining requirements and they are object-oriented. Let's evaluate each of these features as they are supported in each of these languages.

Smalltalk

Concurrent programming in Smalltalk is supported by the more or less standard classes Process, ProcessScheduler, Block, Semaphore, and Context. Methods are provided to spawn threads (e.g., fork), suspend and awaken threads, and support critical sections. Although not a part of the language, the vast majority of Smalltalk implementations provide interfaces to the C programming language, DLLs, etc. There are several forms of Distributed Smalltalk (e.g., HP Distributed Smalltalk, IBM Distributed Smalltalk, DNS CORBA). In addition, there are numerous classes provided to wrap TCP/IP, SNA, and everything under the sun.

Callbacks are supported directly in many fashions. Class DirectedMessage provides a loosely coupled option, and the Smalltalk IdentityDictionary provides a built-in callback mechanism at the root level of the hierarchy (i.e., Object). In addition, Smalltalk provides an ingenious mechanism for handling events as well as a built-in dependency model. In terms of portability, Smalltalk could have been Java. The Java Virtual Machine concept was lifted directly from Smalltalk (several Smalltalk implementations have supported cross-platform binary compatibility for years). Smalltalk can do anything Java can do — and more.

Although Smalltalk is arguably the best, most complete and mature application-level development environment in existence today, it is curiously not as popular as C++, Java, and even Visual BASIC. The popularity of Smalltalk has increased in recent years, but it seems destined to become an afterthought language, a casualty of the popularity of a very similar language — Java. The problem is that Smalltalk never formally standardized the virtual machine,[3] and its vendors ruthlessly slung mud at each other to the ultimate demise of most of the products.

Ada

Ada was the first widely used programming language to provide language-level support for threads. Ada provides two different tasking models to support concurrent programming: one based on C. S. Hoare's communicating sequential processes (Ada tasks) and the other on lightweight threads (Ada protected types). Ada is the only programming language to make guarded *monitors* a part of the language. No other programming language comes close to offering this level of support for concurrent programming.[4]

Ada was built to interface with other languages — in fact, so much so that the support is, again, unmatched. There are packages defined in the language annex that interface with C and COBOL. Further, the framework is in place for other languages. An Ada class can inherit from a C++ class. To date, there are additional mappings to C++ and Java. Callbacks are supported via access types (access to subprograms). Ada also supports distributed programming from the ground up with its Remote Call Interface and Partition Communication Subsystem. Ada is the most portable programming language available today, running on more platforms than any other programming language. Ada has the ability to be run in both a compiled mode as well as in an interpreted garbage collection mode with a virtual machine.

C/C++

You'll note that C and C++ were missing from our original list of languages. This was not a glaring oversight; rather these languages simply do not meet our requirements. But from a practical perspective, their use is pervasive and unavoidable to some extent. No professional programmer today can be considered such without claiming proficiency in at least one of these languages. More importantly, the vast majority of all board-level APIs are provided in C.

Unfortunately, neither C nor C++ supports concurrent programming at the language level. It can be accomplished, but only through either system-level calls (which prohibit portability) or third-party APIs (which, even if portable, lock you into a nonstandard vendor implementation — again prohibiting portability). Neither is distributed programming supported by either language. Both C and C++ support callbacks through pointers and references, respectively.

---

3 Efforts are underway to standardize the language, but it's probably too little, too late.
4 Both Modula and Java also provide some form of monitor mechanism. However, neither of these directly implements a barrier mechanism or balking messages the way Ada does.

Java

Java supports concurrent programming via class Thread and the Runnable interface. Support for interfacing with other languages and distributed programming are provided with native methods and in the Remote Method Interface, respectively. Callbacks are supported with the reflection API or interfaces, and portability is provided with the Java Virtual Machine. In the next section, we explore the features of Java that are of particular interest to telephony programmers.

In summary, there is no technical reason why we could not use Ada or Smalltalk except that neither provides a telephony API as a standard part of the language. However, there is at least one vendor-specific TAPI product in Smalltalk. Proprietary issues aside, one could make a strong argument for using Ada over Smalltalk and even Java because it does not require garbage collection and so is a better performer.

Cynically, one could argue that the world has simply chosen C/C++ and Java to the detriment of other languages and tools. Both languages support telephony APIs, and so that's what we currently have to work with. "Marketing" has always been in the driver seat of the technological automobile, and it always will be. But we are seeing an unprecedented cooperation among software vendors working to make this "Java thing" a reality. If Java does succeed, the success will be attributable to both the cooperation among these industry giants and to an unprecedented grass roots effort among programmers. It is all of these things working together in harmony that offer the promise of Java.

So say we pick Java. Besides basic language capabilities, what other criteria are useful for selecting Java in a telephony context?

Why Java for Telecom?

The most important features of the language in terms of telephony programming are its *packages*, *interfaces*, its clean *thread model*, its built-in *portability*, the *Reflection* API, Java *Events*, the *Remote Method Interface* (RMI), and its support for *native methods*. Java also provides *inheritance* through the **extends** keyword. This is not necessarily a requirement[5] for telecom programming, but programming without an option for extension is like having to plug a phone into a wall socket before each call.

Packages

Java (and C++) lifted the concept of packages directly from Ada. While not quite as advanced as Ada packages and hierarchical library units, Java packages serve roughly the same purpose and are functionally equiv-

---

5 We do not cover the benefits of extension here; rather they are assumed.

alent to C++ namespaces. Coupled with the ability to specify inner classes, packages provide an excellent protection against pollution of the namespace.

Using Packages in Java

Java packages allow programmers the ability to organize classes into module level groups. Packages may be organized in any manner (see **Listing 3.1**). For example, you might want to arrange your packages by company structure or by functionality offered or both.

Listing 3.1 *Declaring Java Packages*

```
// organized by company
package titus.frameworks;

// organized by functionality - in another class file
package engineering.math;
```

Unlike Ada's hierarchical library units, however, the hierarchical ordering of the Java packages do not affect visibility in a transitive sense. For example, importing package javax.telephony does not provide automatic visibility to packages below (such as javax.telephony.callcontrol). Likewise, importing package javax.telephony.callcenter does *not* import package javax.telephony. In other words, each package must be explicitly imported regardless of where it is positioned in the package tree. In this sense, packages are nothing but a convenient grouping mechanism (aside from their use as namespace import tools).

Using Packages in JTAPI

At the top level, Java's packages are organized in the same manner as those of Ada. Those modules essential for using the language are categorized as "core" packages. Additional packages are defined as "standard extensions." The core packages are shown in **Figure 3.1**.

JTAPI is one of several *standard extension packages*, another concept borrowed from Ada. Later, we delve much deeper into the contents of some of these packages, most notably the package javax.telephony.

Interfaces

Interfaces allow Java programmers the ability to provide the functional equivalent of *multiple inheritance* to their design. More importantly, interfaces provide the ability to create *polymorphic routines* and *callbacks* without requiring inheritance at all.

Figure 3.1 *Java's Core Packages*

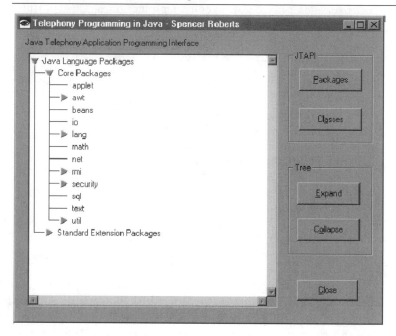

Multiple Inheritance

Java does not support multiple inheritance directly, but a similar effect can be gained by using interfaces coupled with idioms (see Chapter 10). When a programmer inherits from one class and implements the signatures of one or more other interfaces, he can achieve the same effect as if he had inherited from all the "classes" involved.[6] This feature is important because one can gain the benefits of extension without inheriting extra baggage unnecessarily. It allows a sort of "cross-hierarchy" inheritance. The problem is, interfaces don't allow the declaration of instance variables (unless they are constants). Further, interfaces do not allow the specification of protected or private methods. In other words, extension can only occur at the public visibility level. Although interfaces require much more work than multiple inheritance and are less powerful, this technique is nevertheless useful. It is used extensively throughout the JTAPI libraries to specify the JTAPI call model.

Polymorphism

Look, Ma — no OO required! Although polymorphism is commonly discussed in conjunction with object-oriented design and programming, it can be achieved without OO (i.e., without requiring inheritance). Simply stated,

---

6 Referred to in other programming languages (like Ada) as "mixin classes."

polymorphism is accomplished when two or more software entities implement the same *function signature*. A modern example of this is Microsoft's COM specification.

From a telephony programmer's perspective, this Java feature is useful in implementing messaging protocols. If different types of components "understand" the same message, they can be processed in the same manner even if they react differently when processed. Java's interfaces not only allow this, they define exactly what polymorphism is in a clear unambiguous manner.

Callbacks

In C and C++, callback functions are implemented using function pointers and method pointers, respectively. In Java, this can be accomplished using either the Method class (reflection) or interfaces. Interfaces are *usually* the preferred mechanism. This subject is covered in depth in Chapter 10. Callbacks are *essential* to telephony programming.

Java's Thread Model

Programming threads has traditionally been a "black art." While it remains possibly the most difficult skill to master in programming, Java eases the burden considerably. Java specifies a thread model that provides the programmer a primitive set of components and a simple API with which they can build more powerful abstractions. It allows library programmers a standard way to provide *reentrant functions* and *asynchronous notification schemes*. This is good news for telephony programmers, who in the past have usually had to master proprietary APIs or resort to operating system primitives to implement concurrency. We cover threaded programming topics throughout the remainder of this book. Stay tuned...

Portability

Java's creators, Sun Microsystems, tout the phrase "Write Once, Run Anywhere™." In fact, the phrase itself is a trademark! While this marketing slogan seems to be swallowed whole by development managers everywhere, experienced programmers know better. However, the concept of *binary portability* is attractive, even though it is rarely a true requirement. It has also been accomplished in the past with Smalltalk, so even jaded programmers may come to appreciate this capability. If truly portable software can be written for telephony applications, it can probably be written for any vertical market!

True portability requires nothing of a JTAPI implementation except a Java virtual machine running on the platform of choice. It is portability from an application programmer's perspective. In order for a library programmer to provide **true portability**, nothing special is required of Java applications and library implementations except for one thing — reliance on native methods must be kept to a minimum. As we'll see, this is not a very practical approach when it comes to implementing JTAPI libraries on multiple platforms. So instead of true portability, we will come to accept what is defined here as ***practical portability***. Practical portability requires (in addition) the particular telephony library JTAPI is implemented "on top of." If instead a proprietary library is used, the drivers must be provided. For example, on Windows platforms, it makes sense to implement JTAPI on top of Microsoft's TAPI. This compromise is seen as a reasonable one, because a platform telephony interface is not the only additional component required of telephony applications (specialized hardware is also required anyway). But more importantly, it allows JTAPI to take advantage of the underlying platform capabilities which may or may not be present on all platforms. And so a "practically portable" solution requires a JTAPI implementation of a particular vendor's hardware for each board on the box in addition to a Java virtual machine. In addition, it may also require the platform's telephony library if they do not conform to a standard platform API such as TAPI.

The Reflection API

The Java Reflection API provides meta-programming along the lines of Smalltalk and, to a lesser degree, CLOS/LISP.[7] Telephony programmers may also use the reflection API to implement callbacks for use in asynchronous calls and to write generic code (more on this in Chapters 9 and 10). Although JTAPI does not explicitly use these language features, we can develop some reusable components that do. Further, any production-quality JTAPI implementation may require the use of these features.

Java Event Management Models

Java provides two event registration and notification schemes: *dependency/observation* and *delegation*. Delegation is a marginally useful event management model based on methods defined in two classes: java.awt.Event (for UI objects) and java.util.EventObject (for non-UI worker objects). Programmers may extend these classes to create their own specialized events. Telephony applications should probably avoid this type of notification due to the lack of functionality provided (unless, of course, you enjoy writing event management models from scratch[8]). Of more practical use is the Observation Model. Understanding this form of notification is critical to effectively using JTAPI, and so we cover it in detail in Chapters 6 and 9.

Due to their asynchronous nature, message management models require the specification and use of events. Many telephony-specific events are

---

7 The meta-programming features of CLOS/LISP are in fact superior to both Smalltalk and Java.

8 Although there are compelling reasons to do just this due to some limitations of the Java event model. More on this later.

predefined and therefore standardized in JTAPI, freeing the programmer from this task. This event standardization is perhaps the most compelling reason to use JTAPI (or at least a subset of it). Since events are decoupled from implementations by definition, they may be used separately from a particular event management model. This component-based approach also allows for maximum flexibility.

A third form of event management (not specified by Java) is based on a more canonical implementation of events allowing a clean implementation of asynchronous notification schemes used in telephony programming. We will develop just such a set of classes in this book in Chapters 6 and 9.

Remote Method Interface (RMI)

The RMI is useful in implementing multitier architectures in a portable fashion — it is Java's built-in support for network programming. In addition, Java can be seamlessly integrated with other mechanisms for executing in a remote address space such as CORBA. It is important to understand that remote execution is not *directly* tied to telephony programming. Rather it is an implementation detail enabled by the selected *data transport protocol*. But the fact that Java supplies the capability is a plus. In short, RMI may be used to provide the data transport protocol.

Native Methods

Native methods (also referred to as the Java Native Interface — JNI) allow Java programmers to call routines written in other languages (most notably C). This language feature is indispensable in implementing JTAPI bindings — an unfortunate task we also tackle in this book. Ideally, Java application programmers will use COTS JTAPI implementations and native methods will be useful (i.e., required) only for *library programmers* providing JTAPI implementation code. We will find in practice, that a programming language interface is helpful but is insufficient alone for combining libraries in a productive manner — and that's where native method support will come in handy.[9]

Why Not Java for Telecom?

Enough from the Java fan club. Although you'd never know it by the intense interest it has mustered, Java is not necessarily the best (or even an acceptable) option for telephony programming in some cases. There are two primary reasons why (or why not!):

- Garbage collection
- Performance

---

9 For the most complete tour of JNI available, get Rob Gordon's book *Essential JNI*.

Garbage Collection

Any programming language lacking support for pointer types requires garbage collection (of one kind or another). This includes all interpreted[10] languages like Smalltalk, LISP, Prolog, Java, and even BASIC. There are several reasons for this. First, many objects must be allocated at runtime. In most cases, there is no way for an application to know a priori how many objects are required. Even if this is determinable, the lifetime (resolved by scope and execution time) is usually not. Second, the runtime size of many objects (especially container types) is often not known. The third reason is the manner in which all objects are allocated at runtime by computer systems. Whether or not a particular programming language supports pointers, memory is always allocated on the heap (or the so-called "free store") through the use of pointers in Von Nueman computer architectures. If the programming language does not provide this support, the runtime system must. For example, the **DIM** statement in BASIC requires a pointer-based implementation in the runtime libraries even though such support is not directly available (or even visible) to the programmer.

Nondeterminism

Programming languages that provide pointer support (like C, C++, and Ada) allow the programmer the ability to determine when the memory for dynamically allocated objects can be freed for use by the system. This capability is removed from the hands of the programmer in an interpreted, garbage-collecting environment. Many argue that garbage collection is a benefit. But it is the biggest potential problem with using interpreted languages in some environments — nondeterminism as to exactly *when* garbage collection will take place and, even more important, *how long it will take*.

Latent Memory Leaks

There may also be a false reliance on the garbage collector. Granted, automatic memory management is definitely a boon to programmer productivity. However, the vast majority of telephony libraries are (and always will be) written in C. Since the Java-to-C-and-back translation may involve memory leaks due to either programmer error or runtime bugs, a 100% reli-

---

10 Over the years, the distinction between what constitutes an interpreted language has been confused somewhat. For example, both Smalltalk and Java run compiled byte code through an interpreter where early versions of BASIC interpreted each line of code at runtime. Further, some "compiled" runtimes use p-code. However, this distinction is simplified if we take the term "interpreted" to mean any code that is not translated into 100% machine code for a target platform.

able widespread pure Java solution for telephony programming is simply not very realistic.

Now this is not necessarily a catastrophic condition — telephony applications are not usually life critical.[11] Further, the asynchronous messaging model employed by most telephony applications mitigates the impact of nondeterminism. Mechanisms to increase atomic processing (such as critical sections) can reduce nondeterminism within a single process. However, garbage collection will always add some element of potential unpredictability and even instability to software written without the proper considerations made for temporal issues. When the tools necessary to detect and manage temporal issues are not provided, this may be an impossible task for some implementations.

Performance

A more obvious reason for not using interpreted languages (like BASIC and Java) is, of course, speed. It is simply not now, nor will it ever be possible for an interpreted language to match the speed of a compiled language. Native machine code will always execute faster than byte code. Interpreted code is typically ten to thirty times slower than compiled code. This compiled code/interpreted code execution speed (C/I) ratio has been relatively constant in programming language history and will not likely change. Of course, as processor speeds increase, the ratio is certainly less noticeable, and this is a very good thing — but it is *still there*.

Techniques for Improving Java Performance

For applications where performance is an overriding requirement, *source code optimization* can provide dramatic improvements in performance. This is true of all programming languages, not just Java. Although most source code optimization is performed "by hand," there are tools that can analyze source code and point out areas where optimization techniques may be applied. Some of these techniques (a.k.a. idioms) are presented in Chapter 10. Once all that can be done to the Java source is accomplished, we can turn to *automated* methods such as JIT compilers.

Just-In-Time?

One area of confusion often encountered in performance-related Java discussions is that of so-called "just-in-time" (JIT) compilers. What these compilers do is essentially convert cached byte code to machine code. They work kind of like a runtime profiler, sensing which areas of code are accessed most often and compiling that code into the native instruction set.

---

11 This may be news to some parents of teenagers.

Once the code is compiled, the next access to that same address (where the code is stored) will trigger the execution of the native code instead of the interpreted code. For certain types of applications, this technique can make a significant improvement in performance — after the first execution of cached code. If an application runs most of the time in just a few sections of code (as a profiler can point out) and these sections can be converted to machine code, all is groovy. But caching requires resources, and many applications do not fall into this model. It is a promising technology, but again, it's nothing new.[12] Contrary to vendor doublespeak, JIT compilers will not improve the C/I ratio significantly for all Java code. Further, they add yet another element of nondeterminism to the telephony processing model.

However, there are alternatives. In addition to native methods, some Java compilers even provide C++ language mappings. Java can be automatically compiled to C++ object code on a particular platform.[13] If a Java application can execute trusted, statically compiled object code for time-critical elements and keep dynamic memory allocations to a minimum, the side effects of garbage collection can be mitigated. But they can never be eliminated.

Having said this, there needs to be a distinction made between *static optimization* and *dynamic optimization*. Static optimization is performed at compile time and is the only type currently performed using statically compiled languages like C++. There are, however, some operations that simply cannot be optimized in a static context. For example, consider most any dynamic allocation of, say, a large container of objects (as opposed to native types like ints). A JIT compiler could at runtime convert, say, a Vector of Integer objects into an Array of ints prior to a CPU-intensive calculation once the runtime element values and the Vector size are known. This example is somewhat contrived, but you get the point. In this sense, dynamic optimization may hold some promise for Java, but it will never be "faster than" a static language coupled with a runtime engine that performs the same calculations.[14]

But the truth is that any such compiler optimizations can (and probably should) be performed by hand (i.e., in the source code) for those circumstances where it is appropriate. It is always better to have source code that clearly states what will happen at runtime rather than relying on an automated runtime solution that may or may not occur (because the JIT decision to optimize or not in a particular circumstance is outside the control of the programmer).

---

12 The creators and implementers of Smalltalk have already dealt with this issue for a few decades.

13 This practice is functionally equivalent to the manner in which Eiffel programs are compiled into C object code.

14 In this case, the performance would be the same.

Summary

In summary, we advise against the notion of using proprietary telephony application generators for all but the most trivial of applications.[15] Instead, we recommend using standard programming languages coupled with whatever telephony libraries are available. Although it may take a little more time to get the application up and running, it will be more maintainable, flexible, and robust.

As far as programming languages go, we come to the conclusion that there are compelling reasons to use Java for telephony programming that may or may not outweigh the costs of using it. If the benefits of code maintainability and thread management are high, they may offset the associated costs of performance and nondeterminism.

---

15 However, an application generator that generated code in any of the languages covered in this chapter (Ada, Smalltalk, C++, or Java) and featured the capability to link in DLLs and link arbitrary code would be the best of all worlds.

Chapter 4

A CLOSE LOOK AT JTAPI

More than a standard library, *standard extension packages* take a programming language into territory previously occupied exclusively by third-party vendors. JTAPI is one such standard extension package. Although third-party vendors are still required to implement the standard extension package (in this case, JTAPI), the application programmer's interface is vastly simplified if only because it *is* standardized. A standard API that is used by programmers and supported by vendors can "assimilate" the vast (and unnecessary) array of different APIs that do the same thing.

It doesn't take a rocket scientist to see the overwhelming benefits to such an approach in terms of programmer productivity. However, the ease of use of such an interface can still leave much to be desired if it is not defined in an intuitive and clear manner. This is where you get to see for yourself whether or not JTAPI succeeds for your needs.

In this chapter, we are introduced to JTAPI. After this, we break down the contents of each telephony package and examine the functionality provided by each component. In this effort, we describe JTAPI in terms of its *modularity*, its degree of *object orientation*, the *events* it defines, and the error-processing capabilities it provides by way of *exceptions*.

JTAPI — Sun's Java Telephony Application Programming Interface

The standard C++ language definition follows a now well-known specification approach. The language is defined by a *core language definition* augmented by a set of *standard libraries*. These libraries specify a standard set of capabilities to be provided by language implementers (i.e., compiler vendors) covering capabilities such as I/O, container classes, strings, and other useful software component specifications. Standardizing these capabilities is important — without such standardization, each compiler vendor may provide a different interface for core capabilities resulting in needless compatibility problems across implementations.

This "language extension" concept did not originate with C++; rather it originated with the C programming language standard library extensions.[1] In 1983, Ada expanded this concept to include standard package definitions called *annexes* for higher-level abstractions like database access, low-level programming, distributed programming, etc. The 1995 Ada revision added standard extensions for programming language interfaces and encouraged the standardization of vertical market packages by industry consortiums. This is exactly what Sun Microsystems is doing with the standard extensions to the Java language — only this time it is being initiated by the language designers as opposed to industry consortiums. In other words, they're not waiting for industry to catch up. Instead, they are initiating the process and then turning it over to industry consortiums as they emerge (or so we are led to believe).

The Java Standard Extension APIs

Following in the footsteps of Ada, Java has a set of its own standard extension packages. The package javax.telephony is but one of several of these standard extension packages specified as a part of the Java language definition. All extension packages begin with the package name "javax" (x for extension, presumably). These so-called "extension" packages effectively extend the Java language beyond fundamental programming language-specific capabilities to encompass functionality required of *entire industries*. Not only is there an API for telephony, there is one for financial transactions, embedded systems, consumer electronic devices, and so forth. To explore all of these in their current state, visit the "API Overview" section on the Java Web site.

All Java standard extension APIs are organized in the same manner. Each API is given a name and is a combination of a set of **standard extension packages** plus a set of **core language packages** used to implement the API. For example, JTAPI is the API that includes the standard

---

1 It can also be argued that standard libraries began with COBOL intrinsic functions.

extension package `javax.telephony`, all of its subpackages (e.g., `javax.telephony.callcontrol`), and the portions of the core language packages (e.g. `java.util`, `java.lang`) required for implementing the API.[2] The following is a list all of the current standard extension APIs.

EmbeddedJava™

JavaBeans™

Java Commerce (Java Wallet)

Java Enterprise

    Java Database Connectivity (JDBC)

    Java Remote Method Invocation (RMI) & Object Serialization

    Java Interface Definition Language (IDL)

    Java Naming and Directory Service (JNDI)

Java Foundation Classes (JFC)

    Swing Set

    Accessibility

    Java2D

Java Help

Java Management

Java Server

    Java Server

    Java Servlet

Java Media

    Java2D

    Java3D

    Java Media Framework (JMF)

    Java Sound

    Java Speech

    Java Telephony (JTAPI)

PersonalJava™

JavaCard™

---

2 An example of one such core capability would be any core classes used to build a JTAPI implementation that are specified in the standard extension interfaces.

Many of these APIs are still on the drawing board. Further, there is no guarantee they will even remain. Fortunately, the JTAPI API will not likely disappear as it is the Media API furthest along in development.

We can see where JTAPI fits in the overall scheme of API things. The JTAPI API is a subset of the Java Media API. Of all of the standard extension APIs, the APIs that are directly relevant to telephony programming at this level of specification are the Java Media APIs, PersonalJava™, EmbeddedJava™, and JavaCard™. We will discuss the latter three APIs in Chapter 12. For now, let's take a look at where JTAPI fits into the Media API.

The Java Media API

The Media API is presented in **Figure 4.1**. It is comprised of the following APIs: Java Speech, Java Media Framework (JMF), Java Collaboration, Java Animation, Java2D, Java3D, and Java Telephony (our very own JTAPI). The Media APIs of specific interest to telecom programmers are Java Speech, JMF, Java Collaboration, and of course JTAPI. The Media API is designed to provide most forms of interactive media over the Web. As defined by Sun, telephony is just one of these forms of media.

Figure 4.1 *The Java Media APIs*

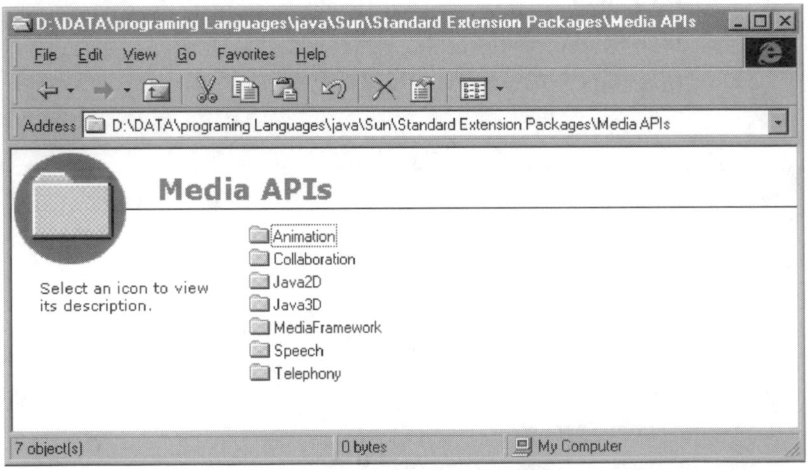

Although the other API sets comprising the Media API may be presented in a telephony application, certain ones stand out. In other words, there is nothing stopping a telecom programmer from receiving and then displaying animation or two- and three-dimensional graphics within a telephony program as the result of data transmission over a telephone connection. To do so portably, one should use the respective APIs presented here or the subpackage interfaces to these APIs defined in the proper package of interest.[3] But the Speech, Collaboration, and JMF APIs are more closely coupled to telephony with respect to the functionality they provide. Let's take a quick look at why these specific "sibling APIs" may be of interest to telephony programmers.

Media Framework API (JMF)

JMF provides a common messaging protocol for the playing, capture and conferencing of various media (e.g., speech, video). The JMF is in turn comprised of three more APIs: Java Media Player, Java Media Capture, and Java Media Conference (see **Figure 4.2**).

Figure 4.2 *The Java Media Framework APIs*

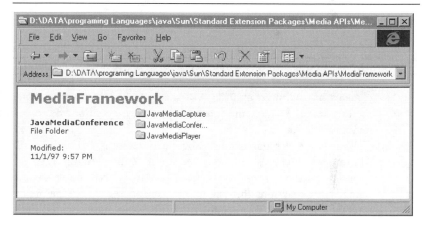

For more information on Java Media Player, Java Media Capture, and Java Media Conference, see the book *Essential JMF* by Rob Gordon (1998) in this same Prentice Hall *Essential* series.

Java Collaboration API

Although the information for the collaboration specification is sketchy at this point in time, the descriptions available imply that this API will provide support for interactive two-way, multiparty communications over a wide array of network architectures. This API may provide a superset of

---

3 Often a functional package has its own interface to other higher-level packages in the form of subpackages. For example, package javax.telephony of JTAPI includes a subpackage javax.telephony.media. This subpackage is actually a wrapper interface to the sibling media packages under the Media API. It includes not all, but only the most common interfaces to the other media services as they relate to telephony data streams of a telephone call. Only enough of the media interface is exposed to provide core functionality at that level of abstraction.

the capability normally associated with conference calls, perhaps including such capabilities as live video feed for teleconferences used in, say, corporate meetings.

Java Speech API

The Java speech API provides automatic speech recognition (record) and speech synthesis (converting text to speech) capabilities. This would presumably come in handy in advanced speech-recognition programs as well as in the playback of recorded messages so common to telecom applications.

In summary, these APIs are to be used in the same manner that a TAPI application may make use of the Win32 Comm API or the MCI API. Now let's drill down the API tree to examine the architecture of JTAPI itself.

The JTAPI Specification

JTAPI itself has gone through a number of revisions as it has matured. Standard APIs are just as susceptible to deprecated methods as the core Java language definition — JTAPI is no exception here. However, the changes have slowed and the API seems to have brewed to an acceptable mellow level. In fact, the latest changes are so minor as to be virtually unnoticeable.

The major changes occurred between versions 1.0 and 1.1 of the API. The biggest changes between version 1.1 and version 1.2 involved the renaming of the core package (from java to javax), the removal of a large number of exceptions thrown, and the introduction of dynamic capabilities (and the subsequent deprecation of the previous static capabilities).

JTAPI Architecture

The JTAPI architecture is based on a simple client call model implemented in package `javax.telephony`. The design suggests an implementation of the *dependency* notification model as it applies to core telephony capabilities.[4] As one would expect, the primary capabilities provided in the call model are the abilities to place a call, hang up a call, and answer a call. The Call, Connection, and TerminalConnection objects provide these capabilities, respectively.

The JTAPI packages define a set of *domain objects* and their behavior that are fairly common in telephony applications. Most objects are implemented as *finite state machines* that generate predefined events upon state transition. These objects will be examined in detail in the section "JTAPI Core Components" later in this chapter.

---

4 This implementation is not required or even necessarily the best option (as we shall see later), but it is implied by the API design.

Each subpackage under package `javax.telephony` builds on this fundamental call model by adding or specializing core objects (usually specified as Java interfaces), states, exceptions, events, and primary capabilities. When an application requires more extensive support than the core provides, extensions to the basic call model are supplied that offer capabilities for implementing server-side call center applications. For example, functionality is provided for routing, ACD grouping, predictive dialing, media extensions, and interfacing with switches.

There is a similarity between this approach and that of the service levels provided by Microsoft's TAPI. Just as Microsoft's TAPI library has a set of core functionality in the basic telephony service level required of all telephony applications, JTAPI requires the implementation of the JTAPI core package (`javax.telephony`). In the same manner that extension *service levels* build on the basic service level in TAPI, *auxiliary packages* build upon the JTAPI core package. Although it appears very different on the surface, there is little doubt that the functional design of the JTAPI architecture was heavily influenced by TAPI. We will study TAPI in depth in Chapter 5, "Telephony API Overview."

JTAPI Security

The JTAPI security model is centered around the Java "sandbox" model. The runtime system determines whether objects invoking JTAPI methods are "trusted" or "untrusted" and allows or disallows access to system resources accordingly. In addition to following this standard model, a simple user name and password scheme may be used to gain access to a provider's implementation through the JtapiPeer object. Additional security capabilities may be added by an implementation. This is covered later in this chapter.

JTAPI Package Hierarchy

Part of the JTAPI API is the set of extension packages that define the functionality of the API. The JTAPI package hierarchy is presented in **Figure 4.3**. Each package is defined below the standard telephony package javax.telephony — and so each class, exception, interface, and constant is subject to Java's package visibility rules.

Figure 4.3 shows JTAPI at the highest level of abstraction. Each folder is a subpackage under package `javax.telephony`. Next, we will examine the contents of package `javax.telephony` as well as that of each subpackage.

Figure 4.3 *Packages Contained in JTAPI*

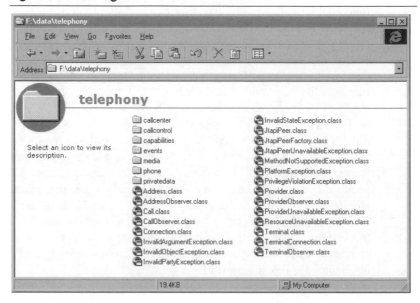

JTAPI — A Modular API

Recall that the JTAPI API set is comprised of a related set of classes, events, interfaces, exceptions, and constants. These API components are organized into a hierarchical set of packages (modules) organized primarily by the telephony functionality offered. The root of this package tree begins at package `javax.telephony`.

JTAPI Packages

The package `javax.telephony` is referred to as the *core* package of JTAPI (see **Figure 4.4**). Earlier, we saw how it "contains" seven other telephony-related packages. From a functional perspective, however, it is related *directly* to only two of these subpackages: `package javax.telephony.capabilities` and `package javax.telephony.events`. In fact, all subpackages are organized in this same manner. *Each subpackage contains its own subpackage of both events and capabilities.* Events correspond to state transitions. We will be exposed to their functional use as we examine the life cycles of the various JTAPI Core Components. We will examine events in more depth in the section called "JTAPI — An Event-Driven API," later in this chapter. Capabilities are explained in the section on JTAPI Capabilities.

In addition to these packages, each `javax.telephony` package also houses a set of classes, events, interfaces, exceptions, and constants of its

Figure 4.4 *Package* `javax.telephony`

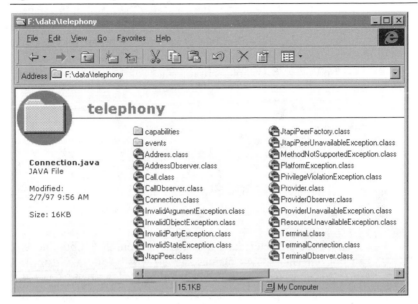

very own (e.g., `Address.java` through `TerminalObserver.java` of `javax.telephony`). But what is meant by the term "core package"? Earlier, we presented a different definition. JTAPI itself is not a core package. It is an extension package, right?

What Is a Core Package?

A core package is one that contains the minimal set of functionality required to perform a set of services. The term "core" is *relative to the context of the services presented.* At the Java language level, core packages relate to a programmer's use of the language — and so the core packages are `java.io`, `java.lang`, and so forth. All packages defined as core packages *at that level* offer functionality relevant to general programming. At the telephony (JTAPI) level, however, we are presented telephony packages — and so the core package at this level is `javax.telephony` even though the package and all subpackages are actually extension packages in a Java programming language context.

Understanding this concept is fundamental to getting a practical handle on the expressive power of the packaging paradigm. This modular organization vastly simplifies an API by enhancing the programmer's understandability of the API.

To properly use and implement the services provided by JTAPI, we must first understand the Observation Model provided by Java. This asynchronous notification model is presented in depth in Chapter 9 of this book. For now, it is sufficient to understand that the primary interfaces in JTAPI are broken down into two camps: those that generate events and are therefore *observable*, and those that care about or report on the occurrence of these events. These interfaces are called *observers*.

The primary observable core interfaces of `javax.telephony` are:

- Address
- Call
- Connection
- Terminal
- TerminalConnection
- Provider

Yes, these are interfaces, not classes. There are important ramifications to using interfaces over classes, which will be addressed throughout this book. For now, we may think of them as classes. Briefly, an Address is a phone number, a Terminal is the phone itself, a Call is a telephone call, and a Connection models the communication path between a Call and an Address. A TerminalConnection is analogous to a telephone line. A provider may be thought of as a telephone service provider like MCI.

In addition to their own inherent behavior, these interfaces are to generate the telephony events defined in the subpackage `javax.tele-phony.events` and implement the capabilities in subpackage `java.capabilities`.[5] Any class that extends a class that implements these capabilities and events, of course, inherits this functionality. Subclasses may then also be observed by any class that implements the interfaces provided by the observer interfaces either directly or through polymorphism. Telephony application programmers are expected to follow this model, just as MFC programmers are expected to subclass MFC classes. Before we delve into a description of these interfaces, let's address the *use* of interfaces.

JTAPI Interface Specification Practice

A cursory examination of the components provided in the JTAPI API shows that the vast majority of these are specified as Java interfaces instead of concrete or abstract classes. Readers coming from a programming background other than Objective-C or Ada will find this a curious practice.

---

5 This same pattern of a subpackage for capabilities and events is repeated for each subpackage under javax.telephony.

Why was the API specified in this manner? In order to answer this question, we require a brief review of exactly what an interface is.[6] Interfaces are the chameleon of the Java language in that they provide many different capabilities. In one sense, an interface is a promise to implement a set of public method signatures. In fact, that is all an interface is: a grouping of function signatures (and possibly other constants). In this sense, interfaces are very *functional* in nature. A class that implements an interface will provide an appropriate implementation of the functions specified in an interface for the behavior of that class.

From an Interface to a Class

Because everything in Java must ultimately be implemented as a class, interfaces alone provide no functionality. In other words, a class somewhere must implement them. Okay, fine. But in order to turn an interface into a class, there may be instance variables involved — how do we know what those are to be? For that matter, how do we know if there are to be any instance variables at all? This is largely a vendor's design issue, but let's take a look at the methods required of a sample JTAPI interface to elicit some clues. Go ahead and look forward a few pages to **Listing 4.2** at the methods required for interface `javax.telephony.Address`. We'll wait.

The first place to look is at the return values and parameters required of the signatures. For example, the method `getName()` returns a String. Although no methods *require* an instance variable to operate, the only alternative would be to either construct a new String to return every time the method is called or to return a reference to a static variable.[7] So it's probably safe to assume that a private or protected instance variable representing the name of the Address of type String is *implied by* this interface. Parameters offer clues in a similar manner. The same logic would be used of the other return values and parameters of the remaining methods.

The Extension Curse

Okay, so now we know the general methodology for converting interfaces to classes — so why didn't Sun do this to begin with like Microsoft and others have for their class libraries? One answer is that Java does not provide multiple inheritance. Microsoft doesn't need to because C++ does support multiple inheritance. Since interfaces are the next best thing, Sun specified the classes as interfaces instead. Using Java, this makes a lot of sense. Had they *not* taken this approach, Sun would have subjected all JTAPI application programmers to the "extension curse" (where Java's lack of support for multiple inheritance forces a design compromise). We have some fun with this concept throughout the book.

---

6 We assume the reader knows what concrete and abstract classes are.

7 This last option makes little sense since each instance will have a different name.

It can also be argued that interfaces allow for more flexible vendor implementations and are therefore more appropriate for vertical market API specifications such as JTAPI. But back to business — let's explore the JTAPI components in more depth.

JTAPI Core Components

One of the most important skills we can obtain or discover as programmers is that of being able to properly identify *layers of abstraction*. This helps us to design modular code by organizing specification from implementation. It also helps us to model the real world in our code, which makes it more understandable and, therefore, maintainable. Dividing software components into physical and logical layers helps us to know intuitively when to use which class. Further organizing components into functional groups is another viable approach.

In this spirit, the primary interfaces and classes of package `javax.telephony` may be categorized into those that are *observable* and those that are *observers*. Further, some of these interfaces may be grouped into those that are *logical* and those that represent *physical* abstractions. We will adopt this approach[8] in an attempt to gain a more functional understanding of this portion of the API. First, we'll divide package `javax.telephony` into three groups — Observable Core Telephony Interfaces, Observer Core Telephony Interfaces, and Peer Core Telephony Interfaces. The first category will be even further subdivided into two groups — The Logical Core Telephony Interfaces and The Physical Core Telephony Interfaces. This categorization is shown as follows:

JTAPI Core Classes

  Observables

    Logical Abstractions

      Call

      Address

      Connection

    Physical Abstractions

      Terminal

      TerminalConnection

---

8 These categorizations are in no manner official — they are the author's artifacts used here in order to clarify the design of the library. We believe, however, that they are clearly implied by the design of the API.

Observers

    AddressObserver

    CallObserver

    TerminalObserver

    ProviderObserver

Peers

    Provider

    JTAPIPeer

    JTAPIPeerFactory

Most of us are pretty clear on the distinction between logical and physical abstractions, but what does it mean to say that an entity is *observable* or that it is an *observer*? This issue is covered in great detail in Chapter 9. Suffice it to say that JTAPI is based on an event registration and notification scheme comprised primarily of objects that register for notification (observers) of the state-changes of other objects (observables). For now, this event management model can be treated as an implementation detail. In short, observables notify observers by sending events every time their state changes.

Observable Core Telephony Interfaces

The logical observable interfaces are Address, Call, and Connection. The physical observable abstractions are the interfaces Terminal and TerminalConnection. In this section we will describe each of these design entities in terms of a general description, the life cycle of an instance, and the operations allowed. Life cycles will be portrayed in terms of state transitions. Deprecated methods will not be presented.

The Logical Core Telephony Interfaces

The core logical interfaces represent the conceptual telephony entities at the highest layer of abstraction. People place phone calls (implementations of interface Call) using phone numbers (implementations of interface Address). The call is made over a phone line, which connects the Address to the Call. The logical component of this connection is modeled as implementations of interface Connection. The relationship between these entities is depicted in **Figure 4.5**.

The first thing to notice about these objects and their relationships is that their operations probably depend heavily on the current states of the objects involved. They do. In fact one of these objects (namely, Connection) exists solely for the purpose of modeling the current state relationship between an Address and a Call. Let's look at the simplest component first, namely, Address.

Figure 4.5 *Calls, Connections, and Addresses*

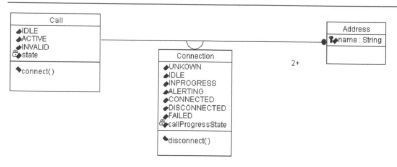

Address Interface

The Address interface is a logical mnemonic representation of a phone call's origination and/or termination points — a phone number. It is the *logical* endpoint[9] of a Call. However an address isn't *required* to play the role of a phone number. In some designs it may be represented as some other type of identifier (say an IP address). This notion of an Address is identical to that of TAPI.

An Address has no state — it is merely a name. An Address can be connected to at most one Call at a time, even though a Call may clearly be connected to more than one Address[10] simultaneously. Address objects are responsible for providing both present and historical information about their telephone calls within the Provider's domain. The relationship between an Address and a Terminal will be discussed later.

Life Cycle of an Address

Because an Address has no state, its life cycle is constant. In other words, an Address exists for as long as an instance of it exists in an application. Let's take a look at how an address is created. A sample instantiation of an Address object is provided in **Listing 4.1**.

Listing 4.1 *Instantiation of an Address*

```
import sroberts.telephony.*;
// altered Sun class per JTAPI spec...
import javax.telephony.JtapiPeerFactory;

public class TestAddressInstantiation {
    public static final void main(String args[]) {
        SDRProvider sdrProvider = null;
```

---

9 A Terminal is the physical endpoint of a Call. More on this later.
10 In fact, it must be or there would be no Call or Connection!

Listing 4.1 (cont.) *Instantiation of an Address*

```
try {
    SDRJtapiPeer icsPeer =
        (SDRJtapiPeer)JtapiPeerFactory.getJtapiPeer( null );
    sdrProvider = (SDRProvider)icsPeer.getProvider( null );
    System.out.println( "Provider name is: "
        + sdrProvider.getName() + "\n" + "Object id: "
        + sdrProvider.hashCode() + "\n");
} catch (Exception e) {
    System.out.println("PeerFactory or Provider call failed:
        "+ e.toString() +"\n" );
    System.exit( 0 );
}

    SDRAddress anICSAddress = null;
    // acts like new... obtain a phone number from the
    //  provider...
    try {
        anICSAddress = (SDRAddress)sdrProvider.getAddress(
                        "1234567" );
    } catch (Exception e) {
        System.out.println( "Address call failed: "+
            e.toString()");
        System.exit( 0 );
    }

    // had better return "1234567"...
    String phoneNumber = anICSAddress.getName();

    SDRProvider referenceTosdrProvider = null;
    // had better return same instance of sdrProvider...
    referenceTosdrProvider = (SDRProvider)
                        anICSAddress.getProvider();

    String providerName = referenceTosdrProvider.getName();

    System.out.println( "Got Phone Number "+ phoneNumber
        +" from : " + referenceTosdrProvider.hashCode() + "
        --> " + providerName );
    }
}
```

(2)

(1)

(3)

Although we have created an instance of the simplest objects in JTAPI, there is quite a bit of base JTAPI functionality built in.[11]

Note first that the Address object must be obtained by the Provider; it cannot be instantiated on its own ([1] of **Listing 4.1**). Before that, the Peer provided the Provider in turn ([2] of **Listing 4.1**). **Figure 4.6** depicts this "chain reaction" of instantiations.

Figure 4.6 *Creating an Address Instance*

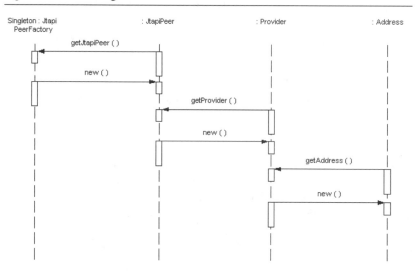

We will describe these objects and the reasoning behind this later. For the time being, it is sufficient to understand that we asked the JTAPI system for an Address object and the system produced that object from its inventory of phone numbers ([1] of **Listing 4.1**).

Next, we make sure that the Address instance is properly matched with its Provider ([3] of **Listing 4.1**). This is not a necessary step; rather it is a test to make sure our implementation is functioning properly. This is accomplished by matching hash codes.

Operations Allowed on an Address

Listing 4.2 lists the public operations allowed on an Address. Most functions are setters and getters and are self-explanatory. Where pre- and postconditions apply, they are noted in comments.

---

11 Or at least there will be once a JTAPI implementation is provided!

Listing 4.2 *Operations Allowed on an Address*

```
public String getName() throws PlatformException;

public Provider getProvider() throws PlatformException;

public Terminal[] getTerminals() throws
 PlatformException;

public Connection[] getConnections();
// Pre-conditions for: getConnections()
//      associated Provider state == IN_SERVICE
// Post-conditions for: getConnections()
//      all connections returned state != DISCONNECTED

public void addObserver(AddressObserver observer)
   throws ResourceUnavailableException,
         MethodNotSupportedException;
// repeated attempts to add the instance of the same
// observer will silently fail
// Post-conditions for: addObserver ()
// observer is an element of this.getObservers()
// Exceptions: ResourceUnavailableException =>
// The resource limit for the number
// of observers has been exceeded
// Exceptions: MethodNotSupportedException =>
// observer can't be added right now

public AddressObserver[] getObservers();

public void removeObserver(AddressObserver observer);

public void addCallObserver(CallObserver observer)
   throws ResourceUnavailableException,
         MethodNotSupportedException;
// automatically attach an observer to each Call in
// which this Address is included. The CallObserver is
// removed from the call when the Call leaves this
// Address.
// repeated attempts to add the instance of the observer
// will silently fail
// Exceptions: same as above

public CallObserver[] getCallObservers();

public void removeCallObserver(CallObserver observer);

public AddressCapabilities getCapabilities();
```

The `getName()` method would presumably return the phone number. Note that there are no corresponding set methods for every get method (e.g., no `setName()` method). This is because only the Provider may set these attributes. This makes sense — the phone company would not be very effective if we were allowed to change our own phone number at will! Most of the other operations reflect the relationships to other objects.

The only somewhat unusual operations allowed on an Address is the querying, addition, and removal of call observers on behalf of Call object instances. This capability enables observers to automatically monitor all calls associated with an address.

Probably the most important thing to remember about Addresses is that they may be associated with at most one Call (and hence one Connection) at a time. This makes perfect sense — we don't carry on two phone calls at the same time (unless we have a lousy connection), even though more than two parties may be *connected* at the same time. Of course, the Call itself may be associated with multiple Addresses, but only through a series of one-to-one relationships between Addresses and Connections.

Let's examine the next basic interface in JTAPI, the Call.

Call Interface

The Call interface represents the logical abstraction of the phone call itself. A Call is not active until at least two Addresses are associated with it (via two Connections). Unlike the Address, the Call is heavily state-oriented. Where an Address is a relatively static object (phone numbers don't change very often — and hopefully not in the middle of a call!), the Call is a relatively dynamic one. In fact, the Call's very usefulness depends on its state and that of at least one Connection.

While an Address can be connected to only one Call at a time, a Call may be connected to multiple Addresses simultaneously. Once the definitions are understood, this relationship is obvious. Note that both a "normal" phone call as well as a multiparty call exhibit this characteristic.

Life Cycle of a Call

Let's look at the life cycle of a Call in terms of a *state transition diagram*. All calls begin in an IDLE state and are created via the `Provider.createCall()` method. Optional parameters may be set upon creation that will affect the subsequent behavior of the Call. Once one or more connections are made, the Call is considered ACTIVE. When all connections disconnect (everyone hangs up), the Call moves into an INVALID state. Once inactivated, a Call instance cannot be used again. These state transitions are depicted in **Figure 4.7**.

Figure 4.7 *State Transitions of a Call*

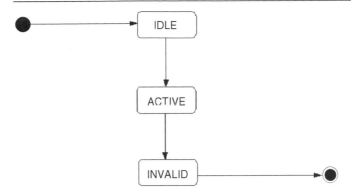

The states in **Figure 4.7** are defined in **Listing 4.3**.

Listing 4.3 *Call Interface State Definitions*

```
public static final int IDLE = 0x20;
// initial state of all Call objects.
// indicates the Call has zero Connections

public static final int ACTIVE = 0x21;
// indicates the Call has one or more Connections,
// none of which are in the DISCONNECTED state

public static final int INVALID = 0x22;
// indicates the Call has lost all of its Connections.
// A Call in this state cannot be used further.
```

When a Call is first created, it is by definition in the IDLE state. At this point, no Connections are associated with it (because it has just been created). It is possible, however, for a single Connection to be associated with a Call in the IDLE state when the Connection itself is in the IDLE state.

When a dial tone is received and then a successful Connection is made between two Addresses (usually by invoking the `Call.connect()` method), a Call becomes ACTIVE and a pair of Connection instances are associated. This relationship is depicted in **Figure 4.8**.

The ACTIVE state of a Call may involve more than one Connection (although it must have at least one Connection in order to be ACTIVE). To avoid the confusion between the state of a Connection and that of a Call, it is helpful to think of all Calls as being candidates for multiple party conference calls (even if they do not truly possess this capability). Although one or more parties (via connections) may become DISCONNECTED, the Call is still ACTIVE until *the last two* parties have signed off. Disconnected Connections are not referenced by the Call.

Figure 4.8 *Life Cycle of a Call*

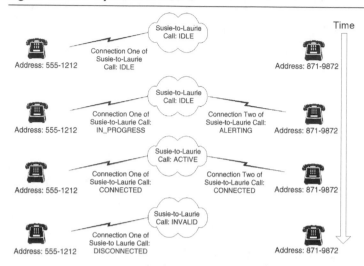

At this point, you may be wondering how a Call can be considered ACTIVE if there is only one Connection involved. Recall that even though a Call has three valid states, a Connection exists to model the state of a Call with respect to a *single particular* Address. But more importantly, a Connection is by definition "connected" when two or more Addresses are associated to each other by way of a Call. We'll revisit this concept later when we examine Connections in more detail.

It is instructive to reflect upon the extremely transient nature of a Call. Intuitively, a Call is a unique single telephone call that can never be repeated. Even if the conversation is taped, the Call itself is gone forever when the parties go *on hook* (i.e., they hang up).

Creating a Call

Creation of a Call instance is identical to that of an Address in that a Call can only be "created" by a Provider. A new Call instance is returned from a Provider in the IDLE state. This is slightly different from an Address in that an Address has no state. The Call creation process is depicted in **Figure 4.9**.

Intuitively, we might want to think of an idle Call as the point where one Address obtains a dial tone. However, this is not the case. A Call in the IDLE state can do nothing except move to another valid state of either ACTIVE or INVALID. All the "action" of getting a dial tone and answering the call occurs with the `Call.connect()` method. The distinction between a dial tone and other intuitive[12] Call states (like RINGING) are modeled at a lower level of abstraction through the TerminalConnection object.

---

12 We call these intuitive because they are not valid Call states; rather they are states one might "expect" a Call to enter without understanding the model.

Figure 4.9 *Creating a Call Instance*

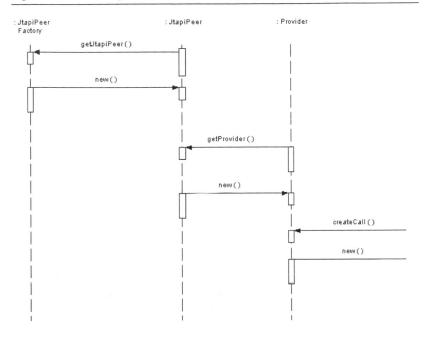

Therefore, a Call delegates some of its operations and state to lower-level objects in the JTAPI call model, in this case, the TerminalConnection. This pattern recurs throughout the JTAPI design. Recognizing it is fundamental to understanding the JTAPI architecture.

Operations Allowed on a Call

The operations a Call may perform are shown in **Listing 4.4**. Most are setters and getters and as such are self-explanatory. Where pre- and post-conditions apply, they are noted.

Listing 4.4 *Operations Allowed on a Call*

```
public Connection[] getConnections();
// Pre-conditions for: getConnections()
//      associated Provider state == IN_SERVICE
// Post-conditions for: getConnections()
//      all connections returned state != DISCONNECTED

public Provider getProvider();

public int getState();

public void addObserver(CallObserver observer)
```

Listing 4.4 (cont.) *Operations Allowed on a Call*

```
        throws ResourceUnavailableException,
            MethodNotSupportedException;
// Pre-conditions for: addObserver ()
//      Call state == IDLE or ACTIVE


public CallObserver[] getObservers();


public void removeObserver(CallObserver observer);


public CallCapabilities getCapabilities(
        Terminal terminal, Address address)
    throws InvalidArgumentException;
// null Terminal parameter returns general provider-wide
// Call capabilities


public Connection[] connect(
        Terminal origterm, Address origaddr, String dialedDigits)
    throws ResourceUnavailableException,
        PrivilegeViolationException,
        InvalidPartyException, InvalidArgumentException,
        InvalidStateException,
        MethodNotSupportedException;
// Pre-conditions for: connect()
//      associated Provider state == IN_SERVICE
//      Call state == IDLE (no existing Connections)
// Post-conditions for: connect()
//      Call state == ACTIVE
//      Two new Connections created (for origaddr &
//      dialedDigits).
//   Each state == IDLE
```

The most interesting operation for the Call interface (and perhaps the entire JTAPI API) is the connect() method. As you might guess, this is the function that attempts a call connection from the Terminal (the phone) and Address (the originating phone number) to the name of the destination Address housed at another Terminal. Note that all of these objects associated with the originating Call are in fact parameters passed to the connect() method.

Upon successful completion of the method, two new Connection instances are returned in the Connections[] array and three events are generated. The Call interface generates a CallCreatedEv event for the Call itself and two ConnCreatedEv events, one for each of the two Connections created. Any registered CallObservers receive these events. The connect() method ultimately generates a large number of events and spawns the creation of several objects. We will return to a discussion of this method after we've been introduced to the majority of the JTAPI components.

In terms of the dynamic states of the call model, the Call is the highest level of abstraction. The state of all Calls, Connections, and Terminal objects may be obtained through the Call interface. Call instances in turn must be queried through the Provider interface. For example, to find all the calls in the MCI network, one would have to query the MCI Provider object for all available Call instances. The Provider is responsible for returning all instances even if they existed before the Provider instance was instantiated. Before we examine the Provider, let's take a look at a Connection.

Connection Interface

The Connection interface is an ***association*** entity modeling the relationship between an Address and a Call. Recall that associations are special kinds of objects that link two objects together. These linked objects may be of the same type or they may be of different types. Because associations model relationships *between* objects, they are not usually considered "first class objects" in their own right, even if they are implemented as such.[13] Rather than modeling the state of the Address (which makes little sense), a Connection object is created to model the states between a Call and an Address explicitly. One could argue that the Connection just models the state of the Call, but a Call has its own states that are distinct and more abstract. An Address is required for a Connection to make sense anyway.

There is one Connection object for each and every Call/Address pair. Again, an Address can only be connected to one Call at a time, but a Call can be connected to many Addresses. In fact, a Call *must be* associated with at least two Addresses in order for any communication to occur, right? Because each of these Connections may be in different states, a Connection instance is required for each Call/Address pair.

Each Connection is a separate object that exists solely to describe the relationship in terms of states between a Call and an Address. The associated Call and Address references are immutable for the life of the Connection (i.e., they cannot change). In a similar sense, a Connection instance cannot be used for more than one Call.

The very existence of a Connection instance implies that a particular Address instance is connected to a particular Call instance in a particular state. Further, it implies the intent of at least one other Connection/Address pair to be associated with this very same call. This makes sense. Two or more Connections and Addresses sharing (i.e., pointing to) the same Call instance are part of a telephone conversation. In fact, the relationship between these three kinds of objects *defines* what a telephone conversation is.

---

13 This is exactly what Connection and TerminalConnection association interfaces are in JTAPI — full-blown objects.

One distinguishing feature of Connections is that they may act as a query interface between Calls and Addresses. An Address may obtain Call information through a particular Connection and vice versa. As far as the JTAPI call model is concerned, a Connection is the *only* valid relationship between a Call and an Address.

Probably the most important thing to remember about Connections is that they are really objects that model not the state of the entire Call (which has its own higher level states), but rather the state of a *particular* Address participation in a *particular* Call. Again, the metaphor of a multiparty Call is helpful. A particular Connection may be in several different states while the state of the entire Call remains ACTIVE. In a very real sense, the very existence (as well as the state) of a Call is dependent upon the very first and the very last Connection made. Before the first Connection is made, the Call is barely useful and after the last Connection becomes DISCON-NECTED, the Call is no longer valid.[14]

Life Cycle of a Connection

Like Calls (and unlike Addresses), Connections are heavily state-oriented. In fact they are one of the most state-aware objects in the JTAPI model. Each state represents the actions possible on a Connection at any given point in time. In terms of states, a Connection is at a lower level of abstraction than a Call. A connection moves in and out of several states, while a Call remains ACTIVE. Like a Call, a Connection's life cycle is best described by means of a state transition diagram. A pictorial view is provided in **Figure 4.10**.

As the number of states and transitions increases, the pictorial representation tends to be less useful than a textual representation, especially for programmers. The textual representation of a state transition diagram shows for each state what the valid state transitions are. It also best describes the life cycle of a Connection by its ordering. This is provided in **Listing 4.5**.

Listing 4.5 *Textual Representation of the State Transitions of a Connection*

```
IDLE -> ALERTING | CONNECTED | DISCONNECTED | FAILED | INPROGRESS
INPROGRESS -> ALERTING | CONNECTED | DISCONNECTED | FAILED
ALERTING -> CONNECTED | DISCONNECTED | FAILED | UNKNOWN
CONNECTED -> DISCONNECTED | FAILED | UNKNOWN
DISCONNECTED -> UNKNOWN
FAILED -> DISCONNECTED | UNKNOWN
```

---

14 It is expected to be reclaimed by the garbage collector.

Figure 4.10 *Connection State Transitions and Events*

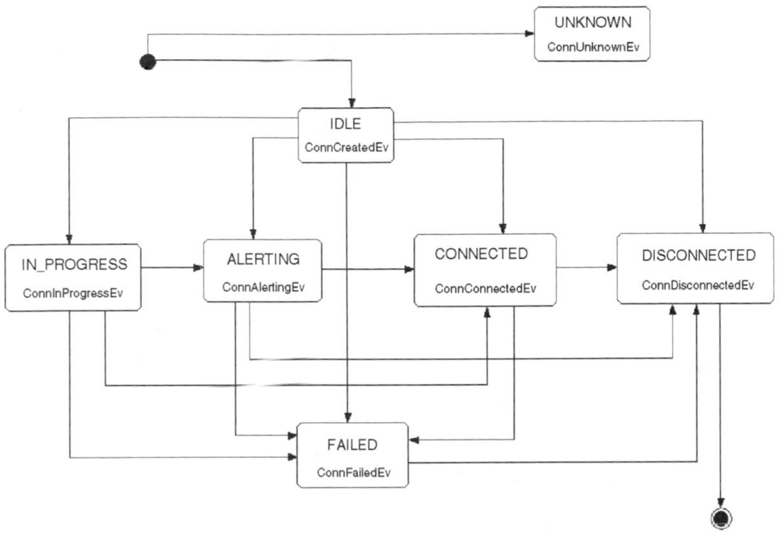

It is helpful to think of the initiation of the Connection life cycle in terms of pairs of Connections. For a phone conversation to take place, at least two Connection instances (and therefore at least two Addresses) must be pointing to the same Call instance *and* their states must be CONNECT-ED. This requires an origination and a termination Address (i.e., the caller and the callee). When a Connection is first instantiated, it is created in the IDLE state associated with an initiating Address and a Call in the IDLE or ACTIVE[15] state (this is true for both the origination and destination). As a Call is attempted with a destination Address instance, both Connection states transition to IN_PROGRESS. Once a dial tone is received on the destination Address, the phone rings and the destination Connection transitions to the ALERTING state while the origination state remains IN_PROGRESS. If the call is answered, the state of the Connection becomes CONNECTED and the Call instance state changes to ACTIVE. If not, the Connection state becomes FAILED for the destination Connection and the state of the Call does not change (this can occur if the caller gets a busy signal). When either party discontinues the call, the state of the Connection instance becomes DISCONNECTED and the Call becomes INVALID (if there is only one other associated Connection at that time). At this point, both the Connections and the Call are to be released to the garbage collector and not to be reused by any other Call/Address pair.

---

15 The Call might already be active if, say, there are already other Connections established for the Call.

Creating a Connection

Unlike Addresses and Calls, Connections are not instantiated directly. Rather they are designed to be returned as the result of a successful `Call.connect()` invocation. `Call.connect()` requires an originating and a termination/destination Address and so implies that a Connection for each is involved. Indeed it is, and that is exactly what is returned by the invocation: exactly two Connection instances (see **Figure 4.11**).

Figure 4.11 *Creating a Connection*

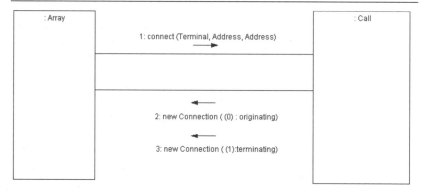

We need an Array instance to hold the two Connections because they are returned as a pair.

Operations Allowed on a Connection

```
public int getState();

public Call getCall();

public Address getAddress();

public TerminalConnection[] getTerminalConnections();
// Pre-conditions for: getTerminalConnections ()
//       TerminalConnection state != DROPPED

public void disconnect()
    throws PrivilegeViolationException,
           ResourceUnavailableException,
           MethodNotSupportedException,
           InvalidStateException;

public ConnectionCapabilities getCapabilities();
```

The Connection interface specifies only two methods of any real interest. The first is called `getTerminalConnections()`, and it returns the TerminalConnections that are not in the DROPPED state. TerminalConnections are examined in the following section.

Just like the `connect()` method was the most important method on a Call, the `disconnect()` method is the most important method of a Connection. You may be tempted to ask why a Call is able to initiate to a Connection, yet the Connection is the object that actually disconnects the Call. Again, it can be argued that this is actually a more intuitive model of the problem space. Calls cannot disconnect themselves. A party on one or the other end of the telephone line must physically depress a hook switch in order to disconnect the call. This action breaks the logical Connection as well as the physical TerminalConnection. The Connection moves into the DISCONNECTED state, the TerminalConnection into the DROPPED state. Further, a Call can remain ACTIVE even when an associated Connection disappears. This is possible, again, when there remain at least two Connections after the subject Connection disconnects!

A disconnected Connection generates two events: ConnDisconnectedEv and TermConnDroppedEv. Any object that implements the CallObserver interface (and, of course, bothers to register) receives these events. But what about the other Connections involved in the Call? Do they remain connected? The answer is that JTAPI does not directly specify what happens in this case. However, the model implies that at least two valid Connections must remain in order for the Call to remain active. Otherwise, we believe it is up to the implementation to handle this case and properly terminate the other Connection if only two remain at the time of the disconnection and one of those two disconnects. Let's drop down to the physical layer.

The Physical Core Telephony Interfaces

The core physical interfaces represent the actual physical telephony entities at the lowest layer of abstraction. These are the interfaces Terminal and TerminalConnection. Any classes created from these interfaces are to be made observable. A (logical) phone Call is connected via two or more physical terminals (implementations of interface Terminal). But why is a Connection instance considered to be a logical abstraction — isn't the connection a physical one? Good question; here's the answer. To the person making the call, there is only one logical connection on either end of the Call. They either successfully place the call or they do not. But the actual Connection may require more than one physical connection. In fact an entire network of physical connections and even potential connections (implementations of interface TerminalConnection) may take place to render one logical Connection.

Understanding the (sometimes subtle) underlying differences between these levels of abstraction aids the programmer in determining which objects to use in which circumstances. It is perfectly conceivable that a client-side application may never be concerned with the physical core telephony interfaces at all — only the logical ones. Likewise, a server-side application may be responsible for providing for the programming of switches. And so they may primarily be concerned with the physical core interfaces.[16] However any application requiring the ability to place a Call will have to know about Terminals (as we'll soon see).

Figure 4.12 *Relationship Between Physical Observable Core Interfaces*

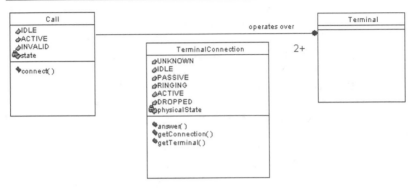

The relationship between the primary physical interfaces is shown in **Figure 4.12**. In the same manner that a Connection models the state relationship between a Call and an Address, a TerminalConnection models the state relationship between a Call and a Terminal. The big difference is that these states model physical events, not logical ones. At any one point in time, a Terminal can only be associated with one Call. However, a Call *must* be connected to at least two Terminals (and by definition, therefore, at least two TerminalConnections).

During the duration of this call, the Call (or a Connection participating in the Call) may be forwarded or transferred to another Terminal using the extended CallControl interfaces. This is another example of how a Call may be associated with multiple Terminals.

Terminal Interface

The Terminal interface represents a physical terminal; it is an *endpoint* in the telephone network. Intuitively, we might think of a Terminal as the thing you hold in your hand and push with your fingers when making a telephone call, although this is not quite accurate. Why? The telephone receiver (where the handset rests when not in use) may also be thought of as a kind of Terminal, but we do not believe that is the intent of the design.

---

16 Of course, a server-side application must concern itself with both levels of abstraction if it is to maintain the mapping between the two. Indeed, it is difficult to imagine a server-side application that would not make use of both abstraction layers — physical and logical.

A Terminal is *both* of these things at the same time. Even though a Terminal is usually thought of as a telephone set, it may in fact be any device that can generate a phone call — for example, a computer. Although a Terminal generally represents a physical abstraction, it may be a *set* of physical devices that implement the services specified in the Terminal interface. The Terminal is a higher level of abstraction than a one-to-one mapping of hardware.

Certain fundamental characteristics are required of a Terminal that are not specified by JTAPI. For example, to be able to place a call requires that a device be able to generate DTMF tones. The model assumes these capabilities.

Life Cycle of a Terminal

In life cycles, we are concerned with state transitions. However as we've seen, some JTAPI objects simply have no state. The Address was one; the Terminal is another such object. The Terminal's state is modeled entirely with the TerminalConnection object it is associated with on a Call. So it really has no state of its own. Per the JTAPI call model, a Terminal is an inert hardware device (or set of devices) that is inactive until a Call is associated with it. Even then, it has no state that is not entirely dependent on a Call.

Again, just as a connection models the state of a Call with respect to a particular Address, a TerminalConnection models the state of a Call with respect to a particular Terminal. We will examine the TerminalConnection in the next section.

Creating a Terminal

Like an Address and a Call, programmers may not directly create instances with the new operator. So how does one go about creating instances of a Terminal? Before we answer that question, we might ask why we would create a Terminal instance in first place. The answer is that we cannot make a call without a Terminal any more than we can make a telephone call without using a telephone! In fact, we need both a Terminal instance as well as an Address instance in order to place a call.[17]

Terminal instances are "known by" Address instances. The only way to obtain a Terminal instance is by querying an Address instance or a Provider instance. Actually, this makes sense when answering an inbound call. Intuitively, we would ask ourselves from which telephone we would be able to receive calls for a particular Address. For example, in order to receive phone calls for my residence number, I need to be at a location with Terminals that are already set up to receive calls made to that Address (my home number). Normally, these Terminals are the telephone sets in my

---

17 Recall that this requirement is specified by the `Call.connect()` method signature.

house, but I could have forwarded my calls to another set of Terminals in another location. Or consider a business number at my office — the Address initiates ringing at the Terminal at my desk, but the Call is then forwarded to the administrative Terminal set. Both of these Terminals are known by my business Address. Let's create some Terminals using an Address (see **Listing 4.6**).

Listing 4.6 *Creation of a Terminal*

```
// assume that a Peer and a Provider instance
// are already instantiated...
try {
   Address origaddr = myprovider.getAddress("5551212");

   // get all the Terminals available for this Address...
   Terminal[] providerTerminals = origaddr.getTerminals();

   // or, get all the Terminals available for this Provider...
   Terminal[] addrTerminals = myprovider.getTerminals();

   // check out my Provider choices...
   for ( int i = 0; i < providerTerminals.length; i++ ) {
      System.out.println ( "Terminal choice " + i
           + " is: " + providerTerminals [ i ].getName() );
   }
   // check out my Address choices
   // (should be a subset of the Provider list)...
   for ( int i = 0; i < addrTerminals.length; i++ ) {
      System.out.println ( "Terminal choice " + i
             + " is: " + addrTerminals [ i ].getName() );
   }
} catch (Exception excp) {
   // Handle exceptions;
}
```

Operations Allowed on a Terminal

The interesting methods that are provided by Terminal instances have to do with how they're to be uniquely named and the additional observation capabilities provided on behalf of Call instances. All of the operations are listed in **Listing 4.7**.

Listing 4.7 *Operations Allowed on a Terminal*

```
public String getName();

public Provider getProvider();
```

Listing 4.7 (cont.) *Operations Allowed on a Terminal*

```
public Address[] getAddresses();

public TerminalConnection[] getTerminalConnections();

public void addObserver(TerminalObserver observer)
    throws ResourceUnavailableException,
          MethodNotSupportedException;

public TerminalObserver[] getObservers();

public void removeObserver(TerminalObserver observer);

public void addCallObserver(CallObserver observer)
    throws ResourceUnavailableException,
          MethodNotSupportedException;

public CallObserver[] getCallObservers();

public void removeCallObserver(CallObserver observer);

public TerminalCapabilities getCapabilities();
```

Cardinality and the Terminal-Address Relationship

Like Addresses, each Terminal must have a unique name within a Provider's domain. Like all observable interfaces, Terminals provide the capability to add and remove observers. In addition to those Terminal observers, Terminal instances also provide this functionality for the Call with which a Terminal instance is associated. This way, a CallObserver can preregister for calls before they happen. This capability is important because Calls are dynamic objects. We have already seen the same functionality supplied on behalf of Calls for an Address. Now Calls are covered from both ends (i.e., logical and physical).

We have already described a cardinality[18] relationship whereby many Terminals may be aware of a single Address. Indeed, all the phones in your home probably ring when an outside call references your home Address (phone number). This many-to-one relationship with respect to Terminals and Addresses is supported by the `getTerminals()` method of the Address interface and is depicted in **Figure 4.13**.

However, it is also very common for office telephones to be able to "answer" calls to multiple addresses. This one-to-many relationship with respect to Terminals and Addresses is supported by the `getAddresses()` method of the Terminal interface and is depicted in **Figure 4.14**.

---

18 Cardinality is addressed in gory detail in Chapter 11.

Figure 4.13 *Appearance Relationship Between a Terminal and an Address*

Figure 4.14 *Service Relationship Between a Terminal and an Address*

Although not explicitly specified in JTAPI, these two Terminal-Address relationships can be combined into a single many-to-many association between Terminals and Addresses as depicted in **Figure 4.15**.

Figure 4.15 *Terminal-Address Relationship*

From an application programming perspective, this relationship is probably only of interest to applications managing or reporting on the transfer of Connections during a Call. However, the Provider must internally (and probably persistently) map this relationship in order to provide a list of destination Addresses for a Terminal that supports multiple Addresses. And because the same Address may appear on more than one Terminal, the provider has a need for a full-blown associative object. This is actually an argument for extending the JTAPI core model.

In Chapter 11, "Organizing a Large-Scale Telecom Development Project," we claim that all many-to-many relationships *must* be resolved. However, this relationship is not reflected directly in the JTAPI model. What gives? This interface is probably not modeled in JTAPI because it is considered an implementation detail. It is a *persistent* relationship outside the scope of JTAPI, which is largely transient in nature. It is the provider's responsibility to implement the functionality required, but it may be modeled in any way they see fit.

Let's do some mental cement work. When placing a phone call, there's a certain sequence one must follow. First, a JTAPI implementation must exist in the form of a JTAPIPeer. Next, a Provider must exist. The Provider acts as a runtime source for the entire JTAPI implementation. The Provider can provide instances of Addresses and Terminals, which may then be associated with Calls. Next, a telephone device must be located. This device is the Terminal.[19] Every Terminal comes with one or more Addresses assigned to it in that an incoming Call will ring that Terminal only for the so-called originating Address(es) it is associated with. Next, a destination Address must be selected for outgoing calls. Once the destination digits are dialed and another party answers, we have two Addresses connected by two Connections on one Call using two Terminals.

Four down, one to go... What is a Terminal Connection?

TerminalConnection Interface

A TerminalConnection is the physical analogy to the logical Connection interface with an added dependency. It not only models the state relationship between a Call and a physical device or set of devices (a Terminal), the TerminalConnection entity itself is dependent on a Connection for its very existence. The particular Connection instance that the TerminalConnection is associated with must be related to an Address that belongs to the set of valid Addresses serviced by the particular Terminal the TerminalConnection is related to (got that?). In other words, it doesn't make sense for an Address to be involved in a Connection where the Terminal or Terminals used do not service that Address!

Similar to the manner in which a Call may be associated with more than one Terminal, a Connection may refer to zero or more TerminalConnections (see **Figure 4.16**). A Connection does not necessarily require a TerminalConnection. The reverse, however, is not true — a TerminalConnection requires a Connection.

Figure 4.16 *Logical and Physical Connection Relationships*

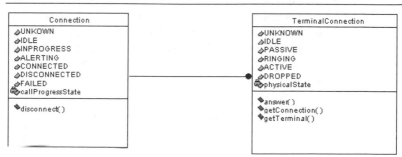

---

19 Of course, the Terminal may really be comprised of not just the phone device, but also a telephony board, an internal switchboard, and even a human operator!

Note the differences in the names of the allowable states between a Connection and a TerminalConnection. Most states seem to map pretty much one-to-one. In this relationship, the logical state of the Connection may correspond to the physical state of the TerminalConnection as depicted in **Listing 4.8**.

Listing 4.8 *Relationship Between Connection and TerminalConnection State Transitions*

```
Connection      TerminalConnection
----------      ------------------
IDLE            --> no connection states may exist
INPROGRESS      --> no connection states may exist
ALERTING        --> RINGING
CONNECTED       --> PASSIVE | ACTIVE | DROPPED
DISCONNECTED    --> DROPPED
FAILED          --> DROPPED
UNKNOWN         --> UNKNOWN
```

From **Listing 4.8**, we can see that there is a clear link between the states of a TerminalConnection and that of the Connection it is associated with. **Listing 4.8** shows the allowable state transitions of a TerminalConnection given those of a Connection.

Because the TerminalConnection exhibits perhaps the most complex state transitions in JTAPI, we defer further discussion of the life cycle until later.

Creating a TerminalConnection

Unlike its logical counterpart Connection, the TerminalConnection is not created as the result of an application-level action (e.g., an invocation of `Call.connect()`). Instead, it is to be created internally as the result of a Connection instantiation. This action is of course the responsibility of the JTAPI implementation.

The creation of a TerminalConnection is not mandatory for an outgoing[20] call. In fact, a JTAPI implementation might instantiate one only if there are observers registered for the events it generates. On the other hand, a JTAPI vendor might decide to go ahead and create one anyway in order to provide a consistent call model framework.

Operations Allowed on a TerminalConnection

The allowable operations on a TerminalConnection are presented in **Listing 4.9**.

---

20 It is implied, however, that a TerminalConnection is implied for an incoming call. More on this shortly.

Listing 4.9 *Operations Allowed on a TerminalConnection*

```
public int getState();

public Terminal getTerminal();

public Connection getConnection();

public TerminalConnectionCapabilities getCapabilities();

public void answer()
   throws PrivilegeViolationException,
          ResourceUnavailableException,
          MethodNotSupportedException,
InvalidStateException;
```

Clearly, the most interesting method provided for the TerminalConnection object is the answer() method. Similar to the manner in which a Connection object may *disconnect* a call, a TerminalConnection object may *answer* a call. In order for the answer method to be invoked, both the Connection and the TerminalConnection objects must be in a certain state. The Connection object must be in the ALERTING state and the TerminalConnection object must be in the RINGING state. If the call is successfully answered (i.e., a ringing switch goes off-hook), the TerminalConnection transitions to the ACTIVE state and the Connection moves to the CONNECTED state. All of this is to occur simultaneously upon completion of the answer() method.

Earlier we noted that a TerminalConnection instance is not necessary for an outgoing call — but what about an incoming call? Since the only method prescribed in the JTAPI API for answering a call belongs to a TerminalConnection, it seems that they are required for incoming calls.

Life Cycle of a TerminalConnection

Like its logical counterpart the Connection, a TerminalConnection exists for the sole purpose of describing the physical *state relationship* between a Call and a Terminal. Also like its logical counterpart the Connection, the TerminalConnection is a state-oriented dynamic object. The allowable states and their respective state transitions are modeled in **Listing 4.10**.

Listing 4.10 *State Transitions of a TerminalConnection*

```
IDLE --> PASSIVE | RINGING | ACTIVE| DROPPED | UNKNOWN
PASSIVE --> ACTIVE | DROPPED | UNKNOWN
RINGING --> DROPPED | PASSIVE | ACTIVE | UNKNOWN
ACTIVE --> PASSIVE | DROPPED | UNKNOWN
DROPPED --> no state transition allowed.
UNKNOWN --> IDLE| PASSIVE | RINGING | ACTIVE | DROPPED
```

As one would expect, the physical Call states of a TerminalConnection are at a lower layer of abstraction than those of the logical Connection. Not too surprisingly, these states have to do with things the Terminal can do while it is associated with the Call. For example, a TerminalConnection starts up in an IDLE state. When the proper signal is applied to the Terminal device, the telephone begins to ring and the TerminalConnection moves into the RINGING state. Once the call is acknowledged, the TerminalConnection usually moves into a PASSIVE or an ACTIVE stage (depending on the implementation). When the Connection is disconnected, the TerminalConnection moves into a DROPPED state and the Call is terminated. The TerminalConnection states and their associated events are modeled in **Figure 4.17**.

Figure 4.17 *TerminalConnection States and Events*

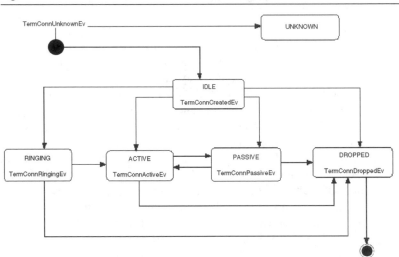

Suppose we think of a particular phone conversation as being a set of two Connections between two different Addresses which are all part of a Call that is currently being implemented from two particular handsets in two separate rooms.[21] Let's walk these components through a scenario in order to better flush out their behavior.

A Terminal Connection Scenario

Suppose a Call comes in and a successful set of Connections are made. Susie took the call in the living room over by the television. She and Claire are making plans for a summer vacation somewhere in

---

21 We are assuming no mobile/cellular phone for simplicity.

the Mediterranean with their families. Ignoring the initialization steps, the Call and the TerminalConnection are now in the ACTIVE state; the Connection is in the CONNECTED state. This situation is depicted in terms of the current states of the objects involved in **Figure 4.18**.

Susie wants to put Claire on hold[22] for a minute while she moves to another phone in a more private room (see **Figure 4.18**). The Call is still ACTIVE, the Connection is now INPROGRESS, and the original TerminalConnection becomes PASSIVE. The interesting thing to note here is that the Call will remain ACTIVE during the entire process of swapping out the underlying TerminalConnection. This is indeed an accurate portrayal of this particular telephony scenario — Susie never hung up the phone and so the Call is indeed still ACTIVE. She asks the home office operator to ring the phone in the other room until she picks it up. The original TerminalConnection is DROPPED. A new TerminalConnection is created in the IDLE state, quickly moving to the PASSIVE and then the RINGING state. At the same time, the associated Connection is moved to a new state of ALERTING.

Figure 4.18 *Transferring TerminalConnections from a Connection*

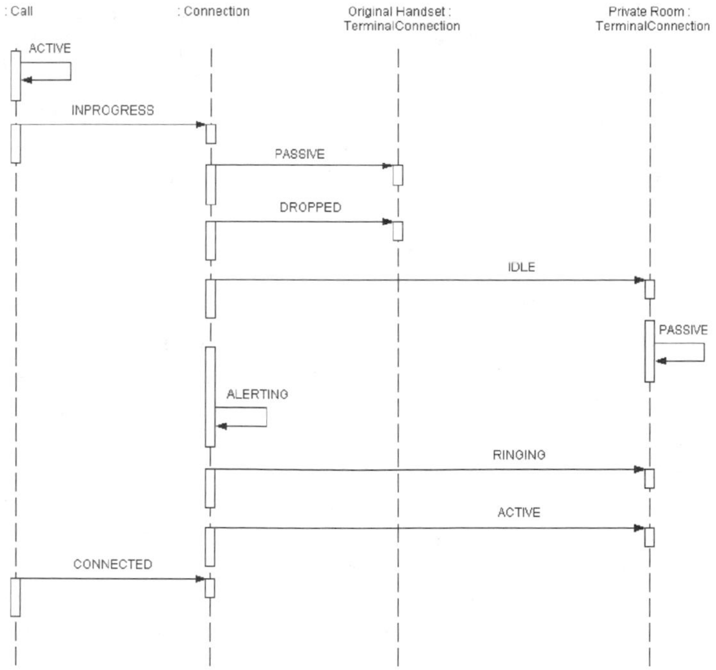

When Susie picks up the phone, all is as before except she has a new TerminalConnection for the same original Connection.

---

22 Hold functionality is addressed in Chapter 8 when we examine the Call Control interfaces.

Return to Pooh Corner

Now that we have been thoroughly exposed to all of the *observables*, its time to walk them through a successful call completion. As promised, we now return to the `Call.connect()` method. Recall that the `Call.connect()` method had just returned us two new Connection instances and had generated the appropriate events. As the Call is actually placed shortly after a successful `connect()` invocation, more objects are created and more events are generated (surprise!).

The originating Connection[0] moves from the IDLE state into the CONNECTED state. A TerminalConnection is created in the ACTIVE state between the originating Terminal and the Call. This triggers a ConnConnectedEv event from the originating Address and both a TermConnCreatedEv and a TermConnConnectedEv event from the newly created TerminalConnection. More TerminalConnection instances may be created in the PASSIVE or DROPPED state if the Address is associated with more Terminals (presumably this allows for the subsystem to prepare these lines for eavesdropping[23]). These in turn would generate more events of their own (i.e., another TermConnCreatedEv and a TermConnDroppedEv or a TermConnPassiveEv for each associated Terminal, if any).

As the destination Address responds, the destination Connection[1] moves from the IDLE state into the INPROGRESS state, then quickly into the ALERTING state as the Connection attempts to alert all available TerminalConnections on the destination side. These state transitions generate yet another set of events called ConnInProgressEv and ConnAlertingEv. Beginning to see a pattern here?

Next, a TerminalConnection object is created between the Call and every Terminal object associated with the destination Address (if they weren't created already). Each of these TerminalConnections are in the RINGING state and so generate first TermConnCreatedEv events, then TermConnPassiveEv and then TermConnRingingEv events. If the call is answered, both Connections move into the CONNECTED state and deliver ConnConnectedEv events. In addition, the destination TerminalConnection, which actually answered the call, moves into the ACTIVE state and generates a TermConnActiveEv event. The other TerminalConnections (if any) move into either the PASSIVE or DROPPED states depending on the implementation (i.e., the behavior of the switch at the destination point). In either case, they generate the appropriate event (either TermConnPassiveEv or TermConnDroppedEv). Finally, the Call itself moves into the ACTIVE state and generates a CallActiveEv event.

This completes our investigation of the core *observable* JTAPI components. We will revisit the `connect()` method when we implement the code on the Windows platform in Chapter 7. Earlier we spoke of events

---

23 Just kidding. Really, these occur if there are multiple phones that may respond to the incoming call, which is a very common case.

being delivered, but we didn't say to whom or how this is accomplished. At this point, you may be asking how these state changes are sent back to an application. Glad you asked — the answer is provided in the next section where we discuss the *role of observers.*

Observer Core Telephony Interfaces

The remaining core interfaces are referred to as *observers.* Observers *receive event notifications* from *observables.* The observer core interfaces are:

- AddressObserver
- CallObserver
- TerminalObserver
- ProviderObserver

Note that these observer interfaces do not correspond one-to-one with the observable interfaces. This is because the CallObserver interface reports on all Connection interfaces as well as TerminalConnection interfaces (i.e., this makes a separate interface for Connection-type observers unnecessary). This makes sense since neither a Connection nor a TerminalConnection can really exist without a Call — they are association interfaces. Both the Connection and the TerminalConnection interfaces exist only to model and to report the states and state transitions between Calls, Addresses and Terminals. To observe these 'state monitoring' classes would be like going to the Super Bowl and observing the reporters instead of the game.

Recall the distinction between interfaces that are observable and those that are observers. Any class implementing the Observer interface will be notified of the state of a previously registered observable interface change provided they follow the appropriate protocol. This protocol consists of a simple registration process of invoking the **addObserver( )** method of the observable interface of interest. Deregistration is accomplished by invoking the **removeObserver( )** method on the same instance. In both cases, the observer passes itself as an argument. The process is the same for all four types of observers.

Life Cycle of an Observer

The life cycle of an observer is completely dependent on the application. The JTAPI model does not in any way control or suggest *when* or even *how* an observer should be created or destroyed. However, observers are the *only* mechanism for querying telephony objects as specified in JTAPI. And so, to not create observers is to not be able to use telephony information — not a very effective approach.

Observers are probably the highest level of abstraction presented in the JTAPI model. They are application-level abstractions that *use* the services of underlying telephony components like Calls and Addresses.

Any object can be an observer. All they have to do is implement the observer interface. This means you are free to use whatever object you want. Good design would map this functionality to an appropriate existing object only if there is one. Otherwise, just create an observer instance and use it. For example, suppose that an interest in phone calls is an intrinsic characteristic of teenage girls. Clearly, all of these instances should implement the CallObserver interface as follows:

```
public class TeenAgeGirl extends Girl
   implements CallObserver { }
```

If extension is either inappropriate or unavailable, a CallObserver implementation as an instance variable in a has-a relationship can be an effective compromise.

```
public class TeenAgeGirl extends Girl {
   private CallObserver myCO;
}
```

Which observer interface should be implemented? It depends on exactly what the application needs to monitor. **Table 4.1** shows which observer interfaces monitor which JTAPI components.

Table 4.1 *Core Components Observed by Core Observers*

This Interface...	Monitors This JTAPI Core Component
AddressObserver	Address
CallObserver	Call, Connection, TerminalConnection
TerminalObserver	Terminal
ProviderObserver	Provider

Operations Allowed on an Observer

Intuitively, observers are just objects interested in possibly[24] reacting to changes in the state of observable objects. For example, a reporting application may want to log every phone call that comes in. In this case, a CallMonitor object may be designed that registers itself with the Call, one or more Addresses, one or more Terminals, or all of the above, etc. We would simply swap out the CallMonitor for the TeenAgeGirl above.

In order to register for events, the observer invokes the `addObserver()` method on the object they wish to observe. For example,

---

24 We are tentative here because an observer may "decide" not to react to all events, just some.

an AddressObserver would invoke the `Address.addObserver()` method to register for events for an Address object. Once these observers have been registered, they can be queried with a method called `XXX.getObservers()` where XXX is the name of the observable class. For example, one would query all Address observers for a particular Address by invoking the method `Address.getObservers()` on that Address instance.

Every time the appropriate events occur, the observers are notified and respond accordingly (i.e., they respond however you program them to respond). This response is implemented when the observer provides an *event handler* to capture and handle these events. This event handler takes the form of a method specified in the relevant interface. All of these event handlers follow a common protocol. Each handler accepts an array of event objects that are specific to the observable that generated the event.[25] For example, the AddressObserver interface specifies the method:

```
addressChangedEvent( AddrEv[] adrrEvents )
```

When notification is no longer desired, an observer simply invokes the `removeObserver()` method on the observable they are observing and the spigot of events is turned off. And so, in the case of Address objects, the AddressObserver invokes the `Address.removeObserver()` method. In addition, the underlying implementation (or JTAPI runtime) may send an XxxObservationEndedEv event (where Xxx is either an Address, a Call, a Provider, or a Terminal). This action has the same result, it is just sent by the system instead of the application. So an Address might receive an AddrObservationEndedEv event when the system is no longer able to report on the Address for, say, internal reasons rather than for any application-specific reason.

Here's a look at the observer interfaces and the events they respond to.

AddressObserver Interface

```
package javax.telephony;
import  javax.telephony.events.AddrEv;

public interface AddressObserver {
    public void addressChangedEvent(AddrEv[] eventList);
}
```

Legal AddressObserver Events

```
javax.telephony.events.AddrEv
javax.telephony.events.AddrObservationEndedEv
```

---

25 There are two exceptions (Connection and TerminalConnection events) to this "rule" that are covered later. These exceptions do not violate the design; rather they complement it.

There is only one event (potentially) generated from an Address and that is the AddrObservationEndedEv event. This is not too surprising in that an Address has no state of its own and therefore no events to generate because it has no state transitions for an AddressObserver to report on. What about AddrEv — isn't it generated as well? No. AddrEv is an abstract interface that all Address-related events are to extend. This same pattern of an abstract event interface plus an ObservationEndedEv is repeated (at a minimum) for each type of observer interface (i.e., Provider, Terminal, and Call).

TerminalObserver Interface

```
package javax.telephony;
import   javax.telephony.events.TermEv;

public interface TerminalObserver {
  public void terminalChangedEvent(TermEv[] eventList);
}
```

Legal TerminalObserver Events

```
javax.telephony.events.TermEv
javax.telephony.events.TermObservationEndedEv
```

Like an AddressObserver, a TerminalObserver doesn't have much going on. It is observing a physical device (a Terminal) that kind of just sits there. The dynamic activity of a Terminal is modeled in the TerminalConnection, not the Terminal itself. Again we find a base event class to extend all Terminal events (TermEv) as well as an ObservationEndedEv event (TermObservationEndedEv) that may be generated by either the application or the runtime system.

ProviderObserver Interface

```
package javax.telephony;
import   javax.telephony.events.ProvEv;

public interface ProviderObserver {
public void providerChangedEvent(ProvEv[] eventList);
}
```

Legal ProviderObserver Events

```
javax.telephony.events.ProvEv
javax.telephony.events.ProvInServiceEv
javax.telephony.events.ProvOutOfServiceEv
javax.telephony.events.ProvShutdownEv
javax.telephony.events.ProvObservationEndedEv
```

A ProviderObserver is a little more exciting than an AddressObserver or a TerminalObserver, but not much. In addition to the normal two events we have an event representing each possible state transition that a Provider may move out of. These correspond one-to-one to the states a Provider may be in (see **Figure 4.20**). This relationship between events and state transitions will be further discussed in the section called "States, Events, and State Transitions," later in this chapter.

CallObserver Interface

```
package javax.telephony;
import   javax.telephony.events.CallEv;

public interface CallObserver {
  public void callChangedEvent(CallEv[] eventList);
}
```

Legal CallObserver Events

```
javax.telephony.events.CallEv
javax.telephony.events.CallActiveEv
javax.telephony.events.CallInvalidEv
javax.telephony.events.CallObservationEndedEv
javax.telephony.events.ConnEv
javax.telephony.events.ConnAlertingEv
javax.telephony.events.ConnConnectedEv
javax.telephony.events.ConnCreatedEv
javax.telephony.events.ConnDisconnectedEv
javax.telephony.events.ConnFailedEv
javax.telephony.events.ConnInProgressEv
javax.telephony.events.ConnUnknownEv
javax.telephony.events.TermConnEv
javax.telephony.events.TermConnActiveEv
javax.telephony.events.TermConnCreatedEv
javax.telephony.events.TermConnDroppedEv
javax.telephony.events.TermConnPassiveEv
javax.telephony.events.TermConnRingingEv
javax.telephony.events.TermConnUnknownEv
```

Well, finally — some events we can sink our teeth into! Like the ProviderObserver, the CallObserver receives notification of events that relate to state transitions on its associated core telephony object (namely, a Call) in addition to the standard two events. The big difference here is that a CallObserver receives state transition notifications not only from Calls, but also from other types of objects, namely, Connections and TerminalConnections. This erases the need for a ConnectionObserver interface and a TerminalConnectionObserver interface; hence there are none provided in JTAPI.

Notice that the signature of the `callChangedEvent()` method takes an array of CallEv instances as a parameter. How then is the function able to report on Connections and TerminalConnections events? The most practical approach to implementing this capability would be to have all Connection and TerminalConnection events simply extend the CallEv interface. And they do.

From the preceding definitions, it is clear that events play an important role in the JTAPI notification scheme. They provide the "glue" that binds application entities with the JTAPI runtime system. Exactly what they are and how they are to be used is covered in more detail later in the section titled "JTAPI — An Event-Driven API" in this chapter.

Observer Convenience Methods on Core Telephony Objects

As we have seen, there is a common pattern for all core telephony objects whereby they may "add observers to themselves." For example, an Address has a method called `addObserver()`, which takes an AddressObserver instance as an argument, a Call exports a method called `addObserver()`, which takes a CallObserver instance as an argument, and so on. Each of these methods enables the delivery of events to the object passed in as a parameter.

However, each observer must usually be of the same "type" as the core interface. For example, a Terminal can only add observers of Terminals, right? Usually, but not exactly. These corresponding types are not the *only* types that a core interface may accept. There are exceptions to this pattern in the case of CallObservers. Convenience methods are placed on Addresses and Terminals that allow for the preregistration of CallObservers on Addresses and Terminals.

To see why this is so, imagine writing a JTAPI application. If these convenience methods were *not* provided, a Call instance would always have to be created before any observers could be registered for incoming calls. Because Calls occur at unpredictable times, a mechanism to store registration requests (i.e., observers) would have to be maintained by the application and registered only as Calls come in. To avoid this, the JTAPI designers shifted this common coding burden onto the JTAPI implementation and away from the application programmer by allowing an operation whereby CallObservers can be passed to Addresses and Terminals before any Calls associated with either that Address or that Terminal come in. The CallObservers are automatically removed when the Call leaves that Address or Terminal, respectively. Cool, huh?

Peer Core Telephony Interfaces and Classes

The remaining three core components provided in `javax.telephony` allow programmers the capability to create what are referred to as "peer" objects. These three interfaces are directly related by way of a *chained instantiation* process. In short, programmers initially interface with an entity called a ***JtapiPeerFactory***, which produces an instance of a ***JtapiPeer***. Through the JtapiPeer, they gain access to a ***Provider*** that allows them to create or locate instances of telephony components. The instantiation relationship between the peer interfaces and classes is depicted in **Figure 4.19**.

Figure 4.19 *Peer Instantiation Relationship*

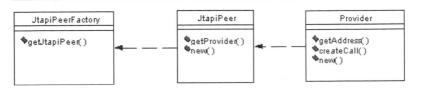

The JTAPI runtime system is initialized by way of this "trinity" process. In fact, no telephony objects can exist without this system in place. Let's start with the factory.

JtapiPeerFactory Class

The JtapiPeerFactory class is the "granddaddy" of all of the peer classes and interfaces. It serves as a namespace manager of packages and different implementations among the same or different vendors. Every JTAPI vendor must supply an implementation of this class.

JtapiPeerFactory operates like a singleton providing a set of static methods. Before any JTAPI API calls to peer objects can be made, a call to the `getJtapiPeer()` method must be made. Since programmers are not allowed to create instances of certain objects (including JtapiPeerFactory instances), a mechanism is required that allows them access to these instances and other operations provided by so-called "provider" objects (i.e., instances of class Provider). The JtapiPeerFactory interface provides this capability by first returning a JtapiPeer object that in turn provides a Provider object. The Provider in turn provides the keys to the JTAPI kingdom.

Managing the namespace of packages is vitally important to JTAPI vendors. Since most of JTAPI is provided as a set of interfaces, vendors are forced to provide unique names for their classes that implement these interfaces or they must force users to disambiguate their names from the JTAPI names and those of other vendors. To avoid this confusion (at least for JtapiPeer objects), Sun imposes a voluntary name-mangling scheme for the fully qualified name of the JtapiPeer class provided by the vendor. This scheme is called "reverse domain name." For example, Titus Corporation has a domain name of `titusoft.com`. They would then provide a class named `com.titusoft.xxx.xxx`, where `xxx.xxx` is any object hierarchy of their choosing. A fully compliant version might have the name `com.titusoft.javax.telephony.DefaultJtapiPeer`.

Life Cycle of a JtapiPeerFactory

The JtapiPeerFactory is the only class in JTAPI that is not an Exception (i.e., all other JTAPI entities are interfaces). The reason for this is that all of its methods are static.

Operations Allowed on a JtapiPeerFactory

JtapiPeerFactory exists for the sole purpose of returning an instance of interface JtapiPeer. It only allows one public method call — getJtapiPeer().

```
public synchronized static JtapiPeer
    getJtapiPeer(String jtapiPeerName)
        throws JtapiPeerUnavailableException;
```

The name string passed must be a fully qualified Java class name as described above. If no name is supplied and instead the value **null** is passed (because the programmer won't bother finding out or doesn't care what the name is), the JtapiPeer interface will provide a default instance by providing a class named DefaultJtapiPeer or by overriding the private getDefaultJtapiPeer() method.

JtapiPeer Interface

Exactly what is a peer? In a general sense, a peer object operates as a mirror object. It shadows the operations of another object. A peer is functionally similar to a proxy in that a peer object operates on behalf of another object.

In Java, however, the term takes on a similar, yet slightly more specific meaning. The term peer means "any platform-specific implementation of a Java interface or API." Each vendor supplies a set of peer objects that implement the JTAPI API. These objects are by definition platform-dependent.[26] Because almost all JTAPI abstractions are interfaces, the classes a vendor supplies would be the set of peer classes. For example, ICS Inc. might create a class called ICSAddress that implements the Address interface. This class would be a peer. Note the similarity between this and the *service provider* role required of TAPI implementations.[27]

The JtapiPeer interface serves three purposes. First, it represents and provides access to a particular vendor's implementation of the JTAPI API. Second, it provides a security interface requiring that users (and even programmers) log in to the runtime system in order to obtain permission to use and create components. Third, the interface provides a means of identifying the services provided by a particular JTAPI implementation.

---

26 This does not mean that the JTAPI code is platform dependent — it is not.
27 TAPI service providers are discussed in Chapter 5.

Life Cycle of a JtapiPeer

The life cycle of a JtapiPeer is static because it has no state (at least as far as the call model is concerned). No events are generated as a result of state transitions because no states exist. It is basically a *service object* used to obtain instances of class Provider. The class itself is obtained via the JtapiPeerFactory class.

Vendors are required to provide a means of placing their implementation of class JtapiPeer in the CLASSPATH on the local machine where JTAPI is to run. Usually, the name of this class is DefaultJtapiPeer.

Operations Allowed on a JtapiPeer

```
public String getName();

public String[] getServices();

public Provider getProvider(String providerString)
   throws ProviderUnavailableException;
```

The getName() method is regularly used as an argument to the JtapiPeerFactory.getJtapiPeer() method as follows:

```
JtapiPeer jtp = new JtapiPeer();
try { jtp = JtapiPeerFactory.getJtapiPeer(
   jtp.getName( "PBX Peer" ) ); }
catch( JtapiPeerUnavailableException jtpe ) {}
```

The getServices() method returns an array of strings describing (i.e., giving service names for) the services that a JTAPI implementation has to offer.

```
// continued from above...
String[] services = jtp.getServices();
```

Presumably, one of these strings would ultimately be passed as an argument to the most interesting method, namely getProvider(). This method takes the string as a required argument and also allows other optional arguments, which can be used in any manner the implementation chooses. Here's a simple example:

```
// continued from above...
Provider p = null;
try { p = jtp.getProvider( services[0] ); }
catch( ProviderUnavailableException pue ) { }
```

If optional arguments are passed, the implementation would parse the input string following a standard format of name/value pairs as follows:

```
// continued from above...
try { p = jtp.getProvider(
    "a Service; type=longDistance; duration=5" ); }
catch( ProviderUnavailableException pue ) { }
```

Of course, the Provider must be in the IN_SERVICE state (otherwise, the ProviderUnavailableException is thrown). There is currently only one standard argument set that may be passed that is used for implementing security, and that is the name/value pair of login:/value and password:/value. These would be used as follows:

```
// continued from above...
try { p = jtp.getProvider(
    "a Service; login:=sroberts; password:=t34w" ); }
catch( ProviderUnavailableException pue ) { }
```

Now that we have obtained a Provider instance, let's see what it can do with it.

Provider Interface

Intuitively, Providers provide things. A provider may be thought of as an abstraction of a combination of a firewall mechanism and a business entity providing telephony services (e.g., MCI, Inc.). In a less abstract and more physical sense, Providers wrap telephony subsystems such as telephony boards or possibly a PBX system.

Providers control the availability and even the creation of most telephony objects (e.g., Call, Address, Terminal). In other words, programmers cannot create instances of any of these objects using the **new** operator. Just as we must obtain permission to use telephone numbers from telephone companies, telephony programmers using JTAPI must obtain instances of these and other entities through the Provider interface. This architecture forces the JTAPI implementation to manage any resource contention issues that may occur.[28]

The Provider interface allows for a built-in mechanism for implementing security and resource utilization for all telephony components. When an instance of a Provider is returned, all necessary communication mechanisms are to be in place. The Provider maintains an active list of all Call instances in all states except INVALID. In addition, they must maintain similar lists for all Terminals and Addresses.

---

28 Of course, the implementation may just pass this responsibility off to a telephony board or an external system and rely on that as a resource manager.

Although it is not forbidden, Providers are not required to interoperate with each other. No API support is given where, say, one provider's Call instance would be able to add a Connection to an Address from another Provider. Each Provider must maintain a unique name since this is the only means of distinguishing one from another in the same application. It is assumed that an URL-style naming convention will allow for this.

Life Cycle of a Provider

Like most other telephony components, a Provider is at all times in a particular state. These are pretty much self-explanatory and are diagrammed in **Figure 4.20**. As indicated by the diagram, the OUT_OF_SERVICE state may be a temporary state (because it may move back into an IN_SERVICE state). However, a Provider in the SHUTDOWN state may not be used again.

Figure 4.20 *Provider State Transitions*

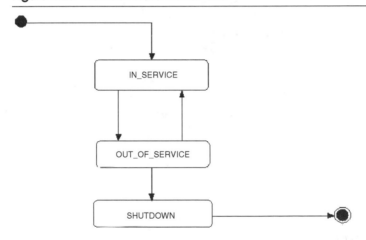

Providers follow (what should be by now) a familiar pattern where state changes trigger events that are sent to observers. The events are ProvInServiceEv, ProvOutOfServiceEv, and ProvShutdownEv. In addition, an observation termination event (ProvObservationEndedEv) is generated by the Provider and sent to all observers when the Provider becomes unobservable.

Operations Allowed on a Provider

```
public int getState( );

public String getName( );

public Call[ ] getCalls( )
    throws ResourceUnavailableException;
```

```java
public Address getAddress(String number)
    throws InvalidArgumentException;

public Address[] getAddresses()
    throws ResourceUnavailableException;

public Terminal[] getTerminals()
    throws ResourceUnavailableException;

public Terminal getTerminal(String name)
    throws InvalidArgumentException;

public void shutdown();

public Call createCall()
    throws ResourceUnavailableException,
           InvalidStateException,
           PrivilegeViolationException,
           MethodNotSupportedException;

public void addObserver(ProviderObserver observer)
    throws ResourceUnavailableException,
           MethodNotSupportedException;

public ProviderObserver[] getObservers();

public void removeObserver(ProviderObserver observer);

public ProviderCapabilities getProviderCapabilities();

public CallCapabilities getCallCapabilities();

public AddressCapabilities getAddressCapabilities();

public TerminalCapabilities getTerminalCapabilities();

public ConnectionCapabilities getConnectionCapabilities();

public TerminalConnectionCapabilities
       getTerminalConnectionCapabilities();

public ProviderCapabilities getCapabilities();
```

Unlike a `getCalls()` method, the list of Addresses returned from `getAddresses()` is static for the duration of the lifetime of the Provider instance that spawned the list. This means that if a new address is somehow added to the list (say a new phone number is installed), a new Provider instance must be generated to reflect this. At first glance, the reason for this restriction seems unclear. It would seem that Addresses should behave in the same manner that Calls do in that successive invocations of methods that return lists may have different contents depending on when the invocation is made. Further reflection reveals the probable answer — because Addresses have no state, there is no way for the API to construct the list based upon, say, an INVALID state.

At this point, we have a pretty concrete understanding of what the major JTAPI core components of `javax.telephony` are and how they behave. All of the remaining (noncore) components operate in the same manner but in a more specialized fashion. For example, package `javax.telephony.callcenter` also contains a subpackage of events relative to that subpackage and a subpackage of Capabilities. These specialized interfaces are covered in Chapter 8, "Extensions to the Core Package." But what are "capabilities"?

JTAPI Capabilities

As mentioned earlier, all JTAPI packages contain a single subpackage containing a set of interfaces called "capabilities." This Capabilities package relates to the enclosing package in the hierarchy. So, for example, the Capability interfaces found in package `javax.telephony.media.capabilities` relates to the components defined in package `javax.telephony.media`.

When implemented, Capabilities are essentially methods that answer questions about the capabilities of an object as implemented by a particular provider. All Capability interfaces return a boolean value indicating whether or not an instance is capable of performing a given method or "capability." And so if we have an object called HumanBeing that can *eat, drink,* and *be merry,* we would expect its related Capabilities interface to be comprised of "questions" such as `canEat`, `canDrink`, and `canBeMerry`. This idiom is useful for all kinds of implementations including JavaBeans™. Let's take a look at an interface in package `javax.telephony.callcenter` in order to flesh out this concept (**Listing 4.11**).

The CallCenterCallCapabilities interface specifies capabilities of objects that implement the CallCenterCall interface. To be complete, these methods should include all methods specified in the public interface of interface CallCenterCall. Sure enough, they do (compare the methods in **Listing 4.11** with the public interface of interface CallCenterCall in Chapter 8). But they don't always; some capability interfaces are a subset of the entire component interface. When this occurs, it is usually setters and getters that are left out. In earlier JTAPI releases, they sometimes didn't match the component interface at all!

Listing 4.11 *JTAPI Version 1.2 CallCenterCallCapabilities Interface*

```
package javax.telephony.callcenter.capabilities;
import javax.telephony.capabilities.CallCapabilities;


public interface CallCenterCallCapabilities extends
      CallCapabilities {
   public boolean canConnectionPredictive();
   public boolean canGetTrunks();
   public boolean canHandleApplicationData();
}
```

As an example of a nonmatching capability, consider the following definition of the CallCenterCallCapabilities interface as it existed prior to version 1.2.

Listing 4.12 *JTAPI Version 1.1 CallCenterCallCapabilities Interface*

```
package javax.telephony.callcenter.capabilities;
import
javax.telephony.callcontrol.capabilities.CallControlCall
   Capabilities;


public interface CallCenterCallCapabilities
   extends CallControlCallCapabilities {
      public boolean canConnectionPredictive();
      public boolean canSetApplicationData();
      public boolean canGetTrunks();
      public boolean canHandleApplicationData();
}
```

Rather than extending the capabilities of the interface above it in the package hierarchy, the CallCenterCallCapabilities interface extended a *sibling* interface with respect to the package hierarchy. Using an inheritance mindset, we would expect interface CallCenterCallCapabilities to extend the interface of CallCapabilities as it does in release 1.2. Instead, it extended the interface of CallControlCallCapabilities. Why? Because CallCenterCall extends the CallControlCall interface. What we found is that the capabilities inheritance tree generally matched the component inheritance tree, but did not necessarily match the *package* tree. This is actually not very surprising; there is no particular reason why we would expect it to. Nevertheless, even advanced programmers sometimes get confused about the relationship between inheritance and packaging.

Static and Dynamic Capabilities

Exactly what are the semantics of a capability return value? Does canGetTrunks() return false if the instance implementing the interface is *currently* unable to get trunks? Or does it return false if the instance is *always* unable to return trunks? The answer is both. Capabilites can be of two forms — static and dynamic. Which one depends on which object invokes the Capability — a Provider or any other core interface.

Static capabilities have to do with the *application's* functional capability as opposed to a specific object instance. Static capabilities are returned from the family of getXxxCapabilities[29]() methods provided on the Provider object. In other words, canConnect() when invoked from a Provider instance means "Does the XYZ company's JTAPI implementation of component interface Call possess the capability to connect()?" In this sense, Capabilities are also metadata in that they report information about the capabilities of the software implementation as opposed to capabilities of the problem space. This interesting approach to specifying APIs has ramifications. The first issue is one of compliance. Allowing false return values implies that Capabilities are optional. Of what use is a JTAPI implementation of say, a CallControl package that does not implement the connect() method?

The second ramification is a positive one. Any application can test for *dynamic* capabilities without actually invoking the methods they report on. Dynamic capabilities are returned with the getCapabilities() family of calls supported on all core components. Rather than reporting the capabilities of the application, they report the capabilities of a particular instance. For example, one can "ask" a Call instance whether or not it can connect without actually attempting a connect — and therefore risking the overhead of a successful call or invoking error processing for a failed call. There are of course temporal issues here (i.e., potential race conditions are likely if the implementation does not provide a means of serializing access between a query about a capability and a subsequent request for that capability). Further, a successful test in no way guarantees that the dynamic state will hold.

Let's take a look at the core Capabilities interfaces.

---

29 Where Xxx represents the name of the core component. For example,
    Provider.**getCallCapabilities**() or Provider.**getConnectionCapabilities**().

JTAPI Core Capabilities

Recall that the core component interfaces of package `javax.telephony` are Call, Address, Connection, Terminal, TerminalConnection, and Provider.[30] Given this, we should see Capabilities interfaces that mirror the component interfaces — and we do. The relevant Capabilities package `javax.telephony.capabilities` contains the interfaces CallCapabilities, AddressCapabilities, ConnectionCapabilities, TerminalCapabilities, TerminalConnectionCapabilities, and ProviderCapabilities. All of the core Capabilities interfaces are listed in **Listing 4.13**.

Listing 4.13 *Package* `javax.telephony.capabilities`

```
package javax.telephony.capabilities;

public interface AddressCapabilities {
    boolean isObservable();
}

public interface TerminalCapabilities {
    boolean isObservable();
}

public interface ProviderCapabilities {
    boolean isObservable();
}

public interface CallCapabilities {
    boolean canConnect();
    boolean isObservable();
}

public interface ConnectionCapabilities {
    boolean canDisconnect();
}

public interface TerminalConnectionCapabilities {
    boolean canAnswer();
}
```

Note, however, that again not all of the methods defined in the interfaces of the component classes match those of the capabilities interfaces. In fact,

---

30 Even though we earlier grouped Provider as a Peer class, it is also a component class in that all internal and external processes require access to it. Neither of these groupings is official in any sense; rather they are abstractions of the author.

the first three interfaces listed are comprised of a single method each — isObservable( ). And this does not match the component interface at all!

In summary, we have seen how JTAPI is organized into modules centered on the functionality provided. This is accomplished primarily by using packages. Java's package mechanism provides for a logical separation of the namespace. Packages also allow for a convenient grouping of telephony components.

JTAPI — An Object-Oriented API?

JTAPI differs from TAPI and other APIs in a very important respect. JTAPI is object-oriented — or is it? If it is, then from a programmer's perspective we should be able to use it like we use the Microsoft Foundation Classes (MFC). In other words, the process of implementing a program using the API should be an exercise of extending the API classes and of behavior specialization.

But there is one important difference — almost all of the components are defined as interfaces, not as classes. Therefore, we cannot *inherit* from these components. We must instead *implement the interfaces* — or we must use classes *provided by others* that implement these interfaces. This latter approach is what standard extension packages are all about. Software vendors are expected to implement the interfaces defined and then provide them to programmers. It is highly unlikely that compiler vendors will provide these packages as a part of the compiler package.

So what does a JTAPI implementation look like? There are two fundamental approaches to implementing a JTAPI library one is likely to encounter. The first is to provide a set of classes that implement the interfaces. Let's call this approach the "extension" approach. The second (and less intuitive) approach is to provide interface implementation source code that may be linked into a programmer's application code (let's call this the "linked interface" approach). Let's examine the most common approach first.

Implementing JTAPI Using Extension

Suppose we wanted to provide our own JTAPI implementation using the extension approach. How would we go about this task? Clearly, we would implement the interfaces defined by package javax.telephony and all subpackages. This being the case, what exactly is it that we would provide as a product to developers? A set of implemented interfaces? Unfortunately, this is not possible in Java. Recall that interfaces cannot contain private or protected members — nor can we inherit from them to create objects because they are not classes. We can only use them once they are implemented in a specific class because that is the nature of interfaces. Besides, we are interested in the implementation of interfaces — not the interfaces themselves (interfaces are mere shells of their potential use).

So, it is important to understand that even though JTAPI is defined as a set of interfaces, users of JTAPI will most likely be required to deal with a set of classes that implement these interfaces — not the interfaces themselves. Telephony programmers are likely to use classes provided by a particular vendor similar to the class defined in **Listing 4.14**. And so we see that unless you are providing a JTAPI implementation, JTAPI will most likely be presented as an object-oriented API and may be used like MFC or any other object-oriented (OO) API.[31]

Listing 4.14 *A Possible Implementation of Interface Address*

```
package javax.telephony.ICS;
import javax.telephony.*;
public class ICSAddress extends Observable
implements Address {
    protected CallObserver[] callObservers;
    protected Connection[] connections;
    protected String name;
    protected Observer[] observers;
    protected Provider provider;
    protected Terminal[] terminals;
    public void addCallObserver(CallObserver co);
    public void addObserver(Observer obs);
    public AddressCapability[] getCapabilities();
    public CallObserver[] getCallObservers();
    public Connection[] getConnections();
    public String getName();
    public Observer[] getObservers();
    public Provider getProvider();
    public Terminal[] getTerminals();
    public void removeCallObserver(CallObserver co);
    public void removeObserver(Observer obs);
}
```

(7) and *(8)* mark the protected instance variable declarations in the listing.

Because the use of interfaces does not allow for specification of instance variables, this is accomplished in [7] – [8] of **Listing 4.14**. At a minimum, we would expect vendors to declare instance variables that hold state information and static relationships among other objects.[32] For example, an Address has a name and is related to a set of Connections — so we provide a String to hold the name and an array of Connections in our implementation.

Notice that the class ICSAddress defined in **Listing 4.14** not only implements the Address interface — it also extends the Observable class. The

---

31 It is also possible that JTAPI could be presented as a set of adapter classes.
32 Of course they may provide other instance variables related to their implementation.

approach we take will assume that a vendor extends class Observable for the observable components and implements the Observer interface for observer components. Why is this? Certainly, it is not a requirement for any vendor to do this, but it is an obvious candidate given the notification scheme implied in the Sun documentation.[33] But it is not the only option. Other implementations are certainly possible and we explore some of these later in the book. But for the sake of understandability, we have provided a possible class hierarchy for classes that implement the `javax.telephony` interfaces using the Observation Model. We describe this model in detail in Chapter 9, "Event Management in Java."

A Possible Object Diagram for `javax.telephony`

From the hints given by the design of JTAPI, we can construct class hierarchies and static object diagrams. **Figure 4.21** depicts a possible implementation of package `javax.telephony` in the form of an OMT object diagram. It is a conceptual JTAPI class hierarchy similar to that which would be provided by a telephony vendor using the extension approach.

Figure 4.21 *A Possible Object Diagram for Implementing Package* `javax.telephony`

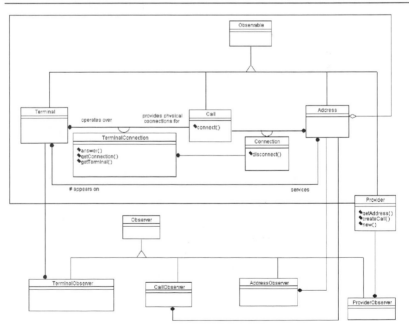

---

33 Actually, we'll find later that extending class Observable is not such a great idea after all. But for the purposes of understanding the call model, it is helpful for now.

The implementation depicted in **Figure 4.21** is easy to understand and use. To create an instance of an Address we would simply instantiate an Address class and use it[34] or we might hang onto an instance variable as in **Listing 4.15**.

Listing 4.15 *Using a Vendor's JTAPI Class*

```
public class MyClass {
    private ICSAddress addr_;
    // other code...
}
```

If we wanted to extend the capabilities of the vendor's implementation, we simply extend the classes they provide.[35] However, unlike an MFC API, such extension is not mandatory or even advisable.

But suppose we wanted the vendor's classes to inherit capabilities common to all objects in an application? Unfortunately there are compromises that must be made in our design. If a vendor implements the observer pattern suggested by the JTAPI API by extending the Observable class, we simply cannot alter the extension tree because they have already "used up" the one chance we had at extension by inheriting from class Observable. The best we can do is to *not* extend the class. The other alternative is to specify an instance variable of the vendor's type in our code and go from there. This is in fact the preferred approach.

The relationships between the components in the object diagram of **Figure 4.21** also depict what is referred to in the Sun documentation as the JTAPI *call model*. A call model is a telephony term used to describe how telephony components interoperate to complete a call.

Implementing JTAPI Using Linked Interfaces

The second approach that may be used by vendors to provide JTAPI capabilities is much less intuitive (and potentially error-prone if not automated). However, it does provide a more flexible approach to using the library in that the class that implements the JTAPI interface can freely extend any other class (i.e., it is not required to inherit from class Observable if that is the implementation that the vendor chooses).

The reason we call this approach "linked interfaces" (other than for lack of a better name) is that the code is provided in source format as opposed to class files, inserted into the application code, and then compiled and linked into the application program as in **Listing 4.16**.

---

34 Of course its name would not be "Address," it would be whatever the vendor called it. Instead, it might be ICSAddress. The same methodology would be used for the other classes.

35 We are not advocating this practice, merely pointing out a potential option.

Listing 4.16 *Linked Interface Code Implementation*

```
class MyClass extends WhateverClassChosen implements Address {
    // insert pre-named instance variables here as necessary...
    private Vector cos_;

    // add your favorite instance variables here...

    // insert vendor's JTAPI interface implementation code here...
    public void addCallObserver(CallObserver co)
        { cos_.add( co ); };

    // rest of Address interface...

    // continue on with MyClass code...
}
```

It is important to note that not all JTAPI classes are faced with this "extension curse" — only those that are subject to inheriting from class Observable. For package `javax.telephony`, this list boils down to the following classes only:

```
Terminal
Call
Address
```

However, subpackages of `javax.telephony` may add to this list. For example, the subpackage `javax.telephony.callcenter` has the class ACDAddress, which is also a candidate for the extension curse because it extends the Address interface. In short, any object that acts as a source of events is a potential candidate.

A variation of this "linked interface" approach would be to require that application programs implement the JTAPI interfaces by wrapping the vendor's implementation. In this scheme the application programmer would declare an instance variable of the vendor's type and then implement the JTAPI interfaces by simply calling the vendor's methods from within the wrapper code as in **Listing 4.17**.

Listing 4.17 *Wrapping a Vendor's JTAPI Implementation*

```
class MyClass extends WhateverClassChosen implements Address {
    // insert an instance of the vendor's class...
    private IC3Address addr_;
    // other code...
    // wrap vendor's JTAPI interface implementation code here...
    public void addCallObserver(CallObserver co)
        { addr_.addCallObserver( co );}
}
```

Again, these processes could (and probably should) be automated.

A Small Soapbox

In all of these cases, what we are really doing is getting around Java's lack of support for multiple inheritance. It is interesting to note that if multiple inheritance were provided in Java, the limitations imposed on an application programmer's design would not be an issue. Again we point out that interfaces are a useful feature — in fact a nice addition in functionality for an OO language that supports single inheritance only (like Java and Objective C). But interfaces are *not an improvement* over multiple inheritance. On the contrary one could argue that interfaces are a step *backwards* in OO technology (Bertrand Meyer, the creator of Eiffel, would certainly agree!). What is really going on here is that the burden of dealing with the issue of multiple inheritance has been shifted from the compiler vendor directly to the Java programmer.

On the other hand, multiple inheritance has not been necessary in object-oriented code in more than a quarter of a century. There are always ways around using multiple inheritance. These techniques may not be as easy to use or as productive,[36] but it's not the end of the world! The problem with the previous approach is that the design relied on extension rather than a component-based approach. Later we will investigate alternative approaches that may be used instead of or in conjunction with extension.

Now that we have seen a sample of what a JTAPI implementation might look like, let's turn our attention to another aspect of the JTAPI API — events.

JTAPI — An Event-Driven API

Telephony generally lends itself well to an asynchronous processing model, especially for server tasks. Events are used to signal asynchronous processing. In JTAPI, all asynchronous processing requires the use of events to notify interested parties of occurrences. JTAPI attempts to standardize these events for each and every state a telephony component may enter.

JTAPI Events

Events are the heart of the JTAPI call model. They are designed to model the state transitions of every observable component. This is important in telephony programming where the current state of an object is everything. This is because telephony objects often go through a series of initialization steps and require the services of many other "state-heavy" objects in order to operate.

---

36 Productivity is lost because code that could have been inherited must now be written.

Figure 4.22 Package `javax.telephony.events`

Java Telephony Event Hierarchy

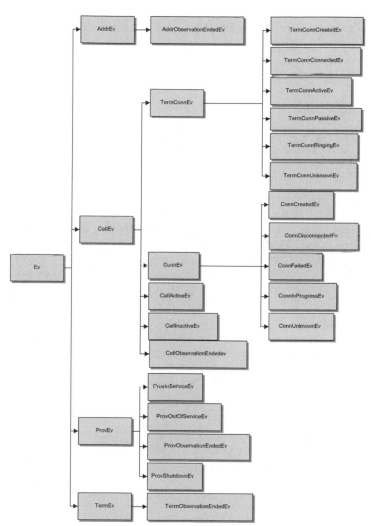

Like almost all components in the JTAPI architecture, events are specified as interfaces. **Figure 4.22** shows the events defined for package `javax.telephony`. Note that there are several layers of interface extension involved. Note also that each classification of events corresponds to an observable interface defined in the core package `javax.telephony` (Address, Call, Provider, Terminal, Connection, and TerminalConnection) as well as the state of a particular object. For example, the TermConnPassiveEv event corresponds to an instance of a

TerminalConnection when in the PASSIVE state. This same relationship between events, states, and observable components carries on for each subpackage in JTAPI.

Earlier we used state transitions to follow the life cycle of JTAPI components. Here we go into a little more detail to ensure we understand the relationship between the state of an object, its transition path, and the events that are generated as a result of a state transition. We also delve into the design concepts surrounding a state model like JTAPI.

States, Events, and State Transitions

In JTAPI, observable objects are modeled as *finite state machines* (FSM). Each observable object transitions from one state to another state along a conceptual arc. In the canonical FSM model, events may either trigger state transitions or they may signal the occurrence of a state transition. JTAPI uses the latter approach. In other words, events are generated "post-mortem" as the *result* of state transitions. For example, a Connection interface signals a connConnectedEv (connection connected event) *after* it enters the CONNECTED state. This concept is so important we reiterate it here.

JTAPI Rule to Remember 1:

Events do not *cause* state transitions. Events *report* state transitions.

Events are reported when they are passed to the relevant event handler, where they are either ignored or code is written to *react to* the event occurrence.

States are implemented as static final ints (i.e., constants) in the interface from which they are generated. For example, the Connection interface defines the seven allowable states it may enter (see **Listing 4.18**).

Listing 4.18 *Sample Logical States as Modeled in JTAPI*

```
public interface Connection {
    public static final int IDLE = 0x30;
    public static final int INPROGRESS = 0x31;
    public static final int ALERTING = 0x32;
    public static final int CONNECTED = 0x33;
    public static final int DISCONNECTED = 0x34;
    public static final int FAILED = 0x35;
    public static final int UNKNOWN = 0x36;
    /* public methods … */
}
```

Events are defined as event objects in JTAPI (extensions of interface EV) and are covered in the next section. State transitions are not modeled explicitly, but one approach is to place the object in the UNKNOWN state during transitions, if this is an important design issue.

The Relationship Between Events and States

There is a one-to-one relationship between states and events. Each event generated represents the completion of a single state transition. For example, the occurrence of a TermConnRingingEv signals the completion of a Terminal entering the RINGING state. We feel another axiom coming on…

JTAPI Rule to Remember 2:

For *each* and *every* state, there is a single unique corresponding event representing the completion of a state transition.

Absorbing this concept will go a long way toward increasing your understanding of the JTAPI model. The entire JTAPI architecture is based primarily upon states, events, and state transitions.

The relationship between events and states is best modeled visually by state transition diagrams.[37] We have already seen many of these. Each observable object is always in at most one state at any point in time, or they are in the process of transitioning between states. An action of some kind triggers the transition from one state to another. At that point, the relevant event is generated so that interested preregistered objects may be notified of the change. State transitions may (or may not) themselves be modeled as states by subclasses.

The Distinction Between Logical and Physical States

The states modeled in **Listing 4.18** represent a logical abstraction for the Connection interface. Because the TerminalConnection interface is a physical interface, we might expect to see physical states modeled. Indeed, we do (see **Listing 4.19**).

Listing 4.19 *Sample Physical States of a JTAPI Interface*

```
public interface TerminalConnection {
    public static final int IDLE = 0x40;
    public static final int RINGING = 0x41;
    public static final int PASSIVE = 0x42;
```

---

37 States are circles and the transitions between them are arcs.

Listing 4.19 (cont.) *Sample Physical States of a JTAPI Interface*

```
    public static final int ACTIVE = 0x43;
    public static final int DROPPED = 0x44;
    public static final int UNKNOWN = 0x45;
    /* public methods ... */
}
```

Observable classes that implement the JTAPI interfaces may of course define additional states. In doing so, it would be wise to choose static values that are "far away from" the values assigned in JTAPI. For example, a class implementing the TerminalConnection interface might define its constants beginning with the value of say 0x500 instead of picking up where JTAPI left off (at 0x46). This way we can be more confident that expansions to the list of states in future revisions of JTAPI will not adversely affect our code.

States of JTAPI objects affect the allowable transitions to other states from within that same object. For example, the current state of a Connection object affects the allowable state it may transition to next. When the Connection instance is ACTIVE, it can only move to one of three different states: PASSIVE, DROPPED, or UNKNOWN.

More importantly, the state of one type of object can affect the allowable states of another. States of JTAPI objects affect not only the allowable transitions from within an object they also affect the legal states other objects may be in given a particular context. For example, the states of a Connection object also affect the states a TerminalConnection may be in and vice versa. For example, when the Connection instance is ACTIVE, a TerminalConnection instance can only be in one of three different states: PASSIVE, ACTIVE, or DROPPED. As another example, the current state of a Provider object affects the allowable state a Call may transition to next. A Provider must be IN_SERVICE for an IDLE Call to move into the ACTIVE state. The sum of all the current states of all active objects at a given point in time defines the *current state of the call model*. These interrelationships are documented further in the comments of the relevant interface code of the JTAPI API itself.

Now that we have seen how events are *used*, let's see how they are to be *defined*.

JTAPI Core Events

In the last several sections, we were exposed to events from a functional perspective. In this section, we take a closer look at the properties of events. We begin by examining core events (i.e., those events defined in the core package `javax.telephony.events`).

Events represent the latest change to the call model (i.e., a change to the state of one of the objects participating in the call model). The six primary core events are based on those core classes that support observers: AddrEv, CallEv, TermEv, ProvEv, ConnEv, and TermConnEv. All of these interfaces extend the Ev interface. Other core events extend these six interfaces further. In fact, all JTAPI events *must* extend the Ev interface. Let's look at the base interface, Ev.

Ev Interface

The Ev interface is the root interface of all JTAPI events. It's kind of like a base class except that it is an interface. Therefore when we speak of common functionality supplied of all JTAPI events, we are speaking of the Ev interface.

All JTAPI events are associated with a ***cause code*** that describes what caused the event to fire and an identifier that uniquely determines the event type.[38] For example, the CAUSE_CALL_CANCELLED cause code indicates that a caller terminated a call without going on-hook. The id is apparently supplied so that programmers may switch on event id rather than having to use instanceOf calls. This is a strange pollution of an otherwise clean interface,[39] but hey it's there.

Event Generators and Receivers

All JTAPI objects may generate events. However, there are only four[40] types of JTAPI observer objects that may *receive* events — observers of Calls, Addresses, Terminals, and Providers. Therefore all events are grouped into one of these four types. Observers that match these same four types receive events. Two of these observers (AddressObserver and TerminalObserver) actually do not receive events, but subclasses of them may and so this capability is provided.

Event Meta-Codes

In addition to cause codes, all events support a mechanism for associating events with a single higher-level code called a *meta-code*. Where cause codes apply to a specific event, meta-codes apply to a group of events. There are several predefined meta-codes for different event types, as follows:

META_CALL_STARTING

META_CALL_PROGRESS

META_CALL_ADDITIONAL_PARTY

---

38 The id is not an object id. It is more like a class id. All instances of a given type of event share the same id.

39 A decent compiler could easily optimize these kinds of statements to be equivalent.

40 Recall that this is because the CallObserver handles events on behalf of both the Connection and TerminalConnection objects.

```
META_CALL_REMOVING_PARTY

META_CALL_ENDING

META_CALL_SNAPSHOT

META_CALL_UNKNOWN
```

The `META_CALL_STARTING` code signifies that a new call has been initiated in the ACTIVE state with at least one valid Connection associated. The `META_CALL_PROGRESS` code indicates that a call is in progress and that TerminalConnections may have been added. The `META_CALL_ADDITIONAL_PARTY` code notifies an application that a new Connection has been added. When *a single* Connection moves to the DISCONNECTED state, the `META_CALL_REMOVING_PARTY` code is generated. When *all* Connections are disconnected, the `META_CALL_ENDING` code indicates that. The `META_CALL_SNAPSHOT` code signals an implementation-defined group of arbitrary events, and the `META_CALL_UNKNOWN` is just that.

All of these meta-codes apply to individual calls. The following additional meta-codes apply to multiparty calls:

```
META_CALL_MERGING

META_CALL_TRANSFERRING
```

The need for meta-codes is evident when one considers the rate at which events may be generated. Meta-codes allow an application programmer to ignore lower-level events and focus on which higher-level actions are occurring and generating the lower-level events.[41] A Call object may be generating multiple events that an application can ignore if it instead is written to monitor meta-codes. For example, the presence of any event with a `META_CALL_ENDING` meta-code signifies the end of a call. However, the following lower-level events occur in order to effect a call ending. First, the Call moves to an INVALID state generating a CallInvalidEv event. Next, all of the Connections involved in the call move to the DISCONNECTED state (thereby generating a ConnDisconnectedEv event). Last, all of the TerminalConnections move to the DROPPED state (which generates a TermConnDroppedEv event). An application can save a lot of time by exercising the meta-code and then moving on.

JTAPI implementations supporting meta-codes are required to deliver lower-level events with the same meta-code in *batch order*. In other words, events generated that belong to one meta-code must be sent together. They are presumed to have occurred at the same time as far as the application is concerned. However, it is possible that groups of events may be received that are described by the same meta-code, yet belong to different event sets over time. This raises an obvious question — Where do groups of events with the same meta-code start and stop? The answer is supplied in the form

---

41 This also implies that some core objects may not even have to be instantiated.

of a call to the method `isNewMetaEvent()`. An implementation would presumably set this method to return a positive boolean value (i.e., true) for the most recent meta-group set.

As mentioned earlier, the six primary core events are AddrEv, CallEv, TermEv, ProvEv, ConnEv, and TermConnEv. Again, all of these extend the Ev interface. Each of these events is in turn a base interface for further specialization. These core events also share the common property of returning a reference to the object they are associated with. For example, the CallEv event has a single method `getCall()`, which returns a reference to the Call the CallEv event is associated with. Likewise, an AddrEv has a `getAddress()` method. In Chapter 7, "Application Programming with JTAPI," we will see how this simple method is critical when implementing asynchronous notification.

Let's take a look at each of these seven event objects.

AddrEv Interface

Addresses don't usually generate events (they certainly do not in the core package!). However, the AddrEv interface is supplied as a *partition interface* so that subclasses may provide events if necessary. If any AddrEv events are defined, they are reported through the AddressObserver interface. As expected, the single method `getAddress()` returns the source object that generated this event.

CallEv Interface

The CallEv interface supplies a single method `getCall()`, which returns the source. The interfaces that extend the CallEv interface are CallActiveEv, CallInvalidEv, and CallObservationEndedEv. The first two model the transition of a call into the ACTIVE and the INVALID states, respectively. The CallObservationEndedEv state signifies that an application will no longer receive notification from the call instance previously observed. All CallEv events are reported through the CallObserver interface. Note that the ConnEv and TermConnEv extend the CallEv interface as well.

ConnEv Interface

The ConnEv interface provides a base interface for all Connection-related events even though it extends the CallEv interface.[42] The method `getConnection()` returns the source. Extension interfaces are named of the form ConnXxxEv, where Xxx represents the name of the state the Connection is currently in. For example, interface ConnConnectedEv represents the connected state for a Connection; interface ConnFailedEv repre-

---

42 Clearly, Connections are not a kind of Call, so what gives here? Stay tuned.

sents a connection failure. These states and events represent the states of a logical connection and were previously depicted in the state transition diagram of **Figure 4.10**. All ConnEv events are reported through the CallObserver interface

TermConnEv Interface

Not surpisingly, the TermConnEv interface provides a base interface for all TerminalConnection-related events. This class also extends the CallEv interface. Recall that TerminalConnections represent physical connections. In a manner similar to that of previous event interfaces, extension interfaces are named TermConnActiveEv, TermConnCreatedEv, TermConnDroppedEv, TermConnPassedEv, TermConnRingingEv, and TermConnUnknownEv. Of course this interface supplies a `getTerminalConnection()` method to return the source. All TermConnEv events are reported through the CallObserver interface.

TermEv Interface

Terminals may generate events, but not from the core package. If any TermEv events are defined, they are reported through the TerminalObserver interface. For the same reason (extension) that the AddrEv interface is supplied, the TermEv interface is also supplied. The source is returned from the method `getTerminal()`.

ProvEv Interface

Anyone "spying on" a Provider will receive events that extend the ProvEv interface. As usual, each of these events map one-to-one to the states a Provider may be in. The method `getProvider()` returns the source, and all events are reported through the ProviderObserver interface.

Is a Connection Event a Call Event?

Earlier we saw where the ConnEv class of events extended the CallEv interface. This use of inheritance may be used to spark a lively debate. Purists might argue that a Connection is *not* a kind of Call and so a ConnEv should not extend a CallEv interface because there is no `isa` relationship between Connections and Calls.

However, further examination proves this argument to resemble Swiss cheese (in that it has a lot of holes in it). Both a CallEv and a ConnEv are events, not the objects they indirectly refer to (i.e., Calls and Connections, respectively). Because there is no compelling reason *not* to use extension for utilitarian reasons, the authors of JTAPI chose to do so by providing a simple mechanism whereby events for Connections and TerminalConnections could be reported by CallObservers. This mechanism is extension. By making events use extension in this manner, they can become polymorphic in that all subclasses may be passed as a parameter to the same method. This method is the `callChangedEvent()` method on class CallObserver, which takes an array of CallEvs. Pretty clever, no?

We've seen how events are defined and how they are used — but how are they *generated*? This is actually an implementation detail covered at great length in Chapters 7 and 9. For now, it is enough to know that they are created in the implementation code of observable objects and passed to observers via a common protocol.

JTAPI — An Exception-Aware API

Exceptions are an important component of the Java arsenal. It can be successfully argued that exceptions add measurably to the reliability and maintainability of code. Unfortunately, most telephony software does a pretty poor job of recovering from catastrophic failure — all the more reason for using exceptions! Exceptions can be designed to allow systems to operate in a degraded mode.

Clearly, error processing is an important part of telephony programming. There is, however, a cost associated with using exceptions. First of all the use of most exceptions is not optional. If a method declares one or more checked[43] exceptions in its definition, client calls *must* be placed in try/catch/finally blocks because the compiler will not compile code that doesn't properly respond to methods that may throw checked exceptions. In other words, try/catch/finally blocks are required of any calling code that invokes methods defined with a throws clause listing checked exceptions.[44] If checked exceptions are defined as part of a standard library (as they are in JTAPI), all implementations must pay the additional overhead whether they want to or not.

"What additional overhead?" you ask. A lot has been written about the additional overhead of exceptions, especially in the worlds of Ada and C++. Anytime an exception is thrown the runtime system must unwind the stack from the point of the exception occurrence all the way back to the point of the call. If the exception is not handled there, it may be *reraised* all the way back to `main()` and eventually to the operating environment from which it was invoked.[45] This stack-unwinding process forces the runtime software to keep track of the current thread of execution and the context of each method stack at a minimum. If there is more than one thread executing, there is more to keep track of. It is easy to see how such monitoring can bloat the size of the runtime image.

---

43 Checked exceptions are any user-defined classes that *directly* extend the class Exception (all others are unchecked).

44 This same behavior is similar in any programming language supporting exceptions (e.g., Ada, Eiffel, C++)

45 By definition, the exception thrown must exist somewhere in the calling chain.

In Java, however, the situation may not be quite as bad as it first seems. In a garbage-collecting environment, the runtime must keep track of all object references anyway. While adding additional information to each of these references (if they throw exceptions) will certainly grow the memory footprint, it does not necessarily negatively affect execution speed because most if not all of the information needed to unwind the stack is available statically[46] (i.e., at compilation time). But there is definitely a cost involved.

On the other hand, there is a clear benefit to defining standard exceptions in that all implementations behave in the same manner with respect to error processing. Code is more maintainable in that error processing is clearly separated from normal processing in a standard fashion. Further, any *other* type of error processing (e.g., return codes) will also add to the size of the image. Many complaints about code bloat from exceptions come from those who never test the return values from most of their code anyway! Let's measure apples with apples, huh?

As an aside, the JTAPI exceptions *could have* been defined optionally by simply extending the Throwable class instead of class Exception. This would have made all JTAPI exceptions unchecked thereby allowing callers the option of whether or not to wrap code in try/catch/finally blocks. We are not advocating this approach, merely observing it as a design option.

Let's take a look at the exceptions defined as a part of JTAPI.

JTAPI Exceptions

JTAPI provides a set of standard exceptions. Definitions for these exceptions are encapsulated in each package as appropriate. Some exceptions merely extend the Exception class; others add specific instance variables and type identifiers that are to be used in returning information about the exception thrown. For your convenience, we have organized all JTAPI exceptions into two categories that mirror this concept for each JTAPI package. This will help you in coding try/catch blocks — no sense in tying to ferret out information that is not provided. We'll call the first class of exceptions **null implementation** exceptions. The second category will be referred to as **full-bodied** exceptions.

Exceptions for Package `javax.telephony`

Figure 4.23 shows the exception classes that are defined for package `javax.telephony`.

---

46 This is not true of code using reflection techniques, but this is rare and probably not an issue using the JTAPI library.

Figure 4.23 *Exceptions for Package* `javax.telephony`

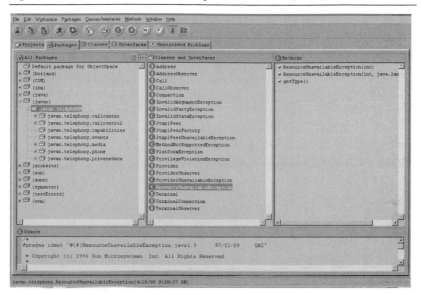

In package `javax.telephony`, the so-called null-implementation exception classes InvalidArgumentException, JtapiPeerUnavailable-Exception, MethodNotSupportedException, and PlatformException do nothing but extend the Exception class with definitions such as:

```
public class InvalidArgumentException extends Exception {
    public InvalidArgumentException();
    public InvalidArgumentException(String s);
}
```

These classes provide constructors, but nothing else. Presumably the information that any of these types of exceptions were thrown is considered sufficient information. The remaining so-called full-body Exception extension classes define specific standard values as constants encapsulated within each class as follows.

Exceptions of type InvalidStateException return constant values identifying which object type is in an invalid state (see **Listing 4.20**). Vendors would presumably extend these classes to specify any specialized types they create.

Listing 4.20 *Class InvalidStateException*

```
public class InvalidStateException extends Exception {
    private int    _type;
    private int    _state;
    private Object _object;
    public static final int PROVIDER_OBJECT = 0;
```

Listing 4.20 (cont.) *Class InvalidStateException*

```
    public static final int CALL_OBJECT = 1;
    public static final int CONNECTION_OBJECT = 2;
    public static final int TERMINAL_OBJECT = 3;
    public static final int ADDRESS_OBJECT = 4;
    public static final int TERMINAL_CONNECTION_OBJECT = 5;
    public InvalidStateException(Object object, int type, int
        state);
    public InvalidStateException(Object object,
       int type, int state, String s);
    public Object getObject();
    public int getObjectType();
    public int getState();
}
```

The next JTAPI exception (**Listing 4.21**), InvalidPartyException, specifies whether it was the originating or the destination party that triggered the exception or whether the source is simply unknown.

Listing 4.21 *Class InvalidPartyException*

```
public class InvalidPartyException extends Exception {
  private int _type;
  public static final int ORIGINATING_PARTY = 0;
  public static final int DESTINATION_PARTY = 1;
  public static final int UNKNOWN_PARTY = 2;
  public InvalidPartyException(int type);
  public InvalidPartyException(int type, String s);
  public int getType();
}
```

Exceptions of type PrivilegeViolationException indicate that a security violation has occurred in either an origination, a termination, or an unknown context.

Listing 4.22 *Class PrivilegeViolationException*

```
public class PrivilegeViolationException extends Exception {
  private int _type;
  public static final int ORIGINATOR_VIOLATION = 0;
  public static final int DESTINATION_VIOLATION = 1;
  public static final int UNKNOWN_VIOLATION = 2;
  public PrivilegeViolationException(int type);
  public PrivilegeViolationException(int type, String s);
  public int getType();
}
```

A ProviderUnavailableException signifies what its name implies — that a Provider instance was requested in the IN_SERVICE state, yet none existed at that time. This exception is also to be thrown by the runtime system any time the Provider moves into the SHUTDOWN state. The method `getCause()` returns the reason why the Provider was unavailable at the point of the call.

Listing 4.23 *Class ProviderUnavailableException*

```
public class ProviderUnavailableException extends
       RuntimeException {

    public static final int CAUSE_UNKNOWN = 0xA0;
    public static final int CAUSE_NOT_IN_SERVICE = 0xA1;
    public static final int CAUSE_INVALID_SERVICE = 0xA2;
    public static final int CAUSE_INVALID_ARGUMENT = 0xA3;
    private int _cause;

    public ProviderUnavailableException();
    public ProviderUnavailableException(int cause);
    public ProviderUnavailableException(String s);
    public ProviderUnavailableException(int cause, String s);
    public int getCause();
}
```

And finally, exceptions of type ResourceUnavailableException (**Listing 4.24**) signal the lack of availability or capacity threshold exhaustion of any resources internal to the JTAPI implementation.

Listing 4.24 *Class ResourceUnavailableException*

```
public class ResourceUnavailableException extends Exception {
    private int _type;
    public static final int UNKNOWN = 0;
    public static final int ORIGINATOR_UNAVAILABLE = 1;
    public static final int OBSERVER_LIMIT_EXCEEDED = 2;
    public static final int TRUNK_LIMIT_EXCEEDED = 3;
    public static final int OUTSTANDING_METHOD_EXCEEDED = 4;
    public static final int UNSPECIFIED_LIMIT_EXCEEDED = 5;
    public static final int NO_DIALTONE = 6;
    public static final int USER_RESPONSE = 7;
    public ResourceUnavailableException(int type);
    public ResourceUnavailableException(int type, String s);
    public int getType();
}
```

Note that some classes inherit from class RuntimeException instead of class Exception. The reason for this is that these exceptions may then be thrown from any JTAPI method (as opposed to just those that name the class in the **throws** clause). In other words, the exception does not have to be declared. Interestingly, there are no further standard exceptions defined in any of the subpackages of `javax.telephony`. Presumably, these are left to implementers of JTAPI if necessary.

Summary

We have covered a lot of ground in this chapter. Walter Mondale fans wondering where the beef was may have found it in abundance here. The core interfaces we have examined provide the foundation of all further JTAPI programming. In Chapter 8, these core packages will be extended with packages that will add more functionality.

In the next three chapters, we take a break from the admittedly dry "software engineering" subject matter of this chapter and venture off into the world of the cowboys. After we study TAPI in Chapter 5, we dive under the hood and write code to make the specification presented in this chapter work in Chapter 6. We will essentially implement the interfaces specified here with Java and Win32 C code. In Chapter 7, we write a Java application that uses this code.

But before we get our boots dirty, we must understand the library we are to wrap. In order to do this we should gain not only an understanding of the target native API, but an appreciation for APIs in general.

PART III

IMPLEMENTING *JTAPI*

In software development literature, two schools of thought have emerged over the years as to which approach is better suited to producing quality software. Residing in their ivory tower, the *software architects* believe that all software can be specified precisely *before* it is written. They believe that the development of software is, in fact, an engineering discipline that can be successfully repeated by adherence to repeatable processes. They believe in software development methodologies, use cases, and quality assurance. But most profoundly, they believe that the design and implementation of software are two distinctly different activities that may be performed by different people. Further, they believe that programming languages and APIs are implementation tools and that software design is to a large part programming language (and API) independent. Software architects will like JTAPI.

On the other side of the valley live the *cowboys*. These hard-core programmers work "in the trenches" every day. They have gained a sense of wisdom simply unattainable by those who produce documentation and stick figures but rarely, if ever, write code. They believe that it is *impossible* for quality software to be the result of those who do not know how to write software. They live by a creed of rapid application development and prototyping software. They believe in self-management and the adherence to a code of honor among programmers based on *pure competence*. But most profoundly, they believe that the design and implementation of software is a single process that will result in disaster if performed by different people. Further, they believe that programming languages and APIs are design and implementation tools whose choice drastically affects the development of quality software. Cowboys may learn to like JTAPI, but first they'll have to pull their heads out of whatever telephony documentation they are currently mired in.

The truth lies somewhere between these two hypothetical extremes. Hopefully, the reader has a foot in each of these camps. The authors do; yet in this section, we lean a little to the cowboy side. We cover two areas — Telephony Application Programming Interfaces (TAPIs) in Chapter 5 and the implementation of a JTAPI-Win32 binding in Chapter 6. As software architects, we examine the manner in which an API or an implementation may be used to specify quality software. With our cowboy hats on, we reckon how an approach to library development may profoundly affect the manner in which telephony applications may perform.

Chapter 5   *TELEPHONY API OVERVIEW*

"It must be done, because we must do
everything that is right."

Jesus Christ, Matthew 3:15

In this part of the book, we look at implementing a Java telephony library so that the construction of telephony application programs using JTAPI is possible. We begin by examining telephony APIs in general to gain an understanding of the nature of the beast. In this process, we study the impact an API can have on the application and library development process.

This chapter is provided as background material required for the major task presented in the next chapter. There, we construct a Win32-JTAPI binding also known as a JTAPI *implementation.* In order to produce a JTAPI implementation, we must bind it to a *platform library.* A platform library is a platform-specific API (accompanied with device drivers as necessary) required to get a telephony board to operate on a specific platform (e.g., Microsoft Windows). Our platform library of choice is TAPI. As a part of this process, we implement the extension packages designed to support core telephony processing, namely, the JTAPI package `javax.telephony` and the associated subpackages `javax.telephony.capabilities` and `javax.telephony.events`.

In this chapter, we discuss various popular API sets used in telephony applications. Becoming familiar with these APIs is essential to *implementing* a JTAPI library, but not *using* one. Uninterested readers may wish to skip ahead to Chapter 7, "Application Programming with JTAPI," to see JTAPI code in action, or to Chapter 8, "Extensions to the Core Package," to get the rest of the JTAPI specification picture. We take an API-centric approach to choosing our tool set (as opposed to the programming language–centric approach taken later in the book).

In the first section, we investigate the utility of standard APIs. Next, we set up some design requirements for both general-purpose APIs and tele-phony-specific APIs. Last, we present a survey of the leading telephony APIs in wide use today. We address the TAPI, TSAPI, and ECTF APIs as well as one vendor proprietary API.

We begin the first steps of coding our JTAPI library by taking a look at how the underlying API of choice (TAPI) is designed. We then begin exercising the TAPI API in working code that implements the varying service levels offered by TAPI. This preliminary exposure to service levels is critical to understanding how to best map these services to the corresponding JTAPI interfaces, events, and data structures.

What Is a Standard API?

APIs have been around for a long time. An API is, of course, nothing but a library of functions. APIs come in many different formats and serve many different purposes. However, most API sets may be categorized into a few broad areas. Most often, APIs are developed for:

- Programming Languages

- Commercial Software Libraries (a.k.a. third-party libraries)

- Operating Systems

- Device Manufacturers

Although it is still a common practice to use proprietary API sets provided by telephony board manufacturers, standard API sets are becoming more widespread in their acceptance and use. It is universally recognized that *standard* APIs are a "good thing." But what constitutes a standard API? Some define a standard API as any that is adhered to by more than one vendor. Others consider them to be standard only if blessed by a formal standards committee (e.g., ISO, ANSI). Unfortunately, there is no standard (pun intended) definition of what the term "standard" really means with respect to an API. In other words, the semantics of the term "standard" may be in the eyes of the programmer — it is clearly a relative term.

In some cases an API becomes standard by association. For example, the standard C library (an API) is standard because the C programming language is formally standardized. Likewise, an operating system API (e.g., Win32) is standardized in both the kernel and user modes — indeed little application software could be written if it were not.

Historically vendors have had little incentive to comply with standard API sets. Many application-level APIs[1] are not standard. These so-called *proprietary* APIs[2] are nonstandard for one of three reasons: it is either economically unfeasible to standardize them, it is economically feasible *not* to standardize them, or the vendor simply doesn't care (i.e., there is no financial incentive for standardization). In telephony programming, the most common reason is probably due to the lack of financial incentive, but it really doesn't matter. The fact is that in computer telephony, proprietary APIs are the norm. Although there are some third-party vendors who would like their APIs to become *de facto* standards (because they are in the business of selling APIs), most telephony programmers are used to coding to the API provided by the telephony board manufacturer (a device manufacturer).

The interesting thing is that this situation is beginning to change (or at least the potential for it to change is becoming more widely available). One reason is the immense popularity of the Microsoft Windows platform and the wide number of APIs that surround it. Not to be outdone, Sun Microsystems has embarked upon an API spree of its own,[3] one of which is the major focus of this book (i.e., JTAPI).

So now we can agree on a loose definition of what constitutes a standard API — but why should we as telephony programmers care?

Why Use Standard APIs?

There are many good reasons for using standard APIs, which we address shortly. But are there any drawbacks?

The Problem with Standards

Of course with any good, there is also bad. Although the benefits of complying to a standard API set are somewhat obvious, there are certain cases where adherence really buys nothing except increased cost and time-to-market! Although capabilities that are commonly provided by standard APIs (e.g., portability) are often a laudable objective, their importance can be overemphasized to the detriment of a project's success.

In addition, compliance to a particular API constricts *freedom of design*. All APIs force design tradeoffs to one extent or another. For example, issues such as the programming language supported, calling conventions,

---

1 An application-level API is one used by application programmers outside a particular programming language library API.

2 A proprietary API may be thought of as one that is implemented for a particular platform or device without regard for its use out of that context.

3 There is, however, a huge difference in the nature of the APIs coming out of these two companies. The difference is in capability. Sun is providing platform-neutral language-specific (Java) API specifications, while Microsoft is providing both specifications *and* implementations for a specific platform.

byte ordering, caller versus library allocation and deallocation of resources, reentrancy requirements, thread safety, underlying messaging protocol support, operating system feature support, and others can severely restrict a vendor's ability to produce a product in the manner desired. In the telephony industry, hardware vendors have traditionally produced boards with accompanying APIs to provide application programmers a programming interface to the specific capabilities of the board. They could give a rip about industry standards if such standards restrict their capability to provide the best possible implementation of a service sent to market in the shortest period of time. And who would have it any other way?

Then there is a *performance tradeoff*. Any vendor-supplied API will outperform a standard API set (unless, of course, the vendor writes the API). This is no small consideration in telephony programming as every application is essentially a distributed system subject to temporal issues. If the use of a particular API increases a latency factor with no perceived benefits, its use is detrimental.

Lastly, there is the *control* issue. Today, there are more APIs than ever before. There is an interesting inverse trend going on between programming languages and APIs — as the viable choices for languages decline, the number of available APIs are increasing. In one sense, it can be argued that this plethora of APIs leads to less coding work and therefore enhanced productivity and commonality. These gains, however, can be offset by the reality that APIs are really just additional tools provided by vendors — in short, language extensions. Even in cases where APIs have been adopted as de facto standards, changes to that API can wreak havoc on existing applications. If a company goes under, will the API survive? Can a company struggling to break even in a fiercely competitive marketplace afford to wait while some standards board argues over an API issue? The reality is that all this has been done before with another programming language — Ada. Was it successful? We submit that the results are not yet in. Only time will tell whether this approach will work for Java.

The Benefits of Standards Compliance

Even though there are certainly many risks and potentially adverse consequences of using standard API sets, many of these risks are shared when using the alternative (i.e., a proprietary API). For instance, a company can still go under no matter which approach is taken!

Standard APIs provide several benefits, but the single most important one is probably *enhanced programmer productivity* over time. The use of standard APIs leads to a reduced learning curve for programmers. From a software maintenance perspective, there is arguably little benefit to learning multiple API sets that accomplish essentially the same task.[4] This benefit

---

4 Although some programmers (present company included) actually enjoy exploring new
  APIs, it is rumored to be an illness resulting from excessive exposure to Dilbert managers.

extends not only to the application programmer who uses the API, but also to the library programmer who implements it. When service-level APIs are standardized (e.g., Microsoft's TSPI), even systems programmers benefit.

Assuming we buy into the notion of considering a standard API for use, what are the criteria for evaluating the quality and usability of a standard API? Let's put together a wish list for the ultimate API by imposing a set of general design requirements.

Design Requirements for an API

The functional requirements for an interface (e.g., a telephony board instruction set) become design requirements for an API. Some of these requirements can be met rather easily; others are actually *inversely related* to each other. When this conflict occurs, it forces a compromise in the API design. In any case, the architecture team must first examine general API requirements (i.e., those required of any API), prioritize among those features that hinder each other, and then tailor the API to its specific set of users — in this case, telephony application programmers. Before we study the telephony APIs, it is helpful to review certain characteristics of all APIs in order to gain a clear perspective.

General API Requirements

A good API will exhibit characteristics to varying degrees in the following categories:

- Usability
- Compatibility
- Extensibility
- Flexibility
- Reliability
- Portability
- Scalability
- Language Interoperability
- Support
- Unobtrusiveness

Usability

Usability is defined here as any feature that enhances the clarity and ease of use of an API. Object-oriented (OO) APIs have gone a long way toward increasing the understandability of APIs by simply publishing the public interface of all the objects involved in the API. The Ada concept of packages has led to the organization of code into functionally understandable modules. All modern OO APIs are following this model. Functional interfaces (e.g., TAPI and TSAPI) may be much more difficult to grasp and therefore use. OO APIs do, however, require a firm understanding of OO concepts — and sometimes much more. For example, the JTAPI API requires an understanding of other computer science concepts such as finite state machines and event notification schemes. An advanced programmer with formal training may find these APIs easier to use where a less experienced programmer may be completely lost, at least initially.

Compatibility

A compatible API is one that remains consistent between releases of the API. This is accomplished by keeping the function signatures unaltered between releases. Although this may seem fundamental, there are many examples in API lore where vendors have completely overhauled APIs between releases, leaving programmers and entire projects beached on the shores of system desperation.

Bertrand Meyer introduced the concept of *contracts* with the Eiffel programming language — where a signature along with its stated pre- and postconditions is guaranteed not to change. Fortunately, no one has made this a *legal* requirement for library providers, but the likelihood of change is something to be seriously considered. The Ada programming language standard went even further by introducing the ability to compile interfaces (package specifications), opening the door for the OO API sets we see today. These types of APIs (which Java employs) encourage the stability of an API set. When APIs are actually extensions to a programming language, compatibility seems assured, right? Well, certainly more so than with vendor APIs, but recent experience with deprecated language features in Java between releases shows that even these APIs change more often than we would like.

Extensibility

An extensible API allows for future enhancements. This is best accomplished by designing function signatures as *generically* as possible. There are three primary techniques for accomplishing this: *typeless parameters*, *common signatures*, and *parameter lists*.

Typeless Parameters

An excellent example of typeless parameters may be found in the LPVOID parameter and similar structures of Microsoft's Win32 interface. This technique can be simulated in Java APIs by using some of the techniques for writing generic code. We explore this topic further in Chapter 10, "Idioms and Patterns in Telephony."

Typeless parameters require casting (either at the point of the call or within an implementation), yet they provide the most extensible interface possible. When typeless parameters are used, periodic changes to data types no longer affect the API specification because there are no data types to change!

Common Signatures

The Win32 API is full of common signature examples. For example, it requires some exported callback functions to have a maximum parameter size of 12 bytes. Because pointers in a 32-bit operating system (OS) are typically four bytes in size, this leaves room for three parameters in the function signature. If the underlying OS can rely on this fact, the kernel code to handle callbacks can be vastly simplified. But most importantly the OS can save machine cycles. This places a constraint on the design of callback functions for the application programmer, but it creates a very flexible and fast messaging architecture.

Parameter Lists

One technique used in the design of extensible APIs is where parameter lists are used whenever possible (as opposed to explicit parameter types). For example, pass an array of values rather than a separate parameter for each value. This way, new parameters can be added without having to change underlying callback handling interfaces. An example of outstanding design in this respect may be found in OTI's callback mechanism for IBM's VisualAge for Smalltalk API. By designing a generic and flexible signature format that may be used for a large category of functions, all similar signatures may be handled in the same manner. By specifying a flexible, compact, yet complete signature, one can implement a generic callback scheme using function pointers for non-OO code and using polymorphism for OO code (like Java and Smalltalk).

Extensibility is one of those attributes of an API that costs something in that there is a clear tradeoff involved. An extensible API is extremely attractive to library programmers, yet is often much less desirable to application programmers because it is more difficult to use and comprehend. Many application programmers perceive parameter lists as just plain "ugly." Another downside is that the parameters must be programmatically added or removed from a list before they can be used. This is additional overhead, another example of a tradeoff — this time *performance* for extensibility.

Flexibility

A flexible API provides alternative mechanisms for doing the same tasks. For example, a function may provide a synchronous and an asynchronous version, a thread-safe version as well as a single threaded version, or perhaps a function with multiple signatures, constructors, and the like.

Portability

An API is portable if it allows software to be written with little or no changes regardless of the platform on which it is deployed. Portability generally falls into two categories: *source code portability* and *binary portability*. Source code portability simply requires a recompile on any target platform. Binary portability does not.

It is, of course, very difficult to provide a portable API using a programming language that is not itself portable, but the degree to which an API is portable goes beyond the programming language chosen. Indeed, the lack of portability of an API may be entirely hidden from the programmer. If library programmers access the OS (i.e., they drop below the programming language level API) to provide functionality for an extra measure of performance, portability is diminished if that same functionality is not available on all platforms. This, of course, defines the so-called least common denominator problem.[5]

Reliability

If a product doesn't work well, people won't use it. Even if an API is quite elegant in every other respect, a poor implementation doesn't bode well for developers or users. This almost goes without saying, but we say it anyway.

Language Interoperability

The ability of the API implementation to provide interoperability with multiple programming languages is certainly desirable. Normally however, this function is provided by the programming language the API is implemented in rather than by the API itself. However, there are API libraries that provide built-in support for programming language neutrality. For example, the Microsoft COM specification provides built-in support for programming language interoperability, albeit for the Windows platform only. Of course, the Common Object Request Broker Architecture (CORBA) is the ultimate in this sense in that with CORBA we gain language interoperability as well as platform independence.

Operating System Support

An API that offers strong OS support provides capabilities and/or hooks into functionality provided in the underlying operating environment. This does not necessarily mean that it must provide every capability the OS

---

5 The *least common denominator problem* occurs when an implementation is compromised in order to provide a solution that satisfies multiple divergent specifications. In other words, when you try satisfying the many, you run the risk of lowering the quality for the few.

does; rather that the programmer is either given some window into the capabilities provided or it is directly supported by the API, as appropriate. Some important considerations in modern API sets with respect to support are the concepts of *backdoors* and *thread safety*.

The Backdoor

Because the vendor is the same, the programming language is the same, and the environment is the same, the so-called backdoor is fully available when writing a TAPI-compliant Windows program. The entire Win32 API is at one's disposal, and it may be freely mixed with TAPI source code. You can even mix application architectures (MFC and Win32) and programming languages to a certain extent (C and C++). However, certain constraints may be imposed by particular elements of the TAPI API in the form of required callback functions.[6] Because these must be static functions, the only way you can hook into the current thread is by either passing it as a parameter or by relying on system global static functions that return pointers to thread instances and windows. Fortunately, the MFC and Win32 APIs provide these capabilities.

JTAPI library providers are less fortunate. They are stuck with the unenviable task of either providing such a capability or of designing a Java class library so powerful that such capabilities are never required (fat chance!). Luckily, there may be a way out by leaning on the JNI specification and a good JNI implementation or perhaps a third-party low-level toolkit like the OSObject class in IBM Smalltalk.[7] Unfortunately, we see later that the JNI is not all it's cracked up to be (at least on Windows platforms). Fortunately, we find there are other alternatives available.

Reentrancy and Thread Safety

All modern operating systems either offer thread support (e.g., UNIX, NT, OS/2), are attempting to add it (e.g., Apple Rhapsody), or are of little use to telephony application programmers (e.g., DOS). When an API is implemented on a platform that supports threads, the library must be made *thread-safe*. Alternatively, a thread library may be used on top of a platform whether or not it supports threads (e.g., DOS and some flavors of UNIX).

A thread-safe API by definition consists of reentrant functions. Reentrant functions are inherently thread-safe. A function is said to be *reentrant* when a context switch can occur without corrupting data. Corruption can occur when multiple threads attempt to modify shared data.

---

6 We revisit this issue in code when we write some TAPI applications later in this chapter.

7 This API provides C style memory management functions in Smalltalk — an extremely powerful tool for mixed-library programming. If Java is to truly become a world-class development tool, it needs class libraries like this one.

Even when data is not written, logic errors can be introduced at the application layer if values read in are relied on but then change (the so-called dirty read). If there is no shared data (as is the case if a function uses only local variables), the function is by definition thread-safe. But many functions share data at some level, and so the programmer must serialize access to static data. An API that provides fully reentrant functions is, not surprisingly, called a reentrant API. This is not only desirable, it is quickly becoming a standard requirement. Indeed, to provide a nonreentrant library on a platform that supports threads is not only ignorant, it is financial suicide.

Unobtrusiveness

An unobtrusive API does not interfere with the capabilities of any other software on the target system. There are three general manners in which an API can be obtrusive. The first is when the API implementation requires a particular set of drivers that are *not in conformance* with the target platform. An example would be a runtime library that requires a Terminate-and-Stay-Resident (TSR) program.

The second form of obtrusiveness comes when an API *interferes with* the capabilities of the underlying platform. For example, Windows NT provides a system-level thread model. An API that implemented its own tasking mechanism might disallow or interfere with correct operation of threads in NT. One way this can occur is when an NT library implementation does not take into account peculiarities with the manner in which user interface threads interoperate with worker threads.

The final form of obtrusiveness occurs when an API actually *disables* certain system functionality. This is rare but not unheard of (it is even rarer to find it documented!). This can be particularly annoying, to say the least.

Now that we've examined some of the more common design characteristics for an API, we will spend the next section discussing a topic that is crucial in distributed programming — the issue of *scalability*. Exactly how an API is related to scalability is not always clear. Indeed, sometimes the best support for scalability is no support at all. Nevertheless, it is important that we understand exactly what a scalable architecture looks like as well as what we can do to at least avoid *hindering* a scalable architecture.

Scalability

An API is scalable if it supports seamless migration from single box to multiple box operation. Multibox operation means what its title implies: in short, a distributed API should be able to run effectively on multiple computers simultaneously. In addition, it should support *fat or thin clients* and *multitier software architectures*. It should not restrict and should, in fact, support *remote procedure calls* and other such distributed software idioms. But before we can assess API support for scalability, we must first agree on what scalability is. Let's start with some fundamental categories.

In terms of scalability, software processing distribution architectures may be divided into four increasingly scalable categories: *link*, *client/server*, *peer-to-peer*, and *multitier*. All of these architectures are really a combination of both a physical and a logical model. This relationship is depicted in **Figure 5.1**.

Figure 5.1 *Architecture Complexity and Scalability*

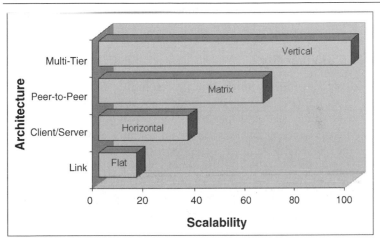

As **Figure 5.1** implies, the level of scalability increases as the complexity of the architecture increases. But this added complexity often increases the flexibility of the architecture. The scalability quotient moves from *flat*, then *horizontal*, then *matrix*, and then to *vertical* scalability. A proper evaluation of an API in terms of scalability requires an understanding of how these architectures provide scalability.

But what exactly is scalability? Scalability is one of those terms that is thrown around a lot (i.e., it is a buzzword), yet it is rarely if ever properly defined. One definition (the one we will use hereafter) is as follows:

> **Scalability** — the degree to which a system supports expansion in both software and hardware components with minimal impact on both system performance and existing software maintenance

In short, a system is said to be scalable if it exhibits constant or decreasing *marginal cost of expansion*. An API is scalable if it supports such expansion.

Link Architecture

The Link architecture is the least scalable of our categories. The physical model simply links two or more computers together via an I/O channel or a specialized bus. It is a rather archaic architecture that is rarely used except in specialized circumstances. However, it is useful to examine the most primitive scalability approach so that we may better understand the higher-level architectures.

A standalone computer can be made to communicate with other computers in a number of ways to implement a Link architecture. The most common is through the serial port over a null modem cable. Of course, this is impractical for most applications, but it is certainly possible. This type of communication requires nothing special of an API, but a reasonable one would include operations to connect with and monitor remote boxes as well as the capability to pass information between them.

Functionality

Using the Link architecture, you're pretty much on your own when it comes to defining a logical model (some architecture, eh?). One way to scale an application would be either to roll your own kind of token ring-type message-passing scheme or to design a master/slave architecture. In other words, you need to write your own communications protocol (although it needn't be as complex as, say, TCP/IP). You also need to either rely on a library or programming language with serial port support or, again, write your own communications layer. If you've ever attempted to program a UART, you'll understand why this approach is not really practical. Even though one could concoct and code such a system, the sheer effort required would likely bust any development schedule. Further, the addition of more boxes would likely add an unacceptable latency factor.

Scalability

In reality, this type of configuration is not really scalable at all; it is said to be *flat* (see **Figure 5.2**). Although additional boxes can be added, the logical model is for all practical purposes nonexistent.

Figure 5.2 *Link Architecture*

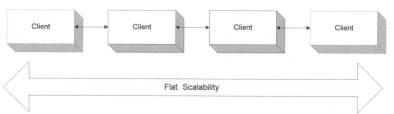

In short, the link architecture is unnecessary given the low cost and high availability of transport protocols such as TCP/IP and SNA. These protocols were developed in part so that application programmers would not be burdened with such details. Further, telephony products and APIs generally mask this level of complexity from the application programmer.[8] The remaining scalability options assume such protocols exist and are in use.

Client/Server Architecture

The next rung up in the food chain of scalability is the client/server (C/S) architecture. A reasonable implementation of the physical model would utilize an Ethernet or Token Ring LAN. More typically it might be a database system with a front-end client that wraps the communication layer altogether.

The canonical C/S model has been around for a long time. Mainframes, in fact, may be thought of as a client/server configuration (although they are not usually referred to as such). Some might argue that the so-called dumb terminal mainframe approach is merely taking a CPU and moving the monitor to another location, but the UNIX-based X Window System is not entirely unlike the mainframe model. As defined here, they are both C/S architectures.

The C/S architecture is often referred to as a *two-tier* architecture. It is two-tiered both physically and logically; the host machine (physical) houses the server (logical), and the remote desktop terminals (physical) house the clients (logical).

Functionality

The key difference between C/S systems and link (standalone) systems in terms of functionality is that the server must be able to handle multiple simultaneous remote client (terminal) requests, regardless of the content of the requests. In addition, C/S systems require the management of resource contention (i.e., serialization of access to shared resources), and so we would expect the API to successfully handle multiple calls to the same remote resources.

Scalability

The C/S architecture is scalable in the *horizontal* sense (see **Figure 5.3**). In other words, the server can seamlessly add multiple clients (or clients may attach to the server) with little or no noticeable system degradation.[9] In either case, each client is communicating with a single remote server at any one point in time.

Horizontal scalability is fundamental to the C/S model.

---

8 ... although telephony board vendors deal with these issues regularly.
9 Of course, degradation is inevitable at some point. However, it is a function of resource contention endemic to the client/server model.

Figure 5.3 *Client/Server Scalability*

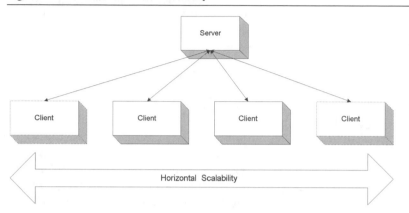

Memory Footprint

Here, we inject the concept of a memory footprint because we will find that certain scalability options may affect the memory footprint. As the name implies, a memory footprint is simply the size in bytes that an application occupies at runtime. It is not usually measured precisely. Rather, it is a term used to express the relative size given different physical implementations. In other words, one scalability option may lead to a larger or smaller memory footprint than another.

When evaluating scalability options, discussions about memory footprints usually center on the client. When the C/S architecture came into wide use, a term was introduced that came to be known as *fat client*. What this means is that the memory footprint on the client is relatively large compared to, say, a network computer configuration. For example, a simple small-scale 4GL C/S application to query a relational database is typically implemented as a fat client. The request for data is made to the server, who in turn returns the entire set of data to the client. The fattest of fat clients use dynamic SQL queries. Less obese versions execute the operation on the server in the form of stored procedures and optionally using database cursors. In either case, potentially large amounts of data go over the wire and are stored in memory on the client. But most importantly, a large amount of application code resides on the client. The C/S architecture is by definition a fat client implementation of distributed processing because there is nothing "built into" the architecture that specifies any level of control over the size of the memory footprint. We see an example of what is called a *thin client* when we discuss the multitier architecture.

Application of Client/Server Architecture

In terms of telephony programming, the implications of a fat client vary depending on the application. If the size of the messages that traverse the client server boundary are small and relatively infrequent, then a fat client implementation is not a problem. This is characteristic of most telephony applications — it is rare to retrieve a million-row result set in a telephony application. Clients usually pass small messages or requests for services across the C/S interface rather than large amounts of data.

There are, however, valid uses for the C/S architecture in telephony. An example of this would be a voice-mail application where the *voice response unit* (VRU) is the client and provides all of the telephony services. The host is the database server, which holds all of the mailbox/account information. An architectural diagram is provided in **Figure 5.4**.

Figure 5.4 *Telephony Application of C/S Architecture*

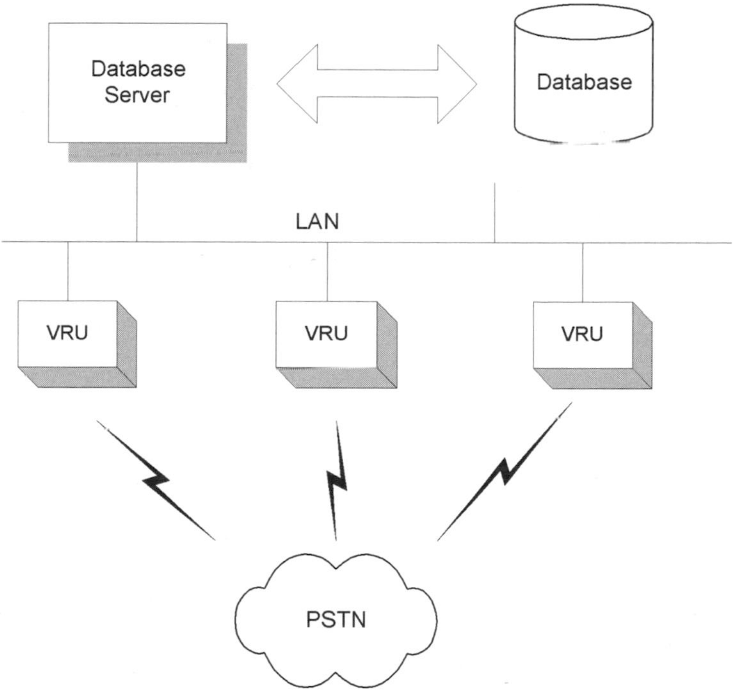

Peer-to-Peer Architecture

From the physical perspective, a peer-to-peer configuration allows any box on the network to assume the role of either client or server or both simultaneously (see **Figure 5.5**).

The peer-to-peer architecture encourages a network approach to processing. In most telephony software there is a server component to both the client and server machines and so this architecture is usually more appropriate than C/S in that it is more applicable to a wider range of applications.

In the peer-to-peer architecture, a software component is a *client* when it requests services of another software component. It is a *server* when it provides services to other software components.[10]

Figure 5.5 *Peer-to-Peer Matrix Scalability*

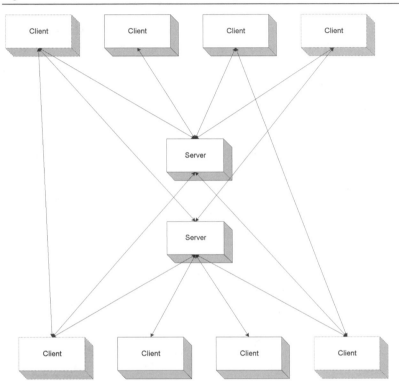

Functionality

From a logical perspective, the previously examined C/S architecture is really just a specialization of the peer-to-peer architecture where specific constraining roles are played by the software components — and so an API supporting peer-to-peer should support (or at least not hinder) C/S as well. But the peer-to-peer architecture goes beyond C/S because there needn't be a dedicated host machine — clients can communicate directly with other clients.

---

10 Of course, we must define the term "services." The definition presented here is meaning-less if we define services to be analogous to the public interface of an object. And so services must be defined in the context of the problem space. Here, services would mean "telephony services."

Scalability

In the peer-to-peer architecture, both the client and the server are horizontally expandable; hence, it is scalable in a *matrix* sense. Because the peer-to-peer architecture is more scalable than the C/S does not mean it is the better solution in all cases. For example, an application that requires a central repository of information might run the risk of data anomalies if it allowed the server subsystem to reside on multiple boxes. In other words, the advantages of a trusted single server may be lost or (at the very least) complicated by a peer-to-peer architecture. Nevertheless, the peer-to-peer architecture offers several advantages over the C/S architecture in terms of overall scalability.

Memory Footprint

The memory footprint of the peer-to-peer architecture is the same as the C/S architecture — it just depends on which software entity is currently playing the role of the client and which entities are servers. Indeed, a memory footprint could grow quite large unless these components are managed well. Just like the C/S architecture, there is nothing inherent in the peer-to-peer architecture to control the size of the memory footprint.

Internally, a PBX is an example of a peer-to-peer architecture. Although most are configured with hardware, PBX systems play the role of both a client and a server on the same "box." When they answer and route telephone calls, they are servers. When they dial an internal line, they are clients.

Multitier Architecture

The multitier architecture is the Cadillac of distributed processing architectures. Intuitively, it introduces a middle layer to the peer-to-peer architecture as depicted in **Figure 5.6**.

Being a Cadillac does not always translate to being the best option in all situations; there are many where a used Jeep may be the best solution. However, nothing can match the scalability and per-object caching flexibility that the multitier architecture provides. More often than not, this can lead to increased overall performance for large distributed systems.

Functionality

In the C/S architecture, processing is initiated on the client and is passed to the server; each has its own box. In the peer-to-peer architecture, the role of client and server may be performed by the same entity on the same or different boxes. In the multitier architecture, some processing may be moved to an intermediate layer and executed there on behalf of a client, server, or both. The client and the proxy are always on the same box. A simple example of this functionality is in "store and forward" processing.

Figure 5.6 *Multitier Architecture*

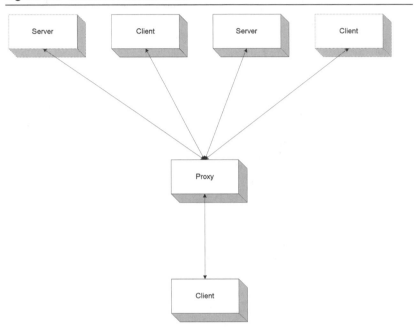

Multitier architectures provide the capability to handle features the other architectures are unable to support in an effective and efficient manner. These services include transaction processing, load balancing, and performance monitoring.

Scalability

Advanced implementations of the multitier architecture allow the processing agent to migrate among an arbitrary number of middle layer tiers. This architecture holds incredible promise for telephony application programmers — it is distributed programming at its apex!

The so-called three-tier architecture used in much of today's distributed object middleware is a specialization of the multitier architecture. Three-tier distributed objects operate on the principle of a *proxy*. Here's how it works: A proxy acts as an *agent* for a remote object. In a sense, the original object requesting a service is split into three components — a *client*, a *proxy*, and a *remote object*. Together, these three components request the services of a server tier. The remote object itself is split again into three components — the remote object, its proxy, and the server object. This relationship is depicted in **Figure 5.7**.

Figure 5.7 *A Three-Tier Architecture*

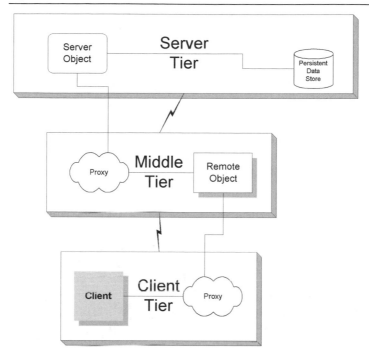

From the client tier (tier 1), the proxy is instantiated in the address space of the client software that initiates the request. The remote object in the middle tier (tier 2) implements the caller's method on behalf of the proxy. The remote object's method call is in turn implemented by a call to a proxy in its address space, which invokes services on either a server tier (tier 3) or another "client" proxy.[11] All three tiers may reside on three different boxes. Perhaps the best alternative in terms of performance is for the second and third tiers to reside on the same box.[12] However, it makes little sense for all three tiers to reside on the same box (in this case, a three-tier approach adds nothing but overhead!).

Why is this approach widely held as the most scalable? Let's return to our original definition of scalability to find out. It is not difficult to see how this architecture supports almost unlimited expansion in both software and hardware components. Because software can play any role, can be placed on any box, and can even be split into smaller pieces, scalability in this sense is higher than in any other approach we've seen.

---

11 In a multitier configuration, both the client and the server may contain proxies and there may be more than three logical layers.

12 Using the computer's bus *directly* as the communication medium is almost always faster than slapping RPC calls between two or more computer buses!

Whether or not there is minimal impact on both system performance and existing software depends on the quality of the software, the bus bottleneck and how fast the processors are, and the effective bandwidth of the transport mechanism (e.g., the telephone network, the LAN). If all of these components are operating in prime form, scalability is logically infinite.[13]

Assuming fast processors can be acquired and network throughput can be maximized, what does it take to write multitier software? Well, this subject (distributed objects) has filled many books and so any attempt to address it here is superficial at best. However, the fundamental concepts are relatively straightforward if the right methodologies and tools are used.

Writing Scalable Software

Scalable software is software properly organized into functional subsystems. For example, there are subsystems for user interface, persistent stores and data access, common data structures, communications, print services, and so forth. Of course, what we're really describing here is the development of modular software. Modular subsystems enable scalability because they can be placed on separate boxes or swapped out for different implementations. In terms of telephony, writing scalable software normally entails the specification of a clean separation between application software and communication software. Writing or wrapping a proxy mechanism to handle all server requests is one way to implement this separation.

When writing the proxy portion of scalable software, there are two general approaches that may be taken. You can write everything from scratch (using remote procedure call (RPC) APIs or some messaging scheme) or you can use proprietary or standardized distributed object middleware. The first approach would be a significant undertaking and so is not advised. The second approach may be accomplished using distributed object API technology such as Java's Joe or RMI, CORBA, Ada's Distributed Systems Annex, DCOM, DSOM, Distributed Smalltalk, and other such component middleware. Although the benefit of an object-oriented implementation is realized using these latter approaches, the performance penalty is roughly the same for most applications.

Memory Footprint

Unlike all the previous architectures, the multitier architectures are designed to address the size of the memory footprint. The memory footprint is dramatically smaller for the client using multitier architectures. This is made possible because the proxy effectively becomes a pointer to the "real" object in the middle tier. The proxy is not, however, a panacea; rather, it should be used judiciously.

---

13 Of course, there are performance constraints and engineering trade-offs that mitigate (and at some point overtake) the benefits of scalability.

It is important to note that both overall memory requirements (i.e., overhead) and system latency may be increased using multitier architectures. This *must* be offset by the reduction of local instantiations and invocations, or the approach should not be undertaken. No matter how clever the algorithm, remote calls are many times more expensive than local calls and so should be used sparingly. This is where the design comes in. Not all objects can afford a proxy implementation. Most tools that provide proxy capability also provide a caching option for specifying when and where a proxy mechanism may be used.

However, the increased overhead of multitier architectures should be compared to the relative distributed alternatives (such as a C/S or an RPC implementation). The proxy mechanism can be a much better performer than RPCs if the final remote/server object resides on the same box as the persistent store. In some cases, average system throughput is actually decreased as the number of clients increases! On the other hand, the performance may be no better than invoking stored procedures. The benefit in this case is the issue of control. Even if performance is the same, the programmer can fine-tune the cache on a per-object basis.

Applications of a Three-Tier Architecture

A typical implementation of a three-tier architecture is a Java applet running in a Web browser communicating with a database. The browser (and the Java virtual machine) is allocated to the first tier to manage the *presentation layer*, the Java code resides on the middle tier to handle *business logic*, and the *persistent store* is placed in tier 3. Again, this software architecture does not specify the allocation of these software resources to hardware processors and boxes. It does, however, imply that at least two boxes are to be involved. It is more scalable precisely because this allocation will have less of a negative impact on performance than any of the other architectures. In fact, one of the largest justifications for implementing multitier architecture is to improve overall system performance.

One of the most sophisticated and interesting implementations of multitier architectures is that of *mobile agents*. Mobile agents are intelligent distributed objects that roam from box to box carrying out duties similar to the UNIX Gopher facility. System latency is not really an issue because these objects only perform workflow-like activities. Generally, these activities do not require long-term access to shared resources.

A company called Interactive Communications Systems (ICS) provides a "real-world" example of a three-tier architecture. ICS has developed what they call a **Unified Service Platform** (USP) for telephony applications.[14] This implementation takes advantage of many industry standard specifications and Commercial Off-The-Shelf (COTS) products to implement an

---

14 "Unified Services Platform," ICS, Inc., January 1998.

extensible and truly scalable telephony-processing environment. Having already developed "The Mother of All CT PC Apps,"[15] ICS has gone on to develop a reliable, fault-tolerant infrastructure capable of handling the largest telephony processing the world has to offer.

ICS has addressed scalability from both the hardware and software perspectives. To properly address true scalability, this approach is absolutely necessary (i.e., you can't have hardware scalability without software scalability, and vice versa). The software architecture separates processing into three primary subsystems: an *application server* on tier 1, a *component server* on tier 2, and a *media server* on tier 3. In addition, ICS provides an API to manage the platform. The hardware architecture[16] supports scalability by integrating cluster-awareness into all software and hardware components.

Intuitively, it would seem that multitier architecture would add overhead, thereby decreasing overall system performance. This is, however, not the case. In fact, performance is usually *increased* when the middle tier is implemented properly. For example, ICS found a 25% increase in performance over a two-tier approach by using Microsoft Transaction Server for the middle tier.

Mix and Match

Having now investigated four scalability architectures, it is important to note that these architectures may be mixed within a particular application. For example, the database services may be implemented as a C/S and the asynchronous messaging subsystem may be implemented as a peer-to-peer. And so it is not necessarily a requirement that a particular API support all architectures if it is designed well to support any particular one.

Now let's take a look at more specific API requirements, but this time purely from a telephony programmer's perspective.

Telephony-Specific API Requirements

A telephony interface will have API requirements beyond the general requirements we just examined. Many of these mirror the requirements we imposed on programming languages earlier, but they take on slightly different manifestations with respect to an API set.

Asynchronous Notification

We expect a telephony library to provide synchronous (blocking) and asynchronous (nonblocking) versions of many routines. For example, we may want to be able to place a call and wait for a response in a synchronous

---

15 See *Computer Telephony* magazine, January 1997 issue.

16 Both software and hardware architectures are discussed in Chapter 11, "Organizing a Large-Scale Telecom Development Project."

mode or be able to place a call and be asynchronously notified when the connection is made. This support is critical in, for example, predictive dialer-type applications.

Interruption and Graceful Termination

When a device driver issues I/O commands on a single processor computer, it usually hogs the processor or intentionally blocks all other operations to that device. This makes programmer-initiated interruption a difficult task unless the API is designed to support *interrupt service routines* (ISRs). For example, we would like to be able to cancel a call in the middle of dialing, line negotiation, or whatever. If the API provides no hooks into ISRs and the application requires it, you're toast.

Graceful termination seems to be a tall order for most telephony systems today. For any of you that have had the pleasure of working with hardware on a PC, it is clear that the area of hardware and software integration needs a lot of work. We have crashed Windows 3.1; Windows 95, Windows NT, and OS/2 several times by simply swapping out a modem. Plug and Play becomes Unplug and Pray. It is very easy to completely hang all of these operating systems with a single telephony function call. Let's hope this situation improves soon (we believe it will because it simply *has* to).

Thread Support

At the application programming level, using threads is generally a desirable feature in telephony applications, although a similar asynchronous effect can be achieved using sequential messages across address spaces (e.g., communicating sequential processes, shared memory, and the like). However, at lower service levels, threads can only be effectively supported if the particular telephony device is designed to work well in a threaded environment. For example, a box with one line device used to convey real-time audio or video feeds may suffer undesirable side effects if its playback thread can be interrupted by other threads in the system (which they clearly can on a system employing a round-robin scheduling policy). In this case, the playback thread may have to implement synchronized buffering mechanisms. In any case, the more of this type of functionality provided with a telephony API, the better.

Integration with Other API Sets

It would be nice if telephony APIs were built to interoperate each other. This is not a realistic requirement — it is more of a wish list item. While the proprietary nature of most telephony implementations generally precludes their ability to interoperate, it is not an impossibility. In fact, it is entirely possible depending upon the API used. JTAPI provides this promise.

Distributed Programming

Support for distributed programming capabilities like remote procedure calls is rare among API sets not specifically designed as such. For example, we would expect telephony API to provide a mechanism to place a call from our client box, but would we expect the API to provide the capability to have this box tell another box to make a call?[17] In most advanced telephony environments, the answer is "yes!" Modern APIs provide such support through *location transparency*.

Portability of Telephony APIs

In order to levy a portability requirement, we must define the term as it pertains to a typical telephony API. We have already discussed portability in a general sense as it applies to JTAPI (and we will certainly discuss it more); but how do APIs become portable? In terms of an API, portability means *there should be no platform-specific data types required in the public interface or function signature of any API call*. For example, an API like Win32 requires Windows handles as arguments to be passed to many functions. In addition, platform-specific types are returned.

In contrast, JTAPI does not follow this proprietary model. The data types required of all formal parameters and return types are purely portable. However, to say that a JTAPI application can be made *truly* portable (i.e., binary-compatible on all platforms) is somewhat of a misnomer. Even though the API itself is completely portable, it requires nonportable components to operate!

We will use these criteria as we examine the telephony APIs. As is so common in software design, there are engineering trade-offs that must be made in order to accommodate an API's emphasis on supporting one or more of these requirements over another. So let's get started.

A Survey of the Leading Telephony APIs

In this section, we survey the leading telephony APIs. These are Microsoft's Telephony Application Programming Interface (TAPI), Novell and AT&T's Telephony Services Application Programming Interface (TSAPI), and Sun's Java Telephony Application Programming Interface (JTAPI). We also look at a leading vendor's proprietary API to get a flavor of what the market has produced over time in the absence of standard telephony APIs.

But first we take a look at an industry organization that is very influential in the telephony API business — the ECTF.

---

17 In a sense, this is exactly the definition of third-party call support.

Enterprise Computing Telephony Forum APIs

The Enterprise Computing Telephony Forum (ECTF) is an organization formed to formulate industry interoperability agreements for computer telephony convergence and interoperability. They view the current state of the computer telephony industry (CTI) as a real impediment to market growth. They seek to develop or find an approach that will allow an application developer to harness all of the diverse CTI technologies and create new CTI applications. They believe that this new generation of applications should not only span the existing domain of known uses of CTI technology, but also extend the range into new territories without requiring the developer to learn all of the various proprietary interfaces that are associated with the existing application-specific CTI devices.

The ECTF views their role as an advisory one that specifies the functional and performance requirements for a universal telephony framework. This framework includes the functional capability to provide the following types of systems:

- Interactive Voice Response
- Voice Mail
- Automatic Call Distributors
- Predictive Dialers
- Fax-on-Demand
- Departmental PBX
- Enterprise PBX
- Intelligent Conference Bridges
- Voice Dialing

There are other requirements as well as specifying the need for integration with existing systems; platform independence, software architectures (e.g., C/S), resource sharing (including telephone calls), media extensibility, customization, scalability, modularity (application independence), fault tolerance, and management of security, performance, and configuration.

Does this standards body matter? Absolutely. All of the APIs in this book are considered to be ECTF-compliant at some level. For example, S.100 spec functionality is incorporated into Java Media spec (which includes JTAPI). There are other telephony architectural specifications not covered here, most notably TINA.

FCTF Architectural Components

The ECTF has defined a set of CTI architectural components that can be used to provide all of the functionality required for the list of applications described above. These components are

- **ECTF Telephony Server** — hardware platform providing telephony support for all CTI applications

- **CTI application** — software applications that control the telephony servers

An example of a telephony server is a PBX. CTI applications provide services to users by implementing the functionality of the framework. In short, application programmers develop applications that communicate between these two types of servers using the S.XXX series of telephony APIs, which in turn define how CTI applications request services of ECTF telephony servers. All APIs are categorized into a series of APIs that specify interfaces to core functionality at varying levels. The S.XXX series are basically software specs, the H.XXX are hardware specs, and so forth. For example, TAPI, TSAPI, and JTAPI are S.100 CTI Application specs; TCP/IP qualifies as an S.200 Telephony Server specification. The architectural components of ECTF are shown in **Figure 5.8**.

Figure 5.8 *ECTF Architectural Components*

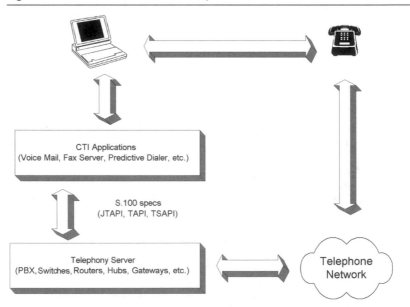

The basic idea is that an API that is written to one of these ECTF specs includes the capability to interoperate with another API by a different vendor that implements another ECTF spec category. For example, a Microsoft TAPI implementation ought to be able to use a TCP/IP transport protocol from another vendor. More information on ECTF may be found at http://www.ectf.org.

Novell and AT&T's Telephony Services Application Programming Interface

In this section, we briefly examine Novell and AT&T's Telephony Services Application Programming Interface (TSAPI). Although we describe its main capabilities, we do not analyze this API in significant detail for two reasons. The first reason lies in its lack of similarity to JTAPI. TSAPI does not keep track of state changes. Both TAPI and JTAPI do. The second reason lies in the fact that the use of Novell as a telephony platform is far less pervasive than that of Windows.[18] Although a JTAPI implementation may certainly be constructed directly from the TSAPI API specification (and it has been), we leave that exercise to the reader (or more likely to some telephony vendor).

TSAPI is based on the Computer Supported Telephony Applications (CSTA) specification developed by the European Computer Manufacturer's Association. From an ECTF perspective, TSAPI provides direct support for telephony servers and indirect support for CTI applications. TSAPI only runs on Novell networks.

TSAPI Functionality

TSAPI provides a set of services as follows:

- **Control Services** — Functions for controlling channels and querying devices from the Novell NetWare telephony server.

- **Switching Functions** — The core set of services provided for controlling switches from an external computer. Like TAPI, TSAPI provides support levels in the form of a Basic service level in a Supplementary service level (we cover this concept in detail when we examine TAPI).

- **Status Reporting** — An API for retrieving event status information from a specific device.

- **Snapshot Services** — An API for retrieving status and affirmation of a software entity or function. Similar to status reporting except at a higher level of abstraction.

- **CSTA Computing Functions** — Application-level functions such as call routing.

- **Escape and Maintenance** — The "back door." Similar to JTAPI's Private Data.

- **Network Loadable Module (NLM) Interface** — Device drivers for the physical medium used to interface with the telephony server.

---

18 Although there are many PBX vendors that support the TSAPI, the popularity of the TAPI API due to its existence on Windows platforms delegates TSAPI to a secondary consideration.

From a portability perspective, TSAPI suffers the same limitations as TAPI does. Both APIs are clearly proprietary interfaces designed to operate on specific platforms only — Novell and Windows environments, respectively. The fundamental difference lies in the fact that a Novell network is primarily designed around a network API. Windows, on the other hand, is an operating system with built-in networking capabilities (at least with NT).

From a telecom programming perspective, these two APIs compete with one another. Although it is possible to run a JTAPI/TSAPI implementation on top of Windows, TAPI is already resident on a Windows box — and it is free. There is, however, at least one JTAPI implementation developed for TSAPI by Lucent technologies. However, the TSAPI spec itself is not as complete as, say, TAPI because it primarily supports call control functions of a switch-to-host link and nothing more. Additional capabilities must be provided through the CSTA interface.

A Dialogic Application Programming Interface

Before investigating our chosen platform library (i.e., TAPI), we examine a popular vendor's proprietary interface implemented on the DOS platform. This will give us a flavor for what traditional telephony programming looks like. Granted, there are later releases of the Dialogic API that support both TAPI and Windows. But the point of this section is to examine how telephony programmers get along in the absence of standard APIs (and for that matter, without threads!).

The API we discuss is the Voice Programmers Guide for MS-DOS, released in 1995. This API is representative of the kinds of APIs most telephony programmers typically deal with. It provides base capabilities as well as complete control of the telephony board it is designed to support. It is implemented in C.

Most interesting is its implementation of simulated concurrency through its complete support for both synchronous and asynchronous channel control on a platform that does not support threads. It is an example of how the lack of support provided for critical services of an operating system (in this case, the lack of thread support on MS-DOS) can lead to the proliferation of nonstandard APIs *by necessity*.

All the functions provided in this API fall into one of two categories: multitasking and nonmultitasking functions. Multitasking functions, of course, return to the caller immediately. The application then waits for some kind of event notification from the runtime system that the multitasking operation has completed. In the meantime, the channel affected by that same asynchronous operation is blocked from use by other functions.[19] However, the application itself is free to initiate function calls on other available channels.

---

19 An application is made aware of this situation by examining the state of the channel. It is "busy" during an asynchronous call and "idle" otherwise.

As might be expected, two methods are provided to determine the state of a channel: a *polling mode* and an *event mode*. In polling mode, the application must periodically make calls to a function that checks the state of a given channel. In event mode, the application queries an event queue that essentially performs a destructive read on the queue removing the requested event. Events are stored in FIFO (first-in first-out) order. The negative implications of using polling over event notification are obvious. However, all programmers appreciate having the option to use whatever mode suits them.

The design of the event notification scheme used in this proprietary API is representative of a common pattern used in telephony programming. This pattern is the Finite State Machine (FSM). Throughout this book, we revisit this pattern over and over again as we note how it is implemented in various APIs.

Microsoft's Telephony Application Programming Interface

Telephony Application Programming Interface (TAPI) is Microsoft's telephony API for Windows applications and platforms. The Windows NT operating system is fast becoming the telephony platform of choice, and so we can expect the popularity of this API to grow. TAPI supports both speech and data transmission. It allows for a variety of terminal devices and supports complex connection types and call-management techniques such as conference calls, call waiting, and voice mail. TAPI allows all elements of telephone usage from the simple dial-and-speak call to international e-mail to be controlled within applications developed for the Microsoft Win32 application programming interface. TAPI allows for the following functionality:

- Connect directly to the telephone network from within a C/C++ Windows application (later versions support COM).

- Dial phone numbers automatically.

- Transmit documents as files, faxes, or electronic mail.

- Access data from news retrieval and other information services.

- Set up and manage conference calls.

- Receive, store, and sort voice mail.

- Use caller-ID to automate the handling of incoming calls.

- Control the operations of a remote computer.

- Compute collaboratively over telephone lines.

To write applications making use of TAPI, you need at a minimum a Windows operating system (Windows 3.11, Windows 95 or 98, or Windows NT), a Windows C/C++ compiler, a Windows-compatible modem, and the TAPI software components outlined in **Table 5.1**.

TAPI Architecture

TAPI is designed around the Windows Open System Architecture (WOSA), as are the related Microsoft API sets MAPI (Messaging API) and SAPI (Speech API). All of these APIs are implemented using the C language. None of them are explicitly thread-safe.

WOSA

WOSA is Microsoft's long-term architectural solution for interoperability of software and device drivers designed to run on Microsoft platforms. Ultimately, these platforms will converge to Windows NT; for now, this architecture is designed to support Windows 3.1, Windows for Work Groups, Windows95, Windows98, and Windows NT.

Presenting WOSA as an "open" architecture is somewhat misleading. It is designed to support Microsoft operating systems only. Although Microsoft programmers can communicate with other types of systems (DCE, for example), DLLs do not run on UNIX boxes! However, a consistent, published interface is of benefit to developers and the clever manner in which Microsoft has specified the architecture is an example of how a little forethought and ingenuity can lead to extensible software.

The WOSA architecture is divided into three components: two programming interfaces and a DLL library. All WOSA-compliant APIs (including MAPI, SAPI, and TAPI) conform to this same architecture. The two interface components (the Client Application Interface and the Server Provider Interface) are separated by a DLL interface with which they each communicate. By communicating with only this common DLL component, each interface component can change without affecting the other's interface.

Required Software Components

To run on a box, TAPI requires the software components listed in **Table 5.1**.

Table 5.1 *TAPI Components*

Software Component	Function
TAPI32.dll	Application programmer's telephony service interface
TAPISRV.exe	Telephony Server. Translates TAPI calls to vendor TSPI implementations
Vendor-specific drivers	Implement TAPI calls vis-à-vis TSPI interface

From a programmer's perspective, you code to one of two interfaces, either TAPI for application code or Telephony Service Provider Interface

(TSPI) for implementing the TAPI calls using the vendor board.[20] TAPI calls go directly into the source code of the application, and TSPI calls use the TSPI interface to hook device driver calls into the TAPI framework when called by the Telephony Server (TAPISRV).

The Client Application Interface — TAPI

The TAPI version of the WOSA client interface is the TAPI API itself. This is the interface used by application programmers seeking to add telephony capabilities to their applications. You simply include the right header files, make the calls, and you're off!

The Service Provider Interface — TSPI

The hardware vendor provides the Telephony Service Provider Interface *implementation*. It is the telephony systems programmer's API window into the functions provided by the device and is used to implement the client interface (TAPI) on this operating system (Windows) using this manufacturer's telephony device. The components in **Table 5.1** interact as depicted in **Figure 5.9**.

Figure 5.9 TAPI Component Interaction

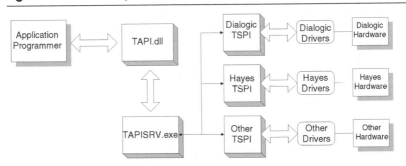

When an application calls a TAPI function, the TAPI dynamic-link library validates the parameters of the function and forwards the call to `TAPISRV.exe`. TAPISRV (the Telephony Server/Service) processes the call and routes a request to the appropriate previously registered service provider. To receive requests from TAPISRV, the service provider must implement the TSPI. This in turn is called in the body of the TAPI functions by TAPISRV. It's callback city…

This pattern of implementing an API for use by application programmers will be revisited many times over in this book. It is essentially the

---

20 This latter task is the job we define in Chapter 11 as a *library programmer*.

same task that must be accomplished in providing a JTAPI implementation. Meanwhile, let's take a closer look at the services TAPI provides in order to gain an understanding of what we're up against.

TAPI Service Levels

A service provider using the TSPI interface can provide three different levels of the service provider interface: *basic*, *supplementary*, or *extended* (Microsoft essentially provides the first level, called "assisted"). For example, a simple service provider might choose to provide basic telephony service, such as support for incoming and outgoing calls only. This is analogous to your typical modem software that comes with a modem. A more sophisticated provider might provide a full range of more advanced support such as caller id, fax services, voice mail, and the like.

There are actually four levels of telephony support that are grouped into two broad categories: Assisted Telephony and Full Telephony Support.

Assisted Telephony Support

Assisted telephony support provides a simple mechanism for sending either voice or data over a POTS connection. Assisted telephony is the easiest and most efficient way to give an application limited telephonic functionality. However, assisted telephony applications cannot manage calls. They essentially provide an interface to a "real" telephony application. In other words, you can pass a phone number (a.k.a. an address) to place phone calls, but you can't do any further processing. Functionality beyond dialing such as the transmission and reception of data would require additional data-transfer APIs, including the communications functions of the Win32 Comm API. Assisted telephony is designed to make applications "telephony-capable," but only in the most limited sense. Let's call one of these weaklings an assisted-telephony–enabled application (ATEA). The ATEA does not actually make the call; rather, it registers a call request with the TAPI subsystem using the `tapiRequestMakeCall` function. The TAPI subsystem queues the request, then invokes a previously registered call manager application to make the call and manage it on behalf of the ATEA. This process is depicted in **Figure 5.10**.

The call to `tapiRequestMakeCall` is asynchronous in that it returns upon successful registration, *not* when the call manager application is actually signaled. If there are no call manager applications to handle the request, a TAPIERR_NOREQUESTRECIPIENT error is returned instead. If, however, one exists and it never gets around to handling the request, the call request stays queued until a call manager application handles it. So if everything seems cool but the application just sits there, the call manager application probably just forgot to register itself with the TAPI subsystem on start-up.

Figure 5.10 *TAPI Assisted Telephony*

There are only two functions in the assisted service level. We've already covered `tapiRequestMakeCall`. The remaining function is an informational function called `tapiGetLocationInfo`. It provides the country code and city (area) code, which the user has previously set in the current location parameters in the Windows Telephony Control Panel. To see how assisted telephony works on your system, generate an MFC application and add event handler code (as in **Listing 5.1**) to make a call to `tapiRequestMakeCall`.

Listing 5.1 Assisted Telephony API Call Using MFC in C++

```
void CAssistedDlg::OnDialButton() {
    char str[60]; char which[15]; LONG ret;
    const char* s = ">> SUCCESS! <<";
    const char* f = ">> FAILURE! <<";
    if (ret = tapiRequestMakeCall( m_PhoneNumber, NULL, NULL, 0)
            != TAPIERR_NOREQUESTRECIPIENT )
                ::strcpy( which, s );
    else ::strcpy( which, f );
    ::sprintf( str, "%s tapiRequestMakeCall() returns ==> %d",
        which, ret);
    AfxMessageBox( str );
}
```

(1) marks the line `if (ret = tapiRequestMakeCall( m_PhoneNumber, NULL, NULL, 0)`

(2) marks the line `AfxMessageBox( str );`

I created a very simple dialog application called `assisted.exe` that does just this. The full source code is provided in Appendix A. The only thing the `assisted.exe` application really does is ask any available call manager application to place a call. The MFC AppWizard generates the `OnDailButton` method skeleton. In **Listing 5.1**, [1] actually makes the TAPI call. The rest of the code inspects the return value and reports it to the user. When you run the application, you can visually see that the call returns asynchronously (i.e., immediately).

First, the main dialog appears (see **Figure 5.11**). Once the "Dial ..." button is pushed, the informational dialog [2] of **Listing 5.1** appears immediately. On my machine, TAPI invokes an instance of the PhoneDialer application provided by Microsoft as a part of NT (this is the third dialog on the bottom of the diagram in **Figure 5.11**). The point of this demonstration application is to show exactly what assisted telephony is but also, more importantly, what it is not.

Figure 5.11 *TAPI Assisted Telephony Application*

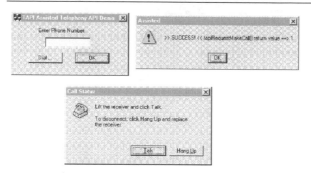

Full Telephony Support

Full telephony support comes in three further categories: Basic, Supplemental, and Extended. Each service level builds on the previous one in terms of capabilities offered. Any real telephony programming is done using these three service levels. A telephony application developed with any of these API sets might be invoked from an assisted telephony call to `tapiRequestMakeCall` in place of PhoneDialer. These are the APIs one would use to bind JTAPI to Win32 platforms.

Basic Telephony

All so-called service providers[21] are required to implement the basic telephony service level. These services correspond approximately to those offered on POTS networks. Application programmers in turn use their implementations through the standard TAPI API to create telephony applications. I created an application to place an outbound call using basic telephony called `Basic.exe`. It also tracks the status of messages sent to the application by the TAPI subsystem.

The creation of a TAPI basic telephony application is a two-step process involving *TAPI subsystem initialization* and *TAPI event handling* by the application. Here's TAPI basic service level programming in a nutshell: First, you must initialize the TAPI subsystem. Next, you get a handle to the line and/or device(s) on your system. Last, you exercise the API. But before you can do any of this, you must either implement and register a callback function that will receive and respond to all messages sent to your application by the TAPI subsystem, or you must essentially provide a threaded architecture (more on this approach later). This callback architecture can get a bit ugly because your design is naturally constrained by the design of the callback signature. However, it is no more ugly than any other

---

21 A service provider is a third party that provides a TSPI implementation for a device or board.

Win32 program — they all make extensive use of callbacks anyway. Besides, we can get to any information we need by passing void pointers or by making system calls. Further, the Win32 API was not designed for our ultimate purposes — to be wrapped by a higher-level API! But back to the code ...

`Basic.exe` is another MFC-generated application. Because we are using MFC, it is a curious blend of C and C++ code that only an MFC programmer playing with a Win32 API can appreciate. I must confess that I love programming in MFC and moping around with the Win32 API — there's such a feeling of accomplishment when you are through! It is not, however, the most productive or intuitive environment around, especially for a die-hard Smalltalk programmer. This is the promise of Java — to reduce some level of the complexity in application development and therefore increase productivity (for those of us who like seeing our families at the end of the day). You can be the judge of whether or not that goal is ultimately accomplished. Hopefully, this book will shed some light on some of the issues.

`Basic.exe` is a simple modal dialog-based application that dials a phone number and displays TAPI state messages during the duration of the call. In Chapter 7, "Application Programming with JTAPI," we map some of these messages to JTAPI events. For now, let's take a look at the application and of course, the code. First, we'll look at the initialization process, then at event handling.

TAPI Subsystem Initialization

Like any good MFC programmer, we place all (or at least the majority of) of our initialization code in the `CWnd::OnCreate()` method of the main window of the application. In this case, we are using a dialog box as the main window, so the proper initialization method is `CDialog::OnInitDialog()`. In **Listing 5.2** we initialize the TAPI subsystem in the first part of `OnInitDialog()`. The TAPI function calls are in *italics*.

Listing 5.2 *Basic Service Level TAPI Initialization*

```
BOOL CBasicDlg::OnInitDialog()
{
   CDialog::OnInitDialog();
   SetIcon(m_hIcon, TRUE);
   SetIcon(m_hIcon, FALSE);
   // TODO: Add extra initialization here
   m_pListBox = (CListBox*)GetDlgItem(
              IDC_LISTTapiMessages );
   // initialize TAPI...
   m_tapiLineAppHandle = NULL;
   m_tapiLineHandle = NULL;
```

Listing 5.2 (cont.) *Basic Service Level TAPI Initialization*

```
      m_tapiCallHandle = NULL;
(3)   if ( LONG answer = lineInitialize(
          &m_tapiLineAppHandle,
(4)       AfxGetApp()->m_hInstance,
(5)       (LINECALLBACK)&CBasicDlg::tapiMessageHandler,
          "Basic Telephony",
          &m_LinesOnMachine ) < 0 ) {
             ::AfxMessageBox(
             "ERROR initializing TAPI subsystem. Exiting
                Application.");
             PostMessage(WM_CLOSE);
      }
      else {
          char msg[50];
          ::sprintf( msg, "TAPI subsystem initialized.
             Return: %d, # lines: %d", answer,
                m_LinesOnMachine );
          ::AfxMessageBox( msg );
      }
// continued in Listing 5.3
```

After we create some member variables to hold onto TAPI information, we make our first TAPI invocation [3]. The parameters of interest here are the second and third parameters ([4] and [5], respectively). TAPI needs to know which application is initializing the line, and it needs a pointer to the callback function to invoke upon receiving line information from the line device. Next, we specify the API version range acceptable to use [6] and actually open the line for calls [7] in **Listing 5.3**.

Listing 5.3 *Basic Service Level TAPI Line Opening*

```
// find an acceptable API version & line to use...
      char verBuf[70];
      LONG ans;
// this code works only if there is one TAPI device on the
// computer. If there are more, place the call to
// lineNegotiateAPIVersion in a loop...
      if ( (ans = lineNegotiateAPIVersion( m_tapiLineAppHandle, 0,
(6)          MAKELONG(3,1), MAKELONG(4,1),
          &m_APIversion, &m_LineExtensionId )) < 0 ) {
             ::sprintf( verBuf, "ERROR negotiating API version.
                      ret: %d. Exiting Application.", ans );
             ::AfxMessageBox( verBuf );
             PostMessage(WM_CLOSE);
```

Listing 5.3 (cont.) *Basic Service Level TAPI Line Opening*

```
      }
      else {
         char verBuf[50], finalBuf[75];
         longToVersionNumber( m_APIversion, verBuf );
         ::sprintf( finalBuf,
            "Found version %s of TAPI on this machine", verBuf );
         ::AfxMessageBox( finalBuf );
(7)      if ( (ans = lineOpen( m_tapiLineAppHandle, 0,
               &m_tapiLineHandle,
            m_APIversion, 0, (DWORD)this,
            LINECALLPRIVILEGE_OWNER | LINECALLPRIVILEGE_MONITOR,
            LINEMEDIAMODE_DATAMODEM, NULL )) != 0 ) {
               ::AfxMessageBox( "ERROR opening line." );
               PostMessage(WM_CLOSE);
      }
      else {
         char buffedOut[128];
         ::sprintf( buffedOut, ">> SUCCESS << opening line.
                              Line Handle: %d", m_tapiLineHandle );
         ::AfxMessageBox( buffedOut );

         // set the LINEPARMS struct. This is NOT optional,
         // as the docs say it is...
            ::memset( &m_tapiLineCallParms, 0, sizeof
               ( LINECALLPARAMS ) );
            m_tapiLineCallParms.dwTotalSize = sizeof
               ( LINECALLPARAMS );
            m_tapiLineCallParms.dwMinRate = 9600;
            m_tapiLineCallParms.dwMaxRate = 9600;
            m_tapiLineCallParms.dwMediaMode =
               LINEMEDIAMODE_DATAMODEM;
      }
   }
   m_pListBox->InsertString( -1, "TAPI subsystem
      Initialized!!");
   return TRUE;
}
```

Initialization is complete — the system is now adequately prepared to place and accept calls. But how do we know when a call is placed? We accept events from the TAPI subsystem and handle them.

Handling Events from TAPI Notification

We now address the heart of the matter — the TAPI callback function. The primary purpose of the callback function (called a *lineCallbackFunc*) is to handle all notification from the TAPI subsystem. This occurs when the calling application invokes the `GetMessage()` function. This callback mechanism is one of three notification mechanisms supplied by TAPI. Basically, you provide an implementation of the callback and tell your application what to do as each message type comes in — you write event handlers for each event. Part of this notification is a class of messages defined in `tapi.h` of type "LINE_CALLSTATE". Not surprisingly, these messages model the state of the line device (e.g., when it is busy, dialing, disconnected, and so forth). This will come in rather handy when we map the API to JTAPI later on.

Let's go ahead and implement part of the callback. Like any callback in C, you can name it anything you like as long as the parameters match those required by the API (i.e., the function signature is identical). Ingeniously, I called mine `tapiMessageHandler`. For now, we'll just implement some of the LINE_CALLSTATE group of messages. Let's start with the one called "LINECALLSTATE_CONNECTED" ([9] in **Listing 5.4**). This particular state is critical in that once a call is in the connected state, information can be transmitted over it.

Listing 5.4 *A TAPI Event Handler Callback Function*

```
void CALLBACK CBasicDlg::tapiMessageHandler(
                        DWORD   hDevice,
                        DWORD   dwMessage,
                        DWORD   dwInstance,
                        DWORD   dwParam1,
                        DWORD   dwParam2,
                        DWORD   dwParam3)
{
    switch ( dwMessage ) {
        case LINE_CALLSTATE: {
            switch ( dwParam1 ) {
                case LINECALLSTATE_CONNECTED: {
                    LPVARSTRING lpVarString;        LONG answer;
                    int msgSize = sizeof(VARSTRING) + 2048;
                    stuffTapiListBox( "-> LINECALLSTATE_CONNECTED" );
                    if ( (lpVarString =(LPVARSTRING)::LocalAlloc( 0,
                            msgSize ))
                        != NULL ) {
                        lpVarString->dwTotalSize = msgSize;
                        if ( (answer = lineGetID( 0,
                                    0, (HCALL)hDevice,
```

(8)
(9)
(10)

Listing 5.4 (cont.) *A TAPI Event Handler Callback Function*

```
                              (DWORD)LINECALLSELECT_CALL,
                              lpVarString, "comm/datamodem"
                              )) != 0 ) {
                  char buffy[256];
                  ::sprintf(
                    buffy, "ERROR >> 0x%x << getting lineID",
                       answer );
                  ::AfxMessageBox( buffy );
                }
                else ::AfxMessageBox( ">> SUCCESS << Got line
                  ID" );
                s_tapiCommHandle = *((LPHANDLE)lpVarString);
                char buffy[256];
                ::sprintf( buffy,
                    "s_tapiCommHandle >> %d <<",
                       s_tapiCommHandle );
                ::AfxMessageBox( buffy );
                ::LocalFree( lpVarString);
              }
            break;
            }
          break;
          }
      // other LINE_CALLSTATE type code…
      break;
      }
    }
}
```

Label (11) appears at the line `s_tapiCommHandle = *((LPHANDLE)lpVarString);`

From [8] of **Listing 5.4**, we can safely assume that all LINE_CALL-STATE messages arrive in the `dwParam1` parameter. Of particular interest is the third parameter, `dwCallbackInstance`. This argument may be used to pass callback instance data. This is a convenient mechanism for obtaining instance-specific application data in the callback function (i.e., getting around the fact that the callback must be a static function). In this toy application, we simply obtain the line device identifier ([10] of **Listing 5.4**) and snag the comm file [11]. In addition to these operations, in a real application we might notify other systems, write to a log file, fire an event, or, say, change state variables. When we implement JTAPI, this is exactly what is required at strategic points of state transition as specified by the JTAPI architecture.

Finally we place the call ([12] of **Listing 5.5**).

Listing 5.5 *Placing an Outbound Call Using TAPI Basic Telephony*

```
void CBasicDlg::OnDialbutton()
{
    // TODO: Add your control notification handler code here
    LONG answer;
    GetDlgItemText( IDC_EDITPhoneNumber, m_PhoneNumber );
    if ( m_PhoneNumber.GetAllocLength() < 7 ) {
        ::AfxMessageBox("ERROR: phone number not big enough");
        return;
    }
    else {
        ::AfxMessageBox("About to Dial number: " +
            m_PhoneNumber);
        // make the call...
        if ( (answer = lineMakeCall( m_tapiLineHandle,
            (LPHCALL)&m_tapiCallHandle,
            (LPCSTR)m_PhoneNumber,
            0,
            &m_tapiLineCallParms )) < 0 ) {
            char buffy[256];
            ::sprintf( buffy, "ERROR >> 0x%x << dialing number:
                %s",
                    answer, m_PhoneNumber );
            ::AfxMessageBox( buffy );
        }
        else {
            ::AfxMessageBox(">> SUCCESS << requesting number: "
                + m_PhoneNumber + " to be dialed.");
        }
    }
}
```

(12)

The complete source code for `Basic.exe` may be found in Appendix A.

The Basic Application

Let's take a look at what this application (i.e., `Basic.exe`) does. In short, it starts out pretty much like its sister, the assisted telephony application. But this time instead of relying on another TAPI-aware application like `PhoneDialer.exe` to do the dialing for us, `Basic.exe` does the dialing itself. First, a few dialogs are displayed verifying the initialization of TAPI. Next, the installed version number and the line handle received (see **Figure 5.12**) are presented to the user. Once a valid phone number is retrieved by the application, it is passed on to the TAPI layer.

Figure 5.12 *A Basic Service Level TAPI Application*

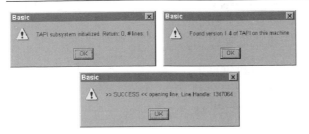

When the line device receives a response, TAPI invokes the callback passing the info in as parameters to the function through a function pointer. The application then executes the message handling code, updating the status display list box along the way (see **Figure 5.13**).

Figure 5.13 *TAPI Basic Service Level Callback Invocation*

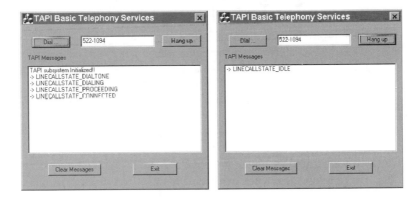

The status messages in the dialog snapshot on the left correspond to TAPI messages generated as a result of pressing the Dial button. When the Hang Up button is pressed, the line goes idle as depicted in the dialog on the right.

In terms of notification, there are two other methods supported by TAPI 2.x and beyond: Win32 events and I/O completion ports. These may be used in place of the hidden window callback mechanism just described. For a truly threaded implementation, we recommend using either Win32 *events* or *completion ports*. However, due to context switching, telephony events may be received out of order if multiple threads are waiting on a single event or completion port. This may or may not be an issue depending on the type of application.

At this point, we could go on and on mired in the marvelous complexity of Win32 notification schemes in an attempt to provide the remaining two options. However much fun it would be, it is not the purpose of this book.

Instead, we will stop coding our sample TAPI applications and focus our efforts on preparing to convert the TAPI API into JTAPI Java code in Chapter 6, "Construction of a JTAPI Library." But for completeness, we finish this section with a brief explanation of the remaining TAPI service layers. A full understanding of these is required before implementing a complete JTAPI-TAPI binding.

Supplemental Telephony

The supplemental telephony service level provides for advanced features like holding, parking, conferencing, and transferring calls. It also supports ISDN and PBX services. Service providers are not required to implement any of these services; they are optional. They are, however, necessary if these types of server-level applications are to be developed using TAPI.

Extended Telephony

The extended telephony API allows service-provider vendors to extend the telephony API using device-specific extensions. Extended telephony services are also referred to as device-specific services. These services include all extensions to the API defined by a particular service provider. The API defines the extension mechanism only. Therefore, the definition of the extended telephony service behavior must be completely specified by the service provider.

The extension mechanism of TAPI allows service-provider vendors the capability to define new data structures and extend most existing ones. This is accomplished by utilizing a locally generated unique extension identifier that is assigned to a set of extensions (but not to each instance of those extensions). This allows the TAPI subsystem a mechanism for uniquely identifying a vendor's services so that they may be distinguished from another vendor's implementation of an extended TAPI service.

Related Microsoft APIs

The remaining WOSA APIs cover other types of media interfaces. These are called MAPI (Messaging Application Programming Interface) and SAPI (Speech Application Programming Interface). Java provides similar APIs in their media API set. Why do we care? It turns out that while TAPI controls the transmission of information over the telephone network, it does not actually manage the content of the message. Instead, the APIs for media stream are used. These are the Communications, WAVE, and MCI services. This fact does not simplify the task of providing a Win32 JTAPI binding unless JTAPI itself is similarly decoupled. It turns out that JTAPI is indeed decoupled in this exact same manner by way of the other related Java Media APIs referenced in Chapter 4.

TAPI Programming Concepts

It is beyond the scope and the intent of this book to completely cover programming in TAPI. For those interested, see the Microsoft press release "Communications Programming for Windows95." There are, however, some important concepts we will investigate because they have correlating design entities or concepts in JTAPI. These are the concepts of *call ownership* and *call state transitions*.

Call Ownership

TAPI applications control telephone calls based upon *call ownership*. When one or more applications own a call, only then may they affect the state of the call. All other interested applications may only *monitor* the call (i.e., log information and query the state of the call). Ownership is initially set to only one application. This application may subsequently hand off ownership to another application at which point it is encouraged to release ownership to avoid race conditions. Call monitor applications are notified of every new call owner. Ownership hand off does not affect the state of the media — this must be controlled separately. We can use this information in our mapping design. TAPI call ownership may be mapped to JTAPI notification. Monitor applications may be analogous to JTAPI observer objects. Other Java Media APIs handle MAPI and SAPI calls (we will get a glimpse of these APIs in Chapter 8).

Events and Call State Transitions

Both TAPI and JTAPI are *event-driven* APIs. In fact, all Win32 applications are essentially event-driven. Event-driven environments are inherently asynchronous and directly support the implementation of finite state machines (FSM). It is universally accepted that this is the best model for telephony programming. Both TAPI and JTAPI provide predefined events that model telephonic occurrences and domain object state transitions. These kinds of models are often represented visually using *state transition diagrams*. **Figure 5.14** shows a traditional state transition diagram used in modeling FSMs.

Like all objects, telephony objects generally are in a specific state at any given point in time. In telephony programming, the most important object is the logical call itself. As a call is established, processed, and then terminated, it transitions through many different states. Events are the mechanisms that cause these states to change — the occurrence of an event is used to force a call object to transition from one state to another.

Figure 5.14 *A Typical State Transition Diagram*

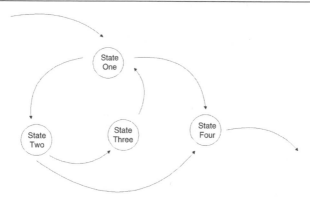

Because interested monitor applications are notified of the new state of the call, they can infer the next potential event if they know the call model. Further, they can predict the next set of likely state changes given the current state of the call. Whenever a call changes state, TAPI reports the new state to the application in a message. JTAPI does the same thing, although the implementation is not specified. States are also used as preconditions to certain types of operations. Again, it is interesting to note that JTAPI was designed in exactly the same manner. This should hopefully ease the mapping between the two APIs.

This completes our examination of some of the most popular APIs on top of which JTAPI may be implemented. We've now seen JTAPI and most of the APIs it may encapsulate on the Windows platform. But how does JTAPI itself measure up in terms of our earlier examination of APIs? We finish this chapter with an examination of this issue.

Does JTAPI Measure Up?

In light of our earlier API criteria, how well does JTAPI fare? Or is this even a fair question? Although many of the API design issues we covered are important, in some senses they simply don't seem to apply to an API like JTAPI. This is because it is defined at such a high level of abstraction that many of these concerns are to be assumed by lower levels of software. If this is true, it raises another issue — is JTAPI defined at a level too high to be of any use in telephony programming? It certainly leaves a lot of work to the JTAPI vendor. That is another issue we discuss later. For now, let's grade its performance.

First, we examine JTAPI suitability to the general API requirements. In review, we identified these as usability, compatibility, extensibility, flexibility, reliability, portability, scalability, support, reentrancy and thread safety, and unobtrusiveness. Next, we examine the telephony-specific requirements as they are satisfied by JTAPI.

JTAPI and General API Requirements

Category: Usability
Grade: A+
We find JTAPI to be an extremely programmer-friendly API — especially for an OO programmer. We believe it is, in fact, a new *kind of* API — one that captures design entities and the essence of the problem space as well as the functionality.

Category: Compatibility
Grade: B
So far, JTAPI has remained fairly consistent between releases of the API. Of course there is not much history to go on here between three releases (1.0, 1.1, and 1.2). Nevertheless, all Java APIs are subject to change and language extension packages even more so. However, the changes between the last releases were so minute that compatibility seems not to be much of an issue here.

Category: Extensibility
Grade: B
Earlier we saw an extensible API as one that allows for future enhancements. In general, JTAPI employs neither typeless parameters nor parameter lists to provide extensibility. Instead it adopts another novel mechanism for extending the API — inheritance and package extensions. In this macro sense, it is well-suited for extension.

JTAPI also supplies an interface that seems well suited for the "backdoor" capability in package `javax.telephony.privatedata` (see Chapter 8, "Extensions to the Core Package"), although it is not clear why a vendor would choose this mechanism over extension.

Category: Flexibility
Grade: C
Recall that we defined a flexible API as one that provides alternative mechanisms for doing the same tasks. In this sense, JTAPI is not very flexible. There are virtually no overloaded methods. On the other hand, it is not clear that this feature is appropriate for this kind of API. Flexibility is important for systems level APIs, but not necessarily for vertical market APIs. However, such a feature might have been very useful applied to the notification API.[22]

---

22 A blocking form of Call.connect() might be useful as well as a guaranteed nonblocking event notification API.

Category: Reliability
Grade: N/A
Reliability will depend 100% on JTAPI vendors. There is nothing inherently reliable or unreliable about the JTAPI specification alone. Reliability can only be measured with working implementations.

Category: Portability
Grade: B
JTAPI is as portable as Java is. However, we will see in Chapter 6, "Construction of a JTAPI Library," that this level of portability requires individual JTAPI implementations for every platform and sometimes every board supported on that platform. It is, however, as portable as device-dependent software gets.

Category: Scalability
Grade: B
Where does JTAPI fit into this picture? Right on top, of course. JTAPI is scalable in that there is nothing in the definition of the API that *prohibits* scalability. Although the JTAPI documentation enumerates support for two general architectures (Network Computer and C/S), the truth is that the API itself neither directly supports nor disallows any such architecture. JTAPI may safely be used no matter *what* the underlying data transport protocol is. In addition, it may be used with any of the distributed architectures we examined: the link architecture, the C/S architecture, the peer-to-peer architecture, or the multitier architecture.

On the other hand, there is nothing inherent in JTAPI that explicitly *enhances* scalability. Is this a problem? We submit that it is not. The design approach behind all of the Java APIs (not just JTAPI) is that they are to be *complementary* to one another. If an application requires scalability, it would look to another Java standard API to fulfill this need in a manner similar to the way JTAPI supports media (more on this in Chapter 8).

Category: Operating System Support
Grade: N/A
At first glance, it would seem that this category is simply not applicable to JTAPI. And in one sense, it is not. We neither require nor would we desire JTAPI to be sprinkled with system-level call support. However, JTAPI does in fact provide a backdoor for telephony implementations by way of the `privatedata` package (see Chapter 8) and its methods. Some might argue that this is in fact all that is necessary and appropriate for a telephony API, and they're probably right.

Category: Reentrancy and Thread Safety
Grade: N/A
Because JTAPI is specified almost entirely as a set of interfaces, reentrancy simply does not apply (i.e., we cannot determine the capability of software that does not have any code).

Category: Unobtrusiveness
Grade: N/A
There is no way that JTAPI could be considered intrusive as we have defined the term. It is simply specified at too high a level.

JTAPI and Telecom-Specific API Requirements

Let's turn now to the more telephony-specific characteristics an API may or may not support.

Category: Asynchronous Notification
Grade: A+
Although there is no implementation, JTAPI support for asynchronous notification is provided in a clear and unambiguous manner in the JTAPI observer design. This design is, in turn, supported well by the JTAPI event model, and call state transitions are supplied as comments in the interface code itself.

Category: Interruption and Graceful Termination
Grade: A
JTAPI supports interruption and graceful termination vis-à-vis standard Java exceptions and extensions to the exception classes. Although it is still up to an implementation to provide the glue code that ties board capabilities to these exceptions, the exception support is a well-thought-out and integrated part of the design of the API.

Category: Thread Support
Grade: B
When we chose Java as our implementation language, one of the language-selection criteria was the support for threads. So, how are threads used with JTAPI? Is JTAPI a thread-safe API?

Strictly speaking, JTAPI is not a threaded API. Why? Because none of the objects used in the specification are *required* to implement the Runnable interface. Recall that unless a class does implement this interface, it cannot be used with threads.

This raises an interesting question: When is it appropriate to specify a Runnable interface? Well, it would seem that a class should inherit from class Thread when threaded behavior is an intrinsic part of an object's behavior *in all cases*. This is simply not so with telephony objects.

However, specifying a `Runnable` interface *enables* a class to run in a separate thread — it does not *require* it to. And so, in most cases, specifying a `Runnable` interface is more flexible and therefore desirable.

The decision of whether or not to use threads for telephony programming is largely an implementation issue — if it is a library requirement to provide both a sequential and a thread-safe version of the model. Clearly, we do not want to have to pay for the overhead of threads if we do not need them. However, we must have them available for a threaded implementation on platforms that provide threads. So it seems that the decision to leave this open in the JTAPI specification is indeed an appropriate one. This is probably true of all extension packages. However, the specification of the `Runnable` interface could have been supported with no additional burden on the application programmer. It is easy to provide a null implementation and therefore leave the option open in a different manner by requiring the interface but not requiring an implementation.

The bottom line is that JTAPI can be made to be thread-safe. The lack of specification of a `Runnable` interface does not preclude an implementation from providing one. Because all JTAPI implementations must ultimately provide concrete classes for a JTAPI implementation, they are free to either add a `Runnable` interface to these classes, inherit from class Thread, or to provide other synchronization techniques (e.g., synchronized methods, instance variable locks).

Note that it is also possible to make the API threadsafe at a lower level. In other words, thread safety can become an implementation issue. Microsoft provides such an option with their Java VM implementation. This level of granularity may or may not be appropriate for all levels of concurrent programming, especially as it applies to telephony boards.

Category: Integration with other API Sets
Grade: A
JTAPI is designed from the ground up to interoperate with other Java APIs. A good example of this is the package `javax.telephony.media` covered in Chapter 8.

Category: Distributed Programming
Grade: B
There are two general approaches for supplying remote method invocations with JTAPI. Distributed programming is not supplied directly by JTAPI. Instead, it may be implemented by using any of the standard mechanisms for distributed programming with Java (e.g., RMI, CORBA), or the underlying platform library may support it.

Category: Portability of Telephony APIs
Grade: A
We covered this earlier. Java data types, return values, and parameter values arc completely portable.

Summary

In this chapter we have investigated APIs from both a general and a specific context in order to understand the functionality they provide. We may have also gained an understanding of how to encapsulate various telephony APIs within a JTAPI implementation. This will be useful in the next chapter, where we use this information to begin the construction of a Win32-JTAPI binding.

Chapter 6

CONSTRUCTION OF A JTAPI LIBRARY

"The Emperor wears no clothes."
Unknown

When we began this project, we were hoping to be able to use a JTAPI vendor implementation. Unfortunately, none existed, and so we were faced with the task of creating our own. Actually, this makes for a more interesting book, and so we were happy to oblige. This chapter documents part of that process and may be of some use to JTAPI library implementers. For the rest of us application programmers, we'll get to see a practical use for quasi-native methods in Java as well as applications for synchronization when we discuss a threaded implementation.

As explained earlier, a JTAPI implementation is not available from Sun Microsystems or as a component library provided with any Java compiler. It is only available as telephony vendors implement and provide it. This fact has dismayed a large number of potential users of the API who are used to being provided implementations along *with* specifications. To them, the emperor indeed wears no clothes! What is *not* commonly understood is the fact that the null implementation model of vertical APIs specified as Java interfaces is an *intentional* design decision borrowed from the Ada programming community. When the reasons behind this model are better understood, some might come to the conclusion that the emperor may not *need* any clothes.[1]

---

1 Or, more accurately, you supply the clothes.

As we have also said, JTAPI is a scalable API designed to "sit on top of" other telephony APIs like TAPI and TSAPI. So in the first part of this chapter, we deal with all these issues and write our own (partial) JTAPI binding to Microsoft Win32 on top of TAPI. In doing so, we discover some rather unsettling news — that the binary portability mantra is pure, unadulterated trash, at least from a telephony library programmer's perspective!

The purpose of this chapter is to provide an implementation of a JTAPI library we call "JTAPI-Lite." It is not, however, to provide a *complete* JTAPI binding. It is to show one approach toward creating one. Providing a complete JTAPI binding is a monumental task that is complicated by the fact that platform-level libraries (e.g., Microsoft TAPI) are themselves changing very rapidly. But a methodology is presented that may be used to complete the task.

In the next chapter (Chapter 7, "Application Programming with JTAPI") we create a telephony application using this JTAPI library implementation. The library itself is then put to use.

A Library Design Methodology

In one sense, the task at hand is rather like an exercise in the laboratories of Dr. Frankenstein (hopefully the outcome will be more successful). We are gluing together pieces of code to implement a rather loose, yet well-defined specification. In order to make the final product a little more appealing to Frankenstein's bride, it is best to formulate a methodology to follow, both for the design and for the implementation of our product.

Deciding Upon a Design Approach

First of all, we know that we must implement the interfaces of the chosen JTAPI package. The design of the services and the interaction between the prime design entities has already been provided for us in the form of the respective interfaces themselves. There are, however, pieces missing. For example, we know that we must be able to respond to and generate events — but how exactly are we supposed to accomplish this? In addition, we must provide a means to call into TAPI services in order to provide JTAPI functionality on Windows platforms. Here is the approach we chose for proceeding from a design perspective:

- Decide which interfaces to implement
- Decide which notification scheme to employ
- Map out a security policy
- Choose the methods that need to be declared native (i.e., implemented in TAPI)

Now that we know *what* to do, let's figure out *how* we want to do it.

Choosing an Implementation Approach

First, we provide concrete no-op implementation classes for every interface (because these are interfaces, this step is required anyway). This will provide a "top-down" compiled framework from which to build. Next, we implement the service layers of *security*, *messaging*, and *platform bindings*. These service layers provide an infrastructure, if you will.

Once the infrastructure is in place, we provide implementations for all our no-op methods in Java using this infrastructure layer (a bottom-up approach). The Peer classes require a security policy that will be provided by our security layer. For methods that generate or respond to events, we delegate that functionality to the messaging service. Lastly, we hook in those method implementations that require use of native methods (i.e., those that actually invoke TAPI code) as our platform binding. Let's expand each of these areas.

JTAPI Library Architectural Components

Each of the tasks identified corresponds to the construction of a particular *architectural component*. **Figure 6.1** depicts these tasks: implementation of the proper *interfaces*, provision of a *messaging architecture*, a *security policy*, and construction of a *platform binding*. Further, these components may be grouped into two higher-level service layers where the messaging architecture, security policy, and the platform binding make up the *infrastructure layer* and the interface implementation makes up the *API layer*. The API layer is what the application programmers instantiate in their application code. The application programmer never sees the infrastructure layer. It is only used for implementing the API layer above it.

Figure 6.1 *Architectural Components of a JTAPI Implementation*

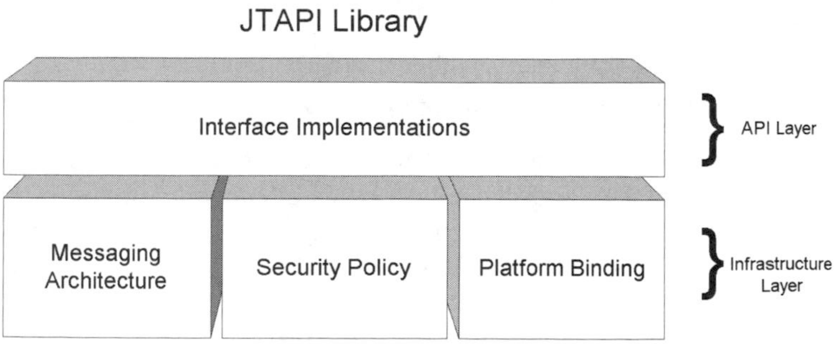

JTAPI Library

These library components will constitute "JTAPI-Lite." From the application programmer's perspective, it will consist of the set of classes (i.e., interface implementations) specified by the interfaces in package `javax.telephony`:

Address

Call

Terminal

Connection

TerminalConnection

Provider

JtapiPeer

The following interfaces will be supplied in Chapter 7. They are to be implemented by application programmers *using* our JTAPI library:

AddressObserver

CallObserver

TerminalObserver

The following classes are provided by JTAPI and require no implementation:

JtapiFactory

InvalidArgumentException

InvalidPartyException

InvalidStateException

JtapiPeerUnavailableException

MethodNotSupportedException

PlatformException

PrivilegeViolationException

ProviderUnavailableException

ResourceUnavailableException

In addition, we must also provide concrete classes for the interfaces specified in the associated subpackages of *capabilities*, *events*, and optionally *privatedata*. If we provide these as well, we need to implement the additional interfaces as follows:

Package javax.telephony.capabilities:

AddressCapabilities

CallCapabilities

TerminalCapabilities

TerminalConnectionCapabilities

ProviderCapabilities

`Package javax.telephony.events:`

AddrEv

AddrObservationEndedEv

CallActiveEv

CallEv

CallInvalidEv

CallObservationEndedEv

ConnAlertingEv

ConnConnectedEv

ConnCreatedEv

ConnDisconnectedEv

ConnEv

ConnFailedEv

ConnInProgressEv

ConnUnknownEv

Ev

ProvEv

ProvInServiceEv

ProvObservationEndedEv

ProvOutOfServiceEv

ProvShutdownEv

TermConnActiveEv

TermConnCreatedEv

TermConnDroppedEv

TermConnEv

TermConnPassiveEv

TermConnRingingEv

TermConnUnknownEv

TermEv

TermObservationEndedEv

Package javax.telephony.privatedata:

PrivateData

The implementation of these interfaces requires the use of the three remaining architectural components (messaging, security, and binding) that will be implemented as a set of *helper classes*. The JTAPI interface implementations (i.e., our API Layer classes) will then make use of these infrastructure classes as appropriate.

The Infrastructure Layer

Let's begin at the bottom by implementing the *infrastructure layer*. One approach to this effort is to break into four teams — one programmer for each implementation. This is a practical approach because the functionality of each of these architectural components is fairly orthogonal. We'll start with the security policy and follow with the messaging architecture and the platform binding. Once these are all in place, we will implement the core interfaces by plugging these service layers in where appropriate and writing code to provide the functionality specified or implied by the JTAPI specification.

Constructing a Security Policy

Security policies can get quite complicated. Many security systems provide functional security, data level security, or both. In addition, there are other issues to consider such as encryption,[2] validation duration, and challenge response policies. The security policy we will put in place for JTAPI-Lite will have none of these characteristics. We will implement a lightweight policy that will not be suitable for commercial use. The purpose of this policy is to demonstrate how security may be plugged into the JTAPI architecture, not to provide a commercial implementation.

At a minimum, we must maintain some kind of list of valid users. Each user has a unique name and a password that grants them access to the Provider through the JtapiPeer interface. Once an instance of a provider is created, we will grant access to all of the system functionality. In other words, we are implementing functional security at an extremely high level of granularity as opposed to granting it on a per-function or per-object basis. **Listing 6.1** presents our first helper class[3] — SecurityMonitor.

---

2 Java provides some level of security functionality vis-à-vis the Java Security API. The major functional focus is on cryptography.

3 Recall that all helper classes are not a part of JTAPI. They are, however, typical of the kinds of classes that vendors will likely provide along with their JTAPI libraries. They are free to do this because these classes are to be implementation details outside the scope of the JTAPI specification.

Listing 6.1 *Helper Class SecurityMonitor*

```java
package sroberts.util.singleton;
import java.util.*;

public class SecurityMonitor extends SDRSingleton {

    final private String STANDARD_JAVA_PROVIDER_LOGIN_TOKEN =
        "login";
    final private String STANDARD_JAVA_PROVIDER_PASSWORD_TOKEN =
        "passwd";
    private Hashtable userList_ = new Hashtable();
    private String masterName_;
    private String masterPassword_;
    private boolean securityIsSet_ = false;
    private String mainToken_;

    // must provide only package visibility to ctor...
    SecurityMonitor() { super(); }

    SecurityMonitor( String mainToken ) {
        this(); mainToken_ = mainToken; }

    public void setUpSecurity(
        String mainToken,
        String masterName,
        String masterPassword ) {
            if ( !securityIsSet_ ) {
                mainToken_ = mainToken;
                masterName_ = masterName;
                masterPassword_ = masterPassword;
                securityIsSet_ = true;
            }
        }

    public boolean okayToProceed( String name, String password )
{
        if ( userList_.containsKey( name ) ) {
            if ( userList_.get( name) == password ) {
                return true; }
        }
        return false;
    }
```

Listing 6.1 (cont.) *Helper Class SecurityMonitor*

```java
public boolean isMaster( String password ) {
    if ( masterPassword_ == password ) { return true; }
    return false;
}


public void addUser( String name, String password ) {
    userList_.put( name, password );
}


public boolean removeUser(
    String masterPassword, String name, String password ) {
    // only allow removal if they know master password & user
    // password!
    if ( !isMaster( masterPassword ) ) return false;
    if ( okayToProceed( name, password ) ) {
        userList_.remove( name );
        return true;
    }
    return false;
}


public boolean parseJtapiPeerProviderString( String str ) {

    StringTokenizer semicolonParseList = new
        StringTokenizer(str, ";");
    while ( semicolonParseList.hasMoreTokens() ) {
        String nextTokenToProcess =
            semicolonParseList.nextToken();
        // first process service name...
        if ( !(nextTokenToProcess.compareTo( mainToken_ ) ==
            0) ) {
            return false;
        }
        // next process login...
        else if ( nextTokenToProcess.substring(
                1,nextTokenToProcess.length()- 1)
                == STANDARD_JAVA_PROVIDER_LOGIN_TOKEN ) {
            StringTokenizer loginChars =
                new StringTokenizer( nextTokenToProcess, "=" );
            // push past "login=" string to get to login
            // value...
            loginChars.nextToken();
```

Listing 6.1 (cont.) *Helper Class SecurityMonitor*

```
                if (loginChars.nextToken().compareTo(
                    masterName)==0 ) {
                    return false;
                }
            }
            // now process passwd...
            else if (nextTokenToProcess.substring(
                    1, nextTokenToProcess.length()-1 )
                        == STANDARD_JAVA_PROVIDER_PASSWORD_TOKEN ) {
                StringTokenizer loginChars =
                    new StringTokenizer( nextTokenToProcess, "=" );
                // push past "passwd=" string to get to the
                // passwd value...
                loginChars.nextToken();
                if (loginChars.nextToken().compareTo
                    (masterPassword_)==0) {
                    return false;
                }
            }
        }
    }
    return true;
    }
}
```

Class SecurityMonitor is a toy class that provides a minimal set of security operations to allow for the secure creation of Provider objects. This class will be created by our implementation of the JtapiPeer class and will be used to provide security services throughout the call model. Let's move on to the next infrastructure piece, the messaging architecture.

Implementing the Messaging Architecture

In Chapter 4, "A Close Look at JTAPI," we were exposed to events as they relate to the JTAPI call model. Events require some kind of asynchronous messaging architecture in order to ensure their delivery to registered objects. In Chapter 9, "Event Management in Java," we present a thorough discussion of the many ways in which a messaging architecture may be implemented in Java. In this section, we actually implement a message management scheme based upon some of the concepts covered in Chapter 9.

Figure 6.2 shows a simple diagram depicting the life cycle of the Smalltalk Observer Pattern as it is implemented in the Java language standard. The way this works is that when something changes in the Observable object, it notifies any preregistered Observers of this fact by calling their update() method. Later, any registered Observers may deregister, at which point they will receive no more notifications. The Observer Pattern is one of many possible *message management models*.

Figure 6.2 *Smalltalk's Observer Pattern Implemented in Java*

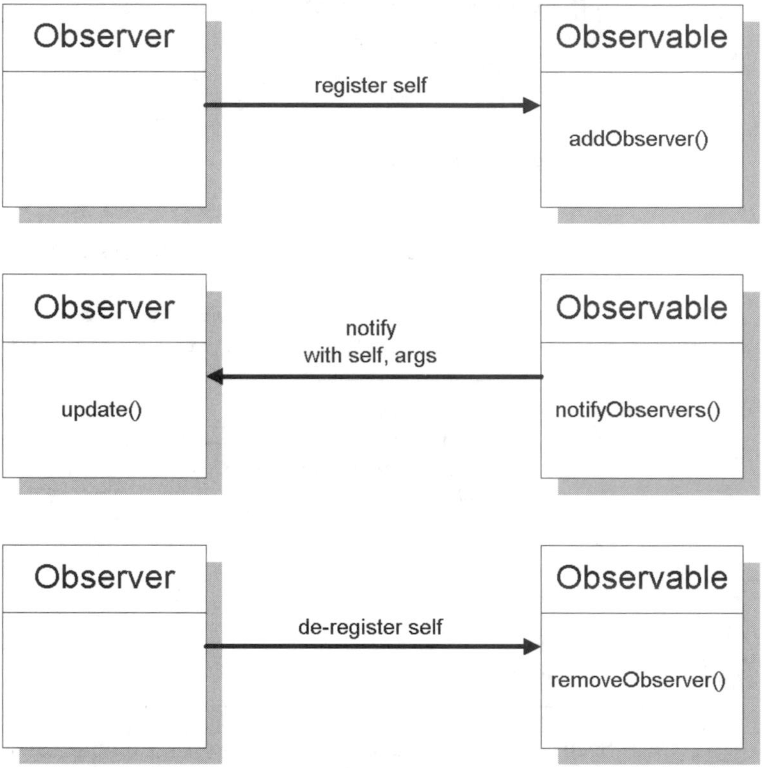

The JTAPI message management model implies a messaging architecture almost identical to the Observer Pattern. However, there are some problems with using the Java implementation of the observer pattern "out of the box." Not the least of these is the fact that the notification interface is different than that specified in JTAPI. Again, the trade-offs and options available for implementing a JTAPI message management model are covered in Chapter 9. Here, we cover the implementation we've chosen for the purposes of this book.

The JTAPI message management model specifies a separate notification interface for every type of event. So instead of a generalized messaging architecture capable of handling many different types of events, the model specifies only the types of events on which a particular observer may report. For example, CallObservers must implement the `callChangedEvent()` method and AddressObservers must implement the `addressChangedEvent()` method instead of both just implementing the `update()` method. In short, each type of notification object gets its own "observer pattern." A discussion of whether or not this is good or bad is deferred until Chapter 9. Ignoring the deregistration process, **Figure 6.3** shows the JTAPI message management model for the Call Observer Pattern.

Figure 6.3 *The Call Observer Pattern of JTAPI*

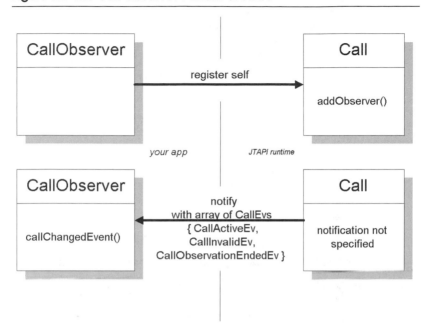

We have the opportunity to define a message management model and its associated architecture precisely *because* the notification mechanism is not specified. However, the framework and the design are specified, so it's up to us to properly implement it. Whatever we come up with will be used throughout the call model and on just about every object. But before we implement it, we have to understand it! Let's use the Call classes (i.e., Call and CallObserver) as an example.[4]

The `callChangedEvent()` method is essentially an *event handler* that application programs are to implement. This handler is called for all registered CallObservers every time any kind of CallEv occurs (i.e., specifically, a CallActiveEv, a CallInvalidEv, or a CallObservationEndedEv). The notification process itself is the responsibility of the JTAPI library. In implementing the messaging architecture, there are two major design areas to address: *implementing the event handler* and *implementing the asynchronous notification mechanism*. Let's take each of these in turn.

Implementing the Event Handler

In implementing the event handler (e.g., `callChangedEvent()`), there are two possible approaches. The first is to do as the JTAPI specification suggests and simply require application programmers to implement the

---

4 The same methodology applies to the Provider, Address, and Terminal classes.

event handler by responding to every type of event that it may receive. This approach is the simplest for the JTAPI vendor to implement; yet it lays the entire burden of event handling upon the application programmer. Let's call this approach the **Specification Approach**. The second method is a more **User-Friendly Approach**, but it flip-flops the event-handling burden from the application programmer to the vendor. It also violates the JTAPI standard, but hey, vendors do that all the time, right?

Event-Handling by the Book — The Specification Approach

The Observer examples that come with the JTAPI documentation use the Specification Approach. On the surface, it seems that it is easy to understand and to implement — and it is — for toy examples. But as the complexity of using the more powerful features that events provide emerge, this approach can become quite cumbersome. Let's take a look in **Listing 6.2** at a sample call listener for an example of this approach.

Listing 6.2 *Event Handling Using the Specification Approach*

```
public class GoodOldCallObserver implements CallObserver {

   public void callChangedEvent(CallEv[] evlist) {
      for (int i = 0; i < evlist.length; i++) {
         if (evlist[i] instanceof CallEv) {
            Call call = ((CallEv)evlist[i]).getCall();
            String msg = "Call is ";
            if (evlist[i].getID() == CallActiveEv.ID) {
               System.out.println(msg + "ACTIVE");          }
            else if (evlist[i].getID() == CallInvalidEv.ID) {
               System.out.println(msg + "INVALID");          }
            else if (evlist[i].getID() ==
                  CallObservationEndedEv.ID) {
               System.out.println(msg + "NO LONGER OBSERVED");
            }
         }
      }
   }
}
```

This approach seems pretty straightforward once you get a handle on the JTAPI call model. The application programmer implements the event handler by creating a switch statement with a case for every possible event type[5] it is allowed to process. While a bit tedious, it can be argued that this

---

5 This is not to say they *must* respond to *all* event types in every event handler. Rather, they only need to "case out" those they care about.

approach has the benefit of being easy to understand, at least from a methodological perspective.

"Waiter, There's a Fly in My Soup ..."

The downside of the Specification Approach is that it is more tedious (and possibly error-prone) because every CallObserver must reimplement the switch code. In the toy example of **Listing 6.2**, we simply examined each event for its type. But an event may also have a *cause code* or it may belong to a series of other events forming a *meta-code*. More tedium is introduced when consideration is made for cause codes and meta-codes (see Chapter 8, "Extensions to the Core Package"). To handle each of these cases requires more levels of switch statements with corresponding case statements for each legal cause code and meta-code combination — yuk!

User-Friendly Event Handling

The User-Friendly Approach follows a more loosely coupled pattern because it delegates the responsibility for responding to each event type to a separate method. Instead of writing switch statements, the application programmer simply implements the corresponding predefined event handler method.[6] One method is supplied for each type of event (see Listing 6.3). Although this approach requires redefining, replacing, or augmenting the CallObserver interface, it is more in line with most object-oriented (OO) commercial libraries where programmers subclass and override the vendor supplied methods.

Listing 6.3 *An Alternative Approach to Event Handling in JTAPI*

```
interface DelegatedCallObserver {
    abstract public void onActiveCall( CallActiveEv ev );
    abstract public void onInvalidCall( CallInvalidEv ev );
    abstract public void
        onCallObservationTermination( CallObservationEndedEv ev );
}
```

In short, the application programmer never implements the single `callChangedEvent()` method. Instead, they implement only the event handler methods they require. This approach of course runs into the same issue as the Specification Approach when consideration is made for cause codes and meta-codes. However, the solution is a little more elegant — we just create another interface for the application programmer to implement (see **Listing 6.4**).

---

6 The manner in which this implementation occurs depends on how the enhanced observer is presented. If it is an interface, the programmer implements it. If it is a class, they override the default implementation provided (which should be null).

Listing 6.4 *Butchering the JTAPI Specification to Achieve a Simpler API*

```
interface CauseCodeCallObserver {
    abstract public void onActiveCallCauseNewCall( CallActiveEv ev );
    abstract public void onActiveCallCauseNormal( CallActiveEv ev );
    abstract public
        void onCallObservationTermination(CallObservationEndedEv ev );
}


interface MetaCodeCallObserver {
    abstract public void onActiveCallCallStarting( CallActiveEv ev );
    abstract public void onActiveCallCallProgress( CallActiveEv ev );
    abstract public void onActiveCallCallAddingParty
        ( CallActiveEv ev );
    abstract public void onActiveCallCallRemovingParty
        ( CallActiveEv ev );
    // other meta code / cause code / active call combinations...
    abstract public void onInvalidCallUnknown( CallInvalidEv ev );
    // other meta code combinations...
}
```

Further user convenience can be added by creating *adapter classes* just like the `java.awt.events` package does. Instead of requiring the application programmer to implement interfaces, we might require them to extend and override a class definition. In this case, the DelegatedCallObserver might be presented as an adapter class as in **Listing 6.5**.

Listing 6.5 *An Adapter Class Version of an Observer Interface Implementation*

```
public class CallObserverAdaptor implements
        DelegatedCallObserver {
    public void onActiveCall( CallActiveEv ev ) { null; }
    public void onInvalidCall( CallInvalidEv ev ) { null; }
    public void onCallObservationTermination(
        CallObservationEndedEv ev ) { null; }
}


// use it like this...
public class MyCallObserverAdaptor extends CallObserverAdaptor {
    public void onActiveCall( CallActiveEv ev ) {
        // your override code goes here...
    }
    public void onInvalidCall( CallInvalidEv ev ) {
        // same here, as necessary...
```

Listing 6.5 (cont.) *An Adapter Class Version of an Observer Interface Implementation*

```
    }
    public void
        onCallObservationTermination( CallObservationEndedEv ev ) {
        // and so on...
    }
}
```

It should be pointed out that each approach really requires the same amount of work, except the requirement for large switch statements in every event handler is eliminated. It is really a question of *who does* that work — the application programmer or the library programmer. The user-friendly approach is easier for application programmers to implement because they never have to write switch statements and they never even have to check the event parameter coming in. In this sense, it is also more *strongly typed* than the JTAPI version.

"Waiter, This Isn't the Soup I Ordered ..."

By now you should be feeling a little nervous about our cavalier approach to mucking with a standard. Indeed, code written using the so-called User-Friendly Approach will not normally run using other vendors' JTAPI implementations. One of the main reasons for using JTAPI is the potential for what we have called "practical portability." By easing the burden of the application programmer, we have rendered their code nonportable — this is the trade-off. However, in our implementation, we might choose the best of both worlds — an application programmer may choose either approach. This is accomplished by chaining all of the interfaces in an *extension chain*[7] so that the final implementation of our CallObserver class supports all of the interfaces[8] (i.e., both those specified in JTAPI as well as these new "convenience" methods we have introduced). This extension chain is shown in **Listing 6.6**.

The chain is created because MetaCodeCallObserver extends the CauseCodeCallObserver interface, which in turn extends the DelegatedCallObserver interface, which extended the CallObserver interface. By extending JTAPI interfaces like CallObserver, application code can use either the event model as specified in JTAPI, or they may use our home-grown "easy interface," albeit at the expense of rendering the code nonportable. To see how they are prepared for use, see **Listing 6.7**.

---

7 A fancy name for a class hierarchy.
8 Actually, we won't support them all, we leave that exercise to a vendor. But we would if we were supplying a commercial library and we chose to offer this support.

Listing 6.6 *Using an Extension Chain to Ensure Compatible Polymorphic User Code*

```
interface DelegatedCallObserver extends CallObserver {
   // abstract methods...
}
interface CauseCodeCallObserver extends DelegatedCallObserver {
   // abstract methods...
}
interface MetaCodeCallObserver extends CauseCodeCallObserver {
   // abstract methods...
}
```

Listing 6.7 *Keeping Our Options Open*

```
public class SDRObserver implements MetaCodeCallObserver {
     // code to implement both types of interfaces...
}
```

This approach can also be made to work with standard JTAPI by the vendor implementing all reporting methods (e.g., `callChangedEvent()`) so that they in turn call these user-friendly methods.

Implementing the Asynchronous Notification Mechanism

Just as there were two possible approaches to implementing the event handler, there are at least two[9] for implementing asynchronous notification — the code that essentially invokes the event handler. Both approaches shown here have to do with *where* to launch the notification thread — from the vendor's **Call** or from the application programmer's **CallObserver** (see **Figure 6.4**).

Figure 6.4 *Launching the Notification Thread*

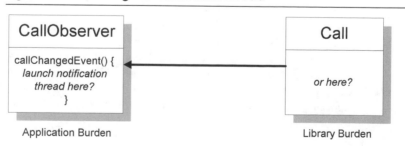

Application Burden   Library Burden

---

9 Actually, there are quite a few more, but we will only consider two here.

We have labeled these two approaches based upon who becomes the "beast of burden" in launching the thread. If the application programmer is responsible, that is the **Application Burden Approach**. Otherwise, the library programmer is responsible and we use the **Library Burden Approach**.

So far, we have spoken of *where* to launch the thread, but not *why*. Again, we defer a detailed discussion until Chapter 9, "Event Management in Java," but for now, suffice to say that the launching of the thread will allow the caller to return immediately. That way, they won't have to wait for the object on the receiving end to complete their processing before continuing on. Anyway, let's examine the two approaches. We address the Application Burden Approach first.

The Application Burden Approach

JTAPI library vendors will prefer the Application Burden Approach. This is not surprising because this approach places the entire burden for initiating the notification upon the application programmer who uses the JTAPI library. In this approach, ibrary programmers simply invoke the `callChangedEvent()` method on the list of call observers and they're done. Application programmers, on the other hand, must follow an idiomatic approach to implementing notification. In short, they launch a thread from within their implementation of the `callChangedEvent()` method so as not to tie up the caller (i.e., the Call instance they are observing). This is demonstrated in **Listing 6.8**.

Listing 6.8 *Forcing Your Customer to Do Your Work ...*

```
public void callChangedEvent( CallEv[] eventList ) {

    for ( int i=0; i < eventList.length; i++ ) {

        if (evlist[i] instanceof ConnEv) {

            // TO DO: instantiate any final data here ...

            Runnable r = new Runnable() {
                public void run(){
                // TO DO: your ConnEv handler code goes
                // here...
                };
            };
            Thread t = new Thread(r);
            t.start();
        }
    }
}
```

This approach is easy to follow. However, we're again faced with a choice between *following an idiom* (which might become clumsy), and simply *using a fully capable, thread-safe library*. Let's go there instead.

The Library Burden Approach

As the name implies, the Library Burden Approach places the notification burden entirely on the JTAPI library. A sample implementation is demonstrated in **Listing 6.9**.

Listing 6.9 *A Sample implementation of the Library Burden Approach to Notification*

```
public void notifyObserversOfEvent( Ev event ) {

    final CallEv[] callEvent = new CallEv[ 1 ];
    callEvent[ 0 ] = (CallEv)event;
    final Call source = ((CallEv)event).getCall();

    try {
      Thread localNotificationThread = new Thread() {
        public void run(){
          finalCallObserver[] callObservers =
            ((CallObserver[])(source.getObservers())));
          for ( int i = 0; i < callObservers.length; i++ )
            { callObservers[ i ].callChangedEvent( callEvent );
            }
        };
      };
      localNotificationThread.start();
    } catch ( Exception e ) {
      System.out.println( " <<FAILED>>" );
      e.printStackTrace();
    }
}
```

While only marginally more difficult to implement for library programmers than the Application Burden approach, this proposal has a large number of advantages for application programmers. Primarily, the user no longer has to worry about following an idiom of any kind. If the Application Burden Approach is simple, this approach is even more so. All they have do is what the JTAPI specification says they have to do; and that is to simply implement the appropriate event handler (in this case, callChangedEvent()).

As we have mentioned, there are other approaches besides these two that may be used to implement the notification mechanism. Again, we refer the reader to Chapter 9. So how did we choose to provide event notification in JTAPI-Lite? We used the Library Burden Approach. We created a common interface for all notification classes to implement and then a class for each type of event. The common interface is presented in **Listing 6.10**.

Listing 6.10 *Common Notification Interface*

```
package sroberts.telephony.events;
import javax.telephony.events.*;


interface JtapiEventNotifier {
    abstract public void notifyObserversOfEvent( Ev event );
    abstract public void notifyObserversOfMetaEvents( Ev[]
        events );
}
```

The notification class we created for Call objects is presented in **Listing 6.11**.

Listing 6.11 *Event Notifier for Calls*

```
package sroberts.telephony.events;

import javax.telephony.*;
import javax.telephony.events.*;


public class CallEventNotifier implements JtapiEventNotifier {

    // normal event...
    // see listing 6-8...

    // series of meta-events...
    public void notifyObserversOfMetaEvents( Ev[] events ) {

        // assume all events are from the same source...
        final Call source = ((CallEv)events[0]).getCall();
        final CallEv[] callMetaEvents = (CallEv[])events;

        try {
            Thread localNotificationThread = new Thread() {
                public void run(){
                    final CallObserver[] callObservers =
                        ((CallObserver[])(source.getObservers()));
                    for ( int i = 0; i < callObservers.length; i++ ) {
```

Listing 6.11 (cont.) *Event Notifier for Calls*

```
                    callObservers[ i ].callChangedEvent(
                        callMetaEvents );
                }
            };
        };
        localNotificationThread.start();
    } catch ( Exception e ) {
        System.out.println(
            "CallEventNotifier::notifyObserversOfMetaEvents
                <<FAILED>>" );
            e.printStackTrace();
        }
    }
}
```

How does this work? Each JTAPI object being observed hangs on to an instance of the appropriate notifier class. They use this guy to perform their notification for them. Whenever a state change occurs in the observable class (e.g., Call), an event is created and passed to the notifier. The notifier then notifies all observers as in **Listing 6.12**.

Listing 6.12 *Using a JtapiNotifier*

```
// callEventNotifier_is an instance variable of class Call...
state_ = ACTIVE;
callEventNotifier_.notifyObserversOfEvent( new
    SDRCallActiveEv(this) );
```

This same pattern is to be repeated for classes Terminal, Provider, and Address.

As we have indicated, implementing a JTAPI API involves four primary steps: implementing the JTAPI interfaces, creating an underlying messaging architecture, constructing a security policy, and implementing the native methods required to either hook into an existing telephony API or to write one from scratch. We've covered two of the three steps for implementing our JTAPI infrastructure. Before we move on to actually implementing the interfaces of the API layer, let's check out the final infrastructure step — implementing a Win32-JTAPI binding.

What Is a JTAPI Binding?

Good question. We know what JTAPI is (from Chapter 4), and we know what TAPI is (from Chapter 5). On a Windows platform, a *JTAPI binding* is essentially an API that sits between the two. We prefer to think of it as a Library Programming Interface (LPI). Application programmers never invoke a JTAPI binding; rather it is glue code that implements the JTAPI specification "on top of" another API — in this case TAPI (see **Figure 6.5**). It is an API that is developed internally to bind one API to another.

Figure 6.5 *JTAPI Bindings*

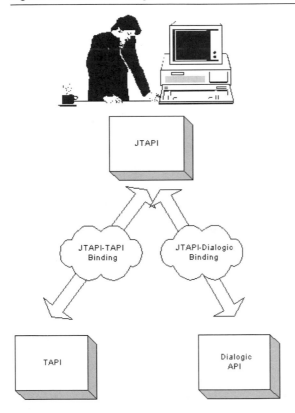

As **Figure 6.5** shows, JTAPI does not *have to* wrap another platform telephony API like TAPI or TSAPI. It may be implemented instead by invoking proprietary vendor APIs (e.g., Dialogic). What does an LPI look like? Just like a normal API. The difference lies not necessarily in their structure, rather in *where* and *by whom* they are invoked. LPI functions are always used to implement the functionality of a higher-level public interface.

In one sense, JTAPI and TAPI are competing APIs. Although one is a platform-independent Java API and the other a Win32 C API, this is irrelevant in terms of how they may be used in an application. Application programmers write telephony applications using both APIs in roughly the same manner because they provide roughly the same functionality. However, TAPI is a much lower-level API. The JTAPI function calls are much more loosely coupled than are those of TAPI. The designers of the

JTAPI specification essentially leveraged this characteristic to create a scalable and portable API that performs the same functionality yet at a much higher level of abstraction. Application programmers like that. Although scalable in an architectural sense, TAPI may be described as exceedingly complex and could never be described as being designed for portability. Which leads to our next subject ...

Portability in a Binding Context

Before the process of creating a JTAPI implementation commences, let's be clear on exactly what it is we are creating in terms of portability. Earlier, we described code developed using a JTAPI implementation as "practically portable." So how portable is a JTAPI binding? Well, not at all. However, JTAPI *enables portability* for Java applications that *use* the API exclusively. Obviously this comes at a cost. The cost is the development of JTAPI bindings for each and every platform. This is worth restating:

JTAPI Rule to Remember 3:

A different JTAPI binding is required for each and every platform on which JTAPI is implemented.

A partial list of some of the required bindings is depicted in **Figure 6.6**.

Figure 6.6 *Write How Many Times, Run Anywhere?*

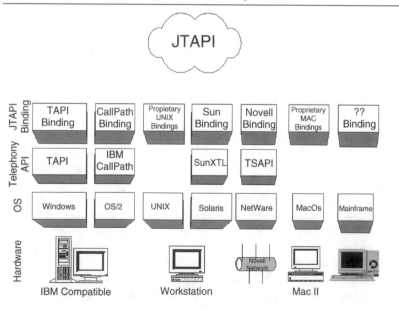

Although our JTAPI-Lite is implemented on top of Microsoft's TAPI API, it will be portable to any computer that has a Microsoft Java virtual machine *and* any telephony board that implements TAPI (i.e., provides a TSPI implementation) *for that platform*. In other words, our implementation is not portable *at all* beyond Windows platforms!

This is not a design flaw — it is inherent in the nature of device-dependent APIs. The lack of "true portability" lies in the manner in which we have chosen to implement the library (TAPI) and the characteristic that telephony invocations are always platform- and device-specific anyway. In order for JTAPI-Lite to be *truly* portable (i.e., to achieve binary compatibility) a *platform binding* must be provided for each operating system, API, and device supported on a given computer. For example, a vendor may have to provide one binding for TAPI for each board, one for TSAPI for each board, one for each version of a proprietary API, one for Macs, and one for any other vendor under the moon (as is depicted in **Figure 6.6**). Of course, the portion of the Java code visible to application programmers calling JTAPI interfaces will be portable with a recompile, but the underlying layers of software bindings must be provided as well. This intermediate API (or LPI) is what we refer to here as a *JTAPI binding*.

What Is a Platform?

The term "platform" is relative. For example, application programmers are used to using the terms "platform" and "operating system" interchangeably. Most application programmers are familiar with terminology such as "the software runs on Windows and Unix platforms." Statements like these are fairly common for many types of applications, but they are a mouthful for telephony applications! To say that a piece of telephony software runs on a single operating system is a monumental claim. To support multiple operating systems is even more difficult. The reason, of course, is that telephony applications are device dependent. The hardware required to operate the software is not standardized for a single operating system, let alone *across* operating systems. If you found **Figure 6.6** daunting from an implementation perspective, take a look at **Figure 6.7**!

Figure 6.7 is essentially a hypothetical explosion of *one section* of **Figure 6.6**. It demonstrates the proliferation of bindings required to support disparate boards on a *single* operating system. Clearly, the term "platform" takes on a different meaning in the device-specific context. When speaking of Windows platform support in the telephony context, we must be more specific (unless of course, we support *all* possible windows board configurations). So we might refer to JTAPI support for the TAPI, Dialogic/Windows, and Lucent/Windows platforms. For the purposes of this book, we are only implementing a *piece* of *one* of these platforms.

Figure 6.7 *Proliferation of "Platforms" Required for a Single Operating System*

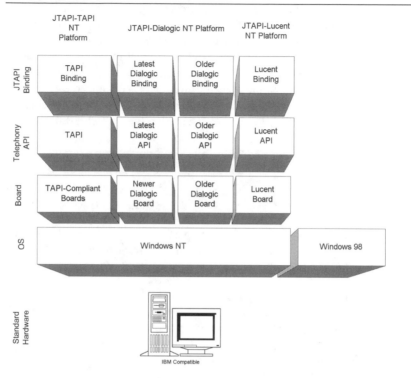

From Java to C

Provided we are willing to accept nonbinary portability as a practical constraint (which we must), we can attempt to provide the cleanest possible interface between the Java JTAPI invocations and the TAPI functions implemented in C. This goal can be best accomplished if we use a standard mechanism for defining data type declarations and passing parameters at runtime. That is exactly the goal of the JNI — to provide binary compatibility of native method libraries across all Java VM implementations on a given platform.

What we will find is that the success of this goal is mitigated when a large number of different devices and manufacturers are involved and even more so when each provides their own object libraries to call. But more importantly, we find that JNI is not easily implemented on the Windows platform. Bummer — let's proceed anyway.

Implementing the Java Native Interface

From a language standard perspective, native methods are those that conform to the JNI specification. For a given platform, the JNI allows Java code that runs inside any fully compliant JVM to interoperate with applications and libraries written in other programming languages, even Assembler.[10] For our purposes, however, we are going to broaden the definition of a native method by loosening the restriction that an implementation conform to the standard JNI specification.

Briefly, recall that native methods are best used for the following reasons:

- The standard Java class library does not support the platform-dependent features needed.

- There exists a library written in another language.

- A portion of time-critical or deterministic code is to be implemented in a lower-level language such as C or Assembler.

For our project, the second reason applies. The TAPI interface can be made to be accessible to Java code through native methods if we can just figure out how to do it! Turns out there are two primary approaches: JNI or J/Direct (more on this later). Before we get bogged down in implementation details, let's see where we're going.

Assessing the Job at Hand

The first thing to recognize about the native method effort required is that not *all* JTAPI method implementations are required to be native. In fact, for package `javax.telephony`, only a few native methods are required. The implementation of these methods will not alter the public interface so as not to expose the platform interface to the caller. This is how we will maintain a *practically portable* implementation.

Specifically, we'll need to map all the calls in JTAPI that "do something telephonic" with those in TAPI that provide essentially the same telephony service. In core JTAPI, this equates to providing native methods for the methods `Call.connect()`, `Connection.disconnect()`, and `TerminalConnection.answer()`. We go hunting for the TAPI functions that provide the same functionality and then write glue code to piece them together. But before we begin, we must become familiar with some of the platform peculiarities of the Win32 API.

Win32 Native Method Considerations

Java aficionados hope that the native method API will someday become a set of deprecated language features. In our opinion, this is not likely in the near future, if at all. As long as people implement Java code on Windows platforms, native methods will be needed — especially for library program-

---

10 This is not intended to be an exhaustive foray into the ins and outs of native methods. For that, see the JNI specification and another book in this same series — Rob Gordon's *Essential JNI*, Prentice Hall, 1998.

mers. Further, because Java does not support pointers and is interpreted (and therefore garbage-collected), there will always be some set of functionality Java will not be able to provide.

Implementing native methods under Win32 is quite a bit more complicated than compiling a native "hello world" `stdout` response for a Win32 console or TTY UNIX application. The reason these complications arise is because they are created by API-specific extensions (in this case, Win32 API requirements).

Native methods are designed to interface with programming languages, not platform-specific behavior per se. In other words, Java can talk to C++ through JNI, but how do we get Java to talk to existing DLLs? The JNI answer is: "Convert all DLL data types and interfaces to C++ and then to Java byte code." This means wrapping each data type and function call with native methods and native data type declarations. Fortunately, there are alternatives if we are willing to trade a degree of portability for convenience. At the risk of implementing a "nonstandard" solution, we will adopt one of these workarounds shortly.

Other sources of Win32 complexity are DLL-thread interaction, storage-class attributes, structured exceptions, callbacks, and calling conventions. Their use does not preclude us from interfacing with Win32, they just make the job much more difficult. Let's look at each of these in turn.

Dynamic Link Libraries and Threads

To begin with, properly written DLLs work within the Win32 system *thread model*. Because the DLL has no control over what type of environment it will be loaded into, it must be programmed using a *defensive posture*. This typically involves allocating some **thread local storage** and monitoring callers. Further, any static data must be synchronized — in short, the DLL must be made thread-safe. This may not pose a problem as long as the Java runtime implements their thread model using Win32 system primitives. If, however, the runtime uses their own thread library, it must be written to successfully interact with Win32 threaded system calls. Another thread complication comes with the Java garbage collector interaction with native code.[11] Any time a DLL is released that is not thread safe, it is simply unreliable software — period.

Storage-Class Attributes

Storage-class attributes are, in fact, Microsoft-specific keyword extensions to the C and C++ languages. The extended attribute syntax for qualifying storage-class information is commonly used when declaring data types and

---

11 Native code is outside the purview of the Java garbage collector. Therefore, memory allocated by native code must be managed separately (e.g., a Java object is freed by the GC, but the underlying C++ object is not).

functions in DLLs (e.g., `__declspec( dllexport )`), although there are other uses. The DLL-related extensions are very helpful in that they eliminate the need for *module definition files* required in previous versions of Windows. Unfortunately, their use is completely nonportable.[12]

Calling Conventions

Win32 calling conventions typically require the FAR PASCAL format. Although this calling convention has been replaced by either WINAPI or CALLBACK, it is really the same thing and is necessary if you are writing a DLL with exported API entry points (i.e., any callback function responding to Windows messages).

What does this mean to a library implementation of Java native code? Clearly a mechanism must be provided for determining which functions are to follow this calling convention — for this is not a standard feature of Java (or any other programming language, for that matter). This shouldn't be too difficult to provide. However, it may require dirtying up our pristine glue code with yet another nonstandard extension!

Structured Exceptions

Both Java and C++ provide exceptions. Of course, C does not. So Microsoft provides us with yet another a platform-specific extension of the C language — *structured exceptions*. This mechanism provides essentially the same functionality as C++ exceptions. Our Java code must be able to handle structured exceptions because they are the primary error-handling mechanism used in Win32. Fortunately, most TAPI errors are instead handled by messages to the main TAPI callback function. However, there is no guarantee that a lower layer of code might not throw a structured exception.

Callback Architecture (Optional)

Depending on how we decide to implement asynchronous calls, a separate callback architecture may be required. Although Windows is designed to handle callbacks in an arguably eloquent manner, implementing a callback mechanism may be more difficult than providing a "normal" API mapping.

Let's return to the issue of using a non-JNI approach. Given the large number of obstacles presented by the Win32 API, it would be nice if we didn't have to deal with all these issues. What we'd like is a Java API that wrapped the TAPI API in Java! Unfortunately, none exist. That's essentially what we must provide. However, this task can be simplified if we can find a Java wrapper for at least the Win32 API. Fortunately, such a wrapping does exist. It's called J/Direct.

---

12 Of course, module definition files have never been "portable" either — they were a *platform requirement*. Now they have been replaced with what amounts to a C *language extension* on Windows platforms!

Raw Native Interface and J/Direct

Microsoft provides an alternative to JNI in four flavors,[13] only two of which we are concerned with here: the *Raw Native Interface* (RNI) and *J/Direct*. Neither of these APIs is an implementation of JNI, but they accomplish essentially the same task, albeit for Windows platforms only. Some believe these technologies were designed as part of an evil plot to splinter the Java language because they provide functionality already provided by JNI. This attitude goes a long way toward fanning the flames of the Java religious wars, but it is easy to see how it occurred. Because Sun initially provided no implementation, they left the door open for Microsoft to do just that. Because JNI is platform-specific anyway, Microsoft saw no compelling reason to support it. Instead, they provided their own implementation and suited it to the needs of Windows programmers. On the surface, we as programmers would like to think we prefer the specification approach. But we often change our tune when we actually try to program with JNI under Windows. Only then do we appreciate having a working product over a specification that requires a lot of tedious work!

With the release of version 2.0 of the Microsoft Java Software Development Kit, Microsoft introduced J/Direct. Essentially, J/Direct is a Java API that wraps the Win32 API. J/Direct is a technology that complements RNI — in fact, the two may be used together. J/Direct is easier to use, but its use comes with some restrictions. In contrast, RNI provides garbage collection synchronization primitives within the native code environment. Fortunately, libraries are free to use both approaches even within the same source file. Tapping into the power of this technology will ease our workload considerably, but not completely. Without this technology, we would be forced to resort to a large amount of tedious glue code. Using J/Direct and RNI, we can reduce the problem set from the entire Win32 API to just that subset of the TAPI API we intend to implement for this book.

To give an idea of how this technology works, let's try to invoke a Win32 MessageBox from Java code. Using J/Direct, this is completely trivial (see **Listing 6.13**).

There are two "nonstandard" extensions to JNI to be found in this code. The first and most obvious is found in [1] of **Listing 6.13**. [1] is essentially a compiler directive telling the linker where to find the code for the native method `MessageBox()` (in this case, the application extension library named USER32.DLL). This syntax (`@dll.import("library name")`) is required of all J/Direct Win32 library definition invocations as well as that of any DLLs you write yourself. Note also that the parameter types and name match exactly to the Win32 name and parameter data types.

---

13 The other two native method mechanisms are ActiveX/Beans Integration and Low-Level Java/COM Integration.

Listing 6.13 *J/Direct Win32 API Call*

```
public class TestMessageBox {

    public static void main(String args[]) {
        try {
            MessageBox(0,"MessageBox called from Win32
                API.", "J/Direct",0);
        } catch (UnsatisfiedLinkError ule) {
            System.err.println("Caught exception: " + ule);
        }
    }
    /** @dll.import("USER32") */
    static native int MessageBox(
        int     hwndOwner,
        String text,
        String title,
        int     style);
}
```

(1)

The other nonstandard feature is far more subtle — can you spot it? Actually, it is a *missing* statement normally required of Java invocations for methods defined outside the current package. It is the Java *import* statement. A third form of source code pollution occurs when we pass or receive parameters and return values. If any Java data types are passed to J/Direct routines, the API requires that they be declared with another compiler directive called @dll.struct.

J/Direct and Portability

So, does J/Direct prohibit portability? Well, yes. It only runs on Windows platforms. However, there is another problem here. It also only runs on virtual machines that support J/Direct. What we have compromised is our ability to run on another virtual machine even on the same platform! Why? It is clear that J/Direct code will not provide the desired result with virtual machines other than the Microsoft VM (unless of course a particular VM chooses to support Microsoft. But if they do, they may be violating their license agreement with Sun!). This is true even though the directive is essentially a comment in the code. The only way around this is if other compiler vendors and VM suppliers support J/Direct. From a code perspective, the changes that would be required of a rewrite are not drastic[14] and clearly provide a much simpler approach than JNI.

---

14 In fact, they are technically unnecessary due to the fact that the directives are essentially code comments.

So what exactly has Microsoft done to accomplish the ability to invoke Win32 functions from within Java? Just what we would have had to do had we done it ourselves. They wrapped each and every data type and function call with the equivalent Java types so the Java compiler and interpreter would "understand" it. That is exactly what the Java SDK is — a set of Java classes.

What remains for us to do? Unfortunately, a bit of tedious work still remains. We must also wrap all the exposed TAPI data types, constants, and APIs in Java. Or do we? More on this when we discuss the design considerations of implementing our library.

Taking J/Direct for a Spin

To test the capabilities of J/Direct in terms of it working with TAPI code, we wrote a quick wrapper for one of the functions we wrote earlier (i.e., the TAPI Assisted Telephony function `tapiRequestMakeCall()` of Chapter 5, "Telephony API Overview"). First, we created a DLL to hold the function so we could point the J/Direct directive at it (see **Listing 6.14**).

Listing 6.14 *Assisted Telephony TAPI Call as a DLL*

```
// wrapAssist.h
#include <windows.h>
#define EXPORT __declspec(dllexport)
#ifdef __cplusplus
    extern "C" {
#endif  /* __cplusplus */
EXPORT void CALLBACK wrapAssist( void );
#ifdef __cplusplus
    }
#endif
// wrapAssist.c
#include <stdio.h>
#include <tapi.h>
#include "wrapAssist.h"
int WINAPI DllMain(HINSTANCE hInstance, DWORD fdwReason,
    PVOID pvReserved)
{
    return TRUE ;
}
EXPORT void CALLBACK wrapAssist( void )
{
    char str[60];
```

Listing 6.14 (cont.) *Assisted Telephony TAPI Call as a DLL*

```
char which[15];
LONG ret;
const char* s = ">> SUCCESS! <<";
const char* f = ">> FAILURE! <<";
if ( ret = tapiRequestMakeCall( "522-1094", NULL, NULL, 0 )
    != TAPIERR_NOREQUESTRECIPIENT )
    strcpy( which, s );
else strcpy( which, f );
sprintf(str,"%s tapiRequestMakeCall() return value ==>
    %d",which,ret);
MessageBox( 0, str, NULL, MB_OK );
}
```

(2)

The code in **Listing 6.14** is identical to the code in **Listing 5.1** of Chapter 5, except for the minor difference that **Listing 5.1** is a C++ MFC application and **Listing 6.14** is a Win32 DLL. Because of this, the calls to invoke message boxes (see **Listing 6.14**, [2]) as well as some of the required header files are different.

Next we wrote a quick wrapper class in Java (TestTAPI.class) to actually test the TAPI function (see **Listing 6.15**).

Listing 6.15 *Testing a TAPI Call in Java*

```
public class TestTAPI {

    public static void main( String args[] )
    {
        try {
            wrapAssist();
        } catch ( UnsatisfiedLinkError ule ) {
            System.err.println("Caught exception: " + ule);
        }
    }
    /** @dll.import("wrapAssist") */
    static native void wrapAssist();
}
```

The results of invoking this application are shown in **Figure 6.8**. This worked like a charm (i.e., just as it did before, using straight C++)!

Now that we've solved the Win32 problem (or at least know how we intend to approach the task), let's see what TAPI obstacles we must overcome.

Figure 6.8 *Invocation of DLL via J/Direct*

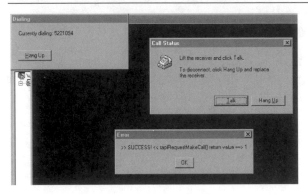

Library Design Considerations

Implementing the JTAPI implementation is a job for *library program-mers*.[15] Just as application programmers must make design considerations for their applications, so must library programmers for their libraries. Just as an application programmer must be concerned with usability and perfor-mance issues for their customer, so must library programmers. However, just as the approach is the same, there are also differences. The customer of the application programmer is the end user; for the library programmer, it is the application programmer. The two primary library design considerations are for *callbacks* and for an awareness of the *Application Programming Boundary (APB)*. Let's begin with callbacks.

Implementation Support for Callbacks

Recall that TAPI notification is implemented using one of three asynchro-nous notification schemes. Using our earlier example, when certain events occur, the TAPI subsystem notified our application by invoking a static callback function we had previously registered. This is one mechanism for asynchronous communication provided by TAPI; there are two more begin-ning with version 2.0. In addition to static functions as callbacks imple-mented with function pointers, TAPI notification response may be imple-mented using NT events or I/O completion ports. For continuity, we will build on the callback function provided earlier.[16] In a production quality release, we might choose to use either of the other two mechanisms.

Fortunately, J/Direct supplies an elegant mechanism for specifying call-backs — class Callback. Recall that the TAPI callback function signature is

---

15 We'll define this term in Chapter 11, "Organizing a Large-Scale Telecom Development Project." For now, consider a library programmer as one who implements an API (as opposed to an application programmer who uses an API).

16 We'll find later there are problems using this approach.

etched in stone, and so depending on how we write the glue code, we may have to match that signature in Java if we choose the Verbatim APB approach. We would define this interface when we code the Java classes that implement this callback.[17] This strategy is an implementation option, but not necessary using the Encapsulation APB approach. But what are these approaches? And what is an APB?

Application Programming Boundary

Most fundamental from a mapping design perspective is consideration for what we define here as the "Application Programming Boundary." The APB is essentially the interface between the highest-level library calls (e.g., TAPI's `lineMakeCall()`) and the API calls they must implement (e.g., JTAPI's `Call.connect()`). It's like a firewall between the API and the library itself. This relationship is depicted in **Figure 6.9**.

Figure 6.9 *The Application Programming Boundary*

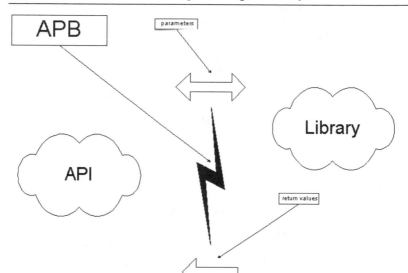

What moves across the APB is data in the form of parameters to library calls and return values from library call invocations. What makes this a design consideration is the manner in which these data values are represented in primary storage (e.g., RAM) and in code (either Java or C). This is reflected by the degree to which these parameters and return values are exposed to the API.

---

17 Actually, there is another approach to implementing callbacks in Microsoft Java called *delegates*. Delegates bring function pointers to Java, but not *standard* Java! This capability is *clearly* a Java language extension.

Let's look at a concrete example in code. Suppose we were to implement a call to the TAPI function `lineMakeCall()` in Java. In implementing this interface, there are two possible extremes. One is to implement the API *verbatim*. The other extreme we'll call the *encapsulation* approach. We'll address both approaches shortly. Here's the JTAPI call we must implement:

```
// from class javax.telephony.Call:

Connection[] connect(
    Terminal origterm, Address origaddr, String dialedDigits );
```

Here's the TAPI call we must ultimately use to implement the JTAPI API call (i.e., the library call):

```
LONG lineMakeCall(
    HLINE hLine,
    LPHCALL lphCall,
    LPCSTR lpszDestAddress,
    DWORD dwCountryCode,
    LPLINECALLPARAMS const lpCallParams
);
```

The job of the library programmer is to convert the various values (i.e., parameters and return variables) back and forth over the APB to satisfy both APIs in a manner that is most efficient and also least intrusive to the application programmer. As a side effect of accomplishing this, storage issues arise regarding data required of the library call but not of the API (and possibly vice versa). For example, consider all of the parameters required of `lineMakeCall()`. Except for the third parameter *lpszDestAddress*, none of these other values is required of JTAPI.[18] Yet they must come from somewhere and be stored somewhere in order to be passed to the TAPI call. The operative question is "Where will they be stored — in the application programmer's storage area or that of the library programmer?"

The Verbatim APB Approach

Using the *verbatim approach*, we would write a Java native implementation of the TAPI function using JNI or J/Direct and then pass the required parameters to it. For example, we would write Java code as follows:

---

18 This is not entirely true — the lphCall and hLine parameters should probably be mapped to a Call instance and a Terminal instance, respectively. But we'll ignore this detail at the moment for the sake of presentation clarity.

```
public long lineMakeCall(
    hLine int[],
    lphCall int[],
    lpszDestAddress StringBuffer,
    DwCountryCode int[],
    lpCallParams String[]
);
```

All parameters must be mapped in both Java and C. These values would likely be stored in a set of private Java helper classes attached to JTAPI domain objects of type Call and Connection. In past projects, we have used what we call *shadow classes* to accomplish this. These shadow classes are essentially private instance variables whose values change as the domain object's state changes. These shadow instances are visible only to the underlying implementations of public methods and are used to satisfy calls to external interfaces that implement the public methods.

The problem with the verbatim approach is twofold. First, it creates a maintenance nightmare. Changes to the underlying library API (in this case, TAPI) force changes to the Java *application* code. Of course, the code would be written in such a manner so as to localize it, but the maintenance issue remains. The second problem is more physical in nature. The verbatim approach pollutes the namespace and the storage space of the application program. Fortunately, the namespace problem is easily solved in Java using packages. But the one-to-one mapping of parameters and return types across the APB may also lead to *slower execution* as this translation must occur upon every method invocation. In many cases, there is simply no choice because either access to the source is not provided or the interface is to an external system. In that case, all that can be done is to be sure to properly insulate the application as much as possible. But with TAPI, we do have a choice.

The Encapsulation APB Approach

Using the *encapsulation approach*, the need to store this transient information in the application is mitigated or eliminated altogether. As much of this parameter information as possible would be kept local to the library binding DLL, eliminating them from the Java interface altogether, if possible. The library programmer's job is to shift the APB line as far to the left (toward the application programmer's JTAPI API cloud in **Figure 6.9**) as possible. In short, we do the dirty work in C instead of in Java.

The advantage of this approach is threefold. First, the required mapping of data types between Java and C is mitigated. This solves the runtime overhead performance issue of passing data across the APB. Second, the Java interface is vastly simplified. This eases the task of making library API invocations; it makes the library API more palatable to application programmers. But third, and arguably most important, future changes to the underlying library API (in this case, TAPI) will have far less impact on the Java application code. The cost is an extra layer of C/C++ code to wrap the library interface, as necessary. Ideally, this overhead is more than offset by the lack of required instantiation and translation of these values across the APB.

Upon examination of the TAPI call APIs, it is clear that either approach is possible. Because the calls are made at a fairly atomic level relative to the JTAPI API, the parameters required of the `lineMakeCall()` function could indeed be stored in application storage between TAPI function invocations. However, many of them can also be combined in order to place a call if we simply move all of this processing to the library. In other words, the variables used to store the line and call handles can be held in memory in the library storage space until they are needed. This is in contrast to returning these values to the application storage to be later passed in again.

However, using the encapsulation approach, there is still one other design consideration. As good object-oriented programmers, we have become very accustomed to expressing software entities in the form of classes and objects. Because we are now also aware of the design in JTAPI, we have an almost knee-jerk reaction. Our first instinct is to map the Java JTAPI telephony classes directly to C++ classes in order to increase the understandability of the underlying library code. Sounds reasonable — let's give it a whirl.

The TAPI Foundation Classes (TFC)

We are now at the point where we can begin to encapsulate a subset of the TAPI API into a set of C++ classes. TAPI is a Win32 API — therefore it is a C API, not a C++ API. This exercise will be similar to what the Microsoft team must have gone through to create the Microsoft Foundation Classes (MFC) albeit at a much smaller scale. The purpose is to provide a cleaner mapping of C++ to Java. There are two reasons for this:

1. Enhanced code maintenance

2. Encapsulation

Code maintenance is improved primarily through *design clarity*. As the TAPI API changes, changes must be made to this layer of glue code. The more understandable it is from a design perspective, the easier it is to maintain. Second, we can use some of the features of the C++ language to encapsulate many of the lower-level platform-specific extensions of the TAPI environment, thereby reducing the number of data types we must expose to the Java native interface. Our goal is to completely eliminate the need to map TAPI data types to Java. But where do we start?

Just as there are similarities in the standard events between TAPI and JTAPI, there are also similarities between the TAPI structs and the JTAPI domain objects. Attempting to map the functionality required of JTAPI classes to TAPI function calls helps to identify these similarities. For example, we might encapsulate many of these structs as private data inside classes like TFCAddress, TFCCall, and TFCConnection. Let's get started.

But wait a minute. What in the world were we thinking? We were thinking with the mindset of an application programmer — not a library programmer! The practice of mapping the Java classes directly to C++ classes may be elegant, but it is actually unnecessary. It is, in fact, kind of stupid. Think about it. We can still provide the desired encapsulation by simply placing all the code in a single module. On Windows platforms, this is a DLL.[19] Although using C++ classes in addition seems like a good idea, from a practical perspective, all we would be adding is more overhead and more code to maintain! And so we abandon this exercise immediately. Sorry for the detour, but we wanted to make a point. Anyway, let's move on.

Let the Mapping Begin ...

At a higher level of abstraction, both TAPI and JTAPI support the concept of a logical abstraction for a telephone call, but from fairly different perspectives. The JTAPI abstraction is much more obvious — there is an object (`javax.telephony.Call`) which represents this design entity. TAPI has no such animal, and so we must glean the TAPI abstraction from our understanding of the API. Perhaps the best place to start is to look at the state transitions that are modeled as a part of the APIs.

The standard messages defined for TAPI when a call is in progress represent events that are generated as the state of line devices change. In TAPI, this is as close to a phone call object abstraction as we get. However, there are some clear similarities between the TAPI states and the JTAPI states. In both APIs, the "action" doesn't really get started until either a line device (TAPI) or a Call (JTAPI) is in the CONNECTED state. In TAPI, this occurs with the `lineMakeCall()` function; in JTAPI with the `javax.telephony.Call.connect()` method. And so our first task at hand is to implement the `javax.telephony.Call.connect()` method *in terms of* the TAPI `lineMakeCall()` function.

A commercial-quality JTAPI implementation would analyze both APIs and determine which JTAPI objects should hold what TAPI information. For example, the line identifier and the comm handle supplied by TAPI probably belong in the Terminal object, and the destination and originating addresses obviously belong in two separate Address instances. But for the purposes of a clarified demonstration of binding techniques, we will build on work already done recognizing that a better implementation is ultimately required.

---

19 On most UNIX platforms, we would use a shared library.

Recall that in Chapter 5, "Telephony API Overview," we wrapped all of the TAPI functions in a method named `callConnect()`. In order to accomplish encapsulated APB for the `Call.connect()` method, one approach is to combine the following TAPI functions:

LineNegotiateAPIVersion( )

LineOpen( )

LineMakeCall( )

LineGetID( )

In addition, we must initialize the `tapiLineCallParms` struct with the proper values. In short, we must create a *tight coupling* between the initialization and call initiation processes. One way to do this is to use the encapsulation capabilities of DLLs. So let's write a DLL that places a call. But we already did this work when we created the `call.dll` library! Therefore, we can just use that library to demonstrate a JTAPI binding approach. Before we do, let's backtrack a bit to get a clearer idea of the process used in determining exactly which library functions mapped to which API functions.

Recall that it took three TAPI functions to implement a single JTAPI method. Although this may not be what a commercial-quality implementation would look like, this is not unusual. In fact, most library APIs exhibit a many-to-one relationship between the function calls required to implement a single API function at the application level. Although in some cases there may be a one-to-one mapping, a library API is usually at a lower level of abstraction than the application API. In cases where this relationship is reversed, we have a real problem. Indeed, we have an impedance mismatch between the APIs. We might begin to question the design of the application API if it is in fact at a lower level of abstraction than the library API it is attempting to wrap.

Now that we've covered all the design issues and theoretical bases, let's get started writing some code!

Let's Go!

Okay — where do we start? It's helpful to group the tasks into categories dealing with the kind of information we are working with. To that end, we've provided four categories. Let's enumerate the required steps here:

A. Subprogram Identification

   1. Determine which JTAPI methods we are to implement
   2. Determine which library functions (in this case, TAPI) must be invoked to implement each application API method

B. Data Mapping

3. Determine which parameters and return values must be passed across the APB, if any

4. Determine which transient data must be instantiated between library function invocations, if any

C. Encapsulation

5. Encapsulate all the library function calls and transient data into a code module (e.g., a C/C++ file)

6. Compile the code module from Step 5 into a platform library (e.g., a DLL, an x.so file)

D. Wrapping

7. Wrap the code module from Step 6 into a single[20] Java native method

8. Wrap the native method(s) from Step 7 with the application API method or, better yet, encapsulate all native code into separate classes first

This process is repeated for every method in the application API requiring a native mapping. Of course, the last step is to write drivers to test the implementation. Let's take each of these steps in turn.

A) Subprogram Identification

For the `javax.telephony.Call.connect()` method, we've already accomplished the first two steps in our earlier discussion. We have identified exactly which library functions map to the API function we are trying to implement. This identification was based upon the functionality these functions provided. Here's the tally so far:

Step 1: `javax.telephony.Call.connect()` from JTAPI

Step 2: `lineNegotiateAPIVersion()`, `lineOpen()`, `lineMakeCall()`, `lineGetID()` from TAPI[21]

B) Data Mapping

In Step 3, we actually map the data moving across the APB. The goal is to add no *additional* data to cross the APB, if at all possible. This means that the only data passed or returned should be determined entirely by the application API (in this case, the method `connect()`). In the case where this is

---

20 It is possible and indeed sometimes necessary to provide more than one native method, but this is again a last resort.

21 Again, a "real" JTAPI binding would probably decompose these in a different manner. The approach, however, is the same.

not possible, one or more extra layers of wrapper code may be necessary on the Java side. However, this can usually be avoided.

A determination must be made as to which parameters from the application API can be used to pass data to the library functions. Likewise, those data structures provided by the library API that can be used to initialize the application API objects are identified.[22] In addition, the calling convention of each parameter must be determined. Each parameter is passed in as a copy (IN) or a pointer (INOUT). Return values are always of type OUT.

Step 3a: Application API parameters:
   Terminal origterm **IN**, Address origaddr **IN**, String dialedDigits **IN**

Step 3b: Application API returns:
   Connection[ ] **OUT**

Step 3c: Library API parameters:
   HWND hwnd, **const char*** destAddr, **char*** statusStr

Step 3d: Library API returns:
   long

Let's start with the application API. For incoming parameters, the first question we ask is, "Does the library API need any or all of the information these parameters supply?" The answer is, "Yes, the wrapped TAPI function `callConnect()` requires a destination address string, a status string, and a handle to a Window."

But how do we actually map this data? In other words, how in the world do I convert an HWND Windows C data type from a Java application? The answer is, "Read the J/Direct documentation."[23] It's all there. For example, a DWORD maps to a Java **int**[ ]. In our example, an HWND maps to a Java long integer, a **const char*** maps to a Java String, and a **char*** maps to a Java StringBuffer (the code to demonstrate this is shown in Step 7).

In Step 4, we consider the data required for library invocations. This is pretty straightforward and is determined by the data required of all the library API calls. In this case, the only data is a C struct called **tapiLineCallParms**. There are, however, other parameters required for the library invocations from Step 3. For ease of maintenance, these may all be grouped into one data structure.

Step 4:   Initialize tapiLineCallParms struct

C) Encapsulation

Steps 5 and 6:   **Listing 6.16** shows a code module and a DLL
   (`callrep.c` and `callrep.dll`) that satisfies these steps.

---

22 As much as possible, we would endeavor to place this initialization in either constructors or a static initialization function, as appropriate.

23 Any other native method mechanism (e.g., JNI) must also by definition supply a mapping of C types to Java types and back.

Listing 6.16 *Encapsulating the Call's C Representation in a DLL*

```
// header file...
#include <windows.h>

#ifndef EXPORT
#define EXPORT __declspec(dllexport)
#endif


// Wrapped TAPI Error codes...
#define lineInitializeERROR -1
#define lineNegotiateAPIVersionERROR -2
#define lineOpenERROR -3

//other errors...
#define DLLinUseERROR -1


#ifdef __cplusplus
extern "C" {
#endif  /* __cplusplus */


// TAPI functions which will be native methods in Java...

EXPORT long pvtCallConnect( DWORD* tapiCallHandle, DWORD*
dwCallbackInstance, const char* destAddr, char* statusStr );

EXPORT int callDisconnect( const char* phoneNumber );

void CALLBACK tapiMessageHandler(
                                DWORD    hDevice,
                                DWORD    dwMessage,
                                DWORD    dwInstance,
                                DWORD    dwParam1,
                                DWORD    dwParam2,
                                DWORD    dwParam3   );

// helper functions...

void dialAway( DWORD* tapiCallHandle );




#ifdef __cplusplus
}
#endif
```

Listing 6.16 (cont.) *Encapsulating the Call's C Representation in a DLL*

```c
// implementation file...
#include <stdio.h>
#include <tapi.h>
#include "callrep.h"

// TAPI variables...
HANDLE tapiCommHandle = NULL;
HLINEAPP tapiLineAppHandle = NULL;
HLINE tapiLineHandle = NULL;
DWORD apiVersion;
LINECALLPARAMS tapiLineCallParms;
LINEEXTENSIONID lineExtensionId;
DWORD dwCallID;
DWORD dwCurrentCallHandle;
DWORD linesOnMachine;

HINSTANCE hInst;
char destinationAddress[ 50 ];


/*
 * The hWnd parameter is unnecessary other than to demonstrate
 * J/Direct conversion of Java int[] to a DWORD*
 */

HWND hWnd;

static BOOL dllInUse = FALSE;
static BOOL okayToGetCallHandle = FALSE;
static int stall = 0;


//********************************************************
int WINAPI DllMain(HINSTANCE hInstance, DWORD fdwReason, PVOID
   pvReserved)
{
   hInst = hInstance;
   return TRUE;
}



//**************************************************************
EXPORT int callDisconnect( const char* phoneNumber )
{
      char lulu[50];
```

Listing 6.16 (cont.) *Encapsulating the Call's C Representation in a DLL*

```
if ( dwCurrentCallHandle == 0 ) {
    sprintf( lulu, "inside disconnectCall(),
                    Call HANDLE %d", dwCurrentCallHandle );
    MessageBox( 0,
    "Call handle not ready yet. Try again when call
        receives reply.", "callDisconnect( const char*
        phoneNumber )", MB_OK);
    return -1;
}

// drop the call...
if ( dwCurrentCallHandle != 0 ) {

    if ( lineDrop( (HCALL)dwCurrentCallHandle, NULL, 0 ) >
        0 ) ;
    else {
        MessageBox( hWnd, "ERROR: dropping call", "",
            MB_OK);
        return -2;
    }
}
else
    MessageBox( hWnd, "tapiCallHandle is NULL", "",
        MB_OK);
    dllInUse = FALSE;
    return 0;
}


//************************************************************
EXPORT long pvtCallConnect( DWORD* tapiCallHandle,
                            DWORD* dwCallbackInstance,
                            const char*  destAddr,
                            char* statusStr )
{

    LONG answer;
    LONG ans;

    okayToGetCallHandle = FALSE;

    if (dllInUse == FALSE) { dllInUse = TRUE; }
    else {
      MessageBox( 0,
      "Call DLL currently in use. Try again later...", "",
        MB_OK);
```

Listing 6.16 (cont.) *Encapsulating the Call's C Representation in a DLL*

```
        return DLLinUseERROR;
    }

    sprintf( destinationAddress, destAddr );

    if ( answer = lineInitialize(
            &tapiLineAppHandle,
            hInst,
            (LINECALLBACK)&tapiMessageHandler,
            "JTAPI Application",
            &linesOnMachine ) < 0 ) {

        return lineInitializeERROR;
    }

    /*
     * Find an acceptable API version & line to use...
     * this code works only if there is one TAPI device on
     * the computer. If more, place the call to
     * lineNegotiateAPIVersion in a loop...
     *
     */

    if ( (ans = lineNegotiateAPIVersion( tapiLineAppHandle,
            0, MAKELONG(3,1), MAKELONG(4,1),
                &apiVersion, &lineExtensionId )) < 0 ) {

        sprintf( statusStr,
          "ERROR negotiating API version. ret: %d. Exiting
             Application.", ans );
        MessageBox( 0, statusStr, "ERROR", MB_OK);
        return lineNegotiateAPIVersionERROR;
    }
    else {

        if ( (ans = lineOpen( tapiLineAppHandle, 0,
                    &tapiLineHandle,apiVersion, 0,
                    (DWORD)dwCallbackInstance,
                    LINECALLPRIVILEGE_OWNER
                  | LINECALLPRIVILEGE_MONITOR,
                    LINEMEDIAMODE_DATAMODEM, NULL )) != 0 ) {
            return lineOpenERROR;
        }
        else {

            // set the LINEPARMS struct.
            memset( &tapiLineCallParms, 0, sizeof( LINECALL
              PARMS ) );
```

Listing 6.16 (cont.) *Encapsulating the Call's C Representation in a DLL*

```
            tapiLineCallParms.dwTotalSize = sizeof(
                LINECALLPARMS );
            tapiLineCallParms.dwMinRate = 9600;
            tapiLineCallParms.dwMaxRate = 9600;
            tapiLineCallParms.dwMediaMode =
                LINEMEDIAMODE_DATAMODEM;
        }
    }
    dialAway( tapiCallHandle );
    return 0;
}


//*********************************************************
void dialAway( DWORD* tapiCallHandle )
{
    LONG answer;
    char buffy[256];
    DWORD dwThisThreadId = GetCurrentThreadId();

    if ( strlen( destinationAddress ) < 7 ) {
      sprintf( buffy, "ERROR: phone number not big enough" );
      MessageBox( hWnd, buffy, "", MB_OK);
      return;
    }
    else {

      // make the call...
      if ( (answer = lineMakeCall( tapiLineHandle,
                          (LPHCALL)&tapiCallHandle,
                          (LPCSTR)destinationAddress,
                          0,
                          &tapiLineCallParms )) < 0 ) {
        sprintf( buffy, "ERROR >> 0x%x << dialing number:
          %s", answer, destinationAddress );
        MessageBox( hWnd, buffy, "", MB_OK);

      }
      else {

        // poor man's block!
        sprintf( buffy,
        ">> SUCCESS << requesting number: %s%s Call HANDLE:
         %p :: %d", destinationAddress, " to be dialed.",
        tapiCallHandle, tapiCallHandle );
        MessageBox( hWnd, buffy,
          "Bug: DO NOT CLOSE THIS DIALOG UNTIL
                          CALL IS CONNECTED", MB_OK);
```

Listing 6.16 (cont.) *Encapsulating the Call's C Representation in a DLL*

```
              }
         }
}


//********************************************************************
void CALLBACK tapiMessageHandler(
                                  DWORD   hDevice,
                                  DWORD   dwMessage,
                                  DWORD   dwInstance,
                                  DWORD   dwParam1,
                                  DWORD   dwParam2,
                                  DWORD   dwParam3)
{
        char buffy[256];

        LPVARSTRING lpVarString;
        LONG answer;
        int msgSize = sizeof(VARSTRING) + 2048;
        DWORD dwThisThreadId = GetCurrentThreadId();

        switch ( dwMessage )
        {
          case LINE_CALLSTATE:
          {
            dwCurrentCallHandle = hDevice;
            okayToGetCallHandle = TRUE;

            switch ( dwParam1 )
            {
            case LINECALLSTATE_IDLE:
               lineDeallocateCall((HCALL)hDevice);
            break;

            case LINECALLSTATE_CONNECTED:

                // public static final int
                // javax.telephony.Connection.CONNECTED = 0x33;
                // this will send a message to JTAPI
                // that a Connection is CONNECTED...
                *(((DWORD*)dwInstance) + 1) = 0x33;

                if ( (lpVarString = (LPVARSTRING)LocalAlloc( 0,
                                      msgSize )) != NULL ) {
                   lpVarString->dwTotalSize = msgSize;
```

Listing 6.16 (cont.) *Encapsulating the Call's C Representation in a DLL*

```
                    if ( (answer = lineGetID( 0,
                                   // m_tapiLineHandle,
                                   0, (HCALL)hDevice,
                                   (DWORD)LINECALLSELECT_CALL,
                                   lpVarString, "comm/datamodem"
                                   )) != 0 ) {

                        sprintf( buffy,
                        "ERROR >> 0x%x << getting lineID",
                        answer );
                        MessageBox( hWnd, buffy,
                            "LINECALLSTATE_CONNECTED", MB_OK);
                    }
                    LocalFree( lpVarString );
                }
                else
                    MessageBox( hWnd,
                     "LocalAlloc FAILED.", ">> ERROR <<", MB_OK);

        break; //LINECALLSTATE_CONNECTED:


        case LINECALLSTATE_ACCEPTED:
            sprintf( buffy, "-> LINECALLSTATE_ACCEPTED" );
            break;

        case LINECALLSTATE_PROCEEDING:
            sprintf( buffy, "-> LINECALLSTATE_PROCEEDING" );
            break;

        case LINECALLSTATE_OFFERING:
            sprintf( buffy, "-> LINECALLSTATE_OFFERING" );
            break;

        case LINECALLSTATE_DIALTONE:
            sprintf( buffy, "-> LINECALLSTATE_DIALTONE" );
            break;

        case LINECALLSTATE_DIALING:
            break;

        case LINECALLSTATE_BUSY:
            break;

        case LINECALLSTATE_DISCONNECTED:
            // public static final int
            // javax.telephony.Connection.DISCONNECTED = 0x34;
```

Listing 6.16 (cont.) *Encapsulating the Call's C Representation in a DLL*

```
                // this should a message to JTAPI that a
                // Connection is DISCONNECTED...
                *(((DWORD*)dwInstance) + 2) = 0x34;

                sprintf( buffy, "->
                        LINECALLSTATE_DISCONNECTED" );
                MessageBox( hWnd, buffy, "inside CALLBACK",
                        MB_OK);
                break;
            }
        }
    }
}
```

D) Wrapping

Step 7:   Wrap the exported function `callConnect()` from
`callrep.dll` in a J/Direct native method. Also provide an
implementation for disconnecting the phone call mapped to the
`TerminalConnection.disconnect()` method.

This native method is found in the class named CallRep (for "call representation") of **Listing 6.17**.

Listing 6.17 *Wrapping Native Methods into a Representation Class
for Clarity*

```
/*
 * This class holds all the native method calls to implement
 * the JTAPI Call class. It wraps a C DLL using the
 * JDirect @dll.import directive for all TAPI code.
 */

package sroberts.telephony.jTAPIimplementations.tapi;

public class CallRep {

    /** @dll.import("callrep") */
    static public native long callConnect(
        int[] tapiCallHandle, String destAddr, StringBuffer
            statusStr )
            throws UnsatisfiedLinkError;

    /** @dll.import("callrep") */
    static public native void callDisconnect( String phoneNumber )

        throws UnsatisfiedLinkError;

}
```

Just for grins, we wrote a quick driver application to test this class, shown in **Listing 6.18**.

Listing 6.18 *A Driver to Test Class CallRep*

```java
import java.applet.*;
import java.awt.*;
import java.awt.event.*;
import sroberts.telephony.jTAPIimplementations.tapi.*;
import JDirect2NativeAppFrame;


public class JDirect2NativeApp
extends Applet implements Runnable, ActionListener
{
    static private final String PHONE = "522-1094";
    private Thread m_JDirect2NativeApp = null;
    private Label message_;
    private boolean m_fStandAlone = true;

    public static void main(String args[])
    {
        JDirect2NativeAppFrame frame =
            new JDirect2NativeAppFrame("JDirect2NativeApp");

        frame.setSize(frame.insets().left +
                frame.insets().right  + 320,frame.insets().top
                + frame.insets().bottom + 240);
        JDirect2NativeApp applet_JDirect2NativeApp =
            new JDirect2NativeApp();

        frame.add("Center", applet_JDirect2NativeApp);
        applet_JDirect2NativeApp.m_fStandAlone = true;
        applet_JDirect2NativeApp.init();
        applet_JDirect2NativeApp.start();
        frame.show();
    }

    public void init() {
        setLayout( new FlowLayout() );
        message_ = new Label("                         " );
        Button dialButton = new Button( "Dial" );
        Button hangUpButton = new Button( "Hang Up" );
        Button exitButton = new Button( "Exit" );
        add( dialButton );
        dialButton.addActionListener( this );
        add( hangUpButton );
```

Listing 6.18 (cont.) *A Driver to Test Class CallRep*

```
      hangUpButton.addActionListener( this );
      add( exitButton );
      exitButton.addActionListener( this );
      add( message_ );
   }

   public void start() {
      if (m_JDirect2NativeApp == null) {
         m_JDirect2NativeApp = new Thread(this);
         m_JDirect2NativeApp.start();
      }
   }

   public void stop() {
      if (m_JDirect2NativeApp != null) {
         m_JDirect2NativeApp.stop();
         m_JDirect2NativeApp = null;
      }
      if ( m_fStandAlone ) System.exit(0);
   }

   public void actionPerformed( ActionEvent ev ) {

      String action = ev.getActionCommand();

      if ( action.compareTo( "Dial" ) == 0 ) {
         message_.setText( "Calling Native Connect()
            for ..." + PHONE );
         int[] hCall = new int[1];
         hCall[0] = 0;

         try {
            CallRep.callConnect( hCall, PHONE, new
               StringBuffer() );
         } catch (UnsatisfiedLinkError ule) {
            System.err.println("Caught exception: " + ule);
            ule.printStackTrace();
         }
      }
      else if ( action.compareTo( "Hang Up" ) == 0 ) {
         message_.setText("Calling Native Disconnect()
            for ..." +PHONE);
         try {
            CallRep.callDisconnect( PHONE );
```

Listing 6.18 (cont.) *A Driver to Test Class CallRep*

```
        } catch (UnsatisfiedLinkError ule) {
          System.err.println("Caught exception: " + ule);
            ule.printStackTrace();
        }
      }
      else if ( action.compareTo( "Exit" ) == 0 ) {
        message_.setText( "Program Terminated by User..." );
        stop();
      }
    }
  }
}
```

Step 8: One approach would be to place a call to the native method from Step 7 inside the JTAPI method Call.**connect**(). However, we chose to provide an extra layer of abstraction (some would say overhead) to our design to provide an easier way to use API. We placed all the C functions that related to a call within the same Java class (CallRep) from Step 7. The JTAPI implementation will now delegate this responsibility to this class from within the Call.**connect**() method (see **Listing 6.19**).

Listing 6.19 *Using the CallRep Class to Implement a Binding*

```
import jTAPIimplementations.*;

public class SDRCall implements Call {

  public Connection[] connect(
    Terminal origterm, Address origaddr, String dialedDigits)
      throws
          ResourceUnavailableException,
          PrivilegeViolationException,
          InvalidPartyException,
          InvalidArgumentException,
          InvalidStateException,
          MethodNotSupportedException {

      // some code...

    CallRep.callConnect( hCall, dialedDigits,
                         new StringBuffer(50) );

      // more code...
  }
}
```

As a final step, we implement the observer interfaces and provide a Java test program to invoke our JTAPI implementation in a Windows environment. We will accomplish this in the next chapter.

Providing a Thread-Safe Implementation

We do not provide a thread-safe implementation of JTAPI-Lite here. Indeed, all the "good advice" we gave earlier is not implemented in `call-rep.dll` for clarity. However, any commercial-quality implementation must. It is impossible to provide a blanket approach to managing concurrency without becoming mired in the details of a particular implementation. For example, the decision of whether to handle concurrency from within Java, C/Win32 or both will depend upon design considerations of a particular implementation approach (of which there are many). The following are some guidelines that may be used in providing such an implementation.

- Use guarded methods in Java
- Use Win32 events in C
- Use RNI in Java

Again, which of these (or other) tools is used for thread synchronization will depend heavily on how the code is implemented. It may be advisable, however, to follow just one approach to managing threads, if possible. For example, only use guarded methods and allocate all thread management to Java code. Or use only Win32 primitives and avoid thread management in Java.[24] This single-minded approach will likely avoid issues that may arise when attempting to combine thread-management libraries.

We have (finally!) completed the infrastructure layer for our JTAPI library. Now let's move on to the API layer.

The API Layer

At last, we turn to the final step in providing a partial JTAPI library. Recall from **Figure 6.1** that the API layer is the top layer of code in our JTAPI library. It is the *only* structural component the user (i.e., the application programmer) will see. What we are doing here is essentially implementing the interfaces specified in the JTAPI specification using the support classes we just developed (i.e., the infrastructure layer).

Implementing the JTAPI Core Interfaces

In this section, we provide the API layer by converting our JTAPI interfaces into real working classes. Before we get started, let's take a look at

---

24 This approach, of course, has the disadvantage of rendering the code workable only on Windows platforms. However, if a telephony vendor only supports Windows, they will likely gain better speed and more control.

the *primary core interfaces* that require an implementation. Excluding the events, capabilities, and exception classes, there are 10 core component interfaces and 1 class that must be implemented in package `javax.telephony`. These are the classes that will be used directly by application programmers using our JTAPI library (the class may be used as is or enhanced by the implementer). They may be categorized[25] as in **Table 6.1**.

Table 6.1 *Categorizing the Call Model Objects of* `javax.telephony`

Peer Components	Business Objects	Association Objects	Observers
JtapiPeerFactory *class*	Address *interface*	Connection *interface*	AddressObserver *interface*
JtapiPeer *interface*	Call *interface*	TerminalConnection *interface*	CallObserver *interface*
Provider *interface*	Terminal *interface*		TerminalObserver *interface*

These components represent *call model objects*. All of the other interfaces supplied in the core package (and the related *capabilities* and *events* sub-packages) are provided in order to *support* these call model objects.

In a design sense, we can classify the call model entities by functionality. There are four types of components as categorized in **Table 6.1**. *Peer components* are used to create business and association objects and to manage their security. *Business objects* are design entities in the telephony *problem space*. *Association objects* model relationships among business objects. *Observers* are to be implemented by the application programmer using the JTAPI library (which we will defer until Chapter 7).

Because nothing can be created until a Provider exists, let's get started with the peer components.

JtapiPeerFactory

We will modify this class as provided by Sun. This is exactly what we are supposed to do if the default implementation provided doesn't do exactly what we want. In this case, we modified it to make the JtapiPeer class a singleton and to provide a default implementation name. The class JtapiPeerFactory is presented in **Listing 6.20**.

---

25 Note that the Business Objects from **Table 6.1** are also "Observables."

Listing 6.20 *A JtapiPeerFactory Implementation*

```
package javax.telephony;
import java.lang.String;


public class JtapiPeerFactory {

    // BEGIN SDR added code...
     /**
    * My JtapiPeerFactory class is a poor man's singleton.
    */
    static private JtapiPeer jtapiPeer_ = null;
    static private Class jtapiPeerClass_;
    // END SDR added code...

    private JtapiPeerFactory() { }

    public synchronized static JtapiPeer getJtapiPeer(
        String jtapiPeerName )
      throws JtapiPeerUnavailableException {

    // BEGIN SDR altered code...
      // I moved these 2 to make them class variables...
      // Class jtapiPeerClass_;
      // JtapiPeer jtapiPeer_;
    // END SDR added code...

        String errmsg;
        if ( jtapiPeerName == null || _jtapiPeerName.length()
            == 0 ) {
          jtapiPeerName = getDefaultJtapiPeerName();
        }

        if ( jtapiPeerName == null ) {
          throw new JtapiPeerUnavailableException();
        }

        // BEGIN SDR added code...
        // implementing the singleton for the jtapiPeer...
        if ( jtapiPeer_ == null ) {
        // END SDR added code...
          try {
            jtapiPeerClass_ = Class.forName( jtapiPeerName );
          try {
          jtapiPeer_ = (JtapiPeer)jtapiPeerClass.newInstance();
```

Listing 6.20 (cont.) *A JtapiPeerFactory Implementation*

```
            }
            catch (Exception e) {
                errmsg = "JtapiPeer: " + jtapiPeerName
                    + " could not be instantiated.";
                throw new JtapiPeerUnavailableException(errmsg);
            }
            return jtapiPeer_;
            } catch (Exception e) {
                errmsg = "\nJtapiPeer: "
                    + jtapiPeerName + " does not exist.\n";
                throw new JtapiPeerUnavailableException(errmsg);
            }
        // BEGIN SDR added code...
        }
        else return jtapiPeer_;
        // END SDR added code...
    }

    private static String getDefaultJtapiPeerName() {
        String JtapiPeerName = new String();
        JtapiPeerName = "sroberts.telephony.SDRJtapiPeer";
        return(JtapiPeerName);
    }
}
```

Many comments are in order. First, notice that we are *modifying a class* instead of *implementing an interface*. This may not seem unusual, but it is the only instance where this is the appropriate approach when implementing a JTAPI library. Usually, we will be creating a class that implements a JTAPI interface. Note that we have placed comments in the code at the points where we modified the original class provided with JTAPI.

Next, the default implementation prepares the JtapiPeerFactory class for receiving a null parameter instead of an actual named string. There is no reason not to use this functionality, so it is not altered. Next we ensure that only one instance of the JtapiPeer class is ever returned from the JtapiPeerFactory. This is not necessary and may be counterproductive for vendors providing different implementations. But this is JTAPI-Lite, and that's all, folks.

We provided our own default JTAPIPeer name, even though this practice is discouraged (born rebels, I guess). Finally, it is the responsibility of the implementer (i.e., you!) to ensure that the fully qualified class name returned from the method `getDefaultJtapiPeerName()` is placed in the CLASSPATH and to ensure, of course, that the class is actually there.

JtapiPeer

The primary purpose (indeed, the *only* purpose) of the JtapiPeerFactory is to provide an instance of the class JtapiPeer. Let's create this puppy in **Listing 6.21**.

Listing 6.21 *A JtapiPeer Implementation*

```
package sroberts.telephony;

import javax.telephony.*;
import java.util.*;
import sroberts.util.*;
import sroberts.util.singleton.*;


public class SDRJtapiPeer implements JtapiPeer {

        private String name_;
        protected SDRProvider provider_;
        protected SecurityMonitor securityMonitor_;
        // hard-code these for now...
        private String masterSecurityName_ = "Noah";
        private String masterPassword_ = "WestonSpencer";

        // ctor
        public SDRJtapiPeer() {

            super();
            name_ = "sroberts.telephony.SDRJtapiPeer";
            securityMonitor_ =
                     (SecurityMonitor)SDRSingletonFactory.create(
                       "sroberts.util.singleton.SecurityMonitor" );
            SDRProvider.createValidProviders( securityMonitor_ );
            provider_ =
                     (SDRProvider)SDRProvider.getDefaultProvider();
            securityMonitor_.setUpSecurity(
                name_, masterSecurityName_, masterPassword_ );
        }

        public String getName() { return name_; }

        public String[] getServices() { return
                                    SDRProvider.getServices(); }

        public Provider getProvider( String providerString )
```

Listing 6.21 (cont.) *A JtapiPeer Implementation*

```
        throws ProviderUnavailableException {

    if ( providerString == null ) {
      return SDRProvider.getDefaultProvider();
    }
    else {

      if ( isValidJtapiPeer( providerString ) ) {

      SDRProvider phoneCo =
        (SDRProvider)SDRProvider.getProviderNamed(
        parseProviderName( providerString ), "Free Access"
        );

      if ( !phoneCo.inService() )
          throw new ProviderUnavailableException();

      return phoneCo;
    }
  }
  return null;
}


public String parseProviderName( String providerString ) {
  // TO DO: code to parse providerString
  return new String();
}


protected boolean isValidJtapiPeer( String providerString ) {

  if ( securityMonitor_.parseJtapiPeerProviderString(
              providerString ) )
    return true;
  else
    return false;
  }
}
```

The primary function of the JtapiPeer is to provide an instance of class Provider. We also use it to initialize the security infrastructure.

Provider

Listing 6.22 presents our implementation of the Provider interface.

Listing 6.22 *A Provider Implementation*

```
package sroberts.telephony;

import javax.telephony.*;
import javax.telephony.capabilities.*;
import java.util.*;
import sroberts.util.*;
import sroberts.util.singleton.*;
import sroberts.telephony.capabilities.*;

public class SDRProvider implements Provider {

    // CLASS section...
    static protected Provider defaultProvider_ = null;
    static private final String DEFAULT_PROVIDER_NAME =
            "Susie says Spencer is a good Provider";
    static protected Hashtable validProviders_ = null;
    static protected Hashtable validLocalAddresses_ = null;
    static protected SecurityMonitor masterSecurityMonitor_ =
            null;
    static protected String[] services_;

    static protected void createValidProviders(
        SecurityMonitor secretAgent )
            throws IllegalArgumentException {

      if ( validProviders_ == null ) {
          services_ = new String[ 6 ];
          services_[0] = DEFAULT_PROVIDER_NAME;
          services_[1] = "Local Service";
          services_[2] = "Long Distance";
          services_[3] = "Caller ID";
          services_[4] = "Mealtime Hassle Service";
          services_[5] = "Telephony Programming";

          String singletonClassName =
              "sroberts.util.singleton.SecurityMonitor";
          masterSecurityMonitor_ =
                  (SecurityMonitor)SDRSingletonFactory.create
                  (singletonClassName);

          if ( secretAgent != masterSecurityMonitor_ )
              throw new IllegalArgumentException();

          validProviders_ = new Hashtable( 6 );
          defaultProvider_ = new SDRProvider(
              masterSecurityMonitor_, DEFAULT_PROVIDER_NAME );
          validProviders_.put( defaultProvider_,
              DEFAULT_PROVIDER_NAME );
```

Listing 6.22 (cont.) *A Provider Implementation*

```
        validProviders_.put( new SDRProvider(
            masterSecurityMonitor_, "Local Monopoly, Inc." ),
            services_[1] );
        validProviders_.put( new SDRProvider(
            masterSecurityMonitor_, "MCI" ), services_[2] );
        validProviders_.put( new SDRProvider(
            masterSecurityMonitor_, "Private Eyes LTD." ),
            services_[3] );
        validProviders_.put( new SDRProvider(
            masterSecurityMonitor_, "Cold Callers, Inc." ),
            services_[4] );
        validProviders_.put( new SDRProvider(
            masterSecurityMonitor_, "ICS" ), services_[5] );

        createValidLocalAddresses();
        createValidLocalTerminals();
        associateAddressesWithTerminals();
    }
}

static public String[] getServices() { return services_; }

static public Provider getProviderNamed( String name,
                                         String passwd )
    throws IllegalArgumentException {

    if ( !masterSecurityMonitor_.isMaster( passwd ) ) {
        throw new IllegalArgumentException(); }

    if ( validProviders_.contains( name ) )
        return (Provider)validProviders_.get( name );
    else throw new IllegalArgumentException();
}

static protected void createValidLocalAddresses() {

    // normally, this method would hook up to some persistent
    // store or a runtime service. Here, we just hardcode
    // some values...

    if ( validLocalAddresses_ == null ) {
        validLocalAddresses_ = new Hashtable();
        validLocalAddresses_.put( "555-1212",
            new SDRAddress(defaultProvider_, true,
            "555-1212" ) );
        validLocalAddresses_.put( "123-4567",
            new SDRAddress( defaultProvider_, true,
            "555-1212" ) );
    }
}
```

Listing 6.22 (cont.) *A Provider Implementation*

```
static protected void createValidLocalTerminals() {

    if ( validLocalTerminals_ == null ) {
        validLocalTerminals_ = new Hashtable();
        validLocalTerminals_.put( "Terminator",
            new SDRTerminal( defaultProvider_, true,
            "Terminator" ) );
        validLocalTerminals_.put( "Office Phone",
            new SDRTerminal( defaultProvider_, true, "Office
            Phone" ) );
        validLocalTerminals_.put( "Bedroom Phone",
            new SDRTerminal( defaultProvider_, true, "Bedroom
            Phone" ) );
        validLocalTerminals_.put( "Mobile Phone",
            new SDRTerminal( defaultProvider_, true, "Mobile
            Phone" ) );
    }
}

static protected void associateAddressesWithTerminals() {

    if ( validLocalAddresses_ != null &
        validLocalTerminals_ != null ) {
        // office phone can dial or answer calls for these
        // phone numbers...
        SDRTerminal officePhone =
          (SDRTerminal)validLocalTerminals_.get( "Office
            Phone" );
        SDRAddress fiveFiveFive =
          (SDRAddress)validLocalAddresses_.get( "555-1212" );
        officePhone.addAddress( fiveFiveFive );
        officePhone.addAddress(
          (Address)validLocalAddresses_.get( "123-4567" ) );
        // fiveFiveFive is associated with this Terminal...
        fiveFiveFive.addTerminal( officePhone );
    }
}

static public boolean ownsAddress( String address ) {
    if ( validLocalAddresses_.containsKey( address ) )
        return true;
    else return false;
}

static protected Address getAddressNamed( String address ) {
    return (Address)validLocalAddresses_.get( address );
}

static public boolean ownsTerminal( String termName ) {
    if ( validLocalTerminals_.containsKey( termName ) )
        return true;
    return false;
}
```

Listing 6.22 (cont.) *A Provider Implementation*

```
static protected Terminal getTerminalNamed(
                                    String termName ) {
    return (Terminal)validLocalTerminals_.get( termName );
}

static public Provider getDefaultProvider() {
    return defaultProvider_;
}

// INSTANCE section...
private String name_;
protected Vector calls_;
protected Vector addresses_;
protected Vector terminals_;
protected Vector providerObservers_;
protected int state_;
protected SecurityMonitor securityMonitor_;
protected SDRStaticProviderCapabilities
            staticProviderCapabilities_;
protected SDRDynamicProviderCapabilities
            dynamicProviderCapabilities_;
protected CallCapabilities callCapabilities_;
protected SDRStaticAddressCapabilities addressCapabilities_;

// ctors...
protected SDRProvider(
        SecurityMonitor securityMonitor, String name ) {
    super();
    name_ = name;
    calls_ = new Vector();
    terminals_ = new Vector();
    addresses_ = new Vector();
    providerObservers_ = new Vector();
    state_ = OUT_OF_SERVICE;
    securityMonitor_ = securityMonitor;
    callCapabilities_ = new SDRStaticCallCapabilities();
    addressCapabilities_ = new
            SDRStaticAddressCapabilities();
    staticProviderCapabilities_ = new
            SDRStaticProviderCapabilities();
    terminalCapabilities_ = new
            SDRStaticTerminalCapabilities();
    connectionCapabilities_ = new
            SDRStaticConnectionCapabilities();
    terminalConnectionCapabilities_ =
        new SDRStaticTerminalConnectionCapabilities();
}

private SDRProvider() { }
```

Listing 6.22 (cont.) *A Provider Implementation*

```
// JTAPI interface **********************************

public int getState() { return state_; }

public String getName() { return name_; }

public Call[] getCalls()
   throws ResourceUnavailableException {

   if ( inService() ) {
      Call[] arrayOfCalls = new Call[ calls_.size() ];
      calls_.copyInto( arrayOfCalls );
      return arrayOfCalls;
   }
   throw new ResourceUnavailableException(
      ResourceUnavailableException.ORIGINATOR_UNAVAILABLE );
}

public Address getAddress( String number )
        throws InvalidArgumentException {

   if ( SDRProvider.ownsAddress( number ) ) {
      return SDRProvider.getAddressNamed( number );
   }
   throw new InvalidArgumentException();
}

public Address[] getAddresses() throws
        ResourceUnavailableException {

   // Remote Addresses are not reported
   // via the Provider.getAddresses() method...
   if ( inService() ) {
      Vector localAddresses = new Vector();

      for ( int i = 0; i < addresses_.size(); i++ ) {
         SDRAddress next =
                 (SDRAddress)addresses_.elementAt( i );
         if ( next.isLocal() )
            localAddresses.addElement( next );
      }

      Address[] arrayOfAddresses =
         new Address[ localAddresses.size() ];
      localAddresses.copyInto( arrayOfAddresses );
      return arrayOfAddresses;
   }
   throw new ResourceUnavailableException(
      ResourceUnavailableException.ORIGINATOR_UNAVAILABLE );
}
```

Listing 6.22 (cont.) *A Provider Implementation*

```
public Terminal[] getTerminals()
            throws ResourceUnavailableException {

    if ( inService() ) {
        Terminal[] arrayOfTerminals =
                        new Terminal[ terminals_.size() ];
        terminals_.copyInto( arrayOfTerminals );
        return arrayOfTerminals;
    }
    throw new ResourceUnavailableException(
        ResourceUnavailableException.ORIGINATOR_UNAVAILABLE );
}

public Terminal getTerminal(String name)
        throws InvalidArgumentException {

    if ( SDRProvider.ownsTerminal( name ) ) {
        return SDRProvider.getTerminalNamed( name );
    }
    throw new InvalidArgumentException();
}

public void shutdown() { state_ = SHUTDOWN; }

public Call createCall()
    throws ResourceUnavailableException,
        InvalidStateException,PrivilegeViolationException,
            MethodNotSupportedException {
    if ( inService() ) {
        Call newCall = new SDRCall( this );
        calls_.addElement( newCall );
        return newCall;
    }
    throw new ResourceUnavailableException(
        ResourceUnavailableException.ORIGINATOR_UNAVAILABLE );
}

public void addObserver( ProviderObserver observer )
    throws ResourceUnavailableException,
        MethodNotSupportedException {

    providerObservers_.addElement( observer );
}

public ProviderObserver[] getObservers() {

    ProviderObserver[] arrayOfProviderObservers =
            new ProviderObserver[ providerObservers_.size() ];
    providerObservers_.copyInto( arrayOfProviderObservers );
    return arrayOfProviderObservers;
}
```

Listing 6.22 (cont.) *A Provider Implementation*

```
public void removeObserver(ProviderObserver observer) {
    providerObservers_.removeElement( observer );
}

public ProviderCapabilities getCapabilities() {
    return dynamicProviderCapabilities_;
}

public AddressCapabilities getAddressCapabilities() {
    return addressCapabilities_;
}

public ConnectionCapabilities getConnectionCapabilities() {
    return connectionCapabilities_;
}

public TerminalConnectionCapabilities
   getTerminalConnectionCapabilities() {
    return terminalConnectionCapabilities_;
}

public CallCapabilities getCallCapabilities() {
    return callCapabilities_;
}

public ProviderCapabilities getProviderCapabilities() {
    return staticProviderCapabilities_;
}

public TerminalCapabilities getTerminalCapabilities() {
    return null;
}

// Enhanced API ******************************************

public void setState( int state, String passwd ) {

    if ( securityMonitor_.isMaster( passwd ) ) {
            state_ = state; }
    else state_ = OUT_OF_SERVICE;
}

public boolean inService() {
    if ( state_ == IN_SERVICE ) return true;
            else return false;
}

public boolean isInThisDomain( String address ) {
    if ( SDRProvider.ownsAddress( address ) )
        return true;
    else return false;
}
}
```

Address

Listing 6.23 shows our implementation of the Address interface.

Listing 6.23 *An Address Implementation*

```
package sroberts.telephony;

import java.util.*;
import javax.telephony.*;
import javax.telephony.capabilities.*;
import sroberts.telephony.capabilities.*;
import sroberts.util.*;

public class SDRAddress implements Address, AddressCapabilities
{

    final public static int LOCAL = 1;
    final public static int REMOTE = 2;
    private String name_;
    protected Provider provider_;
    protected Vector terminals_;
    protected Vector connections_;
    protected Vector addressObservers_;
    protected SDRDynamicAddressCapabilities
            addressCapabilities_;
    protected SDRObservable callObserverObservable_;
    protected SDRObservable thisAddressObserverObservable_;
    protected boolean isLocal_;

    //ctors...
    private SDRAddress() {} // only Providers can create
                            // Addresses...

    SDRAddress( Provider p, boolean isLocal, String number ) {
        this( p, isLocal );
        name_ = number;
    }

    private SDRAddress( Provider p, boolean isLocal ) {
        super();
        provider_ = p;
        isLocal_ = isLocal;
        connections_ = new Vector();
        terminals_ = new Vector();
        addressObservers_ = new Vector();
        callObserverObservable_ = new SDRObservable();
        addressCapabilities_ =
                new SDRDynamicAddressCapabilities( this );
    }
```

Listing 6.23 (cont.) *An Address Implementation*

```
// JTAPI API **********************************************

public String getName() { return name_;  }

public Provider getProvider() {

   if ( provider_ == null & isLocal_ == true ) {
      try {
         SDRJtapiPeer sdrPeer =
            (SDRJtapiPeer)JtapiPeerFactory.getJtapiPeer(
               null );
          return provider_ =
            (SDRProvider)sdrPeer.getProvider( null );
      } catch (Exception e) {
         System.out.println( "SDRAddress—>
             PeerFactory or Provider call failed:
                "+ e.toString() );
         throw new PlatformException();
      }
   }
      else return provider_;
}

public Terminal[] getTerminals() {
   return (Terminal[])SDRUtility.vectorToArray(terminals_);
}

public Connection[] getConnections() {
   return
      (Connection[])SDRUtility.vectorToArray(connections_);
}

public AddressCapabilities getCapabilities() {
   return addressCapabilities_;
}

public void addObserver(AddressObserver observer)
   throws ResourceUnavailableException, PlatformException {
      thisAddressObserverObservable_.addObserver(
         (Observer)observer);
}

public AddressObserver[] getObservers() {
   return
      (AddressObserver[])SDRUtility.vectorToArray(
         addressObservers_ );
}
```

Listing 6.23 (cont.) *An Address Implementation*

```
public void removeObserver(AddressObserver observer) {
            thisAddressObserverObservable_.deleteObserver(
            (Observer)observer);
}

public void addCallObserver(CallObserver observer)
    throws ResourceUnavailableException, PlatformException {
    callObserverObservable_.addObserver((Observer)observer);
}

public CallObserver[] getCallObservers() {
    return
       (CallObserver[])callObserverObservable_.getObservers();
}

public void removeCallObserver(CallObserver observer) {
 callObserverObservable_.deleteObserver((Observer)observer);
}

public boolean isObservable() {
    return addressCapabilities_.isObservable(); }


// enhanced API ******************************************

public boolean isLocal() { return isLocal_; }

public void finalize() {
    thisAddressObserverObservable_.deleteObservers();
    callObserverObservable_.deleteObservers();
}

void addTerminal( Terminal t ) {
    terminals_.addElement( t );
}
}
```

Call

And now, our long-awaited implementation of the Call interface is presented in **Listing 6.24**.

Listing 6.24 *A Call Implementation*

```
package sroberts.telephony;

import javax.telephony.*;
import javax.telephony.capabilities.*;
import java.util.*;
import sroberts.util.singleton.*;
import sroberts.telephony.jTAPIimplementations.*;
import sroberts.telephony.jTAPIimplementations.tapi.*;
import sroberts.telephony.events.*;
import sroberts.telephony.capabilities.*;

public class SDRCall extends SDRJtapiObject implements Call {

    protected String name_;
    protected Provider provider_;
    protected int state_;
    protected Vector connections_;
    protected Vector callObservers_;
    protected Vector validCallSecurityMonitors_;
    protected CallEventNotifier callEventNotifier_;

    //ctors...
    SDRCall( Provider provider )
       throws PrivilegeViolationException,
                   InvalidStateException {

       super();
       if ( TelephonySubsystem.canMakeCalls() ) state_ = IDLE;
       else
          throw new InvalidStateException(
             this, InvalidStateException.CALL_OBJECT, IDLE );
       callEventNotifier_ = new CallEventNotifier();
       provider_ = provider;
       connections_ = new Vector();
       callObservers_ = new Vector();
    }

    private SDRCall() {}

    // JTAPI API *********************************************

    public String getName()
       throws PlatformException { return name_; }

    public Connection[] getConnections() {
       Connection[] array =
                       new Connection[ connections_.size() ];
```

Listing 6.24 (cont.) *A Call Implementation*

```java
        connections_.copyInto( array );
        return array;
    }

    public Provider getProvider() {
        return (Provider)provider_;
    }

    public int getState() { return state_; }

    public Connection[]
        connect( Terminal origterm, Address origaddr,
                String dialedDigits )
            throws ResourceUnavailableException,
                PrivilegeViolationException,
            InvalidPartyException, InvalidArgumentException,
                InvalidStateException, MethodNotSupportedException {

            if ( !((SDRTerminal)origterm).supportsAddress(
                origaddr ) )
                throw new InvalidPartyException(
                    InvalidPartyException.ORIGINATING_PARTY,
                        "Call.connect()" );

            Connection[] newConnections = new Connection[2];
            newConnections[ 0 ] = new SDRConnection( origaddr,
                this );
            TerminalConnection origTC =
                new SDRTerminalConnection( origterm,
                newConnections[ 0 ] );

            Address dialedNumberAddr = provider_.getAddress(
                dialedDigits );
            newConnections[ 1 ] = new SDRConnection(
                dialedNumberAddr, this );

            // add connections to this call's list...
            addConnection( newConnections[ 0 ] );
            addConnection( newConnections[ 1 ] );

            System.out.println(
                "\tInside Call.connect() ADDED 1 of 2
                    Connections..."
                + newConnections[ 0 ] );
            System.out.println(
                "\tInside Call.connect() ADDED 2 of 2
                    Connections..."
                + newConnections[ 1 ] );
```

Listing 6.24 (cont.) *A Call Implementation*

```
            Connection co = findConnectionFor( dialedDigits );

            System.out.println( "\tInside Call.connect()
               findConnectionFor..."
                              + ((SDRConnection)co).getName() );

            int[] hCall = new int[1];
            hCall[0] = 0;

            long ret = callRep_.callConnect(
                   hCall, dialedDigits, new StringBuffer(50) );

            if (ret > 0 ) {
                System.out.println(
                   "Successfully placed asynchronous call...");
                setState( ACTIVE );
                return newConnections;
            }
            else {
                removeConnection( newConnections[ 0 ] );
                removeConnection( newConnections[ 1 ] );
                System.out.println(
                   "callRep_.callConnect() FAILED...");
                return null;
            }
    }

    public void addObserver( CallObserver observer )
       throws ResourceUnavailableException,
          MethodNotSupportedException {
             callObservers_.addElement( observer );
    }

    public CallObserver[] getObservers() {
       CallObserver[] array = new CallObserver[
          callObservers_.size() ];
       callObservers_.copyInto( array );
       return array;
    }

    public void removeObserver(CallObserver observer) {
       thisCallObservable_.deleteObserver( (Observer)observer );
       callEventNotifier_.notifyObserversOfEvent(
          new SDRCallObservationEndedEv( observer, this, 0, 0,
             false ) );
    }
```

Listing 6.24 (cont.) *A Call Implementation*

```
public CallCapabilities
   getCapabilities(Terminal terminal, Address address)
      throws InvalidArgumentException {
         return new SDRDynamicCallCapabilities( this,
            terminal, address );
}

// Enhanced API ********************************

void setState( int s ) {

   state_ = s;
   switch (s) {
      case (ACTIVE):
         callEventNotifier_.notifyObserversOfEvent(
            new SDRCallActiveEv( this ) );
      break;
      case (INVALID):
         callEventNotifier_.notifyObserversOfEvent(
            new SDRCallInvalidEv( this ) );
      break;
   }
}

protected void addConnection( Connection c ) {
      connections_.addElement( c );
}

protected void removeConnection( Connection c ) {
      connections_.removeElement( c );
}

public void setName( String n ) { name_ = n; }
}
```

Terminal

Listing 6.25 contains our implementation of the Terminal interface.

Listing 6.25 *A Terminal Implementation*

```
package sroberts.telephony;
import javax.telephony.*;
import javax.telephony.capabilities.*;
import sroberts.telephony.capabilities.*;
import java.util.*;
import sroberts.util.*;

public class SDRTerminal implements Terminal {
```

Listing 6.25 (cont.) *A Terminal Implementation*

```
final public static int LOCAL = 1;
final public static int REMOTE = 2;
private boolean isLocal_;
private String name_;
protected Vector addresses_;
protected Vector terminalConnections_;
protected Vector myObservers_;
protected Vector callObservers_;
protected Vector terminalObservers_;
protected Provider provider_;
protected SDRDynamicTerminalCapabilities
    terminalCapabilities_;

// ctors...

private SDRTerminal() {} // only Providers can create
    Terminals...

SDRTerminal( Provider p, boolean isLocal, String name ) {
    this( p, isLocal );
    name_ = name;
}

private SDRTerminal( Provider provider, boolean isLocal ) {
    super();
    addresses_ = new Vector();
    terminalConnections_ = new Vector();
    myObservers_ = new Vector();
    callObservers_ = new Vector();
    terminalObservers_ = new Vector();
    provider_ = provider;
    terminalCapabilities_ = new
        SDRDynamicTerminalCapabilities( this );
}

// JTAPI API **********************************************

public String getName() { return name_; }

public Provider getProvider() { return (Provider)provider_;
}

public Address[] getAddresses() {
    return (Address[])SDRUtility.vectorToArray(addresses_);
}

public TerminalConnection[] getTerminalConnections() {
    return (TerminalConnection[])SDRUtility.vectorToArray
        (terminalConnections_);
}
```

Listing 6.25 (cont.) *A Terminal Implementation*

```java
public void addObserver(TerminalObserver observer) {
  myObservers_.addElement( observer );
}

public TerminalObserver[] getObservers() {
  return (TerminalObserver[])SDRUtility.vectorToArray
        (terminalObservers_);
}

public void removeObserver(TerminalObserver observer) {
  myObservers_.removeElement( observer );
}

public void addCallObserver(CallObserver observer) {
  callObservers_.addElement( observer );
}

public CallObserver[] getCallObservers() {
  return (CallObserver[])SDRUtility.vectorToArray
        (callObservers_);
}

public void removeCallObserver(CallObserver observer) {
  callObservers_.removeElement( observer );
}

public TerminalCapabilities getCapabilities() {
  return terminalCapabilities_;
}


// enhanced API ********************************

public boolean isLocal() { return isLocal_; }

public boolean supportsAddress( Address a ) {
  if ( addresses_.contains( a ) )
      return true;
  return false;
}

void addAddress( Address a ) {
    addresses_.addElement( a );
}

void addTerminalConnection( TerminalConnection tc ) {
    terminalConnections_.addElement( tc );
}
}
```

Connection

And the Connection interface is shown in **Listing 6.26**.

Listing 6.26 *A Connection Implementation*

```
package sroberts.telephony;

import java.util.*;
import javax.telephony.*;
import javax.telephony.capabilities.*;
import sroberts.telephony.capabilities.*;
import sroberts.telephony.events.*;
import sroberts.telephony.jTAPIimplementations.tapi.*;


public class SDRConnection extends SDRJtapiObject implements
        Connection {

    static public final String
    CLASS_NAME = "sroberts.telephony.SDRConnection";

    protected Address address_;
    protected Call call_;
    protected Vector terminalConnections_;
    protected SDRDynamicConnectionCapabilities
        connectionCapabilities_;
    protected CallEventNotifier callEventNotifier_;
    private CallRep callRep_;

    // ctors...
    SDRConnection( Address a, Call c ) {
        super();
        state_ = UNKNOWN;
        name_ = a.getName();
        address_ = a;
        call_ = c;
        callRep_ = ((SDRCall)c).getCallRep( CLASS_NAME );
        connectionCapabilities_ =
            new SDRDynamicConnectionCapabilities( this );
        terminalConnections_ = new Vector();
        callEventNotifier_ =
            ((SDRCall)c).getCallEventNotifier();
    }

    private SDRConnection() {}

    // JTAPI API ******************************************

    public Call getCall() { return call_; }
```

Listing 6.26 (cont.) *A Connection Implementation*

```
public Address getAddress() { return address_; }

public TerminalConnection[] getTerminalConnections() {
   TerminalConnection[] array = new TerminalConnection[
      terminalConnections_.size() ];
   terminalConnections_.copyInto( array );
   return array;
   }

public void disconnect()
   throws PrivilegeViolationException,
   ResourceUnavailableException,
   MethodNotSupportedException, InvalidStateException {

   int retVal = callRep_.callDisconnect(
     address_.getName() );

   // Normally, we wouldn't set the state directly here.
   // Rather,we'd let the CallRep thread check the value
   // and alert the Connections. However, the TAPI run
   // time never calls our C callback upon disconnect (at
   // least using this hardware configuration), and so we
   // must rely on the return value and set the state
   // ourselves.

   if ( retVal == 0 ) { setState( DISCONNECTED ); }
   else throw new InvalidStateException( this, 0,
      DISCONNECTED );

   if ( call_.getConnections().length < 3 )
      ((SDRCall)call_).resetConnections();
}

public ConnectionCapabilities getCapabilities() {
   return connectionCapabilities_;
}

// Enhanced API ****************************************

void addTerminalConnection( TerminalConnection tc ) {
   terminalConnections_.addElement( tc );
}

void setState( int s ) {

   super.setState( s );
   switch (s) {
```

Listing 6.26 (cont.) *A Connection Implementation*

```
               case (CREATED):
                 callEventNotifier_.notifyObserversOfEvent(
                   new SDRConnCreatedEv( this, call_ ) );
               break;
               case (INPROGRESS):
                 callEventNotifier_.notifyObserversOfEvent(
                   new SDRConnInProgressEv( this, call_ ) );
               break;
               case (ALERTING):
                 callEventNotifier_.notifyObserversOfEvent(
                   new SDRConnAlertingEv( this, call_ ) );
               break;
               case (CONNECTED):
                 callEventNotifier_.notifyObserversOfEvent(
                   new SDRConnConnectedEv( this, call_ ) );
               break;

               case (DISCONNECTED):
                 callEventNotifier_.notifyObserversOfEvent(
                   new SDRConnDisconnectedEv( this, call_ ) );
               break;
               case (FAILED):
                 callEventNotifier_.notifyObserversOfEvent(
                   new SDRConnFailedEv( this, call_ ) );
               break;
               case (UNKNOWN):
                 callEventNotifier_.notifyObserversOfEvent(
                   new SDRConnUnknownEv( this, call_ ) );
               break;
            }
         }

      public String toString() { return name_; }


}
```

TerminalConnection

The TerminalConnection interface is implemented in **Listing 6.27**.

Listing 6.27 *A TerminalConnection Implementation*

```
package sroberts.telephony;
import javax.telephony.*;
import javax.telephony.capabilities.*;
import sroberts.telephony.capabilities.*;

public class SDRTerminalConnection implements
      TerminalConnection {
```

Listing 6.27 (cont.) *A TerminalConnection Implementation*

```
protected int state_;
protected Connection connection_;
protected Terminal terminal_;
protected SDRDynamicTerminalConnectionCapabilities
        capabilities_;

public SDRTerminalConnection( Terminal t, Connection c ) {
   terminal_ = t;
   connection_ = c;
   capabilities_ = new
     SDRDynamicTerminalConnectionCapabilities( this );
   ((SDRTerminal)t).addTerminalConnection( this );
   ((SDRConnection)c).addTerminalConnection( this );
   terminalConnections_ = new Vector();
}

private SDRTerminalConnection() {}

public int getState() { return state_; }

public Terminal getTerminal() { return terminal_; }

public Connection getConnection() { return connection_; }

public TerminalConnectionCapabilities getCapabilities() {
      return capabilities_;
}

public void answer()
  throws PrivilegeViolationException,
    ResourceUnavailableException,
    MethodNotSupportedException, InvalidStateException,
    PlatformException {

     // implementation left as an exercise for the reader...
}


}
```

A Helper Class

Note that some of our call model business objects extend the class called JtapiObject. This is a simple class that holds on to common instance variables needed for state representation. In addition, it provides a mechanism for hanging on to arbitrary data. This is required due to the asynchronous nature of the messaging mechanism. The class JtapiObject is presented in **Listing 6.28**.

Listing 6.28 *A Helper Class — JtapiObject*

```
package sroberts.telephony;


public class SDRJtapiObject {


    protected Object[] extraObjects_;
    int state_;
    protected String name_;


    public Object[] getData() { return extraObjects_; }
    public void setData( Object[] stuff ) {
       extraObjects_ = stuff; }
    public int getState() { return state_; }
    void setState( int s ) { state_ = s; }
    public String getName() { return name_; }
    public void setName( String n ) { name_ = n; }
}
```

Note the API providing for the storing and retrieval of extra data that may need to be associated with the object. This is provided above and beyond the getXXX() methods required by JTAPI to return the source object (e.g., `getCall()` for `CallEv`) for events. Note that we might have used `PrivateData` for this purpose. However, `PrivateData` operates on Objects, not the more flexible Object[]. An example of why this data may be needed is reserved for Chapter 7 in the `SDRCallObserver` and the `TestJtapiApp` classes.

Implementing the JTAPI Support Classes

The JTAPI interfaces required to support the core interfaces fall into three primary types: *events* (implementers of interface Ev and their subinterfaces), *exceptions*, and *capabilities*. In general, events are used in notification, exceptions report errors, and capabilities provide both a static and a dynamic snapshot of the call model. Let's look at capabilities first.

Core Capabilities

To provide JTAPI functionality for the core interfaces, we are to implement the interfaces specified in package javax.telephony.capabilities. These are:

- AddressCapabilities
- CallCapabilities
- ConnectionCapabilities
- ProviderCapabilities

- TerminalCapabilities

- TerminalConnectionCapabilities

The JTAPI specification states that both static and dynamic versions of each Capability interface are to be supplied. Both versions implement the same interface, even though their semantics are quite different. For example, take the `CallCapabilities` interface. It exports two methods; `canConnect()` and `isObservable()`. In the static sense, `canConnect()` returns true if the application is able to *invoke* the `Call.connect()` method. In the dynamic sense, it returns true if the application can *perform* the `Call.connect()` method. This seems to imply that an implementation is to return true if an implementation for the `Call.connect()` method has been provided, even if at runtime it may not be supported.

In implementing the Capabilities interfaces, there are several possible design approaches. One is to create a single class with the ability to discern between the different semantics of static and dynamic invocation. The approach we took instead was to define a different class for each type of capability. So, for example, we have two classes for the `CallCapabilities` interface: one static and one dynamic. `SDRStaticCallCapabilities` would be used for the Provider calls and `SDRDynamicCallCapabilities` for `Call` capabilities. We chose this approach because we could see no perceivable benefit in using an extension because the implementation of each method would not share any functionality.

CallCapabilities

Listing 6.29 shows the static and dynamic versions of CallCapabilities.

Listing 6.29 *A CallCapabilities Implementation*

```
package sroberts.telephony.capabilities;
import javax.telephony.capabilities.*;


public class SDRStaticCallCapabilities implements
     CallCapabilities {

   public boolean canConnect() { return true; }
   public boolean isObservable() { return true; }
}
   // Here's the dynamic version:
package sroberts.telephony.capabilities,
import javax.telephony.*;
import javax.telephony.capabilities.*;
```

Listing 6.29 (cont.) *A CallCapabilities Implementation*

```
public class SDRDynamicCallCapabilities implements
      CallCapabilities {

   private Call call_;
   private Terminal terminal_;
   private Address address_;

   // ctors...
   public SDRDynamicCallCapabilities( Call c, Terminal t,
        Address a ) {
        call_ = c;
        terminal_ = t;
        address_ = a;
   }

   private SDRDynamicCallCapabilities() {}

   public boolean canConnect() {

        // be sure the terminal can see the address...
        int found = 0;
        Address[] addresses = terminal_.getAddresses();

        for ( int i = 0; i < addresses.length; i++ ) {
           if ( addresses[i] == address_ ) found++;
        }

        if ( found == 0 ) return false;

        // be sure the call is active...
        if ( call_.getState() == Call.IDLE )
        return true;
        else return false;
   }

   public boolean isObservable() {
        if ( call_.getState() == Call.ACTIVE )
        return true;
        else return false;
   }
}
```

AddressCapabilities

Listing 6.30 provides an AddressCapabilities implementation.

Listing 6.30 *An AddressCapabilities Implementation*

```
package sroberts.telephony.capabilities;
import javax.telephony.capabilities.*;


public class SDRStaticAddressCapabilities implements
        AddressCapabilities {


    public boolean isObservable() { return true; }
}
// Here's the dynamic class:
package sroberts.telephony.capabilities;
import javax.telephony.capabilities.*;
import javax.telephony.*;
import sroberts.telephony.*;


public class SDRDynamicAddressCapabilities
    implements AddressCapabilities {
    private Address address_;

    // ctors...
    public SDRDynamicAddressCapabilities( Address a ) {
       address_ = a;
    }

    private SDRDynamicAddressCapabilities() { }

    public boolean isObservable() {

       if ( ((SDRAddress)address_).isLocal() ) return true;
       else return false;
    }
}
```

We provided a method on our implementation of the Address interface for determining whether or not an Address was local. Because remote addresses are not observable, the dynamic call reflects this fact.

ConnectionCapabilities

Listing 6.31 provides a ConnectionCapabilities implementation.

Listing 6.31 *A ConnectionCapabilities Implementation*

```
package sroberts.telephony.capabilities;
import javax.telephony.capabilities.*;

public class SDRStaticConnectionCapabilities
    implements ConnectionCapabilities {

    public boolean canDisconnect() { return true; }
}
// Here's the dynamic class:

package sroberts.telephony.capabilities;
import javax.telephony.capabilities.*;
import javax.telephony.*;
import sroberts.telephony.*;

public class SDRDynamicConnectionCapabilities
    implements ConnectionCapabilities {

    private Connection connection_;

    public SDRDynamicConnectionCapabilities( Connection c ) {
        connection_ = c;
    }

    private SDRDynamicConnectionCapabilities() {}

    public boolean canDisconnect() {

        int connState = ((SDRConnection)connection_).getState();

        if ( connState == Connection.INPROGRESS ||
             connState == Connection.ALERTING ||
             connState == Connection.CONNECTED )
            return true;
        return false;
    }
}
```

ProviderCapabilities

Listing **6.32** provides a ProviderCapabilities implementation.

Listing 6.32 *A ProviderCapabilities Implementation*

```
package sroberts.telephony.capabilities;
import javax.telephony.capabilities.*;


public class SDRStaticProviderCapabilities implements
        ProviderCapabilities {


    public boolean isObservable() { return true; }
}


// Here's the dynamic class:


package sroberts.telephony.capabilities;
import javax.telephony.capabilities.*;
import javax.telephony.*;
import sroberts.telephony.*;


public class SDRDynamicProviderCapabilities
    implements ProviderCapabilities {

    private Provider provider_;

    public SDRDynamicProviderCapabilities( Provider p ) {
        provider_ = p;
    }

    private SDRDynamicProviderCapabilities() {}

    public boolean isObservable() {

        if ( ((SDRProvider)provider_).inService() )
            return true;
        return false;


    }
}
```

TerminalCapabilities

Listing 6.33 provides a TerminalCapabilities implementation.

Listing 6.33 *A TerminalCapabilities Implementation*

```
package sroberts.telephony.capabilities;
import javax.telephony.capabilities.*;


public class SDRStaticTerminalCapabilities implements
        TerminalCapabilities {
    public boolean isObservable() { return true; }
}


package sroberts.telephony.capabilities;
import javax.telephony.capabilities.*;
import javax.telephony.*;
import sroberts.telephony.*;


// Here's the dynamic class:
public class SDRDynamicTerminalCapabilities
   implements TerminalCapabilities {

    private Terminal terminal_;

    public SDRDynamicTerminalCapabilities( Terminal t ) {
       terminal_ = t;
    }

    private SDRDynamicTerminalCapabilities() { }

    public boolean isObservable() {

      if ( ((SDRProvider)terminal_.getProvider()).inService() )
         return true;
      return false;
    }
}
```

TerminalConnectionCapabilities

Listing 6.34 provides a TerminalConnectionCapabilities implementation.

Listing 6.34 *A TerminalConnectionCapabilities Implementation*

```
package sroberts.telephony.capabilities;
import javax.telephony.capabilities.*;

public class SDRStaticTerminalConnectionCapabilities
    implements TerminalConnectionCapabilities {

    public boolean canAnswer() { return true; }
}


// Here's the dynamic class:

package sroberts.telephony.capabilities;
import javax.telephony.capabilities.*;
import javax.telephony.*;
import sroberts.telephony.*;

public class SDRDynamicTerminalConnectionCapabilities
    implements TerminalConnectionCapabilities {

    private TerminalConnection terminalConnection_;

    public SDRDynamicTerminalConnectionCapabilities(
                TerminalConnection tc ) {
        terminalConnection_ = tc;
    }

    private SDRDynamicTerminalConnectionCapabilities() {}

    public boolean canAnswer() {

        int termConnState = ((SDRTerminalConnection)
                            terminalConnection_).getState();

        if ( termConnState == TerminalConnection.IDLE |
             termConnState == TerminalConnection.RINGING |
             termConnState == TerminalConnection.PASSIVE
           )
            return true;
        return false;
    }
}
```

One final note on dynamic capabilities: Clearly, there are *temporal considerations* that need to be accounted for to mitigate race conditions. For example, suppose a Call instance is idle for the duration of the dynamic `CallCapabilities.canConnect()` method but becomes inactive before the `Call.connect()` method is invoked. This is not a good thing, and some manner of controlling the call state needs to be provided by an implementation. This same problem extends to all of the dynamic Capabilities methods.

Core Events

An implementation of the event classes is required in order to enable notification. First, here's our implementation of the granddaddy of all events, class Ev. An Ev implementation is presented in **Listing 6.35**.

Listing 6.35 *An Ev Interface Implementation*

```
package sroberts.telephony.events;
import javax.telephony.events.*;

public class SDREv implements Ev {

    private int id_;
    private int cause_;
    private int metaCode_;
    private boolean isNewMetaEvent_;
    protected Object[] extraObjects_;

    // ctors...
    public SDREv( int id, int cause, int metaCode,
            boolean isNewMetaEvent )
    {
        super();
        id_ = id;
        cause_ = cause;
        metaCode_ = metaCode;
        isNewMetaEvent_ = isNewMetaEvent;
    }

    public SDREv() {
        super();
        id_ = 0;
        cause_ = Ev.CAUSE_UNKNOWN;
        metaCode_ = Ev.META_UNKNOWN;
        isNewMetaEvent_ = false;
    }
```

Listing 6.35 (cont.) *An Ev Interface Implementation*

```
public int getCause() { return cause_; }
public int getMetaCode() { return metaCode_; }
public boolean isNewMetaEvent() { return isNewMetaEvent_; }
public int getID() { return id_; }

// enhanced API **********************************************

public void setData( Object[] stuff ) {
    extraObjects_ = stuff; }
public Object[] getData() { return extraObjects_; }
}
```

As we can see, this class provides basic functionality required of all events, particularly dealing with cause codes and meta codes. Each event class extends the **SDREv** class and implements the appropriate interface. Here's the case for Call objects, CallEv (**Listing 6.36**).

Listing 6.36 *A CallEv Interface Implementation*

```
package sroberts.telephony.events;
import javax.telephony.*;
import javax.telephony.events.*;

public class SDRCallEv extends SDREv implements CallEv {

    private Call call_;

    // ctors...
    public SDRCallEv(
        Call call, int id, int cause, int metaCode,
            boolean isNewMetaEvent )
    {
        super( id, cause, metaCode, isNewMetaEvent );
        call_ = call;
    }
    protected SDRCallEv( Call call ) { super(); call_ = call; }
    protected SDRCallEv() { super(); }
    public Call getCall() { return call_; }
}
```

Can we use CallEv instances? Not yet. One more level of extension is specified by JTAPI. A Call event can be of many different types, one for each state the Call may be in (e.g., ACTIVE). And so we extend the CallEv interface once more for each of these types of events. For Call events, this translates to the interfaces CallActiveEv, CallObservationEndedEv, and CallInvalidEv. They are shown in **Listings 6.37** through **6.39**, respectively.

Listing 6.37 *A CallActiveEv Interface Implementation*

```
package sroberts.telephony.events;
import javax.telephony.*;
import javax.telephony.events.*;

public class SDRCallActiveEv extends SDRCallEv
    implements CallActiveEv {

   // ctors...
   public SDRCallActiveEv(
         Call call, int metaCode, boolean isNewMetaEvent ) {

      super(
         call, CallActiveEv.ID, Ev.CAUSE_NEW_CALL,
         metaCode, isNewMetaEvent );
   }

   public SDRCallActiveEv( Call call ) {
      super( call, CallActiveEv.ID, Ev.CAUSE_NEW_CALL, 0,
         false );
   }

   private SDRCallActiveEv() {}
}
```

Listing 6.38 *A CallObservationEndedEv Interface Implementation*

```
package sroberts.telephony.events;
import javax.telephony.*;
import javax.telephony.events.*;

public class SDRCallObservationEndedEv extends SDRCallEv
    implements CallObservationEndedEv {

   private Object obj2blame_;

   // ctor...
   public SDRCallObservationEndedEv(
      Object obj2blame, Call call, int cause,
      int metaCode, boolean isNewMetaEvent ) {

      super(
      call, CallObservationEndedEv.ID, cause, metaCode,
         isNewMetaEvent );
      obj2blame_ = obj2blame;
   }
   private SDRCallObservationEndedEv() { super(); }
   public Object getEndedObject() { return obj2blame_; }
}
```

Listing 6.39 *A CallInvalidEv Interface Implementation*

```
package sroberts.telephony.events;
import javax.telephony.*;
import javax.telephony.events.*;

public class SDRCallInvalidEv extends SDRCallEv
    implements CallInvalidEv {

    // ctor...
    public SDRCallInvalidEv(
        Call call, int cause, int metaCode,
            boolean isNewMetaEvent ) {
        super( call, CallInvalidEv.ID, cause, metaCode,
            isNewMetaEvent );
    }
    public SDRCallInvalidEv( Call call ) { super( call ); }
    private SDRCallInvalidEv() { super(); }
}
```

This same pattern is repeated for each remaining core object.

Core Exceptions

For our purposes (implementing core functionality), no new exceptions are required. We can just use those provided by JTAPI.

Summary

This chapter has presented a wide array of material mostly aimed at implementing a JTAPI library on the Windows platform. We presented a methodology for doing so along with sample implementations for each class in the core package `javax.telephony`, as well as the necessary ancillary classes found in `javax.telephony.capabilities` and `javax.telephony.events`. In the next chapter, we will use these core objects in an application.

PART IV

TELEPHONY
PROGRAMMING
WITH JTAPI

In Chapter 7, we make use of the lower-level library we constructed in the last chapter, to produce a trivial telephony application using our JTAPI library.

In Chapter 8, we investigate the extension packages provided with JTAPI that allow for the construction of more capable Java telephony programs including Call Control, Call Center applications, and the integration with various forms of media.

Chapter 7

APPLICATION PROGRAMMING WITH JTAPI

Telephones talk to you.

Weston and Spencer Roberts, ages 5 and 8

Women are like telephones.
They like to be held real close and talked to.
And if you push the wrong button, you're disconnected.

Unknown

In this chapter, we finally begin programming an application using JTAPI. We arrive at the point where JTAPI application programmers normally *begin!* Now having a firm understanding of the JTAPI architecture and having built part of a JTAPI implementation from scratch, we can begin to use it somewhat effectively. Of course, no one should have to build a library before they can use it — and JTAPI is no exception. In this book, we can pretend we just bought a modem board that came with a JTAPI library that will allow us to write Java applications using that board. In fact, this chapter should illustrate just how easy JTAPI is to use (where the last chapter may have shown how difficult one may be to build!).

Recall that the JTAPI implementation provided in Chapter 6 was referred to as "JTAPI-Lite." That binding was only part of the picture. In short, we implemented all of the required interfaces except for the observers. We implement the observers here because that is what users of JTAPI will be required to do in order to use a JTAPI binding. Taken together, the classes created in Chapter 6 and this chapter provide a partial implementation of the package `javax.telephony`. As such, users may place and disconnect telephone calls provided they have a TAPI-compliant modem installed, `TAPI32.dll`, and a Java virtual machine.[1] In short,

---

1 Our implementation only works with the Microsoft Virtual Machine for the reasons explained in Chapter 6, "Construction of a JTAPI Library."

you can place and disconnect calls. We leave implementing call answering as an exercise for the reader.

First, we will provide the code necessary to use JTAPI. Every application programmer is expected to supply code to make JTAPI work. But it's not as bad as it sounds. The code they supply is basically the application code they need to supply anyway — only the required format may be a little unusual. However, the effort is no more than what any C++ or seasoned Visual Basic programmer isn't already used to — implementing event handlers. The only difference is that the events aren't coming from a user interface widget (e.g., a button). In JTAPI, they are coming from the call model itself.

Hello World in JTAPI

Well, okay. Maybe JTAPI use isn't quite as simple as K&R's original program, but it's darn near close. The JTAPI specification says that application programmers are to "implement the *observer interfaces*." This is Java-ese for writing code for an event handler. **Listing 7.1** provides the General Form for doing this.

Listing 7.1 *The General Form for Writing Application Code in JTAPI*

```
public class MyObserver implements AjtapiObserver {

   public void someChangedEvent( Ev[] eventList ) {

      // iterate over the events...
      for ( int i=0; i < eventList.length; i++ ) {

         if ( eventList[i].getID() == SomeEv.ID ) {

            // TO DO: Your application code goes here...

         } else if ( eventList[i].getID() == SomeOtherEv.ID ) {

            // TO DO: more application code goes here...
         }
         // etc.
      }
   }
}
```

In short, all the code application programmers write follows this pattern. Contrast this with the approach in **Listing 7.2** using our "home-grown user-friendly" API (see Chapter 6).

Listing 7.2 *A "User-Friendly" Implementation from Chapter 6*

```
// as an interface...
public class MyCallObserver implements DelegatedCallObserver {

    public void onActiveCall( CallActiveEv ev ) {
        // TO DO: your implementation code goes here...
    }
    public void onInvalidCall( CallInvalidEv ev ) {
        // TO DO: and here...
    }
    public void
        onCallObservationTermination( CallObservationEndedEv ev ) {
        // TO DO: and here...
    }
}


// or using inheritance...
public class MyCallObserver extends DelegatedCallObserverAdaptor {

    public void onActiveCall( CallActiveEv ev ) {
        // TO DO: your over-ride code goes here...
    }
    public void onInvalidCall( CallInvalidEv ev ) {
        // TO DO: and here...
    }
    public void
        onCallObservationTermination( CallObservationEndedEv ev ) {
        // TO DO: and here...
    }
}
```

The approach you take will depend on what types of additional observable interfaces (other than the standard interfaces) are offered by the JTAPI vendor and whether or not you believe in the portability mantra with respect to telephony code.

Implementing the Observer Interfaces

Again, the final step in providing a working JTAPI application is to implement the observer interfaces. There are two approaches possible here. The most flexible is to simply create classes that implement the appropriate interfaces and then use them within a main() method. The other approach is to place main() within each observer class,[2] as in **Listing 7.3**.

---

2 This approach is only practical for explanation code.

Listing 7.3 *One Way to Implement the Observer Interface*

```
public class MyApp implements ProviderObserver {

    public static final void main(String args[]) {
        // somewhere in here,
        // this.providerChangedEvent() gets invoked...
    }

    public void providerChangedEvent(ProvEv[] eventList) {

    }
}
```

The better approach is to use the first method and create objects that have the capability to respond to JTAPI telephony objects. Using this approach, the classes can be used over again in many different applications. Our first implementation of an Observer interface uses this approach and is found in **Listing 7.4**.

Listing 7.4 *An Implementation of the ProviderObserver Interface*

```
public class SDRProviderObserver implements ProviderObserver {

    public void providerChangedEvent(ProvEv[] eventList) {

        for ( int i=0; i < eventList.length; i++ ) {
            try {
                String name =
                    ((ProvEv)eventList[i]).getProvider().getName();
                String msg = "Provider named: " + name + " is —>> ";
                if (eventList[i].getID() == ProvInServiceEv.ID) {
                    System.out.println(msg + "IN SERVICE"); }
                else if (eventList[i].getID() ==
                        ProvOutOfServiceEv.ID) {
                    System.out.println(msg + "OUT OF SERVICE"); }
                else if (eventList[i].getID() == ProvShutdownEv.ID) {
                    System.out.println(msg + "SHUTDOWN"); }
                else if
                    (eventList[i].getID() == ProvObservationEndedEv.ID){
                    System.out.println(msg + "OBSERVATION ENDED"); }
                else { System.out.println(msg
                        + "UNKNOWN PROVIDER EVENT"); }
            } catch (Exception excp) {
                System.out.println( "ProvEv Exception occurred...");
            }
        }
    }
}
```

Clearly, this class doesn't really do much. It merely responds to each type of event and prints an identification message to the system output. Any application requiring more substantial responses would require the placement of application-specific code in place of these system output messages. Note that each branch in this "effective switch statement" corresponds to an event generated by the relevant core object. In this case, the object is a Provider and so provides responses to the events ProvInServiceEv, ProvOutOfServiceEv, ProvShutdownEv, and ProvObservationEndedEv. Likewise, a TerminalObserver is expected to respond to terminal events, and so on.

Next is the TerminalObserver (see **Listing 7.5**). There is not really much here to report on since the Terminal really has no state information to report other than one TermObservationEndedEv. Recall that all state information for a Terminal is modeled in a separate object, the TerminalConnection.

Listing 7.5 *An Implementation of the TerminalObserver Interface*

```
package sroberts.telephony;

import javax.telephony.*;
import javax.telephony.events.*;


public class SDRTerminalObserver implements TerminalObserver {

  public void terminalChangedEvent(TermEv[] eventList) {

      for ( int i=0; i < eventList.length; i++ ) {
        try {
          String name =
            ((TermEv)eventList[i]).getTerminal().getName();
          String msg = "Terminal named: " + name + " is —>> ";
          if (eventList[i].getID() ==
              TermObservationEndedEv.ID) {
            System.out.println(msg +"OBSERVATION ENDED");    }
          else {
            System.out.println(msg +
                            "UNKNOWN Terminal EVENT"); }
        } catch (Exception excp) {
          System.out.println( "TermEv Exception occurred...");
        }
      }
  }
}
```

The same goes for the AddressObserver. Again, there is no state information of any real significance here, so the implementation (see **Listing 7.6**) is trivial. Note, however, that we are making full use of the methods implemented for the core JTAPI objects (i.e., `AddrEv.getAddress()`, `Address.getProvider()`, and `Address.getName()`).

Listing 7.6 *An Implementation of the AddressObserver Interface*

```
package sroberts.telephony;

import javax.telephony.*;
import  javax.telephony.events.*;

public class SDRAddressObserver implements AddressObserver {

   public void addressChangedEvent(AddrEv[] eventList) {

      for ( int i=0; i < eventList.length; i++ ) {
         try {
            Address addr = ((AddrEv)eventList[i]).getAddress();
            String provName = addr.getProvider().getName();
            String name = addr.getName();
            String msg = "Address named: " + name
               + " whose Provider is " + provName + " is —>> ";
            if (eventList[i].getID() ==
                  AddrObservationEndedEv.ID) {
               System.out.println(msg +"OBSERVATION ENDED");   }
            else { System.out.println(msg +
                                    "UNKNOWN ADDRESS EVENT");
            }
         } catch (Exception excp) {
            System.out.println("AddrEv Exception occurred...");
         }
      }
   }
}
```

Of course, we save the best for last. Recall that the CallObserver reports not only on Calls, but also on Connections and TerminalConnections. Because these are the most state-laden objects in the call model, this is the most important observer class (see **Listing 7.7**).

Listing 7.7 *An Implementation of the CallObserver Interface*

```java
package sroberts.telephony;

import java.util.*;
import java.awt.*;
import javax.telephony.*;
import javax.telephony.events.*;
import sroberts.telephony.events.*;

public class SDRCallObserver implements CallObserver {

    static public final int CALL_LISTENER = 1;
    static public final int CONNECTION_LISTENER = 2;
    static public final int TERMINAL_CONNECTION_LISTENER = 4;

    private boolean isCallListener = true;
    private boolean isConnectionListener = true;
    private boolean isTerminalConnectionListener = true;

    //constructors...
    public SDRCallObserver( int type ) {
        super();
        determineListenerMode( type );
    }

    public SDRCallObserver() {
        super();
    }

    // jtapi api ************************************************

    synchronized public void callChangedEvent(CallEv[] eventList) {

        String name = null;
        String msg = null;

        System.out.println( "CallObserver NOTIFIED. Report:");
        System.out.println( "****************************");

        for ( int i=0; i < eventList.length; i++ ) {

            if (isCallListener && eventList[i] instanceof CallEv) {
                try {
```

Listing 7.7 (cont.) *An Implementation of the CallObserver Interface*

```
            Call call = ((CallEv)eventList[i]).getCall();
            Connection[] conns = call.getConnections();
            Provider prov = call.getProvider();
            name = prov.getName();
            msg = "Provider named: (" + name + ")
                    owns a Call that is —>> ";
            if (conns == null) {
                System.out.println(msg + "IDLE"); }
            else if (eventList[i].getID() ==
                    CallActiveEv.ID) {
                System.out.println(msg + "ACTIVE"); }
            else if (eventList[i].getID() ==
                    CallInvalidEv.ID) {
                System.out.println(msg + "INVALID"); }
        } catch (Exception excp) {
            System.out.println( "CallEv Exception occurred
                in SDRCallObserver::callChangedEvent()...");
            excp.printStackTrace();
        }
    }
    if (isConnectionListener && eventList[i]
            instanceof ConnEv) {
        try {
            Connection connection =
                (ConnEv)eventList[i]).getConnection();
            Call call = connection.getCall();
            Address addr = connection.getAddress();
            name = addr.getName();
            msg = "Connection to Address: (" + name + ")
                    is —>> ";

            if (eventList[i].getID() == ConnCreatedEv.ID) {
                System.out.println(msg + "CREATED"); }
            else if (eventList[i].getID() ==
                    ConnInProgressEv.ID) {
                System.out.println(msg + "INPROGRESS"); }
            else if (eventList[i].getID() ==
                    ConnAlertingEv.ID) {
                System.out.println(msg + "ALERTING"); }
            else if (eventList[i].getID() ==
                    ConnConnectedEv.ID) {
                Object[] objs = ((SDRCall)call).getData();
                // hang-up button & label...
                ((Button)objs[1]).setEnabled( true );
```

Listing 7.7 (cont.) *An Implementation of the CallObserver Interface*

```java
            ((List)objs[2]).add( msg + "CONNECTED" );
            System.out.println(msg + "CONNECTED");
         }
         else if (eventList[i].getID() ==
                 ConnDisconnectedEv.ID) {
            Object[] objs - ((SDRCall)call).getData();
            // both buttons...
            ((Button)objs[0]).setEnabled( true );
            // dial...
            ((Button)objs[1]).setEnabled( false );
            // hang-up...
            ((List)objs[2]).add( msg + "DISCONNECTED" );
            System.out.println(msg + "DISCONNECTED");
         }
         else if (eventList[i].getID() ==
                 ConnFailedEv.ID) {
            System.out.println(msg + "FAILED"); }
         else if (eventList[i].getID() ==
                 ConnUnknownEv.ID) {
            System.out.println(msg + "UNKNOWN"); }
      } catch (Exception excp) {
         System.out.println( "ConnEv Exception occurred
            in SDRCallObserver::callChangedEvent()...");
         excp.printStackTrace();
      }
   }
   if (isTerminalConnectionListener
          && eventList[i] instanceof TermConnEv) {
      try {
         TerminalConnection tc =
         ((TermConnEv)eventList[i]).getTerminalConnection();
         Terminal term = tc.getTerminal();
         Connection conn = tc.getConnection();
         String addressName = conn.getAddress().getName();
         msg = "Terminal named: " + name
             + "and Connection named: (" + addressName
             + ") owns a TerminalConnection that is ->> ";
         if (eventList[i].getID() ==
               TermConnCreatedEv.ID) {
            System.out.println(msg + "IDLE"); }
         else if (eventList[i].getID() ==
               TermConnRingingEv.ID) {
            System.out.println(msg + "RINGING"); }
```

Listing 7.7 (cont.) *An Implementation of the CallObserver Interface*

```
                 else if (eventList[i].getID() ==
                         TermConnPassiveEv.ID) {
                   System.out.println(msg + "PASSIVE"); }
                 else if (eventList[i].getID() ==
                         TermConnActiveEv.ID) {
                   System.out.println(msg + "ACTIVE"); }
                 else if (eventList[i].getID() ==
                         TermConnDroppedEv.ID) {
                   System.out.println(msg + "DROPPED"); }
                 else { System.out.println(msg + "UNKNOWN"); }
            } catch (Exception excp) {
              System.out.println(
                 "TermConnEv Exception occurred in
                 SDRCallObserver::callChangedEvent()...");
              excp.printStackTrace();
            }
          }
        }
     System.out.println( "******************************");
  }

  // enhanced API *********************************************

  public String toString() {

      String nameToken = "";

      if ( isCallListener ) nameToken = nameToken
            + "CALL_LISTENER ";
      if ( isConnectionListener ) nameToken =
            "CONNECTION_LISTENER ";
      if ( isTerminalConnectionListener ) nameToken =
            "TERMINALCONNECTION_LISTENER";
      return nameToken;
  }

  private void determineListenerMode( int type ) {

      int firstBit = (type&CALL_LISTENER)/CALL_LISTENER;
      int secondBit = (type&CONNECTION_LISTENER)
         /CONNECTION_LISTENER;
      int thirdBit = (type&TERMINAL_CONNECTION_LISTENER)
         /TERMINAL_CONNECTION_LISTENER;
```

Listing 7.7 (cont.) *An Implementation of the CallObserver Interface*

```
      if (firstBit != 1) isCallListener = false;
      if (secondBit != 1) isConnectionListener = false;
      if (thirdBit != 1) isTerminalConnectionListener = false;
   }
}
```

Because the CallObserver class listens for three different *kinds* of events, we must of course filter for these events. However, this filtering process cannot be exclusive of the other types of events. In other words, a CallObserver must be able to listen for call events, connection events, and terminal connection events — not call events *or* connection events *or* terminal connection events. That is the purpose of the additional method `determineListenerMode()` and its associated attributes. By default our CallObserver listens for all three types, yet we provide a constructor mechanism where it can be made to listen to each type or combination of types selectively by "OR-ing" together the values.

Note also that the `callChangedEvent()` method is synchronized. While this exacts a cost in terms of runtime performance, it ensures that the output will appear correctly[3] on the console screen (or whatever output medium we choose). Note also that the JTAPI specification allows for this type of flexibility in JTAPI implementations.

The only other additional code of interest here is the use of the `getData()` method from our helper superclass JtapiObject. By hanging on to pointers to the GUI objects, we are able to change them here in the event response code. Alternatively, we could have set up listeners for the appropriate events, but this accomplishes the same thing in a "quick and dirty" way.

Revisiting the Phone Dialer Application with JTAPI-Lite

JTAPI-Lite is given a test run using an application that wraps a desktop telephone. The functionality from the user's perspective is very similar to a typical phone dialer application. The user is presented with an extremely simple interface that allows him or her to place and disconnect calls.

Back in Chapter 5 we placed a call using Microsoft's TAPI. In this section the same functionality is accomplished using JTAPI. We've created an applet (which may also be run as an application) that allows for the placing and disconnecting of telephone calls on Windows machines. It assumes that a standard TAPI-compliant modem is present on the box. The user interface is presented in **Figure 7.1**.

---

3 Without proper synchronization, calls to this method from multiple threads will scramble the output.

Figure 7.1 *JTAPI-Lite User Interface*

This is essentially the same interface we have been using all along, except we have added a facility to peek a little under the covers to get a look at important internal values as they change (using the "Display Internals" button — more on this later). The code for the application is presented in **Listing 7.8**.

Listing 7.8 *A JTAPI Application/Applet*

```java
package sroberts.telephony;

import java.applet.*;
import java.awt.*;
import java.awt.event.*;
import javax.telephony.*;
import sroberts.telephony.jTAPIimplementations.tapi.*;

public class TestJtapiApp extends Applet implements Runnable,
    ActionListener
{
    static private final String DEFAULT_PHONE_NUMBER =
        "522-1094";
    static private final String OFFICE_TELEPHONE =
        "Office Phone";
    private Thread m_TestJtapiApp = null;
    private boolean callInProgress_ = false;

    // UI stuff...
    private Button dialButton_;
```

Listing 7.8 (cont.) *A JTAPI Application/Applet*

```
private Button hangUpButton_;
private Button exitButton_;
private List listBox_;
private TextField phoneNumberField_;
private Label message_;

// call model objects...
private JtapiPeer jtapiPeer_;
private Provider provider_;
private CallObserver callObserver_;
private Address originatingAddress_;
private Terminal terminal_;
private Call call_;
private Connection[] twoConnections_;
private String destinationNumber_;


// STANDALONE APPLICATION SUPPORT:
// m_fStandAlone will be set to true if applet is run
// standalone
//─────────────────────────────
private boolean m_fStandAlone = true;

public static void main(String args[])
{
    TestJtapiFrame frame =
          new TestJtapiFrame("JTAPI Application");

    frame.setSize( frame.insets().left + frame.insets().right
            + 240,
              frame.insets().top  + frame.insets().bottom
            + 200 );

    TestJtapiApp applet_TestJtapiApp = new TestJtapiApp();

    frame.add("Center", applet_TestJtapiApp);
    applet_TestJtapiApp.m_fStandAlone = true;
    applet_TestJtapiApp.init();
    applet_TestJtapiApp.start();
    frame.show();
}

public String getAppletInfo()
{
```

Listing 7.8 (cont.) *A JTAPI Application/Applet*

```java
    return "Name: JDirect2NativeApp\r\n" +
           "Author: Spencer Roberts\r\n" +
           "Created with Microsoft Visual J++ Version 1.1";
}

public void init()
{
    // TODO: Place additional initialization code here

    setLayout( new FlowLayout() );
    Label leftSpacer_ = new Label( "              " );
    Label rightSpacer_ = new Label( "              " );
    Label textBoxLabel = new Label(
       "Enter a number to dial: ");
    Button internalsButton = new Button(
       "Display Internals" );

    phoneNumberField_ = new TextField( 35 );
    message_ = new Label( "Welcome to JTAPI on Windows");
    listBox_ = new List();
    dialButton_ = new Button( "Dial" );
    hangUpButton_ = new Button( "Hang Up" );
    exitButton_ = new Button( "Exit" );

    // arrange window...
    add( leftSpacer_ );
    add( listBox_ );
    add( rightSpacer_ );
    add( message_ );
    add( textBoxLabel );
    add( phoneNumberField_ );
    add( dialButton_ );
    add( hangUpButton_ );
    add( exitButton_ );
    add( internalsButton );

    // set up listeners...
    dialButton_.addActionListener( this );
    hangUpButton_.addActionListener( this );
    exitButton_.addActionListener( this );
    phoneNumberField_.addActionListener( this );
    internalsButton.addActionListener( this );
```

Listing 7.8 (cont.) *A JTAPI Application/Applet*

```
      hangUpButton_.setEnabled( false );
      dialButton_.setEnabled( false );

      // first, create the JTAPI peer objects...
      try {
         jtapiPeer_ =
         sroberts.telephony.JtapiPeerFactory.getJtapiPeer(null);
         provider_ = jtapiPeer_.getProvider(null);
         ((SDRProvider)provider_).setState(
               Provider.IN_SERVICE, "sierra" );
      } catch ( Exception e ) {
         e.printStackTrace();
      }

      // now the observers...
      callObserver = new SDRCallObserver();

      // now some of the JTAPI call model objects...
      try {
         originatingAddress_ =
            provider_.getAddress( "555-1212" );
         terminal_ = provider_.getTerminal( OFFICE_TELEPHONE );
      } catch ( Exception e ) {
         e.printStackTrace();
      }
   }

   public void destroy()
   {
      // TODO: Place applet cleanup code here
   }

   public void paint(Graphics g)
   {
      // TODO: Place applet paint code here
   }

   public void start()
   {
      if (m_TestJtapiApp == null)
      {
         m_TestJtapiApp = new Thread( this );
         m_TestJtapiApp.start();
      }
```

Listing 7.8 (cont.) *A JTAPI Application/Applet*

```
      // TODO: Place additional applet start code here
   }

   public void stop()
   {
      if (m_TestJtapiApp != null)
      {
         m_TestJtapiApp.stop();
         m_TestJtapiApp = null;
      }

      // TODO: Place additional applet stop code here

      if ( m_fStandAlone ) System.exit(0);
   }

   public void run() { }

   public void actionPerformed( ActionEvent ev ) {

      String action = ev.getActionCommand();

      if ( action.compareTo( "Dial" ) == 0 ) {

         dialButton_.setEnabled( false );
         if ( destinationNumber_.length() < 7 )
            destinationNumber_ = DEFAULT_PHONE_NUMBER;

         try {
            call_ = null;
            twoConnections_ = null;

            call_ = provider_.createCall();
            call_.addObserver( callObserver_ );

            Object[] objs = new Object[ 3 ];
            objs[0] = dialButton_;
            objs[1] = hangUpButton_;
            objs[2] = listBox_;
            ((SDRCall)call_).setData( objs );
```

Listing 7.8 (cont.) *A JTAPI Application/Applet*

```java
            // make the call...
            message_.setText( "About to make a call from "
                    + originatingAddress_.getName() + " to :"
                    + destinationNumber_ );

            twoConnections_ = call_.connect(
                terminal_, originatingAddress_,
                destinationNumber_ );
            if ( twoConnections_ != null )
                message_.setText( "Created two Connections for "
                    + originatingAddress_.getName() + " and "
                    + destinationNumber_ );

        } catch ( Exception e ) {
            e.printStackTrace();
        }
    }
    else if ( action.compareTo( "Hang Up" ) == 0 ) {

        message_.setText( "Attempting Disconnect() for "
            + destinationNumber_ );
        try {
            // for now...
            Connection conn =
                ((SDRCall)call_).findConnectionFor(
                destinationNumber_ );
            if ( conn != null ) {
                conn.disconnect();
                message_.setText( "Disconnected connection for "
                    + destinationNumber_ );
                callInProgress_ = false;
            }
        } catch ( UnsatisfiedLinkError ule) {
            System.err.println("Caught exception: " + ule);
            message_.setText( "FAILED to Disconnect connection
                for " + destinationNumber_ );
            ule.printStackTrace();
        } catch ( Exception e) {
            message_.setText( "FAILED to Disconnect connection
                for " + destinationNumber_ );
            e.printStackTrace();
        }
    }
```

Listing 7.8 (cont.) *A JTAPI Application/Applet*

```
    else if ( action.compareTo( "Display Internals" ) == 0 ){
        message_.setText( "Displaying Internals
                                to output display..." );
        ((SDRCall)call_).displayInternals();
    }
    else if ( action.compareTo( "Exit" ) == 0 ) {
        message_.setText( "Program Terminated by User..." );
        stop();
    }
    else if ( ev.getSource() instanceof TextField ) {
        destinationNumber_ = phoneNumberField_.getText();
        if ( !callInProgress_ ) {
            dialButton_.setEnabled( true );
        }
    }
  }
}
}
```

This application is pretty straightforward. It is set up to run as either an applet or an application as any Java program may be. The `actionPerformed()` method is implemented in order to allow for response to the buttons on the screen. The buttons are used to invoke the JTAPI call model objects, namely instances of the Call and Connection interfaces. Let's walk through a use of the application and examine the output as we go.

Running the Application

The importance of this application is not the application itself, but rather the invocation of the JTAPI call model objects we have built in this book. Because these are not visual objects, their state is reported by calls to the standard output.[4] Along with visual figures showing the application during execution, this is the primary mechanism we will use to explain what is going on with the call model.

When the application is first initialized, the system output shows the following:

System output:

```
SDRSingletonFactory: created the ONLY instance of type
        —>> SDRSingletonFactory for the FIRST time.
```

---

4 Although some GUI objects are updated in the event handler presented in **Listing 7.7**.

```
SDRSingletonFactory: CREATED an instance of type
        —>> sroberts.util.singleton.SecurityMonitor

SDRSingletonFactory: RETURNED the ONLY instance of type
        —>> sroberts.util.singleton.SecurityMonitor
```

This output is merely a result of our decision to implement the SecurityMonitor helper class of Chapter 6 as a Singleton (the Singleton class is presented in Chapter 10, "Idioms and Patterns in Telephony"). Other objects are created that provide no system output, most importantly the JtapiPeer and Provider instances, along with the Address we are calling from and the Terminal we are using. The stage so far represents the application after the init() method is called and the applet is started.[5]

Placing a Call

When the application is first started, the user may enter a phone number to dial. This state is pictured in **Figure 7.2**.

Figure 7.2 *Ready to Dial...*

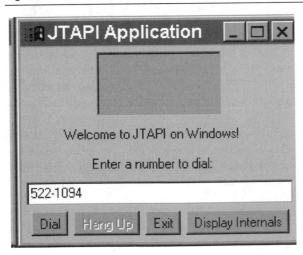

When the user hits the Enter key, the action event is generated from the TextField component (standard Java stuff). This enables the "Dial" button, which will kick off all the action. Once this button is clicked, we create an instance of a Call from the Provider and add the CallObserver we created during initialization to its observer list. This allows the observer to receive events from that Call instance via the JtapiEventNotifier class we built in

---

5 A pictorial view of this state has already been presented in **Figure 7.1**.

Chapter 6. We also create the two Connection instances we will need to return from the `Call.connect()` method. Here's the system output:

System output:

```
Inside Call.addObserver()...
Inside Call.connect() ADDED 2 Connections...
```

Next, we drop inside the `Call.connect()` method. Here we accomplish two tasks. First, we initialize the TAPI callback data in Java that the CallRep helper class uses to keep track of changes in the call model.

System output:

```
Inside CallRep.callConnect()
tapiCallbackData_[0] = 0
tapiCallbackData_[1] = 0
tapiCallbackData_[2] = 0

Inside CallRep.callConnect() worker
thread LAUNCHED on value: 51
```

The CallRep worker thread is launched waiting for the TAPI callback function to change these values through the native interface we built in Chapter 6. The value "51" is the decimal equivalent of hexadecimal 33, the value of the constant Connection.CONNECTED used to signal this state change in JTAPI.

Next, we return from `Call.connect()` and the thread continues to sleep, waking every so often to check if the appropriate value (the second item in the tapiCallbackData array) has changed. In addition, the CallObserver receives notification that the Call is now ACTIVE.

System output:

```
Successfully placed asynchronous call...

CallObserver NOTIFIED. Report:
******************************
Provider named: (Susie says Spencer is a good Provider)
owns a Call that is —>> ACTIVE
******************************

    zzzzzzz CallRep worker thread SLEEPING zzzzzzzzzz
    zzzzzzz CallRep worker thread SLEEPING zzzzzzzzzz
    zzzzzzz CallRep worker thread SLEEPING zzzzzzzzzz
```

If the board were to fail or the TAPI subsystem were to hang at this point, this output would continue on indefinitely (or until the thread was killed) because we have not coded a timeout value. But this is not what we expect to happen, of course. We expect the hardware to notify TAPI that the call was connected by invoking the callback function we so carefully set up in Chapter 6.

When the TAPI system invokes the callback function in the Win32 C DLL `callrep.dll`, and the LINECALLSTATE_CONNECTED value is passed to the *dwParam1* parameter when the *dwMessage* parameter is set to LINE_CALLSTATE, the application data in parameter *dwInstance* are changed. These data are then converted from a C/Win32 DWORD* back into an `int[]` through the J/Direct marshalling process. After this occurs, the next wake-up round from the CallRep worker thread notices the change and initiates the notification process by sending an event through a CallNotifier, which ultimately changes the state of the Connections associated with the Call.

System output:

```
zzzzzzzz CallRep worker thread SLEEPING zzzzzzzzzzz
CallRep worker thread #### SETTING CONNECTIONS STATE ####
setStateOfConnections() SUCCEEDED...
```

Once the states of the Connection objects have changed, standard JTAPI takes over from there and the CallObserver is notified like before — only this time it's a set of Connection events that are sent and so the output is different.

System output:

```
CallObserver NOTIFIED. Report:
******************************
Connection to Address: (522-1094) is —>> CONNECTED
********************************

CallObserver NOTIFIED. Report:
******************************
Connection to Address: (555-1212) is —>> CONNECTED
********************************
```

In addition, the user interface is updated with the appropriate messages in the list box and message line as shown in **Figure 7.3**.

Figure 7.3 `Call.connect()` *Completes ...*

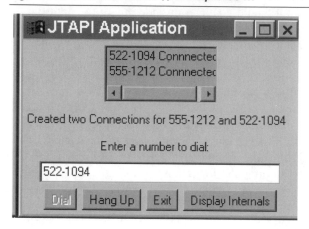

Before attempting to disconnect this call, we'll click the "Display Internals" button in order to examine the state of the internal data structure we passed through JTAPI and J/Direct into the C DLL and back.[6] When the call was connected, it should have set the second item in the list to the value of the constant Connection.CONNECTED (i.e., the value 51). Sure enough, it did.

System output:

```
tapiCallbackData_[0] = 0
tapiCallbackData_[1] = 51
tapiCallbackData_[2] = 0
```

Hanging Up

Having had quite enough of all of this, it's time to hang up the call. Pressing the "Hang Up" button will remove a Connection from the active Call. If it is one of the last two Connections on that Call, both Connections should be disabled and the Call should be dropped. This is in fact the case, and hence the following output results (see also **Figure 7.4**).

System output:

```
CallObserver NOTIFIED. Report:
******************************
Connection to Address: (522-1094) is —>> DISCONNECTED
*******************************
```

---

6 This step is not necessary; rather it is provided for debugging and convenience.

Figure 7.4 *Disconnecting a Connection Through JTAPI*

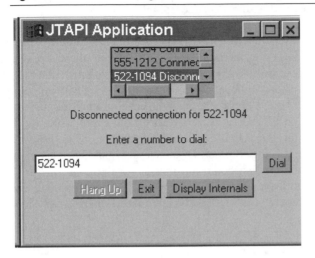

And that's the end of the application programming story in JTAPI. But is it a storybook ending? Well, not exactly.

Glitches

Human beings are fundamentally flawed, and so is this application. There are two sources of these glitches: a bug and what may be considered a design flaw.

Bugs

The application works, but we encountered a bug that requires a work-around or two. It boils down to this — it seems the TAPI runtime does not always generate the events it is supposed to because our TAPI callback function is not always invoked when it should be. In the case of a `connect()`, the callback will not be invoked unless we place a user interface dialog into the calling function and allow it to remain active until the call is connected.[7] If we do this, all is well in connect land. If not, the callback never gets invoked! What we have is essentially a built-in *race condition* (not exactly a reliability feature!).

The second workaround is required upon `disconnect()`. Although the TAPI `linedrop()` function works, our callback is again never

---

7 Recall that the Win32 specifies two types of threads — user interface threads and worker (non-UI) threads. The UI threads are blocking whenever a standard dialog box is invoked. When a dialog is invoked during a worker thread, the worker thread is not completely blocked (the object can still receive function invocations), but the UI thread blocks for user input. Therefore, we can use this technique to effectively "stall" the calling thread without blocking it.

invoked *at all*! In this case, we just use the successful return value from `linedrop()` and set the state accordingly.

It is not clear why these errors are occurring, but it is endemic to working with layers of software and drivers. We're pretty sure it's not our code because we can get our code to work by following these workarounds. In any case, it is not necessarily a bug in the TAPI runtime, either. It could be an omission when the vendor implemented the TSPI interface to the TAPI32 DLL. For example, they might have omitted the generation of a TAPI LINECALLSTATE_DISCONNECTED event when the hardware disconnected the line. Or it could have something to do with the Java/C mapping process using J/Direct. Of course, we could have taken the time to present you with perfect code, but that is not the point of this book. We have chosen to leave the code "as is" for the purposes of discussing the kinds of problems you will likely encounter when using or creating a JTAPI library.

A Design Flaw?

Recall in Chapter 6 we made the choice of proceeding with the callback approach to implementing the TAPI notification process and avoided the other two approaches — I/O completion ports and NT events. Although we may have encountered other problems (either of our own making or that of underlying code) using either of these approaches instead, the problems encountered here would likely disappear. Why? Because both of the other approaches use separate threads to signal completion. In contrast, the callback approach uses the *same thread* for both invocation and notification. So if we block on invocation (during say, `Call.connect()`), we are also blocking the invocation of the callback function!

And so it could be argued that the real flaw was one of design. We made an inappropriate choice of which Win32 service to use to implement our messaging scheme from the beginning.

Summary

In this chapter, we have learned how write application programs using JTAPI. We learned that in order to do so, we must implement the relevant Observer interfaces. In implementing these interfaces, we used the call model objects we built in Chapter 6. Of course, under normal circumstances, the Chapter 6 classes would be supplied by a JTAPI vendor. We also continued along our path of realism, showing workaround solutions, warts and all.

At this point, you are now armed and dangerous. You are ready to create application programs using a commercial JTAPI library from any vendor. In addition some of you are even bold enough to attempt the creation of your own JTAPI library "from scratch." Of course you may have noticed that after all this work, we've really only seen a small amount of telecom functionality. It's not likely that we'll be able to build a call center application from the core capabilities we've seen to this point. In short, all we've really been able to do is place and disconnect calls. Stay tuned. In the next chapter, we take a break from programmatic details and delve once again into the JTAPI library as specified. We examine the "extensions to the extension" — the Java subpackages that allow for more powerful and specialized telephony programming.

Chapter 8   STANDARD EXTENSIONS
TO THE CORE PACKAGE

> For a branch cannot produce fruit if
> it is severed from the vine.
>
> *Holy Bible*, John 15:4

Recall that the core packages provided the minimal set of functionality required for any telephony client application. In short, the core packages offer limited support, primarily for desktop applications. To develop professional applications, we need capabilities far beyond those provided in the core packages. The core extension packages Call Control, Media, Call Center, and Phone build upon the fundamental capabilities provided in the core packages. Server capabilities are also added.

Each JTAPI extension package provides a specialization of the core telephony package (`javax.telephony`) in one manner or another. Additional interfaces, classes, events, capabilities, exceptions, and constants are added to the JTAPI namespace.

Under `javax.telephony` are the core extension packages:

`javax.telephony`
```
javax.telephony.phone
javax.telephony.callcontrol
javax.telephony.media
javax.telephony.callcenter
javax.telephony.privatedata
```

In this chapter, we investigate these subpackages in some detail. We do not, however, implement any of the interfaces as we did for the core pack-

293

age `javax.telephony`. To say that this is left as an exercise for the reader would be masochistic! However, it is an exercise for those JTAPI vendors who choose to implement these packages, and the same methodology that was used to produce our limited library may be used for the extension packages. And so this chapter is primarily a reference for these packages.

Call Control Packages

The core telephony package provided the fundamental capabilities required of every telephone system such as placing and receiving calls. Intuitively, we can think of the call control package as adding to those capabilities for the functional needs of, say, an office telephone set up. Package `javax.telephony.callcontrol` (also referred to as "The Call Control Package") allows for placing calls on hold, transferring telephone calls, and conferencing telephone calls. These services require the underlying services of ANI and DNIS (see Chapter 1), which are assumed to be in place in any implementation of the core package.

Package `javax.telephony.callcontrol` extends the capabilities of the core interfaces Call, Connection, Terminal, Address, and TerminalConnection defined in the core package `javax.telephony`. The Call Control Package also provides an extended set of states (and corresponding events) on the Connection and TerminalConnection objects. These are found in the interface definitions and in package `javax.telephony.callcontrol.events`, respectively. In addition, capabilities interfaces are placed in package `javax.telephony.callcontrol.capabilities`.

Call Control Core Components

The Call Control Core Components are depicted in **Figure 8.1**. This set of objects should look very familiar. They are essentially the same business

Figure 8.1 *Call Control Core Components*

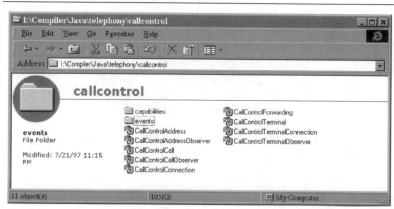

objects as in the core package but with more functionality; namely more control over calls. (The only exception is class CallControlForwarding, which is essentially a helper class.) The JTAPI designers took advantage of a proper use of inheritance here by simply extending the core interfaces as appropriate.

Before we examine all the interfaces that are extended from the core package, let's take a look at the only *class* in the package, CallControlForwarding.

CallControlForwarding

Three of the seven methods specified in the CallControlAddress interface deal with the CallControlForwarding class. As the name implies, the CallControlForwarding class provides or returns information about the call-forwarding characteristics of an Address. This convenient class is used as a specification for a telephone switch providing instructions as to how the switch is to forward incoming calls for an Address.

The CallControlForwarding class has two primary attributes: a *type* and a *filter*. The type specifies *when* to forward calls. There are three type options here:

- **always forward**
- **forward when the address is busy**
- **forward when no one answers**

The filter indicates which type of incoming calls the type applies to. The filter options are:

- *apply to all incoming calls*
- *apply to external calls only*
- *apply to internal calls only*
- *apply only to a specific calling address*

The types and filters are presented in **Listing 8.1**.

Listing 8.1 *Types and Filters of a CallControlForwarding Instruction*

```
//types...
public final static int FORWARD_UNCONDITIONALLY = 0x1;
public final static int FORWARD_ON_BUSY = 0x2;
public final static int FORWARD_ON_NOANSWER = 0x3;
//filters...
public final static int ALL_CALLS = 0x1;
public final static int INTERNAL_CALLS = 0x2;
public final static int EXTERNAL_CALLS = 0x3;
public final static int SPECIFIC_ADDRESS = 0x4;
```

Life Cycle of a CallControlForwarding

Conceptually, a CallControlForwarding is not really a "first class" entity. It is more like a *helper class* that provides information to other classes, most notably the CallControlAddress interface. Its life cycle should depend entirely on the CallControlAddress(es) it is associated with. As we will see shortly, the CallControlAddress exports operations for getting and setting an array of CallControlForwarding instructions. It will not be uncommon to see vendor APIs that take a CallControlForwarding array as an argument to the constructor of a CallControlAddress. This will allow for the convenient predetermination of call-forwarding characteristics to the CallControlAddress.

Creating a CallControlForwarding

The CallControlForwarding class exports four constructors, as shown in **Listing 8.2**.

Listing 8.2 *CallControlForwarding Constructors*

```
public CallControlForwarding( String destAddress ) {
   this.destAddress = destAddress;
   type            = FORWARD_UNCONDITIONALLY;
   caller          = null;
   whichCalls      = ALL_CALLS;
 }


public CallControlForwarding( String destAddress, int type ) {
   this.destAddress = destAddress;
   this.type       = type;
   caller          = null;
   whichCalls      = ALL_CALLS;
 }


public CallControlForwarding(String destAddress,
         int type, String caller){
   this.destAddress = destAddress;
   this.type       = type;
   this.caller     = caller;
   whichCalls      = SPECIFIC_ADDRESS;
 }


public CallControlForwarding(
         String destAddress, int type, boolean internalCalls) {
   this.destAddress = destAddress;
   this.type       = type;
   caller          = null;
   if ( internalCalls ) whichCalls = INTERNAL_CALLS;
   else whichCalls = EXTERNAL_CALLS;
 }
```

Operations Allowed on a CallControlForwarding

The operations allowed on a CallControlForwarding are "read only" in that there are no "setter" methods. This, coupled with the fact that all instance variables are private, means that the constructors are the only means of setting these values (see **Listing 8.3**).

Listing 8.3 *Operations Allowed on a CallControlForwarding*

```
public String getDestinationAddress() { return
   this.destAddress; }
public int getFilter() { return this.whichCalls; }
public String getSpecificCaller() { return this.caller; }
public int getType() { return this.type; }
```

This limitation may be a nuisance — at worst a performance bottleneck. The class specifies that the *type* and *filter* attributes are private, and so any implementation wishing to extend this class for its own use may not use these same attributes in any setter methods it may provide to change the state at runtime.[1] Instead, it must create a new instance passing these values in the constructor. For example, the following code will not compile:

```
public MyCallForwarding extends CallControlForwarding {

   public void setType( int newType ) {
      this.type  = newType;    // generates a compiler error...
   }
}
```

Keeping object creation to a minimum is a crucial factor in improving the performance of Java applications — especially for classes that may be used frequently (we address performance issues in Chapter 10, "Idioms and Patterns in Telephony"). In an application dealing with incoming calls, it would seem that this class *would* be used extensively. Although the same instance could be used for many different CallControlAddress instances, reusing an existing CallControlForwarding instance by resetting its instance variables is not possible. Of course, you are provided the source code and so simply changing the storage specifier of these instance variables from **private** to **protected** is easy enough. This is probably a better approach than adding setter methods to the class as shown previously in this section.

Not to belabor a minor point, but it could be argued that the specification of attributes as private was an intentional design decision (as opposed to a design flaw). By allowing extension classes to set these variables, the JTAPI specification would have violated the Provider's role in creating

---

1 This could have been avoided by simply specifying the storage specifier as *protected* instead of *private*.

JTAPI classes. This argument holds little weight, however, because public constructors *are* provided for this class — and so *any* class may create instances of class CallControlForwarding.

Now let's look at the interface that uses the CallControlForwarding class, namely CallControlAddress.

CallControlAddress

The CallControlAddress interface extends the core Address interface of package `javax.telephony`. And so a CallControlAddress "isa" Address because it is to inherit all of the functions an Address offers.[2] **Figure 8.2** demonstrates this extension relationship.

Figure 8.2 *Extension Relationship Between an Address and a CallControlAddress*

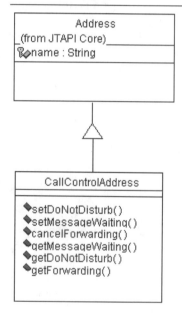

The CallControlAddress interface does not inappropriately extend the interface to allow for capabilities that are not allowed of the Address interface. For example, CallControlAddress inherits the capability to return its name to the caller. However, it is not allowed to set that variable through a public interface such as `setName()`.[3]

---

2 A subtle correction is in order here. Interface extension is not entirely the same as class extension from a design perspective. Although an implementation does actually extend the implementation class by implementing the extended interface, it may also implement other interfaces that may violate the canonical inheritance notion of "isa."

3 Recall that the reason for this is that only Providers may supply Address instances and therefore set their values.

Life Cycle of a CallControlAddress

Like its ancestor the Address, a CallControlAddress has a pretty boring life cycle. Once created, a CallControlAddress just hangs around until it goes out of scope and is reclaimed by the garbage collector. It also has no state information of its own to report, just like an Address.

Creating a CallControlAddress

A CallControlAddress is instantiated in exactly the same manner as an Address (see the Address creation code in Chapter 4, "A Closer Look at JTAPI," and replace the Address instance with a CallControlAddress instance). Just like an Address, both a Provider and a JtapiPeer instance are required to obtain a CallControlAddress.

Operations Allowed on a CallControlAddress

A CallControlAddress is essentially a phone number that allows for the prespecification of certain additional functionality — namely, whether or not the Address can allow any incoming calls, where those calls should go when they come in, and so forth. These options are to be specified to the Provider prior to using a CallControlAddress instance. They are to have no effect upon the instance once it is part of a call. In other words, the functions are *not* dynamic. This makes sense. We can intuitively think of a CallControlAddress as an Address with more capabilities that we can request before we use it. Once we are involved in a call, we cannot change its capabilities any more than we can request a telephone service change from the phone company in the middle of a telephone call ("I'd like to add call-waiting, please"). The CallControlAddress interface is shown in **Listing 8.4**.

Listing 8.4 *Operations on a CallControlAddress*

```
import javax.telephony.*;


public interface CallControlAddress extends Address {
    public abstract void
        setForwarding( CallControlForwarding instructions[] )
            throws
                MethodNotSupportedException,
                InvalidStateException,
                InvalidArgumentException;
    // Each object returned in the array describes a different
    // rule for different types of forwarding.
    public abstract CallControlForwarding[] getForwarding()
        throws MethodNotSupportedException;
    public abstract void cancelForwarding()
```

Listing 8.4 (cont.) *Operations on a CallControlAddress*

```
            throws MethodNotSupportedException,
                     InvalidStateException;
    public abstract boolean getDoNotDisturb()
        throws MethodNotSupportedException;
    public abstract void setDoNotDisturb(boolean enable)
        throws MethodNotSupportedException,
                     InvalidStateException;
    // Precondition: The Provider must in IN_SERVICE
    public abstract boolean getMessageWaiting()
        throws MethodNotSupportedException,
                     InvalidStateException;
    public abstract void setMessageWaiting(boolean enable)
        throws MethodNotSupportedException,
                     InvalidStateException;

}
```

The modifier methods exported from this interface are

`setForwarding()`,

`setDoNotDisturb()`, and

`setMessageWaiting()`.

Each of these methods sends instructions to the switch associated with a particular Address (technically a CallControlAddress, of course). The methods `setForwarding()` and `setDoNotDisturb()` instruct the switch as to how to handle *incoming* calls. The method `setMessageWaiting()` simply tells the switch there is a message waiting at this CallControlAddress. Time for some action. Let's look at JTAPI's version of a Call on steroids — the CallControlCall interface.

CallControlCall

Just as the CallControlAddress interface extends the core Address interface of package `javax.telephony`, the CallControlCall interface extends the core Call interface of package `javax.telephony`. And so a CallControlCall "isa" Call because it inherits all of the behavior a Call offers. **Figure 8.3** demonstrates this relationship.

Life Cycle of a CallControlCall

In order to understand the life cycle of a CallControlCall, we must know the life cycle of a Call (because it extends this interface) and also the *additional* events a CallControlCall generates (because these are reported as a result of state changes in the object). Surprisingly, there are no new events or states that are modeled that pertain directly to a CallControlCall object. Recall

Figure 8.3 *Extension Relationship Between a Call and a CallControlCall*

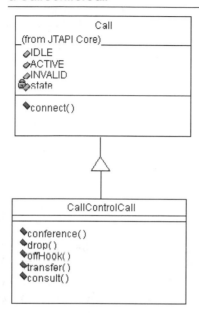

that in the Call interface, every Call state (i.e., ACTIVE, IDLE, INVALID) usually generated a corresponding event (i.e., CallActiveEv, CallInvalidEv, and so forth.). Therefore we might expect to see new states like IN_CONFERENCE, TRANSFERING and the like with corresponding events like, say, CallControlCallConfEv and CallControlCallTransferEv. This design pattern is no longer followed in the case of this extension class. Of course, a CallControlCall is still a Call and as such generates the appropriate Call events. But it generates no additional states and events (at least not directly). We'll try to solve this design puzzle as we move along. For now, let's take a look at how to create a CallControlCall.

Creating a CallControlCall

A CallControlCall is created the same way any type of Call is created — from an invocation of the method `Provider.createCall()`. Just because a CallControlCall is more capable than a normal Call does not necessarily complicate its construction.

Operations Allowed on a CallControlCall

Looking back, it is clear that a Call as provided in the core telephony package is rather simple indeed. Basically, all a Call can do is connect (recall that a Call relies on an associated Connection instance to perform a disconnection on its behalf). In contrast, the CallControlCall offers quite a bit more functionality, much of which is now commonplace in telephone systems, at least in the United States. This functionality includes the capability to conference other calls, to drop a call, to transfer calls, to consult calls, to add parties, and to go "off hook." Let's take each of these in order.

Conferencing

A *conference* is created when one or more calls are *moved* from their associated TerminalConnection to the TerminalConnection of another Call. In a sense, the Call that is conferenced in actually *becomes* the same Call as the target, thereby performing a kind of "kamikaze act" upon itself (for the good of the many we are assured). Each Call that is conferenced effectively turns over control of all its resources (e.g., Addresses, Terminals) to the target Call. The doomed call (more properly referred to as the "second call") must be on hold (i.e., its CallControlTerminalConnection must be in the HELD state) in order for the conference to take place. The implementation provides for merging these Calls one at a time with a method taking the second call as a parameter. At the completion of the operation, the second call is moved into the INVALID state, readying it for the garbage collector.

Here is the abstract interface that must be implemented to provide conferencing:

```
public void conference( Call otherCall )
    throws InvalidStateException, InvalidArgumentException,
        MethodNotSupportedException,
        PrivilegeViolationException,
        ResourceUnavailableException;
```

Transferring

A *transfer* is very similar to a conference except that one or two extra steps are involved. As we have just said, in a conference call, the call being merged (i.e., the "second" call) is assimilated into the Call object the operation is invoked upon. But all of the associated parties stay connected and able to communicate. Just like a conference, a transfer merges the two Calls, but it also forces the initiating TerminalConnection to die. In real world terms, this equates to exactly what happens on a call transfer. Suppose a receptionist answers a call at a business. When she transfers the call, she does not remain on the line as an active participant (at least not in most cases). Instead, she either places the caller on hold or keeps the call active, conferences the caller in and disconnects from the call.[4] In JTAPI terms, her TerminalConnection ceases to exist.

---

4   The order in which these tasks occur is an implementation detail. It is not important as long as the transfer takes place.

There are two abstract interfaces that must be implemented to provide transfer capability. Here's the first:

```
public void transfer( Call otherCall )
    throws InvalidStateException, InvalidArgumentException,
    InvalidPartyException, MethodNotSupportedException,
    PrivilegeViolationException,
    ResourceUnavailableException;
```

Note the obvious similarity here to that of a conference. Functionally, the results are exactly the same as a conference except that the initiating TerminalConnection is destroyed. In JTAPI terminology, this terminal TerminalConnection is called the *transfer controller*. All transfer controllers must be in either the TALKING or the HELD state as defined in class CallControlTerminalConnection. Here's the second method:

```
public Connection transfer( String address )
    throws InvalidArgumentException, InvalidStateException,
    InvalidPartyException, MethodNotSupportedException,
    PrivilegeViolationException,
    ResourceUnavailableException;
```

This interface method essentially overloads the previous one to allow for an additional step of placing a call. In telephony terms, this operation is known as a *single-step transfer* because it places a new call to a destination address and transfers an existing call all in one atomic operation. However, close examination reveals that the semantics are subtly different. The previous method allowed for the *second call* to join the Call object the method was invoked upon. And so an invocation might look something like this:

```
CallControlCall aCallToTransfer = someProvider.createCall();
CallControlCall aCallAllowingTransfer =
    someProvider.createCall();
aCallAllowingTransfer.transfer( aCallToTransfer );
// aCallToTransfer is now INVALID...
```

The transferer was the second call. In the second method, the transferer is the *first* call — the one the method is invoked upon. In the first case, one call object was asking another to transfer it on behalf of itself. In the second case, a call object performs the transfer itself returning a new Connection to the destination Address. Here's a sample invocation:

```
Connection conn = aCallToTransfer.transfer( "853-1212" );
if ( conn != null ) { CallControlCall newCall =
    conn.getCall(); }
```

Presumably, this new Connection should point to a Call instance and be in at least the IDLE state. If no new Connection is returned (i.e., the operation returns **null**), it is presumed that the destination address lies outside the provider's domain and can therefore no longer be traced.

Dropping a Call

Earlier you may have been disappointed in the fact that a Call could not disconnect itself — that it had to rely on a Connection instance to accomplish this task. Well now you can rest easy. Unlike a Call, a CallControlCall has the ability to destroy itself with the method called `drop()`. When a CallControlCall is dropped, it disconnects all associated connections, thereby removing all parties from the call. If more than two parties are connected and just a few want to bow out, each would instead call their respective `Connection.disconnect()` methods. As long as at least two Connections remain, the call will still be ACTIVE and able to accept additional Connections. But if any application points to an instance of a CallControlCall and issues a `drop()`, they're all toast.

The abstract interfaces that must be implemented to drop a call is:

```
public void drop()
     throws InvalidStateException,
         MethodNotSupportedException,
         PrivilegeViolationException,
         ResourceUnavailableException;
```

As you might have guessed by now, dropping a call is exactly the same as disconnecting all of the connections (and in fact may be implemented exactly in this manner).

Consultation

A *consultation* call is one that (usually briefly) allows an IDLE Call to initiate a query of another destination Address. This second Call is said to be "consulted" by the first Call (i.e., the object on which the `consult()` method is invoked). Consultation calls may be used for any purpose the underlying Provider allows for, but most often to prepare for a conference or a transfer. For example, before a conference or a transfer takes place, a consultation may be made[5] as to, say, whether or not certain parties are still on the line.

Consultation is supported by two overloaded methods. Here is the first abstract interface that must be implemented to consult a call:

---

5 Consultation calls are not required prior to a conference or a transfer.

```
public Connection[] consult( TerminalConnection tc,
                             String dialedDigits )
     throws InvalidStateException, InvalidArgumentException,
        MethodNotSupportedException,
        ResourceUnavailableException,
        PrivilegeViolationException, InvalidPartyException;
```

The TerminalConnection and the String passed as arguments are to be related in the form of a new set of Connections. The implementation invokes the `TerminalConnection.getCall()` method and then attempts to connect to the address specified by the dialedDigits String. If successful, the `consult()` method returns a new Connection pair presumably from a successful invocation of the `Call.connect()` method. A simple sample implementation is provided here:

```
public Connection[] consult( TerminalConnection tc, String
                             dialedDigits )
     throws InvalidStateException, InvalidArgumentException,
        MethodNotSupportedException,
        ResourceUnavailableException,
        PrivilegeViolationException, InvalidPartyException {

   Call secondCall = tc.getCall();
   if ( tc.getState() != Call.ACTIVE ) throw new
      InvalidStateException();
   return secondCall.connect( tc, dialedDigits );
}
```

Again, the Call instance from the parameter information returns the associated newly created Connection array. JTAPI does not explicitly specify which Connection is in what order in this array, but it would be reasonable to assume that an implementation would follow the same pattern as the `Call.connect()` method. In that case, the first Connection (i.e., `Connection[0]`) would apply to the Call/Address pair of the TerminalConnection instance and the second (i.e., `Connection[1]`) would point to the Call/Address pair of the dialedDigits String.

The second abstract interface that must be implemented to consult a call is:

```
public Connection consult( TerminalConnection tc )
     throws InvalidStateException, InvalidArgumentException,
        MethodNotSupportedException,
        ResourceUnavailableException,
        PrivilegeViolationException;
```

Although still classified as a consultation, the semantics of this overloaded interface are quite different. When this version is invoked, no Call is made. Instead, only half of the process is completed. Note that this interface returns only a single Connection instead of a pair. This Connection must be in the CallControlConnection.INITIATED state. If so, the caller is to use the returned Connection to place the call himself — presumably by invoking the `CallControlConnection.addToAddress()` method (we'll see this method shortly).

Parties

The JTAPI process of adding a party is referred to in telephony terms as a *single-step conference*. This is perhaps the highest level interface to joining calls together (i.e., conferencing) because it supports adding a destination address to a call in one easy step.

Here is the abstract interface that must be implemented to perform a single-step conference:

```
public Connection addParty( String newParty )
     throws InvalidStateException, InvalidPartyException,
            MethodNotSupportedException,
            PrivilegeViolationException,
            ResourceUnavailableException;
```

Although it is clear what is to occur, the term "newParty" used in the parameter list is a bit confusing. All it really represents is a valid Address name to place a call to — nothing more than the plain old destination address we've seen throughout. Clearly, a party is not the Address name itself. Nevertheless, that's what it says.

Going "Off-Hook"

To go "off-hook" is a popular telephony term. It means exactly what it says — that a handset is lifted off the terminal.[6] In layman's terms, it is receiving a dial tone. Once a phone device is placed in this state, a number may be dialed. All this function does is place the call model in this state.

The abstract interface that must be implemented to go off-hook is:

```
public Connection offHook( Address origaddress,
                           Terminal origterminal )
     throws InvalidStateException, MethodNotSupportedException,
        PrivilegeViolationException,
        ResourceUnavailableException;
```

---

6 Of course, there are other ways of going off-hook depending on the communications device. A portable phone requires the pressing of a button to go "off-hook."

Having obtained a thorough understanding of the JTAPI call model, the previous definition of going off-hook does not provide a satisfactory answer. Your question is "Since a connected Call is made up of at least two Connections, which Connection is the one that goes off-hook? Or do all of them go off-hook? Or are there any Connections at all at this point?" The scenario is pictured in **Figure 8.4**.

Figure 8.4 *An Originating Address Goes Off-Hook*

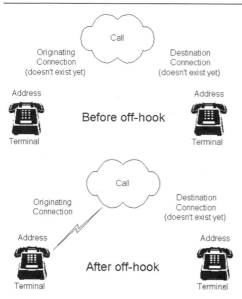

The answer to the first question is that the originating end (i.e., Terminal) of the Call is the one affected. This makes sense as the destination address may be out of the Providers' domain and therefore out of their control. Only one Terminal goes off-hook (this answers the second question). The answer to the third question is "No." There are no Connections affected because they do not yet exist! We know this because the Call is required to be in the IDLE state prior to the method invocation. Since an idle Call can only move to the ACTIVE or the INVALID state (i.e., it may not move back into an IDLE state from another state), the Call has never been connected. In short, what the off-hook method does is provide that first Connection instance by returning it from the `offHook()` invocation. This Connection is returned in the CallControlConnection.INITIATED state.

Because the `offHook()` method provides the "first leg" of a connected Call, it may be thought of as a partial implementation of the `Call.connect()` method. Indeed, that's *exactly* what it is. After the method returns, either a user can manually dial the digits or an application can invoke the `CallControlConnection.addToAddress()` method to proceed with the second leg of the call activation process — dialing.

CallControlConnection

A CallControlConnection "isa" Connection on steroids. This extension relationship is pictured in **Figure 8.5**.

Figure 8.5 *Extension Relationship Between a Connection and a CallControlConnection*

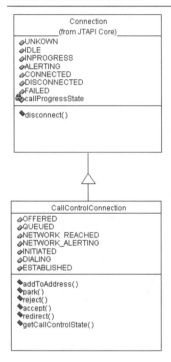

Recall that all a core Connection can do once created is `discon-nect()`. In addition to this behavior, the CallControlConnection provides functionality for accepting, rejecting, redirecting, parking, and partially dialing calls. In exactly the same way that a Connection models the state between an Address and a Call, a CallControlConnection models the state between a CallControlCall and a CallControlAddress.

Life Cycle of a CallControlConnection

The life cycle of the CallControlConnection looks like a spider's web. It includes all the possible state transitions that a Connection has plus several more. A state transition diagram for all the possible states is presented in **Figure 8.6**.

From **Figure 8.6** we can see that there are four transition paths a CallControlConnection can take. These are as follows:

Figure 8.6 *State Transitions of a CallControlConnection*

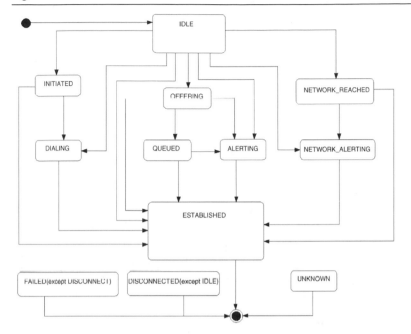

Straight Path

- IDLE → ESTABLISHED

Dial Path

- IDLE → DIALING → ESTABLISHED
- IDLE → INITIATED → ESTABLISHED
- IDLE → INITIATED → DIALING → ESTABLISHED

Queued Path

- IDLE → OFFERING → ESTABLISHED
- IDLE → ALERTING → ESTABLISHED
- IDLE → QUEUED → ALERTING → ESTABLISHED
- IDLE → OFFERING → QUEUED → ESTABLISHED
- IDLE → OFFERING → ALERTING → ESTABLISHED
- IDLE → OFFERING → QUEUED → ALERTING → ESTABLISHED

Network Path

- IDLE → NETWORK_REACHED → ESTABLISHED
- IDLE → NETWORK_ALERTING → ESTABLISHED
- IDLE → NETWORK_REACHED → NETWORK_ALERTING → ESTABLISHED

Of course, any state may move to the FAILED, UNKNOWN, or DIS-CONNECTED state from any other state except that a FAILED state cannot move to a DISCONNECTED state and an IDLE state cannot move to a DISCONNECTED state. All state movements are one way. This means that once a state is reached along a particular transition path, a CallControlConnection cannot move back to the previous state. There is only one exception — the UNKNOWN state. Other states are free to move in and out of the UNKNOWN state.

There is a well-defined relationship between the core Connection interface states and those of the CallControlConnection interface as shown in **Table 8.1**.

Table 8.1 *The Relationship Between the Connection and CallControlConnection States*

If the core connection package state is . . .	then the call control package state . . .
IDLE	Must be IDLE
INPROGRESS	May be **QUEUED** or
INPROGRESS	May be **OFFERED**
ALERTING	Must be **ALERTING**
CONNECTED	May be **INITIATED** or
CONNECTED	May be **DIALING** or
CONNECTED	May be **NETWORK_REACHED** or
CONNECTED	May be **NETWORK_ALERTING** or
CONNECTED	May be **ESTABLISHED**
DISCONNECTED	Must be DISCONNECTED
FAILED	Must be FAILED
UNKNOWN	Must be UNKNOWN

In short, the states with the same name carry the same semantics across both the core Connection and the extended CallControlConnection interfaces. Since this is so, it is not clear why new states were defined in these cases (e.g., Connection.IDLE and CallControlConnection.IDLE). It would seem that by extension this is unnecessary — but hey, that's how it is. Anyway, according to the JTAPI specification, the "new" CallControlConnection states have definitions as presented in **Table 8.2**.

Earlier, we were perplexed that a CallControlCall did not define any states beyond that of a Call. Now we can see why — the CallControlConnection defines enough to go around. Because a CallControlConnection models the Call's state anyway, one might ask why a Call even has a state.[7] In any case, no further states are required beyond the standard Call.IDLE, Call.ACTIVE, and Call.INVALID, at least at that level of abstraction.

Table 8.2 *State Definitions for a CallControlConnection*

State	JTAPI Definition
QUEUED	indicates that a Connection is queued at the particular Address associated with the Connection
OFFERED	indicates than an incoming call is being offered to the Address associated with the Connection
INITIATED	indicates the originating end of a telephone call has begun the process of placing a telephone call, but the dialing of the destination telephone address has not yet begun
DIALING	indicates the originating end of a telephone call has begun the process of dialing a destination telephone address, but has not yet completed
NETWORK_ REACHED	indicates that an outgoing telephone call has reached the network. Applications may not receive further events about this leg of the telephone call, depending upon the ability of the telephone network to provide additional progress information. Applications must decide whether to treat this as a connected telephone call
NETWORK_ ALERTING	indicates that an outgoing telephone call is alerting at the destination end, which was previously only known to have reached the network. Typically, Connections transition into this state from the `CallControlConnection.NETWORK_REACHED` state. This state results from additional progress information being sent from a telephone network that was capable of transmitting that information
ESTABLISHED	similar to `Connection.CONNECTED`, indicates that the endpoint has reached its final, active state in the telephone call

Creating a CallControlConnection

A CallControlConnection is created in the same manner that a Connection is created except that its associated Call may be a CallControlCall instead of a Call. For review, see the code in the standard `Call.connect()` method.

---

7 This rhetorical question is answered, "… because the state of a Call and that of a Connection are at different levels of abstraction."

Operations Allowed on a CallControlConnection

Whereas a core Connection can only disconnect a call, a CallControlConnection can *accept*, *reject*, *redirect,* and *park* a Call. Let's look at each of these in turn.

Accepting a Call

When an incoming CallControlCall is offered to the CallControlAddress associated with a CallControlConnection, that CallControlCall will be accepted when the application invokes the `CallControlConnection.accept()` method. Here's the method signature:

```
public abstract void accept()
    throws InvalidStateException, MethodNotSupportedException,
        PrivilegeViolationException, ResourceUnavailableException
```

What this does is alter the state of the CallControlConnection to that of ALERTING. It will remain in that state until someone answers the phone or the telephony subsystem times out, ultimately forcing a disconnect.

Rejecting a Call

When a Call is rejected by a CallControlConnection, the CallControlConnection immediately moves into the state of DISCONNECTED, never alerting the destination Address with the Call. In short, the Call is DOA (dead on arrival). Here's the public signature:

```
public abstract void reject()
    throws InvalidStateException, MethodNotSupportedException,
        PrivilegeViolationException,
        ResourceUnavailableException
```

Redirecting a Call

A call may be redirected by a CallControlConnection to another Address when the CallControlConnection is in either the OFFERED or the ALERTING state. The CallControlConnection effectively performs a transfer of the Call from its original destination to a new destination *before* the Connection is in the CONNECTED state and the Call is in the ACTIVE state. Here's the public signature:

```
public abstract Connection
    redirect( String destinationAddress )
        throws InvalidStateException, InvalidPartyException,
            MethodNotSupportedException,
            PrivilegeViolationException,
            ResourceUnavailableException
```

The method invocation returns a new Connection between the originating Call and the new destination Address.

Parking a Call

A *parked call* is one that is waiting to be processed. To enter this state, the Connection must first be in the CallControlConnection.ESTABLISHED state. Here's the public signature:

```
public abstract Connection
    park( String destinationAddress )
        throws InvalidStateException, MethodNotSupportedException,
            PrivilegeViolationException, InvalidPartyException,
            ResourceUnavailableException
```

When a call is parked, it is similar to a transfer and a redirect except that the new Connection returned is in a different state — specifically the CallControlConnection.QUEUED state. A parked call can be "unparked" only with an invocation of the `CallControlTerminal.pickup()` method. Let's take a look at this animal.

CallControlTerminal

The CallControlTerminal is an extension to the core Terminal interface (see **Figure 8.7**).

Figure 8.7 *Extension Relationship Between a Terminal and a CallControlTerminalConnection*

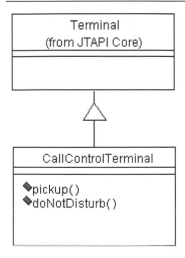

Life Cycle of a CallControlTerminal

Just like a core Terminal, the life cycle of a CallControlTerminal is determined by the Provider that creates it. It really has no state of its own; this state is modeled by the associated CallControlTerminalConnection.

Creating a CallControlTerminal

A CallControlTerminal is created by a Provider in the same manner in which a core Terminal is. In other words, they already "exist," having been either created by a Provider or pointed to by an Address.

Operations Allowed on a CallControlTerminal

The primary additional characteristics offered beyond those of a core Terminal are that a CallControlTerminal can pick up calls and can put up a "do not disturb" sign.

Picking Up a Call

To pick up a call is to either "unpark" a parked call or to answer a Call, which is alerting a different Address than the one with which this CallControlTerminal is normally associated. There are five different function signatures that support call pickups as follows:

```
public abstract TerminalConnection
    pickup( Connection pickupConnection,
            Address terminalAddress )
        throws InvalidArgumentException, InvalidStateException,
            MethodNotSupportedException,
            PrivilegeViolationException,
            ResourceUnavailableException


public abstract TerminalConnection
    pickup( TerminalConnection pickTermConn,
            Address terminalAddress )
        throws InvalidArgumentException, InvalidStateException,
            MethodNotSupportedException,
            PrivilegeViolationException,
            ResourceUnavailableException


public abstract TerminalConnection
    pickup( Address pickupAddress, Address terminalAddress )
        throws InvalidArgumentException, InvalidStateException,
            MethodNotSupportedException,
            PrivilegeViolationException,
            ResourceUnavailableException
```

```
public abstract TerminalConnection
    pickupFromGroup( String pickupGroup,
                    Address terminalAddress )
        throws InvalidArgumentException, InvalidStateException,
            MethodNotSupportedException,
            PrivilegeViolationException,
            ResourceUnavailableException

public abstract TerminalConnection
    pickupFromGroup( Address terminalAddress )
        throws InvalidArgumentException, InvalidStateException,
            MethodNotSupportedException,
            PrivilegeViolationException,
            ResourceUnavailableException
```

As you can see, various combinations of information can be used to retrieve the TerminalConnection instance on which the call will be picked up. This TerminalConnection will be in the CallControlTerminalConnection.TALKING state. All Connections passed in must be in either the CallControlConnection.QUEUED state or the CallControlConnection.ALERTING state. If the Connection is *not* associated with the Address passed in, that Connection is disconnected and a new Connection instance is returned instead. If it is, the same Connection is used. In either case, when the function returns, the Connection is in the CallControlConnection.ESTABLISHED state. Various events are also delivered as a result of a successful invocation, including those signaling the creation of the TerminalConnection returned and those indicating the state changes of Connection involved.

Two of these methods reference a *pickup group*. The pickup group is a code that allows the telephony subsystem to choose which Connection to use rather than the programmer explicitly specifying it as a parameter. This way, the endpoints of the call can be managed by the administration policy of the Provider.

Do Not Disturb

A CallControlTerminal can refuse to take calls when it returns the value true from the `getDoNotDisturb()` method. A boolean instance variable controls this state and can be set by calling the `setDoNotDisturb()` method. The API is as follows:

```
public abstract boolean getDoNotDisturb()
    throws MethodNotSupportedException

public abstract void setDoNotDisturb( boolean enable )
    throws MethodNotSupportedException, InvalidStateException
```

CallControlTerminalConnection

The pattern continues. Just as a CallControlCall specializes the Call interface, a CallControlTerminalConnection specializes a TerminalConnection (see **Figure 8.8**).

Figure 8.8 *The CallControlTerminalConnection Specializes the Core TerminalConnection*

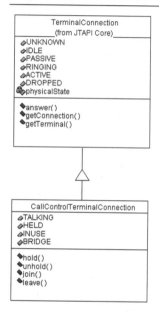

Life Cycle of a CallControlTerminalConnection

Like a TerminalConnection, a CallControlTerminalConnection is a state-laden object. In fact, it exists for the sole purpose of modeling the state between a Terminal and a Connection only at a more specialized level. The state transitions are modeled in **Figure 8.9**.

Figure 8.9 *State Transitions of a CallControlTerminalConnection*

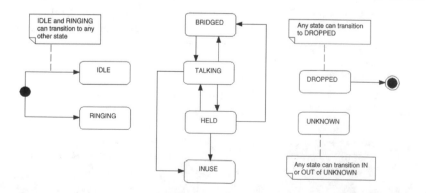

From **Figure 8.9** we can see that there are a multitude of combinations of state transitions that are possible for a given CallControlTerminalConnection life cycle. In terms of the core package TerminalConnection, there is a core-to-call control state relationship just as there is among Connections (see **Table 8.3**).

Table 8.3 *State Relationship Between TerminalConnections and CallControlTerminalConnections*

If the core terminal connection package state is . . .	then the call control terminal package state . . .
IDLE	Must be IDLE
RINGING	Must be RINGING
ACTIVE	May be **TALKING** or
ACTIVE	May be **HELD**
PASSIVE	May be **BRIDGED** or
PASSIVE	May be **INUSE**
DROPPED	Must be DROPPED
UNKNOWN	Must be UNKNOWN

According to the JTAPI specification, the CallControlTerminalConnection states above and beyond those in the core package (for a TerminalConnection) have definitions as presented in **Table 8.4**. These fall into two categories with respect to the core package: ACTIVE (TALKING or HELD) and PASSIVE (BRIDGED or INUSE).

Table 8.4 *Extended CallControlTerminalConnection States*

State	JTAPI Definition
HELD	indicates that a Terminal is part of a Call, but is on hold. Other Terminals which are on the same Call and associated with the same Connection may or may not also be in this state.
BRIDGED	indicates that a Terminal is currently bridged into a Call. A Terminal may typically join a telephone call when it is bridged. A bridged Terminal is part of the telephone call, but not active. Typically, some hardware resource is occupied while a Terminal is bridged into a Call.
INUSE	indicates that a Terminal is part of a Call, but is not active. It may not Call, however, the resource on the Terminal is currently in use. This state is similar to the CallControlTerminalConnection.BRIDGED state, however, the Terminal may not join the Call.
TALKING	indicates that a Terminal is part of a Call. Implies that a Terminal is talking as opposed to being held.

Creating a CallControlTerminalConnection

Like the core TerminalConnection, a CallControlTerminalConnection can only be created as the result of a Connection (or a CallControlConnection) being established.

Operations Allowed on a CallControlTerminalConnection

Recall that the core TerminalConnection object's primary functionality was to `answer()` calls. A CallControlTerminalConnection is a specialized version extending "call answering" capabilities to include the ability to place calls on and off *hold* and to *join* or *leave* an active call (thereby entering or leaving the BRIDGED state). Let's examine each of these operations separately.

Placing a Call on or off Hold

In order to place a call on hold, one must invoke its CallControlTerminalConnection's `hold()` method. Conversely, a call is taken off hold by invoking `CallControlTerminal-Connection.unhold()`. Here's the API:

```
public abstract void hold()
    throws InvalidStateException, MethodNotSupportedException,
          PrivilegeViolationException,
          ResourceUnavailableException
```

```
public abstract void unhold()
    throws InvalidStateException, MethodNotSupportedException,
          PrivilegeViolationException,
          ResourceUnavailableException
```

Joining and Leaving a Call

When a CallControlTerminalConnection *joins* an active call, it leaves the passive BRIDGED state and transitions to an active state (either TALKING or HELD). This passive CallControlTerminalConnection must be in the BRIDGED state — it cannot join a Call if the state is INUSE. When *leaving* a Call, a CallControlTerminalConnection transitions (possibly back) into the BRIDGED state. So when you join a call, you leave a bridge and vice versa. Here is the API:

```
public abstract void join()
    throws InvalidStateException, MethodNotSupportedException,
          PrivilegeViolationException,
          ResourceUnavailableException
```

```
public abstract void leave()
    throws InvalidStateException, MethodNotSupportedException,
        PrivilegeViolationException,
        ResourceUnavailableException
```

These are all the classes that we expect a JTAPI library to implement for us if they implement the Call Control package. What remain are the Call Control Observer interfaces, which may or may not be implemented by the vendor, depending on the approach they take.

The Call Control Observer Interfaces

Recall that we implemented the core observer interfaces in Chapter 7, "Application Programming with JTAPI." There we learned that all observer interfaces exist for the sole purpose of receiving events from the JTAPI run-time. When these events are received, the application can be assured that the call model is in a particular state. All events are sent to one of four event handlers defined in one of the four observer interfaces (AddressObserver, CallObserver, TerminalObserver, and ProviderObserver). This is the way the core observer interfaces work. It is also the manner in which the Call Control observer interfaces work, except that there is no extended call control interface for the ProviderObserver (because none is needed).

Observer classes are in the application programmer's domain even though they are part of JTAPI. Just as the core packages contain observers for Addresses, Calls, and Terminals, so does the Call Control package. Therefore, the Call Control package provides three extended interfaces:

- CallControlAddressObserver, which extends AddressObserver
- CallControlCallObserver, which extends CallObserver
- CallControlTerminalObserver, which extends TerminalObserver

In terms of events, the only difference is in the kinds of events that each package generates and each observer is therefore able to respond to. The core package generates core events (e.g., CallActiveEv) and the Call Control package generates call control events (e.g., CallCtlConnNetworkAlertingEv).

Interestingly, no new methods are added to these extended observers — only event definitions they are expected to respond to. In other words, *by extension* the CallControlCallObserver has a `callChangedEvent(` CallEv) method just like a CallObserver. Presumably this method is overridden to allow for the processing of Call Control events and `super()` is called from within it to ensure that the super-class functionality exists. Although there's not a lot of new conceptual material to cover, let's look at each of these observers in turn.

CallControlAddressObserver

Let's take a look at the CallControlAddressObserver interface:

```
package javax.telephony.callcontrol;
import   javax.telephony.AddressObserver;


public interface CallControlAddressObserver
   extends AddressObserver { }
```

What? That's it? Well, we did say that no new methods were defined —
but of what possible use is an interface that extends another yet provides no
new methods or even constants? Let's see if we can figure this out.

The JTAPI specification says that the three extended observer interfaces
in the Call Control package are in place to "allow applications to signal to
the implementation that they are interested in call control package events."
What does that mean? Well it seems that these kinds of interfaces are what
the Java language specification calls *marker interfaces.*[8] They are defined
in order to partition the namespace for a particular design or implementation policy. The implementation can identify a marker interface by simply
applying the **instanceof** operator to an object. Examples of this principle in
the Java language specification may be found in the interfaces
java.lang.Cloneable and java.io.Serializable.

CallControlCallObserver

The CallControlCallObserver is another marker interface specified like
this:

```
package javax.telephony.callcontrol;
import javax.telephony.CallObserver;
public interface CallControlCallObserver
   extends CallObserver { }
```

Again, there's not much going on here. The marker interface technique
may be of some use depending on how the notification mechanism is
implemented, but it is unnecessary using the approach we took in Chapter
7. In our case, we might implement the CallControlCallObserver interface
as in **Listing 8.5**.

---

8 Marker interfaces are similar in functionality to what OO programmers are used to seeing
   in *partition classes*. A partition class is essentially an empty class that partitions the namespace in a particular hierarchy for classification purposes only. For example, we might have
   some classes inherit from a class BusinessObject, which provides no additional data or
   methods; yet we wish to classify the problem space so that objects may be categorized in
   this manner.

Listing 8.5 *Implementing the callChangedEvent Method of CallControlCallObserver*

```
synchronized public void callChangedEvent( CallEv[] eventList ) {

    super();

    .

    .

    .

    // add for Call Control Support...
    if ( isCallListener && eventList[i] instanceof CallCtlCallEv )
{
        try {
            Call call = ((CallEv)eventList[i]).getCall();
            Connection[] conns = call.getConnections();
            Provider prov = call.getProvider();
            name = prov.getName();
            msg = "Provider named: (" + name
                + ") owns a Call Control Connection that is —>> ";
            if ( eventList[i].getID() == CallCtlConnOfferedEv.ID ) {
                System.out.println(msg + "OFFERED");            }
            else if ( eventList[i].getID() ==
                    CallCtlConnQueuedEv.ID ) {
                System.out.println(msg + "QUEUED");            }
        } catch ( Exception excp ) {
                System.out.println( "CallEv Exception occurred in
                SDRCallObserver::callChangedEvent()...");
                excp.printStackTrace();
        }
    }
}
```

Note that here we are testing class identity on the *event*, not the observer. Because our notification class calls the method `callChangedEvent()`, which is defined on the parent interface CallObserver (and not CallControlCallObserver), the marker interface is of no use to us. Anyway, let's check out the last observer.

CallControlTerminalObserver

Surprise! Another marker interface:

```
package javax.telephony.callcontrol;
import javax.telephony.TerminalObserver;
```

```
public interface CallControlTerminalObserver
    extends TerminalObserver { }
```

Okay, you get the point. Let's move on to the closely related events of the call control package.

Call Control Events

The call control package defines several new events as depicted in **Figure 8.10**.

Figure 8.10 *Call Control Events*

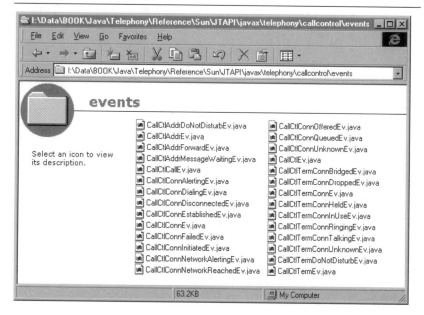

It should be obvious by now that these events correspond directly to the valid states of the relevant call model business objects. For example, you should be able to look at **Figure 8.10** and deduce the fact that the CallCtlTermConnTalkingEv event is generated by a CallControlTerminalConnection when it transitions to the TALKING state. Further, you should know that this event is sent to a CallControlCallObserver because CallObservers receive all events from Calls, Connections, and TerminalConnections of all kinds.

Events are closely related to observers — so much so that they almost have no meaning without each other. Recall that every observer has a list of valid events it is to report on. The following list provides a summary of this information.

CallControlAddressObserver

- CallCtlAddrEv
- CallCtlAddrDoNotDisturbEv
- CallCtlAddrForwardEv
- CallCtlAddrMessageWaitingEv

CallControlCallObserver

- CallCtlCallEv
- CallCtlConnEv
- CallCtlConnAlertingEv
- CallCtlConnDialingEv
- CallCtlConnDisconnectedEv
- CallCtlConnEstablishedEv
- CallCtlConnFailedEv
- CallCtlConnInitiatedEv
- CallCtlConnNetworkAlertingEv
- CallCtlConnNetworkReachedEv
- CallCtlConnOfferedEv
- CallCtlConnQueuedEv
- CallCtlConnUnknownEv
- CallCtlTermConnEv
- CallCtlTermConnRingingEv
- CallCtlTermConnTalkingEv
- CallCtlTermConnHeldEv
- CallCtlTermConnBridgedEv
- CallCtlTermConnInUseEv
- CallCtlTermConnDroppedEv
- CallCtlTermConnUnknownEv

CallControlTerminalObserver

- CallCtlTermEv
- CallCtlTermDoNotDisturbEv

We do not show the actual interfaces for every event (as this makes for extremely boring reading). Please refer to the interface code for reference.

Call Control Capabilities

Just as the core package has an associated *capabilities* subpackage, so does the call control package. The contents of this package are shown in **Figure 8.11**.

Figure 8.11 *Call Control Capabilities*

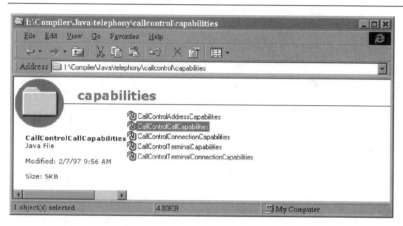

The capabilities interfaces perform the same function in the call control package as they do in the core package. Following are the interface definitions for each of these in turn.

CallControlAddressCapabilities

```
package javax.telephony.callcontrol.capabilities;
import  javax.telephony.capabilities.AddressCapabilities;

public interface CallControlAddressCapabilities
    extends AddressCapabilities {

  public boolean canSetForwarding();
  public boolean canGetForwarding();
  public boolean canCancelForwarding();
  public boolean canGetDoNotDisturb();
  public boolean canSetDoNotDisturb();
  public boolean canGetMessageWaiting();
  public boolean canSetMessageWaiting();
}
```

CallControlCallCapabilities

```
package javax.telephony.callcontrol.capabilities;
import  javax.telephony.*;
import  javax.telephony.capabilities.CallCapabilities;
```

```java
public interface CallControlCallCapabilities
  extends CallCapabilities {

  public boolean canDrop();
  public boolean canOffHook();
  public boolean canSetConferenceController();
  public boolean canSetTransferController();
  public boolean canSetTransferEnable();
  public boolean canSetConferenceEnable();
  public boolean canTransfer(Call call);
  public boolean canTransfer(String destination);
  public boolean canConference();
  public boolean canAddParty();
  public boolean canConsult(TerminalConnection tc,
    String destination);
  public boolean canConsult(TerminalConnection tc);
}
```

CallControlConnectionCapabilities

```java
package javax.telephony.callcontrol.capabilities;
import  javax.telephony.capabilities.ConnectionCapabilities;

public interface CallControlConnectionCapabilities
  extends ConnectionCapabilities {

  public boolean canRedirect();
  public boolean canAddToAddress();
  public boolean canAccept();
  public boolean canReject();
  public boolean canPark();
}
```

CallControlTerminalCapabilities

```java
package javax.telephony.callcontrol.capabilities;
import  javax.telephony.*;
import  javax.telephony.capabilities.TerminalCapabilities;

public interface CallControlTerminalCapabilities
  extends TerminalCapabilities {

  public boolean canGetDoNotDisturb();
  public boolean canSetDoNotDisturb();
  public boolean canPickup();
  public boolean canPickup(Connection connection,
    Address address);
```

```
public boolean canPickup(TerminalConnection tc,
    Address address);
public boolean canPickup(Address address1, Address address2);
public boolean canPickupFromGroup();
public boolean canPickupFromGroup(String group,
    Address address);
public boolean canPickupFromGroup(Address address);
}
```

CallControlTerminalConnectionCapabilities

```
package javax.telephony.callcontrol.capabilities;
import
    javax.telephony.capabilities.TerminalConnectionCapabilities;

public interface CallControlTerminalConnectionCapabilities
    extends TerminalConnectionCapabilities {

    public boolean canHold();
    public boolean canUnhold();
    public boolean canJoin();
    public boolean canLeave();
}
```

Phone Packages

The Phone extension packages are `javax.telephony.phone`, `javax.telephony.phone.capabilities`, and `javax.telephony.phone.events`. These packages are referred to simply as the *phone packages*.

Phone Core Components

The Phone Core Components are depicted in **Figure 8.12**. Note the hardware-centric nature of the objects and their relationship to the physical core component of the core telephony package — the Terminal interface.

Unlike the Call Control package extensions, most of these components are *not* extensions of the core interfaces (because there's nothing similar to extend!). The only exceptions are the PhoneTerminalObserver interface, which extends the TerminalObserver interface in the core package, and the PhoneTerminal interface, which likewise extends the core Terminal interface. Let's start with the only observer in this package, PhoneTerminalObserver.

Figure 8.12 *Phone Components*

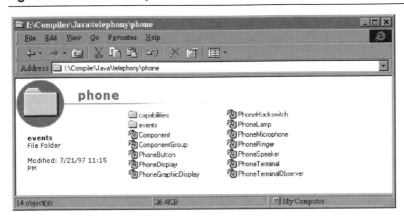

PhoneTerminalObserver

The PhoneTerminalObserver interface is used just like all our other observer interfaces. In this case, it accepts all events for the entire `javax.telephony.phone` package. Like the non–core observers before it, it is also a marker interface:

```
package javax.telephony.phone;
import  javax.telephony.TerminalObserver;
public interface PhoneTerminalObserver
  extends TerminalObserver { }
```

Again, a JTAPI implementation is required to implement this interface if it is providing the phone package. In order to receive events, either the implementation or the JTAPI application programmer must override the `terminalChangedEvent()` method of the Terminal interface in order to properly receive phone events (refer back to **Listing 8.5** for an example of how to do this).

Component

Each type of hardware in the phone package extends the Component interface. This includes the PhoneButton, PhoneDisplay, PhoneGraphicDisplay, PhoneHookswitch, PhoneLamp, PhoneMicrophone, PhoneRinger, and the PhoneSpeaker interfaces. Here's the common parent interface:

```
package javax.telephony.phone;
import  javax.telephony.*;
import  javax.telephony.phone.capabilities.*;
```

```
public interface Component {

  public String getName();
  public ComponentCapabilities getCapabilities();
}
```

Each component is typed by extension and uniquely identified within a class type by a presumably unique name. In addition, the dynamic capabilities are returned for each type. Why this same extension approach was not used in the core telephony package is not clear.[9]

ComponentGroup

A ComponentGroup is simply a grouping of Component objects. A Terminal may optionally be composed of ComponentGroups. Applications query the PhoneTerminal interface for the available ComponentGroups. Once they have a group, this interface is used to determine which components are in the group. Here's the interface:

```
package javax.telephony.phone;
import   javax.telephony.*;
import   javax.telephony.phone.capabilities.*;

public interface ComponentGroup {

    // component group types...
    public final static int HEAD_SET = 1;
    public final static int HAND_SET = 2;
    public final static int SPEAKER_PHONE = 3;
    public final static int PHONE_SET = 4;
    public final static int OTHER = 5;

    public int getType();
    public String getDescription();
    public Component[] getComponents();

    public boolean activate();
    public boolean deactivate();
    public boolean activate( Address address )
       throws InvalidArgumentException;
    public boolean deactivate( Address address )
       throws InvalidArgumentException;
    public ComponentGroupCapabilities getCapabilities();
}
```

---

9 Specifically, many of the core business objects (e.g., Address, Terminal) carry a name, and all of them require the same ability to return information about dynamic capabilities.

The ComponentGroup interface defines a few component types (e.g., HEAD_SET). These definitions might be considered a little awkward in that they use **int** types instead of extension like the other phone components do. In other words, there is an obvious benefit to classifying component groups by type, but why not let vendor implementations simply extend this interface to accomplish this? Using this approach we would expect an interface called HeadSetComponentGroup that extended the ComponentGroup interface. Instead we are presented with an incomplete list of possible component group types as **int**s. Of course, this does not prevent extension, but it makes it a little ugly. It seems as though the encouraged approach is to instead extend the interface and add new **int** types.

The only other interesting feature of this interface is the activation and deactivation functionality. What this allows for is the enabling and disabling of events or media streams between all the components in a component group. We'll learn more about media streams when we visit the media package later in this chapter. Let's look at the only other core extension interface, PhoneTerminal.

PhoneTerminal

```
package javax.telephony.phone;
import   javax.telephony.*;

public interface PhoneTerminal extends Terminal {

    public ComponentGroup[] getComponentGroups();
}
```

Although this interface extends the core Terminal interface, all it really allows for is the return of the component groups associated with this Terminal. All the remaining interfaces are extensions of the Component interface.

PhoneButton

```
package javax.telephony.phone;
import   javax.telephony.*;

public interface PhoneButton extends Component {

    public String getInfo();
    public void setInfo( String buttonInfo );
    public PhoneLamp getAssociatedPhoneLamp();
    public void buttonPress();
}
```

PhoneDisplay

```
package javax.telephony.phone;
import  javax.telephony.*;


public interface PhoneDisplay extends Component {

   public int getDisplayRows();
   public int getDisplayColumns();
   public String getDisplay( int x, int y )
      throws InvalidArgumentException;
   public void setDisplay( String string, int x, int y )
      throws InvalidArgumentException;
}
```

PhoneGraphicDisplay

```
package javax.telephony.phone;
import  javax.telephony.phone.Component;
import  javax.telephony.PlatformException;
import  java.awt.Graphics;
import  java.awt.Dimension;


public interface PhoneGraphicDisplay extends Component {

   public Graphics getGraphics();
   public Dimension size();
}
```

PhoneHookswitch

```
package javax.telephony.phone;
import  javax.telephony.*;


public interface PhoneHookswitch extends Component {

   public static final int ON_HOOK = 0;
   public static final int OFF_HOOK = 1;

   public void setHookSwitch( int hookSwitchState )
      throws InvalidArgumentException;
   public int getHookSwitchState();
}
```

PhoneLamp

```
package javax.telephony.phone;
import   javax.telephony.*;


public interface PhoneLamp extends Component {

   public static final int LAMPMODE_OFF          = 0x0;
   public static final int LAMPMODE_FLASH        = 0x1;
   public static final int LAMPMODE_STEADY       = 0x2;
   public static final int LAMPMODE_FLUTTER      = 0x3;
   public static final int LAMPMODE_BROKENFLUTTER = 0x4;
   public static final int LAMPMODE_WINK         = 0x5;

   public int[] getSupportedModes();
   public void setMode( int mode )
      throws InvalidArgumentException;
   public int getMode();
   public PhoneButton getAssociatedPhoneButton();
}
```

PhoneMicrophone

```
package javax.telephony.phone;
import   javax.telephony.*;

public interface PhoneMicrophone extends Component {

   public static final int MUTE = 0;
   public static final int MID = 50;
   public static final int FULL = 100;

   public int getGain();
   public void setGain( int gain )
      throws InvalidArgumentException;
}
```

PhoneRinger

```
package javax.telephony.phone;
import   javax.telephony.*;

public interface PhoneRinger extends Component {

   public static final int OFF  = 0;
   public static final int MIDDLE  = 50;
   public static final int FULL = 100;
```

```
public int isRingerOn();
public int getRingerVolume();
public void setRingerVolume( int volume )
   throws InvalidArgumentException;
public int getRingerPattern();
public int getNumberOfRingPatterns();
public void setRingerPattern( int ringerPattern)
   throws InvalidArgumentException;
public int getNumberOfRings();
}
```

PhoneSpeaker

```
package javax.telephony.phone;
import   javax.telephony.*;

public interface PhoneSpeaker extends Component {

   public static final int MUTE = 0;
   public static final int MID = 50;
   public static final int FULL = 100;

   public int getVolume();
   public void setVolume( int volume );
}
```

Aside from our type-versus-extension comments about ComponentGroups, we have a few more things to say about the design of the phone interfaces.[10] First of all, these interfaces make poor use of extension. Specifically, many of these Components return a state value that is represented as an int. Since this functionality is the same for most if not all Components, why not just have a method on the Component interface called `getState()` (and a corresponding `setState( int )`) that accomplishes this?[11] Instead, we are presented with different method *names* that essentially do the same thing. What's the big deal? Well, this lack of commonality reduces the opportunity to perform *polymorphic processing*[12] on all Components. This is *not* what OO is all about.

---

10 If you respect well-crafted OO designs, you too should be squirming in your seat about now!

11 The same can be said of many of the core package interfaces as well.

12 Specifically, if we can write server code that calls the `getState()` method for all components, a lot of switch code can be eliminated that first determines the instance type, then calls the correct method. Polymorphic processing not only increases the maintainability of the code by reducing code and properly delegating common functionality, it increases *performance* because fewer instructions are required (due to the reduced number of switch statements).

Second, there are several interfaces (e.g., PhoneSpeaker, PhoneRinger, and PhoneMicrophone) that encapsulate identical functionality with respect to processing volume. Again, proper use of extension would factor this behavior out into a parent (or simply a plain) interface, say, VolumeControl as in **Listing 8.6**.

Listing 8.6 *An Alternative Approach to Specifying Volume Functionality*

```
package javax.telephony.phone;

public interface VolumeControl {

   public int getVolume();
   public void setVolume( int volume )
      throws InvalidArgumentException;
}
```

Each Component would then implement this interface (or inherit from the parent implementation) as required. For example, the PhoneRinger interface might then look like this:

```
package javax.telephony.phone;
import  javax.telephony.*;

public interface PhoneRinger extends Component
   implements VolumeControl {

   public static final int OFF  = 0;
   public static final int MIDDLE  = 50;
   public static final int FULL = 100;

   public int isRingerOn();
   public int getVolume();
   public void setVolume( int volume )
      throws InvalidArgumentException;
   public int getRingerPattern();
   public int getNumberOfRingPatterns();
   public void setRingerPattern(int ringerPattern)
      throws InvalidArgumentException;
   public int getNumberOfRings();
}
```

Of course the tradeoff is in the name. Programmers would have to refer to "microphone gain" and "ringer volume" as simply "volume." But in reality, they really are the same things. So we might argue that the tradeoff of polymorphic processing for accurate naming is worth the cost, at least in this case. But we can also have it *both ways*! This can be accomplished by factoring out the interface as we have and leaving the original method names alone as *convenience methods.*[13] That way, the *application* can make the determination as to which API is more suitable to their needs. A sample implementation of this technique is provided in **Listing 8.7**.

Listing 8.7 *Using Interfaces to Factor Out Common Behavior*

```
package javax.telephony.phone;

public class OurVolumeControl implements VolumeControl {

    private int volume_;

    public int getVolume( return volume_; );
    public void setVolume( int volume )
       throws InvalidArgumentException {
       volume_ = volume;
    }
}


package javax.telephony.phone;
import   javax.telephony.*;

public class MyPhoneRinger implements PhoneRinger {

    // implement other methods...

    // helper class...
    private VolumeControl v_;

    public int getRingerVolume() { return v_.getVolume(); }
    public void setRingerVolume( int volume )
       throws InvalidArgumentException
              { v_.setVolume( volume ); }
}
```

An important point to understand here is that it is not *necessarily* the actual specification of the VolumeControl interface that potentially saves the day here. (After all, OO languages have gotten along for years implementing polymorphism without the aid of interfaces.) All that is really nec-

---

13 Presumably, the implementation would implement the common interface (e.g., VolumeControl) and then use these atomic methods in the implementation of the convenience method (e.g., getRingerVolume).

essary is that all operations that do basically the same thing use the same name (i.e., `getVolume()` and `setVolume()`).

Okay, it's capability time again!

Phone Capabilities

Just as the core package and the call control package have an associated *capabilities* subpackage, so does the phone package. The contents of this package are shown in **Figure 8.13**.

Figure 8.13 *Phone Capabilities*

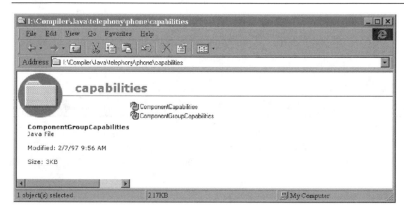

Here are the interfaces:

ComponentCapabilities

```
package javax.telephony.phone.capabilities;

public interface ComponentCapabilities {

    public boolean canControl();
}
```

ComponentGroupCapabilities

```
package javax.telephony.phone.capabilities;
import   javax.telephony.Address;

public interface ComponentGroupCapabilities {

    public boolean canActivate();
    public boolean canActivate( Address address );
}
```

Phone Events

The phone package events are listed in **Figure 8.14**.

Figure 8.14 *Phone Events*

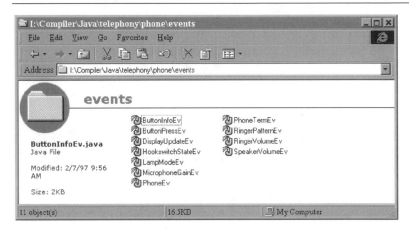

All phone events are required to extend both the PhoneEv and the TermEv interface through the PhoneTermEv interface. This enables them to be first identified as phone events and second to be processed by a PhoneTerminalObserver.

PhoneTerminalObserver

- PhoneEv
- PhoneTermEv
- ButtonInfoEv
- ButtonPressEv
- DisplayUpdateEv
- HookswitchStateEv
- LampModeEv
- MicrophoneGainEv
- RingerPatternEv
- RingerVolumeEv
- SpeakerVolumeEv

Not to belabor a point, but we find some of the same design problems here as we did in the call control package (and for that matter, the core telephony package as well). We see more missed opportunity for polymorphic processing as a result of improper extension policies only this time with events.[14]

Media Packages

The telephony Media package is a subset interface to the core level Media APIs provided by Java Speech, JMF, and Java Collaboration. The media interface is intended to support all of the various types of media present in telephony applications such as fax, voice, video, etc.

Media Core Components

The Media Core Components are depicted in **Figure 8.15**. There are two interfaces provided: MediaCallObserver and MediaTerminalConnection. Why do you suppose only the core telephony components of Call and TerminalConnection are involved? Why not between a Call and a Connection (i.e., Why the physical abstraction and not the logical one)?

Figure 8.15 *Media Core Components*

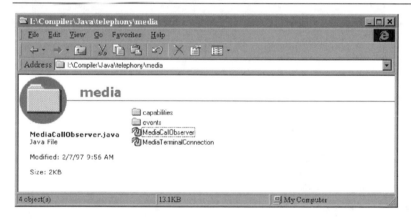

With a little deduction this relationship makes sense. First, a Connection is between a Call and an Address. Since an Address may be present on multiple Terminals, which one is it? We can only tell by identifying the specific telephone device (Terminal) that has the ability to physically answer and disconnect the call (i.e., the Terminal holding the Address that is actually connected to the call). Media is only relevant as it relates to a specific call to a specific terminal connection. The terminal is the physical device sending and receiving data and so is the only place in the model where actual signals can be captured.

---

14 Specifically, every event has an ID to get and set as well as the potential to retain cause codes and meta codes.

Media such as voice and data are passed as streams over a terminal connection. Since the TerminalConnection monitors the state of the Call-to-Terminal relationship, that is the lowest level of abstraction able to generate events that a MediaCallObserver may register for and respond to. This design also allows for each MediaTerminalConnection to have its own media stream. Let's take a look at each of these interfaces individually.

MediaTerminalConnection

The MediaTerminalConnection interface extends the TerminalConnection interface. A MediaTerminalConnection is essentially a specialized TerminalConnection with added media playing and recording capabilities. This extension relationship is modeled in **Figure 8.16**.

Figure 8.16 *A MediaTerminalConnection "isa" TerminalConnection*

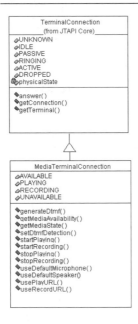

Life Cycle of a MediaTerminalConnection

Basically a MediaTerminalConnection can move from any state to any other state (see **Figure 8.17**).

In fact, a MediaTerminalConnection may be in two states simultaneously! The fact that both RECORDING and PLAYING state transitions generate the same event may seem odd at first. However, media may be being played and recorded at the same time (hopefully in different threads!). This is indicated by the *bitmask* value returned from the `getMediaState()` method. As usual, events are generated upon completion of state transition.

Figure 8.17 *MediaTerminalConnection State Transition Diagram*

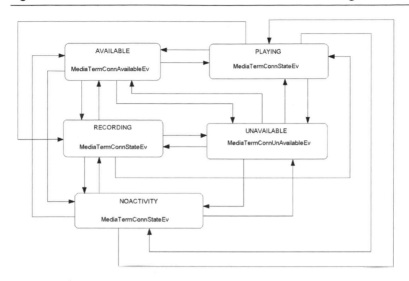

Operations Allowed on a MediaTerminalConnection

In addition to the operations provided by the base class TerminalConnection, MediaTerminalConnection objects can play audio files and record audio signals for output to either the default system microphone or to a file. Playing includes *starting, stopping,* and *rewinding.* In addition the interface supports DTMF *tone detection.* Here's the interface:

```
package javax.telephony.media;
import  javax.telephony.*;
import  java.net.URL;

public interface MediaTerminalConnection
  extends TerminalConnection {

  public static final int AVAILABLE = 0x80;
  public static final int UNAVAILABLE = 0x81;
  public static final int PLAYING = 0x01;
  public static final int RECORDING = 0x02;
  public static final int NOACTIVITY = 0x0;
  public int getMediaAvailability();
  public int getMediaState();

  public void useDefaultSpeaker()
    throws PrivilegeViolationException,
      ResourceUnavailableException,
      MethodNotSupportedException;
```

```
public void useRecordURL( URL url )
  throws PrivilegeViolationException,
    ResourceUnavailableException,
    MethodNotSupportedException;

public void useDefaultMicrophone()
  throws PrivilegeViolationException,
    ResourceUnavailableException,
    MethodNotSupportedException;

public void usePlayURL(URL url)
  throws PrivilegeViolationException,
    ResourceUnavailableException,
    MethodNotSupportedException;

public void startPlaying()
  throws MethodNotSupportedException,
    ResourceUnavailableException,
    InvalidStateException;

public void stopPlaying();

public void startRecording()
  throws MethodNotSupportedException,
    ResourceUnavailableException,
    InvalidStateException;

public void stopRecording();

public void setDtmfDetection( boolean enable )
  throws MethodNotSupportedException,
    ResourceUnavailableException,
    InvalidStateException;

public void generateDtmf( String digits )
  throws MethodNotSupportedException,
    ResourceUnavailableException,
    InvalidStateException;
}
```

Now for the final interface in the media package, MediaCallObserver.

MediaCallObserver

The MediaCallObserver extends the appropriate observer interface, as any good observer does. In this case, it is the core CallObserver interface.

Again, this enables the delivery of events to a MediaCallObserver by way of the extended `callChangedEvent()` method. Here's the beef:

```
package javax.telephony.media;
import  javax.telephony.*;


public interface MediaCallObserver extends CallObserver { }
```

Oh, yeah — almost forgot. Observers at this level have no beef (they are marker interfaces)!

Media Capabilities

Just as the core package, the call control package, and the phone package have an associated *capabilities* subpackage, so does the media package. The contents of this package are shown in **Figure 8.18**.

Figure 8.18 *Media Capabilities*

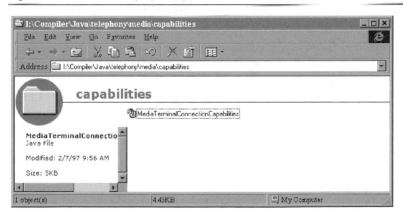

Here's the interface:

```
package javax.telephony.media.capabilities;
import  javax.telephony.capabilities.*;


public interface MediaTerminalConnectionCapabilities
extends TerminalConnectionCapabilities {

    public boolean canUseDefaultSpeaker();
    public boolean canUseDefaultMicrophone();
    public boolean canUseRecordURL();
    public boolean canUsePlayURL();
    public boolean canStartPlaying();
    public boolean canStopPlaying();
```

```
public boolean canStartRecording();
public boolean canStopRecording();
public boolean canDetectDtmf();
public boolean canGenerateDtmf();
}
```

Media Events

In addition to the events presented earlier that map to the state transitions, events are defined and generated that map to the receipt of a DTMF tone. Interestingly, we seem to have lost events that signal the creation of instances (in this case, a MediaTerminalConnection instance might have generated a MediaTermConnCreatedEv). In practice, however, this is not a problem since the superclass event for TerminalConnection creation should suffice. Just be sure to place the event generation in the constructor if possible. This will eliminate the need to worry whether or not the methods were called for the subclasses.

All media events are shown in **Figure 8.19**.

Figure 8.19 *Media Events*

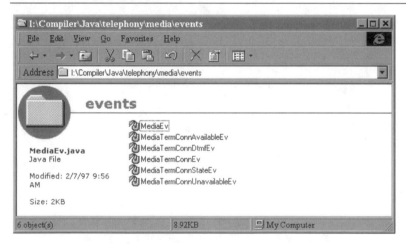

All media events are required to extend both the MediaEv and the TermEv interface through the MediaTermEv interface. This enables them first to be identified as media events and second to be processed by a MediaTerminalObserver.

Call Center Packages

In this section we investigate the packages `javax.telephony.call-center`, `javax.telephony.callcenter.capabilities`, and `javax.telephony.callcenter.events`. These packages make up what are known as the JTAPI *call center packages*.

The call center packages are one of the most powerful packages presented in the JTAPI specification. These packages model a large portion of the telephony vertical market.

Call Center Core Components

The call center core components are found in package `javax.telephony.callcenter`. The entities modeled in this package include support for two primary applications found in the telephony problem space. Support is provided for *automated call distribution* (ACD) and for *call centers*. In order to provide this support, building block entities are specified — these are *agents* and *routing plans*. The core call center interfaces are depicted in **Figure 8.20**.

Figure 8.20 *Call Center Core Components*

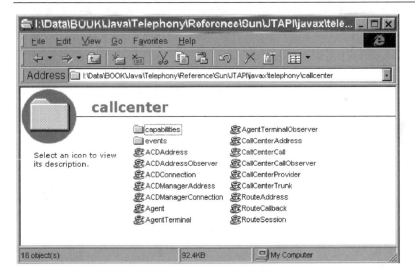

Agents and routing entities are to be used throughout the call center package. Let's check out these "building block" interfaces first.

Agent Support

Call center package support for agents is provided in three interfaces:

- Agent
- AgentTerminal
- AgentTerminalObserver

Agent

An Agent is a person who handles telephone calls at a particular set of Addresses. More accurately, an Agent is a *role* a person plays. A person and an Agent are not the same things since a person can represent many different Agents. Agent identity at multiple Addresses is resolved by ensuring that the same person may play the role of many different Agents, one for each Address.

One example of Agents is those thoughtful folks who call around dinnertime. Not surprisingly, Agents are associated with Addresses and Terminals (endpoints of a Call). The associated Address is a normal Address, the Terminal an AgentTerminal.

An Agent belongs to an ACD Group. A person who plays the role of an Agent may "belong to" multiple ACD Groups, but the Agent itself belongs to only one ACD Group. An ACD Group is called an ACDAddress in JTAPI terminology.[15] An Agent may be logged into one or more ACDAddresses over time, but only one at a time. Logging into an ACDAddress signals the implementation that the Agent is ready to handle Calls that may come into that ACDAddress.

Life Cycle of an Agent

As usual, the valid states and state transitions determine the life cycle of an object. The Agent states are defined by the JATPI specification as shown in **Table 8.5**.

Table 8.5 *State Definitions for an Agent*

State	JTAPI Definition
LOG_IN	indicates the Agent is logged into an ACDAddress.
LOG_OUT	indicates the Agent has logged out of an ACDAddress.
NOT_READY	indicates the Agent is not available to handle Calls because it is busy with other non–call servicing related tasks.
READY	indicates the Agent is available to service Calls.
WORK_NOT_ READY	indicates the Agent is not available to service Calls because it is busy with other call-servicing related tasks.
WORK_READY	indicates the Agent is available to service Calls and is also performing other call-servicing related tasks.
BUSY	indicates the Agent is not available to service Calls because it is busy with another Call.
UNKNOWN	indicates the state of the Agent is currently not known.

---

15 This is an extremely poor choice of a name for an ACD Group. More on this later.

Most of the states have to do with whether or not an Agent is logged on to an ACD Group and, if so, their current work status. Call centers will use these state transitions to gather statistics on the efficiency of their agents and pay them accordingly (economics at its finest).

The state transition diagram in **Figure 8.21** illustrates the valid state transitions for the Agent as well as the events that are generated as a result of these transitions.

Figure 8.21 *State Transition Diagram for an Agent*

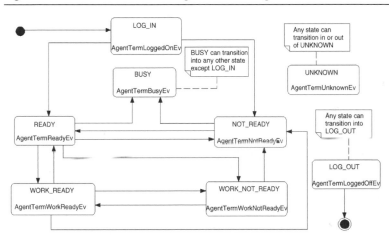

Creating an Agent

Agents are created and associated with an ACDAddress using the `AgentTerminal.addAgent( ACDAddress )` method. Every Agent has a (presumably unique) identifier. Exactly how this identifier is to be used is not specified. Note that this API provides no means for the application to add a *persistent agent* whose identifier may be used repeatedly during a session. Therefore, the creation and management of these identifiers is left to the implementation. Even though most implementations will automatically assign the next available Agent to the AgentTerminal, an overloaded version of this method providing for an additional parameter for the Agent identifier would have proven a more flexible model. Agent instances are destroyed using the `AgentTerminal.removeAgent()` method.

Operations Allowed on an Agent

Here's the Agent interface:

```
package javax.telephony.callcenter;
import javax.telephony.*;
```

```
public interface Agent {

    public static final int UNKNOWN = 0;
    public static final int LOG_IN = 1;
    public static final int LOG_OUT = 2;
    public static final int NOT_READY = 3;
    public static final int READY = 4;
    public static final int WORK_NOT_READY = 5;
    public static final int WORK_READY = 6;
    public static final int BUSY = 7;

    public void setState( int state )
        throws InvalidArgumentException, InvalidStateException;
    public int getState();
    public String getAgentID();
    public ACDAddress getACDAddress(); // really an ACD Group...
    public Address getAgentAddress();
    public AgentTerminal getAgentTerminal();
}
```

The only possible confusion about these methods is the potential ambiguity presented by the `getACDAddress()` and the `getAgentAddress()` methods. The ACDAddress is the Address (or ACD Group queue) the Agent is currently logged into. The other Address is the Address associated with the AgentTerminal itself. In other words, it is a real Address, not an ACD Group.

AgentTerminal

The AgentTerminal interface extends the core Terminal interface in order to provide support for ACD and Agent features.

Life Cycle of an AgentTerminal

Just like a core Terminal, the AgentTerminal has no state of its own. Instead, its state is encapsulated by the TerminalConnection with which it is associated with respect to a particular Call instance.

Creating an AgentTerminal

An AgentTerminal is created in the same manner as a core Terminal — from the implementation (as opposed to the **new** operator).

Operations Allowed on an AgentTerminal

The only real difference between a core Terminal and an AgentTerminal is that the AgentTerminal manages a list of associated Agents. Here's the interface:

```
package javax.telephony.callcenter;
import  javax.telephony.*;

public interface AgentTerminal extends Terminal {

    public Agent addAgent( Address agentAddress,
                           ACDAddress acdAddress,
                           int initialState, String agentID,
                           String password)
        throws InvalidArgumentException, InvalidStateException,
            ResourceUnavailableException;

    public void removeAgent( Agent agent )
        throws InvalidArgumentException, InvalidStateException;
    public Agent[] getAgents();
}
```

Note the "password" parameter to the `AgentTerminal.addAgent()` method. The JTAPI spec says this parameter "authorizes the application to log in as an Agent." Whether this password is to be unique per Agent is not clear. However, there is nothing in the API preventing such use and so it would seem that this is an appropriate way to use the parameter, if desired.[16]

AgentTerminalObserver

Every good event generator (e.g., an observable like Agent) has at least one associated observer, and an Agent is no exception. In fact, an Agent has two observers: an AgentTerminalObserver and an ACDAddressObserver. We'll see the ACDAddressObserver later when we look at ACD functionality. Here's the AgentTerminalObserver interface:

```
package javax.telephony.callcenter;
import  javax.telephony.TerminalObserver;
public interface AgentTerminalObserver
    extends TerminalObserver { }
```

What do you know — another marker interface. By now you should see this marker interface and know instinctively that Agent events are reported to the `terminalChangedEvent()` method. To see which events go where, see the section on Call Center Events later in this chapter.

Routing Plan Support

A well-known feature of any call center is support for the routing of Calls to possibly different destination Addresses than the original one intended for the Call. This is a fundamental capability of telephony server processing

---

16 The underlying implementation would then manage the list of valid passwords for each Agent.

and should be used in ACD support. A typical application would be where a customer calls an 800 number for a company and the Call is routed to the next available service representative (who obviously resides at a different Address than the one the customer dialed). Such rerouting is accomplished based on what are called *routing plans*.[17]

JTAPI provides routing plan support in the form of three interfaces:

- RouteAddress
- RouteCallback
- RouteSession

The static relationship between these interfaces is depicted in **Figure 8.22**.

Figure 8.22 *Object Model for Routing Plan Support in Call Center Package*

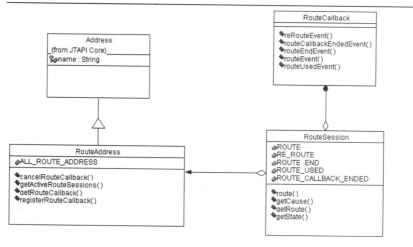

In short, a RouteSession exists in the context of a single RouteAddress and potentially multiple RouteCallbacks.

RouteSession

The JTAPI specification says that a RouteSession represents "an outstanding route request of a Call." In other words, applications make requests to the JTAPI runtime to route a Call in a particular manner as specified in a callback (called a RouteCallback) they register with a RouteAddress. The RouteSession essentially uses one or more RouteCallbacks (a.k.a. routing plans). Although RouteCallbacks are static entities in that they are just pointers to blocks of code to execute, they are processed in a dynamic manner. A RouteSession basically selects from among a set of registered RouteCallbacks for a Call and uses the one that "got there first."

---

17 A routing plan is literally a plan to route Calls.

Life Cycle of a RouteSession

Being dynamic in nature, a RouteSession has a current state. This state represents the state of a Call with respect to the routing plans (callbacks) that have been requested by the application. **Table 8.6** shows the possible valid states along with their official JTAPI definitions.

Table 8.6 *Valid States for a RouteSession*

State	JTAPI Definition
ROUTE_USED	indicates that a destination has been selected for a Call. This destination is one which the application had selected during its routing of the Call.
ROUTE_END	indicates that the routing of a Call has terminated.
RE_ROUTE	indicates that an application has been requested to select another destination for the Call.
ROUTE_CALLBACK_ENDED	indicates that all RouteCallback objects have been removed from this routing session. There are no more routing callbacks associated with this session. This is the final state for the RouteSession interface.

The state transitions for a RouteSession are modeled in **Figure 8.23** along with the events that are generated as a result of each state transition.

Figure 8.23 *State Transitions for a RouteSession*

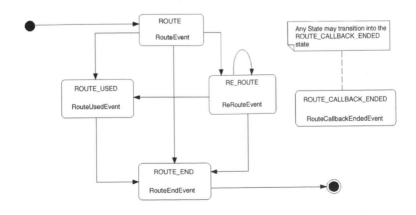

Creating a RouteSession

Clearly, a RouteSession must be instantiated prior to completion of the registration of a RouteCallback. The JTAPI specification says that a new

RouteSession is created for every Call associated with the relevant RouteAddress, based upon requests to register RouteCallbacks. Therefore, every invocation of the `RouteAddress.registerRouteCallback()` method can conceivably lead to the creation a new RouteSession if one is not already in place for that Call associated with that RouteAddress (by way of a Connection, of course). Likewise, no RouteSession can exist unless a callback has been registered for a particular RouteAddress.

Like many JTAPI interfaces, no constructor is specified and it is assumed that the manner of creation is up to the implementation. Because many such registrations may occur for a particular Call over time, a RouteSession may be associated with many RouteCallbacks at once.

Operations Allowed on a RouteSession

RouteSessions are used to manage an application's routing plans for a Call to a particular RouteAddress. The routing process involves two steps: *registration* and *selection*. Here's the RouteSession interface:

```
package javax.telephony.callcenter;
import   javax.telephony.MethodNotSupportedException;

public interface RouteSession {

    public static final int ROUTE = 1;
    public static final int ROUTE_USED = 2;
    public static final int ROUTE_END = 3;
    public static final int RE_ROUTE = 4;
    public static final int ROUTE_CALLBACK_ENDED = 5;

    public static final int CAUSE_NO_ERROR = 100;
    public static final int CAUSE_ROUTING_TIMER_EXPIRED = 101;
    public static final int CAUSE_PARAMETER_NOT_SUPPORTED = 102;
    public static final int CAUSE_INVALID_DESTINATION = 103;
    public static final int CAUSE_STATE_INCOMPATIBLE = 104;
    public static final int CAUSE_UNSPECIFIED_ERROR = 105;

    public static final int ERROR_UNKNOWN = 1;
    public static final int ERROR_RESOURCE_BUSY = 2;
    public static final int ERROR_RESOURCE_OUT_OF_SERVICE = 3;

    public RouteAddress getRouteAddress();

    public void selectRoute( String[] routeSelected )
        throws MethodNotSupportedException;
```

```
public void endRoute( int errorValue )
    throws MethodNotSupportedException;

public int getState();
public int getCause();
}
```

The routing process works like this: First, at least one invocation by an application to the method `RouteAddress.register-RouteCallback()` must be made to ensure not only that a particular callback will be used to route the Call, but that a RouteSession exists for that Call. Registration is now complete. Next, an invocation is made to the `RouteSession.selectRoute()` method to begin the selection process. This allows for a list of destination addresses to be sent to the session that will be called, in order to implement the routing plan. This list is processed in FIFO order based upon the indexing scheme of arrays (i.e., list[0] is tried first, then list[1], and so on). In order for selection to occur, the RouteSession must be in one of either of the states ROUTE or RE_ROUTE. Upon successful completion, the RouteSession transitions to the state of ROUTE_USED.

RouteAddress

The RouteAddress interface extends the core Address interface as we saw in **Figure 8.22**. It adds methods to allow applications the ability to implement routing plans.

Life Cycle of a RouteAddress

A RouteAddress contains no state information.

Creating a RouteAddress

Just as in the case of an Address in the core package, a RouteAddress is created and then returned by the Provider (in this case, possibly a CallCenterProvider). The method `CallCenterProvider.get-RouteableAddresses()` returns an array of all available RouteAddresses from which an application may choose.

Operations Allowed on a RouteAddress

Here's the interface of a RouteAddress:

```
package javax.telephony.callcenter;
import  javax.telephony.*;

public interface RouteAddress extends Address {
```

```
public static final String ALL_ROUTE_ADDRESS =
    "AllRouteAddress";

public void registerRouteCallback( RouteCallback
    routeCallback )
  throws ResourceUnavailableException,
    MethodNotSupportedException;

public void cancelRouteCallback( RouteCallback
    routeCallback )
  throws MethodNotSupportedException;

public RouteCallback[] getRouteCallback()
  throws MethodNotSupportedException;

public RouteSession[] getActiveRouteSessions()
  throws MethodNotSupportedException;
}
```

The primary method exported by this interface is `registerRouteCallback()`. This method makes use of a callback architecture[18] not unlike the TAPI message handler function we wrote in Chapter 6. The RouteAddress simply uses an object you supply to implement the routing plan. This object must implement the RouteCallback interface. Once this object is registered with the RouteSession (a side effect of the invocation to the `registerRouteCallback()` method), the JTAPI runtime simply uses this instance and invokes the appropriate method of that object at the appropriate time.[19] Again, we see the familiar pattern of essentially implementing an event handler (or a set of handlers) that respond to predefined events.

One more point: What's an ALL_ROUTE_ADDRESS? ALL_ROUTE_ADDRESS is a special name given to a particular unique Address created by the Provider. If `registerRouteCallback()` is invoked upon this special Address, the callback object passed as a parameter will receive every single routing request (for all RouteAddresses) within the Provider's domain.

RouteCallback

The RouteCallback interface is used by applications to receive routing requests for a particular RouteSession. A RouteCallback is simply any object that implements the RouteCallback interface. By doing so and then

---

18 For more information about writing callbacks in Java, see Chapter 10.
19 Specifically, when it receives any kind of RouteEvent passed to any of the methods implemented in the RouteCallback interface.

registering that object with the `RouteAddress.register-RouteCallback()` method, the RouteCallback instance will receive routing events from the RouteSession. Whatever code they place to handle these events will be invoked upon event receipt.

Life Cycle of a RouteCallback

The life cycle of a RouteCallback may begin before it is introduced into the JTAPI runtime code. Applications create polymorphic instances of this interface and register these instances whenever they see fit. A RouteCallback may live beyond when JTAPI is through with it. As long as an object reference is held somewhere by the application, the instance will be alive. And so JTAPI controls neither the creation nor the destruction of a RouteCallback.

Although a RouteCallback may indeed have a current state (because it can be any arbitrary object), as far as JTAPI is concerned, there is no state information to maintain or monitor.

Creating a RouteCallback

The creation of a RouteCallback is not specified in JTAPI. In fact, there's no way it should be specified. By design, a RouteCallback can be any arbitrary object at all as long as it implements the RouteCallback interface. And so construction is none of JTAPI's business. And we like it that way!

Operations Allowed on a RouteCallback

Here's the RouteCallback interface:

```
package javax.telephony.callcenter;
import  javax.telephony.callcenter.events.*;


public interface RouteCallback {

    public void routeEvent( RouteEvent event );
    public void reRouteEvent( ReRouteEvent event );
    public void routeUsedEvent( RouteUsedEvent event );
    public void routeEndEvent( RouteEndEvent event );
    public void routeCallbackEndedEvent( RouteCallbackEndedEvent
        event );
}
```

As you can see, each method in this interface is reserved for a specific kind of event. This interface is very much like the "user-friendly" interface we presented in Chapter 6. No need to write sloppy switch statements here against an array of different kinds of events — just implement the method you use and go!

So where's the observer? The RouteCallback takes the place of the observer, more or less filling that role in the call model for routed calls.

Call Center Support

In the most general sense, a Call Center is just that — a center that receives (and places) calls. Of course the center itself doesn't place and receive the calls. Neither do the people working there. A call center is automated to some degree or another. The main components of the call center package are shown in **Figure 8.24**.

Figure 8.24 *Main Components of Call Center Package*

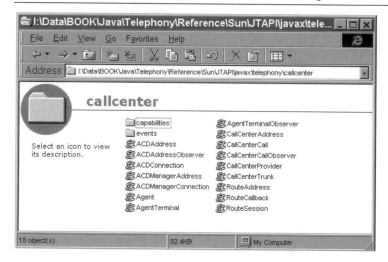

Call Center support involves five interfaces:

- CallCenterProvider
- CallCenterAddress
- CallCenterCall
- CallCenterTrunk
- CallCenterCallObserver

CallCenterProvider

Recall that a Provider is responsible for creating instances of Addresses and Terminals from within its domain. A CallCenterProvider specializes this concept to include capabilities to return created Addresses of types other than the "plain vanilla" brand offered by the core telephony package. These types are RouteAddresses, ACDAddresses, and the ACDManagerAddresses. We've already seen the RouteAddress; this section covers the other two.

Life Cycle of a CallCenterProvider

Nothing here out of the ordinary. In terms of life cycle, this class behaves the same as its super-class Provider.

Creating a CallCenterProvider

A CallCenterProvider is created in the same manner as a core Provider.

Operations allowed on a CallCenterProvider

Here's the interface:

```
package javax.telephony.callcenter;
import  javax.telephony.*;

public interface CallCenterProvider extends Provider {

    public RouteAddress[] getRouteableAddresses()
        throws MethodNotSupportedException;

    public ACDAddress[] getACDAddresses()
        throws MethodNotSupportedException;

    public ACDManagerAddress[] getACDManagerAddresses()
        throws MethodNotSupportedException;
}
```

CallCenterAddress

A CallCenterAddress "isa" core Address that overrides the parent method `addCallObserver()`. It is the base interface for the other two Addresses in the call center package (i.e., ACDAddress and ACDManagerAddress).

Life Cycle of a CallCenterAddress

Same as parent interface.

Creating a CallCenterAddress

Same as parent interface.

Operations Allowed on a CallCenterAddress

Here's the interface:

```
package javax.telephony.callcenter;
import javax.telephony.*;


public interface CallCenterAddress extends Address {

  public void addCallObserver( CallObserver observer,
      boolean remain )
    throws ResourceUnavailableException,
      PrivilegeViolationException,
      MethodNotSupportedException;
  }
```

The overloaded method `addCallObserver()` allows applications to monitor Calls just like in the core package. The difference is that this monitoring may now continue beyond the lifetime of the Address and may last instead for the lifetime of the Call. In other words, the ability to monitor the Call does not end when the Address is no longer associated with the Call (through a Connection). This means that an observer can continue to monitor a call after the Address they "rode in on" goes away, provided there is at least one Connection alive.

CallCenterCall

A CallCenterCall extends the core package interface Call. Recall that a Call's most important method was `connect()`, which simply places a call to a destination Address from a given Terminal. The CallCenterCall interface extends this concept to provide for the placing of specialized calls made by *predictive dialer* applications. In addition, support is provided for an application to pass arbitrary data to the CallCenterCall and to query it for any associated Trunks.

Life Cycle of a CallCenterCall

No new state information is maintained by a CallCenterCall beyond those found in the core package (e.g., ACTIVE, INACTIVE, and so forth.).

Creating a CallCenterCall

Same as the core Call interface.

Operations Allowed on a CallCenterCall

Connecting a Call for a predictive dialer is subtly different than the core case because the destination Connection is created first and placed in a state favorable to the application, depending on its requirements. This is all accomplished with the method `connectPredictive()`. Only when the victim on the other end of the call answers is the other Connection activated.

Remember the get/setData() methods we attached to our helper class JtapiObject that allowed our SDRCall class the ability to pass around arbitrary data? That's essentially what the getApplicationData() and setApplicationData() methods are for.[20] We used GUI components but you can use any object. The JTAPI specification suggests using objects that contain data such as customer information. Here's the interface:

```
package javax.telephony.callcenter;
import javax.telephony.*;

public interface CallCenterCall extends Call {

  public static final int MIN_RINGS = 2;
  public static final int MAX_RINGS = 15;

  public static final int
    ANSWERING_TREATMENT_PROVIDER_DEFAULT = 1;
  public static final int ANSWERING_TREATMENT_DROP = 2;
  public static final int ANSWERING_TREATMENT_CONNECT = 3;
  public static final int ANSWERING_TREATMENT_NONE = 4;

  public static final int ENDPOINT_ANSWERING_MACHINE = 1;
  public static final int ENDPOINT_FAX_MACHINE = 2;
  public static final int ENDPOINT_HUMAN_INTERVENTION = 3;
  public static final int ENDPOINT_ANY = 4;

  public Connection[] connectPredictive(Terminal
            originatorTerminal, Address originatorAddress,
            String destination,
            int connectionState,
            int maxRings,
            int treatment,
            int endpointType)
    throws ResourceUnavailableException,
      PrivilegeViolationException,
      InvalidPartyException, InvalidArgumentException,
      InvalidStateException, MethodNotSupportedException;

  public void setApplicationData( Object data )
    throws ResourceUnavailableException,
        InvalidArgumentException,
        InvalidStateException, MethodNotSupportedException;
```

---

20 In retrospect, we certainly could have used the CallCenterCall interface instead of the core Call interface, but we didn't want to complicate the train of thought at the time. So instead, we hacked up the namespace with a nonstandard extension. Shame on us.

```
public Object getApplicationData()
  throws MethodNotSupportedException;

public CallCenterTrunk[] getTrunks()
  throws MethodNotSupportedException;
}
```

Note the various constants defined to allow more control over the Call. Note also that these are related to call center activities such as giving up if no one answers (e.g., MAX_RINGS), recording the fact that a fax answered (e.g., ENDPOINT_FAX_MACHINE) instead of a human, and so forth.

CallCenterTrunk

A Trunk is a communication line between two switching systems (e.g., a PBX and a central office). It is a low-level, hardware-specific feature that is required in order for, say, an incoming telephone call to be answered by any telephone within a particular system. When an application can control a trunk, more capability is available for call control and processing. The JTAPI animal for a trunk is the CallCenterTrunk interface.

A CallCenterTrunk is associated with a single Call, yet a Call can be associated with many CallCenterTrunks.

Life Cycle of a CallCenterTrunk

A CallCenterTrunk has only two states: VALID_TRUNK and INVALID_TRUNK. The state transitions are not documented in JTAPI, so it is unclear whether a CallCenterTrunk is allowed to move freely among the two states or if, instead, state transitions are one-way.

Creating a CallCenterTrunk

It is assumed that the Trunks are managed by the JTAPI subsystem and that the only means of gaining access to them is through the CallCenterCall.getTrunks() method.

Operations Allowed on a CallCenterTrunk

Here's the interface:

```
package javax.telephony.callcenter;
import javax.telephony.Call;

public interface CallCenterTrunk {
```

```
public final static int INVALID_TRUNK = 0x1;
public final static int VALID_TRUNK = 0x2;

public final static int INCOMING_TRUNK = 0x1;
public final static int OUTGOING_TRUNK = 0x2;
public final static int UNKNOWN_TRUNK = 0x3;

public String getName();
public int getState();
public int getType();
public Call getCall();
}
```

CallCenterCallObserver

Finally we come to a familiar friend — the observer. Again we find a marker interface and again the `callChangedEvent()` method is to accept yet another gaggle of events from a subpackage. By now our Chapter 6 concerns about a very large switch statement should be starting to sink in. If all the core subpackages are implemented by a vendor, the `callChangedEvent()` method implementation is about a mile long by now. Here's the interface:

```
package javax.telephony.callcenter;
import  javax.telephony.CallObserver;

public interface CallCenterCallObserver
  extends CallObserver { }
```

ACD Support

ACD support is based on providing services to what is known as an ACD Group. An ACD Group is a list of phone numbers that are to be called when the Agents at AgentTerminals that service those numbers are ready to take, say, the next customer Call. In order to "belong" to an ACD Group, Agents must log on to a system that manages that group. Once "in the system," Calls can be routed to the Agents if the appropriate application requirements are met (as defined by each application). If not, each Agent who is not prepared has his phone number (Address) queued until the Agent is available to take the call. Of course, that same Call may be taken first by another Agent who is a member of that same (or another) ACD Group before the original Agent becomes available. ACD support involves five interfaces:

- ACDAddress
- ACDManagerAddress

- ACDConnection

- ACDManagerConnection

- ACDAddressObserver

Figure 8.25 shows the relationships between the primary components of `javax.telephony.callcenter` as they relate to ACD support.

Figure 8.25 *Primary Design Entities for ACD Support in the Call Center Package*

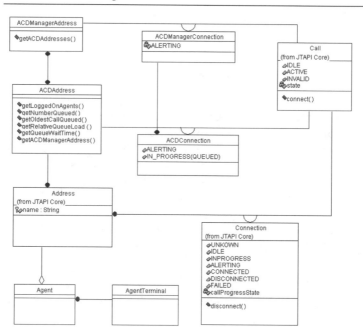

We should warn the reader ahead of time that we believe that the portion of the call center package dealing with ACD support could have been better designed. Most of the JTAPI API has been very well thought out and designed. This package, however, has some major problems, most of which have to do with the inappropriate extension of core interfaces and the poor choice of names for both interfaces and states. We'll try to steer the reader through this minefield as we go.

ACDAddress

The ACDAddress interface ultimately extends the core Address interface adding functionality related to the queuing of Calls destined for Agents who are members of an ACDAddress at a call center. Its immediate parent interface is CallCenterAddress. This extension chain is shown in **Figure 8.26**. If a picture paints a thousand words, we're in for an essay.

Figure 8.26 *Inappropriate Extension for ACD Support*

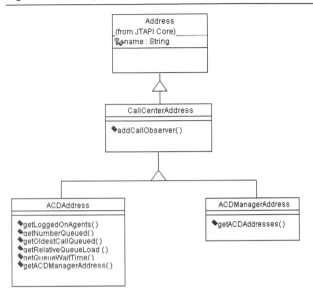

The ACDAddress interface is meant to model an ACD Group. We'll examine this functionality soon, but first we feel compelled to discuss the architecture in general terms because there are some fundamental design problems with the specification of this interface. Let's see what the spec says:

> *ACDAddresses differ from Addresses. Some important differences between ACDAddress and Address are:*
>
> - *An ACDAddress cannot have Terminal objects associated with it.*
>
> - *An ACDAddress is not a logical endpoint of a call in the same sense as an Address, rather it models a queuing process whereby the selection of a logical endpoint is deferred.*
>
> - *ACDConnections to an ACDAddress do not enter into a CONNECTED state.*
>
> - *It is not returned on Provider.getAddresses(), but is available through CallCenterProvider.getACDAddresses().*

Okay. The ACDAddress interface extends the core Address interface. This implies that an ACDAddress is to be thought of as a *kind of* Address. Yet we are told it is not a case of *pure* specialization. In fact we are told that some of the fundamental relationships between other call model objects held in the generalized case no longer hold true. Where I come from, this is a case for *avoiding* extension, not using it. If a class called Thing derives from a class called Car but it cannot be driven, it's probably not a specialization of Car. In fact, the second statement says it all. What we have here is an ACDAddressQueuingPolicy or an ACDGroup, not an ACDAddress. In any case, let's move on.

But how can we proceed if we cannot even describe what it is we are looking at? Let's get a better handle on this thing — this so-called ACDAddress. First of all, it represents a collection[21] of Agents' Addresses known in the industry as an *ACD Group* — the specification even says so. Incoming calls are sent to the Addresses in that group. If no Agents are available, the Call is placed on a queue where it sits for a time until an Agent is able to process the Call. As the Agents signal to the application that they are prepared to accept a Call, Calls are then sent to the Agents in the group, typically in FIFO order.

Life Cycle of an ACDAddress

There are no "getter methods" suggesting instance variables that hold state information, yet the return values of some of the methods may paint a picture of the current state of the queue. And so a state model is *implied*, but not specified as it is for other call model objects. There is, however, a modeling of state information between the ACD Group and the Calls it monitors. Specifically, the ACDConnection interface models the state relationship between an ACDAddress and a particular Call.

Creating an ACDAddress

Unlike the core Address, an ACDAddress is returned from a CallCenterProvider. In other words, the "normal" Provider does not manage ACDAddresses — only a CallCenterProvider may do so. The list of available ACDAddresses is returned from the method `CallCenterProvider.getACDAddresses()`.

Operations Allowed on an ACDAddress

Even a cursory glance at the ACDAddress interface reveals that this interface is poorly named (and improperly extended). Clearly, this is not a telephone number of any kind. Granted, it has a name (by extension from Address) and as such may be *used* as a telephone number, but contrary to what the specification implies, the object itself is not a telephone number.[22]

---

21 Right away we know that whatever this thing is, it's not an Address because a Collection can never specialize a single object!

22 Now it is certainly possible that an ACD Group "has-a" Address; and so Calls could be placed to this *associated* Address. Perhaps that is what the API designers were thinking. But this does not mean that an ACD Group "isa" Address any more than I *am* a telephone number because you can place Calls to me!

```
package javax.telephony.callcenter;
import javax.telephony.*;

public interface ACDAddress extends CallCenterAddress {

    public Agent[] getLoggedOnAgents()
        throws MethodNotSupportedException;
    public int getNumberQueued()
        throws MethodNotSupportedException;
    public Call getOldestCallQueued()
        throws MethodNotSupportedException;
    public int getRelativeQueueLoad()
        throws MethodNotSupportedException;
    public int getQueueWaitTime()
        throws MethodNotSupportedException;
    public ACDManagerAddress[] getACDManagerAddress()
        throws MethodNotSupportedException;
}
```

The ACDAddress is really an object that manages Calls intended
for Agents. The interface exports operations for querying the state
of a call queue. It is not really an Address itself; rather it is a
manager of a list of Addresses. So when an application invokes
`CallCenterProvider.getACDAddresses()`, it is sent all of the
lists being managed at a call center, not all the Addresses, as the name of
both the object and this method implies.

There was a change introduced between versions 1.1 and 1.2 of this portion of the specification that should be noted. Note the method
`getACDManagerAddress()`. The specification says the following
regarding this method:

> **FOR JTAPI 1.2** *Returns the ACDManagerAddesses (was a
> single ACDManagerAddess) associated at system administra-
> tion time with this ACDAddress.*

The first thing to note is merely a typo; clearly the method should be
named `getACDManagerAddresses()` — no big deal. But more
importantly there is now implied a many-to-many relationship between an
ACDAddress and an ACDManagerAddress. This means that not only can
an ACDManagerAddress manage many ACDAddresses (ACD Groups),
but that these groups may be managed by more than one
ACDManagerAddress. More on this later.

ACDConnection

An ACDConnection is an object that models the state between a Call and
an ACDAddress. Unfortunately, because of the confused definition of the

ACDAddress, the ACDConnection has become a willing partner in this design debacle. Although an ACDConnection extends the Connection interface, it is really not a Connection at all. It is merely a relationship between an ACDAddress (ACD Group) and a Call. Granted, it models the state between two objects like a Connection, but this is hardly a characteristic unique to Connections! What is worse, in order to make an ACDConnection *seem like* a Connection, both classes use the same states. For example, both a Connection and an ACDConnection may be in the ALERTING state, but the semantics are actually quite different, including the rules under which this state is valid for each class. But the object of this book is to clarify, not ridicule, and so we will do our best to try to explain what's going on here. We believe that the functionality of the design is sound, in that ACD support requires objects that manage lists of Addresses and that these Addresses are those of Agents, etc. But the naming of the objects, the "overloading" of states, and the improper use of extension is not only confusing, it may lead to the outright rejection of this subpackage by the programming community. Most programmers we know will find it difficult to *want to* work with a design that is just plain wrong.

Life Cycle of an ACDConnection

An ACDConnection exists until an Agent on an ACD Group takes the Call. At that point, the ACDConnection is disconnected and a new Connection is created between the Call and the Address of the Agent that takes the Call. In this sense, we may have been a little harsh in our dislike of the ACDConnection definition. It is conceivable that one might think of a Call as being "connected to" an ACD Group until such point as it is ready to become a real Connection — then the two "connections" swap places. One remains and the other (the ACDConnection) dies.[23] If we are to use JTAPI ACD support, that's clearly the way we should be thinking.

The life cycle of an ACDConnection emulates that of a normal Connection except that there is no CONNECTED state and the semantics of the INPROGRESS and ALERTING states differ slightly. An ACDConnection cannot become CONNECTED because it delegates that responsibility to a normal core `Call.connect()` invocation. In other words, that's the job of a *real* Connection! The INPROGRESS state means that the Call associated with the ACDConnection is queued at an ACDAddress (so why not give the ACDConnection its own states and call this state QUEUED?). The ALERTING state has the same semantics (except that it's alerting an Agent number), but the rules are different. Not

---

23 In this case, the problem lies not in the definition of what *is* and what *is not* a Connection — we might be able to swallow that. But we're still stuck with the problem of the original definition of a Connection (which should change) if we are to accept this use. If so, a Connection would have to be defined as modeling the state between a Call and any Object, not a Call and an Address. Why? Because again, an ACDAddress is not really an Address!

just any ACDConnection can even enter the ALERTING state — only those that have no connection to an ACDManagerConnection. The reason for this restriction is unclear.

Creating an ACDConnection

An ACDConnection is to be created whenever a Call is placed on an ACD Group list (i.e., to an ACDAddress).

Operations Allowed on an ACDConnection

After all this discussion, all an ACDConnection can really do is point to its parent ACDManagerConnection, if it has one.

```
package javax.telephony.callcenter;
import   javax.telephony.*;

public interface ACDConnection extends Connection {

  public ACDManagerConnection getACDManagerConnection()
    throws MethodNotSupportedException;
}
```

The conditions under which an ACDConnection can be associated with an ACDManagerConnection are explained in the section describing an ACDManagerConnection. There we hope to also further clarify this object (the ACDConnection).

ACDManagerAddress

If an ACDAddress is a manager of Calls to Agents, an ACDManagerAddress is a manager of these managers.[24] Applications can rely on an ACDManagerAddress to automatically route a Call to the appropriate ACD group (ACDAddress) without having to specify the ACDAddress directly. The reader may want to refer back to **Figure 8.25** for a refreshed view of this relationship.

Life Cycle of an ACDManagerAddress

Like all Addresses, there is no specific state information held by an ACDManagerAddress.[25] Instead, the associated connection interface

---

24 Again, naming is getting us into trouble. We believe a more suitable name for this interface might have been something like "ACDGroupManager."

25 The fact that no state information is held in this class relies on the associated connection class, but not because it resembles an Address in any way — it doesn't. It just so happens that this API deals with state objects (like Connection and TerminalConnection) which model the state between two other types of objects.

ACDManagerConnection maintains state information about the ACDManagerAddress with respect to a particular Call.

Creating an ACDManagerAddress

The JTAPI specification is silent on creation of an ACDManagerAddress. However, it is safely assumed that they are returned from an invocation of `CallCenterProvider.getACDManagerAddresses()`.

Operations Allowed on an ACDManagerAddress

All an ACDManagerAddress really does is point to the list of ACDAddresses that it manages. Here's the interface:

```
package javax.telephony.callcenter;
import  javax.telephony.*;
public interface ACDManagerAddress extends CallCenterAddress {
    public ACDAddress[] getACDAddresses()
        throws MethodNotSupportedException;
}
```

Earlier, we made mention of the many-to-many relationship between an ACDManagerAddress and an ACDAddress. The one-to-many relationship between an ACDManagerAddress and an ACDAddress is intuitive — managers often manage multiple things. The other side of this relationship is more interesting and less intuitive.[26] The one-to-many relationship between an ACDAddress and an ACDManagerAddress implies that many different ACDManagerAddresses may manage an ACD Group at the same time. This option provides a lot more flexibility in implementations.

ACDManagerConnection

Just as an ACDAddress relies on an ACDConnection to model its relationship to a Call, so does an ACDManagerAddress rely on an ACDManagerConnection for the same functionality. Of course the same design problems exist, but if you can follow us to this point, this "connection" relationship has essentially the same semantics as it does for an ACDConnection.

Life Cycle of an ACDManagerConnection

Similar to an ACDConnection, an ACDManagerConnection models the state between an ACDManagerAddress and a Call. When an

---

26 This lack of intuition for one of the M:N sides of the relationship is not at all uncommon — usually one side "hurts" to think about! You can read a lot of gory detail about these types of relationships in Chapter 11.

ACDManagerConnection is no longer needed (when an ACDAddress takes over responsibility for the Call), the ACDManagerConnection is placed in the DISCONNECTED state. Again, the allowable states generally mimic those of a core Connection with some changes. Specifically, there is no INPROGRESS state and the ALERTING state holds true between an ACDManagerConnection and an ACDManagerAddress.

Creating an ACDManagerConnection

Just as an ACDConnection is to be created whenever a Call is placed on an ACD Group list (i.e., to an ACDAddress), an ACDManagerConnection is created whenever a Call is associated with an ACDManagerAddress.

Operations Allowed on an ACDManagerConnection

```
package javax.telephony.callcenter;
import  javax.telephony.*;

public interface ACDManagerConnection extends Connection {
  public ACDConnection[] getACDConnections()
    throws MethodNotSupportedException;
}
```

The JTAPI specification implies that an implementation can "decide" when it is appropriate to either initiate an ACDManagerConnection between a Call and an ACDManagerAddress or to instead issue an ACDConnection between an ACDAddress and a Call. "Lucy, you got some 'splainin' to do …"

Some applications may explicitly place a Call onto a known ACD Group (ACDAddress). In some cases, however, the application may not know which group to use, while in others, a chosen group's relative queue load or wait time may be unacceptable. In these cases, the JTAPI runtime is supposed to manage the Call by either finding the correct ACD group to use or passing by the Call onto an acceptable ACD Group other than the one initially specified by the application.

ACDAddressObserver

Earlier we saw how Agent events were reported to the ACDTerminalObserver interface. They are also reported to this ACDAddressObserver interface. Here it is:

```
package javax.telephony.callcenter;
import  javax.telephony.AddressObserver;
public interface ACDAddressObserver extends AddressObserver { }
```

As usual, this interface is to be implemented for applications requesting notification of state changes for an ACDAddress (i.e., an ACD Group).

Before we move on to the remaining subjects of call center capabilities and events, we feel a need to apologize to the reader for our basting of the ACD design. While some may feel it is a sport to tear apart the design of others, that is not the intent here. Others may feel the opposite — that the quality of a software design is in the eyes of the beholder and that we are way out of line in criticizing this design. While there may some truth to both of these extremes, our basic goal is to explain this API. When we first saw JTAPI, we were very impressed by the overall architecture — and we still are. However, it is only fair that we expose areas where it may be improved and in doing so, clarify what we believe to be the intent of the design so that even if you don't *like* it, you can still *use* it.

Call Center Capabilities

Figure 8.27 lists the capabilities interfaces for the call center package.

Figure 8.27 *Call Center Capabilities*

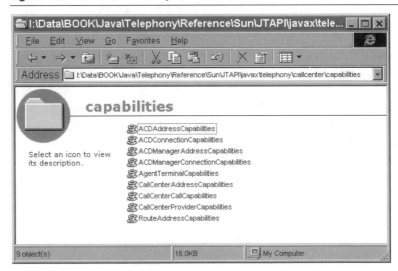

Rather than listing all of these here, we refer you to the JTAPI source. Basically, these interfaces do what all capabilities interfaces do — tell whether or not a feature is implemented.

Call Center Events

The phone package events are listed in **Figure 8.28**.

Figure 8.28 *Call Center Events*

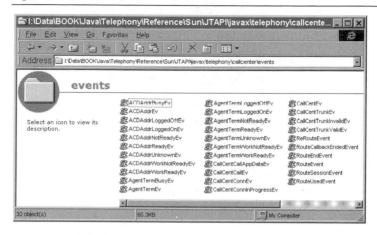

Recall the close relationship between events and observers. The following is the mapping of which observers are to respond to which events for the entire Call Center package.

ACDAddressObserver

- ACDAddrEv
- ACDAddrBusyEv
- ACDAddrLoggedOffEv
- ACDAddrLoggedOnEv
- ACDAddrNotReadyEv
- ACDAddrReadyEv
- ACDAddrUnknownEv
- ACDAddrWorkNotReadyEv
- ACDAddrWorkReadyEv

CallCenterCallObserver

- CallCentCallEv
- CallCentTrunkValidEv
- CallCentTrunkInvalidEv
- CallCentCallAppDataEv
- CallCentConnInProgressEv

AgentTerminalObserver

- AgentTermEv
- AgentTermBusyEv

- AgentTermLoggedOffEv

- AgentTermLoggedOnEv

- AgentTermNotReadyEv

- AgentTermReadyEv

- AgentTermUnknownEv

- AgentTermWorkNotReadyEv

- AgentTermWorkReadyEv

Private Data Packages

Private Data is intended to be the backdoor of JTAPI. It allows for platform-specific functions to be called and provides a partitioning space for platform-specific data definitions. Of course, any use of these functions is nonportable, even across otherwise portable JTAPI implementations, due to the proprietary nature of the data sent and received across this interface.

Private Data Core Components

The Private Data Core Components are depicted in **Figure 8.29**. Package Private Data contains only one interface, PrivateData. Implementations are expected to implement this interface for platform-specific data definitions and nonstandard platform calls.

Figure 8.29 *Private Data Core Components*

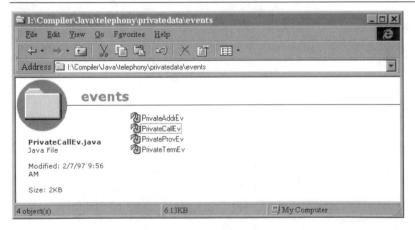

The PrivateData interface exposes two methods: `setPrivateData()` and `sendPrivateData()`. Each of these methods takes a single parameter of type object. If more than one piece of data is required in the call, the object would pass some list type (e.g., a vector) containing the appropriate data for the call. Note how this idiom provides for the return of data as well (just change the data in the list).

The primary benefit of this class is to provide a consistent interface for partitioning platform-specific data and behavior. This practice enhances maintainability primarily by localizing code and making it easily identifiable. For example, device-specific data can be defined in one place (or in one set of classes) in the code. In short, PrivateData is used here as a *partitioning* mechanism.

If there is no platform-specific data to pass to a platform function, some might argue that the utility of this interface is questionable. From a functional perspective it is not clear what added benefit a platform-specific wrapper class provides. All platform-specific behavior can be hidden in the implementation of any given method. And so some (primarily cowboys) may feel that an interface like this may add nothing to an implementation except a slight overhead. Nevertheless, its use is optional and so for those who find it useful (software engineers) it is available. Let's take a closer look at the methods provided. Here's how the interface looks:

```
package javax.telephony.privatedata;
import   javax.telephony.*;


public interface PrivateData {

    public void setPrivateData( Object data );
    public Object getPrivateData();
    public Object sendPrivateData( Object data );
}
```

Let's look at each method individually. First, let's pass some data to an underlying library.

Sending Data to the Underlying Native Platform

The JATPI specification says this can be done in one of two ways. The first approach simply passes some data that the underlying native implementation is expecting using a single call to `sendPrivateData` () as in **Listing 8.8**.

Listing 8.8 *Sending Private Data, Option 1a*

```
//assume the implementation implements this ctor...
SDRPrivateData pd = new SDRPrivateData();
// the native interface expects the integer 31...
pd.sendPrivateData( new Integer( 31 ));
```

In this case, the underlying implementation is simply expecting a particular value of a particular type and we just pass it on. For example, the receipt of the integer 31 may cause some action on the telephony board such as system initialization.

Most interfaces, however, are not as simple to use as this. Specifically, many APIs require multiple parameters. In this case, we might simply pass a Vector of values as required by the interface[27] as in **Listing 8.9**.

Listing 8.9 *Sending Private Data, Option 1b*

```
// this native interface expects the integer 31
// followed by a string...
Vector v = new Vector(2);
v.addElement( new Integer(31));
v.addElement( "Welcome to the Machine..." );
pd.sendPrivateData( v );
```

Note that we are using either new instances (i.e., we are not relying on static data or instance variables) or we have created local variables to pass as parameters. This is what is meant by the term "immediate." It is not necessary to synchronize these methods so that multiple threads can't botch the data before it is sent because if we follow this idiom, these methods are reentrant.[28] Clearly this supports non–object-oriented APIs, which are common for native platform functions.

The second way to send data is to do it in stages. Some APIs require the initialization of some data prior to calling a function. Using this approach, we first initialize the data with a call to `setPrivateData()`. Next, we call `sendPrivateData()` (just as in the first approach), which may or may not require additional data. In short, we use the API with pairs of calls to these methods. This approach is shown here:

```
try {
    SDRPrivateData pd = new SDRPrivateData();
    pd.setPrivateData( data );
    pd.sendPrivateData( otherData );
} catch ( Exception e ) {
    // handle exceptions...
}
```

The pair-wise calls are required. The code in **Lisiting 8.10** may be erroneous.

---

27 This technique is covered in more detail in Chapter 10.
28 Recall that reentrant functions are inherently thread-safe because they use only local data.

Listing 8.10 *A Questionable Invocation of* `sendPrivateData()`

```
try {
   Integer data = new Integer( 25 );
   Integer otherData = new Integer( 26 );
   Integer yetOtherData = new Integer( 27 );
   SDRPrivateData pd = new SDRPrivateData();
   pd.setPrivateData( data );
   pd.sendPrivateData( otherData );
   // if this next call relies on data, it's toast...
   pd.sendPrivateData( yetOtherData );
} catch ( Exception e ) {
   // handle exceptions...
}
```

Note that we said the code *may be* erroneous *if* the second call relied on the prior data. That's because the interpretation of which platform function to invoke is entirely dependent on the data sent. If the entire underlying API required data initialization prior to the invocation of any function, the second call to `sendPrivateData()` would certainly fail in some platform-specific manner (which of course may or may not send failure notifications to the JTAPI runtime!). Otherwise, it may or may not fail depending on what "yetOtherData" means to the native platform.

We can see how private data can be sent to peripheral devices. But how is data received? Enter Private Data Events.

Private Data Events

Private Data Events are used not only for notification, but also for transmission of private data. This is a subtle departure from the "normal" JATPI way of doing things using specialized observers, but is conceptually the same and identical with respect to event processing. Currently, JTAPI provides four events as shown in **Figure 8.30**.

Each of these objects extend the proper event object (i.e., AddrEv, CallEv, ProvEv, and TermEv, respectively) and provides one additional method as follows:

```
public abstract Object getPrivateData()
```

Here are the interfaces in order:

```
package javax.telephony.privatedata.events;
import javax.telephony.events.*;

public interface PrivateAddrEv extends AddrEv {
   public static final int ID = 600;
   public Object getPrivateData();
}
```

```
public interface PrivateCallEv extends CallEv {
  public static final int ID = 601;
  public Object getPrivateData();
}

public interface PrivateProvEv extends ProvEv {
  public static final int ID = 602;
  public Object getPrivateData();
}

public interface PrivateTermEv extends TermEv {
  public static final int ID = 603;
  public Object getPrivateData();
}
```

Notice anything missing? It's the observers. Unlike all the other previous packages, the private data package defines no new observer. So how do we get the data if there are no observers defined?

Figure 8.30 *Private Data Events*

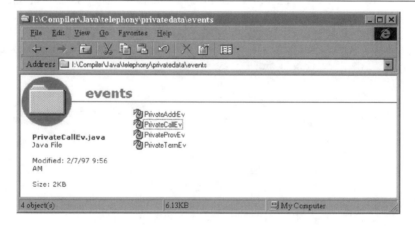

Retrieving Data from the Underlying Native Platform

No observer is necessary because we already have many that understand how to process (i.e., accept as parameters) the parent interfaces of all the private data events. Thus we can cleverly use extension to gather private data in a regular old application. **Listing 8.11** shows how.

Listing 8.11 *Retrieving Data from the Platform Interface Using Private Data*

```
package sroberts.telephony;

import javax.telephony.*;
import  javax.telephony.events.*;


public class SDRCallObserver implements CallObserver {

synchronized public void callChangedEvent( CallEv[]
        eventList ) {

    String name = null;
    String msg = null;

    System.out.println( "CallObserver NOTIFIED. Report:" );
    System.out.println( "****************************" );

    for ( int i=0; i < eventList.length; i++ ) {

        if (isCallListener && eventList[i] instanceof CallEv) {
          try {
             Call call = ((CallEv)eventList[i]).getCall();
             Connection[] conns = call.getConnections();
             Provider prov = call.getProvider();
             name = prov.getName();
             msg = "Provider named: (" + name + ")
                   owns a Call that is —>> ";
             if (conns == null) {
                System.out.println(msg + "IDLE");    }
             else if (eventList[i].getID() ==
                   CallActiveEv.ID) {
                System.out.println(msg + "ACTIVE");    }
             else if (eventList[i].getID() ==
                   CallInvalidEv.ID) {
                System.out.println(msg + "INVALID");    }
             else if (eventList[i].getID() ==
                   PrivateCallEv.ID) {
                System.out.println(msg + "PRIVATE DATA:");    }
                Integer i =
                   (Integer)eventList[i].getPrivateData();
          } catch (Exception excp) {
             System.out.println( "CallEv Exception occurred
                in SDRCallObserver::callChangedEvent()..." );
             excp.printStackTrace();
```

Listing 8.11 (cont.) *Retrieving Data from the Platform Interface Using Private Data*

```
            }
        }
        if (isCallListener && eventList[i] instanceof
            PrivateCallEv) {
          try {
            System.out.println(msg
                + "PRIVATE DATA: instanceof approach");}
            Integer i =
                (Integer)eventList[i].getPrivateData();
          } catch (Exception excp) {
            System.out.println(
                " PrivateCallEv Exception occurred in
                SDRCallObserver::callChangedEvent()...");
            excp.printStackTrace();
          }
        }
      }
    }
}
```

Clearly this design encourages an event-oriented approach whereby the target object receives an event and then queries it for data, if any. As we have learned, events are designed to support asynchronous processing, which is essential in telephony programming. We see that events can also be used to transport data, and that is a good thing as well.

Private Data Capabilities

The standard capabilities specified for private data are listed in **Figure 8.31**. There is only one interface in this package as follows:

```
package javax.telephony.privatedata.capabilities;

public interface PrivateDataCapabilities {

  public boolean canSetPrivateData();
  public boolean canGetPrivateData();
  public boolean canSendPrivateData();
}
```

Figure 8.31 *Private Data Capabilities*

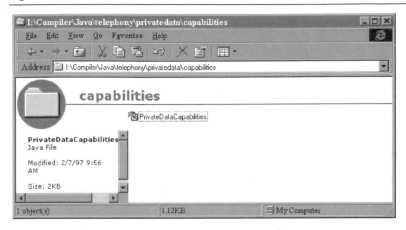

Summary

In this chapter, we have covered all of the standard extension packages defined in JTAPI. These are all the subpackages under `javax.tele-phony` except for packages `javax.telephony.capabilities` and `javax.telephony.events` (which actually belong with the core package and were covered in Chapter 4).

This completes Part III, and hence our coverage of JTAPI. In the remaining chapters, we delve into areas concerning general telecom development in a Java environment. The techniques and idioms in the following chapters may be useful in any JTAPI program or implementation.

PART V

REAL WORLD TELEPHONY PROGRAMMING

In this part, we shift gears. We investigate processes that generally lead to the construction of more productive and reusable software. We also get real. We move from the instructional examples of the previous section (which are useful for demonstrating implementation techniques) to more industrial strength software construction and design concepts used professionally. We take a fairly critical look at some of the practices and idioms of the day and attempt to cast the light of truth upon them .

Many in software development would like to believe that software tools work as advertised right out of the box. From experience, we know this is not, nor will it likely ever be, true — even with Java. Professional programmers often find themselves spending time creating infrastructure layers to support the shortcomings of a particular tool set (and even programming language!). In the long run, it is always more productive to spend time early on analyzing libraries and organizing software into functional layers for the purpose of creating an architectural back-plane for a successful development effort. To pretend that any library is designed so well that it suits all needs for all application development efforts for all time is simply a myth. We will find that this is true even for JTAPI.

In Chapter 9, we initiate the construction of an infrastructure layer of reusable code that will prove useful for any Java development effort. The motivation for creating these components will be driven by the needs of generic telephony applications. For example, all telephony applications require an effective notification mechanism. If we were using C/C++ and MFC or the Win32 API, we would use NT events. If we were using Smalltalk, we would use Smalltalk's built-in event notification mechanism or its dependency model. But because we are using Java, we will use Java's dependency mechanism and will attempt to use Java events. If we find that any of these built-in capabilities are insufficient for our needs, we will roll our own mechanisms.

Next, Chapter 10 provides an examination of some common idioms that may be used in Java code that are of particular interest to telephony programmers. Components will be enhanced to implement various telephony patterns we have discovered. Many of these are skeletons from the education closet or born from sheer observation. Others are from the frustrating annals of experience. We will examine many common issues in telephony programming and provide solutions in Java. Finally, in Chapter 11, we take a look at common pitfalls in telephony development and examine some practices that may be of use for large-scale application development in a telecom environment.

Chapter 9

EVENT MANAGEMENT IN JAVA

"Talk amongst yourselves — I'll give you a topic."
Coffee Talk, on *Saturday Night Live*

In this chapter, we investigate three[1] forms of event management possible in Java: ***dependency***, ***delegation,*** and ***message management***. Recall that our motivation is either to discover or to provide a flexible and extensible asynchronous notification model for use in telephony programming. In fact, JTAPI *requires* the use of an event management implementation of some kind. We have seen how the JTAPI design seems to imply an implementation using one of these mechanisms — namely, dependency. But other notification mechanisms may be used instead. Here, we dig into how dependency and delegation are implemented and introduce the concept of message management.

Event management could be classified as either an idiom or a pattern. Indeed, Gamma et al. describe one of these notification models (dependency) as a pattern called "Observer" because it may be implemented in an indirect fashion using any object-oriented language. However, we chose to classify it as an idiom because it is supported in a direct fashion by the programming languages Java and Smalltalk, yet its proper use may still require some understanding of the underlying design.

---

1 We'll also briefly investigate the use of CORBA events, but not in any detail.

Event Management in a Nutshell

At a minimum, event management involves three primary kinds of objects: a *source*, an *event* and one or more *targets*. The model involves a two-step process: event *registration* (asking to be notified) and event *notification* (actually being notified). Before notification can occur, each target must register in advance for a particular event (see **Figure 9.1**). Later, the source (or another) object generates the event, which notifies the target as in **Figure 9.2**. The target may also cancel (deregister for) this notification request.[2]

Figure 9.1 *Event Registration*

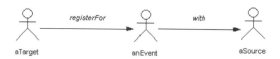

In one sense, event management is by definition asynchronous in that event *registration* is disengaged from event *notification*. It is particularly well suited to telephony programming because most telephony objects communicate best in an asynchronous environment. Intuitively, event registration is similar to mailing a letter. You mail the letter, then go about your business (i.e., one does not sit at the mailbox waiting for a response before continuing on). However, event notification is *not* like periodically checking your mailbox (essentially polling), it's more like receiving a phone call. Event notification is a generalization of the concept of interrupts. Recall that interprocess communication (IPC) of all kinds require that the target object be interrupted by an event of some kind. This is the same general idea.

Figure 9.2 *Event Notification*

Notification may be provided in two fundamental ways. In the ***broadcast*** form, all events are sent to all registered targets. In the ***targeted*** form, notification is delivered based upon some other criteria (i.e., notification is filtered in some way — only a subset of the registered targets is notified). These approaches may be combined.

---

2 In one sense, deregistration may be presented as a third step. However, deregistration is simply the opposite of registration and the semantics are obvious so will not be discussed further.

The target's reaction to the notification from the event is either *explicit* or *polymorphic*. In other words, the target either explicitly passes some form of a *callback* to be invoked upon notification, or it implements a well-known *common signature* that is invoked upon the occurrence of the event. In either case, this "reaction function" is referred to as an *event handler*. An event handler is simply a function that contains code to be executed upon event delivery — it *handles* the event.

In an object-oriented setting, it is instructive to realize how event notification differs from *synchronous* notification. In this context, the term "synchronous notification" is just another name for a typical subprogram invocation. Normally, one object directly invokes the method of another (or one of its own). The source always knows who the target is, and the target always responds in the same manner. With events, the source does not necessarily need to directly know the identity of the target, nor does it necessarily care.[3] Although it may be processed in the same thread[4] just like a normal subprogram call, the invocation method (event handler) is never called *directly*. In addition, each target may be of a different type, and so may respond to the same event in a different manner — or not at all. There is an inherent natural beauty to this form of communication in that it seems to model many real world occurrences and behaviors.

A Brief Illustration

Suppose we have an object called CallCenter[5] and we employ the broadcast form of notification. CallCenter generates three events called UP, DOWN, and ON_FIRE. The semantics are as follows: UP means it can process calls, DOWN means it cannot, and ON_FIRE means it is in trouble. When the CallCenter enters certain states, it triggers these events. Two target instances register for notification of types Caller and Fireman, respectively. We can intuitively guess that each of these targets will react in a different manner to the occurrence of these events. The Fireman would probably ignore the UP and DOWN events and would hopefully invoke a method like `putOutFireAt( CallCenter cc )` when notified of an ON_FIRE event. Likewise, the Caller would attempt to place a call only if the CallCenter were UP; it might invoke a cowardly method `stayAwayFrom( CallCenter cc )` in response to the ON_FIRE event.

So, using broadcast we find that the target registers for notification of *all* events the source (in this case, CallCenter) generates. When these events

---

3 Some implementations require that the source know the target, but this is not a design requirement.

4 Implementing notification from the same thread is possible but can be highly problematic and is not recommended. More on this later.

5 The example classes used here are not to be confused with the JTAPI interfaces of the same name. They are used for illustration only.

actually are generated, they are sent to the registered targets (in this case, both Fireman and Caller). Each target then inspects which event was sent and decides what to do in reaction to that event occurrence.

If, instead, a targeted form of notification were employed, the process would be different. In this case, the source would keep track of which objects registered for which specific events the source generates and not necessarily *all* of them. In other words, registration is *selective*. Likewise, notification is not broadcast; rather, it is also selective.

In this case, both the Firemen and the Caller would register only for those events they are interested in. The Fireman would register for the ON_FIRE event and the Caller would register for all three events (ON_FIRE, UP and DOWN). The source would then send ON_FIRE events only to the Fireman so she doesn't waste time on checking for events she doesn't care about (e.g., UP and DOWN). On the other hand, both the Caller and the Fireman are interested in the ON_FIRE event (for different reasons) and this event would be sent to the Caller as well.

A Set of Event Management Model Design Requirements

Before we investigate the various event management models, let's enumerate a set of requirements necessary for telephony asynchronous notification — a kind of telephony programmer's wish list, if you will:

- *Asynchronous Registration* — We need a built-in mechanism for objects to register for and then receive notification of the occurrence of predefined events in an asynchronous fashion. In other words, we don't want to have to write a lot of code to gain event functionality.

- *Arbitrary Object Notification and Registration* — We'd like to be able to have an *arbitrary* object (a target) notified when something occurs (an event). In other words, we want *all* types of Objects to exhibit registration and notification behavior – not just *some* classes

- *Nonaltered Interface* — We'd like to be able to register for an event occurrence and receive notification without changing the interface of the source or the target. Their reaction to an event occurrence should already be a part of their behavior. Therefore, we do not want to be required to alter this behavior just to register for or to react to an event occurrence.

- *Source Identification Option* — In some circumstances, we may want to register for event notification without regard to the source; in others, we may only be interested in notification from a particular source. We want it both ways.

- *Event Filtering* — We'd like to be notified only about those events we registered for, not all events. In other words, we'd like the option of using a targeted notification mechanism, not just broadcast.

- *Different Targets and Registrars* — We'd like to have the flexibility of having one object perform event registration on behalf of another target object.

- *Asynchronous Notification* — We'd like the source object to be able to trigger an event and then go about its business without having to wait for all targets to be notified. Further, we do not want to be forced to wait for all responses to run to their completion before continuing on.[6]

Let's examine what Java offers and see how we can use what's already provided for us. We begin with the Java implementation of dependency — namely, the Observation Model.

Dependency — The Java Observation Model

Java provides a lightweight event management mechanism sometimes called the Observation Model (lifted directly from Smalltalk) that allows for a simple form of event processing. In Smalltalk, this support is called *dependency*. The designers of Java chose to incorrectly credit the design patterns book as the originators of this "observer pattern" although it has been a feature of Smalltalk since its inception.[7] In Java, the abstract class Observable implements the dependency mechanism in conjunction with the abstract interface called Observer.[8] Their static relationship is depicted in **Figure 9.3** in the form of an OMT object diagram.

Understanding the Observation Model

The Observation Model is an event management scheme of the broadcast form. It allows **observers** to register their interest in the *entire state* of an **observable** object. The observer cannot specify which particular change it is interested in. All the observer knows is that something changed in an object it's concerned with. It cannot determine exactly what that change is until it actually receives the change notification.[9] At that point, they must examine the "event" to determine whether or not it wishes to respond. Typically, the event itself is not implemented as a different type of object in

---

6 This requires the use of some form of IPC (e.g., threads).

7 There is a recurring tendency among language designers to steal features from other programming languages and then pretend they got the information from some other source. For example, advocates of C++ have always pretended that Ada generics did not influence the concept of C++ templates (which, of course, is nonsense). This grand tradition continues with Java.

8 In Smalltalk, it is implemented in the root of the hierarchy — class Object. It is not clear why this capability is not provided in Java for all Objects — instead we are forced to subclass and implement interfaces.

9 This is why it is called "dependency" — the target is *dependent* on the state of the source.

it's own right; rather it is a copy of the source itself or some ***aspect***[10] of the source.

Figure 9.3 *Dependency — The Java Observation Model*

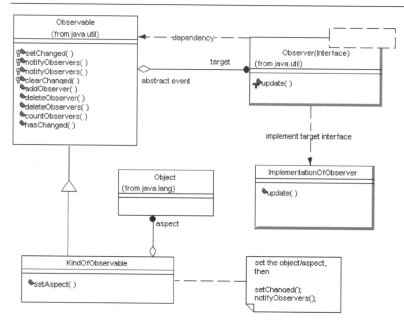

An Exercise in Anthropomorphism

At the risk of committing a literary crime, let's create anthropomorphism from telephones and girls in order to illustrate the implications of the Observation Model. Suppose eight girls live in a dorm with only one telephone. Clearly, they are all interested in the state of the telephone; they are all *observers*. The telephone itself (or its incoming call) is the observable object. All girls register their interest in the state of the telephone by staying in close proximity to it so they can hear it ring or be notified (in verbal relay fashion) when the telephone's state changes. It rings. Five run to it. One observer wins. When its state changes to ANSWERED, each girl wants to query it further to find out if the call is for her (or not!).

When the phone rings, the telephone invokes each girl's `update()` method passing some information as a parameter. After finding out that the event is a phone ring by examining the state of the telephone, some girls will choose to attempt to answer the phone, others will ignore the ring, instead waiting for verbal notification from whoever does answer the phone. Still others might just let the answering machine take the call.

---

10 In either case, it is an instance variable or a copy of some value. It had better be enough information for the observer to react to.

Others might rather sleep no matter who calls. But the point is that no observers have a choice — they must examine all events anyway. Why? Because *all* events are broadcast to *all* observers.

When the state becomes ANSWERED, the telephone again invokes every girl's `update()` method; again passing some information as a parameter. Presumably the telephone call would contain information about for whom the call was intended. Only after each girl examines the call can she determine for herself how she will react to it — if at all.

It is important to note that the observers are unaware of the kind of event that has occurred until they examine it — that's why they *must* examine every event from the source. Further, all observers must examine every event, even those they may not be interested in (after all, Susie doesn't really care that much that Heather's distant aunt called, but she had to examine the ANSWERED event anyway), first to determine it was indeed an answered phone call, and second who called. The sleepy girl should have called the `removeObserver()` method passing herself as a parameter. This is the essence of the dependency/observation model.

Implementing the Observation Model

An object makes itself "observable" by allowing "observers" to register their interest in the state of the object. As in the general model, the target registers with the source. The observer is the target, the observable the source. When the state of the observable object changes (typically by a change to the value of an instance variable), the observer is notified. Here's how it works. First, the Observable abstract class is extended to a concrete class (presumably the source) and the Observer interface is implemented to play the role of the target. For those instance variables the observable source object publishes as being changed (called aspects), the programmer invokes the notification API immediately *after* changing that instance variable (see **Listing 9.1** [1]–[3]).

Listing 9.1 *An Observable Source Object*

```java
import java.util.*;
public class KindOfObservable extends Observable
    private int aspect = 0;
    public int getAspect() { return aspect; }
    public void setAspect( int a ) {
        if ( aspect != a ) {
            aspect = a;
            // here's the notification API…
            setChanged();
            notifyObservers();
            clearChanged();
        }
    }
}
```

(1)
(2)
(3)

Next, the target object implements the Observer interface providing an `update()` method that queries the state of a source object which is passed as a parameter (**Listing 9.2** [4]). The target is then registered with the source by invoking the `addObserver( Observer aTarget )` protocol. Registration is complete — on to notification.

Listing 9.2 *An Observer Target Object*

```
import java.util.*;
public class ImplementationOfObserver implements Observer {
    public void update( Observable obs ) {
        // now that we have obs, we can examine its state
        if ( obs.getAspect() == 12 ) {
            doSomething();
        }
    }
}
```

(4)

(5)

When the event is triggered, the source object[11] itself (or a copy) is passed to the observer(s), they examine the attributes they are interested in and respond accordingly (see **Listing 9.2** [5]).

The dependency mechanism (or some derivative thereof) seems to be an obvious candidate for implementing event management in JTAPI. In fact, the fit is so good that this implementation design is almost *implied by* the API design. But does the Observation Model satisfy our general requirements? Let's see.

We can certainly have an object notified when something occurs, but neither party involved can be an *arbitrary* object. First, the source must inherit from class Observable. Next, the target must implement the Observer interface (i.e., it must change its interface). This means that any class participating in this form of notification *must* implement the required interfaces and modify its inheritance hierarchy. *Strike One ...*

The dependency mechanism allows registration with a particular source, but not without regard to that source. The registration is instance based (as opposed to class based or arbitrary). We must register with a *particular* source — we don't have a choice. In some designs, this may be exactly what we want. In others, we might not care who the source is. In still others, we may want to register before the identity of the source is even known. *Strike Two ...*

When we register for notification, we cannot specify which aspect we are interested in unless we register with a particular event instance (more on this later). In other words, the Observable object decides which methods and aspect changes trigger notification, not the observer. *Foul Ball ...*

---

11 Actually, any Object may be passed. But to make the protocol work, it must refer somehow to the observable of interest. The easiest way to accomplish this is to simply pass a pointer to the observable.

The Observer will be notified if *any* notification-aware attribute changes, not just those they may have wanted to be registered for. There is no way to *not* be notified of all events that are triggered by the source. This is because the design is a broadcast model where all dependents (observers) are notified of all changes. They then react or ignore each such notification. *Strike Three ...*

There is no standard mechanism to filter the event notification based upon target criteria at runtime. *We're out ... Why are we still at the plate?*

Well, we still haven't seen if dependency can be used to implement JTAPI notification. The problem is, we can't. Why? The issue is the event handler signature. When we examine the function signature required of an Observer, we see that it differs from any of those required for JTAPI Observers. For example, a CallObserver must implement an event handler for `callChangedEvent()`. In contrast, the dependency Observer is to implement the `update()` event handler. Therefore, we cannot use the dependency interface directly, nor should we.[12]

Swallowing the Pill

Besides the fact that we can't use it with JTAPI, let's take a moment to digest all of the ramifications this architecture imposes on our code. First, being forced to inherit from Observable is probably something we can swallow, although it may present a real problem for some designs.[13] For example, my normal OO programming practices of inheriting all my objects from my class IdentifiableObject must be abandoned in order to use the dependency classes provided in Java.[14]

Fortunately, Java provides a simple (although inferior) solution if I am willing to recode my classes as interfaces (see **Listing 9.3**).

Listing 9.3 *An Object Becomes an Interface*

```
public interface Identifiable {
    public int getId();
    public void setId( int newId ) ;
    public String getName();
    public void setName ( String n );
}
```

---

12 Of course, we *could* implement any JTAPI Observer in terms of the dependency Observer interface (by invoking it in the implementation). But what would this buy us? Nothing but an extra layer of overhead because in either case, we'd have to override the `update()` method. Further, it would require some heavy casting.

13 Had the language designers made notification a feature of class Object, we would not be in this boat.

14 It may be argued that the language designers broke a fundamental rule of language design — interfering with the programmer's prerogative. This is one reason many programmers may opt **not** to use the observable classes.

Unfortunately, interfaces don't allow the declaration of instance variables (just constants). So each class that implements the interface outside a particular class hierarchy must not only provide an identical implementation, but must also declare the affected instance variables over and over again (as in **Listing 9.4**). This is tedious, some would even say stupid. It negates one of the prime benefits of inheritance, namely, code reuse. In short, we want to inherit method implementations and instance variables, not just signatures!

Listing 9.4 *The Redundancy of Interfaces*

```
class IdentifiableObject implements Identifiable {
    private int id;          // must re-declare these
    private String name;     // in each hierarchy
    public int getId() { return this.id; };
    public void setId( int id ) { this.id = id; };
    public String getName() { return this.name; };
    public void setName ( String name ) { this.name = name; };
}
```

This is an example of why it is important that language designers take great care when designing class hierarchies in languages that do not support multiple inheritance. Contrary to popular trade rag magazines from self-appointed industry gurus, Java interfaces are not a more "elegant solution" to the "multiple inheritance problem." In this context, interfaces are a less-than-optimal work-around, at best (Eiffel, CLOS, and C++ programmers would call it a hack). But we can get around this (slightly) by following yet another idiom. Bjarne Stroustrup and James Coplien discuss various multiple inheritance and specification-from-implementation separation techniques like *implementation inheritance* and *concrete and abstract types*. These idioms may be transferred to Java and are presented in Chapter 10, "Idioms and Patterns in Telephony." In short, the general idea is that you go ahead and create a class that contains the appropriate instance variables required of the interface. You may provide getters and setters for each instance variable (thereby fully encapsulating them), or you may declare them public. Finally, this implementation class is made an instance variable of the class implementing the interface.

This idiom can be extended to further reuse. If the implementations are not identical but the data types are, the "interface mixin" class can be made abstract so that implementations can vary. Or the data types can be made Objects and cast to the appropriate type for each circumstance. There are benefits to using this approach. Indeed, it is the only practical idiom to use in this case. But it is clearly not a "superior" approach over multiple inheritance. Using this technique, we can mitigate the adverse impact to code reuse, but we cannot eradicate it. Anyway, back to events ...

As far as the Observer interface goes, we can probably also live with that interface requirement. Even though we'd rather not alter our interface, there is only one method `update()` we must implement (an arguably small price to pay for target participation in an event management scheme). Yet it is instructive to take a moment to digest the impact of forcing an object to alter its interface to receive notification. Why in the world should it? Do we change the shape of our ears to receive a telephone call? Thankfully, no. Neither should our code.

However, even if we are willing to "swallow the altered interface pill," the Observation Model as implemented in Java still doesn't satisfy all the requirements set forth. In short, we have failed all of them save one and a half. The Java Observation Model works well for some cases, but its shortcomings are evident. First, it encourages switch type processing in the target implementation of `update()` because there is only one event handler per class for all possible events. Second, the dependency mechanism supports a broadcast model and so does not allow for a standard way of altering the timing notification among multiple dependents nor for adding additional processing or constraint checks (e.g., pre- and postconditions) before and after the occurrence of an event. Further, it does not allow for the coordination of notification among dependents. The broadcast mechanism is also inefficient in that it blindly notifies every object that has registered, regardless of what they were registering for;[15] and each target must usually query the "event" twice: once for identification and again for content. And finally, there is no *standard* way to ack/nak the notification back to the source to ensure that the target has received the notification event.

Requirements Satisfaction Using the Observation Model

So far, we can use the Observation Model to satisfy only one of our requirements (see **Table 9.1** for the status).

Does this mean we cannot use dependency? Absolutely not. If we are willing to live with the design restrictions, it will suffice in a large number of cases. But it is not in and of itself powerful enough or flexible enough for general-purpose use. It obviously involves a lot of potentially needless target interruption for events about which they may not care. In fact, if the notification process is single-threaded, this may pose a serious performance bottleneck problem for some types of applications. Later, we will modify the Observable Model mechanism to support most of the required behavior, including a nonblocking notification mechanism. First, let's take another approach by trying to use Java's event delegation model "off-the-shelf."

---

15 Programmers can pass an aspect by using the `notifyObservers( Object )` protocol, but this still requires (at a minimum) a type check on the part of the Observer if it's registered with more than one observable source.

Table 9.1 *Observation Model Requirements Satisfaction*

Requirement	Status	Reason
Asynchronous registration	Satisfied[16]	Fully supported by Observation Model
Arbitrary object notification and registration	Unsatisfied	Observation Model requires both extension and interface implementation
Nonaltered interface	Partially Satisfied	Source object okay,[17] but target must implement update() protocol
Source identification option	Unsatisfied	Observation Model forces the source to be the responsible party for notification
Event filtering	Unsatisfied	Observation Model supports only the broadcast form of notification
Different targets and registrars	Unsatisfied	Observation Model forces the target to be the same object as the registrar
Asynchronous notification	Unsatisfied	Observation Model provides no async option

Delegation — The Java Event Model

The Java delegation model was created in reaction to the inadequacies of the Java 1.0 model of event processing. In short, the old model was based entirely on a widget-oriented architecture that required programmers to subclass visual components in order to implement event processing.[18] This model worked but coupled the event handling code with the visual component. It also introduced potential performance problems as events were essentially pushed up inheritance hierarchies searching for an event handler.[19]

---

16 Actually, the degree of synchronicity depends on the implementation of the notification mechanism. If the entire notification process is implemented within a single thread, it is technically synchronous. It is only asynchronous in that registration is separated from notification. Each of these processes may be implemented asynchronously.

17 Actually, the source is not really okay because the interface was altered through extension!

18 Many other commercial OO widget architectures have used this model (e.g., zApp, Zinc).

19 Performance hits could be mitigated by explicitly consuming events, but this approach was still awkward.

To solve these shortcomings, Java 1.1 introduced another Smalltalk concept called *delegation*. Delegation is the process by which one class delegates some or all of its responsibility to another class. The delegated class then performs that action on their behalf. In general, this decoupling allows for the event handler to be reused by other components. It also allows for (but does not specify) an ideal "jettison point" for worker threads. Many believe this model to be an improvement for user interface processing. However, does it work for general-purpose event management — will delegation work for telephony programming? And why should event management be different for visual components than for any other kind of object? We'll explore these issues shortly. First, let's get our bearings.

Understanding the Delegation Model

Conceptually, the Delegation Model is essentially the same general event management model with slightly different terminology. The source is still a source, the event is now an explicit class (an instance of class EventObject), and the target is called a *listener* (an object that implements the EventListener *marker interface*). The target still registers with the source. However, there are major differences as well. Because they are not specified in the model, the implementation of the target's reaction and the notification mechanism may be implemented in many different ways. For example, one implementation has the source (rather than the target) determine the kind of event that occurred. In any case, the target may eliminate the event type check altogether because the context of the call is now explicit (i.e., the target knows the identity of the event). The target now explicitly registers for an event, not a general state change in the source. The source then calls the appropriate event handler of each event listener only when that particular event is fired. Rather than just passing information about itself, the source actually generates an event and passes that instead. There is no loss of flexibility because the event holds a pointer back to the source. And finally, the delegation model supports a targeted form of notification rather than a broadcast form.

◀

Back to the Dorm...

The phone rings again. George answers it. It's for Heather. Susie called (again...). Before George could even hear the phone ring, he invoked its `addListener()` method[20] with himself as a parameter (this is a requirement of all boys entering the girl's dorm as well as this idiom!). He was then able to receive the event when the phone

---

20 This method is functionally equivalent to the `addObserver()` registration method of the Observation Model.

invoked his `onRing()` event handler. Once the phone was ANSWERED, the `onAnswered()` method of each answer listener was invoked. The sleepy girl never bothered to register for RING notification, but she did for ANSWER notification — for that she was willing to open an eye.

Implications of the Delegation Model

The notification mechanism is the same as in the Observation Model in that the source object hangs on to a collection of interested listeners (previously called observers in the Observation Model). The difference here is that there may be multiple lists of listeners, one for each type of event supported in the source. This is called *multicast event delivery* and is strongly advised (the corresponding *unicast event delivery* is discouraged). It is also different in the implementation of the notification mechanism. Instead of having all listeners (targets) implement a single `update()` method, the Delegation Model requires the listener to implement a single method for each type of event the source is able to generate. So for the RING event in our latest dorm incident, each listener is required to implement an `onRing`[21]`()` method whether or not they care about answering the phone. An implementation for the `onAnswered()` interface method must also be provided. However, the difference is they don't *have to* do anything in response to any event (i.e., although interface bodies are required, they may be empty[22]). In terms of performance, the advantage of this approach over that of the Observation Model is the savings of an event type-check in the listener. Although the source may still have to make the check before the call in some implementations,[23] there are almost always more targets than sources; and so it's better for the source to take the performance hit. However, the listener method is still invoked, even if it has no body.

Trouble on the Horizon

On the surface, it seems like we've made some headway. Unfortunately, there are problems with the Java implementation of the Delegation Model that render it useless for general-purpose event management without extreme modification. It's not that it can't be made to work — it can. The biggest problem with Java events is that they don't really *do* anything. There is no built-in mechanism to fire events and for listeners to respond to

---

21 Actually, the name may be anything, not just onXX where XX is the event name. But it is good practice to follow a naming convention of some kind.

22 Empty interface implementations are called "no-op" methods in that they provide "*no operation*" in the event handler — they simply do nothing! Classes that provide one or more no-op methods are called "adapter classes."

23 This source check can be eliminated by using the reflection API or another approach altogether. More on this later.

them. Programmers must code these by hand by following guess what – an idiom! In fact, we must follow an entire set of idioms.

Worse yet, one popular approach to implementing the Java Delegation Model requires any object registering for an event to drastically alter their interface (more so than in the Observation Model). Believe it or not, in order to be able to receive notification from a source that generates multiple events in this implementation of the Delegation Model, the target/listener has to implement an event handler for each event type triggered, *whether they use them or not*. It's kind of like registering for a raffle and having to permanently change into clothes that may not fit in order to do so — and then never taking them off! When the Observation Model required us to change our ear to receive messages, we only changed it once and in the same manner for every case (with the `update()` method). The Delegation Model forces us to change it in a different way for each kind of telephone call we may receive! Java's inner classes are often touted as the "solution" to this design fiasco. In reality, they are no help either. All they do is localize the event handling code. Another "Band-Aid" approach is to write a bunch of so-called adapter classes that provide no implementations for interfaces so you don't have to write this same useless code repeatedly. This approach can help, but it again interferes with the programmer's design. In the context of performance-sensitive telephony programs, adapter classes can only be used in trivial cases. We address this situation later.

An Important Bunny Trail — True Events

The problem with Java is that it's not Smalltalk. Even though Java has lifted many language features from Smalltalk implementations,[24] some are not implemented in the same way, nor do they behave in exactly the same manner. Three important capabilities that Smalltalk provides are sorely missed (or are implemented in an inferior manner) in Java. Let's cover the two that are missing first.

Smalltalk provides support for passing around arbitrary blocks of code (along with the context of their stack) as objects. This is an extremely powerful feature giving the programmer a level of control over dynamic behavior that is not easily achievable in Java.[25] This could come in very handy for telephony applications where we're always throwing around a lot of context-specific, state-oriented stuff. Smalltalk is also typeless, where Java is strongly typed. Although some would (correctly) argue that type safety is an important language feature, it can get in the way of writing generic code by requiring excess casting. The bottom line is that we can get along without these neat features, or we can usually simulate them in a manner suffi

---

24 (For example, even JavaBeans™ are implementations of wrapper classes taken from Digitalk Smalltalk.)

25 Although we take a stab at it later in the book (see Chapter 10).

cient to gain a close proximity to their functionality. It's another story altogether when a language feature is implemented in an incomplete manner. Such is the case with Java events. To understand their shortcomings, let's look at how to do it right.

The Smalltalk Event Mechanism

In Smalltalk (and beginning in Java 1.1), event management is built into the language by way of the class library provided. In Java, we are speaking of `java.util.EventObject` and its subclasses; in Smalltalk, class Object. Earlier we saw how both Smalltalk and Java support dependency mechanism as a form of event management. In this sense, they are more or less equivalent (except for the unfortunate subclassing requirement in Java). What makes Smalltalk superior to Java in this respect is the ease of use, the lack of required interface alterations, and the loose coupling of the objects involved. All of this is accomplished by simply placing the functionality in the root class instead of requiring the extension of another class.

In another more powerful form of Smalltalk notification typically referred to as "event management," the programmer communicates with the Smalltalk runtime system. Events are defined in a number of ways, and their scope is related to the manner in which they are defined. In Smalltalk, an event is not an object, it is just a name; a symbolic constant representing the fact that something just happened.[26]

To register for event notification, all one has to do is specify an event by name and then specify the callback or event handler to be invoked upon event occurrence. In general, the event registration protocol is as follows:

```
self when: #anEvent perform: #aCallback with: args
```

This registration is usually done by the target object, the one who wants to be notified (or in Java terminology the "listener" or "observer"). But it doesn't *have to* be. Registration can also occur elsewhere — even from an unrelated object! Event notification is accomplished by simply signaling the event from the source object. For example, the protocol is invoked as follows:

```
self signalEvent: #anEvent
```

Note that the object requesting notification (i.e., registering for the event occurrence) is not required to alter its interface in any way. It is supplying an existing method to be invoked; there is no requirement (or need) to code a special event handler.

---

26 This is only partially true! Because everything in Smalltalk is an object and events are implemented as instances of class Symbol, they are, in fact, objects. They do not, however, contain behavior that is used in the event management scheme.

The Smalltalk event management protocol is preferred over dependency due to its flexibility and maximum loose coupling. Any object can signal an event and any object can be a target/listener without altering its interface. More elaborate notification schemes may be built on top of these primitive operations.

Is this beautiful, or what? We'll revisit this notion later when we actually implement it in Java. For now, let's continue our investigation of Java events.

The Java Event Mechanism

In Java, enabling the delegation form of event management is not quite as transparent to the programmer as it is in Smalltalk.[27] A programmer doesn't just *use* the services provided; *he has to code them first!* Further, delegation does not resemble the Java dependency or the Smalltalk event model at all. This would not be a problem if the alternative worked in approximately the same manner without side effects. Unfortunately, we will find that this is not the case with Java events.

Just What Is a Java Event, Anyway?

A casual perusal of the public interface of the original class `java.awt.Event` (version 1.0) provides an excursion into the outer limits of questionable design. There is nothing inherent in an event that would lead one to assume that they should apply only to *visual* elements. Taking an extension approach, clearly the proper technique would have been to define a generic event and then subclass it for visual events.[28] This was corrected in version 1.1 of the language (see **Figure 9.4**).

Unfortunately, the new and improved definition of an event may also be confusing. In Java, events are full-blown objects. Our encapsulation instincts tell us this is good, but further examination reveals an awkward implementation (at least in the context it is normally presented in). Let's take a look at the standard presentation of events — another idiom.

All events using delegation are to inherit from class EventObject. In general, there are two types of events: visual and nonvisual. Most event tutorials present examples of visual widget-oriented event usage. Visual events come with lots of predefined adapter classes and constants. Although this use of events is perfectly acceptable, telephony programming generally requires the use of nonvisual events — the use of events in JavaBeans™ correlates more closely to what we are interested in. Unfortunately, this approach requires developers to construct the entire registration and notification mechanism from scratch.[29] We'll do just that

---

27 This is an extreme understatement.

28 Or at the very least, name the class something like WidgetEvent.

29 Actually, this may be considered a blessing in disguise after examining how visual events are implemented in Java.

using two different implementations. The first will involve a typical implementation we'll call the "Source Event Delegation (SED)" approach to implementing the Delegation Model. This is the approach normally encouraged when using visual events. We'll call the second approach "Decoupled Event Delegation (DED)."

Figure 9.4 *EventObject Class Hierarchy*

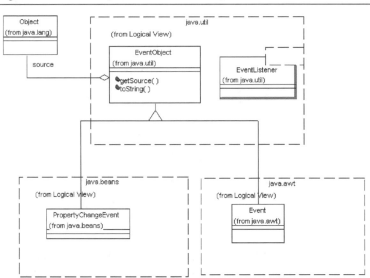

Source Event Delegation Approach

With SED, event types are defined and grouped in the context of their use by sources. For example, all events generated by a CallCenter[30] source object would be grouped into one EventObject class called, say, CallCenterEvent. Each type of CallCenterEvent would then be defined as a constant integer value. This is the event definition approach used in the `java.awt.event` package. For example, all types of mouse events are grouped into class `java.awt.event.MouseEvent`. Many different event definitions are defined in one class. In this model, event classes do not represent *atomic* events at all — they are portrayed as objects that can generate multiple *kinds of* events. Instead of using type extension (i.e., inheritance) to distinguish event types, presumably unique identifiers are passed upon instantiation.

So how does this SED architecture work? The event idiom is to use public instance variables (usually ints) as the definition of actual event *types* (see **Listing 9.5**) and then to provide matching event handlers by implementing the EventListener interface; one handler for each event type. In

---

30 Again, these are *not* JTAPI classes!

this way, the event handling code is encapsulated in the interface of the target and away from the source, while at the same time event definitions for a particular source are localized within one class. Public constants allow an easy mechanism for declaring variables to be used for the instantiation of instances of each event type and for type-checking their identity prior to notification. Let's revisit the CallCenter example we created when discussing the Observation Model and apply SED.

Listing 9.5 *Event Definition Using Delegation*

```
public class FireworkEvents extends java.util.EventObject {
    public static final int FIRE = 1;      // event "type"
    public static final int EXPLODE = 2; // another event "type"
}
```

Using the SED delegation model approach, we cram all of our event definitions into a single class and provide a public method for each event type in the interface implementation (see the CallCenterEvent class and the CallCenterListener class in **Figure 9.5**, respectively) of the target. Per SED, the generic CallCenterEvent class enumerates all possible event types a source can create (i.e., UP, DOWN, and ON_FIRE).

Figure 9.5 *Source Event Approach to the Delegation Model (SED)*

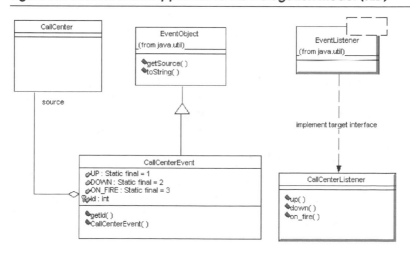

Next, sources are enabled to hang on to lists of listeners. This is easily accomplished by adding a collection type (such as a vector) to hold each type of listener required and is demonstrated in **Listing 9.6**, [6] and [8]. If another type of list is used (e.g., an Array as in [7]), care must be taken to ensure that list operations are synchronized to prevent update anomalies.

Listing 9.6 *Delegation Source Specification*

```
public class CallCenter {
(6)       protected Vector upListeners_;
(7)       protected Object[] downListeners_;
(8)       protected Vector fireListeners_;
          public void addUpListener(CallCenterListener ccl);
          public void
              removeUpListener(CallCenterListener ccl);
          public void synchronized
              addDownListener(CallCenterListener ccl);
          public void synchronized
              removeDownListener(CallCenterListener ccl);
          public void
              addFireListener(CallCenterListener ccl);
          public void
              removeFireListener(CallCenterListener ccl);
          public void route(CallCenterEvent evt);
(9)       protected void notifyUpListeners(CallCenterEvent evt);
(10)      protected void notifyDownListeners(CallCenterEvent evt);
(11)      protected void notifyFireListeners(CallCenterEvent evt);
}
```

Providing a single notification method for each event type supported enables notification. These methods also correspond one-to-one for each listener list ([9]–[11]). We may also optionally add an event routing method that will switch on incoming events and fire one of the three notification methods `notifyXXX()`, where `XXX` is the type of listener (for example, `notifyUpListeners()` has `XXX` equal to "UpListeners"). The routing method is actually an unnecessary extra step, but adds the maintenance benefit of placing all notification code in the same location.

Listing 9.7 *SED Event Routing Invocation*

```
import someTelephonyPackage.events.*
// defines CallCenterEvent as well as the event constant UP
      .
      .
      .
if ( initOkay() == 1 ) {
(12)     CallCenterEvent evt = new CallCenterEvent( this, UP );
         // notify upListeners
(13)     route( evt );
}
```

When a source wants to fire an event, it may create an event instance and pass it to a routing method as in **Listing 9.7** [13]. The source is passed to the event constructor via the **this** keyword along with an event "type" indicator ([12]).

During notification (when an instance of type CallCenterEvent is created), the event is always of one of the types available in the class definition (e.g., UP). This type discrimination allows the source notification process a means of identifying which set of listeners to notify. Note that type discrimination is *not* used as an event identification mechanism by the target upon event receipt. This is now unnecessary since the event is known beforehand because there is a typed event handler for each registered event in the target.

Listing 9.8 *Possible Event Routing Implementation for a Source*

```
public void route( EventObject e) {
   if e.getId() == CallCenterEvent.UP {
      notifyUpListeners ( e );
   }
   if e.getId() == CallCenterEvent.DOWN {
      notifyDownListeners ( e );
   }
   if e.getId() == CallCenterEvent.ON_FIRE {
      notifyFireListeners ( e );
   }
}
```

A notification mechanism from the source to the target listeners is then implemented. This notification is either called explicitly at the point of the event occurrence or called within a general routing method (as in **Listing 9.8**).

Each notifyXXXListeners() method sends the XXX() method of each type of listener to all registered listeners of type XXX. For example, the notifyUpListeners() method invokes the up() method to all upListeners; the notifyDownListeners() method invokes the down() method to all downListeners (see **Listing 9.9** [14] and [15], respectively). This is what is meant by the earlier term "typed event handler"; a different target method is invoked for each type of event. Of course, the same goes for "fireListeners" ([16]).

Event handler code for each event type supported by the source (e.g., up(), down(), and on_fire()) is then implemented in the target. The bodies of these methods depend on the target behavior, of course. It may be the same or it may be different between any two targets. If the implementation is identical for all handlers, you can inherit from an adapter class. If it is identical for some but not others, you can always use those methods you need from a local instantiation of an adapter class in the body of an implementation or hang on to an adapter class instance variable and use that.

Listing 9.9 *Delegation Notification Implementation*

```
public void notifyUpListeners ( EventObject e ) {
    for( int i=0;i<upListeners.size;i++ ) {
        upListeners.elementAt(i).up( e );
    }
}
public void notifyDownListeners ( EventObject e ) {
    for( int i=0;i<downListeners.size;i++ ) {
        downListeners.elementAt(i).down( e );
    }
}
public void notifyOnFireListeners ( EventObject e ) {
    for( int i=0;i<fireListeners.size;i++ ) {
        fireListeners.elementAt(i).on_fire( e );
    }
}
```

(14)

(15)

(16)

Note that each listener of the same listener type may be a different type of object as long as they implement the appropriate interface. For example, recall that both Callers and Firemen registered for ON_FIRE notification, and they will respond differently (i.e., the bodies of their `on_fire()` methods will be different). This makes intuitive sense; they didn't register based on the type of object they were. Rather they registered based upon the type of event they wanted to be notified about. This is the same polymorphic concept used in the `update()` method of the Dependency Model. As long as each listener understands the notification protocol, this scheme works.

The astute reader may by now have gained an uneasy feeling of "overidiomization." Indeed, it is difficult to ignore how much of the Delegation Model is based entirely on idioms like naming conventions and similarly named interfaces as opposed to language features or pure library functionality.[31] Actually, it seems to be a recurring design theme for Java. For example, the entire JavaBeans™ architecture is based primarily on naming conventions. Whether this is "good" or "bad" depends on the developer's perspective, but only time will tell whether it will be widely used successfully.

So what's wrong with this picture? Nothing really, except for a few awkward requirements we have imposed on fellow programmers. The first problem has to do with the manner in which events are defined. The SED approach we've shown favors grouping all events generated by a source into one class, namely classes like CallCenterEvent and MouseEvent. Although this localizes the definitions and clarifies their context, it negatively affects reusability. Why?

---

31 This focus on conventions is why we generally consider this an idiomatic approach as opposed to a pattern approach.

Sharing Events

First, it may be "unnecessary overkill" to couple the source with the event. Since the target rarely cares about the identity of the source, of what benefit is this coupling? In cases where source identity is important, the target can always determine the source anyway, so again, why couple the definitions? Why not allow different sources the ability to generate *the same* event? Remember, we are not sharing implementations, only interfaces. Let's try to separate them by taking a different approach.

Decoupled Event Delegation Approach

Even though this coupling is by name only, it would certainly be confusing to implement an up() interface defined in a class called CallCenterListener for use in an Elevator class that needed to go up() in response to an elevator button being pressed. If we decouple the names of these entities, events can be reused by many different sources as well as targets. [17]–[19] of **Listing 9.10** show a redefinition of these classes to support such decoupling.

Listing 9.10 *Polymorphic Event Listeners in a Target*

```
(17)   public class UpEvent extends EventObject{ }
(18)   public class DownEvent extends EventObject{ }
(19)   public class OnFireEvent extends EventObject{ }
       // a target object
       public class CallCenterAgent implements UpListener,
               DownListener {
         public void up( UpEvent evt ) {
         // code to react to a call center being up
         }
         public void down( DownEvent evt ) {
         // code to react to a call center being down
         }
       }
       public class Elevator implements UpListener, DownListener {
         public void up( UpEvent evt ) {
         ///code to make elevator go up
         }
         public void down( DownEvent evt ) {
         ///code to make elevator go down
         }
       }
```

An Elevator object can now implement the UpListener interface as well as a CallCenter can using the very same event (i.e., UpEvent, DownEvent, or OnFireEvent). A renaming facility (like that provided for the Ada programming language) would be of tremendous help here, but we won't hold our breath.

No-Op Methods

The second problem with the SED approach is much more problematic. Recall that each target type may respond to each event in a different manner (e.g., the Fireman runs *to* the fire, the Caller *away* from it!). This is supported well by the Delegation Model in that one merely has to implement the particular interface method for the particular event type in the target. The real problem shows up with what turns out to be no-op methods. The Fireman could care less if the CallCenter is UP or DOWN — she only cares if it is ON_FIRE. The Fireman must pollute her interface with up( ) and down( ) methods even though they will never be invoked. And so, we must reimplement no-op implementations for each of the events she is not concerned with for each different type of target. At first glance, this seems like no big deal, but if the set of events is large and the targets diverse, this can get old very quickly. It may not be a show-stopper in all cases, but it's at least a little ugly to have EventListener interface operations prescribed in a public interface when they are not even used! And it is extremely wasteful. The DED alternative approach solves this problem cleanly and simply. Precisely because events are decoupled from sources, there is no need to implement interfaces just because they are part of a coupled event definition.

The DED approach is modeled in **Figure 9.6**. Using this approach, each event is a distinct type implemented through extension. Their respective event handlers are presented as individual interfaces (there is never to be more than one method per interface). Because each interface requires that users provide an implementation anyway, this approach capitalizes on that fact. In doing so, it eradicates the need for no-op interface implementation because event definitions are no longer grouped together.

Figure 9.6 *Decoupled Event Approach to the Delegation Model*

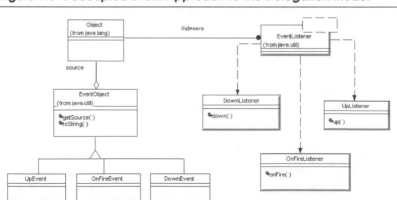

The implementation of this approach is identical to that of the SED approach except in those places where events and listener interfaces are created and processed. The implementation is trivial and so is not provided here.

Altered Interfaces Abound

A major problem with either approach to the Delegation Model has to do with the fact that we are modifying the public interface of target objects at all. Although this problem is mitigated using the DED approach, there is no avoiding this side effect using the Delegation Model.[32] Granted, we need event handlers. But wouldn't it be better to just use an object's *existing behavior* to respond to events? Why not have a Person object handle an ON_FIRE event by invoking a method `Person.run()`? Instead, we are expected to wrap this behavior inside event handlers (e.g., `Person.on_fire()`), one for each event type in the source. Why? For what purpose? Well, in one sense, it is a more evident mechanism of notification. By using an idiom of matching the name of the event handler with that of the event clarifies the code (recall that the `update()` method in the Observation Model hid the event handling code). This is a weak argument, at best. Clearly, it would be better to use the existing public interface of the target directly to respond to events. Stay tuned ...

We've covered notification, but how is registration provided in the Delegation Model? Well, you get to code that, too (i.e., it is simply *not provided!*). Again, we follow an idiom. The source is to maintain a list of listeners and not only notify them when an event is fired, but also provide access and synchronized update operations for each list supported. So, delegation is not really an event management mechanism at all — it's an explicit, hand-coded set of calls to a series of subroutines following a naming convention idiom! In summary, the delegation model as implemented (or not!) in Java is useless to us, at best. We can certainly *make* it useful, but there is no need to use the "standard" classes provided to do so — they don't really do much for us.

Requirements Satisfaction Using the Delegation Model

If we have the time and patience to do so, we can implement the Delegation Model. Unfortunately, it satisfies none of our requirements unless we use the DED form (see **Table 9.2** for the status).

---

32 Note that the Observation Model (a.k.a. dependency) suffers from this same deficiency, but on a much smaller scale — only one method must be added to the object's interface: `update()`.

Table 9.2 *Event Management Requirements Satisfaction Using the Delegation Model*

Requirement	Status	Reason
Asynchronous registration	Partially Satisfied	Partially supported by Delegation Model, but largely enforced by idiom with no "built-in" registration or notification support
Arbitrary object notification and registration	Unsatisfied	Delegation Model requires both extension and interface implementation, but only in the event and the target. The source is freed and may be an arbitrary object. However, the source must know about and be able to process different kinds of events
Nonaltered interface	Unsatisfied	Event class defines event types. Target must implement event handler protocol for each event type defined in the event class used by the source
Source identification option	Unsatisfied	Delegation Model frees the source, but provides no a priori source identification mechanism for registration. Nor does it allow for blind event registration
Event filtering	Partially Satisfied	Delegation Model does not implement a broadcast form of notification; rather all notifications are explicit by event type. However, each such notification must be coded by hand
Different targets and registrars	Unsatisfied	Not supported at all
Asynchronous notification	Unsatisfied	Delegation Model provides no async option

Using the Delegation Model without alteration, it seems we are worse off than with the Observation Model. It's as if we've taken a few steps forward, but several steps backward. The biggest problem with the delegation model is the excess reliance on idiom forced by a lack of functionality provided by the Java language. If we have to code the registration and notification mechanism ourselves, then the Delegation Model isn't much of a model after all. Actually, this last statement is incorrect — it is *only* a model, nothing more. If this were all it was presented as, then fine. Instead, we must deal with all the "standard" classes, adapters, constants and nonfunctional interfaces that come with the model. Fortunately, this is only true of visual events. Because no such predefined entities exist for nonvisual events, we have the option of using the DED approach and still maintaining language standard compliance.

To SED or to DED — Is **That** *the Question?*

Not really. In evaluating the Delegation Model, one has to question why the language designers provided (or feigned) any support for event management at all. Actually, *there is no support* — just a suggested framework that is half-baked, at best. In retrospect, it might have been more prudent to provide it all, or to provide none of it. Instead, we are forced to use idioms, or more likely to forgo the entire model and just implement our own event management mechanism. This approach is taken later when we introduce the Message Management Model.

The other big problem with the Delegation Model is the acceptance and unchecked proliferation of no-op methods in the target. The SED approach to implementing the Delegation Model is inelegant at best probably more aptly described as a mess than an architectural model. Although seemingly very popular, use of the SED approach encourages this excess reliance on no-op interfaces. This forces an awkward implementation that does more to hog the namespace than to solve the problem at hand. The introduction of inner classes and adapter classes seems to merely add more confusion, complexity, and certainly runtime overhead to the solution.

We have shown that taking the DED approach can largely solve the excess reliance on no-op interfaces. The DED approach makes the Delegation Model an attractive alternative to the Observation Model because targets no longer have to type-check events upon notification. The cost is a much more extensive impact on target interfaces, but far less than the SED approach requires.

Actually, the DED approach may be rather useful. In fact, we can use it to implement JTAPI notification. Unlike the Observation Model, the event handler signature is not fixed (we can create any callback signature we want) and so it may be used right along with the JTAPI Observers. In general though, can't we do better? What if we could combine the Observation and Delegation Models? Let's try it.

Morphing the Delegation Model into the Observation Model

To merge the two models, we begin by simply making the event class represent one and only one event type as in the DED approach (see class DedicatedEventObject **Figure 9.7**). Now a target can pick and choose from among the events it will implement — if it doesn't respond to an event, then it needn't implement an interface for it. However, it still has to alter its interface just to be able to respond to an event. Specifying a single common protocol all Event Listeners can implement so listeners can be notified in the same way can minimize this inconvenience. Let's call it `update( EventObject eo )`.

Figure 9.7 *The Morphed Delegation Model*

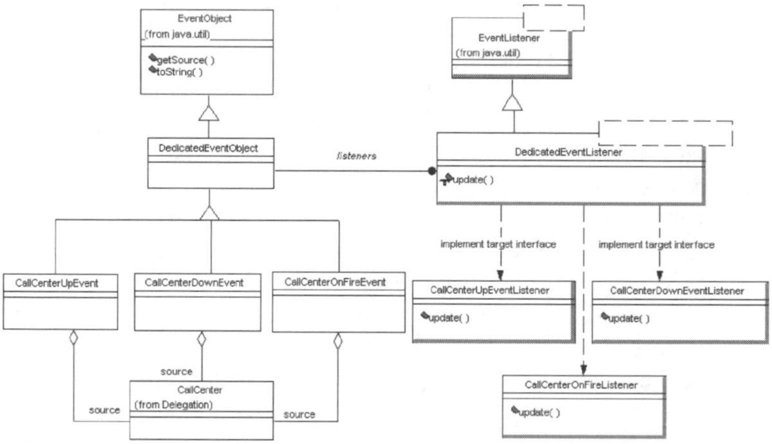

Look familiar? It should. We have effectively implemented the Observation Model in terms of the Delegation Model! But are we any better off, or are we largely back to where we left off with the Observation Model? It seems we are better off in that the source may be disengaged from the inheritance requirement — it can be an arbitrary object as long as it instantiates an event and fires it at the appropriate time. But we have not alleviated the dual type-check problem discovered in the Observation Model — targets must still check the event type upon notification. Worse, if the target depends somehow on the source type, two checks are necessary instead of the single one required in the DED approach. And as far as JTAPI goes, we're hosed with the common `update()` signature. So we're back to square one.

Requirements Satisfaction Using Morphed Delegation

So far, we can use the morphed Delegation Model or the DED approach to satisfy the same number of requirements (see **Table 9.3** for the status) as the Observation Model.

Table 9.3 *Event Management Model Requirements Satisfaction Using Enhanced Delegation Model*

Requirement	Status	Reason
Asynchronous registration	Satisfied	Same support as the Observation Model
Arbitrary object notification and registration	Unsatisfied	No change from original Delegation Model
Nonaltered interface	Partially Satisfied	Must implement update() protocol in the target, but the source is freed
Source identification option	Partially Satisfied	Source identification is not directly supported, but aggregating the source to the event opens the door for providing this capability
Event filtering	Unsatisfied	Back to broadcast land …
Different targets and registrars	Unsatisfied	Same as before
Asynchronous notification	Unsatisfied	No async option

Let's see if we can do better — again!

Enhancing the Observation Model

When we examined the support for dependency in the Observation Model earlier, we said we couldn't register for specific events defined within an ObservableObject. We got all of the changed state of an object that presumably triggered multiple "events" and then had to examine the source aspect to see which event was fired before proceeding. But that assumed that the Observable object was not itself an atomic event. Suppose it was — we might have exactly what we're looking for! If we make all our *events* observable, allow only one event definition per class and make them associated with the source classes they "work for," observers can register for those particular event instances and voila! We have the beginnings of a workable design (see **Figure 9.8**).

Figure 9.8 *Relationship Between Event and Source Objects*

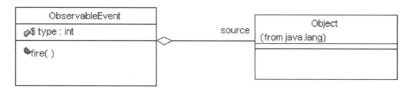

Note that this is a combination of the `java.util` classes EventObject and Observable. It models the relationship between the source and the event through aggregation rather than inheritance. But there's still a problem — one of *cardinality*. Sure, an event may be associated with a source object, but why just one? Can't an event instance be associated with multiple source objects simultaneously? And why can't a source object generate multiple events? Well, they certainly should be able to, but this is not reflected in the Observation (or the Delegation) Model. And so we introduce a class that provides this capability among others — the EventNotifier.

In this "Enhanced Observation" Model (**Figure 9.9**), we allow Observers to register with ObservableEvents through the registration protocol of an EventNotifier. This class provides both registration and notification. Observers can register for an event regardless of the source or they may specify the source explicitly. Telephony Objects (or any other object, for that matter) then trigger the events through the EventNotifier in the implementation of their methods. This triggering comes with an option that allows for *truly* asynchronous notification. If this option is selected, the call returns immediately. The EventNotifier then fires the appropriate events on behalf of the Telephony Objects in a worker thread.

Asynchronous Notification

Neither the Observation Model nor the Delegation Model addresses asynchronous notification. While this may be considered by some to be an implementation issue, it has major repercussions on the usability of the model if it is prevented or not supported by a certain implementation. Asynchronous notification is defined here as simply returning from the notification call immediately (i.e., when the source or designated notifier notifies the target). This approach requires using a multithreaded implementation.[33] Without a separate thread to either implement the notification or process waiting notifications, the caller thread must wait until all

---

33 Technically, either signals or interrupts of some kind could also be used, but both are fraught with problems that are overcome rather nicely using threads.

Figure 9.9 An Enhanced Java Observation Model

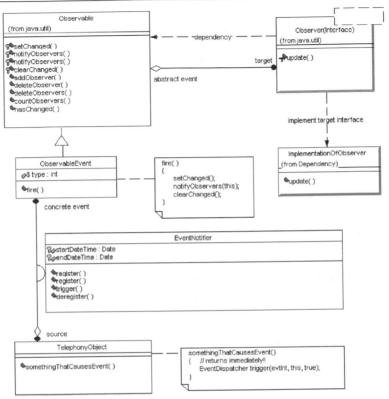

listeners/observers finish their processing in order to return. While this may suit some designs, it is certainly disastrous for others. For example, suppose we are implementing a traffic light management system. The traffic management subsystem must control light processing at several intersections simultaneously. If the manager (playing the role of the source) must wait for each car (listener/observer) waiting at a light to complete its processing before it can move on to notify listeners at another intersection, this simply will not work (unless planned pileups are part of some sadistic traffic design!).

Clearly, the Delegation Model may be implemented using asynchronous notification. Since we must write the notification methods ourselves, we can control not only the concurrency, but the granularity of that concurrency as well. Using the Observation Model, we may be able to implement similar behavior by controlling the implementations of the `update()` method. However, such control may affect the signature of the method or the design of the source classes (i.e., we may be forced to pass an additional parameter or to have the source point to some kind of semaphore). This again may force a design compromise. We address this situation by looking at a few ways to implement this in Chapter 10.

Enhanced Dependency Requirements Satisfaction

So far, we can use the Enhanced Observation Model to satisfy almost all of our requirements (see **Table 9.4** for the status).

Table 9.4 *Event Management Model Requirements Satisfaction Using Enhanced Dependency*

Requirement	Status	Reason
Asynchronous registration	Satisfied	Enhanced to support asynchronous notification
Arbitrary object notification and registration	Partially Satisfied	The source can be an arbitrary object, but the target must still implement the Observer interface
Nonaltered interface	Unsatisfied	Must implement `update()` protocol
Source identification option	Satisfied	By using the services of the EventNotifier, any object can register for notification
Event filtering	Satisfied	Registrars register for specific events. Source discriminant is optional
Different targets and registrars	Satisfied	By using the services of the EventNotifier, any object can register for notification and specify another target in the process
Asynchronous notification	Satisfied	Async option provided

The Enhanced Observation Model will cover most any circumstance of event management we can conceive of. We can also alter the Delegation Model so it works just like the Enhanced Observation Model. Note that the original interfaces or super-classes of either model do not address many of these issues.

Even though we have not satisfied all of the requirements we set out to, we have a couple of extremely flexible models that are relatively easy to implement. Using the last model, we've solved the problem of not being able to discern between source objects on registration and notification by transferring this behavior from the event to a third party (the EventNotifier) who knows about both. We've satisfied all requirements save one and a half.

The only remaining drawback is that Observers must implement `update()` and perform switch processing on incoming events. We fix this in the next section by introducing a new model. Again, what we'd like to see is a mechanism that does not require the target class to modify their interface. Turns out this is not possible using either the Delegation or the Observation Model. In fact, both of these models *depend upon* targets altering their public interfaces. So there is no way we can meet the "nonaltered interface" requirement following proposed idioms or using standard Java classes. In the next section, we see if we can come up with a model to support the remaining requirement.

Take a deep breath. If you've made it through the preceding discussion with a clear understanding of the issues presented, you are probably a library programmer at heart. If you did so in one sitting, you are either now asleep or you are a true nerd.

We have seen that the Java dependency and delegation models "out of the box" are useful tools but may be inadequate for general event management purposes without extreme modifications. For those cases where these architectures do not suit our needs, we must roll our own. In short, we must use our own idiom to make Java a better Java. Let's go for it.

A Java Message Management Idiom

The Java Message Management Model (MMM) as presented here takes a different approach than either the Observation or the Delegation Model. Rather than beginning with a tight coupling between sources, events, and targets, it strives for a *loose coupling*. Rather than relying on language mechanics like inheritance and aggregation, it is a *component-based* model.[34] Rather than requiring objects to alter their interfaces and write a bunch of code to handle and register for events, the process is transparent and the interfaces remain intact. It assigns specific classes the responsibility for registration and notification without requiring inheritance, aggregation, or altering the interfaces of objects involved in the service. Further, it explicitly supports the separation of the registrar from the target and alleviates the requirement that the target know the identity of the source.

Understanding the Message Management Model

Recall our original discussion of a general event management model (see Event Management in a Nutshell). We follow the same general model, but with a few distinguishing feature changes.

---

34 By the term "component-based," we do not mean as it is used in the JavaBeans™ model. Rather we are referring to loosely coupled objects using the services of other objects without using inheritance or aggregation, just local instantiation and invocation. This is also referred to as dependency in other OO literature; but to use that term would collide with the Smalltalk notion of dependency!

Registration Under Message Management

Rather than assuming that targets register for notification, the MMM assumes any object can play the role of a *registrar*. This can also be accomplished with either the Observation or the Delegation Model. The difference is that the MMM registrar does not even have to know the identity of the source in order to register on behalf of a target. **Figure 9.10** diagrams this notion.

Figure 9.10 *Registration Using the Message Management Model*

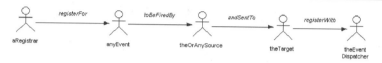

Notice how much more general the registration process is. It is also more flexible in that most of the objects involved can play the role of any other. For example, any of the objects involved (except for the event itself) can register or be a source or a target.

Notification Under Message Management

The MMM notification process (see **Figure 9.11**) is similar to that of the previous models, yet there are some crucial differences. Once the source generates the event, they are on their way. It is an inherently asynchronous process. It is, of course, possible (and potentially desirable) to provide a synchronous/blocking version, but that is likely the exception rather than the rule.

Figure 9.11 *Notification Using the Message Management Model*

Animal House

Back at the dorm, things have deteriorated very rapidly. All the girls have left in sheer disgust at the boys' behavior. The problem is that the boys are now answering the girls' phone calls. Using MMM, there is no need for the boys to change their behavior by implementing an event handler. This is a good thing, as most of them are in no shape to do so. All they have to do is tell the registration process which method of theirs to call when a phone event they care about occurs. Those who do not wish to be bothered with the RING event needn't be. Those who want someone else to answer the phone for them in response to the ANSWERED event may specify this. Using MMM, the boys can be more selective ahead of time when registering for phone calls. They can register in advance based upon any criteria supported by the source. For example, if John wants to accept all calls for Sarah except those from her father, he may do so.

Implications of the Message Management Model

This idiom will take the form of three new objects — the DirectedMessage class, the GeneralEvent class, and the EventDispatcher class. The DirectedMessage class is lifted directly from Smalltalk. The EventDispatcher class is an enhancement of the EventNotifier class we built in the Enhanced Observation Model. Likewise, the GeneralEvent class is an enhancement of the previous ObservableEvent class. We will implement these classes using the Java reflection API (a concept also lifted from Smalltalk!). Here's how it works. An object of any kind registers an interest in a particular event occurrence with an EventDispatcher by identifying the kind of event, a method to call when the event occurs, and, optionally, a source discriminant. When the event occurs, the method is called. Pretty simple — and we don't have to change our personality (i.e., interface) to implement it! Let's start with the DirectedMessage class.

Implementing the Message Management Model

Smalltalk provides a class called DirectedMessage (or some close facsimile thereof). It does exactly what it says — it directs a message to a particular object. In short, it is the Smalltalk implementation of a callback mechanism. This class will be the building block of our event management scheme in Java. We will use it in favor of either "standard" Java event mechanism, because however useful they are, both models force programmers to alter their designs (i.e., they require alteration of the target interface, at a minimum).

Listing 9.11 *Class DirectedMessage*

```
package sroberts.eventManagement;
import java.lang.reflect.*;
public class DirectedMessage {
    private   Object target;
    private   String method;
    private   Vector args;
    public DirectedMessage( Object o, String s, Vector v );
    public void send();
}
```

A DirectedMessage (**Listing 9.11**) is a very simple object that holds three instance variables: an object instance to call or notify (the target), the callback to use upon notification, and an optional list of arguments required to be passed to the callback, if any. The target must of course implement the callback, but *it is already a part of the object's interface.* In other words, we don't have to alter the object's behavior or create unnecessary additional wrapper interfaces or adapters simply to register for event notification (as we must under normal Java event circumstances and even using the Observation Model). We respond with behavior *already present* in the target.

The benefits of this particular design feature cannot be underestimated. *The manner in which an object responds to an event should correspond directly to its inherent behavior.* In other words, there should already be a public method to invoke in response to an event that we can just *use* as an event handler. If not, we need to alter the object's behavior to support such an event, not wrap it, provide adapter classes, inner classes, or any other nonsense. Let's not let the model itself get in the way of appropriate object-oriented design.

Next is the definition of the class GeneralEvent (see **Listing 9.12**). This class will replace the Observation Model's Observable class as well as the delegation model's EventObject class. It may be extended if a particular design calls for it. Class GeneralEvent models exactly one event.

Listing 9.12 *Class GeneralEvent*

```
package sroberts.util.events;
import sroberts.util.callback.*;
public class GeneralEvent {
    protected Vector targets;
    public GeneralEvent();    // ctor
    public void fire();
    public synchronized void addTarget( DirectedMessage msg );
    public synchronized void deleteTarget( DirectedMessage msg );
    public void notifyTargets();
    public void notifyTargets( Object callData );
}
```

(20)
(21)

Last, we specify the EventDispatcher. It is very similar to the EventNotifier class except that it takes a DirectedMessage as an argument. This one simple design change buys us a large degree of freedom — it frees us from the necessity of having to implement the Observer or the EventListener interface. This means that *any* object can register for notification (not just Observers and EventListeners)! Further, it can specify whatever response behavior it wishes, and even one that is not its own![35] It also eliminates the need for switch processing in the target implementa-

---

35 In short, registrars can delegate notification to any object, not just EventListeners or Observers.

tion. But if we don't need Observers, why do we need Observables? We don't, and so sources can now be made arbitrary. But we still need the notification functionality they provide. So we move that into GeneralEvent in the form of the `notifyTargets()` methods (**Listing 9.12** [20] and [21]). Now back to EventDispatcher.

The EventDispatcher (see **Listing 9.13**) is essentially a traffic cop that accepts registration requests from targets and triggers their callbacks on behalf of sources when events occur. It also plays the role of an association class resolving the many-to-many cardinality between source objects and events (another shortcoming of both models).

Listing 9.13 *Class EventDispatcher*

```
package sroberts.util.event;
import sroberts.util.callback;
import java.lang.*;
public class EventDispatcher {
    protected  Object source;
    protected  GeneralEvent event;
    public EventDispatcher( Object src, GeneralEvent evt );
    public void register( Class kind, int duration,
                            DirectedMessage msg);
    public void register( Class kind, Object source,
                            int duration, DirectedMessage msg );
    public int deregister( Class kind, Object target );
    public void trigger( Class kind, Object from, Boolean aSync );
}
```

(22)

The behavior of EventDispatcher could be placed in the source, but we opt for the most loosely coupled implementation possible. The EventDispatcher maintains the list of registered targets on behalf of each source, along with other information. The actual notification is performed by the event.

Asynchronizing the Message Management Model

Recall our earlier discussion about asynchronous notification. We addressed the importance of providing the capability to return control to the calling thread so that subsequent notification would not block the further processing of events. An asynchronous notification capability is also provided programmatically as a parameter to the method `trigger()` (see Listing 9.13 [22]). Here, the programmer is given an option as to whether notification is to occur synchronously or asynchronously. In an implementation, the default would be asynchronous.

An asynchronous notification capability is absolutely necessary. To see why, imagine an implementation without it. Suppose several thousand

Observers register for notification. When the source object generates the relevant event, all the observers are notified. There is no getting around the overhead of traversing the list of registered observers and passing them the event.[36] However, the source (or delegated "notifier") has absolutely no control over how the targets respond to the events. If we're lucky, the targets all set a local variable to the value they are interested in and return control to the caller immediately.

Unfortunately this policy is not only unenforceable, it is highly unlikely.[37] Most observers will likely do whatever local processing is necessary to respond to the event and ignore the needs of the caller (Wouldn't you?). This means that if the observers choose to calculate primes for the next seven centuries the caller is blocked waiting for the observer to return control. Multiply this possibility by the number of registered observers and we have a real mess on our hands.

There are two ways out of this, but both require the use of threads. To see the solution, visit Chapter 10.

Is it Soup Yet?

The final event management model object diagram is presented in **Figure 9.12**. In practice, we will see how much more powerful this form of event management is than either event model provided for Java. The main benefit to this design approach is that it is *loosely coupled*. It also requires no *interface modification* or inheritance in either the source or target; they both just use the services of the EventDispatcher. Further, it is much more flexible in that the registering object can specify a target other than them, thereby delegating the responsibility of reacting to the event to another object.

The loose coupling of this alternative notification approach is illuminating. As object-oriented designers, we sometimes get carried away with the intoxicating power of inheritance. But sometimes the best approach is to use a component-based (uses-a) approach instead of extension (is-a) or aggregation (has-a). In other words, it may be best to simply model the capabilities required and then to design classes that provide these services. This is especially true of lower-level service-oriented classes designed to support capabilities like event management.

This model can of course be extended. The behavior of EventDispatcher may be distributed across several classes if the design criterion warrants. In other words, one might partition a separate EventDispatcher subclass for each source class or perhaps one based upon the number of participants. For simplicity, we have implemented a global Singleton that operates not unlike the Smalltalk runtime engine itself.

---

36 Note that there is no compelling argument for assigning this responsibility to sources only.

37 We may have no control over the source of the object that registers for notification.

Figure 9.12 *Java Message Management Model*

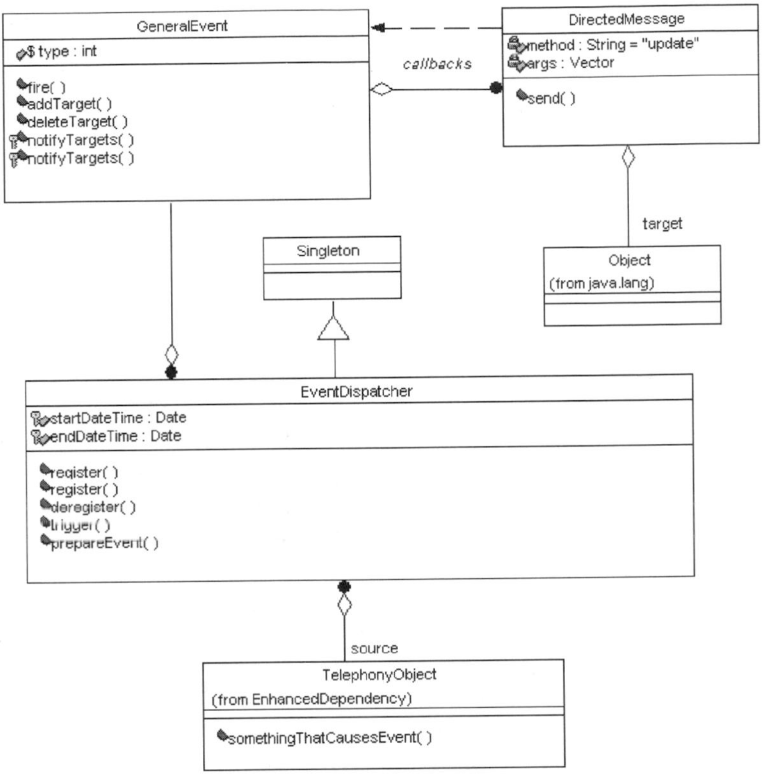

The CORBA Event Services

Now that we've gone to all the trouble to design this event model, there is yet another one that may be used instead. The CORBA 2.0 specification provides Event Services that define both a *push* and a *pull* mode of operation. The push mode most closely resembles the kind of behavior we are looking for.

Technically, the CORBA push model is not a *true* asynchronized notification scheme,[38] but it can be made to behave like one if it is correctly implemented. In short, the CORBA event model employs the same general design approach we used in our message management model. There are three main objects involved: a *push supplier* (the source), a *push consumer* (the target), and an *event channel* (similar to our EventDispatcher). By now, you get the picture as to how these operate. For details, see the CORBA Event Services specification or the documentation that comes with any CORBA product that supports event services.

---

38 A true asynchronous notification CORBA Messaging Service is under consideration now.

Event Management in a Bombshell

The skeptical reader may find our message management model "design excursion" a bit disturbing. Believe me, so do the authors. However necessary, we find the need to second-guess the design of a programming language library a less than productive use of our time. But the Java core classes are supposed to comprise an extensible, reusable library standardized across all code for all time. With all due respect, it is our humble opinion that the implied event management implementations (and some models) provided for Java fail this test.[39] In contrast, the event management implementations and models of dependency and directed messages in Smalltalk have survived the test of time and refinement by some of the brightest minds in object-oriented development since 1980. Since the idea was clearly lifted from Smalltalk, perhaps the implementation should have been followed exactly. When Bjarne Stroustrup designed C++, he deliberately steered clear of this kind of "OO design on steroids." His approach was to instead allow libraries to mature over time with those who use them. In retrospect, this was probably not such a bad idea.

One may also question the entire "model specification" approach encouraged by some Java advocates. This approach is pervasive across all extension packages, including JTAPI. Some may question whether it is really wise to assume that a group of programmers can sit down and codify a set of cooperating classes and interfaces that will be so well crafted that they will suit every possible use. Won't this approach hinder future alternative designs? This is an ambitious undertaking, to say the least. Recall that these design entities are not always "foundational" in nature — many are targeted at entire application-level problem spaces, not essential programming services. More than twenty years of experience with languages that are more expressive and powerful than Java (e.g., Smalltalk, Ada, and C++) have not yet yielded any conclusive favorable results in this arena. The same approach has been embraced by the OMG with CORBA, again, showing little measurable progress (in fact, some of the adopted CORBAdomain vertical specifications are simply unusable).

While the exercise of discussing these models is certainly beneficial and necessary from a design perspective, the benefits of *standardizing* the results of this process may be overblown, even counterproductive! Despite all the hype, the programming community at large seems to be understandably cautious about embracing the latest version of the Silver Bullet. On the other hand, there are some very compelling arguments for *attempting* to provide common interfaces for an industry the size of telecom. We trench programmers are used to working in a vacuum — rewriting code over and

---

39 An example of just how far one has to go in writing excess code to implement the delegation model may be found in most popular Java user interface tools. These products automatically generate a very large number of event handlers, adapters, and inner classes just to handle, say, a mouse click.

over again no matter what the specifications and best wishes of the day are. If the interfaces provided are general enough to provide reuse yet complete enough to be functionally useful, how could we *not* advocate their widespread use?

Further, the innovative approach from Sun Microsystems of specifying APIs using Java interfaces allows for flexibility in implementations. Notice how we were able to provide at least three different implementations of message management with JTAPI. This is possible precisely *because* the API is defined using interfaces!

Summary

In summary, we have presented three alternative forms of event management in Java suitable for use in asynchronous processing in most any telephony application. Unfortunately, the Delegation Model is not usable in professional-quality telephony application development without extensive modification and massive "idiomization." One of the most widely used approaches (SED) is seriously flawed in this respect. The other approach (DED) is an effective alternative but requires much effort on the part of the developer. (The provision of two base classes or interfaces that do nothing but hold onto another object and hog the namespace is less than a productive contribution for developers used to gaining functional utility from class libraries.) However, if we are willing to code the registration and notification ourselves and implement the DED approach, the Delegation Model can work. The Observation Model is much more useful "out of the box," yet it forces a compromise in design in order to use the services it offers. There may also be performance issues, depending on the implementation of the notification mechanism and possibly even the frequency of messaging. More importantly, dependency simply cannot be used to implement JTAPI notification due to the function signature problem. And last but not least, CORBA provides at least one set of services that is designed to support asynchronous notification.

All of these models are demoted to mere idioms when we are forced to modify or drastically enhance them in order to use them effectively. Perhaps future versions of the Java language will incorporate classes similar to the ones developed here (which are lifted, again, from Smalltalk). Or perhaps these types of services are best left to be implemented in any manner the developer sees fit. In either case, using interfaces to define an API seems like a good idea.

In the next chapter, we fill in some of the details exposed in this chapter and move into other ways of improving our Java telephony code.

Chapter 10

Idioms and Patterns in Telephony

> "Please ignore the man behind the curtain."
>
> *The Wizard of Oz*

When first programming, it is possible to form some misconceptions about how things really work. Once the mountain of learning a programming language (like C) is scaled, you figure you are well on your way to becoming a "real programmer."

Then comes the Windows API, the X Window System, OS/2 Presentation Manager, concurrent programming, the Relational Model and Normalization, C++ idioms, artificial intelligence, the Booch components, the software development life cycle, software engineering, TCP/IP and the OSI model, OOA/OOD/OOP, generics, design patterns, UML — the list goes on. You discover that programming languages, however vital to the formula, are only part of the picture.[1] In order to program effectively, there is a need to learn far more than proper syntax and debugging techniques — there are tool sets programmers use and common practices they follow in order to write *effective* software. Looking back, it is clear that we are always either implementing an ***idiom*** or following a ***pattern***.

Idioms and patterns are specifications software engineers may use to improve software "ilities" (e.g., reliability, reusability, scalability, and

---

1 We do not mean to imply that programming is somehow "less important" than design. To the contrary, mastering design concepts without gaining programming proficiency is a useless exercise. The point is that the two go hand in hand.

423

others). They are usually exercised during the design and construction phases of software development. Oftentimes it is difficult to tell whether a technique is an idiom or a pattern. The primary difference seems to be that idioms are usually born out of necessity; some would even argue inadequate programming language functionality where patterns are born out of an explicit effort to improve and to reuse overall program design. Another distinguishing feature is that patterns are programming language-independent where idioms generally are not. But the distinction between the two is really not that important — the point is that we learn to recognize, develop, and use them. In order to write quality software (including telephony software), we must master some of these. This chapter presents some idioms and patterns that we believe are essential to producing a commercial-quality JTAPI implementation.

Idioms

All programming languages require the use of idioms — some more than others. Modern programming languages not saddled with the burden of supporting legacy semantics of prior versions are usually coherent and well designed; therefore, they do not require the use of a large number of idioms (this inverse relationship is depicted in **Figure 10.1**). Examples are Ada, Eiffel, Smalltalk, and of course, Java. In contrast, languages born with requirements to support legacy functionality (and sometimes explicit memory management) are always more complex.[2] Examples are OOCOBOL and the champion of perversity in semantics,[3] C++. And then there are dinosaur languages that are poorly designed altogether (e.g., FORTRAN).

But exactly what is an idiom? In the context of programming, an idiom is defined here as:

> *a practice commonly put into place to enforce a consistent semantic representation of a programming language construct.*

Idioms are things programmers sometimes expect to have to implement, but should never be imposed by language designers.[4] An excellent example of an idiom is the use of *smart pointers* in C++. Recall the use of dynamic allocation in C++: If an exception is thrown, it is possible for the memory segments of dynamically allocated objects to be lost on the free store, thereby creating a memory leak. There are many more idioms required to

---

2 There are exceptions; Ada's design includes a clean model of memory management.

3 Don't get me wrong, I love C++ just as much as the next guy. But one must admit that it is a bit complicated, especially when a single symbol or operator can mean different things in different contexts — and that is my point.

4 The worst thing a language designer can do is provide *incomplete* or *insufficient* support for some set of functionality as a part of the language design — this *forces* the use of idioms. Better to leave it out than to get it wrong.

make C++ a more *reliable* language, many which fill entire books.[5] However, not all idioms are in place to "fix" holes in programming languages. Some are just ways of operating that allow better implementations. For example, the fact that Java does not directly support generics (a.k.a. templates) is irrelevant if we can learn a technique for writing generic code in Java.

Figure 10.1 *Programming Languages and Required Idioms*

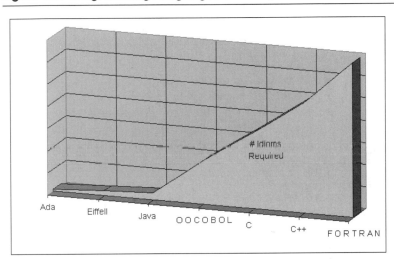

Idioms in Java

There are very few (if any) real "traps, pitfalls, and gotchas" to find in Java. Java is a very clean and straightforward language for four primary reasons: first, it was derived from clean languages (most notably Ada and Smalltalk); second, it is object-oriented; third, it has no prior legacy language baggage to carry around; and finally there is no memory management. Nevertheless, we can still do fabulously ridiculous things with Java, just as we can with any language. Java just makes us work a little harder to do it! So what we'll cover here are those things that are relatively unusual about Java as well as some Java design idioms that may be used to write better and more useful telephony code. We're going to look at idioms for:

- **Basic utility operations**
- **Performance**
- **Simulating multiple inheritance**
- **Generics**

---

5 Scott Meyers' *Effective C++* and sequels and Stan Lippman's *C++ Primer* are examples.

- **Implementing asynchronous notification using threads**
- **Callbacks**

All of these idioms are useful for any JTAPI implementation. In fact, a clean JTAPI implementation is simply not possible without using the majority of these idioms. A little time spent studying design patterns and developing reusable quality components will go a long way toward saving time in future telephony development efforts. We begin with what we call basic utility operations.

Basic Utility Operations

Before initiating any development project, I always provide a set of base classes I know will be needed. First, I always make sure I can find the objects I create! This sounds fundamental — it is. Yet the root class Object provides no identification scheme (other than hashcodes), and so I do. Most of my objects inherit from this guy. It takes the form of a very simple class with two attributes: *id* and *name* (see **Listing 10.1** for a Java version).

Listing 10.1 *Class IdentifiableObject*

```
class IdentifiableObject extends Object {
    private int id;
    private String name;
    public int getId() { return id; };
    public void setId( int id ) { this.id = id; };
    public String getName() { return name; };
    public void setName ( String name )
        { this.name = name; };
    public void String toString() { return name; };
}
```

Although most runtime code relies on object references (and in Java, hashcodes) to enforce uniqueness among object instances, there are two very good reasons for having an additional identification scheme. The first is *persistence*. Although not all objects are persistent, when they are this class provides a place to hold object ids, primary keys, and names. The other reason is more subtle. Once the name is set, an overridden toString() method allows for automatic presentation. This is extremely useful for debugging and displaying objects in listboxes and other components because they call toString() by default. The IdentifiableObject class may also be enhanced to provide reflection methods to determine its type and comparison methods to allow, for example, sorting.

In addition to the IdentifiableObject, I also provide an ObjectIdGenerator class to generate numbers at runtime (it may also be seeded with a start value) and a utility class typically called Utility. It mostly contains static convenience functions for things like conversion, bit manipulation, basic persistence, and the like. None of these are absolutely necessary for telephony programming per se, but they are useful nonetheless and so are identified here.

Performance Idioms

Performance considerations are critical in telephony applications primarily because there is always a user of some type waiting for an operation to complete. Simply put, the longer the user has to wait, the less favorable his reaction will be to the software. In Chapter 2, "Telephony Bus Architectures," we spoke briefly of the requirement to improve the performance of Java software. In this section, we revisit the subject and provide some specific source code idioms for generating faster Java byte code.

Some Rules of Thumb

As with any programming language, accessing data in Java uses machine cycles. Some means of accessing data use more cycles than others. **Figure 10.2** shows some relative access times given different means of access.

Figure 10.2 *Different Access Times for Different Access Types*

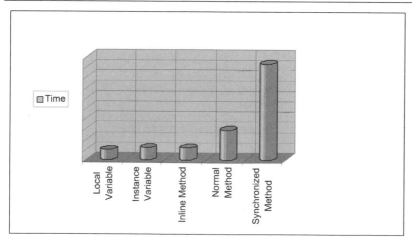

The results depicted in the figure are not very surprising. Method invocations are more expensive than variable instantiations and synchronized methods are indeed very expensive. The basic idea in optimization is to avoid the more expensive types of access, if practical. For example, the following rules of thumb apply when performance is tantamount:

- Prefer the use of *local variables* over instance variables.

- Use *inline methods* whenever possible over normal methods.
- Use synchronized methods only when absolutely necessary.

Other tactics for reducing runtime overhead are using a JIT compiler, setting the appropriate optimization settings, and running a profiler on code to pinpoint hot spots of execution.

In addition to these practices, the following idioms may be used to increase performance. Of course, many of these idioms are counter to common coding practices that lead to what is generally considered well-written software. Before using many of these, it is assumed that the higher performance gained is worth the cost in maintainability, encapsulation, and so forth.

Inline Methods

Declare any performance-critical methods as either private or final access. Because methods declared with these access privileges cannot be overridden, the compiler is free to optimize where it is capable of doing so.

Local Variables

When a method returns a value, it is better to hold on to a copy of that value than to call the method repeatedly. This may seem obvious, but this simple optimization technique is missing in most code I have read in my professional career. For example, consider the (rather contrived) code in **Listing 10.2**.

Listing 10.2 *Reducing Method Invocation Overhead Using Local Variables*

```
SomeObject o = new SomeObject();
for ( int i = 0; i < o.getId(); i++ ) {
    int answer = o.getId();
}

// is better re-written as:
int question = o.getId();
for ( int i = 0; i < question; i++ ) {
    int answer = question;
}
```

Even when a method is called only twice, the overhead of declaring a local variable and assigning the result will almost always execute faster than invoking the same method twice. The more often that same variable is used, the stronger the argument becomes.

Increment and Decrement Operators

Some Java compilers generate tighter byte code for the increment and decrement operators than they do with arithmetic operators used in assignment. For example,

```
int i = 0;
i++;        // this code will often generate tighter byte code
i = i + 1; // than this code...
```

It might be argued that this kind of performance penalty is to be expected for an interpreted language. This is, of course, hogwash. In reality, there is no good reason for this situation. The interpreter executes compiled byte code, not each line individually. Since the result of both operations is identical and easy to spot, there is no *valid* reason why a decent optimizing compiler would be unable to detect this situation and generate the same byte code in both circumstances. Although we can argue about this, it is largely a stylistic issue. In short, why not just use the arithmetic operator just in case the compiler stinks?

Loops

Loop optimization is (and always has been) a favorite target for optimization. Any decent JIT compiler will recognize loops and automatically generate efficient byte code. Is yours a decent JIT? Run benchmarks to find out.

Synchronization and Lock Scope

Synchronization is absolutely necessary in threaded code. It is, however, expensive in terms of performance. A synchronized method is not only slower in execution speed, it also uses up scarce kernel resources that other synchronized methods may need concurrently. The rules?

Provide synchronization only as needed — At the risk of overstating the obvious, we present this rule.

Reduce lock scope to atomic levels — Don't synchronize an entire method if only part of the code actually requires resource protection. Instead use local variables, block scope, or instance variables as locks. If appropriate, use condition variables to test for the need to synchronize first.

If possible, avoid using locks from within any loop — It is easy to control this from within your own code — don't invoke any synchronization code from within a loop. It is impossible, however, to predict if or when users of your code might place your synchronized methods in a loop of their own!

Protected Variables

Wherever possible, use protected variables instead of private accessor methods to access variables from within a class hierarchy. In extreme cases, place the related classes in the same package[6] or use public variables (an extremely unpopular option). As a compromise, another option is to go ahead and write (or generate) accessor methods as usual, but don't use them in subclasses — instead refer directly to the protected (or package scope) variables.[7]

Container Classes

Use Arrays whenever possible. Although the classes Vector and Hashtable are much more powerful, they are also generally slower.[8] Of course, either of these two classes may be converted to an Array after using their useful operations.

Class Vector also provides an operation `trimToSize()` which should be called whenever the final size is known. In addition, Vectors should be "reused" by calling the `setSize(0)` method, which sets the size to zero rather than creating a new Vector. However, be careful to check if other code relies on a null value for, say, an instance variable. If some code is relying on a null value you have "optimized away" by calling `setSize(0)` instead of setting an instance variable to null, this can be a subtle bug to catch because it is a *logical* error, not a syntax or runtime error.

Object Construction and Destruction

Although often touted as a "pure" object-oriented language, Java breaks this mold by supporting both reference types *and* primitive types. Pure OO languages (e.g., Smalltalk) treat all data types as full-blown objects. Java, however, also supports what are known as "built-in" types in other languages (e.g., int). On the surface, it may seem that this decision would somehow "enhance" the performance of some operations. In practice, however, just the opposite can occur.

Sometimes Java bites off its nose to spite its face. The decision to support primitive types is one such case (at least in terms of performance). Rather than making all objects reference types, primitive types force some objects to perform extra object initializations in order to comply with the Java object model. For example, consider the most often used container

---

6 This has the same general effect as a **friend** in C++.

7 Again, this *should be* unnecessary given a decent optimizing compiler. Clearly, `someObj.getId()` should be converted to `someObj.id` by the compiler. Is it?

8 Class Vector is especially slow because each addition or removal of an element to the list is synchronized. This valuable (and sometimes absolutely necessary) feature can be a performance *pig*.

class, Vector. A Vector can only hold reference types. Therefore, any code that uses primitive types must first convert these values back and forth in order to use a Vector. Again, use Vectors with care and prefer Arrays over Vectors whenever possible.

Simulating Multiple Inheritance in Java

Throughout this book we have time and again visited the problem of the *extension curse* (where Java's lack of support for multiple inheritance has forced a design compromise). We see it again here with class IdentifiableObject in that the class is designed to provide functionality of all objects, yet third-party libraries (or our own application libraries) may use classes that already hog the single extension capability provided in Java.

Actually, this curse occurs all the time in most other OO languages that do not provide interfaces, most notably Smalltalk and Ada. The solution using these languages is simple — and it is the same solution we should use in Java. The answer should not always be a knee-jerk turn to interfaces,[9] rather we simply hold onto an instance variable that provides the desired capability and add the class name to the **implements** clause list as in **Listing 10.3**.

Listing 10.3 *Simulating Multiple Inheritance in Java*

```java
// 1. First, define an interface to match the capability desired

interface ObjectIdentifier {
    public int getId();
    public void setId( int id );
    public String getName();
    public void setName (String name);
}
// 2. Next, implement this interface using a class...

class IdentifiableObject implements ObjectIdentifier {

    private int id;
    private String name;
    public int getId() { return this.id; };
    public void setId( int id ) { this.id = id; };
    public String getName() { return this.name; };
    public void setName ( String name )
        { this.name = name; };
}
```

---

9 Actually it should, but in conjunction with another idiom.

Listing 10.3 (cont.) *Simulating Multiple Inheritance in Java*

```
// 3. Last, add the interface to the class implements clause
//     and declare an instance variable of the class that
//     implements the interface at the top of every inheritance
//     tree that requires the functionality

class MyFavoriteKindOfObject implements ObjectIdentifier {

    private IdentifiableObject  identifiableObject_;

    public int getId() { return identifiableObject_.getId(); }
    public void setId( int id )
        { identifiableObject_.setId( id ); }
    public String getName() { return
        identifiableObject_.getName(); }
    public void setName { identifiableObject_.setName( name ); }
}
```

All we're really doing here is wrapping a helper class. When we wrap the helper object's public interface (e.g., IdentifiableObject) by adding it to our **implements** clause, we are indeed reimplementing its interface. By utility the class MyFavoriteKindOfObject in **Listing 10.3** "isa" IdentifiableObject or an ObjectIdentifier even though extension was not used. Using this idiom the effect is essentially the same as using extension, since all subclasses inherit the instance variable and the capabilities provided. It is a combination of a composition approach and an inheritance approach.

This approach promotes reuse because the *mixin class* (i.e., IdentifiableObject) can be reused in many different multiple inheritance hierarchies without requiring the code to be rewritten every time. In contrast, using Java interfaces without this idiom *does* require redundant implementation code.

Callbacks — Reflection Versus Interfaces

Callbacks are essential in telephony programming wherever there is a need to implement asynchronous notification (in other words, always!). Callbacks are provided in most other languages (e.g., Ada, C, C++) by the support of *function pointers*. Java does not support function pointers. In Java, there are two other primary mechanisms for implementing callbacks: *reflection* and *interfaces*.

In some circles, it has been stated that reflection is an inappropriate method of implementing callbacks. Instead, interfaces are said to be the preferred implementation and are even claimed superior to reflection. This display of "conventional wisdom" exposes a surprising level of ignorance.

As is true so many times in programming, the decision about which approach to be used should be dependent more upon the implementation requirements than on some self-appointed "guru's" attitude. The truth is one approach is not necessarily any better than the other given the circumstances. Rather they are two different ways of accomplishing approximately the same task with different costs and benefits for each approach. Experienced programmers use the appropriate tool for the appropriate task.

In review, let's first examine how interfaces support callbacks. In short, a minimum of two classes and one interface are required to implement a Java interface implementation of a callback mechanism. Let's start with the interface first. In **Listing 10.4**, we first create an interface (in this case, CallbackFunctions) that specifies one or more of the callback functions to be invoked. In Step 2, we create one or more classes that implement that interface (class SampleCallbackClient) so that a third class (CallbackServer) can invoke the callback functions in an asynchronous fashion on behalf of the client class SampleCallbackClient.

Listing 10.4 *Implementing Callbacks Using Java Interfaces*

```
// step 1: create the callback interface...
public interface CallbackFunctions {
   public void callbackOne( CallbackServer server );
   public void callbackTwo( CallbackServer server,
      Object[] obj );
}


// step 2: implement the callback interface with one
// or more classes...
public class SampleCallbackClient
implements sroberts.callback.CallbackFunctions {

   private Object callbackServer_;
   public SampleCallbackClient () {
      SampleCallbackClient[] allRequests =
         new SampleCallbackClient[1];
      allRequests[0] = this;
      callbackServer_ =
         new sroberts.callback.CallbackServer( allRequests );
   }
   public void callbackOne( CallbackServer server )
      { // some code... }
   public void callbackTwo( CallbackServer server,
      Object[] obj ) { // some other code... }
   }
```

Listing 10.4 (cont.) *Implementing Callbacks Using Java Interfaces*

```
// step 3: provide a server in a separate thread to invoke
// the callback on behalf of all implementers of the
// callback interface (i.e. the clients)...

public class CallbackServer implements java.lang.Runnable {

    private sroberts.callback.CallbackFunctions[]
        callbackClients_;
    private java.lang.Thread thisThread_;

    public CallbackServer(
        sroberts.callback.CallbackFunctions[] cbfArray ) {
        callbackClients_ = cbfArray;
        thisThread_ = new Thread( this );
        thisThread_.start();
    }

    public void run() {
        while ( true ) {
            try { thisThread_.sleep( 1000 ); }
            catch ( InterruptedException ie ) {}
            for ( int i = 0; callbackClients_.length < i; i++ ) {
                callbackClients_[ i ].callbackOne( this );
            }
        }
    }
}
```

In this example, CallbackServer's sole purpose in life is to sit around and invoke the methods of clients (in this case, the method `callbackOne()` of any clients that implement the CallbackFunctions interface). Class CallbackServer can, of course, either implement the Runnable interface or extend the Thread class (in this example we chose the former approach).

When Interfaces Are Not Enough: Providing Anonymous Callback Capability

This interface approach certainly allows for the use of callbacks in one sense, but it disallows one very important feature C, C++, and Ada programmers use callbacks for — the invocation of different functions that share a common function signature but use *different function names*. For this type of support, Java interfaces no longer suffice. For example, the callback mechanism created in **Listing 10.4** will support any class that implements the CallbackFunctions interface.[10] It will *not*, however, support any class that implements the callbackOne and callbackTwo function signatures *alone* (i.e., using a name other than `callbackOne()` or `callbackTwo()`). The difference is that the callback in Java *must use the same name* for the method that is specified in the interface. Take the first callback, `callbackOne()`. Any class that implements the CallbackFunctions interface and uses the same name *and* function signature for their calls (i.e., `callbackOne()` taking an instance of a CallbackServer as a parameter) can use Java's interface approach. But they can't use another function name that also only takes a CallbackServer as a parameter (say, `myFunction( CallbackServer cs )`). This limitation eliminates an entire class of very powerful generic programming from consideration.

Suppose we want to provide a notification scheme that does *not* rely on a well-known name (like "update"). Instead we require the most generic interface imaginable — a function taking an array of Objects. This architecture still imposes a design constraint on Observers, but assume for now that this is an acceptable tradeoff. In C/C++, we might create a function pointer for all "updates" as follows:

```
typedef void ( *funcTakingAnArrayOfObjects ) ( void* );
```

We could then pass an instance of this function pointer to our server as follows:

```
void run( funcTakingAnArrayOfObjects func, void* objList ) {

    for ( int i = 0; observers_.length < i; i++ ) {
        observers_[ i ].func( objList );
    }
}
```

Using C/C++ function pointers, *the function can have any name* as long as it complies with the prescribed function pointer interface. This kind of capability is simply not available in Java. In order to add full function pointer-like capability in Java, we *must* turn to reflection. Using reflection, we can discover the name used in an implementation and call that different name at runtime. This is not quite the same as function pointers in that there is an additional amount of overhead required in the name lookup, but it achieves the same goal. In fact, it is the only possible way in which this

---

10 This is the same as saying that either the callbackOne or callbackTwo function signatures are supported.

anonymous call capability can be achieved in Java — but at least it is possible. We have already seen reflection used in this manner in our class DirectedMessage (see Chapter 9, "Event Management in Java"). In fact, that's exactly what class DirectedMessage is — a threaded reflection callback mechanism.

In summary, an interface implementation for callbacks provides for faster execution and type safety at the cost of generic use. In contrast, a reflection implementation provides for the more powerful anonymous callback capability at the cost of a slight performance hit and the potential for runtime errors due to lack of type checking.

Generics in Java

The keyword `generic` is reserved in Java, though not currently used. Like every other feature of Java, the concept came from somewhere else. In this case, both the concept and keyword were lifted from the Ada programming language.[11] Without being mindreaders, we can pretty safely assume that if the language designers intend to add *parameterized type* support to the language, this is the keyword they will use. This is appropriate, because parameterized types are usually thought of as being synonymous with Ada's *generics* or C++ *templates*.

Recall that generic code is code that does not rely on the intrinsic properties of the representation of the data types used in an algorithm. The canonical example is the proverbial `swap( )` function (see **Listing 10.5**).

Listing 10.5 *Generic Code in C*

```
void swap( int* a, int* b ) {
    int temp = *a;    *a = *b;    *b = temp;
}
```

Two items are initialized with values and then passed into the `swap( )` function. Upon returning from the call, the first actual parameter now contains (i.e., points to) the value of the second; the second contains the value of the first. The point is that the code inside the body of the function qualifies as being *generic* — it is an algorithm that does not rely on any characteristics of the underlying *data types* being swapped. As long as the data passed in "understand" the operations performed, this scheme works.

In the `swap( )` function, the only requirement is that every data type passed in "understand" the assignment operator. The goal is to write as much code as we can in this fashion. If we do, the algorithm can be used on many different data types (or interfaces and classes) without alteration.

---

11 C++ also borrowed the concept from Ada and called it *templates*.

A Bunny Trail — Parameter Passing and Assignment in Java

Let's try this in Java. Knowing what we do about the assignment operator, what do you suppose happens? Here's a first stab at the same code in Java (**Listing 10.6**).

Listing 10.6 *The Wrong Way to Swap in Java*

```
public static void swap ( int a, int b ) {
    int temp = a;
    a = b;
    b = temp;
}
```

This code works just fine within the scope of the method — the swap takes place. But as soon as we return from the call, the values of a and b have *not* changed — not exactly what we had hoped for. And so we see that this "magic assignment pointer" (i.e., the assignment operator) is not a true pointer mechanism after all. It only works within the scope of an enclosing call. So even though values seem to be passed by reference, assignment doesn't work for *all* values passed as parameters to a method. The same is true in Smalltalk. In fact, the Smalltalk compiler *won't even allow* assignment to parameters passed into a method[12] (the code won't compile)! In C/C++, we can "fix" this problem by passing a pointer or a reference. In Java, we must resort to idioms. First we'll present the solution, then we'll come back to the problem.

There are two ways to simulate this behavior (in both Smalltalk and Java). The first is to create a new instance from within the method and return one or more of them in a container class[13] (as in **Listing 10.7**).

Listing 10.7 *Implementing Parameterized Types in Java Returning a Container*

(1)
```
public static Object[] swap( Object a, Object b )
    throws CloneNotSupportedException {

    Object[] array = new Object[2];
    Object temp;
    try {
        temp = a.clone();
        a = b.clone();
```

---

12 This occurs because overloading of the assignment operator is not allowed in Smalltalk (although overloading of all other operators is).

13 This is not to suggest that actual parameters passed into a method cannot be altered — in fact, they can, but only by using public methods defined on the object, not by using the assignment operator!

Listing 10.7 (cont.) *Implementing Parameterized Types in Java Returning a Container*

```
      b = temp;
   }
   catch ( CloneNotSupportedException cnse )
      { throw cnse; }
   array[0] = a;
   array[1] = b;
   return array;
}
```

The array now contains objects that point to the correct values. Another way of accomplishing the same objective is to pass the arguments in a container in the first place as in **Listing 10.8**.

Listing 10.8 *Implementing Parameterized Types in Java by Passing a Container*

```
public static void swap( Object[] twoObjects )
   throws CloneNotSupportedException {

   if ( twoObjects.length ) != 2 return;
   Object temp;
   try {
         temp = twoObjects[0].clone();
         twoObjects[0] = twoObjects[1].clone();
         twoObjects[1] = temp;
   }
   catch( CloneNotSupportedException cnse )
         { throw cnse; }
}
```

Using this idiom, it is not necessary to create and return a container from within the implementation; instead the onus is placed on the caller to pass in the container. Another option would be to pass in two arrays, each holding a parameter (in general, one array for each parameter passed). This "container idiom" is easy to remember and works the same way no matter what type of reference object is passed. It works best when you don't want to bother converting data types.

But isn't there an alternative? And why is this necessary in the first place? The answer is that built-in types like ints (technically called *primitive types*) are second-class citizens in Java. The key is to always pass a *reference* type[14] that defines mutator methods[15] as in **Listing 10.9**.

---

14 A reference type is any object that is not a primitive type.

15 A *mutator method* is one that allows for the changing of an object's value (e.g., setName()).

Listing 10.9 *The Right way to Swap in Java*

```
public static void swapNames( SDRCall a, SDRCall b ) {

    SDRCall temp = new SDRCall( a ); // a copy constructor
    a.setName( b.getName() );
    b.setName( temp.getName() );
}
```

In Java, the ability to change the value of parameters depends on the type of object passed and whether or not the operation invoked within the method is defined for that object. If it is, and the object is a *mutable reference type* that provides appropriate mutator methods, the process works as planned. You get the point. Let's get back to the subject — generics.

Usually, generics provide three primary features to a programming language:

- Parameterized types
- Type safety
- Macro expansion

Macro expansion[16] can be useful even in an interpreted language like Java. A generic function might look something like **Listing 10.10**. The pseudo type G is replaced at compile time with a suitable type.

Listing 10.10 *Possible Generic Syntax in Java*

```
generic public static void swap( G a, G b ) {

    G temp = a;
    a = b;
    b = temp;
}
```

In order for generics to work, the compiler must be "smart enough" to determine that each parameter has a suitable mutator method. This has already been accomplished in Ada, Smalltalk, and C++, so it is certainly possible with Java.

In addressing *parameterized types* and *type safety* in more detail, perhaps the best we can do here is observe how the lack of some of these features has affected a similar programming language, namely Smalltalk.

---

16 Recall that macro expansion occurs when the overhead of a function call is replaced by a static compilation of object code placed directly in the program text. This is a tradeoff between program size (i.e., memory footprint) and execution speed.

Parameterized Types

In Smalltalk, parameterized types are easily implemented. Because all formal parameter arguments really have no type, all parameters are essentially parameterized types.[17] Of course, it does not immediately follow that all Smalltalk code is therefore generic. Rather the same care of design must be made to write generic code, but the process relies more heavily on polymorphism than on data types.

In Java, programming for parameterized types can be accomplished by following idioms. We can use interfaces to implement polymorphism, but we cannot rely on a typeless nature for actual parameters at runtime. In other words, we are in for a healthy dose of casting. However, because all reference objects inherit from class Object, we can simulate Smalltalk's typeless nature using extension. This is accomplished by providing class Object as the data type for all formal parameters (see **Listing 10.7** [1]) and then casting all actual parameters to class Object at the point of the call (see **Listing 10.11** [2]).

Listing 10.11 *Using Parameterized Types in Java*

```
import sroberts.util.*;

public class TestSwap {
    public static void main( java.lang.String[] args ) {

        IdentifiableObject i1 = new IdentifiableObject( "joe", 1 );
        IdentifiableObject i2 = new IdentifiableObject( "mary", 2 );
        i1.printName();   i2.printName();
        Object[] array = new Object[2];

        try {
            // cast at point of call…
            array = SDRUtility.swap( (Object)i1, (Object)i2 );
            System.out.println( "i1 = " + i1.getName() );
            System.out.println( "i2 = " + i2.getName() );
            System.out.println( "array at 0 = "
                + ((SDRIdentifiable)array[0]).getName());
            System.out.println( "array at 1 = "
                + ((SDRIdentifiable)array[1]).getName());
        }
        catch ( Exception e ) {
            System.out.println( "Exception thrown: " + e ); }
        }
}
```

(2)

---

17 Indeed, much of the speed attributable to Smalltalk implementations (relative to Java implementations) can be attributed to the fact that type checking is simply not performed!

Of course, this may also require casting back to the original type after the call to retrieve the values, but hey this isn't Smalltalk.

Type Safety

Java is a strongly typed language. The approach just presented to implement parameterized types obviously sidesteps the type-checking mechanism of the language, rendering it somewhat meaningless. We can *reintroduce* this type checking, yet retain the necessary level of abstraction and flexibility by specifying formal parameter types as far down an inheritance hierarchy branch as needed to implement generic code. At the same time, however, we place this type in the hierarchy branch high enough so as not to prohibit subclasses from benefiting from a generic implementation. For example, take the standard class hierarchy found in `java.lang` beginning with class Number (see **Figure 10.3**).

Figure 10.3 *Java Number Class Hierarchy*

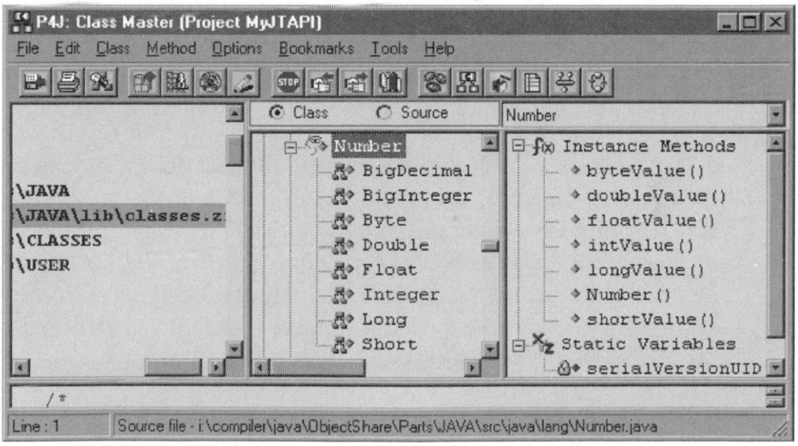

Clearly, some kinds of numerical operations will depend upon the properties common to all numbers, while others will yield different results depending on the type of number operated on (i.e., passed as an actual parameter cast to type Number). For example, a generic algorithm to calculate the number of calls received since midnight will probably yield the same results no matter which subclass of class Number we pass in. And so in this case, class Number may be the best choice for a formal parameter type (see **Listing 10.12** [3]).

Listing 10.12 *Type Safety Balanced with Generic Code*

(3)

```
public void callsMade( Number[] nums ) {
    // do stuff with nums...
    nums[ 0 ] = ...
    return;
}


// now call it...
Number[] nums = new Number[3];
nums[0] = (Number)(new Integer(27));
nums[1] = (Number)(new Float(12));
nums[2] = (Number)(new Long(33));
callsMade( nums );
```

Although the example is a bit contrived, it demonstrates that the function signature doesn't ever have to change if the values (data types) passed in do not adversely affect the outcome. Rather than writing new functions for every different type, this same generic code in function `callsMade()` can be used for any subclass of type Number. The tradeoff is, well, more casting upon invocation.

When Precision Matters

So far we have only considered algorithms that do not depend on the data type used.[18] However, an operation to calculate the present value of an annuity will yield wildly different results when solving for the time period or the internal rate of return, *depending on the precision* of some of the numeric types passed in. In this case, we will likely have to *travel further down the extension tree* to find a suitable formal parameter type to pass in; say, class Float (see **Listing 10.13** [4]).

Listing 10.13 *Adjusting Generic Parameter Types for an Algorithm*

(4)

```
public Float
presentValue( Float futureValue, Float rate,
    Number period ) {
        // some code...
}
```

For those parameters that require precision, precision is supplied. For those that do not (e.g., the third parameter "period"), a tradeoff is made that forces casting at the point of the call in return for more flexibility. Is the code in **Listing 10.13** generic? That's a good question. The answer is "only

---

18 Recall that that was in fact the definition of *generic* code!

partially, at best." Because only the third parameter is generic in any sense, this might be a poor example. It does, however, demonstrate a situation where the technique might be useful.

When Generics Meet Polymorphism

Polymorphism can be used to implement generic code because classes in an object hierarchy already handle the same data types by way of extension. This same concept can (and should) be applied for higher-level abstractions used in telephony programming. The rule of thumb is more or less as follows:

JTAPI Rule to Remember 4:

If the behavior is the same for a particular polymorphic method in an inheritance tree, go as high up the tree as possible to select an appropriate formal parameter class type.

For example, if a particular generic algorithm is designed to operate on objects of type Address, it should only call methods common to all Addresses.[19] If on the other hand it must invoke more specific methods based on specializations of class Address, we must supply classes CallCenterAddress, ACDAddress, ACDManagerAddress, or any subclass as the formal parameter. We also can use these same techniques to operate on instances that implement interfaces and their extensions. Because most JTAPI classes are actually specified as interfaces, this works just fine.

So what's the difference between polymorphic code and generic code? Generic code will work on any data type, period. Polymorphic code will (hopefully) work only on code that either implements an interface or is part of an object hierarchy. The generic code is guaranteed by the compiler to work. In contrast, the polymorphic code may bomb at runtime. Generic invocation code can be statically compiled. Polymorphic invocation code cannot; it uses *late binding* to dynamically determine the proper method to call. There is also a difference in the mindset of the developer. The generic code is intended to run with any data type — it is algorithmic in nature. The polymorphic code takes any generic benefit as a *side effect*. The prime design consideration is the behavior of the object (as it should be).

In summary, we have presented some idioms for increasing the level of genericalness of our code. This is accomplished by making formal parame-

---

19 Technically, we could do a type check on incoming parameters and cast them accordingly, but this is hardly generic coding!

ters to methods as far up an extension tree as possible. The side effect of loosened type-checking may then be offset by moving back down the extension tree (from class Object) until an appropriate level is reached. This idiom should prove useful for implementing generic JTAPI code.

Implementing Asynchronous Notification Using Threads

Throughout this book, we have shown how an asynchronous notification capability is absolutely necessary in telephony programming. In this section we outline a few more possible implementation approaches in Java. Both methods presented here require the use of threads.

The first approach places the burden on the source (let's call it the "source approach"). In this scheme the source (or whoever the notifier is) simply spawns a new thread for each target notification.[20] An example using dependency is shown in **Listing 10.14**.

Listing 10.14 *Threaded Asynchronous Notification Using Dependency*

```
          import java.util.*;
          public class KindOfObservable extends Observable
(5)             implements Runnable
          private int aspect = 0;
          public int getAspect() { return aspect; }
          public void setAspect( int a ) {
            if ( aspect != a ) {
               aspect = a;
               Runnable koo = null;
(6)            try { koo = this.clone() }
               catch ( Exception e ) {
                  System.out.println("Exception caught at clone");
               }
               // here's the notification API...
               setChanged();
(7)            Thread t = new Thread( koo );
(8)            t.start();
               clearChanged();
            }
          }


          public void run () {
(9)          notifyObservers( this );
          }
          }
```

---

20 This is a variant of the notification techniques we used in Chapter 6.

As always, the source must implement the Runnable interface if it is to spawn threads ([5]). Just in case observers want to get cute and alter the source, a copy is made ([6]). This has the fortunate side effect of providing an instance for the new thread invocation ([7]). Finally, [9] provides an implementation of the run() method, which will be invoked when [8] is executed.

Okay, maybe targets can't do *anything* they want. Targets must properly protect any changeable data from concurrent access via threads (i.e., they must synchronize). The reason for this is that the source may later spawn notification to the same target object, or notification may be received on the same method from another thread. Because there is no guarantee of the order of processing or the length of time processing will consume in any target methods using the same data, proper care must be taken. The largest granularity of locking here would be to synchronize the update() method of the target. Smaller granularity can of course be achieved using tighter lock scope in the target using either synchronized helper functions, blocks, or local variables.

The second threaded asynchronous notification approach places the burden on the target. There are no changes required in the source object. Using this "target approach" a thread is spawned from the target instead of the source. This means a new thread is fired from each object receiving notification from the source from inside the target's update() method. An example is shown in **Listing 10.15**.

Listing 10.15 *Asynchronous Notification in the Target*

```java
import java.util.*;
public class ImplementationOfObserver
      implements Observer, Runnable {

   public void update( Observable obs ) {
       // now that we have obs, we can examine its state
       if ( obs.getAspect() == 12 ) {
          Thread t = new Thread( this );
          t.start();
       }
   }

   public void run () {
       doSomething();  // synchronize if any static data
                       // is altered
   }
}
```

Choices, Choices

So which approach is preferred? As usual, you get to decide — but here are the ramifications. The target approach runs the risk of a large proliferation of threads — and so care must be taken to ensure the system can handle such an approach. The associated overhead for each thread invocation and the added system context-switching overhead adds up. However, the potential need to synchronize is made obvious.

The source approach is sort of a middle ground between no *concurrency* at all and no *liveliness*.[21] Fewer threads are spawned and so system resources are not taxed to any alarming degree. On the other hand, concurrency is reduced relative to the target approach because each notification of observers processes an entire list at a time. The notifying object is suspended until all target processing is complete. Should any of these calls take too long to process, the system may appear to be hung when it is not. But we have delegated the notification to another instance and so the source itself is never blocked! If the source is set to run at a higher priority level than the notifiers, this should achieve the desired effect.

In any case both of these idioms are superior to no threads at all. Remember — no threads means no asynchronous notification! Either of these approaches can be used whether implemented using Java dependency; Java events, the Thread Pattern or our homegrown MMM model.

Having investigated several idioms, it is time to now move on to the more fashionable topic of patterns.

Patterns

Java, being in the category of well-designed modern programming languages, requires fewer idioms. Nevertheless, patterns are useful for any programming language. Recall that patterns (first popularized on a grand scale by Gamma et al.'s book *Design Patterns*) are descriptive templates for coding reusable software components. They are like programming language independent *meta-specifications*.

Contrary to popular computer science hype, patterns are really nothing new. By their very nature, patterns are not created, rather they are *discovered*. It is often said that we "go mining for patterns." Our examination of patterns will take us into the discovery of two types:

- *Component patterns useful in telephony applications* implemented in the Java Programming Language
- *Server telephony application patterns* implemented in Java

---

21 Liveliness is the degree to which a concurrent system responds. It is inversely related to safety, a condition by which concurrent anomalies are mitigated. For an excellent discussion of these topics, see Doug Lea's masterpiece *Concurrent Programming In Java* (Addison-Wesley, 1996).

What we mean by the term "component pattern" is that while useful for telephony applications, they may be useful as component patterns in other problem spaces as well. The reason we concentrate on server telephony patterns is that JTAPI has already specified many of the client telephony patterns in its design and in the comments of the standard interfaces.

Java Component Patterns Useful in Telephony

The patterns represented here are not new. We provide implementations because we use them in our telephony code. The patterns implemented here are *Singleton, FiniteStateMachine,* and *Block.* We use an extension of Singleton in implementing our EventDispatcher class in the Message Management Model from Chapter 9 as well as our SecurityMonitor helper class in Chapter 6. Other valid uses in JTAPI are for class Provider and any Peer classes. The FiniteStateMachine pattern is useful in implementing all JTAPI notification (although we did not use this approach, it is yet another pattern for notification in any OO language that supports threads). Block is a class that simulates the Smalltalk mechanism of the same name (albeit not as completely). Blocks are literally blocks of code and are useful in any threaded implementation. And finally, we present an example of using *adapter classes* and *inner classes* to support a JTAPI message management implementation.

Singleton Pattern

The Singleton Pattern involves two cooperating classes. The SDRSingletonFactory class enforces the concept of a single instance. The SDRSingleton class is the superclass of all SDRSingleton instances, which is managed by the SDRSingletonFactory class. Instances of subclasses of SDRSingleton are the singletons themselves.

Creating the Singleton Classes

The general idea is that no matter how many times a new instance is requested, the same instance is returned. Without considerations for inheritance, the implementation is trivial. If, however, the requirement is to provide Singleton capabilities for all subclasses of a class, the implementation requires some sort of factory implementation because a single static variable representing the only instance will not suffice. Instead we must manage a list of such instances.[22] We have assumed such a requirement. Our implementation of the singleton factory is presented in **Listing 10.16**.

---

22 Because Java does not support the Smalltalk concept of "class instance variables," this is the only feasible implementation.

Listing 10.16 *A Singleton Factory*

```
package sroberts.util.singleton;
import java.lang.*;
import java.util.*;


public final class SDRSingletonFactory {

(12)        private static Hashtable singletons_;
            private static SDRSingletonFactory meMyselfAndI_ = null;
            private SDRSingletonFactory();
               // disallow instance creations...
            public static Object create( String className );
               // ctor...
            public static void remove( String className );
            private static SDRSingletonFactory pvtCreate();
               // private ctor...
            public static Enumeration getSingletonNames();
            public static void ttySingletonNames();
}
```

The implementation we provide maintains a static list of all singletons ([12]). The list is maintained automatically by the SDRSingletonFactory class using reflection to keep track of the classes with singleton instances that are currently allocated. If a class has an entry in the list, that same instance is returned. Otherwise a new instance is created, pointed to by the list, and then returned. Subsequent calls to **create()** will return that same instance. The structure of a singleton is shown in **Listing 10.17.** Line [13] hides the object from instantiation outside the singleton package by giving the constructor default package visibility.

Listing 10.17 *A Singleton*

```
package sroberts.util.singleton;

import java.lang.*;
import java.util.*;


public class SDRSingleton {

            // required default package visibility for ctor...
(13)        SDRSingleton () { }

(14)        public void finalize() throws Throwable {
               SDRSingletonFactory.remove( this.getClass().toString() );
               super.finalize();
(15)        }
}
```

Lines [14]–[15] override `finalize()` to ensure that singleton instances are removed from the factory's list[23] before the garbage collector kicks in (i.e., when the object instance is no longer referenced in code).

In order for an object to become a singleton, two idioms are required. First, singleton objects must extend the SDRSingleton class as in **Listing 10.18** [17].

Listing 10.18 *Extending the Singleton Class*

(16)
```
package sroberts.util.singleton;
```

(17)
```
public class AnSDRSingletonForTest extends SDRSingleton { }
```

The second requirement is that the class must be placed in the same package as class SDRSingleton (see line [16]). This provides each class default package visibility to the constructor method to be called by the Singleton class enabling the hidden construction mechanism.

As expected, programmers cannot create instances of singletons.[24] In fact, calls to the new keyword won't even compile! So instead of invoking the new operator, programmers must invoke the class method `SDRSingletonFactory.create()` passing the fully qualified name of the class to "single-ize" (see **Listing 10.19**).

Listing 10.19 *Returning a Singleton Instance*

```
public static Object create( String className )   {
```

(18)
```
    if ( meMyselfAndI_ == null ) {  // make sure the factory
                                    // exists...
      meMyselfAndI_ = pvtCreate();
    }
```

(19)
```
    if ( className == "SDRSingletonFactory" )
        return meMyselfAndI_;

    Object instance = null;
    String classKey = "class " + className;

    if ( singletons_.containsKey( classKey ) ) {
       instance = singletons_.get( classKey );
    }
```

---

23 Of course, `finalize()` may never actually be called, and so some programmers may wish to code and use an explicit destructor instead.

24 Actually, classes inside the SDRSingleton package can, but we ignore that design flaw for expedience sake.

Listing 10.19 (cont.) *Returning a Singleton Instance*

```
        else {
          try {
(20)        instance = Class.forName( className ).newInstance();
(21)        singletons_.put( classKey, instance );
          }
          catch ( Exception e ) {
          }
        }
(22)    return instance;
      }
```

The SDRSingletonFactory class must also maintain a singleton policy on itself! This is accomplished in lines [18]–[19] of **Listing 10.19**. If an instance for this class does not already exist, the factory creates the instance ([20]), places it in the management list ([21]), and returns it to the caller ([22]).

Using the Singleton Classes

Again, instances of singletons are referenced (or created as needed) by a call to `SDRSingletonFactory.create()`. This is demonstrated in **Listing 10.20**. Due to Java's strong typing, all instances must be explicitly cast to the correct type of the caller ([23], [24], and [25] in **Listing 10.20**).

Listing 10.20 *Instantiating a Singleton*

```
String singletonClassName =
"sroberts.util.singleton.AnSDRSingletonForTest";

AnSDRSingletonForTest obj1 =
(23)  (AnSDRSingletonForTest)SDRSingletonFactory.create(singletonClassName);

// try to create another instance...
AnSDRSingletonForTest obj2 =
(24)  (AnSDRSingletonForTest)SDRSingletonFactory.create(singletonClassName);

// and another...
AnSDRSingletonForTest obj3 =
(25)  (AnSDRSingletonForTest)SDRSingletonFactory.create(singletonClassName);

SDRSingletonFactory.ttySingletonNames();
```

All three object instantiations in this listing will return exactly the same object. For a look at how it is used in JTAPI, refer back to our implementation of the Provider interface in Chapter 6, "Construction of a JTAPI Library."

Finite State Machine Pattern

Finite state machines are used in a variety of systems. They are used extensively in the design and even the implementation of many real-time systems. Although it is not an absolute requirement that it be run in a *deterministic* environment, a telephony system may be thought of as a "soft" real-time system.[25]

The objects modeled in JTAPI exhibit classic characteristics found in finite state machines. The entire behavior of many objects may be defined exclusively by a set of states and the transitions between them. This has become obvious in our exploration of states and events in JTAPI. And so here we present yet another implementation of events and their associated notification schemes, this time using finite state machines implemented in Java. **Figure 10.4** shows the primary objects and their relationships to one another.

Figure 10.4 *Finite State Machine Object Model*

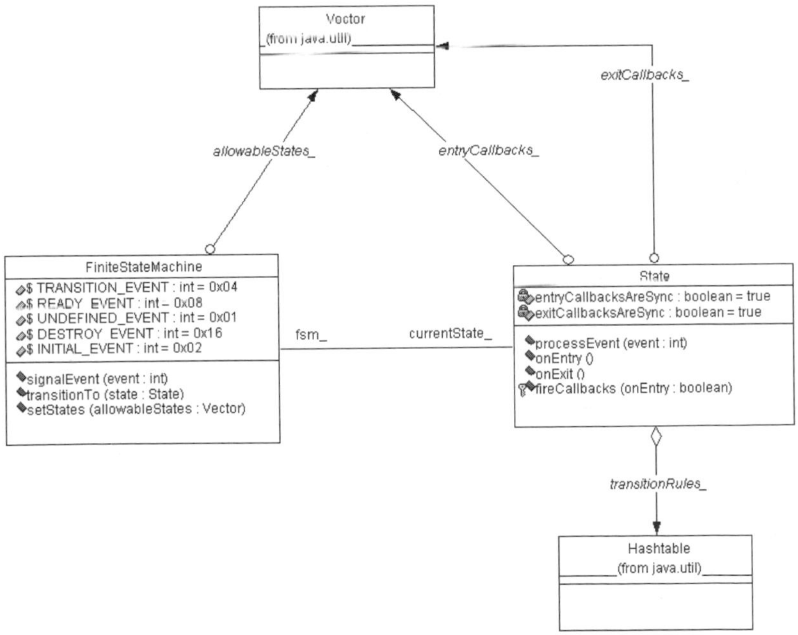

A finite state machine (FSM) is an object with an allowable set of states through which it may transition in and out. These state transitions can occur only when the appropriate event is received by the FSM. When that event is received, the FSM not only transitions to another allowable state, but it may

---

25 In contrast, a "hard" real-time system is one where a missed deadline is considered a failure.

also fire multiple callbacks either upon entry, during, or upon exit from a particular state.

Building the FSM

The FSM is presented in **Listing 10.21**.

Listing 10.21 The Finite State Machine Class

```java
package sroberts.fsm;

import java.util.Vector;

public class FiniteStateMachine {

    // events common to all FSMs...
    static public final int UNDEFINED_EVENT = 0x01;
    static public final int INITIAL_EVENT = 0x02;
    static public final int TRANSITION_EVENT = 0x03;
    static public final int READY_EVENT = 0x04;
    static public final int DESTROY_EVENT = 0x05;

    private Vector allowableStates_;
    private State currentState_;
    private int lastEventFired_;

    public void setCurrentState( State newState ) {
        currentState_ = newState;
    }

    public int getLastEventFired()
        { return lastEventFired_; }

    public void setStates(
            Vector allowableStates, State initialState ) {
        allowableStates_ = allowableStates;
        currentState_ = initialState;
    }
    public void signalEvent( int event ) {
        lastEventFired_ = event;
        currentState_.processEvent( event );
    }
    public void transitionTo( State state ) {
        currentState_ = state;
        state.onEntry();
    }
}
```

The State itself is an object that essentially maintains the list of callbacks to fire as well as the transition rules necessary to ensure that the appropriate callbacks are fired in response to the correct event. The State is presented in **Listing 10.22**.

Listing 10.22 *The State Class Used with Finite State Machines*

```
package sroberts.fsm;

import java.util.*;
import sroberts.eventManagement.*;

public class State {

    static public final int ENTRY = 1;
    static public final int EXIT = 2;
    static public final int SUCCESS = 3;
    static public final int ERROR = 4;

    // a collection of DirectedMessages...
    protected Vector entryCallbacks_;
    protected Vector exitCallbacks_;
    protected Vector successfulTransitionCallbacks_;
    protected Vector errorCallbacks_;

    // a collection of ifEvent/gotoState pairs...
    private Hashtable transitionRules_;
    private FiniteStateMachine fsm_;


    // ctors...
    private State() { }

    public State(
        FiniteStateMachine fsm,
        Vector entryCallbacks,
        Vector exitCallbacks
        )
    {
        super();
        fsm_ = fsm;
        entryCallbacks_ = entryCallbacks;
        exitCallbacks_ = exitCallbacks;
    }
```

Listing 10.22 (cont.) *The State Class Used with Finite State Machines*

```java
protected void fireCallbacks( int callbackType ) {

    Vector callBacks;
    if ( callbackType == ENTRY ) {
        callBacks = entryCallbacks_; }
    else if ( callbackType == EXIT ) {
        callBacks = exitCallbacks_; }
    else if ( callbackType == SUCCESS ) {
        callBacks = successfulTransitionCallbacks_; }
    else if ( callbackType == ERROR ) {
        callBacks = errorCallbacks_; }
        else { return; }  // silently fail...

        if ( callBacks == null ) return;

        Enumeration e = callBacks.elements();
    while ( e.hasMoreElements() ) {
        ((DirectedMessage)e.nextElement()).send();
    }
}

public void onEntry( ) {
    fireCallbacks( ENTRY );
}

public void onExit( ) {
    fireCallbacks( EXIT );
}

public void onSuccess( ) {
    fireCallbacks( SUCCESS );
}

public void onError( ) {
    fireCallbacks( ERROR );
}

public void processEvent( int event ) {
    if ( !transitionRules_.containsKey(
        new Integer(event) ) ) {
        System.out.println( "No such event numbered: "
            + new Integer(event) );
        return;
```

Listing 10.22 (cont.) *The State Class Used with Finite State Machines*

```
      }
      onExit();
      fsm_.transitionTo(
            (State)transitionRules_.get( new Integer(event) ) );
   }
   public void setEntryCallbacks( Vector directedMessages ){
      entryCallbacks_ = directedMessages;
   }
   public void setExitCallbacks( Vector directedMessages ){
      exitCallbacks_ = directedMessages;
   }
   public void setTransitionRules (
         Hashtable transitionRules) {
      transitionRules_ = transitionRules;
   }
}
```

The JTAPI model is built using post-mortem events. In other words, callbacks are fired upon exit from a transition. For example, the `callChangedEvent()` method is invoked *after* a CallEv is received from a CallObserver. And so using these classes to implement the JTAPI model would become an exercise of determining the exit callbacks to be invoked (i.e., the entry callbacks would not be used).

Using the FSM

Using the FSM is a multiple step process as depicted in **Listing 10.23**.

Listing 10.23 *Using the FSM Classes*

```
package sroberts.fsm;

import java.util.*;
import sroberts.eventManagement.*;

public class TestFSM {

   public static void main(java.lang.String[] args) {
   // insert code to start the application here

   FiniteStateMachine fsm = new FiniteStateMachine();

   try {
```

Listing 10.23 (cont.) *Using the FSM Classes*

```
// 1. create the legal states for this fsm...

Vector allowableStates = new Vector();

// 1.a - first create the callbacks...

DirectedMessage initialENTRYCallback;
DirectedMessage initialEXITCallback;
DirectedMessage readyENTRYoneCallback;
DirectedMessage readyENTRYtwoCallback;
DirectedMessage readyEXITCallback;
DirectedMessage destroyedENTRYCallback;
DirectedMessage destroyedEXITCallback;
DirectedMessage inLimboENTRYCallback;
DirectedMessage inLimboEXITCallback;

inLimboENTRYCallback = new DirectedMessage(
    System.out, "println",
        "INVOKED: Entering NOWHERE LAND, man..."
    );
inLimboEXITCallback = new DirectedMessage(
    System.out, "println",
        "INVOKED: Woah dude, leaving the Twilight Zone..."
    );
initialENTRYCallback = new DirectedMessage(
    System.out, "println", "INVOKED: initialENTRYCallback"
    );
initialEXITCallback = new DirectedMessage(
    System.out, "println", "INVOKED: initialEXITCallback"
    );
readyENTRYoneCallback = new DirectedMessage(
    System.out, "println",
    "INVOKED: readyENTRYoneCallback"
    );
readyENTRYtwoCallback = new DirectedMessage(
    System.out, "println",
    "INVOKED: readyENTRYtwoCallback"
    );
readyEXITCallback = new DirectedMessage(
    System.out, "println", "INVOKED: readyEXITCallback"
    );
destroyedENTRYCallback = new DirectedMessage(
    System.out, "println",
    "INVOKED: destroyedENTRYCallback"
    );
```

Listing 10.23 (cont.) *Using the FSM Classes*

```
destroyedEXITCallback = new DirectedMessage(
   System.out, "println",
   "INVOKED: destroyedEXITCallback"
   );

// 1.a.1 - segregate the entries from the exits...

Vector startingStateENTRYCallbacks = new Vector();
Vector startingStateEXITCallbacks = new Vector();
Vector readyStateENTRYCallbacks = new Vector();
Vector readyStateEXITCallbacks = new Vector();
Vector finalStateENTRYCallbacks = new Vector();
Vector finalStateEXITCallbacks = new Vector();
Vector limboStateENTRYCallbacks = new Vector();
Vector limboStateEXITCallbacks = new Vector();


// entries...
startingStateENTRYCallbacks.addElement(initialENTRYCallback);
readyStateENTRYCallbacks.addElement(readyENTRYoneCallback );
readyStateENTRYCallbacks.addElement(readyENTRYtwoCallback );
finalStateENTRYCallbacks.addElement(destroyedENTRYCallback );
limboStateENTRYCallbacks.addElement(inLimboENTRYCallback );

// exits...
startingStateEXITCallbacks.addElement( initialEXITCallback );
readyStateEXITCallbacks.addElement( readyEXITCallback );
finalStateEXITCallbacks.addElement( destroyedEXITCallback );
limboStateEXITCallbacks.addElement( inLimboEXITCallback );

// 1.b - now create the states...

State startingState = new State(
   fsm,
   startingStateENTRYCallbacks, startingStateEXITCallbacks );

State readyState = new State(
   fsm,
   readyStateENTRYCallbacks, readyStateEXITCallbacks );

State finalState = new State(
   fsm,
   finalStateENTRYCallbacks, finalStateEXITCallbacks );
```

Listing 10.23 (cont.) *Using the FSM Classes*

```
State limboState = new State(
   fsm,
   limboStateENTRYCallbacks, limboStateEXITCallbacks );


// 2. create & set the transition state rules for each state
// in this FSM. The semantics are that if an event of a
// certain type is received, which state do we transition to?

Hashtable startingTransitionRules = new Hashtable();
startingTransitionRules.put(
     new Integer(FiniteStateMachine.READY_EVENT),
                  readyState );
startingTransitionRules.put(
     new Integer(FiniteStateMachine.DESTROY_EVENT),
                  finalState );
startingState.setTransitionRules ( startingTransitionRules );

Hashtable readyTransitionRules = new Hashtable();
readyTransitionRules.put(
     new Integer(FiniteStateMachine.INITIAL_EVENT),
                  startingState );
readyTransitionRules.put(
     new Integer(FiniteStateMachine.DESTROY_EVENT),
                  finalState );
readyTransitionRules.put(
     new Integer(FiniteStateMachine.UNDEFINED_EVENT),
                  limboState );
readyState.setTransitionRules ( readyTransitionRules );

Hashtable finalTransitionRules = new Hashtable();
finalTransitionRules.put(
     new Integer(FiniteStateMachine.READY_EVENT),
                  readyState );
finalTransitionRules.put(
     new Integer(FiniteStateMachine.DESTROY_EVENT),
                  finalState );
finalState.setTransitionRules ( finalTransitionRules );

Hashtable limboTransitionRules = new Hashtable();
limboTransitionRules.put(
     new Integer(FiniteStateMachine.INITIAL_EVENT),
                  startingState );
limboTransitionRules.put(
     new Integer(FiniteStateMachine.DESTROY_EVENT),
                  finalState );
```

Listing 10.23 (cont.) *Using the FSM Classes*

```
        limboState.setTransitionRules ( limboTransitionRules );

        // 3. associate the allowable states to the fsm...

        allowableStates.addElement(limboState);
        allowableStates.addElement(startingState);
        allowableStates.addElement(readyState);
        allowableStates.addElement(finalState);

        fsm.setStates( allowableStates, limboState );

    }
    catch( NoSuchMethodException nsme ) {
        System.out.println( "ERROR: from prgram TestFSM -> " );
        nsme.printStackTrace();
    }
    catch( Exception e ) {
        System.out.println( "ERROR: from prgram TestFSM -> " );
        e.printStackTrace();
    }

    fsm.signalEvent( FiniteStateMachine.INITIAL_EVENT );
    fsm.signalEvent( FiniteStateMachine.READY_EVENT );
    fsm.signalEvent( FiniteStateMachine.DESTROY_EVENT );
    }
}
```

output:

```
I:\DATA\JAVACODE\sroberts\fsm>java TestFSM

INVOKED: Woah dude, leaving the Twilight Zone...

INVOKED: initialENTRYCallback

INVOKED: initialEXITCallback

INVOKED: readyENTRYoneCallback

INVOKED: readyENTRYtwoCallback

INVOKED: readyEXITCallback

INVOKED: destroyedENTRYCallback
```

Because we're all big boys and girls here, we'll assume you can follow the comments in the code to determine what is going on (if not, this isn't the right book for you!). Transforming these classes into a JTAPI implementation is left as an exercise for the reader. In short, we would map events to the JTAPI standard events and callbacks to the Observer class event handlers. States would be mapped to the legal state values in JTAPI (e.g., ACTIVE, INVALID) and off we would go.

Block Pattern

One of the most powerful tools in the Smalltalk arsenal is an object called a *block*. The class called Block is an object just like everything else in Smalltalk. When Smalltalk programmers speak of everything being an object, they're not merely paying lip service to some object-oriented feelgood mantra. In Smalltalk, everything *literally* is an object. This includes not only so-called built-in types like integers and strings, but the entire programming environment, the compiler, the processor that runs the development environment, all windows and pointing devices attached to the computer, indeed even the source code itself! This notion of the code being an object is unique to Smalltalk. This is *very* cool.

The class called Block represents a block of source code. All nondeclarative programming languages support this notion. A block of code is enclosed by some kind of "begin" statement and an "end" statement. For example, in Ada, Pascal and BASIC, the symbols used to create the block are actually the keywords `begin` and `end`. In C and Java, they are the two famous curly braces (i.e., { and }) and in Smalltalk,[26] the symbols [and].

Blocks provide several important features in Smalltalk. Any arbitrary piece of code can be enclosed in a block and executed "on the fly." What this means is that the code can be passed as a parameter to a function, can be stored in containers like arrays, and can even be processed concurrently by "forking" the block. The following code snippets show some of the ways in which Smalltalk blocks can be declared and used.

```
[ 1 + 1 ]                                "a block of code..."
[ | :a :b | | y | y := b * a. ]          "block accepting 2
                                          parameters"
b := Block new.                          "an instance of Class
                                          Block..."
b value: [ | :x | x doIt ].              "give it some code…"
c := b value.                            "execute the code.
                                          c now = 2"
d := SomeObject new; acceptBlock: b.     "a block passed as a
                                          parameter to a
                                          function..."
```

---

26 Smalltalk Blocks can also be represented and declared as variables; instances of class Block.

b fork.   "code in block b is
                                           executed in a separate
                                           thread..."

Java programmers will notice a similarity in this notion of "running code" with the concept of the class Thread. In Java, a Thread is an object that runs an arbitrary piece of code in a separate thread. The code itself is not an object, but the Thread is. We supply the code to the thread by overriding the run() method[27] as follows:

```
class myCode2runConcurrently extends Thread {
    public void run() {
        // your code goes here...
    }
}
```

Java does not provide a class called Block, but we can. Of course, this class will not be nearly as powerful as the one provided with any Smalltalk programming environment,[28] but it will provide a mechanism for the same functionality in many cases. Blocks are a powerful tool for writing *generic* code, and generic code is the cornerstone of telephony programming on the server side, especially when handling messages. Anyway, let's build this beast.

Creating the Block Classes

First, we model an arbitrary grouping of source code. We expand the concept of a Block to include parameters, just like Smalltalk. This is nothing more than a series of legal Java statements that may optionally process a set of parameters. Class Code is presented in **Listing 10.24**.

Listing 10.24 *Class Code Used by Class Block*

```
// Subclass this class and implement either the exec() or
// the execWithArgs method. If you need to return values,
// place them in a new Vector. Otherwise, just return a new
// empty Vector.
// Use the args_ instance variable to hold arguments, if any.

package sroberts.block;

import java.util.*;
```

---

27 This is also true, of course, of the Runnable interface.
28 This is because the Block class is tightly integrated into the runtime environment providing hooks into both the runtime and the debugging environment. The entire state of the processor is modeled along with context information.

Listing 10.24 (cont.) *Class Code Used by Class Block*

```java
public class Code {

    protected Vector args_ = null;

    // ctors...
    protected Code() { }

    protected Code( Vector args ) {
        super();
        args_ = args;
    }

    // protocol...
    public Vector execute() {

        if ( args_ == null )
                return exec();
        else
            return execWithArgs( args_ );
    }

    public void addArguments( Vector v ) {

        for ( int i=0; i < v.size(); i++ ) {
            args_.addElement( v.elementAt( i ) );
        }
    }

    // over-rides...
    protected Vector exec() { return null; }

    protected Vector execWithArgs( Vector args ) {
        return null; }
}
```

Class Code optionally holds onto a set of parameters to be passed to the block at runtime. The way this works is that the programmer is to extend this class and override either the `exec()` method or the `execWithArgs()` method (if parameters are to be passed). Now we create a class called Block that hangs onto an arbitrary block of code (see **Listing 10.25**).

Listing 10.25 *Introducing Class Block*

```java
package sroberts.block;
import java.util.*;

public class Block implements Runnable {

    private Code code_;

    // ctors..
    public Block( Code code2exec ) {
        super();
        code_ = code2exec;
    }

    private Block() { }

    // synchronous protocol...
    public Vector value() { return code_.execute(); }

    // asynchronous protocol...
    public Vector fork() {

        Thread t = new Thread( this );
        Vector v = new Vector();
        v.addElement( this );
        t.start();
        return v;
    }

    // runnable protocol...
    public void run() { code_.execute(); }

    // convenience protocol...
    public void addArguments( Vector v ) {
        code_.addArguments(v); }
}
```

Using the Block Classes

Before we can see how a Block works, we have to supply some code to execute. This is accomplished by extending class Code as in **Listing 10.26**.

Listing 10.26 *Extending Class Code*

```
package sroberts.block.test;

import sroberts.block.*;
import java.util.*;

public class TestCode extends Code {

    public TestCode( Vector args ) {
        super( args );
    }

    // over-rides...
    protected Vector exec() {

    System.out.println(
            "\tinside ::exec() : Running TestCode::exec()" );
       return new Vector();
    }

    protected Vector execWithArgs( Vector args ) {

        System.out.println( "\t***************");
        System.out.println(
            "\tRunning TestCode::execWithArgs()");

        for ( int i = 0; i < args_.size(); i++ ) {
           System.out.println( "\tinside ::execWithArgs() : Arg("
                + i + ") -> " + args_.elementAt(i) );
        }
        return new Vector();
    }
}
```

Here's a test program that runs the block class first in synchronous mode, then asynchronously (see **Listing 10.27**).

Listing 10.27 *Testing Class Block*

```
package sroberts.block.test;

import sroberts.block.*;
import java.util.*;

public class TestCodeApp {
```

Listing 10.27 (cont.) *Testing Class Block*

```
public static void main( String args[] ) {

    Vector args2Block = new Vector(2);
    args2Block.addElement( new Integer(1) );
    args2Block.addElement( "Hello World Forked" );

    // plain synchronous block, no args...
    Vector codeBlockReturnValues;
    Block codeBlock = new Block( new TestCode( null ) );
    codeBlockReturnValues = codeBlock.value();

    // asynchronous block with args...
    Vector codeBlock2ForkReturnValues;
    Block codeBlock2Fork = new Block(
        new TestCode(args2Block) );
    codeBlock2ForkReturnValues = codeBlock2Fork.fork();
    }
}
```

output:

```
I:\DATA\JAVACODE\sroberts\block\test>java TestCodeApp

    inside ::exec() : Running TestCode::exec()

    ***************

    Running TestCode::execWithArgs() ->

    inside ::execWithArgs() : Arg(0) -> 1

    inside ::execWithArgs() : Arg(1) -> Hello World Forked
```

Very nice, but how can we adopt this class for use in JTAPI? Suppose you wanted to enforce a policy that all active Calls must behave a certain way consistently throughout an application. Specifically, you want to report to the system output in a consistent manner whenever a Call in the ACTIVE state is reported on. One way to do this is to create a coding rule whereby each programmer repeats the same code in their CallObserver.callChangedEvent() methods as in **Listing 10.28**.

Listing 10.28 *Enforcing a Coding Standard*

```
public class SDRCallObserver implements CallObserver {

    synchronized public void callChangedEvent(
            CallEv[] eventList ) {

      for ( int i=0; i < eventList.length; i++ ) {
         if (isCallListener && eventList[i] instanceof CallEv) {
          // common standard code goes here - or else!!
         }
      }
    }
}
```

This approach will work, but it is kind of stupid given the fact that we can simply place a common output method on our implementation of the CallObserver interface and call that instead as follows:

```
public class SDRCallObserver implements CallObserver {

    synchronized public void callChangedEvent(
            CallEv[] eventList ) {

      for ( int i=0; i < eventList.length; i++ ) {
         if (isCallListener && eventList[i] instanceof CallEv) {
          commonStandardCode();  // everyone call this here
         }
      }
     }

    private void commonStandardCode {
       // common standard code goes here instead
    }
}
```

Okay, but this still requires everyone to place the call to that method in the same place. And even if we override the default behavior of `CallObserver.callChangedEvent()` so that it calls this method for us, each programmer still has to remember to call `super()` before they write their respective override code. As far as placing the code in the same place, there's no getting around that no matter which approach is used. But what if we wanted two versions of the method, one synchronous and the other asynchronous? And what if we wanted to change the reaction code without recompiling the CallObserver? If we did that, we could have a separate team go off and write classes that do nothing but respond to events of a specific type.

That's what Blocks are for.[29] Using Code classes in conjunction with Blocks, we can specify *ahead of time* and *outside the invocation class* what code is to be executed and pass that as a parameter to a Block on construction. We can also choose to hang onto that code and execute it at another location in the source. We can choose to execute it in either a synchronous or an asynchronous fashion. And most importantly, we can change the code and recompile it without affecting the code where it is called. Blocks allow for the separation of the reaction code from the code that invokes it. **Listing 10.29** shows what an implementation of the CallObserver interface might look like using Blocks.

Listing 10.29 *Using Blocks with JTAPI Observers*

```
package sroberts.telephony;

import java.util.*;
import java.awt.*;
import javax.telephony.*;
import javax.telephony.events.*;
import sroberts.telephony.events.*;

public class SDRCallObserver implements CallObserver {

    private Block onActiveCallBlock_;
    // others would follow, say one or InactiveCalls, etc.

    // block ctor...
    public SDRCallObserver( Block b ) {
        super();
        onActiveCallBlock_ = b;
    }

    synchronized public void callChangedEvent(
            CallEv[] eventList ) {

        for ( int i=0; i < eventList.length; i++ ) {

            if (isCallListener && eventList[i] instanceof CallEv) {
                try {
                    Call call = ((CallEv)eventList[i]).getCall();
                    onActiveCallBlock_.addArgument( call );
                    onActiveCallBlock_.fork();
                    //asynchronous version...
```

---

29 To be sung to the tune of Amy Grant's "That's What Love Is For."

Listing 10.29 (cont.) *Using Blocks with JTAPI Observers*

```
        } catch (Exception excp) {
            System.out.println( "CallEv Exception occurred
            in SDRCallObserver::callChangedEvent()...");
            excp.printStackTrace();
        }
    }
}
System.out.println( "*********************************");
    }
}
```

Class Block has gained some significant advantages. The CallObserver now becomes a shell of its former self. It is just a thing that sits around and waits for CallEvs and invokes arbitrary code in response.

This may seem a far-fetched use, but it actually is not at all. This architecture is *perfect* for defining the kinds of code generator applications that are so common in telephony environments. The big difference here is that this one is written in Java instead of some vendor's proprietary mystery language that will go "poof" when the vendor does!

Inner Classes and Adapter Classes for JTAPI

Recall that JTAPI requires the use of *events*. However, the API is presented as a set of interfaces, and so the *implementation* of the event mechanism is not specified. As we pointed out, this leaves room for many different types of implementations, some of which we have provided. One of these approaches is implied by Java's delegation model and is demonstrated here, namely inner classes and adapter classes. This approach is demonstrated in **Listing 10.30**.

Listing 10.30 *Using Package Classes and Adapter Classes for JTAPI Notification*

```
/* Step 1 -  In the class that uses the object to be notified
(could be a main() method), create a method that takes the
appropriate event list as parameter. Then, simply write your
application code as an implementation of this method. As far as
the application programmer is concerned, she's done.
*/

    void callInstance_callChangedEvent( CallEv[] eventList) {
    // TO DO: your application code goes here
    }
```

Listing 10.30 (cont.) *Using Package Classes and Adapter Classes for JTAPI Notification*

```
/* Step 2 - Generate a member inner class in the scope of your
main class that implements the appropriate listener interface
which calls the method in Step 1.

*/

    class MyMainApplet_callInstance_callChangedAdapter
    implements javax.telephony.CallObserver {

      MyMainApplet adaptee;

      MyMainApplet_callInstance_callChangedAdapter(
          MyMainApplet adaptee ) {
        this.adaptee = adaptee;
      }

      public void callChangedEvent( CallEv[] eventList ) {
        adaptee.callInstance_callChangedEvent( eventList );
      }
    }

3. // add the generated class as a listener to the main class

    private Call callInstance = new SDRCall();
    callInstance.addObserver(
      new MyMainApplet_callInstance_callChangedAdapter(
          this ) );
```

The class to be generated by a tool in Step 2 is technically a *member class* (which is a type of inner class). This explains how it can freely reference the top-level class (i.e., MyMainApplet) in which it is defined.

If this idiom seems a bit contrived, that's because it is! We only present it here for completeness. If you share the author's dislike of adapters and inner classes, you will avoid creating maintenance monstrosities such as the one presented here. To be fair, however, there may be an advantage to this approach if the code can be generated as it is in many Java GUI programming IDEs. The advantage is that all of the code is statically compiled, which may have performance advantages over a runtime lookup or registration approach. If the code can be generated and maintained by the development environment, it may also be presented as a more "user-friendly" approach to JTAPI telephony programming. Application programmers may not have to learn JTAPI at all — they just implement methods like the one that is generated in Step 1. This method effectively takes the place of the requirement for implementing the CallObserver interface.

The disadvantage is, of course, the excess amount of code that must be produced and maintained, even if it is all "in one place."

Server Telephony Patterns

In telephony applications, the client applications make calls to an API like TAPI or JTAPI to request services. These services are then provided by the server component. Telephony patterns tend to fall into these two categories of patterns: client and server.

The client telephony patterns are handled well by the JTAPI architecture. Other than the Observer interface (which is essentially a server pattern), all of the architectural entities we have examined in this book essentially support patterns for answering and placing telephone calls. We now have a pretty clear handle on client-side processing. But what about server-side processing? Even the JTAPI interfaces designed to handle server-oriented are at too high a level to suggest a particular implementation. So we examine two of the more common patterns here.

Because the nature of server processing in the telephony environment is to handle incoming and outgoing requests as quickly as possible, synchronous processing is rarely used. Instead, most servers are designed to release control to the appropriate routine and then wait for notification of either successful completion or of an exception. However, even the wait states can be handled asynchronously so as not to delay the processing of more incoming and outgoing messages. There are two alternative patterns commonly used to handle telephony asynchronous server processing: the *State Machine Callback* (SMC) pattern and the *State Machine Thread* pattern. Actually, both of these patterns are variations on the same theme. As would be expected, each of these alternative approaches carries costs and benefits.

Of course, we've seen these finite state machines before. We've seen how finite state machines are excellent tools for modeling event-driven systems. In review, an FSM is a pattern that places an application or an object in one of a finite set of known states based upon incoming messages, external stimuli, or events. In server message processing applications, the processing component generally has only a few states such as INCOMING_MESSAGE, IDLE, and NOTIFYING. The FSM is often implemented as an endless loop with a blocking thread. Optionally, the FSM may execute auxiliary processing if there are no messages to process (i.e., when it is idle). The familiar Microsoft message loop is an example of this pattern. Here's how it works.

In one thread, the FSM waits for incoming messages in a tight loop. If there are none, it pauses or blocks with a delay allowing some other background processing while waiting for a message to arrive. This background processing is typically called an *idle process*. When messages do arrive, the appropriate callback is made in the form of a synchronous call. When control returns from the call, a notification is sent along with some context information to signal the application of success, failure, or to return data as a result of the call. This algorithm is depicted in **Figure 10.5**.

Figure 10.5 *A Lousy Message Notification Algorithm*

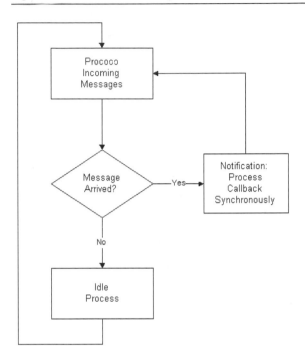

But there's a problem with this approach, isn't there? What happens if the callbacks take a long time to process? Meanwhile more messages arrive and the application cannot process the incoming messages fast enough. (If these incoming messages were actual calls in a telephony system, we call this "dropping calls on the floor.") The main problem is that the *callback processing is synchronous*. Because of this, each subprogram invocation must run to completion before control is returned to the notification application. Clearly, there is a better solution.

State Machine Callback Pattern

We can simulate asynchronous calls by queuing the messages in a buffer and then calling them from another thread. The second thread removes messages from the buffer according to a particular queuing policy (e.g., LIFO, FIFO) and *then* makes a synchronous call. The second thread is represented by a different color. This is depicted in **Figure 10.6**.

Figure 10.6 *The State Machine Callback Algorithm Flow*

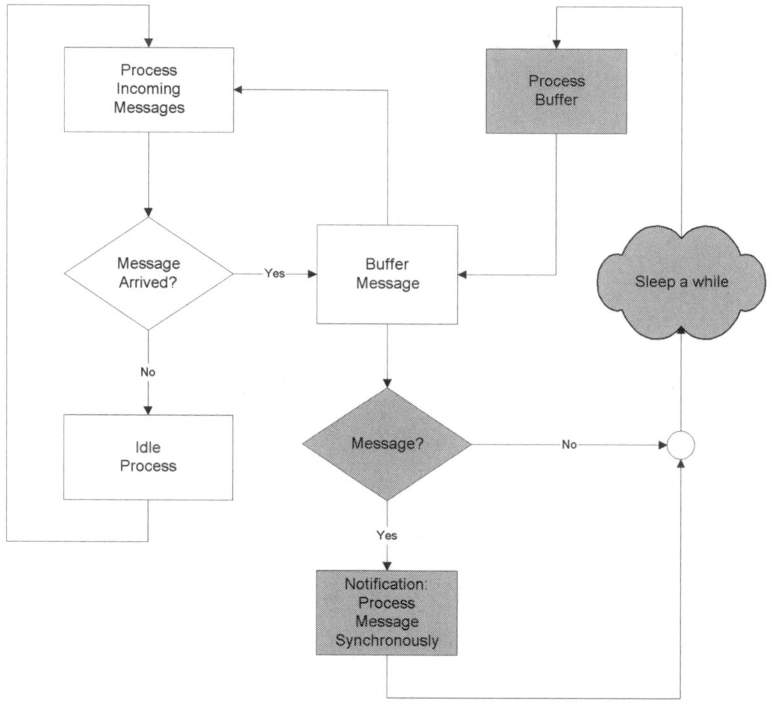

Notification is the second part of the algorithm that is implemented in the second thread. It creates outgoing messages based upon the success or failure of the callbacks. This can be implemented in several ways. One of the more loosely coupled approaches is to have callers register their interest in certain types of messages with a separate registration process. This process is then responsible for notifying the interested parties of the occurrence of the message(s) for which they previously registered.

An important concept to understand about the *notification* portion of the SMC pattern is that it is single threaded. From within the second thread, each callback is processed from beginning to end without a *programmer-initiated* context switch from the processor.[30] This has important benefits in that the overhead of a programmer-initiated context switch is avoided. The downside is that other waiting calls of a lower priority may be starved if any particular function call takes too long to complete. How long "too long" is depends on the application. An alternative pattern that solves this potential starvation problem is the State Machine Thread pattern.

---

30 On operating systems with round robin time-slicing scheduling policies (like Windows NT), the programmer cannot prevent a context switch no matter what. There is, however, the possibility that the notification thread is at a higher priority than that of waiting threads, and these waiting threads may starve.

State Machine Thread Pattern

Threads provide many benefits not possible in single-threaded implementations. First, threads are *by nature* asynchronous. Once a thread is started, control returns immediately to the caller. Second, notification is an integral part of the threaded model, regardless of the platform or programming language used. All threaded APIs provide light-weight IPC mechanisms for notifying other dependent threads. Third, threads can be made to be *fair* — they can be set up to avoid (or at least mitigate) the potential starvation problem we encountered in the SMC pattern.

The State Machine Thread pattern implements asynchronous server processing using threads (as its name implies). Instead of making synchronous notification calls, it launches a new thread for each callback. **Figure 10.7** demonstrates this.

Figure 10.7 *SMT: The Thread Version of a Server-Side FSM*

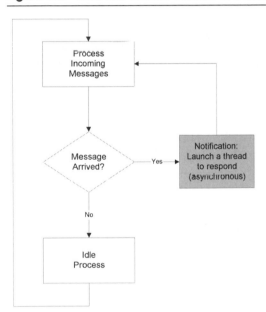

This pattern probably came to mind as soon as we presented the synchronous notification problem. That is a good thing. Some patterns are obvious, yet overlooked until presented. However simple or obvious, more importantly it is a powerful pattern. Of course, this power comes at a cost. Threads can be expensive, especially when the average callback execution duration is small. The difference between the SMC and SMT patterns is in the granularity of the programmer-controlled context switch. In the SMC pattern, the granularity boundary is at the function call level. In the Thread pattern, it is at the most atomic level possible — that of the operating system's scheduling policy for the context switch itself.

Implementing Persistent Graph Structures

Many telephony abstractions may be represented as graphs. Applications that are written to model telephony network components and call paths often follow a component pattern where pieces are made up of one or more other pieces. Further, these pieces may be shared among alternate configurations. The only way to model these types of relationships is to use a directed graph (hereinafter referred to simply as a graph[31]). Here we present two useful telephony patterns based on *graphs*.

Recall that a graph is a collection type object. By definition it "contains" or is "made up of" other objects, which are in turn made up of others. The objects are called *nodes* and the path between any set of objects an *edge*. Many types of common data structures in computer science use graph representations, among them being binary and AVL trees as well as adjacency matrices. This concept is nothing new, but its use has usually been limited to relatively low-level abstractions used in sorting, traversing, and retrieving data. In telephony applications, however, these types of structures are useful for modeling application-level domain objects. From an application programming perspective there are generally two kinds of graphs: *tree* graphs and *vine* graphs.

Tree Graphs

A tree graph is a hierarchical structure where the root node has no parent (an *n*-degree of 0) and each child node may have at most one parent (an *n*-degree of 1). Further, each edge or path is comprised of at most one path from the root node to any child leaf node.[32] A typical tree graph is depicted in **Figure 10.8**.

Figure 10.8 *A Tree Graph*

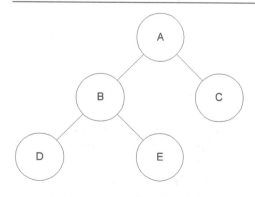

---

31 This simplification is actually incorrect — an undirected graph is not a directed graph. However, the discussion does not render this distinction and so we have simplified the terminology for the sake of clarification.

32 Recall that a leaf node has no children.

Tree graphs are obviously useful for representing hierarchical structures. In enterprise modeling, they are common representations of organizational structures. In the telephony problem space, they can be used to model *non–matrix reporting relationships* and simple *service arrangements*. **Figure 10.9** shows an OMT object model representation of a tree graph.

Figure 10.9 *OMT Object Model of a Tree Graph*

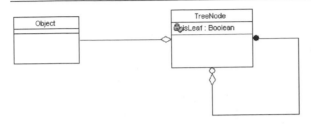

Note the Boolean attribute `isLeaf`. At first glance it would seem that this attribute is unnecessary because one would always be able to determine a leaf node as being one without any child nodes. This is true, but checking for a leaf node in this manner could be an expensive operation relative to a Boolean check depending on how the list is implemented (especially for very large trees). The containing association to an Object reference is necessary if the data structure itself is not a node. For example, suppose we are modeling an organization of people's roles. At the top of the company is the president; below that is a gaggle of vice-presidents. The vice-presidents report only to the president and so this model fits.[33] The role of president itself may be modeled as a true node, but the person playing the role of president is not. This is typical for these types of relationships. The alternative would be to inherit from the node object. This latter approach is a true model for only a very few types of objects.

Persistence and Tree Graphs

Any decent college program in computer science includes at least one course on data structures. To implement a graph all one needs to do is learn how from these sources. It can be quite a different animal, however, to make that structure persistent (say in a relational database) and then to manage the integrity of this structure between a client and a server.

---

33 Note that a tree structure does not properly model a matrix organization. For example, if the VP also reports to the CEO, that role requires two parent nodes — or *another* tree!

An object database can store a tree structure directly.[34] In a relational database there are two issues: one of *storage* and one of *retrieval.* The storage requires mapping the attributes of the object to columns in the database, which is trivial. It is important to note, however, that any reconstruction of the graph can only be implemented with iteration code, which is not supported with SQL. So some kind of procedural code is required. In other words, there is no extensible manner to use SQL alone to retrieve the hierarchy.

Recursion and Tree Graphs

Another important consideration is that relational databases (and most object databases) often have limited support for *recursive* methods. This is important because the natural implementation for many tree graph operations (e.g., exploding a graph) is to use recursion. Even though the nesting recursion level may be configured, it is usually not a runtime feature, requiring a restart of the database at a minimum. This option is also not flexible enough for a telephony environment, because whatever setting is chosen is often *fixed* until the databases are restarted. So from a practical perspective, an implementation may be forced to use nonrecursive algorithms.

Another pattern to be aware of is a *self-related* graph, in which the same instance of an object appears in the graph structure. Generally this is okay as long as the instance does not contain infinitely recursive components. If it is semantically inconsistent from an application perspective (which is entirely possible), mechanisms must be put in place to prevent such constructions. Most problematic is a *recursive graph*, where a node has children that contain another node with all its children and all these nodes are in fact *the same node* (see **Figure 10.10**).

What makes the graph recursive, is represented by the dots below node "E," is the fact that every instance of node "E" contains another node "A," which in turn contains another node "E," and so on. There is no terminating condition to end the recursion. It's pretty clear that the construction of recursive graphs must be prevented. In practice this is not a problem for the simple reason that construction of a nonterminating recursive graph leads to a stack overflow on most computers.[35] Over time, however, it is possible for a recursive graph to be constructed piecemeal if proper instance management techniques are not employed. For example, every node in **Figure 10.10** can refer to items with the same name (e.g., "A"), but they cannot be the *same instance.*

---

34 In this sense, object databases are superior choices for hierarchical data. However, to retrieve ad hoc information about the structure is much more cumbersome and awkward than in a relational database.

35 Hardly an acceptable "feature" to build into an application, eh?

Figure 10.10 *A Recursive Graph*

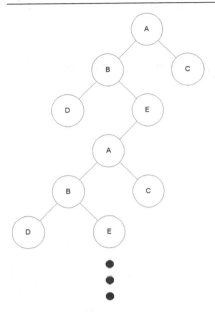

Vine Graphs

In a vine graph each node may have more than one parent node; hence there may be more than one path from the root to some child nodes. A vine graph (also known as a matrix) is not a tree graph, although they look very similar (see **Figure 10.11**).

Figure 10.11 *A Vine Directed Graph*

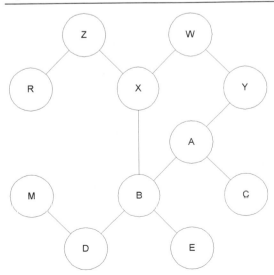

A vine may also contain more than one root node (see items X and B in **Figure 10.11**). This type of data structure provides a true representation of more complex graph structures. It is well suited for matrix reporting and call paths. An OMT object diagram is presented in **Figure 10.12.**

Figure 10.12 *An OMT Representation of a Vine Graph*

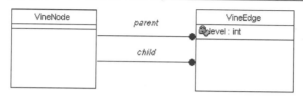

In Chapter 11, "Organizing a Large-Scale Telecom Development Project," we will entertain a discussion about *related requirements*. A vine graph can be used to model requirements of this type.

Summary

In this chapter, we have covered what we hope has been interesting ground. We have peeked into the creative realm of "real-world" telephony programming and discovered that there are many different ways to do the same thing, namely implement the JTAPI interfaces.

We have covered some idioms and patterns that may be used to help make our applications and libraries more robust, reliable, and understandable. If telephony programming has ever struck you as a boring topic, we hope we have changed your mind. We have looked at ways of making Java "a better Java" and our telephony programs, if not better, at least more interesting.

Chapter 11

ORGANIZING A LARGE-SCALE TELECOM DEVELOPMENT PROJECT

"With software, all things are possible;
yet all possibilities are not advisable."

Titus Corporation Motto

The material in this chapter is presented in order to provide telecom developers and managers with a useful framework for molding successful large-scale telecom projects. The reason we focus on large-scale development is rooted in a belief that JTAPI makes practical large-scale development possible for telephony projects. For the first time telephony programmers have a high-level API available that is not mired in the complexities of low-level serial communications and complicated proprietary callback mechanisms.

We take a brief excursion to discuss issues important to project management such as requirements gathering, life cycle issues (analysis and design), documentation, different programming skill sets, and project roles. Those not interested in such "management material" may want to skip ahead to the next chapter, although this chapter also contains some useful design information.

There are many entire books covering the topics we touch on in this chapter, such as analysis and design methodologies. This chapter is no substitute for a thorough understanding of these topics, yet we seek to highlight those aspects that have become typical stumbling blocks and to emphasize practices that are actually necessary from experience.

Project management is approached from a programmer's perspective. As creative engineers (is that an oxymoron?), we'd like to think we have a choice in selecting our tools and in contributing to a successful product development effort by managing our own time and resources. As it is said, "manage or be managed." This section encourages a self-management metaphor. It is based on the assumption that programmers are mature adults who can gather, understand, and implement requirements with little supervision from "management."

In the first part of this chapter, we present a *process management model*[1] called RAF (Requirements, Architecture, and Fabrication). The goal of the RAF model is to close the primary loopholes found in modern software development processes. During this process, we present some fundamental, yet often misunderstood aspects of software design. Finally, we categorize skill sets and programming disciplines in an effort to provide a background for properly staffing and organizing work products for a telecom development project.

Project Management in a Nutshell

Conventional wisdom is to organize the development of software into the following phases:

- Requirements gathering
- Analysis
- Design
- Programming
- Test

This canonical methodology pattern speaks to an iterative process whereby these five phases proceed more or less linearly;[2] yet they are to be iterated over (i.e., repeated) in a so-called *spiral model*.[3] This is all fine and good, but we prefer to put our own spin on the development process. There is nothing wrong with the canonical model. However, it has been our experience that attempts to implement the spiral model may lead to a lack of focus on other critical areas besides what we call *product fabrication* (the activity of building the product). This occurs despite the fact that the spiral model was a risk-driven process model designed to mitigate such problems.

---

1 A *process management model* is distinguished from a *software development methodology*. The former is a model used to manage the development process itself. The latter is a method to follow when creating the software.

2 While the normal progression is linear, each phase may be traversed backwards one or more phases as appropriate. For example, the process normally proceeds from analysis to design to programming. It is perfectly acceptable (and often necessary), however, to move from programming back to design and even back to analysis before proceeding.

3 See Barry Boehm's, "A Spiral Model of Software Development and Enhancement," *IEEE* May 1988.

The spiral model addresses product fabrication issues well but leaves unattended architectural tasks and does not explicitly address the criticality of proper *requirements specification*. It is not that these additional activities cannot be incorporated into the spiral model. Indeed, we have done just this for many years, and we believe the author assumed they would be. However, the problem has really become one of focus, priorities, and concurrency. If architectural and requirements issues are buried in the fabrication process or are given less than primary focus, they become "secondhand citizens." And so we present a new project management model we believe is better suited to large-scale telephony programming and possibly other vertical markets. We call it the RAF Project Management Model. RAF is not a radical departure from the traditional spiral model; rather it is a concurrent refinement of it.

Requirements, Architecture, and Fabrication: The RAF Project Management Model

RAF stands for *requirements, architecture,* and *fabrication*. Conceptually, *requirements* may be thought of as *written line items against a software development contract*. They are to specify in an unambiguous and accurate manner exactly what the proposed software system is to do. Usually this is accomplished by stating what *functionality* is to be provided.

Architecture is a blueprint for integrating the proposed system into other systems both internal and external. It also specifies the performance characteristics the system is to fulfill. The system architecture is a set of deployment plans based upon needs for hardware specification, network support for distributed systems, and the allocation of software components to processors. *Fabrication* is the process of actually producing the software.

RAF is organized in a hierarchical spiral with three complementary activities *running concurrently* throughout the development process. The entire development process is broadly categorized into two primary efforts: *requirements discovery* and *product development*.

The second category (product development) is further categorized into system architecture and product fabrication. This leads to three activities that proceed *in parallel* in the RAF Model:

- Requirements discovery
- System architecture
- Product fabrication

The importance of concurrency in the RAF model cannot be understated. Even though the spiral model is an improvement over the *waterfall model*,[4] the process activities are still generally performed in a *linear* fash-

---

4 The so-called waterfall model was the original software process model created by the U.S. Department of Defense (DoD) many years ago. It was primarily a document-driven model as opposed to a risk-driven model.

ion. So even though tasks are revisited many times over, they are always visited linearly, in the same order. Of course, RAF tasks are not *purely* concurrent because to be completely concurrent is to be *unrelated*. When we speak of RAF concurrency, we are doing so at a very high level. In truth, the processes proceed more like *communicating sequential processes* that run concurrently for a time, but then sync up, share information, and then proceed on again, concurrently. In RAF, the level of granularity is lower. So, for example, instead of allowing new or changed requirements to pile up until the next round in the spiral, they are visited upon the development team *immediately*. The benefit of this approach is that team members can assess *for themselves* the impact of these changes. This brief interruption is well worth the time spent down the road recovering from a problem that could have been avoided altogether. I cannot count how many times as a developer I have been "protected" from information that later profoundly affected my work to the point of requiring either design work-around or complete code rewrites.

The RAF project management model emphasizes the three parallel activities of requirements discovery, system architecture, and product fabrication (see **Figure 11.1**).

Figure 11.1 *The RAF Project Management Model*

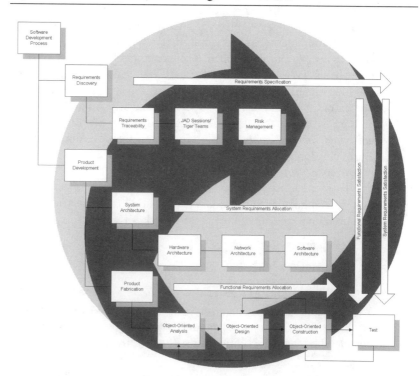

The RAF model is subtly different from the spiral model with respect to requirements. Rather than iterating over a requirements phase, we see to it that the requirements-gathering and validation activity *never ends* for the duration of the project — not even for a moment. Why? We believe that a focus on the three activities of requirements, architecture, and fabrication as *parallel tasks* throughout the development cycle helps to keep the proper focus and allows changes generated throughout the life cycle to propagate effectively. This is not to say that a project requires a gaggle of people hovering over the development team. In fact, the fewer requirements people involved, the better. But we have seen too many projects where the requirements as written bear little resemblance to the system as built. Although it is a popular sport to complain about the lack of valid requirements, few solutions are offered. The RAF model seeks to close this loophole.

Note how the system architecture implements the system requirements and how the product fabrication activity realizes the functional requirements. Although not all requirements are *satisfied* until they are tested, the requirement allocation process is clarified in the RAF model.

Another key deviation from the canonical model is the distinction between *architecture* and *fabrication*. The distinction is again one of focus. Too often architectural issues and their associated *system* requirements[5] are either buried as programmers concentrate on writing code or are allocated to personnel unqualified to properly address them. By the time the architectural issues are adequately addressed it is too late to retrofit the software to accommodate the necessary changes. At best, this often leads to *redundancies* in the system implementation, which adds to both (short-term) development and (long-term) maintenance costs. At worst, it can lead to a system that won't work over time because it won't scale.

An important similarity with the spiral model is found in product fabrication. In this respect, there is really no difference between RAF and the spiral model. Let's take a closer look at each of these activities. We begin with requirements discovery.

Requirements Discovery

Requirements discovery is one of the three parallel activities in the RAF model. As the name implies, the primary purpose of requirements discovery is to *elicit requirements*. We really like the term "discovery" as applied to requirements. It gives the impression and constant reminder how important *impartiality* is to the requirements gathering process. Early on in the

---

5 Remember that system requirements are *different* from functional requirements. Instead of specifying what the system is to do, they specify the manner in which the system must operate in order to satisfy functional requirements. They also tend to be "systemwide" because they affect more than one subsystem. Security is a good example of a system requirement. So are printing services.

life cycle, the programmer/requirements analyst takes on the mindset of an archeologist; he is expected to try to gain as much business knowledge as possible. The goal is to avoid operating primarily on bias gained from prior experience. It is better to take the attitude of knowing nothing of the problem space than to begin by making assumptions.

In RAF, there is urgency about the requirements identification and validation process. There is recognition that requirements discovered too late can have debilitating consequences. Improperly managed software development projects can take on the characteristics of a runaway freight train. Once they get going, they can be stopped — but not without drastic measures and large consequences.

The nature and scope of the project will determine the degree of formality in the requirements gathering process. If end-users are involved, Joint Application Development (JAD) sessions are organized between users and programmers. Customer participation throughout the development process is critical. A system developed without specific and continual customer input will be a useless system. A system specified without programmer input will never be properly implemented.

During requirements discovery we begin to formulate *problem space* terms and create a *data dictionary* of common terminology that can be agreed upon between users and developers. The importance of a common data dictionary cannot be overemphasized. Countless hours can be wasted downstream bickering about terminology that was never properly defined early on. Those items that cannot be formally described become risk items. Their progress is tracked throughout the development process until an acceptable definition can be agreed upon.

In contrast, informal requirements sessions are preferred when the system (or subsystem) is providing lower common service levels in an attempt to satisfy system requirements. Library programmers comfortable with architectural concepts as well as requirements gathering can often move in and out of requirements discovery, analysis, and design at will. This is because infrastructure layers tend to exhibit common patterns that are quickly recognized by experienced programmers. In these cases, too much formality can be a waste of time and actually *hinder* the development process.

Properties of Requirements

Requirements come in two forms — *explicit* and *derived*. This distinction is the *primary property* of a requirement. Explicit requirements are those written down and expressed in terms the customer understands. Derived requirements are those inferred, implied, or otherwise needed to implement explicit requirements. For example, suppose a customer wants to launch a payload into geosynchronous orbit. They describe the payload and levy the requirement that the payload must be safely and successfully delivered into an orbit within a certain time frame. The fact that the customer did not specify the *manner* in which the payload is to arrive at its final destination does not mean a derived requirement to build or procure a spacecraft does not exist.

Programmers and *systems analysts*[6] should determine derived requirements, never customers! If a customer suggests a derived requirement, it should be incorporated into an existing explicit requirement.

Derived requirements are just as valid as explicit requirements, yet an improper diagnosis for derived requirements can prove to be problematic, even irreversible. For example, many projects choose hardware platforms and software implementation packages before the ink is dry on the development contract. This is not requirements satisfaction; rather, it is an example of a solution chasing a problem.

Derived requirements should always be challenged. Those that cannot be mapped back to specific explicit requirements should be reexamined. Derived requirements are tracked just like explicit requirements, yet are to be distinguished by this one property. Therefore a requirement is always spoken of as one of two types — either explicit or derived.

All requirements must be tracked and are subject to approval. This implies that the *current state* of a requirement is a property. This state may be represented as simple Boolean value (e.g., approved or notApproved) or it may be represented as an enumerated list of valid values depending on the extent to which requirements are to be monitored (e.g., approved, pending, disapproved, satisfied, and so forth.). More elaborate schemes may be used, including an entire revision history — a property that effectively places requirements under *configuration management*. In this case, a simple requirements attribute of the current state may be insufficient because we probably need additional information such as when a requirement was approved and by whom. Further, it may not be the requirement itself that needs monitoring — it might very well be a *set of* requirements in a *specific context*. Requirements tracking can get quickly out of hand requiring an automated system just to track the requirements. Because customers are rarely willing to pay for such development, this cost is usually borne by the development organization.[7] In short, the requirements themselves may generate a set of requirements to develop (or use) a requirements tracking system!

Categories of Requirements

In addition to the distinction of primary type and the property of current state, RAF requirements are also categorized in two different ways based upon their *content*. All requirements are classified as either *functional*

---

6 A systems analyst is a nonprogrammer engineer type, whose domain is either requirements or the hardware or network architecture.

7 In some cases, a spreadsheet is sufficient, however, large system development efforts may require more sophisticated tools.

requirements or *system requirements*. Functional requirements are simply textual descriptions of *what the system is to do*. These descriptions should be expressed in terms of what services the system is to provide to its users.[8] It is best to express functional requirements in terms of the word "shall" (e.g., "the system <u>shall</u> provide a mechanism for reporting the organizational structure of the company at arbitrary levels").

System requirements are those that deal with the required *performance characteristics* of the system as a whole and the manner in which the system is to be *deployed*. By their very nature, system requirements cross subsystem boundaries. Some examples of system requirements are characteristics like data transfer rates, network latency, concurrency, deployment geography, fault tolerance, load balancing, data currency, and security. Although the customer may not specify these, it is often because they have not given them much thought. This does not, however, relieve the development organization of the duty of educating the customer in this respect (i.e., system requirements won't disappear if we bury our heads in the sand!). If there are no system requirements, it should be explicitly stated that there are none[9] (which is, of course, ridiculous). It is entirely possible that a system may be fabricated exactly to functional specification ahead of schedule and under budget, yet be a complete failure because the system requirements needed to deploy the system were never considered! This is in fact the rationale behind the RAF practice of separating out System Architecture as a separate parallel activity.

Requirements Allocation

All requirements ultimately become *allocated* and then *satisfied* at some point. To allocate a requirement is to assign it to a system component (software, network, hardware, or all three) in the expectation that the component will satisfy the requirement. Functional requirements are allocated to software components in the RAF product fabrication activity. System requirements are allocated to components in both the product fabrication and the system architecture activities. Both types of requirements are satisfied in the verification and validation (testing) phase of the product fabrication activity.

Subsystem Identification

Before allocating a requirement to a component, it is helpful to break a system down into functional *subsystems*. In a large telecom project, we might create different subsystems for routing, receiving, and placing calls.

---

8 Users can be people or other systems, even machines!

9 Again, system requirements exist whether they are acknowledged or not. But stating their lack of fulfillment contractually can help to satisfy due diligence responsibilities. It also serves to highlight their need.

Likewise, an aircraft system might have separate subsystems for avionics and braking.

Relationships Among Requirements

It is possible for requirements to be related to each other. We have already seen such an implicit relationship among explicit and derived requirements. These two types of requirements are related *by definition* in that a derived requirement exists in order to implement an explicit requirement. It turns out, however, that a derived requirement (or any other requirement) may be used to satisfy more than one explicit requirement and vice versa. In other words, a single requirement may be allocated to multiple components, and one or more of those single components may be used to satisfy more than one requirement. In modeling terminology this is called a *many-to-many relationship*. Some of the semantic confusion that occurs during requirements specification may be attributed to these types of complex relationships among requirements.

One school of thought is that many-to-many relationships among requirements complicate the requirements satisfaction process and so should be avoided whenever possible. This can be accomplished in one of two ways. First, we can simply ignore these relationships or try to remember which are related. If we take a perspective that all must be satisfied anyway, what does it matter? Clearly, this approach can only be used in small development efforts.

The second technique for avoiding multiple references to the same requirement is to constrain the definition of each requirement so that it may relate to *at most* one other parent requirement. For example, a rule stating that all derived requirements may have one and only one parent explicit requirement. When each top-level requirement *must* be orthogonal, this guarantees (at least in theory) less overlap.

The problem with either of these approaches is that they're not easily *enforced*. Why? Requirements are by nature free-form. Because they are nothing more than a series of words, it is difficult to place constraints on their content. Another problem is presented any time an attempt is made to undermine "the truth." Many-to-many relationships do not cease to exist just because we refuse to acknowledge them. And so the best approach to managing referential relationships between requirements is to manage their content "by hand" and to model the true problem space correctly from the beginning.

Requirements Life Cycle

All requirements are alive. It is naïve to assume that requirements don't change at all during the development process. Although it is a necessary endeavor to seek to freeze requirements as much and as soon as possible, it is dangerous to assume that some percentage will not evolve quite frequently —

and quite significantly. Ranking requirements by this attribute is often help-ful. It is better to plan ahead for the 20 percent of the items that are going to bite you.

Those requirements that do evolve cannot be accurately implemented in software unless a flexible process is in place to integrate the dissemination of requirement changes directly to the programmer involved. The only way these types of requirements can be successfully codified is by either direct-ly involving the programmer in the relevant requirements discussions or having a talented programmer on staff as a requirements analyst who may accurately disseminate requirements changes to programmers.

Codifying Requirements (Requirements Traceability)

When the requirements are understood well enough that they may be writ-ten down in a cohesive manner, they are numbered and tracked throughout the remaining life cycle. Because the objects developed during the analysis phase may not match exactly the software that is ultimately produced dur-ing construction, these numbers can be used to track requirements down to the function call level if deemed useful.[10]

Test cases are later developed based upon the requirements with an objec-tive of satisfying one or more requirements. Therefore, it is important that the requirements are written in such a manner that they may be tested. If a requirement cannot be tested, then it cannot be satisfied. Unsatisfied require-ments lead to unhappy customers, which in turn lead to canceled projects.

In order to effectively track requirements the analyst uses a *require-ments traceability matrix*. This is essentially a report in table format speci-fying (at a minimum) all the properties, categories, satisfaction criteria, and current status of each requirement (see **Table 11.1**).

Table 11.1 *A Simple (possibly insufficient) Requirements Traceability Matrix*

# Name	Description	Type	Category	Risk #	Status	Developer Contact	Test Case
1 Company Organization	The system shall provide a mechanism for reviewing and modifying the organizational structure of the company	Explicit	Functional	—	Satisfied	Susie	21
2 Company Organization Concurrent Updates	The system shall provide a means to support concurrent updates of all customer organization information	Derived	System	3	Not approved	Susie	22

---

10 This technique is useful in DoD systems, but less so in commercial telecom systems.

Of course, this matrix should be tailored to suit a project's needs. For example, if there is only one programmer for all requirements, it is of little use to repeat that name over hundreds of rows of data. Or columns may be added to specify any other relevant information for each requirement. The most thorough implementation is to use a database to track the requirements.

Tiger Teams

In large projects, it is helpful to break requirements into functional categories and then formulate "tiger teams" for each functional area. The team is small and is comprised of individuals from requirements specification, testing, and programming. Contrary to popular myth, the tasks of design and programming are rarely successful when accomplished by two different people. The designer *must be* a programmer and the programmer must be a designer. Any other arrangement leads to either software that doesn't do what it should or software that doesn't do what it should but does what it does very well.

Part of the tiger team's job is to learn the lingo of the customer. It is essential that the programmer become at least somewhat immersed in the culture and terminology of the user. Otherwise, they are participating in the construction of a system that will never be used. Again, the best way to handle this is to incorporate critical user terminology into the data dictionary and to ensure the semantics are identical between both developers and customers.

Requirements Satisfaction

The requirement life cycle ends when *satisfaction* occurs. Satisfaction is accomplished when the requirement is tested using the system as *built*.[11] If all that were required were the assurance that a particular requirement was tested, this would be a simple process. However, we have already seen how the relationships between requirements can complicate matters — it turns out that this situation is no different for requirement satisfaction. Specifically, requirements satisfaction may involve the relationships between requirements — a set of requirements in a specific context. This may require the grouping of requirements into "super-requirements" based upon this context.

But why should we mess with requirements relationships anyway? Is there any benefit? It turns out there may be significant benefits. If a proper determination can be made between requirements in meaningful contexts, the satisfaction of a requirement in one context may lead to its satisfaction in others. For example, if a requirement has already been satisfied, why test it again? Of course the context may be different, requiring a regression test

---

11 This process is discussed in the section "Testing" later in this chapter.

but sometimes the knowledge that a test was passed in one context leads to more assurance in another context.

We have covered the main activities found in the requirements discovery process. We now turn to the evil twin — product development. The product development process is where we leave the customer in the dust. It is not that we don't want them to be involved, rather we're driven by the reality that if they do become involved in development issues, nothing but problems will ensue. The design team should take the approach of an independent contractor. Requirements discovery provides a specification that tells them what it is they need to do. In a well-run project, the customer has neither the obligation nor the right to specify *how* that work is to be accomplished. The customer who insists on managing projects in this manner, is probably best advised to hire employees and manage the project himself. This is not to say that the customer should not be kept fully informed and involved during the product development process.[12] The customer is still the customer; he is paying the bill and does have a right to accept or reject any of the products produced. But software product development is for programmers.

Product Development

In the RAF model, product development is categorized into two of the three primary parallel task areas: *system architecture* and *product fabrication*. Although proper adherence to sound product development practices cannot *ensure* the system does what it is supposed to do (that's what accurate requirement capture and satisfaction is for), it can at least lead to an assurance that the systems involved are somewhat well integrated and maintainable. We begin with system architecture.

System Architecture

Any large telecom project requires some understanding of the overall **system architecture**. System architecture is the second parallel activity in the RAF model. It is to be initiated at the same time as requirements discovery and product fabrication. System architecture is comprised of three architectural components: *hardware architecture, software architecture,* and *network architecture.* These three components comprise the system architecture (see **Figure 11.2**).

The system architecture *places constraints on the product fabrication process.* For example, a requirement for concurrent updates will clearly affect the software design. Software design *must* take architectural requirements into consideration from the project's inception.

---

12 In fact, that is precisely why we advocate the ongoing nature of the requirements discovery process in RAF.

Figure 11.2 *System Architecture Components*

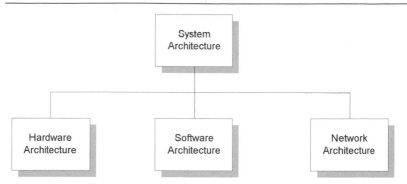

In addition to the effect the system architecture may have on product fabrication, each system architecture component may affect each *other* system architecture component. For example, a network architecture that specifies an Ethernet LAN may not run on an IBM Series 1 without significant modification. Decisions made about any of these components may impact any of the other components, and special care should be taken by project management to identify such areas and to insulate each area from changes in the other. This can only be accomplished by means of proper interface control documentation and good old-fashioned personal communication.

Often the three components of system architecture are intermingled on a project in some kind of confusing mishmash of a document. This helps no one, creates confusion, and wastes time. The best approach here is probably to recognize that each is a very different technical discipline requiring very different kinds of technical involvement. Let's take a closer look at each of these components, beginning with the hardware architecture.

Hardware Architecture

The **hardware architecture** concerns the *capacities* and *capabilities of the machines.* No matter what software is written or how data is distributed, the hardware will ultimately place a set of constraints on system performance. These constraints need to be identified and understood early on. By documenting and, more importantly, *testing* the capabilities of the hardware, it will be much easier to allocate system functionality to either hardware or software or to a certain level of either one. For example, a PBX comes with certain capability built in. Understanding the capabilities and limitations of the existing function set as provided by the hardware "out of the box" will go a long way toward mitigating future improper allocation of system components.

A hardware architecture also provides or refers to an *inventory* describing all the system hardware and where it is physically located. This hardware is then referred to by both the network and software architectures.

Pertinent information may include its version number, the vendor, age, references to installation plans, and so forth. In addition, some systems will require much more information so that timing and sizing requirements can be properly assessed.

How would a hardware architecture affect the requirements discovery and product fabrication activities? This is rather obvious. It is easy to see how the specification of system response time can affect the processor chosen or the specification of an operating system can determine the hardware (e.g., VMS doesn't run on a PC). In some cases, the hardware may be specified before the software is developed. If so, it places a constraint on the system capabilities that needs to be recognized early on.

How would a hardware architecture influence the other two system architectures? Suppose a system must produce postscript output to a factory floor. In this case, there would be an implicit hardware requirement for a postscript-compatible printer that would be identified in the hardware architecture so that this requirement may be properly allocated to that piece of hardware. In addition, the software would have to produce postscript output (a software requirement as well as an allocation for the software architecture) and there may even be a requirement for LAN access to the printer (part of the network architecture).

System reliability is determined to a large extent by the hardware chosen. Operational concerns such as fault tolerance and fail-over are items to be considered. Other practical concerns are vender support, 24 × 7 support, upgrades, capacity, price, and availability.

Clearly, the degree to which hardware control may be exerted varies from project to project. In some cases it may be completely out of our control, such as with the public telephone network. In other cases, you may be developing software for telephone companies. The point here is to find out all you can about the hardware specifications, to document their interface requirements and capabilities/limitations, and then to test them.

Network Architecture

The system **network architecture** involves how data will be moved in the distributed environment. This transportation of data is usually autonomous. In other words, we will not be relying on transport mechanisms under our control or development. We rely on predefined distribution using existing autonomous networks or, at the very least, integrating with them at some point.

Primary issues of concern are *bandwidth* and *load balancing* (the ability or likelihood of alternate paths). We must become familiar with the communications subnet and all of its performance characteristics. Load analysis may reveal the need for additional hardware such as repeaters, routers, bridges, and gateways.

Concerns such as *system latency* and *data availability* are tantamount. The network architecture requires (at a minimum) a *network diagram* depicting the various routers, bridges, and hubs that will be used to transport data as well as which LAN/WAN configurations will be used. The static information on these components would be described or referenced in the hardware architecture, but the dynamic capabilities would be described here in the network architecture.

Of course, the network architecture describes how it impacts the hardware and software architectures. Obviously, the network architecture can impact the hardware architecture by requiring upgraded or new network equipment. It can impact the software architecture depending on the type of data transport required of any particular WAN/LAN implementation (e.g., TCP/IP, Token Ring).

Software Architecture

The last (and arguably most important) component of the system architecture is the *software architecture*. It is not to be confused with software *design*. The principal word here is *scalability*. Software design addresses the proper mapping of software entities to the problem space at multiple appropriate layers of abstraction. Primary concerns are *functionality* and *maintainability*. In contrast, software architecture speaks to the *reusability*, the *reliability*, and the *extensibility* of the software — its ability to process larger amounts of data across disparate operating environments in multiple hardware configurations with minimal impact to system performance. Scalability is particularly important in distributed systems. This subject was addressed in detail in Chapter 5, "Telephony API Overview." Reusability is provided by the enforcement of providing modules that will house common services to be used by all application programmers. For example, all application programmers use the common data access services rather than writing their own from scratch. Reliability can only be enforced by quality code. This only comes from quality programmers who typically cost much more than the average project cannon fodder. There is no free lunch — you get what you pay for.

The same team that develops the software should perform the activity of specifying the software architecture. It is recommended that this task be allocated to the *infrastructure team*.[13]

Distributed systems *require* software architecture. Most telecom projects are part of a distributed system. In some applications, distributed server processing is integral to the service offered. But what constitutes a distributed system? Specifically, how is it different from a network system? Network systems (e.g., LANs) are distributed in the sense that their resources are split or shared among multiple computers. Distributed systems can clearly run alongside of network systems. So what gives?

---

13 Programming teams are covered in the section " Organizing Application Programming Roles" later in this chapter.

Turns out that distributed systems have an additional characteristic not found in network systems. It has to do with the issue of *control*. Generally, distributed systems spread application processing tasks among multiple computers. One or more controlling modules initiate, monitor, and/or control the completion of modifiable user-defined tasks. In contrast, network systems generally operate predefined tasks autonomously — they just go. Although it is possible for a distributed system to include network transmission as a part of the distributed processing, this is neither wise nor necessary.

There is another important difference. Usually, distributed systems are implemented "on top of" network systems. In this sense, they exist at a higher level of abstraction than do network systems. This layered relationship implies an *integration effort* that ties the three architectures together. If the system architecture components (i.e., the network, hardware, and software architectures) are well integrated, the project stands a chance of success. If not, it's time to brush up on that résumé.[14]

Once the system architecture is in place, product fabrication can begin, right? Actually, product fabrication, being a concurrent activity, has already begun, remember? Let's take a look at the first phase of the product fabrication process: analysis. But first, a refresher on product fabrication.

Product Fabrication

Product fabrication is the third and final parallel activity specified in the RAF model. It is to begin concurrently with requirements discovery and system architecture. Product fabrication deals with the *actual construction* of the end product. It is defined entirely in terms of the canonical software development life cycle phases of analysis, design, construction, and test.[15] The fabrication process is generally no different for telecom projects than for any other type of application. This effort requires a coordinated effort among requirements analysts, testers, and programmers.

Product fabrication does not specify a particular development methodology. It is, however, important to follow some kind of *object-oriented* methodology. Arguments can be made extolling the virtues of one over another approach, but having no approach at all is not well advised. We recommend the use of object-oriented methods as opposed to functional methods because the rationale is simply overwhelming for doing so.[16] Therefore, it is advised that either OMT, the Unified Method, or Fusion be adopted and that the UML be used as a model specification language.

---

14 In the past, I have used my assessment of the quality of the system architecture integration effort to gauge when it is time to move on to another project!

15 Note again that requirements gathering is no longer a phase; rather, it is an integral part of each of these phases.

16 Non OO development has now been categorized as an *anti-pattern*.

Object-Oriented Analysis

The primary purpose of the *analysis phase* is to *understand* requirements. In the analysis phase, we determine exactly *what* it is the system is to do based upon our understanding of the requirements gathered so far. We intentionally avoid discussions about how the system is to accomplish those things it is to do. We do not, however, operate in a vacuum. When implementation issues do creep into analysis discussions, we note them as such for future consideration. In any case, how do we go about analyzing a proposed system? We examine the *problem space*.

Describing the Problem Space

Since the early 1980s, a few prominent analysis techniques have emerged. Although early engineering efforts from the likes of Constantine and De Marco and others paved the way for methodologies like Functional Decomposition, the principles of *object-oriented programming* were beginning to have an impact on analysis and design methodologies. The seminal works in this area were summarized in four methodologies developed in the 1990s. These were the Booch Method, Responsibility-Driven Design, the Fusion Method, and OMT. Further refinement efforts have emerged since then (e.g., use cases, patterns, and UML) and surely more are coming, but the principals used for analysis remain fairly constant.

To perform system analysis, we begin by effecting a description of the problem space based upon the functional requirements unearthed in the requirements discovery activity. We try to come up with a few key paragraphs or pages of text that adequately describe what the proposed system is to do at a fairly high level. Once we are comfortable with the output, we tag the nouns of the text as *objects* and the verbs as *operations* performed by those objects. We then walk these objects through as many scenarios as we can think of. Along the way, we discover new objects. For information systems, we try to model the *workflow*. For real-time systems, analysis becomes more temporal in nature as state transitions and critical events are modeled. Once the list is refined and responsibilities are allocated to objects, requirements are mapped and subsystems can be formulated. The process is then repeated until it feels like it is done or we run out of time.

Don't Copy — Reengineer!

Often a new system development effort is contracted in order to replace or significantly enhance an existing system. If this is the case, it is critically important to avoid describing the new system in terms of the system it is to replace. We are to partition our understanding of the existing system — to separate the specification from the implementation. Understand what it does; ignore *how* it does it.

Many times it is best to completely ignore the existing system. If the deployment is phased and requires an integration period prior to full cutover, it may be advisable to defer investigation of the existing system as much as possible so as not to pollute the design of the new system. On the other hand, understanding what an existing system does helps to discern what needs to be done to improve its functionality. It should never be forgotten that users are *used to* that existing system no matter how "bad" it is. And so every proposed improvement in functionality over the existing system that is proposed had better include a description of how and why it improves the user's current situation.

Identifying External Agents

Of course, the analysis process isn't quite as simple as we have depicted it. Although the process itself is rather rudimentary, it actually takes a surprising amount of intuition and experience to elicit proper analysis entities. Some of the best analyses look very simple, even *obvious* once they are complete, but getting there can be quite a task. One key output of proper analysis is the accurate identification of external systems. Distinguishing between what belongs *inside* the system and what *interfaces externally* with the system is a critical part of the analysis phase. We believe the exercise of partitioning the problem space between internal and external actors is best accomplished through *use cases*[17] and formalized with a preliminary interface control document[18] (ICD).

Once several rounds of analysis are complete, we begin to *categorize content.* We concentrate on formulating testable specifications by removing references to implementation and linking high-level functionality to requirements. Functional requirements are further refined into system-specific–derived requirements that are allocated to initial *subsystems.* Then off we go to design.

Object-Oriented Design

Our discussion of design begins with an overview of the design phase and moves into object modeling. Understanding object models is critical to gaining an understanding of the relationships between JTAPI entities. Readers familiar with these fundamental concepts may wish to move ahead to the section on distributed programming.

During the design phase, we further *refine* the objects identified in the analysis phase, and we derive many more objects. We begin to examine in detail the *static*, *dynamic,* and *functional* properties of the proposed system. At a minimum, we assure ourselves that every single entity from the analy-

---

17 Use cases have been incorporated into the Unified Modeling Language (UML) advocated earlier.

18 An ICD is a document that *describes the interface* between two or more systems. The ICD specifies the data types and either function signatures or messages required for communicating between them.

sis phase is present in the design. We add to the data dictionary and begin the process of *data modeling* and s*ubsystem specification.* We introduce for the first time computer implementation subsystems like GUIs, databases, and communication protocols. We begin to assess the impact of system requirements on the software design. We hook up with the system architecture folks to ensure we are getting a solid foundation for the service-level software components to build on. We focus on incorporating OO concepts and object modeling into our design.

Object-Oriented Concepts

Programmers are becoming more accustomed to analysis. However, they have always been aware of the need for design. Pioneered by the Simula and Smalltalk programming languages of the 1960s, OO techniques began to take shape in the technical journals and computer science curricula of the 1980s. The arguments for using object-oriented technology in analysis, design, and programming are so compelling that it is simply irresponsible to advocate a functional approach. Grady Booch demonstrated how the Ada programming language was designed from the ground up to support key OO features and, more importantly, how programming language features could for the first time be used in software design.[19] Although not quite as robust as Ada, languages like C++, CLOS, Smalltalk, and Java also provide support for the key OO concepts of *encapsulation*, *polymorphism*, and *extension*. All of these concepts are important in the development of maintainable and reliable telephony software. Without their use, the software quickly becomes an unmanageable mess.

Encapsulation

The canonical definition of encapsulation is the grouping of data together with operations that act on that data. JTAPI is built on this concept. Object-oriented languages like Java facilitate encapsulation. Encapsulation provides the perfect implementation of an object's state. This is extremely important in telephony applications because they are laden with state-heavy objects.

A more subtle example of encapsulation supported by OO languages is *aggregation*. By hanging onto an object via a private (or protected) instance variable, enclosing objects can reap the benefits of a helper object's services without altering its own interface or "falsely" inheriting. Encapsulation by aggregation is not always as obvious as may be dictated by the object model (e.g., **has-a** relationships). Other service-level uses such as variable scope and lock management sometimes come into play. Encapsulation as provided in OO languages provides a clean implementation for these concepts as well.

---

19 Grady Booch, *Software Engineering with Ada,* Benjamin/Cummings Publishing Company, Inc., 1986.

Polymorphism

In telephony applications, polymorphism is particularly well suited to server code. For example, suppose both an answering machine and a fax machine understand the `answer()` message. Code written to answer an incoming call can invoke the `answer()` method on any object that implements the answer interface. What this means is the server does not have to provide special considerations for varying data types during processing. In other words, the same polymorphic code can be used to support any type of object without modification.

Extension

Extension is also referred to as *inheritance, specialization,* and *generalization.* There are uses for extension other than the obvious use of model-level inheritance (e.g., a car **is-a** vehicle). Inheritance may also be used as *service-level extension* to provide low-level base functionality to higher level objects.[20]

It is interesting to note that all of these OO principles *may* be implemented without the use of OO languages, but the discipline, expertise, and sheer patience to do so is overwhelming. So why not go with the best?

We have described the high-level activities in the design phase at the 30,000-foot level. We now combine all of these features into a practical discussion about the heart[21] of software design — object modeling.

Object Modeling, Data Modeling, Optionality, and Cardinality

Object modeling is the practice of representing the world in terms of classes of objects and the relationships between them. It begins with what has been called "data modeling" (or "entity/relationship modeling") and adds representation of *object behavior.* Peter Chen developed data modeling with roots in E. F. Codd's relational model. *Optionality* and *cardinality* are concepts present in both disciplines. Object modeling is not a *revolution against* data modeling; rather it is an *evolution of* data modeling. Here we will present the basic principles of the data side of object modeling only, along with some of its pitfalls.[22] Go get some coffee — you'll need it.

---

20 For example, all objects in Smalltalk extend from class Object; in MFC they inherit from class CObject. Each of these approaches provides a large degree of built-in capabilities presumably required of all objects. Java is different in this respect. In Java, most but not all classes extend class Object. Also, class Object does not provide much functionality; it is lightweight by design.

21 In the following section we only address principles used in modeling the static relationships between objects. Dynamic modeling as it relates to JTAPI has already been addressed in the design of JTAPI messaging and in Chapter 9.

22 One outstanding reference on the subject of data modeling is the book *Data Model Patterns : Conventions of Thought* by David C. Hay. We have had the privilege of working with David and have helped his data models come to life in the form of objects. Great stuff.

What Is a Data Model?

A data model is concerned with *the relationship between entities in terms of how many of each can "exist" at a given point in time*. The "how many" is called *cardinality*.[23] These entities are best expressed in terms of a single instance (i.e., they are not usually expressed in plurality terms). This is because of the semantics of the word "many," and so it can become confusing to speak of many items which themselves are made up of many others. So one speaks in terms of a student, not students — unless we are expressing a set of students as a whole (e.g., classwide operations). Let's call this the principle of *atomicity*.

From an object-oriented standpoint, we are concerned with relationships between both classes and objects, although a model specifically represents classes. There are three primary characteristics of relationships that must be mastered in order to create an accurate data model: *naming, cardinality*, and *optionality*. Cardinality addresses *how many potential instances of one object can exist relative to the existence of another object*. Optionality addresses whether or not an object is *required* to exist relative to the existence of another object. In terms of classes, one can attach cardinality and optionality anywhere along an inheritance tree. However, specialization affects cardinality, sometimes radically so. It is possible to have one relationship at one level and a similar relationship with very different semantics at a lower or higher level.

Getting the specifics of each relationship correct is critical to an accurate design. Incorrect relationships lead to inefficient processing and update anomalies. One thing to remember about relationships is that they are *always* bi-directional.[24] Just like every story, there are two sides. Further, there are three types of relationships: *one-to-one, one-to-many*, and *many-to-many*.

One-to-One Relationships

Suppose we have a starving student. Being a little short on self-esteem, he can only charm one girl at a time. From his perspective, the relationship between him and his girlfriend is one-to-one (1:1). For expression purposes, we can put names on these relationships as in **Figure 11.3**.

Figure 11.3 *Cardinality Relationship*

---

23 Cardinality is also referred to in literature as *multiplicity*.
24 Even though a relationship may not be implemented in a bi-directional sense, it is, in fact, bi-directional.

The arrow is not part of the normal cardinality notation — it is provided for clarity in this discussion only. The semantics of the relationship are "Each boy may be going with one and only one girl." The relationship name is "has-a," because this childish boy thinks he owns his girlfriend (little does he know it is actually the other way around ...). Fortunately, this student's girlfriend is loyal, and therefore prefers only one student at a time. So from her perspective, the relationship is also 1:1 in that "Each girl may be going with one and only one student (boy)." This *bi-directional* relationship is shown in **Figure 11.4**.

Figure 11.4 *Bi-Directional 1:1 Cardinality Relationship*

The relationship name from this side is "goes-out-with." Again, it is common sense and also good practice to give the relationship a meaningful name. Although this is not strictly required to understand a relationship, it is critical to conveying an accurate model. Note also that although the names of the relationships differ depending on which direction they address, they are really two different ways of saying the same thing. This is because they actually *are* the same thing — a single relationship!

Of course, it may be the case that **GirlFriend** goes out with **Student**'s professor at the same time. To restrict the relationship further, we'd have to move up the inheritance tree of **Student**. We'd express it in terms of, say, a male person. That is, "student/boy" is a subtype of "male person," so the relationship would then be "Each girl may be going out with only one male person." **Student** would then inherit that relationship from **MalePerson** and the "goes-out-with / has-a" relationship would disappear.

One-to-Many Relationships

As another example, our student doesn't have much money save for a few coins in his pocket. We might say that the cardinality relationship between any **Student** and any **Coin** in his possession is said to be one-to-many. We will assume that the relationship remains optional in both directions (i.e., 1:N). Let's look at this from the student's perspective. This relationship exists because *at any one point in time* a student can be associated with many different **Coins** (in **Figure 11.5**, the black ball represents "many"; no ball represents "zero or one").

Figure 11.5 *A 1:N Relationship*

Now let's look at the **Coin**'s "perspective." For any given coin, can it be in more than one person's possession *at any one point in time*? No, this is not possible. So, the relationship between a **Coin** and a **Student** is said to be an optional many-to-one (i.e., N:1). Note that this is *exactly* the same as saying that *Student* has a 1:N relationship to **Coin**; they're two different (bi-directional) ways of saying the *same* thing (see **Figure 11.6**).

Figure 11.6 *Bi-Directional 1:N Relationship*

Many-to-Many Relationships

A many-to-many relationship is the *combination* of two 1:N relationships involving the same classes in opposite directions. Let's take a look at one.

Like any good student, ours attends class. Over the time period of a semester, he may attend many classes offered during that semester. More properly, *any* student can attend *many different* classes over a semester. We are modeling the behavior of all students and classes, not just our own.[25] For the **Student**-to-**Class** relationship, this represents a 1:N relationship as demonstrated in **Figure 11.7**.

Figure 11.7 *Attendance 1:N Relationship Between Student and Class*

---

25 In other words, if our particular student instance is lazy and takes only one class this term, it does not follow that there is a 1:1 relationship. Instead, we consider the number of *potential* classes he or she *could have* taken.

In addition, many different students may attend the same class at the same time. This represents a 1:N relationship in the other direction (remember, this is exactly the same as saying that **Student** has a N:1 relationship to **Class** as in **Figure 11.8**).

Figure 11.8 *N:1 Relationship Between Student and Class*

Thus we have a many-to-many (M:N) relationship as shown in **Figure 11.9**. Note the difficulty of trying to name this relationship. Although the semantics are straightforward ("Each student may be enrolled in one or more classes." + "Each class may be taken by one or more students."), how can we name this as a single relationship? Stay tuned.

Figure 11.9 *M:N Relationship*

Transitively, one may express one part of this relationship as an N:1 from **Student**-to-**Class**; and so by examining the second relationship (between **Class** and **Student**), we sometimes alter the first (between **Student** and **Class**). This highlights the importance of always modeling cardinality from *both* directions. It is not merely a matter of preference; rather

> *a design is rendered erroneous if the bi-directionality of a relationship is not considered.*

It is essential, when modeling, to correctly identify the cardinality of each relationship in *each* direction. This will have profound implications on the system's ultimate implementation and will lead to a proper modeling of the problem space.

Now, an M:N relationship raises a problem. Remembering how earlier we wanted to treat *each* occurrence of an entity, we have no way in an M:N relationship to describe each occurrence of one object being related to another object. Yes, each object of class A can be related to one or more objects in class B and vice versa, but what about each class A object /class B object *combination*?

To clarify this, let's walk through an instance exercise. It's about time we met our student, so let's give him a name — Weston. Weston is taking chemistry, biology, and computer science this semester.

```
Weston    Chemistry
          Biology
          Computer Science
```

Because each student-class pair represents a single instance of the three student-class combinations or relationships, let's show this:

```
Weston    Chemistry
Weston    Biology
Weston    Computer Science
```

This says that Weston is taking the classes of chemistry, biology, and computer science this semester. Weston's brother, Noah, is also taking *the same* chemistry class. So is his girlfriend, Katie (his older brother, Spencer, is taking calculus like his Dad). This is seen in the instance diagram of **Figure 11.10**.

Figure 11.10 *Instance Diagram*

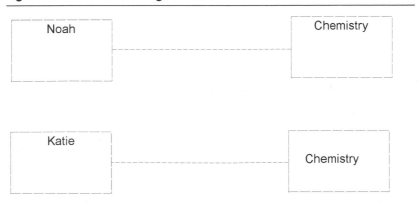

Let's combine all the instances to visualize the multiplicity of this M:N relationship:

```
Weston    Chemistry
Weston    Biology
Weston    Computer Science
Noah      Chemistry
Spencer   Calculus
Katie     Chemistry
```

In other words, another way to model the M:N **Student**-to-**Class** relationship is to think of it as an entity in it's own right. After all, the fact that Weston is taking Chemistry as a **Student** is probably what we're interested in, not just the fact that he *is* a student or that there *is* a class called Chemistry.

In fact, with an M:N relationship, there really is no way to separate this fact. When we speak of Weston as a student, there is certain information we can obtain from the fact he is a student alone. This can be obtained from **Student**. And the fact that a **Class** is offered is very interesting, but probably less interesting if no students enroll in the class! So if we want to find out about the **Class** itself, we can ask it where it is located, its title, any prerequisites required, and so forth. But to find out about **Students** *taking* the class, we *must* ask both **Student** and **Class** — the association between the two.

Recall that an M:N relationship is actually made up of two 1:N relationships in opposite directions. So how do we show this relationship as a stand-alone entity? Let's redraw that relationship by separating them visually, by drawing it as a stand-alone entity that is related to each of the original entities. From **Figure 11.9** we "pull back" the relationship lines to make room for our new entity in **Figure 11.11**.

Figure 11.11 *Preparing To Decompose an M:N Relationship*

Now, place a new entity between the two that represents the instances of each **Student**-**Class** combination. We could call it **ClassStudent** or **StudentClass**. But what exactly is a "studentclass"? This is not a real-world object. What we need is a name that captures what it *means* for a student to take a class. Let's call it **Enrollment**. In doing so, we have created a *compound class* from the association between two M:N classes. If we can add more information about the compound class, it becomes an *associative class, also known as a link class* or an *intersect class*. For example, an attribute like **seatAssignment** is native to the **Enrollment**, although the set of **availableSeats** may be thought of as a part of **Class**.

Note that the relationships are now 1:N between each original object class and this new, associative class. Moreover, note that each occurrence of the associative class *must be* related to one and only one member of each original class. Think about it. The reason the class exists is to represent pairs of occurrences of the other two classes. An occurrence of a pair cannot exist if each of the elements of that pair doesn't exist. Hence, the relationship from the pair to the element is *mandatory* (as opposed to optional).

Figure 11.12 *Decomposing an M:N Relationship into an Associative Class*

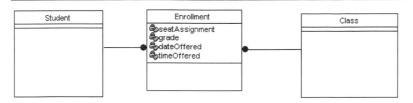

In fact, part of the activity of detailed design is the decomposition of these M:N relationships from Analysis into two 1:N relationships. This helps to flesh their behavior out better because they may be addressed as full-blown *concrete classes*, not just association relationships. This is a subtle but important distinction because association classes are not directly supported in object-oriented languages.[26] So when we go to code this thing, many-to-many associations may become full-blown classes in their own right, depending on the implementation.

An Exercise in Futility

It has been argued that these so-called *link* classes are optional in that "dropping" the opposite side of the link can specify the same relationship (at least from the independent perspective of one or the other object). For example, the **Student** can refer to a collection of **Classes** as shown in **Figure 11.13**.

Figure 11.13 *Student Attends a Collection of Classes*

Similarly, **Class** may refer to the same list of students as in **Figure 11.14**. The problem with this approach is that it is not only imprecise, it is insufficient if the link information is to be stored *persistently*. It is imprecise in that it doesn't truly model the problem space. In terms of persistence, this hack leaves nowhere to store the additional enrollment information (i.e., the attributes grade, setAssignment, etc.) without violating the rules of normalization thereby creating data anomalies. Of course it depends on whether or not the system actually *processes* enrollment infor-

---

26 Indeed, some argue that they should not be anyway.

mation (whether or not the relationship is actually true "in real life"). But usually the full decomposition of M:N relationships into full-blown objects is the correct approach. For nontransient (i.e., persistent) data, it is always the best approach.

Figure 11.14 *Class May Hold a Collection of Students*

Recall that we inserted an associative object called **Enrollment** between two objects participating in an M:N relationship and that it looked pretty cool. But what if we pulled the relationships apart from the other end when we inserted **Enrollment**? In other words, is it wrong to place the end of the relationship with more multiplicity on **Student** and **Class** rather than on **Enrollment** as in **Figure 11.15**? Let's see.

Figure 11.15 *Incorrect Resolution of a M:N Relationship*

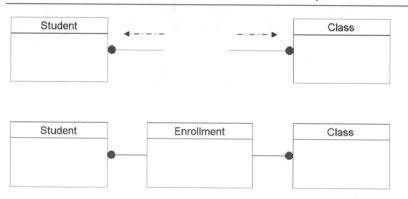

Recall that **Figure 11.9** showed that a **Student** could be related to many different **Enrollments** at the same time. Further, it showed that a **Class** could be referenced in many different **Enrollments**. This represents the relationship from the perspective of the **Student** and the **Class**, respectively. Although **Figure 11.15** says just the opposite, it seems not to matter at first glance. After all, what's the difference of stating that a **Student** is involved in many **Enrollments** and that an **Enrollment** involves many **Students**? We can only answer this question by looking at the other end of the bi-directionality of each link. In other words, look at it from the perspective of the associative object **Enrollment**. **Figure 11.12** showed that an

Enrollment could have *at most* one **Student** and one **Class** per **Enrollment**. This is correct. **Figure 11.15** shows just the opposite — that an **Enrollment** has multiple **Students** and **Classes** at the same time. This is incorrect.[27] And so we see that it *does* matter where the multiplicity is defined.

Normalization and Anomalies

When we introduced the **Enrollment** class, we added a few attributes that better described this "relationship" class, and that made us feel pretty good. But was it accurate? To find out, we must validate each attribute against each associative entity *as a pair of the objects that are associated*. In other words, we look at an **Enrollment** instance as a **Student-Class** pair and determine if each attribute is unique to that pair or if there are other pairs of **Enrollments** instead that share that attribute. Let's start with the attribute **seatAssignment**. Clearly only one **Student-Class** pair can sit in a seat at a time during a class. So this attribute is okay. But what about the attributes representing the date and time offered? Are they unique to a **Student-Class** pair? The answer is "No." To verify this, let's draw another instance diagram in **Figure 11.16**.

Figure 11.16 *Expanding Cardinality to an Instance Diagram*

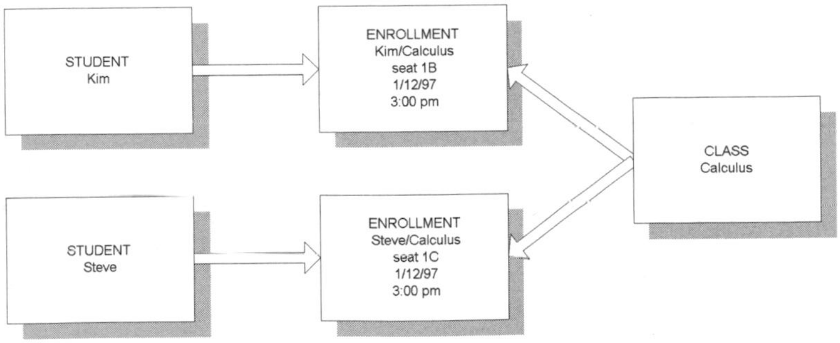

Steve's always late. What would happen if Steve were allowed to change his **Enrollment** time from 3:00 PM to 3:30 PM? Since both Steve and Kim share the same **Class** (Calculus), they share the same time attributes. So a change to Steve's time should also change Kim's time. Clearly something is wrong here.

In data modeling terms, we have initiated an ***update anomaly***. In this case, the problem stems from the fact that the date and time attributes don't really belong in the association class **Enrollment**. They are shared charac-

---

27 It is incorrect unless we redefine the semantics of an Enrollment to be a collection type. But this is a stretch and it violates the singularity of the class relationship — our principle of atomicity. In other words, it is still wrong!

teristics of the **Class**. Or are they? Can't a **Class** be offered at different dates and times? Of course it can. We have discovered the need for two classes (if you'll pardon the expression): **ClassOffering**, which describes the fact that educational material is being presented at a particular place and time, and **Course**, which is the definition of the material to be presented. This modification to the model is presented in **Figure 11.17**.

Figure 11.17 *Refinement of an M:N Relationship*

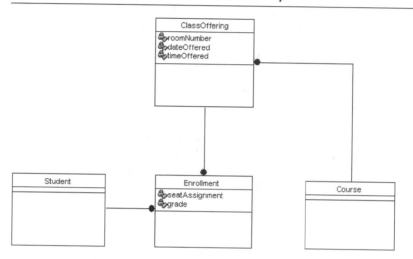

You have now recognized that each course may be presented as one or more **ClassOfferings** (which is to say each class offering must be of one and only one course). The **ClassOffering** and **Course** take the place of **Class** as a further refinement of the model. What we have done is further *normalize* the model. That is, we have more accurately ensured that we have correctly identified what object class an attribute is an attribute of. As happens so often, our model has changed significantly as the result of resolving an M:N relationship. It should be clear now why an M:N relationship cannot be left unresolved.

Transitivity and Navigation

There are a few common mistakes to look out for when creating relationships. One is to fail to define entities correctly. Unless an object is fully and accurately understood, its relationships with other objects cannot possibly be determined with any degree of accuracy. Another common misunderstanding is the confusion between cardinality and the *navigation* among entities. Inexperienced modelers often look at a model showing cardinality and miss the transitivity of the relationships. **Figure 11.18** shows a model with various cardinality traits.

Figure 11.18 *The Transitivity of Cardinality*

Looking at the model in **Figure 11.18**, it should be clear that the entity **LineItem** is specific to a particular customer. In fact, it is specific to a single charge for a certain inventory item on an exact account of a particular customer! Everything to the left of the entity **LineItem** is directly related to a customer. Everything to the right is not — it is related indirectly only *through* the entity **LineItem**. Inexperienced modelers often miss the fact that a cardinality relationship is *transitive*. The navigation tendency is to want to draw a line from, say, **LineItem** or **InventoryItem** directly to **Customer**. This is not only unnecessary, it is incorrect. Cardinality is *not* navigation!

Navigation Exposed

Interestingly, the incorrect relationship depicted in **Figure 11.15** is actually a diagram of ***transient navigation***. In other words, at runtime the class **Enrollment** may need to refer to a list of either all enrolled students, only those in a particular **ClassOffering**, or those in a set of **ClassOfferings**. But these transient references are *not* true characteristics of the static relationships between objects. They are merely means of navigating among objects at runtime to satisfy transient computations. Here's the point:

> *Object and data models **never** represent navigation.*

Now that we have completed discussion of analysis and design, there are two remaining phases in the product fabrication activity: *construction* and *testing*.

Construction

Some but not all ideas must be fleshed out in working code in order to prove their validity. Partial software construction should begin along with design, but probably not during analysis unless project subsystems can be identified early on. In this case, each subsystem may proceed concurrently provided their interface is minimal or very well understood. Some examples where this is appropriate would be lower-level service software developed to support a higher application layer or interfaces with external or legacy systems.

Again we advocate the use of an object-oriented approach. In construction, this translates to an OO language like Ada, C++, Smalltalk, Eiffel, CLOS, or Java.

Testing

The entire purpose of testing is to prove the satisfaction of requirements. Testers *verify* that the system performs to specification by executing test cases. However, it is the responsibility of project management, requirements analysts, and the programmers who wrote the code to *validate* the requirements. Only they can properly determine whether what was specified in the requirements makes sense in the context of what they have actually built!

By following the RAF approach, system validation never loses focus throughout the development cycle because developers are part of the requirements process. When changes in requirements occur, they are the first to know.

Let's do some paperwork (groan ...).

Documentation Requirements

This is everyone's least favorite subject, so we will be brief. Telephony projects do not generally require extensive documentation. In short, we want as little documentation as is necessary to clearly convey requirements and design concepts to all project participants. The smaller and more experienced the team, the less need for documentation. However, documentation is always helpful for maintenance purposes — *if* and *only if* it accurately reflects the design *as-built*!

Documentation requirements for product fabrication are not specified in the RAF model. This is because the development methodology generally determines the documentation requirements and that methodology itself is not specified. Again, RAF provides only a set of guidelines to follow. There are, however, a few documents that fall outside of the product fabrication activity that require documentation. Specifically, the other two parallel activities (requirements discovery and system architecture) rely heavily on the documentation produced. It is in fact the only tangible work product one of these activities (namely, requirements discovery) produces!

RAF Activity Work Products

Each RAF activity may produce output (a.k.a. work products). These products are the result of the successful completion of each activity.

Requirements Discovery Documentation

- High-Level Process Flow Diagrams (optional)
- Data Dictionary
- Requirements Traceability Matrix
- Risk Items

System Architecture Documentation

- Hardware Architecture Plan
- Network Architecture Plan
- Software Architecture Plan

Product Fabrication Documentation

Again, product fabrication documentation requirements will vary with the methodology used. Regardless of the methodology used, product fabrication standards should never be imposed for the sake of following a methodology. Rather they should be used whenever their application is thought by the developers involved to add some utility to the development process. Customer requests for documentation should be countered with guarantees that the documents will actually be read and commented on. There are a few cases, however, where their imposition should be mandatory, and that is where they enhance *communication among developers.* Lack of communication (and more often rampant miscommunication) is the most expensive mistake a project can incur. Misunderstandings about the semantics of a design entity are so common it is alarming. Here are some documentation guidelines organized by development phase.

Analysis

Analysis Document

    Use Cases

    Data Dictionary (updated from Requirements)

    Preliminary ICD from External Systems, if any

    Preliminary Functional Subsystem Descriptions

    Call Model (for telephony projects)

    Object Interaction/Collaboration Diagrams

    State Transition Diagrams

    Data Flow Diagrams

    Low-level Process Flow Diagrams

Design

Final ICD

Object Model

Class Specifications / IDL

Construction

Code

Final Functional Subsystem Descriptions

Test

Cases and Scenarios

Integration Test Reports

A Word on Functional Subsystem Descriptions

A Functional Subsystem Description (FSD) is a small document written by the programmer who wrote the code for a new user of the system under development. It is free-form and meant to convey the design of the relevant subsystem in terms a user can understand. In RAF, this task is not too difficult because the user's terms and the programmer's terminology are identical (at least with respect to problem space entities). The FSD should contain high-level process flows and be laden with terminology with which the user is already familiar. We advocate a two-phase approach to producing FSDs. The first pass should occur before any software is written. The second pass should occur sometime after the software is ready for unit test. At this point, the as-built configuration will give a much more accurate picture of how the system was designed.

Work products should only be updated during the development cycle as such activity measurably adds to the value of a product. In other words, documentation should not be updated solely for the sake of keeping the work products current. It should only be updated as it adds value to the process of developing software.

Alrighty then. We have taken a new, though rather traditional look at the software development process. Hopefully we have addressed the fundamental components and work products necessary for successful completion of a large-scale telecom project. However, we were mostly observing from the canopy level. In the following section, we get down to the roots by examining some of the "nuts and bolts" techniques of managing a successful telecom project.

A Programmer's Perspective

It is important to understand that the art of telephony programming is evolving as you read these words. There have never been programming standards that many of us are used to like TCP/IP, the OSI Seven Layers, Win32, and so forth. Not surprisingly, most telephony APIs are poorly integrated with existing or competing standards, if they are integrated at all.

For application programmers, the practice is beginning to evolve from low-level device coding into an API-centric approach. In other words, telephony programming is fast becoming a matter of mastering an API. The goal of JTAPI is to make that API *one* API so that at least Java programmers don't have to learn a new API for each board vendor that provides basically the same capabilities.

In the first part of this section, we look at programming *skill sets*. For managers, the goal is to understand the fundamental skills required and then to loosely organize the work effort around these skill sets. Better yet, let the programmers organize themselves. The second most important task is to select the right tools — a subject addressed in the last part of this section.

Distributed Programming

Telephony programming is a subset of distributed programming and is therefore subject to many of the same latency and communication issues other types of distributed processing endure. Mastering telephony programming at a professional level requires an understanding of distributed processing and all the complexity that implies.

All distributed systems require some form of *remote communication*. From a programmer's perspective, it is convenient to group remote communication into programming disciplines to better understand the skill sets that must be mastered in order to implement a telephony system. **Figure 11.19** models this relationship in terms of programming categories.

Figure 11.19 *Categories of Distributed Programming*

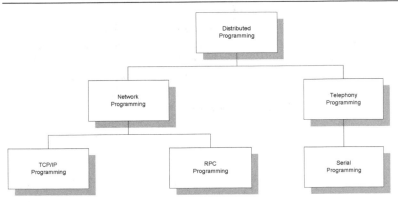

The categories of **Figure 11.19** are not mutually exclusive and in fact are often combined in order to implement a distributed solution. A large telecommunication system will likely employ a mixture of all of these categories; some implemented in terms of others. For example, a server-side telephony persistence subsystem might be implemented over a WAN using

RPC programming, which is built on top of TCP/IP messaging while the client side is implemented using a modem (Serial Programming).

Another important realization must occur in the programmer mindset with respect to the programming categories of **Figure 11.19**. Well-organized telecom projects support the allocation of all of these disciplines away from the *application programmer* and delegates the implementation of these functions to the *library programmer*. What is a library programmer? Let's look at programming from an organizational perspective to see if we can't provide a template for properly layering software and allocating skill sets.

Application, Library, and Systems Programming

Assume there are three kinds of programmers in the world — *application programmers*, *library programmers*, and *systems programmers*. Systems programmers write operating systems and device drivers. Library programmers write software library runtimes and reusable common code typically packaged into modules. Application programmers write everything else.[28] What's interesting (from a project management perspective) is that these programmers often work on opposite sides of an API. The application programmer makes calls to the API, the library programmer implements the API and the systems programmer ties device drivers to the operating system and to specialized I/O hardware (beneath the API).

In the same manner as the task of programming may be categorized as application, library and systems programming, telephony programming may be thought of as being available in these same three flavors. This relationship is depicted in **Figure 11.20**.

Application programmers rely on library programmers who in turn rely on systems programmers. Telephony application programmers use telephony APIs like JTAPI to produce telephony application software. Telephony library programmers implement these APIs. Telephony systems programmers tie the APIs to various hardware for telephony board manufacturer implementations. Whereas telephony application programmers need not be concerned with data transport protocols (indeed, they are hopefully insulated by the API set used), telephony library and systems programmers must be.

Planning a Telecom Project

On a telephony project, the first thing a manager needs to ascertain is which functional components fall into which domains. Of course, the vast majority of project development occurs in the Telephony Application Programmer's Domain. For a typical telephony project, we can assume that we will not be writing device drivers or implementing APIs. We will plan to purchase both and concentrate on the application. We can do this because either the board

---

28 We'll soon break this category down further.

Figure 11.20 *Telephony Programmer's Domains — Programmer's Perspective*

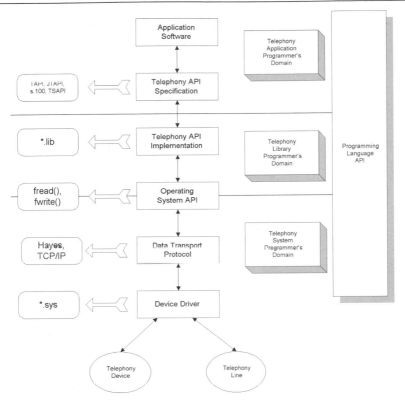

vendor and the telephony API will be supplied by the same vendor or another software vendor will supply the drivers. For example, we might choose a Dialogic telephony board. It comes with drivers and runtime modules without which we would be unable to use the hardware. In addition, the vendor might supply two APIs — their proprietary API and a TAPI-compliant API. This (and a few extra man-months) is all we would need if we were implementing our system in C/C++. We will seek to reduce this schedule and enhance the reliability of the product by using Java. Because we will be using JTAPI, we would expect it with the board, acquire it from a third-party vendor, or write it ourselves.[29] However, writing a full JTAPI implementation may be more than your project can expense. In fact, this is the entire purpose of JTAPI — to eliminate the need for this kind of effort by capitalizing on commercially available implementations. The success of JTAPI will depend largely on the *commercial availability* of quality JTAPI implementations.

---

29 In this case, the project would require library programming skills.

Having addressed the library and systems programming tasks for a typical project, let's get back to application programming. It turns out that no matter the task application programming may be further subdivided into three categories to further refine the skill sets and tasks necessary to complete a successful telecom project.

Organizing Application Programming Roles

The vast majority of programmers are application programmers. Application programming may be further grouped into three categories: *presentation programming*, *domain engineering*, and *infrastructure programming*. This relationship is depicted in **Figure 11.21**.

Figure 11.21 *Telephony Application Programming Roles — Management Perspective*

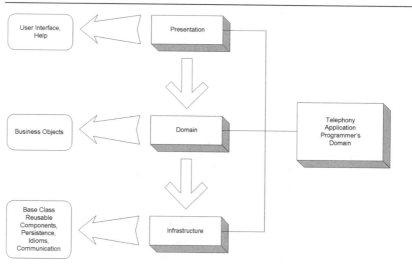

In a manner similar to the relationship between application, library, and systems programmers, the application programming categories of **Figure 11.21** are dependent upon each other. That is to say, *presentation* programmers rely on *domain engineering* programmers, who in turn rely on *infrastructure* programmers. Of course, it can be counterproductive to get too carried away with these categories. This discussion is not meant to encourage the practice of "pigeonholing" programmers into one of these classifications. Rather it is offered as one way of allocating programming resources to the problem at hand. We don't want to get too carried away with classifying talent — especially when we may be unqualified to assess skill sets in the first place! If this is the case, it is better to let the team decide among themselves what pieces they should work on and let it go at that.

All too often, development managers focus entirely on presentation application programming issues. This is understandable given the fact that this is the "top layer" of code. It is the one that will become most visible to the customer (assuming of course, there *is* a user interface!). But for telephony programming, domain level and infrastructure programming is essential. It is, in fact, the "meat" of any nontrivial telephony application. Without proper project focus in these lower-level layers, systems will be developed that will be less scalable and flexible than would otherwise have been the case.

Summary

We have presented a software process model appropriate for large-scale projects called **Requirements**, **Architecture**, and **Fabrication** (RAF). RAF partitions the development process into three parallel activities: *requirements discovery*, *system architecture*, and *product fabrication*. Although RAF may be used for any software project, it is particularly well suited to the fast-paced development cycles of large telecom projects.

Finally, we looked at the development process from both a management and a programmer's perspective. We examined some of the roles programmers can play during development and provided a grouping for programming tasks in six categories as depicted in **Figure 11.22**.

Figure 11.22 *Programming Categories*

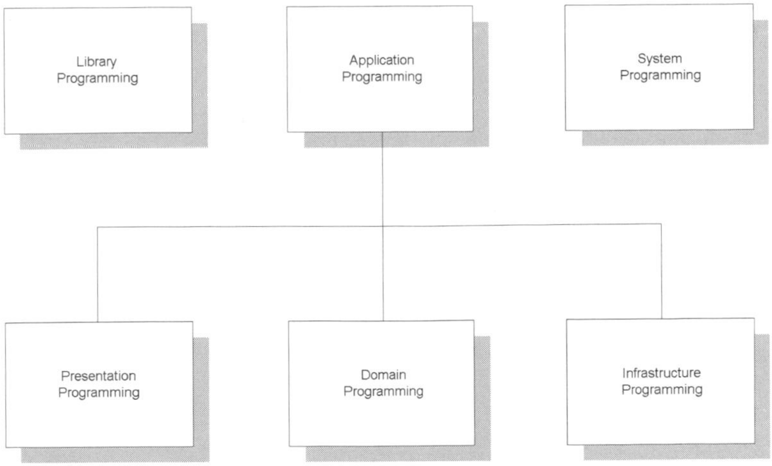

By properly allocating subsystem development efforts to these skill categories, a project can be made more organized and effective.

PART VI

FUTURE TELEPHONY PROGRAMMING IN JAVA

We believe that Java has the potential to have the most significant effect on the future of software development than any other programming language in history (except of course, C/C++). It is not so much the capabilities of language itself that has led to this conclusion. Rather it is the unprecedented commercial acceptance and industry cooperation that has emerged since its inception.

Through interfaces, Java allows for the specification of software components that is absolutely divorced in any way from an implementation. We have worked with this feature throughout this book. Although these same capabilities exist in other programming languages by using abstract classes, these languages have all but been ignored as specification tools. The point here is that through use of these language-specific specifications, industries will be able to "swap out" various media and implementation details while adhering to a common specification. For example, the JTAPI specification will be suitable for all telephony programming whether it is over the traditional telephone network, portable hand-held devices, or IP telephony. In this last chapter, we take a short excursion to peek at future Java telephony implementations, many of which are under development now.

Chapter 12

ALTERNATIVE JAVA TELEPHONY ENVIRONMENTS

"Is this the party to whom I am speaking?"

Lily Tomlin

In this final chapter, we examine some alternative uses for JTAPI. Java is promoted as being usable, even practical in the development of many consumer devices and has been licensed for many embedded systems. This may come as a surprise to many programmers due to its reputation as a relatively slow-executing high-level language. Among the many different types of these systems are consumer devices called Web Phones. These new devices integrate web functionality into telephone service.

By now, we should be able to see how the specification of a high-level API like JTAPI that captures the problem space effectively can lead to software that can be used no matter what the underlying platform is. If vendors can swap out data transport protocols and real-time operating systems (RTOS) without changing the application code base, we are in for a very different world.

By now, though, you should be weary of such claims. Indeed, we have seen firsthand how such support is impossible as long as consumer device vendors continue to manufacture products using proprietary interfaces. Even if they agree to license Java and JTAPI, they will continue to produce device-specific proprietary APIs. To some extent, this is unavoidable because of the nature of lower-level software. It will also continue as long as the market is free and consumers demand continual innovation from vendors (i.e., forever).

Sun however, claims to have solved this problem, at least for devices that run under a Java virtual machine. Their approach is (you guessed it) to use another set of APIs. What's different is that this approach also requires the use of a specialized *execution environment*.[1] We will take a quick look at some of these alternative Java execution and programming environments and try to determine how JTAPI fits into this picture from a development perspective. Only time will tell if their approach will work technically (and more importantly, if the embedded consumer device industry will accept it). If licensing agreements are any indication of the level of acceptance, then they might be on to something here. However, we've seen how uncooperative licensing partners can be, even in the Java arena.

Java and Consumer Devices

Never in the history of the world has a programming language been so heavily promoted as Java. This promotion has gone far beyond that of mere programmers — it has even hit the living rooms of the American consumer. And that's exactly where many companies are hoping the next big commercial wave is — consumer devices. Traditionally, this has not been a very exciting list of tools. Even though some attempts have been made, there are simply not many practical computer applications for irons and toasters (although microwave ovens have been a big hit).

Many would like to believe that the Internet would offer *new types* of consumer devices, thereby ushering in a new wave of demand for products and markets. Through IP technology, many different *integrated* applications are possible. Perhaps the most compelling example of these new consumer devices is the Web Phone.

The Web Phone and Other Consumer Devices

The Web phone is a telephone with a small screen used for accessing the Web. Similar in look and feel to a kiosk, this screen may be used in conjunction with the telephone to perform all kinds of scheduling activities for both work and play. For example, electronic banking, in-house video conferencing, and purchasing tickets to next week's Padres game are some very practical uses. Businesses might want to use them for teleconferencing. Other potential markets where JTAPI can play a role include television set control boxes, game consoles that can access the web, hand-held computers, and, of course, mobile phones.

---

1 This execution environment (and others) is probably why Microsoft views Sun's "programming language" as a threat to their operating system business.

Putting the Pedal to the Metal

But there's still the issue of speed. Isn't Java "too slow"? Again, only time and real products (as opposed to API announcements) will tell. But as real-time access times decrease and network bandwidth and processing speeds increase, Java's interpreted nature will become less of an issue. The real question will be "Is Java's slower execution time noticeable to the customer?". After all, most of today's Smalltalk Windows applications[2] operate at speeds that are indistinguishable to the user. In addition, applications such as easing remote updates and software patches to web-enabled consumer devices may take precedence over slight performance penalties.

Where Does JTAPI Fit In?

Right on top, of course. Although primarily designed for telephony applications, many parts of JTAPI are also useful for integrating telephony capability into other kinds of applications. For example, the lower-level software call center abstractions that add routing capabilities to Addresses offer an ideal solution for many other types of telephone-controlled services. This is possible because they were designed in a flexible manner utilizing callbacks. Many consumer devices are operated with buttons just like a phone. Also, the event services and framework specified in JTAPI can be useful even if not provided directly by the programming language.

Alternative Java Execution and Development Environments

Sun has an alarming number of APIs available for Java covering just about every imaginable market. In order to provide such an array of capabilities many of these APIs build on the core language by creating extension packages like JTAPI. However, there is a world of applications where even the core services of any programming language are "too much." Traditionally, such applications have been programmed using C, Assembler language, and, in the DoD, Ada. While most of these applications fall in the world of *embedded systems*, many are not quite embedded but might still benefit from a smaller memory footprint.

For these types of applications, Sun has devised a few APIs that are effectively *subsets* of the Java language.[3] The way this works is that the core language is listed by package and then capabilities are either included, excluded, or deemed optional. For example, many embedded systems sim-

---

2 Recall that Smalltalk runs compiled byte code just like Java. But these are not consumer devices!

3 Again, this concept is nothing new. Ada has a few formally defined language subsets that are used in many aircraft systems with both military and commercial applications.

ply have no user interface and indeed may not even require the services of a file system. These applications may not require display packages like `java.applet`, `java.awt`, and, say, `java.io` (for file systems). And so, the specifications of these language subsets either exclude or make optional these types of packages as appropriate. The two primary embedded system packages are *PersonalJava* and *EmbeddedJava*.[4]

PersonalJava

PersonalJava (PJ) is a subset specification of the Java language that reduces the core language yet leaves in support for networked applications. Any mobile phone is a candidate for this API. PJ applications must be able to connect with the Internet and download Java applets and applications. Another purpose of PJ is to reduce the cost of porting code across consumer device platforms. This is accomplished primarily by relying on Java's portability features, which (as we have seen) largely do not apply in device-centric arenas! On the other hand, just like a well-written JTAPI application, PJ *applications* are practically portable, even if their device libraries are not.

EmbeddedJava

The EmbeddedJava (EJ) specification is similar to PJ, but even more scaled down. In some sense, the applications for EJ and PJ overlap (e.g., mobile phone). Yet EJ applications may be distinguished by having no user interface or an extremely small or simple UI as well as a small memory footprint. Sample applications include pagers, process control and DSP applications, peripherals, routers, switches, instrumentation panels, watches, decoder rings (seriously!), refrigerators (?), and small mice (just kidding). But you get the picture.

The Java language designers have spoken of Java as being designed for embedded systems from the beginning. For many embedded systems programmers, the statement seems almost ludicrous. In their view, an interpreted language without capabilities for direct memory access and hard real-time requirements satisfaction is not an embedded language, it is a joke. There is, however, some fairly unique and novel capability for embedded system support provided in the EmbeddedJava specification that might help to quiet the laughter, at least for some types of embedded systems.

Dynamic Class Loading

In Java, classes can be loaded dynamically with the standard API. When controlled, this is a feature that can allow for the loading and dismissal of

---

4 There is a third called JavaCard that we will not discuss here.

functionality on demand, thereby providing for a kind of runtime memory footprint optimizer. However, anything dynamic is slower than anything operating in a static mode, and this feature may add to the already present nondeterminism of the Java runtime system.

Reliability

If an application using EJ makes a call to a method that is not supported, the runtime will silently fail rather than throw an exception. This allows for *operating in a degraded mode*, an essential feature of most embedded systems.

Byte Code — Smaller than Machine Code?

There have been claims made that the memory footprint of a Java application can be smaller than that of a statically compiled program. Whether this is true or not is entirely dependent not only on the instruction set of the processor, but also on the use of those instructions in a particular application and the efficiency of the compiler and linker. Nevertheless, it is certainly conceivable that this *could* be the case. Consideration must be made, however, for the size of the JVM required to run any Java code (which would of course not be required using pure object code).

Romlets and Patchlets

The EJ development environment contains tools such as JavaFilter and JavaCodeCompact for configuring different build options and for placing executable code directly into ROM or nonvolatile RAM. Such code is referred to as a *ROMlet*. Real-time software updates are called *Patchlets*.[5]

How Real Is Your Time?

Hard real-time support is simply not possible in Java due to the inherent nondeterminism of garbage collection and dynamic class loading.[6] So when speaking of EJ Java applications running on an RTOS, we are always referring to operation in a *soft* real-time mode.

JTAPI Sits on Top

Earlier we said that JTAPI sits on top of all of these APIs. As **Figure 12.1** shows, this was not just a figure of speech.

---

5 If this naming is getting a little too cute for you, blame marketing.
6 Dynamic class loading can be controlled, but it is an error-prone and not wholly reliable process.

Figure 12.1 *JTAPI Sits On Top*

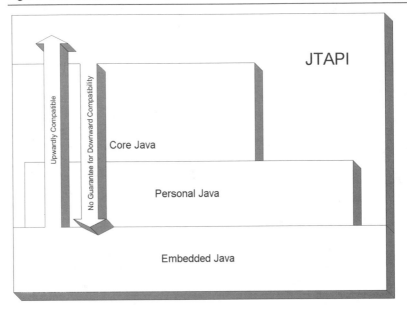

The reason JTAPI can operate just as well over core Java as it can over PersonalJava or EmbeddedJava[7] is simply the fact that the API is specified using interfaces and data types supported on all platforms. A null implementation model *allows* such flexibility where a single class library approach used by most OO class libraries may not.

On the other hand, all JTAPI implementations cannot be *guaranteed* to operate in this fashion because implementations are by definition outside the jurisdiction of the specification. In other words, vendors write the code and if they tie the lower service layers to a particular platform, board, or even API (Java or not), downward API interoperability cannot be guaranteed.

JTAPI and IP Telephony

It's nice when something good and right happens. Something inside all of us roots for the underdog and finds monopolies instinctively offensive. Some believe that the current telecom market situation is not unlike the city of Jericho — that one day the walls will come tumbling down around the feet of the big carriers. If there is any event that is likely to allow this, it is the threat of IP telephony.

---

7 Of course there are other reasons — primarily that the interfaces do not rely on classes that are missing in the lower-level APIs.

Who's Afraid of IP — and Why?

IP telephony is here, right now, today. Barriers to market entry are low, the infrastructure is already in place (the Internet) and the technology superior — hence the perceived threat. Similar to ATM and unlike traditional POTS technology for most of the phones in the world, IP Telephony allows *voice and data to travel over the same line.*[8] The other major benefit is in *bandwidth utilization.* Because audio signals are compressed during transmission, bandwidth requirements are much lower than with normal calls — between 5 and 30 percent lower. If the IP application also suppresses silence (i.e., when one person is listening — or more accurately *not talking*), the utilization rates can be even lower on a full duplex call.

How IP Telephony Works

In short, IP telephony hooks into the public telephone network on one end and the computer world (i.e., the Internet) on the other. Between the two is what is called an *IP Telephony Gateway* that compresses (and possibly digitizes) telephony signals and moves them to their destination using IP as the data transport protocol. Since IP doesn't care what kind of data it is transmitting (bytes is bytes), voice and data can travel on the same line. Just like TCP/IP, the bytes are reassembled at the other end and off we go.

Where JTAPI Plugs into IP Telephony

Java will be the language of choice and JTAPI the API[9] for many IP telephony applications. Because IP telephony is essentially a data transport mechanism, it is at a much lower level than JTAPI. And so "normal" JTAPI applications will be practically portable with any IP telephony application. Because both voice and data can travel to the consumer device, IP telephony will be a boon to consumer device applications dealing with telephone services.

---

8 In fact, it allows any data to travel across the same line — they're all just ones and zeros, right?

9 That is, if JTAPI is accepted by the Java telephony programming community.

TAPI Sᴏᴜʀᴄᴇ Cᴏᴅᴇ

This appendix contains the TAPI source code used throughout the book. References to this code are found in Chapter 5.

Assisted Telephony TAPI Code Sample

Readme.txt

```
=====================================================================
            MICROSOFT FOUNDATION CLASS LIBRARY : Assisted
=====================================================================

AppWizard has created this Assisted application for you. This
application not only demonstrates the basics of using the Microsoft
Foundation classes but is also a starting point for writing your
application.

This file contains a summary of what you will find in each of the
files that make up your Assisted application.
```

Assisted.h
> This is the main header file for the application. It includes
> other project specific headers (including Resource.h) and declares
> the CAssistedApp application **class**.

Assisted.cpp
> This is the main application source file that contains the
> application **class** CAssistedApp.

Assisted.rc
> This is a listing of all of the Microsoft Windows resources that
> the program uses. It includes the icons, bitmaps, and cursors
> that are stored in the RES subdirectory. This file can be
> directly edited in Microsoft Developer Studio.

res\Assisted.ico
> This is an icon file, which is used as the application's icon.
> This icon is included by the main resource file Assisted.rc.

res\Assisted.rc2
> This file contains resources that are not edited by Microsoft
> Developer Studio. You should place all resources not editable by
> the resource editor in this file.

Assisted.clw
> This file contains information used by ClassWizard to edit
> existing classes or add new classes. ClassWizard also uses this
> file to store information needed to create and edit message maps
> and dialog data maps and to create prototype member functions.

///

AppWizard creates one dialog class:

AssistedDlg.h, AssistedDlg.cpp - the dialog
> These files contain your CAssistedDlg **class**. This **class** defines
> the behavior of your application's main dialog. The dialog's
> template is in Assisted.rc, which can be edited in Microsoft
> Developer Studio.

///

Other standard files:

StdAfx.h, StdAfx.cpp
> These files are used to build a precompiled header (PCH) file
> named Assisted.pch and a precompiled types file named StdAfx.obj.

Resource.h
This is the standard header file, which defines new resource IDs.
Microsoft Developer Studio reads and updates this file.

//

Other notes:

AppWizard uses "TODO:" to indicate parts of the source code you
should add to or customize.

If your application uses MFC in a shared DLL, and your application
is in a language other than the operating system's current language,
you will need to copy the corresponding localized resources
MFC40XXX.DLL from the Microsoft Visual C++ CD-ROM onto the system or
system32 directory, and rename it to be MFCLOC.DLL. ("XXX" stands
for the language abbreviation. For example, MFC40DEU.DLL contains
resources translated to German.) If you don't do this, some of the
UI elements of your application will remain in the language of the
operating system.

//

stdafx.h

```
// stdafx.h : include file for standard system include files,
// or projectspecific include files that are used frequently, but arc
// changed infrequently

#if !defined(AFX_STDAFX_H__FCD853A8_27F6_11D1_823C_00207810A20C__INCLUDED_)
#define AFX_STDAFX_H__FCD853A8_27F6_11D1_823C_00207810A20C__INCLUDED_

#if _MSC_VER >= 1000
#pragma once
#endif // _MSC_VER >= 1000

#define VC_EXTRALEAN        // Exclude rarely-used stuff from Windows headers

#include <afxwin.h>         // MFC core and standard components
#include <afxext.h>         // MFC extensions
#ifndef _AFX_NO_AFXCMN_SUPPORT
#include <afxcmn.h>         // MFC support for Windows Common Controls
#endif                      // _AFX_NO_AFXCMN_SUPPORT

//{{AFX_INSERT_LOCATION}}
// Microsoft Developer Studio will insert additional declarations
// immediately before the previous line.

#endif //
!defined(AFX_STDAFX_H__FCD853A8_27F6_11D1_823C_00207810A20C__INCLUDED_)
```

resource.h

```
//{{NO_DEPENDENCIES}}
// Microsoft Developer Studio generated include file.
// Used by Assisted.rc
//
#define IDD_ASSISTED_DIALOG        102
#define IDR_MAINFRAME              128
#define IDC_EDITPhoneNumber        1000

#define IDC_DIALBUTTON             1001


// Next default values for new objects
//
#ifdef APSTUDIO_INVOKED
#ifndef APSTUDIO_READONLY_SYMBOLS
#define _APS_NEXT_RESOURCE_VALUE   129
#define _APS_NEXT_COMMAND_VALUE    32771
#define _APS_NEXT_CONTROL_VALUE    1002
#define _APS_NEXT_SYMED_VALUE      101
#endif
#endif
```

AssistedDlg.h

```
// AssistedDlg.h : header file
//

#if
  !defined(AFX_ASSISTEDDLG_H__FCD853A6_27F6_11D1_823C_00207810A20C__INCLUDED_)
#define AFX_ASSISTEDDLG_H__FCD853A6_27F6_11D1_823C_00207810A20C__INCLUDED_

#if _MSC_VER >= 1000
#pragma once
#endif // _MSC_VER >= 1000
```

```
/////////////////////////////////////////////////////////////////////
// CAssistedDlg dialog

class CAssistedDlg : public CDialog
{
// Construction
public:
    CAssistedDlg(CWnd* pParent = NULL);    // standard constructor

// Dialog Data
    //{{AFX_DATA(CAssistedDlg)
    enum { IDD = IDD_ASSISTED_DIALOG };
        // NOTE: the ClassWizard will add data members here
    //}}AFX_DATA

    // ClassWizard generated virtual function overrides
    //{{AFX_VIRTUAL(CAssistedDlg)
    protected:
    virtual void DoDataExchange(CDataExchange* pDX);    // DDX/DDV support
    //}}AFX_VIRTUAL

// Implementation
protected:
    HICON m_hIcon;

    // Generated message map functions
    //{{AFX_MSG(CAssistedDlg)
    virtual BOOL OnInitDialog();
    afx_msg void OnPaint();
    afx_msg HCURSOR OnQueryDragIcon();
    afx_msg void OnDialbutton();
    //}}AFX_MSG
    DECLARE_MESSAGE_MAP()
private:
    CString m_PhoneNumber;
};


//{{AFX_INSERT_LOCATION}}
// Microsoft Developer Studio will insert additional declarations
// immediately before the previous line.

#endif //
    !defined(AFX_ASSISTEDDLG_H__FCD853A6_27F6_11D1_823C_00207810A20C__INCLUDED_)
```

Assisted.h

```
// Assisted.h : main header file for the ASSISTED application
//


#if !defined(AFX_ASSISTED_H__FCD853A4_27F6_11D1_823C_00207810A20C__INCLUDED_)
#define AFX_ASSISTED_H__FCD853A4_27F6_11D1_823C_00207810A20C__INCLUDED_

#if _MSC_VER >= 1000
#pragma once
#endif // _MSC_VER >= 1000

#ifndef __AFXWIN_H__
    #error include 'stdafx.h' before including this file for PCH
#endif

#include "resource.h"      // main symbols

/////////////////////////////////////////////////////////////////////////////
// CAssistedApp:
// See Assisted.cpp for the implementation of this class
//

class CAssistedApp : public CWinApp
{
public:
    CAssistedApp();

// Overrides
    // ClassWizard generated virtual function overrides
    //{{AFX_VIRTUAL(CAssistedApp)
    public:
    virtual BOOL InitInstance();
    //}}AFX_VIRTUAL

// Implementation

    //{{AFX_MSG(CAssistedApp)
        // NOTE - the ClassWizard will add and remove member functions here.
        // DO NOT EDIT what you see in these blocks of generated code !
    //}}AFX_MSG
    DECLARE_MESSAGE_MAP()
};
```

//

```cpp
//{{AFX_INSERT_LOCATION}}
// Microsoft Developer Studio will insert additional declarations immediately
// before the previous line.

#endif //
  !defined(AFX_ASSISTED_H__FCD853A4_27F6_11D1_823C_00207810A20C__INCLUDED_)
```

stdafx.cpp

```cpp
// stdafx.cpp : source file that includes just the standard includes
// Assisted.pch will be the pre-compiled header
// stdafx.obj will contain the pre-compiled type information

#include "stdafx.h"
```

AssistedDlg.cpp

```cpp
// AssistedDlg.cpp : implementation file
//

#include "stdafx.h"
#include "Assisted.h"
#include "AssistedDlg.h"
#include <tapi.h>

#ifdef _DEBUG
#define new DEBUG_NEW
#undef THIS_FILE
static char THIS_FILE[] = __FILE__;
#endif

/////////////////////////////////////////////////////////////////////////////
// CAssistedDlg dialog

CAssistedDlg::CAssistedDlg(CWnd* pParent /*=NULL*/)
  : CDialog(CAssistedDlg::IDD, pParent)
{
  //{{AFX_DATA_INIT(CAssistedDlg)
    // NOTE: the ClassWizard will add member initialization here
  //}}AFX_DATA_INIT
  // Note that LoadIcon does not require a subsequent DestroyIcon
  // in Win32
  m_hIcon = AfxGetApp()->LoadIcon(IDR_MAINFRAME);
}
```

```
void CAssistedDlg::DoDataExchange(CDataExchange* pDX)
{
    CDialog::DoDataExchange(pDX);
    //{{AFX_DATA_MAP(CAssistedDlg)
        // NOTE: the ClassWizard will add DDX and DDV calls here
    //}}AFX_DATA_MAP
}


BEGIN_MESSAGE_MAP(CAssistedDlg, CDialog)
    //{{AFX_MSG_MAP(CAssistedDlg)
    ON_WM_PAINT()
    ON_WM_QUERYDRAGICON()
    ON_BN_CLICKED(IDC_DIALBUTTON, OnDialbutton)
    //}}AFX_MSG_MAP
END_MESSAGE_MAP()


/////////////////////////////////////////////////////////////////
// CAssistedDlg message handlers

BOOL CAssistedDlg::OnInitDialog()
{
    CDialog::OnInitDialog();

    // Set the icon for this dialog. The framework does this
    // automatically when the application's main window is not
    // a dialog
    SetIcon(m_hIcon, TRUE);             // Set big icon
    SetIcon(m_hIcon, FALSE);            // Set small icon

    // TODO: Add extra initialization here

    m_PhoneNumber = "522-1094";

    return TRUE; // return TRUE  unless you set the focus to a control
}

// If you add a minimize button to your dialog, you will need the
// code below to draw the icon. For MFC applications using the
// document/view model, this is automatically done for you by the
// framework.

void CAssistedDlg::OnPaint()
{
  if (IsIconic())
  {
      CPaintDC dc(this); // device context for painting
```

```cpp
    SendMessage(WM_ICONERASEBKGND, (WPARAM) dc.GetSafeHdc(), 0);

    // Center icon in client rectangle
    int cxIcon = GetSystemMetrics(SM_CXICON);
    int cyIcon = GetSystemMetrics(SM_CYICON);
    CRect rect;
    GetClientRect(&rect);
    int x = (rect.Width() - cxIcon + 1) / 2;
    int y = (rect.Height() - cyIcon + 1) / 2;

    // Draw the icon
    dc.DrawIcon(x, y, m_hIcon);
  }
  else
  {
    CDialog::OnPaint();
  }
}

// The system calls this to obtain the cursor to display while the
// user drags the minimized window.
HCURSOR CAssistedDlg::OnQueryDragIcon()
{
  return (HCURSOR) m_hIcon;
}

void CAssistedDlg::OnDialbutton()
{
  // TODO: Add your control notification handler code here

  char str[60];
  char which[15];
  LONG ret;
  const char* s = ">> SUCCESS! <<";
  const char* f = ">> FAILURE! <<";

  if ( ret = tapiRequestMakeCall( m_PhoneNumber, NULL, NULL, 0 )
     != TAPIERR_NOREQUESTRECIPIENT )
    ::strcpy( which, s );
  else
    ::strcpy( which, f );

  ::sprintf( str, "%s tapiRequestMakeCall()
     return value ==> %d", which, ret);
  AfxMessageBox( str );
}
```

Assisted.cpp

```cpp
// Assisted.cpp : Defines the class behaviors for the application.
//

#include "stdafx.h"
#include "Assisted.h"
#include "AssistedDlg.h"

#ifdef _DEBUG
#define new DEBUG_NEW
#undef THIS_FILE
static char THIS_FILE[] = __FILE__;
#endif

/////////////////////////////////////////////////////////////////////////
// CAssistedApp

BEGIN_MESSAGE_MAP(CAssistedApp, CWinApp)
    //{{AFX_MSG_MAP(CAssistedApp)
        // NOTE - the ClassWizard will add and remove mapping macros
        // here. DO NOT EDIT what you see in these blocks of generated
        // code!
    //}}AFX_MSG
    ON_COMMAND(ID_HELP, CWinApp::OnHelp)
END_MESSAGE_MAP()

/////////////////////////////////////////////////////////////////////////
/////////
// CAssistedApp construction

CAssistedApp::CAssistedApp()
{
    // TODO: add construction code here,
    // Place all significant initialization in InitInstance
}

/////////////////////////////////////////////////////////////////////////
// The one and only CAssistedApp object

CAssistedApp theApp;
```

```
/////////////////////////////////////////////////////////////////////
// CAssistedApp initialization

BOOL CAssistedApp::InitInstance()
{
    // Standard initialization
    // If you are not using these features and wish to reduce the
    // size of your final executable, you should remove from the
    // following the specific initialization routines you do not
    // need.

#ifdef _AFXDLL
    Enable3dControls();      // Call this when using MFC in a shared DLL
#else
    Enable3dControlsStatic();    // Call this when linking to MFC
                                 // statically
#endif

    CAssistedDlg dlg;
    m_pMainWnd = &dlg;
    int nResponse = dlg.DoModal();
    if (nResponse == IDOK)
    {
        // TODO: Place code here to handle when the dialog is
        //  dismissed with OK
    }
    else if (nResponse == IDCANCEL)
    {
        // TODO: Place code here to handle when the dialog is
        //  dismissed with Cancel
    }

    // Since the dialog has been closed, return FALSE so that we exit
    // the application, rather than start the application's message
    // pump.
        return FALSE;
}
```

Basic Telephony TAPI Code Sample

Readme.txt

```
=====================================================================
            MICROSOFT FOUNDATION CLASS LIBRARY : Basic
=====================================================================
```

AppWizard has created this Basic application for you. This application not only demonstrates the basics of using the Microsoft Foundation classes but is also a starting point for writing your application.

This file contains a summary of what you will find in each of the files that make up your Basic application.

Basic.h
   This is the main header file for the application. It includes other project specific headers (including Resource.h) and declares the CBasicApp application **class**.

Basic.cpp
   This is the main application source file that contains the application **class** CBasicApp.

Basic.rc
   This is a listing of all of the Microsoft Windows resources that the program uses. It includes the icons, bitmaps, and cursors that are stored in the RES subdirectory. This file can be directly edited in Microsoft Developer Studio.

res\Basic.ico
   This is an icon file, which is used as the application's icon. This icon is included by the main resource file Basic.rc.

res\Basic.rc2
   This file contains resources that are not edited by Microsoft Developer Studio. You should place all resources not editable by the resource editor in this file.

Basic.clw
   This file contains information used by ClassWizard to edit existing classes or add new classes. ClassWizard also uses this file to store information needed to create and edit message maps and dialog data maps and to create prototype member functions.

//

AppWizard creates one dialog **class**:

BasicDlg.h, BasicDlg.cpp - the dialog
   These files contain your CBasicDlg **class**. This **class** defines the
   behavior of your application's main dialog. The dialog's template
   is in Basic.rc, which can be edited in Microsoft Developer Studio.

//
Other standard files:

StdAfx.h, StdAfx.cpp
   These files are used to build a precompiled header (PCH) file
   named Basic.pch and a precompiled types file named StdAfx.obj.

Resource.h
   This is the standard header file, which defines new resource IDs.
   Microsoft Developer Studio reads and updates this file.

//
Other notes:

AppWizard uses "TODO:" to indicate parts of the source code you
should add to or customize.

If your application uses MFC in a shared DLL, and your application
is in a language other than the operating system's current language,
you will need to copy the corresponding localized resources
MFC40XXX.DLL from the Microsoft Visual C++ CD-ROM onto the system or
system32 directory, and rename it to be MFCLOC.DLL. ("XXX" stands
for the language abbreviation. For example, MFC40DEU.DLL contains
resources translated to German.) If you don't do this, some of the
UI elements of your application will remain in the language of the
operating system.

//

stdafx.h

```
// stdafx.h : include file for standard system include files,
// or project specific include files that are used frequently, but
// are changed infrequently
//


#if !defined(AFX_STDAFX_H__0E04D5DB_28BA_11D1_823D_00207810A20C__INCLUDED_)
#define AFX_STDAFX_H__0E04D5DB_28BA_11D1_823D_00207810A20C__INCLUDED_

#if _MSC_VER >= 1000
#pragma once
#endif // _MSC_VER >= 1000

#define VC_EXTRALEAN        // Exclude rarely-used stuff from Windows headers

#include <afxwin.h>         // MFC core and standard components
#include <afxext.h>         // MFC extensions
#ifndef _AFX_NO_AFXCMN_SUPPORT
#include <afxcmn.h>          // MFC support for Windows Common Controls
#endif // _AFX_NO_AFXCMN_SUPPORT


//{{AFX_INSERT_LOCATION}}
// Microsoft Developer Studio will insert additional declarations
// immediately before the previous line.

#endif //
!defined(AFX_STDAFX_H__0E04D5DB_28BA_11D1_823D_00207810A20C__INCLUDED_)
```

resource.h

```
//{{NO_DEPENDENCIES}}
// Microsoft Developer Studio generated include file.
// Used by Basic.rc
//
#define IDD_BASIC_DIALOG            102
#define IDR_MAINFRAME               128
#define IDC_DIALBUTTON              1000
#define IDC_HANGUPBUTTON            1001
#define IDC_LISTTapiMessages        1002
#define IDC_EDITPhoneNumber         1003
#define IDC_BUTTONClearListBox      1004
```

```
// Next default values for new objects
//
#ifdef APSTUDIO_INVOKED
#ifndef APSTUDIO_READONLY_SYMBOLS
#define _APS_NEXT_RESOURCE_VALUE        129
#define _APS_NEXT_COMMAND_VALUE         32771
#define _APS_NEXT_CONTROL_VALUE         1005
#define _APS_NEXT_SYMED_VALUE           101
#endif
#endif
```

BasicDlg.h

```
// BasicDlg.h : header file
//

#if !defined(AFX_BASICDLG_H__0E04D5D9_28BA_11D1_823D_00207810A20C__INCLUDED_)
#define AFX_BASICDLG_H__0E04D5D9_28BA_11D1_823D_00207810A20C__INCLUDED_

#if _MSC_VER >= 1000
#pragma once
#endif // _MSC_VER >= 1000

#include <tapi.h>

#define DEFAULT_PHONE_NUMBER            "522-1094"


static void stuffTapiListBox( const char* messageStr );


/////////////////////////////////////////////////////////////////////////////
// CBasicDlg dialog

class CBasicDlg : public CDialog
{
// Construction
public:

    static void longToVersionNumber( DWORD num, char* verStr );

    static void CALLBACK tapiMessageHandler(
                DWORD   hDevice,
                DWORD   dwMessage,
                DWORD   dwInstance,
                DWORD   dwParam1,
```

```
                      DWORD   dwParam2,
                      DWORD   dwParam3   );


    CBasicDlg(CWnd* pParent = NULL);    // standard constructor

    CListBox* m_pListBox;



// Dialog Data
    //{{AFX_DATA(CBasicDlg)
    enum { IDD = IDD_BASIC_DIALOG };
    //}}AFX_DATA


    // ClassWizard generated virtual function overrides
    //{{AFX_VIRTUAL(CBasicDlg)
    protected:
    virtual void DoDataExchange(CDataExchange* pDX);    // DDX/DDV support
    //}}AFX_VIRTUAL

// Implementation
protected:

    HICON m_hIcon;

    // Generated message map functions
    //{{AFX_MSG(CBasicDlg)
    virtual BOOL OnInitDialog();
    afx_msg void OnPaint();
    afx_msg HCURSOR OnQueryDragIcon();
    afx_msg void OnDialbutton();
    afx_msg void OnHangupButton();
    afx_msg void OnButtonClearListBox();
    //}}AFX_MSG
    DECLARE_MESSAGE_MAP()

private:

    HCALL m_tapiCallHandle;
    LINEEXTENSIONID m_LineExtensionId;
    DWORD m_APIversion;
    HLINEAPP m_tapiLineAppHandle;
    HLINE m_tapiLineHandle;
    DWORD m_LinesOnMachine;
    LINECALLPARAMS m_tapiLineCallParms;
    CString m_PhoneNumber;
};
```

```
//{{AFX_INSERT_LOCATION}}
// Microsoft Developer Studio will insert additional declarations immediately
// before the previous line.

#endif //
    !defined(AFX_BASICDLG_H__0E04D5D9_28BA_11D1_823D_00207810A20C__INCLUDED_)
```

Basic.h

```
// Basic.h : main header file for the BASIC application
//

#if !defined(AFX_BASIC_H__0E04D5D7_28BA_11D1_823D_00207810A20C__INCLUDED_)
#define AFX_BASIC_H__0E04D5D7_28BA_11D1_823D_00207810A20C__INCLUDED_

#if _MSC_VER >= 1000
#pragma once
#endif // _MSC_VER >= 1000

#ifndef __AFXWIN_H__
    #error include 'stdafx.h' before including this file for PCH
#endif

#include "resource.h"        // main symbols

/////////////////////////////////////////////////////////////////////////////
// CBasicApp:
// See Basic.cpp for the implementation of this class
//

//HANDLE s_tapiCommHandle;   //HANDLE s_tapiCommHandle = 0;

class CBasicApp : public CWinApp
{
public:
    CBasicApp();

// Overrides
    // ClassWizard generated virtual function overrides
    //{{AFX_VIRTUAL(CBasicApp)
    public:
    virtual BOOL InitInstance();
    //}}AFX_VIRTUAL
```

```
// Implementation

  //{{AFX_MSG(CBasicApp)
     // NOTE - the ClassWizard will add and remove member functions here.
     // DO NOT EDIT what you see in these blocks of generated code !
  //}}AFX_MSG
  DECLARE_MESSAGE_MAP()
};



/////////////////////////////////////////////////////////////////////

//{{AFX_INSERT_LOCATION}}
// Microsoft Developer Studio will insert additional declarations
// immediately before the previous line.

#endif //
   !defined(AFX_BASIC_H__0E04D5D7_28BA_11D1_823D_00207810A20C__INCLUDED_)
```

stdafx.cpp

```
// stdafx.cpp : source file that includes just the standard includes
// Basic.pch will be the pre-compiled header
// stdafx.obj will contain the pre-compiled type information

#include "stdafx.h"
```

BasicDlg.cpp

```
// BasicDlg.cpp : implementation file
//

#include "stdafx.h"
#include "Basic.h"
#include "BasicDlg.h"

#ifdef _DEBUG
#define new DEBUG_NEW
#undef THIS_FILE
static char THIS_FILE[] = __FILE__;
#endif
```

```
/////////////////////////////////////////////////////////////////
// CBasicDlg dialog


CBasicDlg::CBasicDlg(CWnd* pParent /*=NULL*/)
   : CDialog(CBasicDlg::IDD, pParent)
{
   //{{AFX_DATA_INIT(CBasicDlg)
   //}}AFX_DATA_INIT
   // Note that LoadIcon does not require a subsequent DestroyIcon in
   // Win32
   m_hIcon = AfxGetApp()->LoadIcon(IDR_MAINFRAME);
}


void CBasicDlg::DoDataExchange(CDataExchange* pDX)
{
   CDialog::DoDataExchange(pDX);
   //{{AFX_DATA_MAP(CBasicDlg)
   //}}AFX_DATA_MAP
}


BEGIN_MESSAGE_MAP(CBasicDlg, CDialog)
   //{{AFX_MSG_MAP(CBasicDlg)
   ON_WM_PAINT()
   ON_WM_QUERYDRAGICON()
   ON_BN_CLICKED(IDC_DIALBUTTON, OnDialbutton)
   ON_BN_CLICKED(IDC_HANGUPBUTTON, OnHangupButton)
   ON_BN_CLICKED(IDC_BUTTONClearListBox, OnButtonClearListBox)
   //}}AFX_MSG_MAP
END_MESSAGE_MAP()



HANDLE s_tapiCommHandle = NULL;



/////////////////////////////////////////////////////////////////
// CBasicDlg message handlers


BOOL CBasicDlg::OnInitDialog()
{
   CDialog::OnInitDialog();
```

```
// Set the icon for this dialog. The framework does this
// automatically when the application's main window is not a
// dialog
SetIcon(m_hIcon, TRUE);                         // Set big icon
SetIcon(m_hIcon, FALSE);                // Set small icon

// TODO: Add extra initialization here


m_pListBox = (CListBox*)GetDlgItem( IDC_LISTTapiMessages );

// initialize TAPI...

m_tapiLineAppHandle = NULL;
m_tapiLineHandle = NULL;
m_tapiCallHandle = NULL;

if ( LONG answer = lineInitialize(
        &m_tapiLineAppHandle,
        AfxGetApp()->m_hInstance,
        (LINECALLBACK)&CBasicDlg::tapiMessageHandler,
        "Basic Telephony",
        &m_LinesOnMachine ) < 0 ) {

            ::AfxMessageBox("ERROR initializing TAPI subsystem.
            Exiting Application.");
            PostMessage(WM_CLOSE);
}
else {
    char msg[50];
    ::sprintf( msg, "TAPI subsystem initialized.
        Return: %d, # lines: %d", answer, m_LinesOnMachine );
        ::AfxMessageBox( msg );
}

// find an acceptable API version & line to use...

char verBuf[70];
LONG ans;

// this code works only if there is one TAPI device on the computer.
// If there are more,
// place the call to lineNegotiateAPIVersion in a loop...
```

```
if ( (ans = lineNegotiateAPIVersion( m_tapiLineAppHandle, 0,
        MAKELONG(3,1), MAKELONG(4,1),
        &m_APIversion, &m_LineExtensionId )) < 0 ) {
            ::sprintf( verBuf,
                "ERROR negotiating API version. ret: %d.
            Exiting Application.", ans );
            ::AfxMessageBox( verBuf );
            PostMessage(WM_CLOSE);
}
else {
        char verBuf[50], finalBuf[75];
        longToVersionNumber( m_APIversion, verBuf );
        ::sprintf( finalBuf,
            "Found version %s of TAPI on this machine", verBuf );
        ::AfxMessageBox( finalBuf );

        if ( (ans = lineOpen( m_tapiLineAppHandle, 0,
            &m_tapiLineHandle, m_APIversion, 0, (DWORD)this,
            LINECALLPRIVILEGE_OWNER | LINECALLPRIVILEGE_MONITOR,
            LINEMEDIAMODE_DATAMODEM, NULL )) != 0 ) {
        ::AfxMessageBox( "ERROR opening line." );
        PostMessage(WM_CLOSE);
        }
        else {

            char buffedOut[128];
            ::sprintf( buffedOut,
                ">> SUCCESS << opening line. Line Handle: %d",
                m_tapiLineHandle );
                ::AfxMessageBox( buffedOut );

            // set the LINEPARMS struct. this is NOT optional, as
            // the docs say it is...

            ::memset( &m_tapiLineCallParms, 0,
                sizeof( LINECALLPARAMS ) );
            m_tapiLineCallParms.dwTotalSize =
                sizeof( LINECALLPARAMS );
            m_tapiLineCallParms.dwMinRate = 9600;
            m_tapiLineCallParms.dwMaxRate = 9600;
            m_tapiLineCallParms.dwMediaMode =
                LINEMEDIAMODE_DATAMODEM;
        }
    }
```

```
    m_pListBox->InsertString( -1, "TAPI subsystem Initialized!!");

    return TRUE;  return TRUE  unless you set the focus to a control
}


// If you add a minimize button to your dialog, you will need the
// code below to draw the icon.  For MFC applications using the
// document/view model, this is automatically done for you by the
// framework.

void CBasicDlg::OnPaint()
{
    if (IsIconic())
    {
        CPaintDC dc(this); // device context for painting

        SendMessage(WM_ICONERASEBKGND, (WPARAM) dc.GetSafeHdc(), 0);

        // Center icon in client rectangle
        int cxIcon = GetSystemMetrics(SM_CXICON);
        int cyIcon = GetSystemMetrics(SM_CYICON);
        CRect rect;
        GetClientRect(&rect);
        int x = (rect.Width() - cxIcon + 1) / 2;
        int y = (rect.Height() - cyIcon + 1) / 2;

        // Draw the icon
        dc.DrawIcon(x, y, m_hIcon);
    }
    else
    {
        CDialog::OnPaint();
    }
}


// The system calls this to obtain the cursor to display while the
// user drags the minimized window.
HCURSOR CBasicDlg::OnQueryDragIcon()
{
    return (HCURSOR) m_hIcon;
}


void CBasicDlg::OnDialbutton()
{
    // TODO: Add your control notification handler code here
```

```
LONG answer;

GetDlgItemText( IDC_EDITPhoneNumber, m_PhoneNumber );
if ( m_PhoneNumber.GetAllocLength() < 7 ) {
   ::AfxMessageBox("ERROR: phone number not big enough");
   //m_PhoneNumber = DEFAULT_PHONE_NUMBER;
   return;
}
else {
   ::AfxMessageBox("About to Dial number: " + m_PhoneNumber);

   // make the call...
   if ( (answer = lineMakeCall( m_tapiLineHandle,
                    (LPHCALL)&m_tapiCallHandle,
                    (LPCSTR)m_PhoneNumber,
                    0,
                    &m_tapiLineCallParms )) < 0 ) {
      char buffy[256];
      ::sprintf( buffy, "ERROR >> 0x%x << dialing number: %s",
         answer, m_PhoneNumber );
            ::AfxMessageBox( buffy );

/*

         possible errors...
         LINEERR_ADDRESSBLOCKED, LINEERR_INVALLINEHANDLE,
         LINEERR_DEARERMODEUNAVAIL, LINEERR_INVALLINESTATE,
         LINEERR_CALLUNAVAIL, LINEERR_INVALMEDIAMODE,
         LINEERR_DIALBILLING, LINEERR_INVALPARAM,
         LINEERR_DIALDIALTONE, LINEERR_INVALPOINTER,
         LINEERR_DIALPROMPT, LINEERR_INVALRATE, LINEERR_DIALQUIET,
         LINEERR_NOMEM, LINEERR_INUSE, LINEERR_OPERATIONFAILED,
         LINEERR_INVALADDRESS, LINEERR_OPERATIONUNAVAIL,
         LINEERR_INVALADDRESSID, LINEERR_RATEUNAVAIL,
         LINEERR_INVALADDRESSMODE, LINEERR_RESOURCEUNAVAIL,
         LINEERR_INVALBEARERMODE, LINEERR_STRUCTURETOOSMALL,
         LINEERR_INVALCALLPARAMS, LINEERR_UNINITIALIZED,
         LINEERR_INVALCOUNTRYCODE, LINEERR_USERUSERINFOTOOBIG.

      */
   }
   else {
      ::AfxMessageBox(">> SUCCESS << requesting number: "
         + m_PhoneNumber + " to be dialed.");
   }
}
}
```

```cpp
void CALLBACK CBasicDlg::tapiMessageHandler(
                          DWORD  hDevice,
                          DWORD  dwMessage,
                          DWORD  dwInstance,
                          DWORD  dwParam1,
                          DWORD  dwParam2,
                          DWORD  dwParam3)
{
   switch ( dwMessage )
   {
      case LINE_CALLSTATE:
      {
         switch ( dwParam1 )
         {
            case LINECALLSTATE_IDLE:
            {
               stuffTapiListBox( "-> LINECALLSTATE_IDLE" );

               lineDeallocateCall((HCALL)hDevice);
               break;
            }

            case LINECALLSTATE_CONNECTED:
            {
               LPVARSTRING lpVarString;
               LONG answer;
               int msgSize = sizeof(VARSTRING) + 2048;

               stuffTapiListBox( "-> LINECALLSTATE_CONNECTED" );

               if ( (lpVarString = (LPVARSTRING)::LocalAlloc(
                  0, msgSize )) != NULL ) {

                  lpVarString->dwTotalSize = msgSize;

                  if ( (answer = lineGetID( 0,    //m_tapiLineHandle,
                           0, (HCALL)hDevice,
                           (DWORD)LINECALLSELECT_CALL,
                           lpVarString, "comm/datamodem" )) != 0 ) {
                     char buffy[256];
                     ::sprintf( buffy, "ERROR >> 0x%x << getting
                        lineID", answer );
                     ::AfxMessageBox( buffy );
                     /*
```

```
                        LINEERR_INVALLINEHANDLE, LINEERR_NOMEM,
                        LINEERR_INVALADDRESSID,
                        LINEERR_OPERATIONUNAVAIL,
                        LINEERR_INVALCALLHANDLE,
                        LINEERR_OPERATIONFAILED,
                        LINEERR_INVALCALLSELECT,
                        LINEERR_RESOURCEUNAVAIL, LINEERR INVALPOINTER,
                        LINEERR_STRUCTURETOOSMALL, LINEERR_NODEVICE,
                        LINEERR_UNINITIALIZED.
                        */
                }
                else ::AfxMessageBox(
                    ">> SUCCESS << Got line ID" );


                s_tapiCommHandle = *((LPHANDLE)lpVarString);

                char buffy[256];
                ::sprintf( buffy, "s_tapiCommHandle >> %d <<",
                    s_tapiCommHandle );
                ::AfxMessageBox( buffy );

                ::LocalFree( lpVarString);
            }

        break;
    } //LINECALLSTATE_CONNECTED:


    case LINECALLSTATE_ACCEPTED:
    {
        stuffTapiListBox( "-> LINECALLSTATE_ACCEPTED" );

        break;
    }


    case LINECALLSTATE_PROCEEDING:
    {
        stuffTapiListBox( "-> LINECALLSTATE_PROCEEDING" );

        break;
    }
```

```
        case LINECALLSTATE_OFFERING:
        {
            stuffTapiListBox( "-> LINECALLSTATE_OFFERING" );

            break;
        }


        case LINECALLSTATE_DIALTONE:
        {
            stuffTapiListBox( "-> LINECALLSTATE_DIALTONE" );

            break;
        }


        case LINECALLSTATE_DIALING:
        {
            stuffTapiListBox( "-> LINECALLSTATE_DIALING" );

            break;
        }

        case LINECALLSTATE_BUSY:
        {
            stuffTapiListBox( "-> LINECALLSTATE_BUSY" );

            break;
        }

        case LINECALLSTATE_DISCONNECTED:
        {
            stuffTapiListBox( "-> LINECALLSTATE_DISCONNECTED" );

            break;
        }

    }

    break;
    }
    }
}
```

```
void CBasicDlg::longToVersionNumber(DWORD num, char* verStr)
{
   WORD low, high;

   low = LOWORD(num);
   high = HIWORD(num);
   ::sprintf( verStr, "%d.%d", high, low );
}




void stuffTapiListBox( const char* messageStr )
{
   ((CBasicDlg*)::AfxGetMainWnd())->m_pListBox->InsertString(
      -1, messageStr );
}




void CBasicDlg::OnHangupButton()
{
   // TODO: Add your control notification handler code here

   // drop the call...
   if ( m_tapiCallHandle != NULL ) {

      if ( lineDrop( m_tapiCallHandle, NULL, 0 ) > 0 )
         ::AfxMessageBox(">> SUCCESS << dropping call");
      else
         ::AfxMessageBox("ERROR: dropping call");
   }
   else ::AfxMessageBox("call handle is NULL");
}




void CBasicDlg::OnButtonClearListBox()
{
   // TODO: Add your control notification handler code here

   m_pListBox->ResetContent( );
}
```

```
// Basic.cpp : Defines the class behaviors for the application.
//

#include "stdafx.h"
#include "Basic.h"
#include "BasicDlg.h"

#ifdef _DEBUG
#define new DEBUG_NEW
#undef THIS_FILE
static char THIS_FILE[] = __FILE__;
#endif

/////////////////////////////////////////////////////////////////////
// CBasicApp

BEGIN_MESSAGE_MAP(CBasicApp, CWinApp)
    //{{AFX_MSG_MAP(CBasicApp)
        // NOTE - the ClassWizard will add and remove mapping macros
        // here. DO NOT EDIT what you see in these blocks of generated
        // code!
    //}}AFX_MSG
    ON_COMMAND(ID_HELP, CWinApp::OnHelp)
END_MESSAGE_MAP()

/////////////////////////////////////////////////////////////////////
/////////
// CBasicApp construction

CBasicApp::CBasicApp()
{
    // TODO: add construction code here,
    // Place all significant initialization in InitInstance
}

/////////////////////////////////////////////////////////////////////
// The one and only CBasicApp object

CBasicApp theApp;


/////////////////////////////////////////////////////////////////////
// CBasicApp initialization
```

```
BOOL CBasicApp::InitInstance()
{
   // Standard initialization
   // If you are not using these features and wish to reduce the
   // size of your final executable, you should remove from the
   // following the specific initialization routines you do not
   // need.

#ifdef _AFXDLL
   Enable3dControls();    // Call this when using MFC in a shared DLL
#else
   Enable3dControlsStatic();   // Call when linking to MFC statically
#endif

   CBasicDlg dlg;
   m_pMainWnd = &dlg;
   int nResponse = dlg.DoModal();
   if (nResponse == IDOK)
   {
      // TODO: Place code here to handle when the dialog is
      //   dismissed with OK
   }

   // Since the dialog has been closed, return FALSE so that we exit
   // the application, rather than start the application's message
   // pump.
   return FALSE;
}
```

INDEX

A
accepting a call, 312
ACD
   see automated call distribution
ACDAddress Interface, 360
ACDAddressObserver Interface, 367
ACDConnection Interface, 363
ACDManager Interface, 365
ACDManagerConnection Interface, 366
Ada, 34, 36, 49
adapter classes, 188
Address
   capabilities implemented, 255
   implementation, 239
   Interface, 62
AddressObserver Interface
   defined, 89
   implementation, 272
   related events, 89
Agent Interface, 342

AgentTerminal Interface, 346
AgentTerminalObserver Interface, 347
ANI, 6
annexes, 49
API
   and general requirements, 129
   and scalability, 134
   as a standard, 126
   Java Collaboration, 53
   Java media, 52
   Java Media Framework, 53
   Java Speech, 54
   layer, 177, 226
application programmer, 514
Application Programming Boundary, 207
architecture
   hardware, 491
   network, 492
   software, 493
   two-tier, 137
   three-tier, 142, 145

aspect, 386
associative class, 504
asynchronous communication
    and threads, 9
    telephony API support for, 146
asynchronous notification
    implementing, 190, 444
    lack of support for, 410
automated call distribution, 343

B

bandwidth utilization, 527
bus
    address, 24
    control, 24
    data, 24
    defined, 24
    signal control, 27

C

C++
    and smart pointers, 424
    language, 34
    language mappings to Java, 46
    namespaces, 39
callback
    and class Callback, 206
    and function pointers, 432, 435
    function in TAPI, 162, 286
    in Java, 38
    in Smalltalk, 36
    reflection vs. interfaces, 432
    state machine pattern, 471
CallCenterAddress Interface, 355
CallCenterCall Interface, 356
CallCenterCallObserver Interface, 359
Call Center Capabilities, 368
Call Center Events, 368
CallCenterProvider Interface, 354
CallCenterTrunk Interface, 358
CallControlAddress Interface, 298
CallControlAddressObserver Interface, 320
CallControlCall Interface, 300
CallControlCallObserver Interface, 320

Call Control Capabilities, 324
CallControlConnection Interface, 308
Call Control Events, 322
CallControlForwarding class, 295
call control policies, 21
CallControlTerminalConnection
    Interface, 316
CallControlTerminal Interface, 313
CallControlTerminalObserver Interface, 321
Call Interface
    capabilities implemented, 253
    `connect()` method, 68, 70, 74, 86,
        199, 213, 286
    defined, 66
    implementation, 242
    state definitions, 67
    state transitions, 67
call model, 12
CallObserver Interface
    defined, 91
    implementation, 273
    in action, 286
    related events, 91
cardinality
    and events, 410
    relationships, 79, 498
cause code, 113, 185
central office (CO), 5
CENTREX, 5
channel, 25, 28
ComponentCapabilities Interface, 335
ComponentGroupCapabilities Interface,
    335
ComponentGroup Interface, 328
Component Interface, 327
computer telephony, 6
concrete class, 505
concurrency
    in Ada, 37
    in general, 35
    in Java, 38
    in requirements, 481
    in Smalltalk, 36
conferencing a call, 302

Connection Interface
  capabilities implemented, 256
  defined, 71
  `disconnect()` method, 75, 199
  event/state relationship 73
  implementation, 248
  state transitions, 72
  when connected, 68
construction phase, 509
consultation call, 304
CORBA
  and language, platform independence,
    132
  Event Services, 419
  service specification model, 17
coverage policies, 8
CTI, 149

D

data modeling, 498
data transport protocol, 18, 21, 43
Delegation Model, 392
dependency
  in Java, 385
Dialogic, 152
distributed programming, 513
DNIS, 6
do not disturb call, 315
domain engineering, 516
domain objects, 54
dropping a call, 304
DTMF tones, 34, 77, 339

E

ECTF, 149
Eiffel
  and contracts, 130
  and multiple inheritance, xx
embedded systems, 523
encapsulation, 497
Ev
  capabilities implemented, 260
  Interface, 113

event
  and cause codes, 113
  and meta codes, 113
  delivery in Java, 394
  general definition, 382
  generation, 116
  handler, 110, 383, 401
  handler implementation in JTAPI, 185
  in CORBA, 419
  in Smalltalk, 395
  lack of adequate support in Java, 407
  management models, 42
  post-mortem, 455
  registration and notification, 61, 382
  relationship to JTAPI state transitions,
    111
exceptions
  overhead of, 117
  structured, 201
execution environment, 522
extension, 498

F

finite state machine
  and event-driven APIs, 167
  and JTAPI observable objects, 110
  objects implemented as, 54
  pattern, 451
  used in an API, 153
functional subsystem description, 512
function signature
  and polymorphism, 41

G

garbage collection
  and Java, 43
generics
  and polymorphism, 443
  in Java, 436
graph structures
  directed, 474
  tree, 474
  vine, 477

I

idiom
    "application burden" approach, 191
    defined, 424
    difference between pattern, 424
infrastructure layer, 177, 180
infrastructure programming, 516
inline methods, 428
interfaces
    abstract, 90
    and classes, 59, 103
    and multiple inheritance in Java, 40
    and polymorphism in Java, 40
    inferior to multiple inheritance, 390
    vs. abstract classes, 519
interrupt service routine, 147
intersect class, 504
IP telephony, 526
IRQ, 26
ISA, 25
ISDN, 5

J

J/Direct, 199, 202
Java
    borrowed language features, 34
    EmbeddedJava. 523
    events, 397
    implementation of Smalltalk observer
        pattern, 184
    interfacing with C, 198
    language subsets, 523
    PersonalJava, 523
    sandbox model, 55
JIT compilers, 44
JNI, 198
joining a call, 318
JTAPI
    and blocks, 465
    and IP telephony, 526
    application/applet, 278
    architecture, 54
    binding, 194
    capabilities, 99
    core components, 60

JTAPI, *(cont.)*
    events, 108, 112
    handler, implementing, 106, 268
    implementation, 15, 125
    incoming call, 14
    introduced, 10
    library, 177
    message management model, 184
    not a threaded API, 171
    outgoing call, 12
    package hierarchy, 56
    scalability, 16
    security model, 55
    specification, 54
    standard exceptions, 118
JtapiPeer
    implementation, 230
    Interface, 94
JtapiPeerFactory
    class, 93
    implementation, 228

L

late binding, 443
leaving a call, 318
library programmer, 208, 211, 514
library programming interface, 194
link class, 504
LISP, 44
listener, 393, 403
liveliness, 446

M

marker interface, 320
Media
    Events, 342
    rewinding, 339
    starting, 339
    stopping, 339
MediaCallObserver Interface, 340
MediaTerminalConnectionCapabilities,
    341
MediaTerminalConnection Interface, 338
memory
    leaks, 44

Message Management Model, 413
meta code, 113, 185
MFC, 157
mobile agents, 145
modems, 17
multiple inheritance
    simulating in Java, 431
multitasking
    functions, 152
    vs. multiprocessing, 9

N

native methods
    and JNI, 198
    overview, 43
navigation, 509
nondeterminism, 43
normalization, 507
notification
    broadcast, 382, 383
    synchronous, 383
    targeted, 382

O

object
    associative, 80
    modeling, 498
    remote, 142
object-oriented
    analysis, 495
    APIs, 10
    design, 496
    methodology, 494
observable, 58, 61
    `addObserver()` method, 87
Observation Model
    in Java, 385
observer, 58, 61
    implementing, 88, 267
    pattern, 184
    removing, 89
    role of, 87
off-hook, going, 306
operating in a degraded mode, 525
optionality, 498

P

package
    core, 12, 49, 57
    extension, 39, 49
    in Java, 38
    javax.telephony, 54, 55, 105, 178, 199
    javax.telephony.callcontrol, 294
    javax.telephony.capabilities, 56, 178
    javax.telephony.events, 56, 107, 179
parking a call, 313
party of a call, 306
patchlet, 525
PBX, 5
PCI, 25
Performance
    idioms, 427
    in Java, 44
PhoneButton Interface, 329
PhoneDisplay Interface, 330
Phone Events, 336
PhoneGraphicDisplay Interface, 330
PhoneHookSwitch Interface, 330
PhoneLamp Interface, 331
PhoneMicrophone Interface, 331
PhoneRinger Interface, 331
PhoneSpeaker Interface, 332
PhoneTerminal Interface, 329
PhoneTerminalObserver Interface, 327
picking up a call, 314
platform
    binding, 177
    binding and portability, 196
    defined, 197
    library defined, 125
polymorphic processing, 332
polymorphism, 498
port, 26
portability
    and least common denominator, 132
    binary, 40
    in a binding context, 196
    practical, 41
    telephony API support for, 148
    true, 40

presentation programming, 516
private data
    capabilities, 376
    events, 373
    retrieving data using, 374
    sending data using, 371
problem space, 4
Prolog, 44
proprietary
    tools, 35
Provider Interface
    capabilities implemented, 257
    defined, 96
    implementation, 232
    state transitions, 97
ProviderObserver Interface
    defined, 90
    implementation, 270
    related events, 90
proxy, 142

R

race condition, 289
recursion, 476
redirecting a call, 312
reflection
    API, 42
rejecting a call, 312
relationship
    association kind, 505
    bi-directionality, 502
    mandatory, 504
    many-to-many, 80, 501
    one-to-may, 500
    one-to-one, 499
    persistent, 80
requirements
    allocation, 486
    explicit and derived, 484
    functional and system, 485
    relationships among, 487
    satisfaction, 489
    traceability, 488
RMI, 43
ROMlet, 525

RouteAddress Interface, 351
RouteCallback Interface, 352
RouteSession Interface, 348

S

scalability
    and APIs, 134
    and software architecture, 493
    and writing software, 144
    defined, 135
SCSI, 27
security
    policy, 180
service arrangement, 475
service provider, 17
single-step conference, 306
singleton
    pattern, 447
Smalltalk
    blocks, 395, 460
    DirectedMessage class, 415
    events, 396
    language, 34
    observer pattern, 183
    support for concurrent programming, 36
source, 382, 387
state transition diagram, 66, 168
subsystem
    allocation to, 496
    identification of, 486
synchronization
    and lock scope, 429
systems programmer, 514

T

TAPI
    architecture, 154
    auxiliary packages, 55
    callback function, 162
    event handling, 158
    placing a call, 164
    service levels, 55, 156
    specification, 35
target, 382, 388
TDM, 28

Telecom
  companies, 3
  programming, 1
Telephone
  network, 5
telephony
  and Java, 38
  and requirements for APIs, 146
  application generators, 34
  bus architecture, 25
  communications medium, 18
  computer-centric configuration, 20
  hardware configurations, 17
  phone-centric configuration, 19
  programming, 1
  protocols, 21
TerminalConnection Interface
  answer( ) method, 83, 199
  capabilities implemented, 259
  defined, 81
  implementation, 250
  relationship to Connection events, 82
  scenario, 84
  state definitions, 84
  state transitions, 83
Terminal Interface
  capabilities implemented, 258
  defined, 76
  implementation, 245
TerminalObserver Interface
  defined, 90
  implementation, 271
  related events, 90

Testing Phase, 510
third-party call control, 21
thread local storage, 200
threads
  and asynchronous notification, 190
  and telephony, 8
  fairness and starvation, 473
  programming language support for, 35
  safety and reentrancy, 133
  state machine pattern, 473
transferring a call, 302
transitivity, 507
TSPI, 35, 155
types
  and precision, 442
  mutable reference, 439
  parameterized, 440
  reference, primitive, 438
type safety, 440

U
UML, 494
Unified Service Platform, 145
update anomaly, 507

V
voice prompt, 34

W
Web phone, 522
WOSA, 154